Electronic Media Law and Regulation
Fourth Edition

Electronic Media Law and Regulation
Fourth Edition

Kenneth Creech

OXFORD AMSTERDAM BOSTON LONDON NEW YORK PARIS
SAN DIEGO SAN FRANCISCO SINGAPORE SYDNEY TOKYO

Focal Press is an imprint of Elsevier Science.

 Recognizing the importance of preserving what has been written, Elsevier Science prints its books on acid-free paper whenever possible.

Library of Congress Cataloging-in-Publication Data

Creech, Kenneth.
    Electronic media law and regulation / by Kenneth Creech.—4th ed.
      p. cm.
    Includes bibliographical references.
    ISBN 0-240-80509-7 (alk. paper)
    1. Television—Law and legislation—United States. 2. Radio—Law and legislation—United States. 3. Mass media—Law and legislation—United States. 4. Internet—Law and legislation—United States. I. Title.
KF2805 .C74 2002
343.7309'9—dc21

                2002035249

British Library Cataloguing-in-Publication Data
A catalogue record for this book is available from the British Library.

The publisher offers special discounts on bulk orders of this book.
For information, please contact:

Manager of Special Sales
Elsevier Science
200 Wheeler Road
Burlington, MA 01803
Tel: 781-313-4700
Fax: 781-313-4882

For information on all Focal Press publications available, contact our World Wide Web home page at: http://www.focalpress.com

10 9 8 7 6 5 4 3 2 1

Printed in the United States of America

Contents

Cases

This list includes all cases cited in this book.

AandM Records Inc. et al. v. Napster Inc. No. 00-16401 DC No.CV-99-05183-MHP (February 12, 2001)

Abrams v. United States, 250 U.S. 616 (1919)

Action for Children's Television, 58 R.R.2d 61 (1985)

Action for Children's Television v. FCC, 821 F.2d 741 (DC Cir., 1987)

Action for Children's Television v. FCC, 852 F.2d 1332 [15 Med.L.Rptr. 1907] (DC Cir., 1988) ("ACT I")

Action for Children's Television v. FCC, 932 F.2d 1504 [18 Med.L. Rptr. 2153] (DC Cir., 1991), cert. denied, 112 S.Ct. 1281 (1992) ("ACT II")

Action for Children's Television v. FCC, 21 Med.L.Rptr. 2289 (DC Cir., 1993)

Action Repair v. ABC (CA 7, 1985) 12 Med.L.Rptr. 1809

Adrian Weiss, 58 F.C.C.2d 342, 36 R.R.2d 292 (1976)

American Communications Association v. Douds, 339 U.S. 382 (1950)

American Civil Liberties Union v. Reno, 1996 U.S. Dist.LEXIS 1617

Anderson v. Fisher Broadcasting Companies (OR Ct.App., 1985) 11 Med.L.Rptr. 1839

Anderson v. Liberty Lobby (U.S. Sup.Ct., 1986) 12 Med.L.Rptr. 2297

Anderson v. WROC-TV, 441 N.Y.S.2d 220 (Sup.Ct., 1981)

Andren v. Knight-Ridder (DC E.Mich, 1984) 10 Med.L.Rptr. 2109

Apple Corp. Limited v. A.D.P.R. Inc. (DC MidTenn, 1993) 22 Med.L.Rptr 1562

Arkansas AFL-CIO v. FCC (8th Cir.CA, 1993) 22 Med.L.Rptr. 1001

Ashcroft v. American Civil Liberties Union (Slip Opinion, No. 00–1293, May 13, 2002)

Ashcroft v. Free Speech Coalition 122 S.Ct. 1389; 152 L. Ed. 2d 403; 2002 U.S. LEXIS 2789 (2002)

Associated Press v. Bell (NY Ct.App., 1987) 14 Med.L.Rptr. 1156

Preface to the Fourth Edition

The fourth edition of *Electronic Media Law and Regulation* has been significantly updated to reflect the ever-changing nature of the discipline. Although new cases and material have been added, the basic structure of the text remains the same; users of previous editions will be familiar with this new edition as they plan courses and syllabi.

New also to this edition are expanded Web support pages. Some adopters have told me that they desire supplemental material so that their students can engage with the original text of cases in greater depth. The Website http://www.kencreech.com will provide that material. It will also provide regular updates to material in the text, as well as links to other information that students, instructors, and professionals may find useful in their study of *Electronic Media Law and Regulation*. Additional Web support may be found at the Focal Press site, http://www.focalpress.com.

I am grateful for the assistance of John Servizzi at WTBU-TV for his work on the illustrations contained in this edition.

I also offer my thanks to those adopters of previous editions, manuscript reviewers, and students at Butler University who provided their assistance and suggestions in the preparation of the fourth edition.

Thanks also to the staff at Focal Press, with whom it has been a joy to work for these many years.

Kenneth C. Creech
Fishers, Indiana

1

□ □ □
□ □ □
□ □ □

Introduction to the Legal System

America is a nation governed by laws, not by individuals. Since the earliest days of the founding of the United States, Americans have attempted to justify actions by applying laws, rather than by relying on the authority of a single ruler. For example, the Declaration of Independence is a beautifully crafted, philosophical, and legal statement that justifies the separation of the 13 colonies from England. The same reliance on the sanctity of law forced the resignation of a president of the United States in 1974 and the impeachment of another in 1999.

The court cases that result from disputes over interpretations of American laws could easily be used as the basis for writing an accurate history of the United States. Court cases reflect the tensions present in American society at a given time. For example, the major cases of the 1790s reflect the growing pains of the new nation. Sedition and the powers of the various branches of government were common topics of litigation during this period. State rights and civil rights issues were common in the 1860s and again 100 years later. Many cases of the late nineteenth century were concerned with child labor, unions, trust-busting, and consumerism. Of course, every war in which the United States was engaged, from the American Revolution to Vietnam, spawned cases that resulted from protests, espionage, and treason.

Similar to court cases, federal and state laws reflect the concerns of the American people during a given period. Laws designed to protect against subversive activity have been passed and repealed throughout our history, depending on the perceived threat. Laws both limiting and expanding the civil rights of individuals have appeared on the books of many states. Issues of gun control, the right to bear arms, the right to abortion, and gay rights have found their way into the legal system and reflect the dynamics of American society.

The law of communication is a relative newcomer to this arena. Most cases that involve judicial interpretation of the First Amendment, which guarantees freedom of speech and freedom of the press, occurred after World War I. The rapid development of mass communication in the twentieth century focused new attention on the meaning of free speech and free press.

Undergraduate students studying communications law as journalism or mass communication majors often find that they lack the proper background in the legal process to understand communications law issues. This background is necessary to comprehend the cases, statutes, and principles involved in shaping communications law and policy. As they study communications law, undergraduate students must realize that they are studying a specialty field that would be encountered in the third year of most law schools. The remainder of this chapter is devoted to providing a point of departure for the study of communications law.

Law and Policy

Policy is a plan or course of action undertaken and designed by society to achieve a set of goals. Ideally, the articulation of a policy should guide the promulgation of laws. *Laws* are passed in the United States to support policies. For example, as a society we have determined that robbery is an undesirable act, thereby creating a policy. The federal government and the individual states have enacted laws designed to deter and punish individuals who violate this policy.

Basically, a law may be defined as a set of rules, promulgated by government agencies with the authority to do so, that attempt to guide, conduct, and subsequently provide sanctions when the rules are violated.

Sources of American Law

The foundation of the American legal system was imported from England. The jury system, development of the common law, and many statutes were adopted by the colonies and retained after the American Revolution. America expanded her legal system with the addition of the Constitution. In all, there are five sources of American law:

- the common law
- equity law
- statutory law
- constitutional law
- administrative law

Common Law

The roots of the common law go back to medieval England. Legal historians trace the common law to the mid-thirteenth century. It is the strongest British legacy to colonial America. In England, common law was distinguished from ecclesiastical law—the law of the Church. Ecclesiastical law used the Church as the basis for all decisions, whereas the common law looked to the people to resolve disputes. Common law is often called *discovered law* because magistrates discovered solutions to disputes by finding out what had been done in similar situations in the past. Judges or legislators do not create common law. Instead, a legal rule is mandated after specific cases are studied. Common law is inductive rather than deductive.

A fundamental concept of the common law is *stare decisis* or "let the decision stand." This means that judges should look to the past to resolve current problems. At first glance, this concept may give the impression that common law is also static law. After all, how can a 200-year-old decision be applied to today's disputes? And what about "bad" decisions? How does the common law keep from propagating an unfair judgment? Needless to say, many factors are taken into consideration by judges who rely on precedent. Rarely is an archaic precedent used as a basis for a judgment.

The common law is dynamic and is usually very responsive to changing times. Judges use precedent only as a guideline in reaching a decision. There is a great deal of room for interpretation and change. For example, when the Supreme Court reviews a case, it relies on previous decisions as guidelines, but many times it overrules what it considers an incorrect interpretation of the law. When this happens, judges in future cases may no longer cite a particular precedent. Therefore, a "weeding out" process occurs in the application of the common law.

Theoretically, of all forms of Anglo-American law, the common law offers the most equitable means of settling disputes. As Justice Oliver Wendell Holmes wrote about the common law,

> The life of the law has not been logic; it has been experience . . . . The law embodies the story of a nation's development through many centuries, and it cannot be dealt with as if it contained only the axioms and corollaries of a book of mathematics. To know what it is, we must know what it has been, and what it tends to become.[1]

Equity Law

Like the common law, equity law also developed in England and was imported to the colonies. Equity law emerged in the fourteenth and fifteenth centuries as a supplement to the common law and as an additional means of settling disputes. The common law courts of England had become somewhat rigid by the year 1400, and many persons seeking to file grievances were turned away. Unable to obtain a hearing before a magistrate, those individuals often petitioned the king to prescribe a solution to their problems.

The king's chief officer, or chancellor, set up courts of chancery to deal with these petitions. All decisions made in chancery court were made on the basis of conscience or equity—fairness. Some states still refer to equity courts as chancery courts.

Equity law retains the common law dependence on *stare decisis*. However, equity law begins where the common law stops. Child custody, divorce, property settlements, and accident claims are examples of issues taken to equity court. Equity cases are not tried before a jury and decisions are rendered in the form of discretionary orders issued by judges. Equity law provides for an injunction or restraining order, which is issued by a judge to stop someone from behaving in a manner that is deemed unfair or damaging to another. Injunctions are often sought in communications law cases.

Statutory Law

Before the Revolutionary War, laws decreed by Parliament bound Americans. Indeed, it was the enforcement of some of these laws that contributed to the Revolution. After the Revolution, America established her own laws in Congress and in state assemblies. These laws are statutory laws and are so named because they prescribe, by statute, the behavior of members of society. A well-constructed statute defines the behavior to be regulated and imposes sanctions for violating the statute. No statutes promulgated in the United States may violate the U.S. Constitution. Any statute that does so is invalid *prima facie* (on its face).

Before 1825, statutory law did not play a large role in the American legal system. Most legal issues were settled via the common law. Between 1850 and 1900, however, a greater percentage of American law resulted from legislative acts rather than from common law tradition. Today, most American law is statutory. The reason for the shift from the common law to statutory law is tied to the steady growth of the United States population. Common law is most effective when dealing with the problems of individuals. Statutes are written to address the problems inherent in governing large groups.

Statutory law can anticipate social problems, but the common law cannot. While the common law is inductive, statutory law is deductive—one rule applies to many situations. All criminal law in the United States is statutory. While common law is based on precedent, statutory law is founded on various federal, state, and local codes. Ideally, statutory law leaves room for less ambiguity in interpretation than does common law. However, construction of a workable statute is often difficult. Sometimes the application of statutory law does not take into consideration individual circumstances. For these reasons, statutes often require interpretation by judges. For example, federal and state statutes make it illegal to distribute obscene materials. However, the judge must determine what is or is not obscene. Statutory law is not always the final word.

Constitutional Law

The United States Constitution is the supreme law of the land. It provides for the organization of our government, outlines the duties and powers of the various branches of government, and guarantees U.S. citizens certain individual rights. The Constitution is the yardstick by which all other actions of government are measured. Any laws that conflict with the Constitution are legally unenforceable.

The student of all forms of communications law should be familiar with the Bill of Rights and subsequent amendments to the Constitution. Most, but by no means all, communications law cases stem from the interpretation of one of three amendments—the First, Sixth, and Fourteenth. The First and Sixth Amendments are parts of the original Bill of Rights, which was ratified in 1787. The Fourteenth Amendment was ratified in 1868 and was primarily designed to limit the power of the readmitted southern states after the Civil War. The first paragraph of the Fourteenth Amendment, known as the due process clause, has an impact on communications law.

The First Amendment states,

> Congress shall make no law respecting an establishment of religion, or prohibiting the free exercise thereof; or abridging the freedom of speech, or of the press; or the right of the people to peaceably assemble, and to petition the government for a redress of grievances.

Of major concern is the interpretation of the freedom of the press and speech clause. Though it is written in absolute terms, most courts agree that the Founding Fathers did not mean that speech and press could never be restrained. The extent and nature of the restraint has been the subject of a plethora of litigation, most of which has taken place since 1919. Of additional concern is how the First Amendment should be applied to cases regarding the electronic media. As we shall see, the debate continues.

The Sixth Amendment states,

> In criminal prosecutions, the accused shall enjoy the right to a speedy and public trial, by an impartial jury of the State and district wherein the crime shall have been committed, which district shall have been previously ascertained by law, and to be informed of the nature and cause of the accusation to be confronted with the witnesses against him; to have compulsory process for obtaining witnesses in his favor, and to have the Assistance of Counsel for his defense.

The Sixth Amendment guarantee of a public trial by an impartial jury sometimes conflicts with the First Amendment guarantee of freedom of the press. Sometimes, press coverage of criminal acts makes it difficult to provide a defendant with an impartial jury. The balancing of First and Sixth Amendment rights has been another major issue facing the courts.

The Fourteenth Amendment, paragraphs 1 and 5, states,

> All persons born or naturalized in the United States, and subject to the jurisdiction thereof, are citizens of the United States and of the State wherein they reside. No State shall make or enforce any law which shall abridge the privileges and immunities of citizens of the United States; nor shall any State deprive any person of life, liberty, or property, without due process of law; nor deny to any person within its jurisdiction the equal protection of the laws.

The Congress shall have the power to enforce, by appropriate legislation, the provisions of this article.

The First Amendment states "Congress shall make no law . . ." abridging various freedoms, but it says nothing about states not making laws that limit freedoms. Consequently, many states passed statutes that limited the freedoms outlined in the Bill of Rights. The Fourteenth Amendment applies the Bill of Rights to the states. For example, the First Amendment is applied to the states, which is of particular interest for students of communications law. As we shall see, none of the freedoms implicit in the First, Sixth, and Fourteenth Amendments are absolute. States and Congress continue to pass statutes that attempt to define or limit those rights. However, the Fourteenth Amendment ensures that all statutes are in keeping with the Constitution, although their interpretation may vary according to the social climate of the day. No state can refuse freedom of speech to an individual or a group based simply on the grounds that it does not like what that person or group has to say.

Administrative Law

The fifth source of American law developed in the late nineteenth century as a means of coping with the growing complexity of the government, administrative law requires knowledge of a specific industry, which is regulated by the government. The regulating body is usually an independent regulatory agency (IRA) created by Congress and staffed by members appointed by the president. The agency has legislative, executive, and judicial powers. An IRA establishes policy and provides sanctions against regulated industries that violate those policies. It makes rules that apply to a particular industry, enforces those rules, and hears initial cases that involve alleged violation of those rules. The agency may levy fines or other punishments against offenders. Decisions of the agencies are checked by judicial review. A court may declare an IRA ruling unconstitutional. Regulated industries may also appeal an unfavorable decision to the U.S. Court of Appeals for the District of Columbia. As we shall see, the U.S. Supreme Court eventually hears some cases that begin with administrative agency hearings.

The first IRA was created by Congress in 1890 to regulate the interstate transport of natural gas through pipelines and was called the Interstate Commerce Commission (ICC). The ICC still exists and has expanded duties that include regulating interstate trucking. The ICC has been joined by a host of other such industry-specific agencies. In 1914, Congress created the Federal Trade Commission (FTC) to deal with unfair trade practices by trusts. The FTC has expanded its role to include the regulation of false and misleading advertising, and for a brief time considered the regulation of children's television advertising. The IRAs operating today include the Nuclear Regulatory Commission, the Central Intelligence Agency, the Peace Corps, and the Postal Service.

Although students of communications law will encounter the FTC in their studies, the agency that most directly affects communications law is the Federal Communications Commission (FCC). Known as "the Commission" by broadcasters, the FCC began as the Federal Radio Commission (FRC) in 1927 when Congress passed the Radio Act, which authorized the five-person Commission to license radio stations in the "public interest, convenience, and necessity." The agency's role was expanded seven years later with the passage of the Communications Act of 1934. The new act created a seven-member FCC.

Like all IRAs, FCC commissioners are appointed by the president and confirmed by the Senate. The FCC has five commissioners, no more than three of which may be from the same political party. Commissioners are appointed for five-year terms, but many do not serve a full term, because IRA appointments are generally thought of as stepping stones, either politically or to the industry that they regulate. Most commissioners are lawyers who, after a stint on an IRA, can build a lucrative clientele and represent the regulated industry in Washington, D.C.

Congress controls the FCC's budget and, as previously stated, agency rulings are subject to judicial review. This series of checks and balances is supposed to ensure that the FCC is insulated from the political process—hence the term *independent agencies*. In reality, Republican presidents tend to appoint Republican commissioners and Democrats tend to appoint

Democrats. If an agency gets too tough on a regulated industry, it may find its purse strings tightened by members of Congress under pressure from special interest groups.

The statutes and rules promulgated by the FCC and all other IRAs can be found in the *Code of Federal Regulations* (CFR). All IRA procedures are governed by the Administrative Procedure Act of 1946, which requires that all IRA actions (including new rulings) be published in the *Federal Register*. Any new rules or changes to existing agency rules must be published as a *Notice of Proposed Rule Making*. Interested persons and parties can file comments with an IRA regarding a particular rule. The IRA is then supposed to consider these comments before implementing the rule.

If an IRA is concerned about a particular issue, such as the effect of children's television advertising on the well-being of juveniles, it publishes a *Notice of Inquiry*. Again, interested persons or parties (usually the affected industry) file comments. A hearing before the Commission is also guaranteed. The IRA then issues a policy statement, called *Report and Order*, that deals with the issue or the proposed rule. All of these actions become part of the *Code of Federal Regulations* and are enacted into laws when they are ruled on by a court (see Figure 1.1).

How the FCC Conducts Business

When the FCC was created in 1934, it consisted of seven members. In 1982, Congress reduced the number of members to five. As previously noted, commissioners are appointed by the president, confirmed by the Senate, and serve five-year terms. No more than three members may be from the same political party, and terms are staggered so that no two terms expire in the same year. None of the members can have a financial interest in any Commission-related business. The chairperson of the FCC is chosen by the president and is responsible for setting the agenda of the FCC. The chairperson plays a major role in FCC actions. For example, when Mark Fowler (1981–1987) and Dennis Patrick (1987–1989) were chairs, much of the deregulation of broadcasting and cable television was undertaken. When Alfred Sikes assumed the chair in 1989, he cut short some of the deregulatory momentum; he spearheaded a 24-hour ban on indecent programming and earned the moniker "Sikes, the Enforcer." When Reed Hundt assumed the FCC chair in 1993, he focused the agenda of the commission on the creation of the "information superhighway" and on the enforcement of cable rate regulation. In 2001 Michael Powell became chair of the FCC; his tenure is likely to be dominated by issues surrounding media mergers, the development of broadband technologies, and the conversion from analog to digital television.

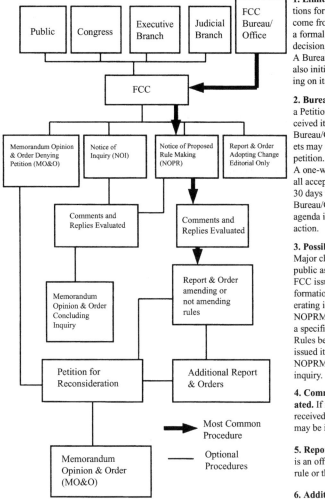

Steps in the Process

1. Limitation of Action. Suggestions for changes to FCC rules can come from outside sources either as a formal petition, legislation, court decision, or informal suggestion. A Bureau/Office within the FCC can also initiate a Rule-Making proceeding on its own.

2. Bureau/Office Evaluation. When a Petition for Rule Making is received it is sent to the appropriate Bureau/Office for evaluation. Dockets may assign a RM number to the petition. A one-week notice is issued listing all accepted petitions. The public has 30 days to submit comments. The Bureau/Office may then generate an agenda item requesting Commission action.

3. Possible Commission Actions. Major changes are presented to the public as an NOI or NOPRM. The FCC issues an NOI when seeking information on a broad subject or generating ideas on a given topic. A NOPRM is issued when there is a specific change to current FCC Rules being proposed. If an NOI is issued it must be followed by an NOPRM or MO&O concluding the inquiry.

4. Comments and Replies Evaluated. If insufficient comments are received, additional NOI or NOPRM may be issued.

5. Report and Order Issued. This is an official statement of an amended rule or that a rule will be changed.

6. Additional Reports. Reconsideration of changes based on comments and other modifications may follow.

Figure 1.1 How FCC rules are made.

The Current Commissioners: Profiles

Michael K. Powell is Chairman of the Federal Communications Commission. He was sworn in as a member of the Commission on November 3, 1997. He was designated Chairman by President Bush on January 22, 2001. Mr. Powell, a Republican, was nominated by President

William J. Clinton on July 31, 1997, and confirmed by the United States Senate on October 28, 1997. He is the son of Secretary of State Colin Powell.

Kathleen Abernathy was appointed to the Federal Communications Commission (FCC) by President George W. Bush in May 2001. In addition to her other responsibilities at the FCC, she chairs the Federal-State Joint Board on Universal Service.

Michael J. Copps was sworn in as a member of the Federal Communications Commission on May 31, 2001, for a term that runs until June 30, 2005. Mr. Copps, a Democrat, was nominated by President George W. Bush on May 1, 2001, and confirmed by the Senate on May 25, 2001.

Kevin Martin was sworn in July 3, 2001. Before joining the FCC, Martin was a Special Assistant to the President for Economic Policy. A Republican, he served on the Bush-Cheney Transition Team and was Deputy General Counsel for the Bush campaign.

Jonathan Adelstein is expected to join the Commission in 2002. A Democrat appointed by President George W. Bush, Adelstein served as an aide to Senator Tom Daschle. At this writing, Adelstein has not yet been confirmed. Please check http://www.fcc.gov for updated information on the filling of this vacancy on the FCC.

Organization of the FCC

The FCC is organized into six bureaus—Media, Wireline Competition, Enforcement, Wireless Telecommunications, Consumer and Governmental Affairs, and International. Each bureau is headed by a bureau chief and various branches report to the chief (see Figure 1.2).

Media Bureau

The Media Bureau is responsible for the policy and licensing programs for media services, including cable television, broadcast television, and radio. It handles matters pertaining to multichannel video programming distribution, broadcast radio and television, direct broadcast satellite service policy, and associated matters. It will conduct rule-makings, resolve waiver petitions and adjudications, and process applications for authorization, assignment, transfer, and renewal of media services, including AM, FM, TV, the cable TV relay service, and related matters.

The Bureau is comprised of staff and functions from the old Mass Media Bureau and Cable Services Bureau and consists of the following organizational units: Management and Resources Staff; Office of Communications

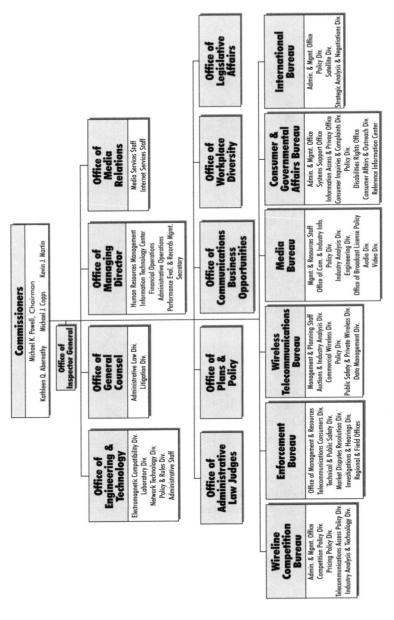

Figure 1.2 The Federal Communications Commission organizational chart.

and Industry Information; Policy Division; Industry Analysis Division; Engineering Division; Office of Broadcast License Policy; Audio Division; and Video Division.

Wireline Competition Bureau

The Wireline Competition Bureau is responsible for the policy programs of communications common carriers and ancillary operations (other than wireless telecommunications services). It conducts rule-makings, resolves waiver petitions and adjudications, determines the lawfulness of carrier tariffs, acts on applications for authorizations, administers accounting requirements for incumbent local exchange carriers, reviews carrier performance, and administers reporting requirements.

The Wireline Competition Bureau is comprised of staff and functions from the old Common Carrier Bureau and has the following organizational units: Administrative and Management Office; Competition Policy Division; Pricing Policy Division; Telecommunications Access Policy Division; and Industry Analysis and Technology Division.

Consumer and Governmental Affairs Bureau

The Consumer and Governmental Affairs Bureau is responsible for the consumer and governmental affairs policies that enhance the public's understanding of the Commission's work and for facilitating the FCC's relationships with other governmental agencies. It conducts rule-makings, interacts with the public, federal, state, local, tribal, and other governmental agencies, oversee the Consumer/Disability Telecommunications Advisory Committee and the Local and State Government Advisory Committee, handles informal complaint resolution, handles consumer outreach and education, and maintains FCC filings.

The Consumer and Governmental Affairs Bureau is comprised of staff and functions from the old Consumer Information Bureau, Cable Services Bureau, and Common Carrier Bureau, and also handles cable services information functions currently performed in the Cable Services Bureau and some related rule-making functions previously handled in the Common Carrier Bureau. It consists of the following organizational units: Administrative and Management Office; Systems Support Office; Information Access and Privacy Office; Consumer Inquiries and Complaints Division; Policy Division; Disabilities Rights Office; Consumer Affairs and Outreach Division; and Reference Information Center.

International Bureau

The International Bureau was realigned along functional lines, with consolidation of the international policy and spectrum rule-making functions, and intergovernmental and regional leadership and planning functions, which had been distributed throughout the Bureau. The International Bureau has the following organizational units: Management and Administrative Staff; Policy Division; Satellite Division; and Strategic Analysis and Negotiations Division.

Other Organizational Changes

The FCC made other organizational changes in 2002. The Enforcement Bureau handles pole attachment complaints and some multichannel video and cable television services complaints that were previously handled in the Cable Services Bureau. It also handles common carrier audit functions. The Wireless Telecommunications Bureau handles instructional television fixed services and multipoint distribution services matters that were handled in the Mass Media Bureau. The Office of Legislative and Intergovernmental Affairs has been renamed the Office of Legislative Affairs.

Other Agencies Affecting Broadcasting and Cable

In addition to the FCC, broadcasters and cable operators must contend with other administrative agencies. The FTC was established in 1914 to regulate unfair competition in commerce. In 1938, with the passage of the Wheeler-Lea amendments, to the Federal Trade Commission Act, the FTC's power was expanded to include regulation of advertising to protect against unfair and deceptive advertising. Although it cannot directly fine broadcasters, the FTC can issue cease and desist orders if false and misleading advertising is suspected.

Broadcasters and cable casters originally paid royalties to the Copyright Royalty Tribunal (CRT), which, until 1993, managed the compulsory licensing scheme for cable television. Congress abolished the CRT in 1993. Now the Librarian of Congress chooses ad hoc panels to review disputes.

The National Telecommunications and Information Administration (NTIA) is the telecommunications policymaking and research arm of the government. It was established in 1978 as a part of the Department of Commerce. The NTIA develops policies that support the development of telecommunications, including radio, television, and cable, and also provides facilities grants to noncommercial broadcasters.

The Civil Rights Act of 1964 created the Equal Employment Opportunity Commission (EEOC). The charter of the EEOC is to eliminate discrimination in employment based on race, color, religion, gender, or national origin. Broadcasters must comply with EEOC and FCC guidelines to obtain or retain their license. Licensees with more than five full-time employees must present the FCC with a model EEO program when applying for a license and must provide annual updates to that program.

The Federal Aviation Administration (FAA) approves tower locations and works with the FCC to ensure that broadcast towers are painted and lighted in a manner consistent with FCC and Agency rules. Broadcasters must notify the FAA if their tower lights fail and must seek IRA approval before changing the height or location of an existing tower or before building a new structure.

The Judiciary—An Overview

Ultimately, serious disputes involving communications law are resolved in court. Technically, there are 54 different judicial systems in the United States—one for each state, the federal court system, and the territorial district courts for Guam, Puerto Rico, and for the Virgin Islands. Fortunately, although the names of the various components may differ from state to state, all courts are organized in a similar manner and owe allegiance to a single source—the Constitution.

The court system in the United States is divided into trial and appellate courts (see Figure 1.3). Each state court system is guided by both a state constitution and the federal Constitution. Each court system is part of the third

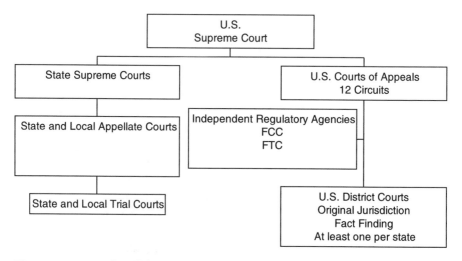

Figure 1.3 Hierarchy of the U.S. court system.

branch of the government (the judicial branch). The states have governors as chief executives and legislatures (or assemblies) who fulfill the legislative function.

Trial Courts

Trial courts are fact-finding courts. They are where most cases begin. It is the function of a trial court to determine exactly what happened in a case. These courts hear testimony from witnesses and establish a factual record of the case. Juries are present in trial courts.

Appellate Courts

After a trial court has rendered its verdict, it may be appealed to the next highest court, which is an appellate court. Appellate courts do not consider facts; they only consider law. On appeal, no more witnesses are called, no more testimony is heard, and no jury is present. A judge looks at the facts established at trial and attorneys argue whether, given the facts, the law was or was not applied properly. Should new evidence emerge, the appellate court may order a new trial.

The Supreme Court

The Supreme Court was established in 1789 and is the oldest federal court. Although other federal courts are created by Congress, the Supreme Court was established by the Constitution and does not serve at the discretion of Congress or of the executive branch of the government. Supreme Court justices, like federal judges, are appointed for life. They are nominated by the president and confirmed by the Senate. Congress establishes the number of justices on the Supreme Court, a number that has changed several times throughout history. The original Supreme Court, headed by Chief Justice John Jay, consisted of six justices—five associate justices and one chief justice of the United States. The total number of judges on the Supreme Court increased to seven in 1807, to nine in 1837, and to ten in 1863. Following the Civil War, in 1866, the Supreme Court was reduced to seven members, and then raised to its current number of nine in 1869. The most recent attempt to change the number of justices on the Supreme Court came in 1937 when President Franklin Roosevelt, frustrated by Supreme Court rulings that declared some of his New Deal programs unconstitutional, proposed that an additional justice be added for each justice reaching the age of 70 and not retiring. Roosevelt's proposal set the maximum number of justices at 15. Although Roosevelt could not persuade Congress to implement his proposal, he ultimately appointed nine men to the Supreme Court—more than any other president, except George Washington. One of Roosevelt's appointees, Justice William O. Douglas, served for 36 years. This is the longest term of any Supreme Court justice. Roosevelt's New Deal influence could be felt as late as 1975, when Douglas retired.

Needless to say, a president will nominate potential justices who can steer the Court in a philosophical, if not political, direction that is in step with the chief executive. Although conservative presidents tend to nominate conservative justices and liberal presidents nominate liberals, sometimes justices do not always vote the way in which they are expected to once they are on the Court. Chief Justice Earl Warren, appointed by Republican President Eisenhower, turned out to be one of the most liberal chief justices in history. Kennedy appointee Justice White was more conservative than one would expect from a justice appointed by a liberal president.

President Reagan appointed three associate justices and elevated President Nixon's appointee William Rehnquist to the position of chief justice when Warren Burger retired in 1986. In 1981, Reagan's first appointee, Sandra Day O'Connor, became the first woman in history to serve on the Supreme Court. The Senate, however, exercised its right of confirmation in 1987 when it rejected the president's second choice for associate justice, Robert Bork. Bork's conservatism and controversial role in the firing of Watergate special prosecutor Archibald Cox in 1973 resulted in the nonconfirmation vote. Reagan's next choice, Douglas Ginsberg, admitted to smoking marijuana while a law professor at Harvard University. This admission drew such strong criticism that Ginsberg withdrew from consideration. At the time of his nomination, Ginsberg was only 41 years old and had the potential of carrying the philosophy of the Reagan years into the twenty-first century. In 1988, the Senate finally confirmed 51-year-old Anthony Kennedy as Reagan's third Supreme Court appointee.

When President George H. W. Bush nominated Clarence Thomas to succeed Justice Thurgood Marshall in 1991, allegations of sexual harassment against Judge Thomas surfaced during the confirmation process. The lengthy hearings were televised, and Americans were riveted to their television sets until the early hours of the morning to hear testimony. Thomas was eventually confirmed, but a heightened awareness of the nature and scope of sexual harassment in society followed him to the Court.

The Current Supreme Court

Currently there are three Reagan appointees, one Nixon appointee (William Rehnquist, who was elevated to chief justice by Reagan), two Bush, Sr. appointees, one Ford appointee, and two Clinton appointees on the Supreme Court. The chief justice of the United States is:

William Rehnquist, born in 1924 in Virginia. Appointed as associate justice in 1972 by President Nixon. Became chief justice in 1986 when Warren Burger retired.

The associate justices of the Supreme Court are:

John Paul Stevens, born in 1920 in Illinois. Appointed in 1975 by President Ford.

Sandra Day O'Connor, born in 1930 in Arizona. Appointed in 1981 by President Reagan. Justice O'Connor is the first woman to serve on the Supreme Court.

Antonin Scalia, born in 1936 in Virginia. Appointed in 1986 by President Reagan.

Anthony Kennedy, born in 1936 in California. Appointed in 1988 by President Reagan.

David Souter, born 1939 in Vermont. Appointed in 1990 by President George H.W. Bush.

Clarence Thomas, born in 1948 in Georgia. Appointed in 1991 by President George H.W. Bush. (After a controversial Confirmation hearing by the Senate Judiciary Committee, Justice Thomas replaced Thurgood Marshall, the first African-American justice on the Court.)

Ruth Bader Ginsburg, born in 1933 in New York. Appointed in 1994 by President Clinton.

Steven Breyer, born in 1938 in California. Appointed in 1994 by President Clinton.

How the Supreme Court Conducts Business

The Supreme Court exercises both original and appellate jurisdiction. Under original jurisdiction, the Supreme Court is the first court to hear a case. It acts like a trial court in gathering facts and deciding law. The Supreme Court rarely exercises original jurisdiction. In fact, it has done so fewer than 150 times—perhaps one or two per year—in the last 200 years.

Much of the law in the United States comes from the exercise of the Supreme Court's appellate jurisdiction (i.e., cases are heard on appeal from a lower court). A case comes to the Supreme Court on appeal in three ways: (1) by direct appeal, (2) by *writ of certiorari*, and (3) by certification.

A direct appeal may be brought to the Supreme Court from a lower federal court or from a state court that has ruled a federal law unconstitutional. The Supreme Court can turn down any appeal by simply refusing to hear the case. If that happens, the case is closed. All legal appeals have been exhausted.

A *writ of certiorari* is a discretionary order issued by the Court when it feels that an important legal question has been raised. The Court asks to hear a case, so that it may issue an opinion to be used as a precedent in similar cases. No one has a legal right to a *writ of certiorari*. The most important requirement that must be met before the Court will issue a writ is that the petitioner must have exhausted all other legal remedies. This means that a case must have gone through the trial court, an intermediate appeals court, and possibly a state supreme or superior court. Then, four of the nine justices must vote in favor of hearing the case in the Supreme Court.

Very few cases reach the Supreme Court by certification. Lower federal courts are permitted to ask questions of the Court regarding matters of law that pertain to cases that the lower court may be hearing. Sometimes the Supreme Court asks that a case be forwarded to it for the final decision.

Hearing a Case

Once the Court agrees to hear a case, the attorneys for both parties prepare their arguments. Arguing a case before the Supreme Court requires months of preparation and is preceded by perhaps five years of litigation in the lower courts. When James Hill sued *Time* magazine for invasion of privacy in 1953, the case reached the Supreme Court 14 years later. In 1967, the Supreme Court ruled that if Hill wanted to collect damages from *Time*, he would have to go back to the trial court and begin again. Hill chose to drop the case.

The nine justices are provided with briefs (prepared by their clerks) of a case at hand. Verbal arguments are then held and each side has 30 minutes to present its arguments. In some important cases, additional arguments are heard from *amici curiae* (or friends of the court). The American Civil Liberties Union often seeks *amici curiae* status in civil rights cases.

The attorneys' arguments are carefully planned and may actually be scripted and read verbatim. During the presentations, the justices listen and often interrupt the attorneys to ask questions. Once the arguments have been presented, the justices move into a closed session and discuss the case. This discussion may last several days or may be relatively short.

Once a decision is reached, the justices prepare opinions. If the decision is not unanimous (and it rarely is), one justice who voted in the majority writes the opinion of the Court. If the chief justice has voted with the majority, he may write the opinion or assign it to another justice. If the chief justice did not vote with the majority, the senior associate justice who voted with the majority selects the justice to write the opinion. The opinion of the Court is then circulated among the Court for revision. This process can be time-consuming. The opinion of the landmark school desegregation case *Brown v. Board of Education* circulated for two years before it was released.

The justices who disagree with the majority opinion may draft a dissenting opinion. The dissenting opinion can be extremely important, especially in close cases. It is often the dissenting opinion that will be used as a basis for reversal in later years. Chief Justice Oliver Wendell Holmes' dissenting opinion in 1919 in *Abrams v. United States* served as the basis for clarifying the Clear and Present Danger Doctrine in later cases. This doctrine outlined conditions that justify abridging an individual's First Amendment rights. Similarly, many of Justice Douglas's dissenting opinions were later used as the basis for majority opinions as the makeup and philosophy of the Supreme Court changed during his 36-year tenure.

A third opinion written by justices is the concurring opinion. Some members of the Court may concur with the majority, but disagree with certain aspects of the decision. For example, in 1957 in *Roth v. United States*, the Court agreed that obscenity (in general) should not be afforded protection by the Constitution, but the process by which the decision was reached was disputed. In Roth and subsequent obscenity cases, members of the Court had difficulty applying abstract definitions of "obscene" to actual materials. Therefore, concurring and dissenting opinions were numerous in these cases.

Other Ways of Disposing of a Case

The Supreme Court may also issue a *per curiam* opinion (or a memorandum order). *Per curiam* literally means "by the court" and is an unsigned opinion drafted by the Court as its collective opinion. A memorandum order simply announces a vote, without giving an opinion. The order may cite an earlier Supreme Court decision as the reason for affirming or reversing a lower court ruling. A tie vote means that the lower court's ruling is sustained. It is rare that the Court issues this type of opinion. However, the Court issued a *per curiam* opinion in 1969 in *Brandenburg v. Ohio*, which struck down Ohio's criminal syndicalism law (i.e., teaching the necessity of or attempting to overthrow an existing government by force), and again in 1971 in the famous "Pentagon Papers" case, *New York Times v. United States*.

After the Decision

The Supreme Court is not empowered to make a final judgment. The Court remands the case to the lower court for the final decision. In reality, the Court has no way to enforce a decision. This can only be done by the executive branch. Public opinion, however, helps ensure that lower courts and the executive branch abide by Supreme Court rulings.

The Federal Courts

Article III, Section I of the Constitution states that "the judicial Power of the United States shall be vested in one Supreme Court and in such inferior Courts as the Congress may from time to time ordain and establish." In other words, except for the Supreme Court, Congress creates the federal courts.

Federal courts hear cases dealing with

- Constitutional questions
- Ambassadors and foreign representatives
- Admiralty and maritime law
- Suits against the United States government
- Disputes between states
- Disputes between a state and a citizen of another state
- Disputes between citizens of different states

The bulk of the cases heard in federal courts involve constitutional issues or disputes between citizens of different states. Both types of cases are typical communications law situations. Many times, the case involves First and Sixth Amendment issues. Libel and invasion of privacy suits often involve citizens of different states. For example, a publication with a national circulation may originate in New York and a resident of Texas may feel libeled by material in that publication. The Texas resident would bring suit in a federal court.

Levels of Federal Courts

The lowest level of federal court is the district court. There are district courts in every state and in Guam, Puerto Rico, and the Virgin Islands. Most business in the federal system begins in a district court. These courts are fact-finding courts. When there is a jury trial, it is heard in a district court. District courts also hear cases when juries are not present.

The second level in the federal court system is the court of appeals. These intermediate-level courts are sometimes called circuit courts, a term coined when judges literally rode the circuit from town to town. Now, federal appellate courts are located in major cities such as Chicago, Boston, San Francisco, and Denver. They serve several states in each region, and cases are tried in the city in which the court is located. There are 11 circuit courts spread across the United States. In addition, a federal circuit court, the court of appeals for the District of Columbia, and a temporary emergency court of appeals are all located in Washington, DC.

Appellate courts, as the name implies, are not trial courts. There is no jury and testimony is not taken. A panel of three judges who review rulings that are usually forwarded from district courts that usually hears cases. The Court of Appeals for the District of Columbia also hears appeals from IRAs such as the FCC and the FTC.

At one time, First Amendment cases were heard by a three-judge district court. This court usually consisted of two district court judges and one appellate court judge. However, in 1976 Congress limited these three-judge panels to hearing questions on activities of members of Congress and reapportionment of congressional districts. However, a three-judge panel heard Turner Broadcasting System's challenge to the must-carry provisions of the Cable Consumer Protection Act of 1992.

Federal Judges

All federal judges are appointed by the president and must be confirmed by the Senate. Appointments are for life, but judges can be impeached if their conduct warrants impeachment. Impeachment means that charges are brought against the individual, who must be found guilty to be removed from office. Only ten federal judges have been impeached in the past 200 years, and only five of these judges were removed from office.

The political affiliation of federal judges is an important factor considered by presidents when making appointments. After all, because a seat on the bench lasts a lifetime, the decisions coming from a federal court can steer the legal interpretation of the law for a generation. It goes without saying that Democrats appoint Democrats and Republicans appoint Republicans.

Judicial Review

Judicial review is the right of any court in the United States to declare any law or official government action invalid because it violates a constitutional provision. The concept has its roots in the famous case of *Marbury v. Madison*, in which Chief Justice John Marshall wrote,

> When the Supreme Court concludes that an act of Congress, or an action of the executive, violates the Constitution, the Court can declare either null and void.[2]

Judicial review is very important in the development of the common law. When abridgments of speech or press occur, judicial review often results in the nullification of these abridgments.

The Lawsuit

The Players

To understand the issues that comprise communications law, the student must be familiar with the process of initiating a lawsuit and the legal names used to refer to the participants in the suit. Most communications lawsuits are civil actions, which are the result of a breach of an individual's rights or duties. Unlike criminal actions, which are punishable by a prison sentence, civil suits award monetary damages to those who win the suit.

The party who initiates a civil action is called the *plaintiff*. The person, or corporation, against whom the suit is brought is called the *defendant*. Libel, slander, invasion of privacy, and other First Amendment issues are called *torts*. A tort is a private or civil wrong done against another resulting from a breach of legal duty. In a tort, a plaintiff may allege that the defendant was negligent, intended to inflict emotional distress, or a similar charge. The civil action for a tort is initiated for the sole purpose of compensating the plaintiff for damages suffered. Criminal actions, on the other hand, are concerned with punishing the wrongdoer and, generally, no compensation is offered to the victim.

Initiating a Lawsuit

To initiate a civil suit, the plaintiff chooses the proper court and presents charges against the defendant in the form of a complaint. The court then summons the defendant to answer these charges. If the defendant fails to appear in court at the designated time to respond to the charges, the plaintiff wins by default and the judge awards damages. If the defendant answers the summons, a hearing is scheduled. At the hearing, the plaintiff and defendant prepare a more detailed argument called a *pleading*. At this point, the attorneys may settle out of court. The plaintiff may settle for less money than originally asked, to avoid the cost and stress of a trial. Similarly, the defendant may compromise and the parties may reach an agreeable settlement.

Defendants may also file for *demurrer*, which is a motion to dismiss the complaint on grounds that the actions charged against them were not illegal. For example, defendants charged with invasion of privacy may attempt to convince the court that what they did was legal. Suppose the plaintiffs charge that the defendant took photographs of them without their consent. If the defendant can convince the judge that the photographs were taken while the individuals were on public property, no invasion of privacy occurred. If demurrer is granted, the plaintiff may appeal.

Before the trial begins, the judge may schedule another conference between the two parties in the case. At this time, the issues are focused and a settlement may be reached. If no settlement is reached, the case proceeds to trial.

If the facts in the case are agreed on by the litigants, no jury will be present. A judge hears the case. If the facts are disputed, a jury will be chosen. The selection of jurors varies from state to state, but most states select jurors from voter registration rolls or lists of property owners. The attorneys and the judge question prospective jurors in a process called *voir dire*. During this questioning, the suitability of jurors is determined. Attorneys attempt to expose potentially prejudiced jurors and seek to retain those who will render an impartial verdict, as required by the Sixth Amendment. Students of communications law will discover that the process of seating an impartial jury is sometimes affected by media coverage of crimes. A major communications law issue is the conflict between the First Amendment right of the press to report on judicial proceedings and the defendant's right to a fair trial by an impartial jury.

The Trial

The trial itself is a rigidly structured, formal proceeding. The attorneys begin with opening statements, which are followed by the plaintiff's argument. In the case of criminal trials, the prosecution presents the state's case. Witnesses are called and testimony is taken to establish the factual record. The plaintiff's argument is followed by arguments by the defendant or, in a criminal trial, by the defense.

Once all evidence and testimony has been taken, the attorneys summarize their case in a closing argument. In criminal cases, the first closing argument is made by the counsel for the defense and is followed by the prosecutor's closing argument.

The judge may then offer instructions to the jury regarding inadmissible evidence and other legal criteria that must be considered by members of the jury as they attempt to reach their verdict. The jury then retires to a room where it attempts to reach a verdict. Once a verdict is reached, the jury returns to court and presents its decision to the judge, who informs the litigants.

The attorney for the losing party may file a motion for appeal. If the motion is granted, the case moves to an intermediate-level or appellate court. The judge awards damages in civil suits and pronounces the sentence in criminal cases. Damages are not awarded until all appeals have been exhausted. Consequently, there have been civil cases in which millions of dollars have been "won" by a plaintiff in trial court but actually have never been received, because of reversals during the appeals process. For example, in 1987 singer Wayne Newton won a $22-million judgment against NBC. However, on appeal, the award was reduced and was later reversed entirely.

The Appeals Process

When a case is appealed, the person seeking the appeal is called the *appellant*, while the other party is called the *respondent*. Appellate courts do not have juries. No new testimony is heard and a judge rules only on matters of law. For example, in a libel case, the defendant may appeal the amount of money awarded to the plaintiff. The appellate judge will then decide whether the award is justified, based on the facts established at the trial. A judge might also decide that information collected at the trial was applied incorrectly and that the defendant is not guilty of libel. If this is the case, the lower court decision may then be reversed.

After being heard in an intermediate-level court, the verdict moves to the next higher court of appeals, which might be a state supreme court, state court of appeals, or, in federal cases, the U.S. Supreme Court. It is not uncommon for the higher level court to overturn the intermediate court's decision and return to the verdict reached by the trial court. Another alternative is to vacate all decisions and return the case back to a trial court for retrial.

As previously stated, the end result in a civil suit is the awarding of monetary damages. Sometimes, law guides the amount awarded. For example, copyright law provides damages equal to the money that would have been earned had an infringement of the copyright not occurred. Some states (e.g., Indiana) limit libel awards to only the actual damages suffered as a result of a libel. In other states, the sky is the limit. For the most part, damages in a civil suit are determined by the amount requested by the plaintiff. Of course, judges reserve the right to reduce damage awards if they believe them to be outrageous or excessive.

The Criminal Case

A criminal case is similar to a civil suit, but instead of the plaintiff bringing suit, a prosecutor on behalf of the state brings charges against a defendant. The federal system requires indictment by a *grand jury*. A grand jury is usually comprised of 23 persons, who are summoned by the Justice Department or other appropriate federal agency to investigate a crime. The grand jury conducts hearings to determine if evidence exists to indict an individual with the alleged crime.

Defendants are arraigned after they are charged with a crime. An *arraignment* is a formal reading of the charge, after which the defendant pleads either guilty or not guilty. If the defendant enters a guilty plea, the judge reads the verdict of the court and may set a date for sentencing. If the defendant pleads not guilty, a trial is scheduled. In most criminal cases, except for murder and some other serious crimes, the defendant may post *bail*. This is money given to the court to ensure that the defendant will appear at trial. Bail is refunded when the defendant appears in court. If defendants cannot post bail, which is set by the judge, they remain in jail until the final appeals are over.

At this point, a preliminary hearing is held. The purpose of this hearing is to determine whether there is enough evidence to try the defendant on the charges that have been made. Sometimes, these hearings are called *probable cause hearings*. Probable cause hearings have been particularly troublesome in balancing First and Sixth Amendment rights. The press maintains a right to attend and report on preliminary hearings, which often generate a great deal of attention, especially when the crime under investigation is a sensational murder. At this point, although the trial has not yet begun, there are often reports of damaging testimony being made against the defendant. Some of this testimony may not be admissible in trial court, but it finds its way into newspapers and news broadcasts. This event is especially problematic, since a jury may have been exposed to biased pretrial publicity.

Judges may choose to grant a *change of venue*, which moves the trial to a location away from where the crime was committed, so that an impartial jury can be picked from a populace less likely to have been influenced by pretrial publicity. The judge may also grant a *continuance*, which postpones the date of the trial in the hopes that impartial jurors will be found more easily. Following the trial, a convicted defendant may appeal the verdict.

How Cases Are Named

The name of the party initiating the lawsuit is listed first in the name of a case. For example, if Doe libels Jones and Jones files suit in 1999, the case goes to court with the name *Jones v. Doe (1999)*. The date follows the name of the case to clarify to which *Jones v. Doe* case a reference is being made. Jones is the plaintiff and Doe the defendant.

Suppose Doe is found guilty of libel and appeals the case. Doe is now the appellant and Jones is the respondent. If the case goes to appellate court a year later, it is named *Doe v. Jones (2000)*. If Doe wins his appeal and Jones is lucky enough to have the case heard by the Supreme Court, the case might bear the name *Jones v. Doe* again, but the date will distinguish it from the earlier case.

Interpreting Legal Citations

When discovering the common law, judges and lawyers must look to previous cases. Students of communications law must also know where to find important cases and statutes. Cases decided by the U.S. Supreme Court are fairly easy to locate by using a case reporter called the *United States Reports* or the *Supreme Court Reporter*. These multivolume works report the entire text of cases in chronological order. Each case is identified by a citation. For example, the famous libel case, *New York Times v. Sullivan*, is cited as 376 U.S. 254 (1964). This means that the text of the decision appears in volume 376 of *United States Reports*, on page 254. The case was decided in 1964.

Other case reporters use similar methods of presenting citations. Probably the most valuable case reporter for communications law students is the *Media Law Reporter*. This loose-leaf publication provides text and summaries for all cases related to media law. Cases are indexed by subject, name, and the court that decided the case. For example, the *Media Law Reporter* cites General William Westmoreland's appeal of his libel case against CBS as *Westmoreland v. CBS (CA 2, 1984) 11 Med.L.Rptr. 1013*. The citation includes the case title, followed (in parentheses) by the court in which the case was decided, and the date of the decision. In this case, "CA 2" means the U.S. Court of Appeals for the Second Circuit. The abbreviation "U.S.Sup.Ct" means U.S. Supreme Court, and so on. Next, the volume number is noted in the citation, which in this case is 11, and is followed by the abbreviation for the reporter and the page on which the case begins. Again, other case reporters follow a similar format when citing cases.

Statutes are found in code books. All federal statutes are indexed in the *United States Code*. Rules and regulations of the IRAs are published in the *Code of Federal Regulations*. State statutes are found in state code books.

Major decisions and actions of the FCC are found in the Commission's official publications, and by searching the FCC Website. All material printed before 1986 is contained in *FCC Reports*. The name was changed in 1986 to *FCC Record*. FCC citations named before October 1986 are referred to by volume number, F.C.C., or F.C.C.2d. *FCC Record* cites by volume number, F.C.C.Rcd., and the page number. Actions proposed by the Commission appear in the *Federal Register*.

Another useful source of FCC decisions is *Pike and Fisher's Broadcast Regulation* and *Pike and Fisher's Cable Television Regulation*. These publications are available online by subscription or are available on CD-ROM. They cover all activities and cases affecting radio, television, and cable communications.

Other Information Online

There are numerous sites and services online and on the World Wide Web that can assist you in finding legal information. Students should exercise caution when conducting research online to ensure that the source is credible. The Website companion to this book, http://www. kencreech.com, offers some suggested online legal research tools.

Summary

The basis of American law was imported from England to the colonies. There are five sources of the law in America: the common law, equity law, statutory law, administrative law, and constitutional law. The Constitution is the supreme law of the land, and no law that violates its provisions can be enforced.

The judicial branch of the government, which includes the Supreme Court created by the Constitution and other federal courts created by Congress, interprets laws in America. State and local governments also provide lower courts.

Most communications law deals with civil cases (i.e., wrongs against private individuals, rather than against the state). Wrongs against the state are tried as criminal cases.

Notes/References

1. Oliver W. Holmes, *The Common Law* (Boston: Little, Brown, 1881), 1.
2. *Marbury v. Madison*, 1 Cranch 137, 2 L.Ed. 60 (1803).

Cases

Abrams v. United States, 250 U.S. 616 (1919)
Brandenburg v. Ohio, 395 U.S. 444 (1969)
Brown v. Board of Education, 347 U.S. 483 (1954)
Marbury v. Madison, 1 Cranch 137, 2 L.Ed. 60 (1803)
Newton v. National Broadcasting Co. (DC Nev, 1987) 114 Med.L.Rptr. 1914
New York Times v. United States, 403 U.S. 713 (1971)
Roth v. United States 354 U.S. 476 (1957)

2

□ □ □
□ □ □
□ □ □

Interpreting the First Amendment

History of Free Speech in America

The English Heritage

The development of the law of free speech and press in the United States, like most American law, has its roots in England. The British model was imported to the colonies and included a tradition that supports punishment for the publication of seditious libel. Prohibition against seditious libel began in 1275 with the enactment of *De Scandalis Magnatum*, which provided for imprisonment of anyone who disseminated false statements about the king that caused discord between the king and his subjects.

The statute of *De Scandalis Magnatum*, as eventually administered by the infamous Star Chamber, was responsible for the evolution of English censorship and seditious libel law. The original Star Chamber was part of the king's council, which sat in a chamber of stars (or *camera stellata*) at Westminster and was first called the Star Chamber during the reign of King Edward III in the fourteenth century. In 1585, the Star Chamber passed an ordinance that required all publications to be licensed and printed by the Star Chamber-sanctioned Stationer's Company. The Star Chamber controlled all printing and publishing in England until it was abolished by the Long Parliament in 1641. During this time, the Star Chamber meted out punishments to violators as it saw fit. In one case, an author who expressed a dislike for acting and actors was fined £10,000, given a sentence of life in prison, branded on his forehead, and had his nose slit and his ears cut off. The Star Chamber viewed the criticism of actors as an insult against the queen (and hence the government) because she had recently taken part in a play.[1]

Although the Star Chamber ceased to exist in 1641, the English Parliament continued to harass printers and publishers through the Stationer's Company and other forms of licensing. No work could be printed legally without the approval of the stationers, who issued licenses. The stationers served as absolute censors and refused to allow publication of material deemed offensive to them. It should be noted that this concept of censorship is not limited to archaic or authoritarian governments. In spite of the First Amendment, censorship of this kind can be found as late as the 1960s in the United States. Some American cities had film-licensing boards that screened motion pictures to determine their suitability for exhibition. Many of these licensing boards exercised capricious judgment and refused to grant exhibition licenses for a variety of reasons. For example, the one-person licensing board in Memphis, Tennessee, refused to allow theaters in that city to show Ingrid Bergman films, noting that her "soul was as black as the soot of hell."[2] The censor found Miss Bergman's bearing of a child out of wedlock to be morally reprehensible.

Under the British Licensing Acts of the colonial period, authors and printers of "obnoxious works" were hanged, quartered, mutilated, or simply fined and imprisoned "according to the temper of the judges."[3] It was in protest of this licensing act that John Milton wrote the famous *Areopagitica* in 1644. Milton's call for a free press in England is important to Americans, because his reasoning served as the philosophical basis for the marketplace-of-ideas theory of First Amendment interpretation. Milton wrote,

> And though all the winds of doctrine were let loose to play upon the earth, so Truth be in the field, we do injuriously by licensing and prohibiting to misdoubt her strength. Let her and Falsehood grapple; whoever knew Truth put to the worse, in a free and open encounter?[4]

The sentiments expressed by Milton in the seventeenth century found their way into American law 275 years later in the dissenting opinion of Justice Oliver Wendell Holmes in *Abrams v. United States*. In Holmes's view, truth is best attained when all ideas are free to compete in the market-place for acceptance. Therefore, any restraints by government tend to obscure the search for truth.

The English Licensing Acts were renewed in 1662, 1685, and again in 1692. Essentially, the acts forbade all printing without a license and gave the king's agents the authority to search all houses and shops in which they suspected unlicensed books were being printed and to seize them.

When the licensing acts expired in 1695, they were not renewed by the British Parliament. Although this signaled the end of press censorship in England, printers were by no means free to publish material that might be deemed seditious or treasonable. Nevertheless, newspapers began to flourish and the press became an outlet for political expression. Because this expression was often critical of those in power, the governing bodies sought new ways to silence the press. A return to licensing was proposed, but rejected. Instead, Parliament adopted a less direct form of censorship when it passed the Stamp Act in 1712.

The Stamp Act was designed to eliminate the small newspapers that published the kind of material most disturbing to the government. The Stamp Act placed a stiff tax on newspapers, pamphlets, advertising, and paper. The act required that publications be registered with the government, which made it easier for those in power to control the dissemination of information. This means of controlling printed material in England continued until 1855.

Punishment for seditious libel continued as common law throughout the eighteenth and the first half of the nineteenth centuries. Publishers were punished for criticizing foreign policy, the conduct of the king, or any other public official. This criticism was thought to weaken the authority of the government. The truth or falsity of the publication was immaterial. Although Fox's Libel Act of 1792 allowed a jury to acquit a publisher charged with sedition if it thought the publication was not seditious, it was not until 1843, with the passage of Lord Campbell's act, that the modern concept of freedom of the press began to formulate. This act made truth a defense in libel claims. This defense was already legal in America at the time. Twelve years later, the Stamp Act was repealed and freedom of the press was realized in England.

The American Experience

The issues of free speech and press in America essentially paralleled developments in England, but moved much more quickly. Licensing in the colonies followed the same pattern as in England. In 1662, Massachusetts appointed two licensers, without whose permission nothing could be printed. In 1664, the colony passed a law that established Cambridge as the only legal site for printing presses, which were regulated by the licensers.

The *Boston News Letter*, which was published between 1704 and 1776, carried the phrase "Published by Authority" under its nameplate. This meant that the paper contained stories approved by the colonial governor. Licensing was also the rule in Pennsylvania and Virginia, where even the laws of the colony could not be printed without a license. Between 1639 and 1776, numerous publishers and editors were prosecuted in the colonies on charges ranging from criticism of religious doctrines to seditious libel. One of the most celebrated trials was that of John Peter Zenger in New York.

Zenger was the printer of the *New York Weekly Journal*, a newspaper devoted to the opposition of controversial New York Governor William Cosby. The *Journal* was the first independent political paper published in America. Oddly enough, although the editor of the paper, James Alexander, wrote most of the material critical of the governor, Zenger (the printer) was jailed for seditious libel. Zenger was charged with printing

... false news and seditious libels, both wickedly and maliciously devising the administration of His Excellency William Cosby, Captain General and Governor in Chief to traduce, scandalize and vilify both His Excellency the Governor and the ministers and officers of the king and to bring them into suspicion and the ill opinion of the subjects of the king residing within the Province. . . .[5]

The *New York Weekly Journal* had been published for about six months before Zenger's arrest. Among the items the governor found objectionable is the following passage:

We see men's deeds destroyed, judges arbitrarily displaced, new courts created without consent of the legislature by which it seems to me trial by jury is taken away when a Governor pleases, and men of known estates denied their votes contrary of the received practice, the best expositor of any law. Who is there then in that Province that can call anything his own, or enjoy any liberty, longer than those in the administration will condescend to let them do it?[6]

Andrew Hamilton, a Quaker lawyer from Philadelphia, defended Zenger. In a surprising move, Hamilton admitted that Zenger had published the materials, but in an eloquent argument to the jury, he asserted that the statements about the governor were true. At this time, truth was not a defense in libel cases; however, so inspiring was Hamilton's argument that the jury returned a verdict of "not guilty."

The *Zenger* case helped widen the growing gap between England and the American colonies, it set a precedent that allowed criticism of colonial governors and other authorities. As Vincent Buranelli points out in his book, *The Trial of Peter Zenger*, no longer could one say that resistance to crown officials was always wrong.[7] America had begun to clear a path leading toward her own legal system.

In reality, the impact of *Zenger* had a more immediate effect on Britain. By 1738, accounts of Andrew Hamilton's address to the jury were apparently gaining much attention in the legal community. The major principles of the case—truth as a defense in libel actions and the jury has the right to decide both "fact" and "law"—became law in Britain in 1792 with the Fox Libel Act. America responded with a federal statute in 1798.

Another major influence on the development of American legal philosophy was the English legal authority William Blackstone. Blackstone's *Commentaries on the Laws of England* was widely read by students and barristers alike in England and in the colonies. Although dismissed by some as elementary, Blackstone's view of liberty of the press served as a benchmark for courts in Britain and America. Blackstone wrote,

The liberty of the press is indeed essential to the nature of a free State, but this consists in laying no previous restraints upon publications, and not in freedom from censure for criminal matter when published. Every free man has an undoubted right to lay what sentiments he pleases before the public: to forbid this, is to destroy the freedom of the press: but if he publishes what is improper, mischievous, or illegal, he must take the consequence of his own temerity. To subject the press to the restrictive power of a licenser, as was formerly done . . . is to subject all freedom of sentiment to the prejudices of one man, and make him the arbitrary and infallible judge of all controverted points in learning, religion, and government. But to punish . . . any dangerous or offensive writings, which, when published, shall on a fair and impartial trial be adjudged of a pernicious tendency, is necessary for the preservation of peace and good order, of government and religion, the only solid foundations of civil liberty. Thus the will of individuals is still left free; the abuse only of that free will is the object of legal punishment.[8]

Blackstone wrote these words in 1769, but they are actually a fairly accurate reflection of twentieth-century American interpretations of the First Amendment. In fact, the Supreme Court relied on Blackstone's concept of no "previous restraint" in the 1931 landmark case *Near v. Minnesota*. In *Near*, the Court ruled that prior or previous restraints on the press violate the First Amendment in most cases. Blackstone also espoused what would later evolve into the Clear and Present Danger Doctrine, when he noted that free speech is not protected when the "peace and good order" are threatened.

In 1791, the states ratified the first ten amendments to the new U.S. Constitution. The First Amendment forbade Congress from making laws that would abridge freedom of religion, speech, and the press. Although written in absolute terms, the First Amendment has never been interpreted by the Supreme Court to mean that individuals have the right to say anything they please, any way they please, anywhere or under any circumstances. In fact, Congress was quick to limit freedom of speech and freedom of the press in the new nation when it passed the Sedition Act of 1798.

The Sedition Act provided punishment for the publication of false, scandalous, and malicious writings against the government, either house of Congress, or the president, if the writings were published with the intent to defame any of these groups or incite the people to rebellion. A companion law, the Alien Act, allowed the president to deport any alien judged dangerous to the security of the United States. The impact of *Zenger* and England's Fox Libel Act were felt, however, because there was precedent for using truth as a defense, and the jury was empowered to determine criminality. This defense was strengthened after the expiration of the Alien and Sedition Acts during the presidency of Thomas Jefferson. Ironically, the defense of truth was used by the editor of a newspaper charged with libeling Jefferson. In another unusual twist, Alexander Hamilton, who generally opposed the First Amendment, argued brilliantly in favor of press freedoms in the case against his adversary, Thomas Jefferson.

The Sedition Act expired in March 1801 and was not renewed. Except for Lincoln's unofficial suppression of critics of his policies during the Civil War, there was no major government action raising free speech issues until the First World War.

The First Amendment in the Twentieth Century

When America entered World War I, Congress passed the Espionage Act of 1917. The Espionage Act was designed to protect against spying by foreign countries and to protect military secrets. The act was amended in 1918 to include what is commonly called the Sedition Act (not to be confused with the Sedition Act of 1798). This amendment dealt more with advocacy, speaking, teaching, printing, and inciting than did the original act. Although the Sedition Act was repealed in 1921, the Espionage Act remained in force into the 1940s.

These especially harsh restraints on press and speech freedoms were the result of internal suspicions during the war with Germany (the number of Americans with a German heritage led some to question their loyalty), the controversy generated over conscription of troops, and the growing threat of Bolshevism. During this time, more than 1900 people were prosecuted for alleged subversion and criticism of the national government.

Why was the suppression of First Amendment freedoms tolerated during this time? Legal scholar Zechariah Chafee writes that it may have been because many Americans viewed the freedoms guaranteed by the Founding Fathers as no more than abstract doctrine.

> The First Amendment had no hold on people's minds because no live facts or concrete images were then attached to it. Like an empty box with beautiful words on it, the Amendment collapsed under the impact of terror of Prussian battalions and terror of Bolshevik mobs. So the emotions generated by the two simultaneous cataclysms of war and revolution swept unchecked through American prosecutors, judges, jurymen, and legislators.[9]

It was during this tumultuous time that the initial First Amendment cases reached the Supreme Court. It was also during this time that the first serious interpretations of the meaning of the First Amendment were attempted. With the development of case law, the First Amendment took on a new character—that of living law. No longer was the First Amendment an ethereal concept untouched by the courts of the land. In *Schenck v. United States*, the Court began the arduous task of shaping concrete images from abstract doctrine.

The Clear and Present Danger Test

Schenck was the first and most influential case dealing with significant First Amendment issues to come before the Supreme Court. In this case, Justice Holmes formulated the "clear and present danger" test for determining when an individual's First Amendment rights may be abridged. Schenck had been charged with violating the Espionage Act of 1917, because he distributed leaflets that urged men not to register for the draft during World War I. Justice Holmes delivered the following opinion of the Court:

Schenck v. United States (1919)

☐   This is an indictment in three counts. The first charges a conspiracy to violate the Espionage Act of June 15, 1917 . . . by causing and attempting to cause insubordination &c., in the military and naval forces of the United States, and to obstruct the recruiting and enlistment service of the United States, when the United States was at war with the German Empire, to wit, that the defendants willfully conspired to have printed and circulated to men who had been called and accepted for military service . . . a document set forth and alleged to be calculated to cause such insubordination and obstruction. The count alleges overt acts in pursuance of the conspiracy, ending in the distribution of the document set forth. The second count alleges a conspiracy to commit an offence against the United States, to wit, to use the mails for the transmission of matter declared to be non-mailable by title 12, section 2, of the Act of June 15, 1917. . . . The document in question upon its first printed side recited the first section of the Thirteenth Amendment said that the idea embodied in it was violated by the Conscription Act and that a conscript is little better than a convict. In impassioned language it intimated that conscription was despotism in its worst form and a monstrous wrong against humanity in the interest of Wall Street's chosen few. It said "Do not submit to intimidation," but in form at least confined itself to peaceful measures such as a petition for repeal of the act. The other and later printed side of the sheet was headed "Assert Your Rights." It stated reasons for alleging that any one violated the Constitution when he refused to recognize "your right to assert your opposition to the draft," and went on "If you do not assert and support your rights, you are helping to deny or disparage rights which it is the solemn duty of all citizens and residents of the United States to retain." It described the arguments on the other side as coming from cunning politicians and a mercenary capitalist press, and even silent consent to the conscription law as helping to support an infamous conspiracy. It denied the power to send our citizens away to foreign shores to shoot up people of other lands, and added that words could not express the condemnation such cold-blooded ruthlessness deserves . . . winding up "You must do your share to maintain, support and uphold the rights of the people of this country."

Of course the document would not have been sent unless it had been intended to have some effect, and we do not see what effect it could be expected to have upon persons subject to the draft except to influence them to obstruct the carrying of it out. The defendants do not deny that the jury might find against them on this point.

But it is said, suppose that was the tendency of this circular, it is protected by the First Amendment to the Constitution. Two of the strongest expressions are said to be quoted respectively from well-known public men. . . . We admit that in many places and in ordinary times the defendants in saying all that was said in the circular would have been within their constitutional rights. But the character of every act depends on the circumstances in which it is done. . . . The most stringent protection of free speech would not protect a man in falsely shouting fire in a theatre and causing a panic. It does not even protect a man from an injunction against uttering words that may have all the effect of force. . . . The question in every case is whether the words used are used in such circumstances and are of such a nature as to create a *clear and present danger* that they will bring about the substantive evils that Congress has a right to prevent. [Emphasis added by the author.] . . . When a nation is at war many things that might be said in time of peace are such a hindrance to its effort that their utterance will not be endured so long as men fight and that no Court could regard them as protected by any constitutional right. It seems to be admitted that if an actual obstruction of the recruiting service were proved, liability for words that produced that effect might be enforced.[10]

Schenk was found guilty of violating the Espionage Act. Justice Holmes articulated the Clear and Present Danger Doctrine as a means of setting the limits of First Amendment rights. In essence, speech could be punished if the utterance of words might bring about "evils that Congress has a right to prevent." The interpretation of "clear and present danger" was still not absolutely clear. In fact, Justice Holmes found himself on the dissenting side of a similar case shortly after Schenck. Holmes disagreed with the majority of the Court's application of the doctrine in *Abrams v. United States*. Abrams and four other Russian-born aliens living in the United States were convicted of violating the Espionage Act. These self-admitted revolutionists were critical of President Wilson's policies and called for the "workers of the world" to rise and put down capitalism. The Supreme Court saw this call as a clear and present danger intended to incite an uprising against the government of the United States. Justice Holmes disagreed.

Abrams v. United States (1919)
Mr. Justice Holmes dissenting:

☐   This indictment is founded wholly upon the publication of two leaflets.

      . . . The first of these leaflets says that the President's cowardly silence about the intervention in Russia reveals the hypocrisy of the plutocratic gang in Washington.

      . . . The other leaflet, headed "Workers—Wake Up," with abusive language says that America together with the Allies will march for Russia to help the Czecko-Slovaks [sic] in their struggle against the Bolsheviki, and that this time the hypocrites shall not tool the Russian emigrants and friends of Russia in America. It tells the Russian emigrants that they must now spit in the face of the false military propaganda . . . and further, "Workers in the ammunition factories, you are producing bullets, bayonets, cannon to murder not only Germans, but also your dearest, best, who are in Russia fighting for freedom." It then appeals to the same Russian emigrants at some length not to consent to the "inquisitionary expedition in Russia." The leaflet winds up by saying "Workers, our reply to this barbaric intervention has to be a general strike! . . . Woe unto those who will be in the way of progress.

      Let solidarity live! [signed] The Rebels."

      No argument seems to be necessary to show that these pronouncioamentos in no way attack the form of government of the United States. . . .

      I do not doubt for a moment . . . the United States constitutionally may punish speech that produces or is intended to produce a clear and imminent danger . . . The power undoubtedly is greater in time of war than in time of peace because war opens dangers that do not exist at other times.

      But as against dangers peculiar to war, as against others, the principle of the right of free speech is always the same. It is only the present danger of immediate evil or an intent to bring it about that warrants Congress in setting a limit to the expression of opinion where private rights are concerned. Congress certainly cannot forbid all effort to change the mind of the country.[11]

Holmes applied the marketplace of ideas concept in *Abrams*. Borrowing from Milton's *Areopagitica* and nineteenth-century philosopher John Stuart Mill's essay *On Liberty*, Holmes wrote,

☐ the best test of truth is the power of the thought to get itself accepted in the competition of the market, and that truth is the only ground upon which their wishes can be safely carried out.[12]

The marketplace-of-ideas theory assumes that all ideas, regardless of how loathsome they may be, should be heard. While Milton might assume that truth will triumph over falsity and that "good" will prevail over "evil," neither Mill nor Holmes are so naive. Both accept the fact that truth may not triumph, but in the words of Mill,

... [T]he peculiar evil of silencing the expression of an opinion is, that it is robbing the human race; posterity as well as the existing generation; those who dissent from the opinion, still more than those who hold it.[13]

In Holmes's view, the only time government should intervene in the process is when these opinions

☐ imminently threaten immediate interference with the lawful and pressing purposes of the law that an immediate check is required to save the country.[14]

Applying the First Amendment to the States

Six years after *Abrams*, the Supreme Court decided *Gitlow v. People of State of New York*. In *Gitlow*, the Court upheld the conviction of Benjamin Gitlow for violating the New York Criminal Anarchy Statute. Although a majority of the Court found New York's law to be reasonable, even the dissenters, Holmes and Brandeis, agreed on the principle that the First Amendment was binding on the states through the Fourteenth Amendment. They disagreed as to how it should be applied.

Gitlow v. People of State of New York (1925)
Justice Sanford delivered the opinion of the Court:

☐ ... For present purposes we may and do assume that freedom of speech and of the press—which are protected by the First Amendment from abridgement by Congress—are among the fundamental personal rights and "liberties" protected by the due process clause of the Fourteenth Amendment from impairment by the States.[15]

Justice Holmes, dissenting, wrote,

☐ Justice Brandeis and I are of the opinion that this judgement should be reversed. The general principle of free speech, it seems to me, must be taken to be included in the Fourteenth Amendment, in view of the scope that has been given to the word "liberty" as there used.[16]

The Balancing Test

Sometimes the courts must balance First Amendment interests against conflicting social and personal interests. In these situations, the court must determine which interest should receive the greater protection. The balancing test was articulated by the Supreme Court in *American Communications Association v. Douds*.

The Fighting Words Doctrine

Although the Clear and Present Danger Doctrine and the balancing test offer methods of adjudicating First Amendment disputes, they are by no means the only methods employed by the courts. Different First Amendment conflicts require different solutions. Therefore, the common sense approach of what was to become the Fighting Words Doctrine evolved in the 1940s. The Fighting Words Doctrine says that words directed at an average person that may provoke a fight are not protected by the First Amendment. The rationale is that a breach of the peace should be avoided over the protection of an individual's right to utter hostile words. The Fighting Words Doctrine stems from *Chaplinsky v. New Hampshire*, a case that involved a Jehovah's Witness and his activities on a street corner in Rochester, New Hampshire.

Chaplinsky v. New Hampshire (1942)

☐ . . . Chaplinsky was distributing the literature of his sect on the streets of Rochester on a busy afternoon. Members of the local citizenry complained to the City Marshal . . . that Chaplinsky was denouncing all religion as a "racket." The Marshal told them that Chaplinsky was lawfully engaged and warned Chaplinsky that the crowd was getting restless. . . .
Chaplinsky made the following remarks to the Marshal outside City Hall: "You are a God-damned racketeer and a damned Fascist and the whole government of Rochester are Fascists or agents of Fascists."

Chaplinsky . . . asked the Marshal to arrest those responsible for the disturbance. But the Marshal, according to Chaplinsky, instead cursed him and told Chaplinsky to come along with him. Chaplinsky was prosecuted under a New Hampshire statute, part of which forbade "addressing any offensive, derisive or annoying word to any other person who is lawfully in any street or other public place."

. . . The statute, as construed, does no more than prohibit the face-to-face words plainly likely to cause a breach of the peace by the speaker—including "classical fighting words," words in current use less "classical" but equally likely to cause violence, and other disorderly words, including profanity, obscenity and . . . argument is unnecessary to demonstrate that the appellations "damned racketeer" and "damned Fascist" are epithets likely to provoke the average person to retaliation and thereby cause a breach of the peace.[17]

In the years following *Chaplinsky*, the Fighting Words Doctrine was seriously weakened. Many state laws were struck down on the grounds that they were overbroad—and that, as constructed, they not only prohibited fighting words but other expression as well. In *Gooding v. Wilson*, a Georgia statute prohibiting the use of "opprobrious words or abusive language tending to breach the peace" was struck down as unconstitutionally vague and overbroad under the First and Fourteenth Amendments.[18]

Citing *Chaplinsky*, the Supreme Court defined "fighting words" as those having a "direct tendency to cause acts of violence by the person to whom, individually, the remark is addressed."[19] This means that the doctrine is not applied when groups of people are provoked.

In *Lewis v. City of New Orleans*, the Court also struck down a New Orleans ordinance making it unlawful to "curse or revile or to use obscene or opprobrious language toward or with reference to" a police officer on duty.[20] The New Orleans ordinance was found to have a "broader sweep" than the constitutional definition of fighting words.

Offensive or indecent words, in and of themselves, are not necessarily fighting words. When Paul Robert Cohen walked into the Los Angeles County Courthouse in April of 1968 wearing a jacket with "Fuck the Draft" printed on it, he was arrested for disturbing the peace. Even though he made no physical disturbance, he was convicted on the grounds that the writing on his jacket might provoke others to acts of violence. In *Cohen v. California*, the Supreme Court overturned his conviction and stated that the four-letter word displayed by Cohen in relation to the draft was not directed to any one person.

☐ . . . No individual actually or likely to be present could reasonably have regarded the words on the appellant's jacket as a direct personal insult. . . . There is . . . no showing that anyone who saw Cohen was in fact violently aroused or that the appellant intended such a result.[21]

The display was protected by the First Amendment, as it was Cohen's opinion of the Vietnam War and the draft.

In 1977, the American Nazi Party was denied a parade permit by village officials in Skokie, Illinois, because they feared that the sight of such Nazi symbols as the swastika might trigger violence and trauma based on the vulnerability of Holocaust survivors to symbolic reminders of past persecution. In April 1977, an injunction prohibiting the Nazi demonstration was obtained, and in the following weeks three ordinances were passed that required permits for which the American Nazis could not qualify. The Nazis obtained the assistance of the American Civil Liberties Union and filed suit against the town on the grounds that the ordinances violated the First Amendment. After a lengthy struggle in the courts in *Village of Skokie v. National Socialist Party*, the Nazis finally won the right to demonstrate.

Village of Skokie v. National Socialist Party (1978)

☐   Plaintiff urges and the appellate court has held, that the exhibition of the Nazi symbol, the swastika, addresses to ordinary citizens a message which is tantamount to fighting words. Plaintiff further asks this court to extend Chaplinsky, which upheld a statute punishing the use of such words, and hold that the fighting-words doctrine permits a prior restraint on defendant's symbolic speech. In our judgement we are precluded from doing so. . . .

. . . The display of the swastika, as offensive to the principles of a free nation as the memories it recalls may be, is symbolic political speech intended to convey to the public the beliefs of those who display it. It does not, in our opinion, fall within the definition of "fighting words" and that doctrine cannot be used here to overcome the heavy presumption against the constitutional validity of a prior restraint. . . . We do not doubt that the sight of this symbol is abhorrent to the Jewish citizens of Skokie, and that the survivors of the Nazi persecutions, tormented by their recollections, may have strong feelings regarding their display. . . . In summary, as we read the controlling Supreme Court opinions, use of the swastika is a symbolic form of free speech entitled to First Amendment protections. Its display on uniforms or banners by those engaged in peaceful demonstrations cannot be totally precluded because that display may provoke a violent reaction by those who view it. Particularly . . . where . . . there has been advance notice by the demonstrators of their plans so that they have become common knowledge and those to whom sight of the swastika banner or uniforms would be offensive are forewarned and need not view them. A speaker who gives prior notice of his message has not compelled a confrontation with those who voluntarily listen.[22]

Although they won a legal victory, the Nazis eventually cancelled their plan to march in Skokie. According to Professor Donald Downs, Frank Collin, the leader of the National Socialist Party, decided against the march because he knew his group would make easy targets for counter demonstrators.

Probably no case involving the First Amendment so tests the fabric of the marketplace of ideas theory as does the *Skokie* case. The parameters of the conflict give new life to Justice Douglas' resurrection of the concept in his dissent in *Dennis v. United States:*

☐ Full and free discussion even of ideas we hate encourages the testing of
our own prejudices and preconceptions. Full and free discussion keeps a
society from becoming stagnant and unprepared for the stresses and
strains that work to tear all civilizations apart.[23]

Hate Speech

In a further refinement of the Fighting Words Doctrine, in 1992
the U.S. Supreme Court struck down a Minnesota law prohibiting "hate
speech." Essentially, the ruling prohibits government from silencing speech
on the basis of its content alone. In *R.A.V v. City of St. Paul Minn., 112 S.Ct
2538 (1992)* the court struck down a Minnesota law that prohibited the
display of a symbol that one knows or has reason to know "arouses anger,
alarm or resentment in others on the basis of race, color, creed, religion
or gender." The court found the law unconstitutional because it imposed
special prohibitions on the speaker. In other words, the law held that one
could argue in favor of racial tolerance, but not against it. Minnesota's "hate
speech" law had the effect of favoring "politically correct" fighting words
over all others, and therefore violated the First Amendment.

Speech and Action

Courts have experienced difficulty in cases involving both
verbal and nonverbal elements. When David Paul O'Brien burned his draft
card on the steps of the South Boston Courthouse (1966), he said he did so in
protest of the war in Vietnam. Although draft card mutilation was a violation
of the Military Training and Service Act of 1948, O'Brien maintained that the
draft card burning was "symbolic speech" and was therefore protected by the
First Amendment. In *United States v. O'Brien (1968)*, the Supreme Court disagreed. Justice Warren wrote,

☐ This Court has held that when "speech" and "nonspeech" elements
are combined in the same course of conduct, a sufficiently important
governmental interest in regulating the nonspeech element can justify
incidental limitations on First Amendment freedoms. . . . The many
functions performed by Selective Service certificates establish beyond
doubt that Congress has a legitimate interest in preventing their wanton
and unrestrained destruction and continuing their availability by
punishing people who knowingly and willfully destroy or mutilate them.[24]

O'Brien could have burned "symbolic" draft cards, but not the real item.

The Supreme Court reached a different decision one year later. Students
in Des Moines wore black armbands to school to protest the Vietnam War.

The Des Moines school system had specifically prohibited the wearing of armbands. Seven of the 18,000 students enrolled in the system wore armbands and no disruption of school operations occurred. In *Tinker v. Des Moines Independent School District*, the Court held that the wearing of armbands was a "symbolic act" protected by the First Amendment.

Twenty years later, a badly divided Supreme Court (5 to 4) ruled that burning the American flag may be symbolic speech. In *Texas v. Johnson*, Justice Brennan delivered the opinion of the Court:

Texas v. Johnson (1989)

☐ . . . While the Republican National Convention was taking place in Dallas in 1984, respondent Johnson participated in a political demonstration. . . . the purpose of this event was to protest the policies of the Reagan administration and of certain Dallas-based corporations. The demonstrators marched through the Dallas streets, chanting political slogans and stopping at several corporate locations to stage "die-ins" intended to dramatize the consequences of nuclear war. . . . [Johnson] . . . did . . . accept an American flag handed him by a fellow protestor who had taken it from a flag pole outside one of the targeted buildings.

The demonstration ended in front of Dallas City Hall, where Johnson unfurled the American flag, doused it with kerosene, and set it on fire. While the flag burned, the protestors chanted, "America the red, white and blue, we spit on you." After the demonstrators dispersed, a witness to the flag burning collected the flag's remains and buried them in his backyard.

Of the approximately 100 demonstrators, Johnson alone was charged with a crime. The only criminal offense with which he was charged was the desecration of a venerated object in violation of Tex. Penal Code. . . . After a trial, he was convicted, sentenced to one year in prison, and fined $2000. The Court of Appeals for the Fifth District of Texas at Dallas affirmed Johnson's conviction, but the Texas Court of Criminal Appeals reversed . . .

Johnson was convicted of flag desecration for burning the flag rather than for uttering insulting words. This fact somewhat complicates our consideration of his conviction under the First Amendment. . . .

Texas conceded that Johnson's conduct was expressive conduct. Johnson burned an American flag as part—indeed, as the culmination—of a political demonstration that coincided with the convening of the Republican Party and its re-nomination of Ronald Reagan for President. The expressive, overtly political nature of this conduct was both intentional and overwhelmingly apparent. . . .

Texas claims that its interest in preventing breaches of the peace justifies Johnson's conviction for flag desecration. However, no disturbance of the peace actually occurred or threatened to occur because of Johnson's burning of the flag. . . . The State's position, therefore, amounts to a claim that an audience that takes serious offense at particular expression is necessarily likely to disturb the peace and that the expression may be prohibited on this basis. Our precedents do not countenance such a presumption. On the contrary, they recognize that a principal "function of free speech under our system of government is to invite dispute." . . .

Nor does Johnson's expressive conduct fall within that small class of "fighting words" that are "likely to provoke the average person to retaliation, and thereby cause a breach of the peace." *Chaplinsky v. New Hampshire 315 U.S. 568 (1942)* . . .

The State also asserts an interest in preserving the flag as a symbol of nationhood and national unity. . . . If there is a bedrock principle underlying the First Amendment, it is that the Government may not prohibit the expression of an idea simply because society finds the idea itself offensive or disagreeable.

We have not recognized an exception to this principle even where our flag has been involved. . . . In short, nothing in our precedents suggests that a State may foster its own view of the flag by prohibiting expressive conduct relating to it. . . .

To conclude that the Government may permit designated symbols to be used to communicate only a limited set of messages would be to enter territory having no discernible or defensible boundaries. Could the Government, on this theory, prohibit the burning of state flags? Of copies of the Presidential seal? Of the Constitution? In evaluating these choices under the First Amendment, how could we decide which symbols were sufficiently special to warrant this unique status? To do so, we would be forced to consult our own political preferences, and impose them on the citizenry, in the very way that the First Amendment forbids us to do so.

There is, moreover, no indication—either in the text of the Constitution or in our cases interpreting it—that a separate judicial category exists for the American flag alone. . . .

We are fortified in today's conclusion by our conviction that forbidding criminal punishment for conduct such as Johnson's will not endanger the special role played by our flag or the feelings it inspires.

. . . The way to preserve the flag's special role is not to punish those who feel differently about these matters. It is to persuade them that they are wrong[25] . . .

In October 1989, President George H. W. Bush signed into law the *Flag Protection Act*. This law provided for penalties of up to one year in jail and a $1000 fine for those who desecrate the American flag. In June 1990, the Supreme Court overturned the law as violative of the First Amendment.

Prior Restraint

Prior restraint means censoring or preventing material from being broadcast or published. Although the presumption against prior restraint in Anglo-American law may be traced back to Blackstone's *Commentaries*, the first major American case did not reach the Supreme Court until 1931. *Near v. Minnesota* involved a Minnesota newspaper called *The Saturday Press.*

A Minnesota statute allowed local prosecutors to enjoin publications judged "malicious, scandalous and defamatory." The county attorney of Hennepin County brought such an action against *The Saturday Press*. It seems that the paper had accused the law enforcement officials in Minneapolis of failing to punish gambling, bootlegging, and racketeering activities. The paper also charged that law enforcement was controlled by a "Jewish gangster."

The state trial court found that the *Press* had violated the Minnesota public nuisance statute and "perpetually enjoined" publication of the paper. The Supreme Court reversed the ruling, finding the Minnesota statute unconstitutional. States are free to provide for punishment after publication, but the Court stressed that freedom to publish must be guarded. In *Near*, the Supreme Court noted that although there was a heavy presumption against prior restraints, there may be times when such action is justified.

No one would question that a government might prevent actual obstruction to its recruiting service or the publication of sailing dates of transports or the number and location of troops. On similar grounds, the primary requirements of decency may be enforced against obscene publications. The security of community life may be protected against incitements to acts of violence and the overthrow by force of orderly government.[26]

The Doctrine of Prior Restraint was tested again in 1971 in what has become known as the Pentagon Papers case. The *New York Times* was restrained from publishing 36 classified papers outlining how America became involved in the Vietnam War. The papers had been obtained from Dr. Daniel Ellsberg, a former Pentagon employee who had become disenchanted with the war.

A temporary restraining order was issued against the *Times*, but when the U.S. government requested a permanent injunction, Judge Gurfein of the Federal District Court for the Southern District of New York refused to grant one. The U.S. Court of Appeals for the Second Circuit reversed, calling for further hearings on the matter. In the meantime, the temporary injunction remained in effect.

Next, the *Washington Post* obtained the papers and planned to publish them. Once again, the government requested a restraining order. Judge Gerhard Gesell of the U.S. District Court for the District of Columbia refused to issue the order and the *Post* was free to publish, while the *Times* could not. The Supreme Court eventually ruled in favor of the *Times*, noting that,

> ☐ Any system of prior restraints of expression come to this Court bearing a heavy presumption against its constitutional validity. . . . The government "thus carries a heavy burden of showing justification for the enforcement of such a restraint." The District Court for the Southern District of New York in the *New York Times* case and the District Court for the District of Columbia and the Court of Appeals for the District of Columbia Circuit in the *Washington Post* case held that the government had not met that burden. We agree.[27]

In the fall of 1990, the Cable News Network (CNN) planned to cablecast tapes of telephone conversations between deposed Panamanian dictator Manuel Noriega, who was jailed in Miami, and his attorneys. Miami, Florida, District Court Judge William Hoeveler issued a temporary injunction against CNN on the grounds that Noriega's Sixth Amendment right to a fair trial might be jeopardized. In spite of the injunction, CNN did cablecast one of the conversations, but eventually turned the tapes over to the court for fair trial consideration. CNN was threatened with contempt charges for the cablecast. On November 18, 1990, the Supreme Court refused to schedule arguments on the merits of the injunction and also refused to give CNN permission to air the taped conversations. On November 28, 1990, Judge Hoeveler lifted the restraining order, saying that after viewing the tapes, he had concluded that Noriega's right to a fair trial would not be impaired. In 1994, CNN was found guilty in U.S. District Court of criminal contempt of court for the airing of the conversations between Noriega and his attorney.

Clear and Present Danger
Doctrine Revisited

After *Schenck* and *Abrams*, the Clear and Present Danger Doctrine fell into disuse. It did not reappear until 1951 and then in a somewhat altered form. In *Dennis v. United States*, the Supreme Court upheld the conviction of Eugene Dennis and ten other persons for violating the Smith Act. The Smith Act made it a crime to conspire to teach and advocate the overthrow of the United States government by force. In a 6-2 decision, the Court convicted the petitioners for conspiracy and advocacy—not for actual violence. A majority of the Court held that the state cannot be expected to wait until violence is imminent before acting. The justices noted that obstructions to free speech and press might be necessary in order to prevent an even greater evil to society. Hence, Dennis presented a clear and present danger.

The doctrine reached its apex with Dennis. An individual's First Amendment rights could be abridged for merely teaching the necessity of overthrowing the government. However, the pendulum quickly began to swing the other way. In spite of the fact that the government brought many prosecutions under the Smith Act after Dennis, by 1957 the act had been overruled. With McCarthyism on the wane, the Supreme Court, in *Yates v. United States*, made a distinction between advocacy of direct action and advocacy of abstract doctrine. The latter, said the Court, was protected by the First Amendment.

The Clear and Present Danger Doctrine was finalized in *Brandenburg v. Ohio (1969)*, in which the Supreme Court held that advocacy may not be banned unless it is directed to inciting or producing imminent lawless action and is likely to incite or produce such action.

Compelled Speech

Up to this point we have examined ways in which speech may be legally restricted by government. It is also important to note that case law also protects individuals from being forced to speak against their will. For example, in *Wooley v. Maynard 430 U.S. 705, 97 S.Ct. 1428, 51 L.Ed.2d (1977)* the Supreme Court held that the state of New Hampshire could not require an individual to display a license plate with the ideological message "Live Free or Die" on their private automobile. Similarly, in *Hurley v. Irish-American Gay, Lesbian and Bisexual Group of Boston 115 S.Ct. 2338 (1995)*, a group representing several gay organizations sought permission from the City of Boston to participate in a parade organized by a private veterans organization. The Supreme Court ruled that the gay groups could be excluded from the public parade because their presence would compel the private organizers to convey a message that they did not wish to convey; thereby violating the First Amendment rights of the veterans.

The First Amendment and Traditional Broadcasting

As we shall study in later chapters, material broadcast over the air is not afforded the same First Amendment protection as printed matter. The underlying assumption of broadcast regulation originally rested on the premise that broadcasters used a scarce public resource—the electromagnetic spectrum. In theory, because there are a limited number of broadcast frequencies available, the FCC was charged with choosing the best applicant from those who applied for a broadcast license. The FCC developed criteria for making that choice, all of which are under the umbrella of the "public interest standard." Unlike newspapers, broadcasters were "public trustees." Although the First Amendment protected publishers, the Supreme Court ruled in *Red Lion v. FCC*, that

> ☐   . . . Because of the scarcity of radio frequencies, the Government is permitted to put restraints on licenses in favor of others whose views should be expressed on this unique medium. But the people as a whole retain their interest in free speech by radio and their collective right to have the medium function consistently with the ends and purposes of the First Amendment. *It is the right of the viewers and listeners, not the right of the broadcasters which is paramount.* [Emphasis added by the author.] It is the purpose of the First Amendment to preserve an uninhibited marketplace of ideas in which truth will ultimately prevail, rather than to countenance monopolization of that market, whether it be by the Government itself or by private licensee. . . . It is the right of the public to receive suitable access to social, political, esthetic, moral and other ideas and experiences which is crucial here.[28]

In spite of the fact that "scarcity" is a creation of the frequency allocation process and that even the FCC has questioned its validity, concern over fairness remains.[29]

The FCC is prohibited from censoring program content. Newspapers and magazines are legally free to publish almost any material that has not been judged by a court to be obscene. Broadcasters do not have that freedom. Because of the pervasive nature of the broadcast media, certain material may not be broadcast over the air, as ruled in *FCC v. Pacifica Foundation (1976)*. The courts and the FCC have ruled that because broadcasting comes into the home, sometimes "uninvited," consideration for the makeup of the audience is in order. Cable operators are not subjected to these restrictions on content.

Unlike newspapers, broadcasters must provide equal time to political candidates, and the rates at which this time can be sold are governed by the Communications Act. Any legislation suggesting that newspapers or magazines be subjected to the same standards would surely violate the First Amendment, which was the case in *Miami Herald Publishing Co. v. Tornillo (1974)*.

Many in the industry see these regulations as unfair burdens that hinder the ability to compete in the marketplace. Others in society believe that regulation enhances the number of voices given access to the marketplace of ideas. In *Turner Broadcasting System, Inc. v. FCC (1994)*, the Supreme Court reaffirmed *Red Lion*'s importance in assessing broadcasters First Amendment rights but refused to apply *Red Lion* to cable television.

The First Amendment and Cable/Satellite Television

Because cable, and by extension satellite television, is not subjected to the "limited spectrum" as are broadcasters, the Courts have generally held that cable television is deserving of greater First Amendment protection than over-the-air broadcasters.[30] The regulation of over-the-air broadcasting and cable, and their respective First Amendment freedoms, has evolved in very different directions. The next two chapters will address these differences.

The First Amendment and the Internet

The courts have applied the First Amendment to the Internet in a similar manner to that of the print media. Efforts to hold the Internet to broadcast-like indecency standards have been repeatedly struck down by the Supreme Court. (See *Reno v. American Civil Liberties Union*, 521 U.S. 844 [1997]). Similarly, the High Court struck down the Child Pornography Prevention Act of 1996, which would have made "virtual images" of certain sexually oriented material illegal. The Act would have banned a range of sexually explicit images, sometimes called "virtual child pornography," that appear to depict minors but were produced by means other than using real children, such as through youthful-looking adults or computer-imaging technology. (See *Ashcroft v. Free Speech Coaltion* 122 S. Ct. 1389; 152 L. Ed. 2d 403; 2002 U.S. LEXIS 2789 [2002]).

In *Reno*, the Supreme Court held that the Communications Decency Act violated the First Amendment because it was "overbroad"—that is, it was not narrowly tailored to address only the harms it was designed to prevent. Congress tried to address the Court's concern with the passage of the Child Online Protection Act (COPA). The COPA addressed only commercial material on the World Wide Web (not the entire Internet) that was found to be "harmful to minors" (see *47 U.S.C.§ 231 (a)(1)*). A Federal District Court issued a preliminary injunction against enforcement of COPA on the grounds that the Act was unlikely to survive "strict scrutiny." The Court of Appeals for the Third Circuit affirmed, but based its decision on the use of the "contemporary community standards" doctrine, borrowed from current obscenity law, see *Miller v. California* (as discussed on page 159 in Chapter 6) to identify material as "harmful to minors."

The Supreme Court heard the case in October of 2001 and held that the COPA's reliance on the "community standards" doctrine did not, by itself, render the COPA "overbroad." The Supreme Court offered no opinion on the constitutionality of COPA as a whole, and sent the case back to the Third Circuit for review. The preliminary injunction preventing enforcement of COPA remains in effect pending action by the lower courts. (See *Ashcroft v. American Civil Liberties Union* No. 00-1293, May 13, 2002.)

Summary

The major cases that dealt with interpretations of the First Amendment did not occur until the twentieth century. Although the First Amendment is written in absolute terms, the courts have developed guidelines that indicate the limitations of freedom of speech and freedom of the press. The interpretations of the First Amendment given by the courts have varied over the years, depending on the philosophical bent of the justices hearing the cases.

Because broadcast media are licensed to serve the public interest and use space on the electromagnetic spectrum, they are held to a stricter standard under the First Amendment than publishers or cable television operators. The courts have rejected a broadcast-like regulatory scheme for the Internet, preferring to treat the medium more like print for First Amendment issues.

Notes/References

1. Edward G. Hudon, *Freedom of Speech and Press in America* (Washington, D.C.: Public Affairs Press, 1963), 11.
2. Donald M. Gillmor and Jerome A. Barron, *Mass Communication Law*, 4th ed. (St. Paul: West Publishing Co., 1984), 738.
3. Ibid.
4. John Milton, *Areopagitica and Of Education*, ed. George H. Sabine (New York: Appleton-Century-Crofts, 1951), 50.
5. Vincent Buranelli, *The Trial of Peter Zenger* (Washington Square: New York University Press, 1957), 95.
6. Ibid., 97.
7. Ibid., 62.
8. William Blackstone, *Commentaries on the Laws of England*, ed. Charles M. Haar (Boston: Beacon Press, 1962), 161–62.
9. Zechariah Chafee, Jr., *Thirty-Five Years with Freedom of Speech* (New York: Roger N. Baldwin, Civil Liberties Foundation, 1952), 4.
10. *Schenck v. United States*, 249 U.S. 47 (1919).

11. *Abrams v. United States*, 250 U.S. 616 (1919).

12. Ibid.

13. J. S. Mill, *On Liberty, Etc.* (London: Oxford University Press, 1969), 24.

14. *Abrams v. United States*, 250 U.S. 616 (1919).

15. *Gitlow v. People of State of New York*, 268 U.S. 652, 45 S.Ct. 625, 69 L.Ed. 1138 (1925).

16. Ibid.

17. *Chaplinsky v. New Hampshire*, 315 U.S. 568, 62 S.Ct. 766, 86 L.Ed. 1031 (1942).

18. *Gooding v. Wilson*, 405 U.S. 518 (1972).

19. Ibid.

20. *Lewis v. City of New Orleans*, 408 U.S. 913 (1972) and *Lewis v. City of New Orleans*, 415 U.S. 130 (1974).

21. *Cohen v. California*, 403 U.S. 15 at 20 (1971).

22. *Village of Skokie v. National Socialist Party*, 373 N.E. 2d 21 (Ill. 1978).

23. *Dennis v. United States*, 341 U.S. 494 (1951).

24. *United States v. O'Brien*, 391 U.S. 367 (1968).

25. *Texas v. Johnson*, Slip op. 88–155 (U.S. June 21, 1989).

26. *Near v. Minnesota*, 283 U.S. 697 (1931).

27. *New York Times v. United States*, 403 U.S. 308 (1971).

28. *Red Lion v. FCC*, 395 U.S. 367 (1969).

29. For additional information regarding this issue, see the *Fairness Report* of 1985, 102 EC.C.2d 143, 58 R.R.2d 1137 (1985) and "Fairness Doctrine Legislation Re-Emerges," *Broadcasting* (January 12,1991): 43.

30. *Turner Broadcasting System, Inc. v. Federal Communications Commission*, Op. 93–44 (U.S. June 27, 1994)

Cases

Abrams v. United States, 250 U.S. 616 (1919)

American Communications Association v. Douds, 339 U.S. 382 (1950)

Ashcroft v. American Civil Liberties Union (Slip Opinion, No. 00-1293, May 13, 2002)

Ashcroft v. Free Speech Coaltion 122 S. Ct. 1389; 152 L. Ed. 2d 403; 2002 U.S. LEXIS 2789 (2002)

Brandenburg v. Ohio, 395 U.S. 444 (1969)

Chaplinsky v. New Hampshire, 315 U.S. 568, 62 S.Ct. 766, 86 L.Ed. 1031 (1942)

Cohen v. California, 403 U.S. 15 at 20 (1971)

Dennis v. United States, 341 U.S. 494 (1951)

FCC v. Pacifica Foundation, 438 U.S. 726 (1978)

Gitlow v. People of State of New York, 268 U.S. 652, 45 S.Ct. 625, 69 LEd. 1138 (1925)

Gooding v. Wilson, 405 U.S. 518 (1972)

Hurley v. Irish-American Gay, Lesbian and Bisexual Group of Boston 115 S.Ct. 2338 (1995)

Lewis v. City of New Orleans, 408 U.S. 913 (1972)

Lewis v. City of New Orleans, 415 U.S. 130 (1974)

Miami Herald Publishing Co. v. Tornillo, 418 U.S. 241 (1974)

Near v. Minnesota, 283 U.S. 697 (1931)

New York Times v. United States 403 U.S. 713 (1971)

R.A.V. v. City of St. Paul, Minn., 112 S.Ct. 2538 (1992)

Red Lion Broadcasting Co., Inc. v. FCC, 395 U.S. 367 (1969)

Reno v. American Civil Liberties Union, 521 U.S. 844 (1997)

Schenck v. United States, 249 U.S. 47 (1919)

Texas v. Johnson, Slip op. 88–155 (U.S. June 21, 1989)

Tinker v. Des Moines Independent School District, 393 U.S. 503 (1969)

Turner Broadcasting System, Inc. v. Federal Communications Commission, Op. 93–44 (U.S. June 27,1994)

United States v. O'Brien, 391 U.S. 367 (1968)

Village of Skokie v. National Socialist Party, 373 N.E.2d 21 (Ill., 1978)

Wooley v. Maynard 430 U.S. 705, 97 S.Ct. 1428, 51

Yates v. United States, 354 U.S. 298 (1957)

3 □ □ □
□ □ □
□ □ □

The Rationale of Broadcast Regulation

I think this is probably the only industry of the United States that is unanimously in favor of having itself regulated.[1]

When Commerce Secretary Herbert Hoover made this statement at the Third National Radio Conference in 1924, he was describing a chaotic industry. The number of radio stations on the air continued to increase, though few frequencies had been allocated for broadcast use. Hoover had designated 833 kHz for broadcast use in 1921 and added 750 kHz in 1922. By 1923, the band was expanded to include frequencies from 550 kHz to 1350 kHz. Every channel was filled and there was considerable interference among stations.

Even to an ardent believer in free enterprise like Hoover, it seemed that the only solution to the problem of radio interference was stricter government regulation. Hoover had already established the groundwork for government intervention into broadcasting when he established frequency allocations, power regulations, and operating schedules. The Commerce Department's authority to regulate radio was the Radio Act of 1912. This act provided for government regulation of the maritime industry, spurred largely by the *Titanic* disaster. Although the Radio Act of 1912 was weak and did not anticipate commercial radio broadcasting as it was to develop in the 1920s, it served as the only radio regulatory legislation passed by Congress until 1927.

Using the 1912 Act as the basis of his authority, Hoover called a series of four radio conferences between 1922 and 1925. Originally, he hoped that the radio industry could work out its problems without government controls. But with each conference that possibility appeared more remote. In 1922, only 22 broadcasters attended the radio conference. By 1925, more than 400 were in attendance. Each year the industry called for the government to step in and straighten out the mess.

Despite the industry's overt cries for regulation, and the obvious need for some form of control over the burgeoning broadcast industry, enacting regulatory measures did not come easily. When Maine's Representative Wallace H. White sponsored legislation in 1922 authorizing Hoover to act as "traffic cop of the air," it was voted down by Congress. In 1923, when Hoover attempted to reduce the overcrowding of the airwaves, the U.S. Court of Appeals for the District of Columbia ruled in *Hoover v. Intercity Radio Co. Inc.* that Hoover had exceeded his authority. The final blow to Commerce Department regulation of radio came in 1926 when a series of court rulings denied Hoover the authority to regulate frequencies, power, or operating hours. This case, *United States v. Zenith Radio Corp. et al.*, led directly to the passage of the Radio Act of 1927 and ultimately to the Communications Act of 1934.

United States v. Zenith Radio Corp. et al. (1926)

After the Fourth National Radio Conference in 1924, the Zenith Radio Corporation applied to the Commerce Department for a permit to build a radio station. A license was granted and Zenith was authorized to operate WJAZ radio on a frequency of 930 kHz. WJAZ was also required to share this frequency with several other stations. Time-sharing was common during this period and served as a somewhat less than optimal solution to the overcrowding problem. Zenith found the two hours per week it was permitted to broadcast to be overly restrictive and applied for a license to broadcast on 910 kHz. This frequency was not available for use by American stations. An agreement between the United States and Canada had limited 910 kHz to Canadian use. Zenith's application for the frequency was denied, but Zenith defiantly changed frequencies anyway. After Zenith "jumped frequency," other stations announced their intention to do the same. The Commerce Department took Zenith to court, but an Illinois federal district court found that the Radio Act of 1912 gave the Commerce Department no authority to establish radio regulations. Therefore, the Commerce Department was powerless to stop Zenith from broadcasting on any frequency it chose.

Judge Wilkerson wrote,

☐   . . . There is no express grant of power in the act to the Secretary of Commerce to establish regulations. The fifteenth regulation prohibits a private or commercial station not engaged in the transmission of bona fide commercial business by radio communication or in experimentation in connection with the development and manufacture of radio apparatus for commercial purposes from using a wave length exceeding 200 meters except by special authority of the Secretary of Commerce. Defendant's license authorizes the use of wave length 332.4 meters on Thursday night

from 10 to 12 PM when use of this period is not desired by the General
Electric Company's Denver station.

Each of the acts of the defendant, relied upon by the United States as
the basis of prosecution, is within the prohibition of the fifteenth
regulation. Each count of the information covers broadcasting on a
wavelength of 329.5 meters at a time not covered by the authority in the
license. Section 4 contains a special provision for penalties for violations of
regulations as follows:

For a violation of any of these regulations, subject to which a license
under sections one and two of this act may be issued, the owner of the
apparatus shall be liable to a penalty of one hundred dollars, which may
be reduced or remitted by the Secretary of Commerce . . . and for repeated
violations . . . the license may be revoked.

Does the operation of the station upon any wave length at any other
time than from 10 to 12 PM on Thursday constitute a violation of section
1? The license provides:

This station to be operated only on Thursday nights from 10 to 12 PM
Central Standard Zone and then only when use of this period is not
desired by the General Electric Company's Denver station.

The provision in section 2 as to stating in the license the hours for
which the station is licensed must be read and interpreted in its relation
to the entire act.

The Secretary of Commerce is required to issue the license subject to
the regulations in the act. The Congress has withheld from him the power
to prescribe additional regulations. If there is a conflict between a
provision in the license and the regulations established by Congress, the
latter must control . . .[2]

The *Zenith* case leaves no doubt that it is Congress that must establish
regulatory procedures to be applied to radio. By 1927, Congress had passed the
Radio Act designed to do just that.

The Radio Act of 1927 was signed into law by President Coolidge on
February 23, 1927. The act created a temporary, five-member Federal Radio
Commission (FRC). The commissioners remained in power from year to year
through various acts of Congress. The 1927 act was eventually superseded by
the Communications Act of 1934. The 1934 act created the Federal Communications Commission (FCC), which was a permanent regulatory agency.

An important feature of the 1927 act was the establishment of the phrase
"public interest, convenience, and necessity" as the standard for licensing
radio stations. The somewhat slippery phrase was borrowed from public
utility legislation and was incorporated into the 1934 act as well. The ambiguity of the public interest standard has served as the basis for much of the

litigation surrounding broadcast law. Since the phrase was incorporated into the Communications Act of 1934, it has been and still is a source of controversy.

Though the Radio Act of 1927 brought an end to the chaos of radio by creating an agency to oversee the development of broadcasting, the act left some aspects of radio and all interstate and foreign wire communication under the control of other federal agencies. The Communications Act of 1934 brought wire and wireless communication under the control of the Commission. The essence of broadcast regulation remained the same, because much of the Radio Act was imported to the Communications Act. Although there have been numerous amendments over the years and several attempts at rewriting the 1934 act, today's broadcast stations are essentially regulated under many of the same provisions that were part of the 1927 act.

The FCC began formal operation on July 11, 1934. The Commission was created by the Roosevelt administration as an independent regulatory commission, like the Interstate Commerce Commission and the Federal Trade Commission. Like the FRC before it, the FCC based its authority to regulate broadcasting on the nebulous "public interest" concept. The phrase "public interest, convenience, and necessity" was borrowed from an 1887 Illinois railroad statute and was later adopted in the Federal Transportation Act of 1920. Legal scholar Don Le Duc wrote,

> Yet, whereas it would seem relatively easy to decide when the extension of a rail line or an increase in shipping tariffs might ultimately serve the needs or interests of its customers, it was far more complex and less precise in outcome to make a similar determination, in terms of audience requirements about factors as sophisticated as subtle programming balance or local orientation.[3]

The Communications Act of 1934

The Communications Act sets the parameters within which the FCC functions. It stipulates the organization of the Commission, outlines the procedures to be followed, defines terms, and states the "charge" of the FCC. The act was originally made up of six "titles." In 1984, Congress passed the Cable Communications Policy Act, so that currently there are seven titles:

Title I—Definition of Terms; Provisions Setting up the Commission
Title II—Common Carriers (Telephone and Telegraph)
Title III—General Powers of the Commission, Licensing, Administrative Sanctions, Public Broadcasting
Title IV—Hearings and Appeals of Commission Decisions

Title V—Penal Provisions and Forfeitures
Title VI—Cable Television (added in 1984)
Title VII—Miscellaneous Provisions; War Powers of the President

Each of these titles is comprised of sections and paragraphs. Some sections of the Communications Act have become so well known that they are referred to by number. For example, Section 315 is the equal time provision, which applies to candidates for public office. Section 326 contains the no censorship clause. It is essential for the student of the law of electronic media to become familiar with these and other provisions of the Communications Act.

No Ownership of Frequency—Title III, Part I, Sec. 301

It is the purpose of this Act, among other things, to maintain the control of the United States over all the channels of interstate and foreign radio transmission; and to provide for the use of such channels, but not the ownership thereof, by persons for limited periods of time, under licenses granted by Federal authority, and no license shall be construed to create any right beyond the terms, conditions, and period of the license.[4]

FCC Can Regulate in the Public Interest— Title III, Part I, Sec. 302

(a) The Commission may, consistent with the public interest, convenience, and necessity, make reasonable regulations governing the interference potential of devices which in their operation are capable of emitting radio frequency energy.[5]

Specific Powers of the FCC—Title III, Part I, Sec. 303

Except as otherwise provided in this Act, the Commission from time to time, as public convenience, interest, or necessity requires shall—

(a) Classify radio stations;
(b) Prescribe the nature of the service to be rendered by each class of licensed stations and each station within any class;
(c) Assign bands of frequencies to the various classes of stations, and assign frequencies for each individual station and determine the power which each station shall use and the time during which it may operate;

(d) Determine the location of classes of stations or individual stations;

(f) Make such regulations not inconsistent with law as it may deem necessary to prevent interference between stations and to carry out the provisions of this Act . . .

(1) (I) Have authority to prescribe the qualifications of station operators . . .

(n) Have authority to inspect all radio installations associated with stations required to be licensed . . . to ascertain whether in construction, installation, and operation they conform to the requirements of the rules and regulations of the Commission . . .

(o) Have authority to designate call letters of all stations . . .

(r) Make such rules and regulations and prescribe such restrictions and conditions, not inconsistent with law, as may be necessary to carry out the provisions of this Act . . .[6]

Power of License Revocation—Title III, Part I, Sec. 312

The Commission may revoke any station license or construction permit—

(1) for false statements knowingly made either in the application or in any statement of fact which may be required pursuant to section 308;

(2) because of conditions coming to the attention of the Commission which would warrant it in refusing to grant a license or permit on an original application;

(3) for willful or repeated failure to operate substantially as set forth in the license;

(4) for willful or repeated violation of, or willful or repeated failure to observe, any provision of this Act or any rule or regulation of the Commission authorized by this Act or by a treaty ratified by the United States;

(5) for violation of or failure to observe any final cease and desist order issued by the Commission under this section;

(6) violation of section 1304, 1343, or 1464[7] of Title 18 of the United States Code; or

(7) for willful or repeated failure to allow reasonable access to or permit purchase of reasonable amounts of time for the use of a broadcasting station by a legally qualified candidate for Federal elective office on behalf of his candidacy.

Equal Time for Political Candidates—
Title III, Part I, Sec. 315

(a) If any licensee shall permit any person who is a legally qualified candidate for any public office to use a broadcasting station, he shall afford equal opportunities to all other such candidates for that office in the use of such broadcasting station: Provided, that such licensee shall have no power of censorship over the material broadcast under the provisions of this section. No obligation is imposed under this subsection upon any licensee to allow the use of its station by any such candidate. Appearance by a legally qualified candidate on any—

   (1) bona fide newscast,
   (2) bona fide news interview,
   (3) bona fide news documentary (if the appearance of the candidate is incidental to the presentation of the subject or subjects covered by the news documentary), or
   (4) on-the-spot coverage of bona fide news events (including but not limited to political conventions and activities incidental thereto), shall not be deemed to be use of a broadcasting station within the meaning of this subsection. Nothing in the foregoing sentence shall be construed as relieving broadcasters, in connection with the presentation of newscasts, news interviews, news documentaries, and on-the-spot coverage of news events, from the obligation imposed upon them under this Act to operate in the public interest and to afford reasonable opportunity for the discussion of conflicting views on issues of public importance.[8]

(b) The charges made for the use of any broadcasting station by any person who is a legally qualified candidate for any public office in connection with his campaign for nomination, or election to such office shall not exceed—

   (1) during the forty-five days preceding the date of the primary runoff election and during the sixty days preceding the date of a general or special election in which a person is a candidate, the lowest unit charge of the station for the same class and amount of time for the same period; and
   (2) at any other time, the charges made for comparable use of such station by other users thereof.

(c) No station licensee may make any charge for the use of such station by or on behalf of any legally qualified candidate for Federal elective office (or for nomination to such office) unless such candidate (or a person specifically authorized by such candidate in writing to do so) certifies to such licensee in writing that the payment of such charge will not violate any limitation . . . of the Campaign Communications Reform Act . . .[9]

"Use" of a Broadcast Facility by a Political Candidate

The equal time and lowest-unit-rate provisions are triggered by "use" of the broadcast facility by the political candidate. "Use" is defined as any nonexempt appearance by a legally qualified candidate. This can be an identifiable picture, or the voice of the candidate. If such an appearance is not a part of a political spot, there is no "use."

Sponsorhip Identification

Each political advertisement must indicate who paid for the spot. Typically, such identifications include audio or visual tags stating the name of the specific organization (i.e., Committee to Re-elect Candidate X) paying for the ad. The tag must also state whether the spot is authorized by the candidate.

Who Is a Legally Qualified Candidate?

Section 315 of the Communications Act only applies to legally qualified candidates for public office. Section 73.1940 of the FCC rules defines a legally qualified candidate as

> . . . [A]ny person who:
> (i) has publicly announced his or her intention to run for nomination or office.
> (ii) is qualified under the applicable local, state or federal law to hold the office for which he or she is a candidate; and,
> (iii) has met the qualifications set forth in either subparagraphs (2), (3) or (4), below. . . .
> (2) A person seeking election to any public office including that of President or Vice President of the United States, or nomination for any public office except that of President or Vice President, by means of a primary, general or special election, shall be considered a legally qualified candidate if, in addition to meeting the criteria set forth in subparagraph (1) above, that person:
> (i) has qualified for a place on the ballot, or
> (ii) has publicly committed himself or herself to seeking election by the write-in method and is eligible under applicable law to be voted for by sticker, by writing in his or her name on the ballot or by other method, and makes a substantial showing that he or she is a bona fide candidate for nomination or office. Persons seeking election to the office of President or Vice

President of the United States shall, for the purposes of the Communications Act and the Rules thereunder, be considered legally qualified candidates only in those states or territories (or the District of Columbia) in which they have met the requirements set for this paragraph (a)(1) and (2) of this Rule: Except, that any such person who has met the requirements set forth in paragraph (a)(1) and (2) in at least 10 states (or nine and the District of Columbia) shall be considered a legally qualified candidate for election in all states, territories and the District of Columbia for purposes of this Act.

(3) A person seeking nomination to any public office, except that of President or Vice President of the United States, by means of a convention, caucus or similar procedure, shall be considered a legally qualified candidate if, in addition to meeting the requirements set forth in paragraph (a)(1) above, that person makes a substantial showing that he or she is a bona fide candidate for such nomination: Except, that no person shall be considered a legally qualified candidate for nomination by the means set forth in this paragraph prior to 90 days before the beginning of the convention, caucus or similar procedure in which he or she seeks nomination.

(4) A person seeking nomination for the office of President or Vice President of the United States shall, for the purposes of the Communications Act and the rules thereunder, be considered a legally qualified candidate only in those states or territories (or the District of Columbia) in which, in addition to meeting the requirements set forth in paragraph (a)(1) above,

(i) he or she, or proposed delegates on his or her behalf, have qualified for the primary or Presidential preference ballot in that state, territory or the District of Columbia, or

(ii) he or she has made a substantial showing of bona fide candidacy for such nomination in that state, territory or the District of Columbia; except that any such person meeting the requirements set forth in paragraphs (a)(1) and (4) in at least ten states (or nine and the District of Columbia) shall be considered a legally qualified candidate for nomination in all states, territories and the District of Columbia for purposes of this Act.[10]

Retention of Political Broadcast Information

(d) See §§73.3526 and 73.3527. Records, inspection. Every licensee shall keep and permit public inspection of a complete record (political file) of all requests for broadcast time made by or on behalf of candidates for public office.[11]

Time Limitations for Equal Opportunities Requests

(e) Time of Request. A request for equal opportunities must be submitted to the licensee within one week of the day on which the first prior use giving rise to the right of equal opportunities occurred: provided, however, that where the person was not a candidate at the time of such first prior use, he shall submit his request within one week of the first subsequent use after he has become a legally qualified candidate for the office in question.

(f) Burden of Proof. A candidate requesting equal opportunities of the licensee, or complaining of noncompliance to the Commission shall have the burden of proving that he and his opponent are legally qualified candidates for the same public office.[12]

Applications of Section 315

Section 315 of the Communications Act has been modified a number of times throughout the years. Prior to 1959, stations were liable for remarks made on the air by candidates, even though broadcasters were forbidden from censoring potentially litigious remarks. In *Farmers Educational Cooperative Union v. WDAY Inc. (1959)* the Supreme Court ruled in a 5–4 decision that broadcasters could not be held liable in defamation suits brought as a result of candidates' remarks. It should be noted that candidates themselves are still liable for potentially defamatory statements.

Another content-related problem of Section 315 occurred when *Hustler* magazine publisher Larry Flynt announced that he would run for President. Flynt said that he would take advantage of his status as a candidate and the Commission's "no censorship" provision by running sexually explicit "announcements" over broadcast television. Legislation was introduced in Congress that was designed to allow broadcasters to refuse to air pornographic materials under Section 315. The FCC indicated that the "no censorship" clause of Section 315 would not apply to obscene or indecent political announcements. In an unrelated incident, Flynt subsequently withdrew as a presidential candidate before the FCC had to deal with the question of sexually explicit political broadcasts.

During the 1992 campaign, several congressional candidates produced graphic anti-abortion ads. Television stations objected to running the ads, but it was unclear whether a station refusal to run the ads violated the "reasonable access" provision of Section 315. One station, WAGA in Atlanta, chose to "channel" a graphic program produced on behalf of candidate Daniel Becker to the "safe harbor" hours between midnight and 6:00 A.M. Becker's program was originally scheduled to air between 4:00 and 5:00 P.M. The U.S. District Court for the Northern District of Georgia held that WAGA could channel the political broadcast into the safe harbor.[13]

Anti-abortion ads resurfaced as an issue in the 1994 elections. WHAS-TV in Louisville channeled ads produced in support of Indiana 9th District congressional candidate Michael Bailey. Bailey claimed that graphic anti-abortion ads were critical to his campaign strategy and asked the FCC to rule on the stations' channeling of the ads. The FCC did not rule on the proceeding; however, other television stations in Indianapolis, Cincinnati, and Louisville did not channel the ads. Many of those stations broadcast a disclaimer before airing the spots. Initially, one Indianapolis station, WTHR, refused to carry the ads in any time period, but later aired them without channeling, but with a disclaimer.[14] In 1994, the FCC issued a ruling that allowed broadcasters to channel abortion ads to times when children are less likely to be in the audience. The Commission noted, however, that a station cannot channel an ad simply because it doesn't like the content of the message.[15]

The Problem of Debates

In 1960, when presidential candidates Richard Nixon and John F. Kennedy planned a series of broadcast debates, Congress suspended Section 315. This questionable application of policy occurred so that the debate would be limited to appearances by Nixon and Kennedy, freezing out any minority candidates. Although this suspension made the debates practical, the move certainly questioned the spirit of Section 315 altogether. One might ask that if Section 315 could be suspended, why was it necessary in the first place?

In 1962, the Commission decided that debates by major candidates sponsored by the news media did not qualify as a "bona fide news event" and was, therefore, subject to Section 315.7. There were no presidential debates broadcast again until 1976. In that year, the FCC ruled that broadcast coverage of a debate by presidential candidates was a news event under Section 315 if it was broadcast live in its entirety and not sponsored or controlled by the broadcaster or the candidate. The Carter–Ford debates were sponsored by the League of Women Voters and were covered live by the networks.

In 1980, the third-party candidacy of John Anderson complicated the broadcast debate process. The League of Women Voters planned a series of debates that included Republican nominee Ronald Reagan, incumbent Jimmy Carter, and challenger Anderson. Carter refused to debate with Anderson. The networks covered a debate between Reagan and Anderson as a news event. Later, the League sponsored a broadcast debate between Carter and Reagan. The League withdrew its sponsorship of presidential debates in 1988, citing demands by candidates for too much control of the debate.

This move was of little importance to the future of presidential debates, however, for in 1983 the FCC reversed its policy and allowed broadcasters to sponsor debates between political candidates without the obligation of providing free time to all qualified candidates. In petitions of Henry Geller et al., the Commission noted that broadcaster-sponsored debates may benefit the public by increasing the number of these events.

Other changes in the FCC policy on debates and political programs included a redefinition of the phrase "on-the-spot" news contained in Section 315. This was originally interpreted as "live" coverage. In *United Church of Christ v. FCC (1978)*, the FCC allowed a broadcaster to tape a political program and air it within 24 hours. This rule was relaxed further in the Geller case when the Commission indicated that broadcasters may use their judgment in deciding how long to hold a taped political program before airing it.

Public Television and Candidate Debates

Public television stations are often licensed to state universities or are part of state-supported networks. This presents additional First Amendment issues in the interpretation of Section 315. In 1992 the Arkansas Educational Television Commission (AETC) sponsored a debate between congressional candidates. The state supported network chose to include only "major" candidates in the televised debate. Third party candidate Ralph Forbes was excluded. He brought suit against AETC, arguing that the state network had violated the First Amendment. The Supreme Court ruled in favor of AETC.

Arkansas Educational Television Commission v. Forbes Certiorari to the United States Court of Appeals for the Eighth Circuit No. 96-779. Argued October 8, 1997 Decided May 18, 1998

☐ Petitioner Arkansas Educational Television Commission (AETC), a state-owned public television broadcaster, sponsored a debate between the major party candidates for the 1992 election in Arkansas' Third Congressional District. When AETC denied the request of respondent Forbes, an independent candidate with little popular support, for permission to participate in the debate, Forbes filed this suit, claiming, . . . that he was entitled to participate under the First Amendment. The jury made express findings that Forbes' exclusion had not been influenced by political pressure or disagreement with his views. The District Court entered judgment for AETC. The Eighth Circuit reversed, holding that the debate was a public forum to which all ballot-qualified candidates had a presumptive right of access. Applying strict scrutiny, the court determined that AETC's assessment of Forbes' "political viability" was neither a compelling nor a narrowly tailored reason for excluding him.

Held: AETC's exclusion of Forbes from the debate was consistent with the First Amendment . . .

Unlike most other public television programs, candidate debates are subject to scrutiny under this Court's public forum doctrine. Having first arisen in the context of streets and parks, the doctrine should not be extended in a mechanical way to the different context of television broadcasting. Broad rights of access for outside speakers would be antithetical, as a general rule, to the editorial discretion that broadcasters must exercise to fulfill their journalistic purpose and statutory obligations. For two reasons, however, candidate debates present the narrow exception to the rule. First, unlike AETC's other broadcasts, the debate was by design a forum for candidates' political speech. Consistent with the long tradition of such debates, AETC's implicit representation was that the views expressed were those of the candidates, not its own. The debate's very purpose was to allow the expression of those views with minimal intrusion by the broadcaster. Second, candidate debates are of exceptional significance in the electoral process. Deliberation on candidates' positions and qualifications is integral to our system of government, and electoral speech may have its most profound and widespread impact when it is disseminated through televised debates. Thus, the special characteristics of candidate debates support the conclusion that the AETC debate was a forum of some type. The question of what type must be answered by reference to this Court's public forum precedents . . . For the Court's purposes, it will suffice to employ the categories of speech fora already established in the case law. The Court has identified three types of fora: the traditional public forum, the public forum created by government designation, and the nonpublic forum . . . Traditional public fora are defined by the objective characteristics of the property, such as whether, "by long tradition or by government fiat," the property has been "devoted to assembly and debate." . . . The government can exclude a speaker from a traditional public forum only when the exclusion is necessary to serve a compelling state interest and is narrowly drawn to achieve that interest. [. . .] Designated public fora are created by purposeful governmental action opening a nontraditional public forum for expressive use by the general public or by a particular class of speakers. . . . If the government excludes a speaker who falls within the class to which such a forum is made generally available, its action is subject to strict scrutiny. . . . Property that is not a traditional public forum or a designated public forum is either a nonpublic forum or not a forum at all. . . . *Access to a nonpublic forum can be restricted if the restrictions are reasonable and are not an effort to suppress expression merely because public officials oppose the speaker's views.* [Emphasis added] The AETC debate was a nonpublic forum. The parties agree that it was not a traditional public forum, and it was not a designated public forum under this Court's precedents . . .

Contrary to the Eighth Circuit's assertion, *AETC did not make its debate generally available to candidates for the congressional seat at issue. Instead, it reserved eligibility for participation to candidates for that seat (as opposed to some other seat), and then made candidate-by-candidate determinations as to which of the eligible candidates would participate in the debate. Such "selective access," unsupported by evidence of a purposeful designation for public use, does not create a public forum, but indicates that the debate was a nonpublic forum. . . .*

AETC's decision to exclude Forbes was a reasonable, viewpoint neutral exercise of journalistic discretion consistent with the First Amendment. [Emphasis added] The record demonstrates beyond dispute that Forbes was excluded not because of his viewpoint, but because he had not generated appreciable public interest. There is no serious argument that AETC did not act in good faith in this case.

. . . reversed. KENNEDY, J., delivered the opinion of the Court, in which REHNQUIST, C. J., and O'CONNOR, SCALIA, THOMAS, and BREYER, JJ., joined. STEVENS, J., filed a dissenting opinion, in which SOUTER and GINSBURG, JJ., joined.

Use by Supporters—The Zapple Doctrine

The Zapple Doctrine (or quasi-equal opportunities), which was the result of the Nicholas Zapple decision, requires that a station making time available to supporters or to a spokesperson for a candidate also make time available to supporters or a spokesperson for the opposing candidate. The Zapple Doctrine does not apply outside campaign periods, nor does it apply to minor candidates. It applies to major party candidates only.

Nonpolitical Appearance by Candidates

It is generally accepted that all appearances by political candidates fall within the definition of "use" in Section 315. Local air personalities running for office usually must leave the air during their candidacy or risk providing regular "free time" to their opponent. When Ronald Reagan ran for the Republican nomination in 1976, the Broadcast Bureau ruled in *Adrian Weiss* that stations showing old Reagan films were obligated to provide as much time to his opponent Gerald Ford. In 1992, the Political Broadcast Rules were modified to exempt nonvoluntary appearances by candidates, effectively overturning Weiss.[16]

In 1985, California journalist William H. Branch, who was running for office, challenged the validity of applying Section 315 each time he appeared on the air reporting a news story. Branch argued that the equal time provision should not be applied each time he appeared on camera, because he was reporting a news story and not making a political announcement. He contended that his appearance was part of a "bona fide news event" as defined in Section 315.

In *Branch v. Federal Communications Commission (1987)*, Judge Bork, writing on behalf of the Court of Appeals for the District of Columbia, noted that

> When a broadcaster's employees are being sent out to cover a news story involving other persons, therefore, the "bona fide news event" is the activity engaged in by those other persons, not the work done by the employees covering the event . . . There is nothing at all "newsworthy" about the work being done by the broadcaster's own employees, regardless of whether any of those employees happens also to be a candidate for public office.[17]

Lowest Unit Rate

Under Section 315(b), broadcasters are required to charge political advertisers no more than the station's "most favored commercial advertisers" would be charged for comparable time. This means that political advertisers may not be charged more than the lowest rate charged for the same class and amount of time for the same period. Recently, the FCC held that preemptible spots and runs of schedule spots constitute a separate class of time for purposes of Section 315. The lowest unit rate is in effect 45 days preceding a primary or primary runoff election and 60 days preceding a general or special election. Recently, the FCC has stepped up enforcement of this provision. In May 1990, the Commission levied a record $10,000 fine against WXIN-TV in Indianapolis for repeated violations of the lowest unit charge requirements.

The "comparable use" rule applies when the lowest unit rate rule does not. This rule provides that charges for use of a station by a legally qualified candidate may not exceed charges made for comparable use of the station by other advertisers.

Reasonable Access

Section 312(a)(7) of the Communications Act requires broadcasters to provide "reasonable access to or to permit purchase of reasonable amounts of time" by candidates for federal elective office. Although Section 31 2(a)(7) applies only to federal candidates, a 1971 FCC ruling states that broadcasters have a public interest obligation to make some time available to non-federal candidates.[18]

CBS Inc. v. FCC (1981)

In 1981, the issue of reasonable access reached the Supreme Court in *CBS Inc. v. FCC*. In December 1979, the Carter–Mondale campaign asked to purchase 30 minutes of air time on the three major television networks. CBS offered to sell 10 minutes of time in 5-minute segments. ABC said that it would not sell political time until January, and NBC denied the request completely. The Carter campaign committee complained to the FCC, which found the network-owned-and-operated stations (O&Os) in violation of Section 312(a)(7). The court of appeals and the Supreme Court agreed. Chief Justice Burger delivered the opinion of the Court.

☐ Broadcasters are free to deny the sale of air time prior to the commencement of a campaign, but once a campaign has begun, they must give reasonable and good faith attention to access requests from "legally qualified candidates" for federal elective office. Such requests must be considered on an individualized basis, and broadcasters are required to tailor their responses to accommodate, as much as reasonably possible, a candidate's stated purposes in seeking air time.

... The Commission has concluded that, as a threshold matter, it will independently determine whether a campaign has begun and the obligations imposed by § 312(a)(7) have attached. . . . Petitioners assert that, in undertaking such a task, the Commission becomes improperly involved in the electoral process and seriously impairs broadcaster discretion.

However, petitioners fail to recognize that the Commission does not set the starting date for a campaign. Rather, on review of a complaint alleging denial of "reasonable access," it examines objective evidence to find whether the campaign has already commenced. . . .

... [P]etitioners assert that § 312(a)(7) as implemented by the Commission violates the First Amendment rights of broadcasters by unduly circumscribing their editorial discretion. . . . petitioners are correct that the Court has never approved a general right of access to the media. . . . Nor do we do so today. . . .

Nevertheless, petitioners ABC and NBC refused to sell the Carter–Mondale Presidential Committee any time counteroffers, but adopted "blanket" policies refusing access despite the admonition against such an approach. . . . Likewise, petitioner CBS, while not barring access completely, had an across-the-board policy of selling only 5-minute spots.

... Section 312(a)(7) represents an effort by Congress to assure [sic] that an important resource, the statutory right of access, as defined by the Commission and applied in these cases, properly balances the First Amendment rights of federal candidates, the public and broadcasters.[19]

No Censorship—Title III, Part I, Sec. 326

Nothing in this Act shall be understood or construed to give this Commission the power of censorship over the radio communications or signals transmitted by any radio station, and no regulation or condition shall be promulgated or fixed by the Commission which shall interfere with the right of free speech by means of radio communication.

The Telecommunications Act of 1996

In February 1996 Congress passed the Telecommunications Act. Essentially, the act relaxes many of the rules that prohibit telephone companies, cable systems, and broadcasters from providing similar services. The act also modifies the multiple ownership rules and directs the FCC to implement rules requiring television receivers to contain V-Chip technology. The V-Chip allows electronic in-home blocking of violent or sexually explicit programming.

Title V of the 1996 Telecommunications Act was known as the Communications Decency Act (CDA). CDA would have applied broadcast-like indecency standards to the Internet. CDA would have prohibited intentional transmission of indecent or "patently offensive" materials to minors over the Internet (see *Communications Decency Act of 1996, Title V, Sec. 502,* available at www.epic.org/CDA/CDA.html). Upon passage of the CDA, the American Civil Liberties Union filed suit against the Justice Department on grounds that the CDA violated the First Amendment. Pending the outcome of the case, the Justice Department did not enforce the provisions of CDA. *ACLU v. Reno (1996,* U.S.Dist.LEXIS 1617) was heard by a three-judge panel. The three-judge panel found the Internet indecency ban unconstitutional, noting that the Internet deserves the broadest possible constitutional protections. Judge Stewart Dalzell likened the Internet to newspapers and magazines, as opposed to more tightly regulated broadcast transmissions. The Supreme Court heard arguments in the appeal *of ACLU v. Reno* in March 1997. In *Reno v. American Civil Liberties Union, 117 S.Ct. 2329, 138 L.Ed.2d 874 (1997)* the Supreme Court held that Communications Decency Act violated the First Amendment.

The U.S. Criminal Code

Originally, the prohibition against broadcasting obscene or indecent language was part of Section 326 of the Communications Act. In 1948, the prohibition was removed and made part of the U.S. Criminal Code. Title 18, U.S.C. 1464 states,

Whoever utters any obscene, indecent, or profane language by means of radio communication shall be fined not more than $10,000 or imprisoned not more than two years or both.[20]

These issues are discussed in greater depth in Chapter 5, "The Broadcast Licensing and Cable Franchising Process."

The Evolution of FCC Authority

Although the Communications Act seems to guarantee broadcasters protection under the First Amendment, application of that right took a peculiar turn. Freedom of speech was to apply to speech deemed to be in the public interest. It was not that the speech of broadcasters was to be protected as much as it was the right of the radio audience to be protected from certain forms of speech. In *KFKB Broadcasting v. Federal Radio Commission*, the Commission revoked the license of the station featuring programs by Dr. J. R. Brinkley. Brinkley answered medical questions on the air and dispensed his medicines, for which he received a fee. The Commission denied renewal to KFKB on grounds that it had not operated in the "public interest." The FRC denied that it had exceeded its jurisdiction and engaged in censorship and the court agreed.

In *Trinity Methodist Church, South v. Federal Radio Commission*, the Commission expanded this doctrine further. Associate Justice Groner wrote,

☐ Appellant, Trinity Methodist Church, South, was the lessee and operator of a Radio Broadcasting station at Los Angeles, Cal., known by the call letters KGEF. The station had been in operation for several years. The Commission, in its findings, shows that, though in the name of the church, the station was in fact owned by the Reverend Doctor Shuler and its operation dominated by him. Dr. Shuler is the minister in charge of Trinity Church. The station was operated for a total of 23 1/4 hours each week.

In September, 1930, appellant filed an application for renewal of station license. Numerous citizens of Los Angeles protested, and the Commission, being unable to determine that the public interest, convenience, and necessity would be served, set the application down for hearing before an examiner . . . upon consideration of the evidence, the examiner's report, the exceptions, etc., the Commission denied the application for renewal upon the ground that the public interest, convenience and/or necessity would not be served by the granting of the application. Some of the things urging it to this conclusion were that the station had been used to attack a religious organization, meaning the Roman Catholic Church; that the broadcasts by Dr. Shuler were sensational rather than instructive; and that in two instances Shuler had been convicted of attempting in his radio talks to obstruct the orderly administration of public justice . . .

. . . The basis for this appeal is that the Commission's decision is unconstitutional, in that it violates the guaranty [sic] of free speech, and also that it deprives appellant of his property without due process of law. It is further insisted that the decision violates the Radio Act because it is not supported by substantial evidence, and therefore is arbitrary and capricious.

. . . [I]t is generally regarded that freedom of speech and press cannot be infringed by legislative, executive, or judicial action, and that the constitutional guarantee should be given liberal and comprehensive construction. It may therefore be set down as a fundamental principle that under these constitutional guarantees the citizen has in the first instance the right to utter or publish his sentiments, though, of course, upon condition that he is responsible for any abuse of that right. . . . But this does not mean that the government, through agencies established by Congress, may not refuse a renewal of license to one who has abused it to broadcast defamatory and untrue matter. In that case there is not a denial of the freedom of speech, but merely the application of the regulatory power of Congress in a field within the scope of its legislative authority.

. . . This is neither censorship nor previous restraint, nor is it a whittling away of the rights guaranteed by the First Amendment or an impairment of their free exercise. Appellant may continue to indulge his strictures upon the characters of men in public office. He may just as freely as ever criticize religious practices of which he does not approve. He may even indulge private malice or personal slander—subject, of course, to be required to answer for the abuse thereof—but he may not, as we think, demand of right the continued use of an instrumentality of commerce for such purposes, or any other, except in subordination to all reasonable rules and regulations Congress, acting through the Commission, may prescribe.[21]

The first broadcasting case to reach the Supreme Court was decided in 1943. Again, the essence of the case questioned the scope of FCC regulatory power. The *NBC* case is worthy of study because it resulted in a greatly expanded role for the FCC in the regulation of broadcast content. It also outlined major issues in broadcast regulation. Along with the public interest standard and the limited broadcast spectrum, issues like multiple ownership, network dominance over programming, antitrust considerations, and economic impact would continue to dot the regulatory landscape long after the Chain Broadcasting Regulations had disappeared.

National Broadcasting Co., Inc., et al. v. United States et al. (1943)

In the late 1930s, the FCC became concerned over the power that the national radio networks exercised over local stations. The Commission perceived that the public interest was not being served because NBC, CBS, and mutual radio networks demanded much of the affiliate stations' time. The principal of localism, among other things, was not being adhered to when a station obtained and broadcast a high percentage of its programming from New York. Of additional concern was the nature of the affiliate agreements. The FCC was concerned that these agreements forced stations to give up control of programming to the networks.

Although the FCC had no direct jurisdiction over the networks themselves, the agency chose a "back door" approach to regulating network affiliate agreements and ultimately to regulating programming. The Commission proposed the Chain Broadcasting Regulations. The Chain Broadcasting Regulations prohibited local stations from entering into network affiliation contracts that resulted in the station surrendering control of is programming to the network. A station that entered into such an arrangement could have its license revoked.

NBC and other networks challenged the FCC's authority to make such rules. The networks contended that the Commission had exceeded the authority given to it by the Communications Act. The *NBC* case found its way to the Supreme Court. The Court ruled in favor of the FCC noting:

☐ The Act itself establishes that the Commission's powers are not limited to the engineering and technical aspects of regulation of radio communication. Yet we are asked to regard the Commission as a kind of traffic officer, policing the wave lengths to prevent stations from interfering with each other. But the Act does not restrict the Commission merely to the supervision of traffic. It puts upon the Commission the burden of determining the composition of that traffic. The facilities of radio are not large enough to accommodate all who wish to use them. Methods must be devised for choosing from among the many who apply. And since Congress itself could not do this, it committed the task to the Commission.[22]

The *NBC* case attempts to clarify the FCC's role in defining the "public interest" standard. Because the case was the first broadcasting case to come before the Supreme Court, it broke entirely new ground for the emerging industry. The nation's highest court had recognized broadcasting as a social institution worthy of its attention.

Justice Frankfurter articulates the limits of the First Amendment rights of broadcasters. He reminds the networks of the "limited spectrum" and the obligation to serve the public interest. These arguments serve as the basis for the regulation of electronic media. Throughout the years, courts and the Commission have assigned varying degrees of importance to the fundamental arguments, but nonetheless, they remain just that—fundamental.

Another result of the *NBC* case was the creation of the American Broadcasting Company in 1945. In 1943, NBC sold the less profitable Blue Network, which then became ABC.

The Supreme Court next considered the FCC's power in 1969. In the intervening years, the Commission's foray into program regulation continued. In 1946, the FCC issued the controversial "Blue Book," so named because of the color of its binding. The Blue Book was officially titled *Public Service Responsibility of Broadcast Licensees* and essentially chastised the industry for failing to provide local programs, for providing an overabundance of commercials, and for the general failure of most programming to serve the "public interest." Although the measures were never really enforced, the report concluded with ways that the FCC would enforce higher programming standards. For example, the FCC urged broadcasters to devote more time to local programming and to sustaining programs. Sustaining programs were programs without commercial sponsorship.

The Rise and Fall of the Fairness Doctrine

From its earliest days, the Commission believed that broadcasters should be fair in their presentation of public issues. As early as 1929, the FRC noted that,

> It would not be fair, indeed it would not be good service to the public to allow a one-sided presentation of the political issues of a campaign. In so far as a program consists of discussion of public questions, public interest requires ample play for the free and fair competition of opposing views, and the commission believes that the principle applies not only to addresses by political candidates but to all discussions of issues of importance to the public.[23]

The concern with fairness was the subject of various FCC cases. In 1940, in the *Mayflower* decision (In the Matter of MayFlower Broadcasting Corp. 8F.C.C.333 (1941)), the Commission prohibited broadcasters from editorializing. In 1949, the Commission issued a report called *In the Matter of Editorializing by Broadcast Licensees.* The report reversed the FCC's policy on editorializing set forth in *Mayflower* and outlined the new Fairness Doctrine by stating,

> . . . [U]nder the American system of broadcasting the individual licensees of radio stations have the responsibility for determining the

specific program material to be broadcast over their stations. The choice, however, must be exercised in a manner consistent with the basic policy of the Congress that radio be maintained as a medium of free speech for the general public as a whole rather than as an outlet for the purely personal or private interests of the licensee. This requires that licensees devote a reasonable percentage of their broadcasting time to the discussion of public issues of interest in the community served by their stations and that such programs be designed so that the public has a reasonable opportunity to hear different opposing positions on the public issues of interest and importance in the community.[24]

In 1959, Section 315 of the Communications Act was amended. The addition of the statement requiring broadcasters to "afford reasonable opportunity for the discussion of conflicting views on issues of public importance" (see section 315, paragraph (a)(4)) appeared to codify the Fairness Doctrine. In 1986, a court ruled that this was not the case. The ruling in *Telecommunications Research and Action Center v. Federal Communications Commission (TRAC v. FCC)* played an important part in the demise of the Fairness Doctrine.

The wording of the 1959 statement still remained vague, and in 1964 the Commission issued what it called a "Fairness Primer," which was titled Applicability of the Fairness Doctrine in the Handling of Controversial Issues of Public Importance. In the primer, the FCC attempted to clarify fairness and delineate it from the "equal opportunities" requirement in Section 315. The Commission provided examples of possible "controversial issues," such as the nuclear test ban treaty, Communism, and civil rights. The FCC offered this additional advice:

While Section 315 thus embodies both the "equal opportunities" requirement and the fairness doctrine, they apply to different situations and in different ways. The "equal opportunities" requirement relates solely to use of broadcast facilities by candidates for public office. . . .

The fairness doctrine deals with the broader question of affording reasonable opportunity for the presentation of contrasting viewpoints on controversial issues of public importance. Generally speaking, it does not apply with the precision of the "equal opportunities" requirement.[25]

In 1967, the Commission added two more aspects to the Fairness Doctrine—the personal attack rules and political editorializing. Before the end of the decade, the issue of fairness in broadcasting would come before the Supreme Court in *Red Lion*. At issue was not only the validity of the Fairness Doctrine, but also the extent of the Commission's power.

☐ *Red Lion Broadcasting Co. Inc. et al. v. Federal Communications Commission et al. (1969)*

Justice White delivered the opinion of the Court.

☐ The Red Lion Broadcasting Company is licensed to operate a Pennsylvania radio station, WGCB. On November 27, 1964, WGCB carried a 15-minute broadcast by the Reverend Billy James Hargis as part of a "Christian Crusade" series. A book by Fred J. Cook entitled "Goldwater—Extremist on the Right" was discussed by Hargis, who said that Cook had been fired by a newspaper for Communist-affiliated publication; that he defended Alger Hiss and attacked J. Edgar Hoover and the Central Intelligence Agency; and that he had now written a "book to smear and destroy Barry Goldwater" . . . When Cook heard of the broadcast he concluded that he had been personally attacked and demanded free reply time, which the station refused. After an exchange of letters among Cook, Red Lion and the FCC, the FCC declared that the Hargis broadcast constituted a personal attack on Cook; that Red Lion had failed to meet its obligation under the fairness doctrine . . . to send a tape, transcript, or summary of the broadcast to Cook and offer him reply time; and that the station must provide reply time whether or not Cook would pay for it. On review in the Court of Appeals for the District of Columbia Circuit, the FCC's position was upheld as constitutional and otherwise proper. 127 U.S.App. D.C. 129, 381 F.2d 908 (1967).

    . . . Not long after the Red Lion litigation was begun, the FCC issued a *Notice of Proposed Rule Making* . . . with an eye to making the personal attack aspect of the fairness doctrine more precise and more readily enforceable . . . the regulations read as follows:

    "Personal attacks; political editorials.

    (a) When, during the presentation of views on a controversial issue of public importance, an attack is made upon the honesty, character, integrity or like personal qualities of an identified person or group, the licensee shall, within a reasonable time and in no event later than 1 week after the attack, transmit to the person or group attacked (1) notification of the date, time and identification of the broadcast; (2) a script or tape (or an accurate summary if a script or tape is not available) of the attack; and (3) an offer of a reasonable opportunity to respond over the licensee's facilities."

    Believing that the specific application of the fairness doctrine in Red Lion, and promulgation of the regulations . . . are both authorized by Congress and enhance rather than abridge the freedoms of speech and press protected by the First Amendment, we hold them valid and constitutional. . . .

It is the right of the viewers and listeners, not the right of
broadcasters, which is paramount. . . . It is the purpose of the First
Amendment to preserve an uninhibited marketplace of ideas in which
truth will ultimately prevail, rather than to countenance monopolization of
that market, whether it be by the Government itself or a private license
. . . In view of the scarcity of broadcast frequencies, the Government's role
in allocating those frequencies, and the legitimate claims of those unable
without governmental assistance to gain those frequencies for the
expression of their views, we hold the regulations and ruling at issue here
are both authorized by statute and constitutional.[26]

The Supreme Court upheld both the Fairness Doctrine and personal
attack rules. The latter are not applied to attacks on foreign groups, or individuals, or to statements made by legally qualified candidates for public
office. Other exemptions are similar to those found in Section 315, such
as bona fide newscasts, news interviews, and so forth. (See 47 C.F.R. 73.123
for the complete text of the personal attack rules. Available online at
www.access.gpo.gov/cg1-bin/cfrassemble.cg1?title/199847.)

In *Red Lion*, the court relied on the "spectrum scarcity" rationale to base
its decision. That is, because there are a finite number of broadcast channels
available, those granted a broadcast license must operate in the public interest. The FCC was to act as proxy for those who would present different views
by giving them access to broadcast facilities through the Fairness Doctrine.
Broadcast licensees had an affirmative duty to seek out these contrasting
viewpoints.

Application of the Fairness Doctrine *after* Red Lion

The first station after Red Lion to have license renewal denied
for failure to adhere to the Fairness Doctrine was WXUR. In 1972, in
Brandywine-Main Line Radio Inc. v. Federal Communications Commission,
the court upheld the Commission's decision to deny renewal based on Fairness Doctrine violations and lack of candor. The operator of WXUR was the
Faith Theological Seminary. The Reverend Carl McIntire presided over the
seminary. In 1965, a group headed by McIntire applied for transfer of control
of WXUR, and the application was opposed by community groups. The FCC
approved the transfer only after the McIntire group pledged they would
provide an opportunity for the expression of opposing viewpoints on controversial public issues.

At license renewal time, citizens groups decided that McIntire had
not honored his pledge. The station manager was finally fired as a result of

anti-Semitic remarks that had been made on the air. Other personal attacks had been made, and WXUR had established no guidelines for providing notice and response as required by the *Red Lion* ruling. The license renewal was denied by the FCC.

Commercials

The Fairness Doctrine played a major part in the congressional ban of cigarette advertising from the airwaves. In 1967, the FCC held that, because of the health concern involved, cigarette smoking constituted a controversial issue of public importance. Therefore, the broadcast of cigarette advertisements were affected by the Fairness Doctrine. Broadcasters were required to devote time to opposing viewpoints. In 1968, in *Banzhaf v. Federal Communications Commission*, the Commission ruled that equal time was not required for anti-smoking spots, but balanced coverage was expected. In 1969, the FCC proposed to ban cigarette ads from radio and television completely.

Broadcasters, led by the National Association of Broadcasters (NAB), favored a gradual phasing out of cigarette ads. They argued that self-regulation was the most effective way of dealing with the issue. Congress beat the Commission to the punch. In 1970, cigarette broadcast advertising was banned by statute. The law went into effect January 2, 1971. In 1986, Congress banned smokeless tobacco products, such as snuff and chewing tobacco, from the airwaves in the *Comprehensive Smokeless Tobacco Health Education Act of 1986*. Cigars and pipe tobacco are not included in the ban.

The FCC would have preferred to treat cigarette ads as a special situation and not apply the Fairness Doctrine to advertising. In *Friends of the Earth v. Federal Communications Commission*, the Commission refused to require broadcasters to present contrasting views in response to automobile ads. The petitioners argued that gasoline and high-powered engines contributed to air pollution and therefore were within the definition of a "controversial issue." They argued that these ads were in the same vein as cigarette ads. The U.S. court of appeals agreed and ordered the FCC to be consistent.

Faced with the possibility of a staggering number of fairness complaints, the Commission modified its policy. The FCC applied the Fairness Doctrine to advocacy or editorial advertisements, but not to product ads. It left the regulation of deceptive advertisements to the Federal Trade Commission. The reversal of the policy was challenged by public interest groups, but was upheld by a federal court in 1975 in *Public Interest Research Group v. Federal Communications Commission*.

Political Campaigns

Section 315 of the Communications Act was designed to cover appearances of political candidates but did not address appearances of a candidate's supporters. This was left to be addressed in the Fairness Doctrine. In "Letter to Nicholas Zapple," the Commission noted that the 1959 amendment to Section 315 recognized that the Fairness Doctrine applied when a candidate's own appearance was exempt from Section 315. This letter is the basis of the Zapple Doctrine, which states that if broadcasters give or sell time to supporters of one political candidate, they must do the same for supporters of the opposing candidates for the same office. The Zapple Doctrine remains in effect today.

The Supreme Court ruled in *CBS v. Democratic National Committee* that there is no First Amendment right of access to broadcast facilities. The Fairness Doctrine no longer applied to editorial advertising, but the Cullman Doctrine might apply. The Cullman Doctrine required the licensee to provide free time if needed to ensure a balanced presentation.

Abolition of the Fairness Doctrine

Although the Fairness Doctrine was held to be constitutional in Red Lion, the policy was not without its critics. Many believed that the doctrine did not promote the discussion of conflicting viewpoints as intended, but rather inhibited that discussion. In 1985, the Commission issued a report concluding that the Fairness Doctrine was no longer justified. The *1985 Fairness Report* stated that the diversity of opinions sought by the doctrine was being served by the "multiplicity of voices in the marketplace."[27]

The report concluded that the Fairness Doctrine actually inhibited robust discussion of ideas and restricted the journalistic freedom of broadcasters. The Commission was concerned that it was too involved in evaluating viewpoints and that continued enforcement of the doctrine increased government interference in the editorial process of broadcast journalists. The FCC noted that a large percentage of its staff time was needed to deal with fairness complaints and that it had received more than 6700 complaints in 1984. The Commission argued that the costs associated with enforcement were unnecessary, because the tremendous increase in information sources had made the doctrine obsolete.

The scarcity rationale used as the basis of *Red Lion* also was attacked. The Commission stated that the dramatic increase in the number of radio and television outlets since *Red Lion* had made that argument moot. Again, the FCC relied on the marketplace to ensure that the public was exposed to controversial issues of public importance.

The Commission did not act to eliminate the Fairness Doctrine, preferring to wait until Congress had the opportunity to respond to the *1985 Fairness Report*. In the meantime, the Commission announced that it would continue to enforce the Fairness Doctrine.

In 1984, the Commission ruled that the Meredith Corporation's WTVH had violated the Fairness Doctrine. The station had presented a series of commercials discussing a proposed nuclear power plant. The FCC found that the station failed to present balanced coverage with contrasting points of view. The Meredith Corporation appealed the Commission's ruling and relied heavily on the *1985 Fairness Report* as a defense. In *Meredith Corp. v. Federal Communications Commission*, Circuit Judge Silberman maintained,

☐   . . . The Commission's *1985 Fairness Report* quite clearly determined that the Fairness Doctrine as embodied in its regulations no longer serves the statutory public interest Congress charges the Commission with advancing and further states that if it were up to the Commission it would hold the Doctrine unconstitutional. . . . An agency is not required to reconsider the merits of a rule each time it seeks to apply it. . . . Here, however the Commission itself has already largely undermined the legitimacy of its own Rule. . . . If time and changing circumstances reveal that the "public interest" is not served by the application of such regulations, it must be assumed that the Commission will act in accordance with its statutory obligations. ". . . Accordingly we remand the case to the FCC with instructions to consider the Petitioner's constitutional arguments."[28]

The court tossed the issue back into the lap of the Commission, where it might have lagged if not for the Telecommunications Research and Action Center, or TRAC, decision. In this case, the court of appeals found that the 1959 amendment to Section 315(a) did not codify the fairness doctrine:

☐   We do not believe the language adopted in 1959 made the fairness doctrine a binding statutory obligation; rather, it ratified the Commission's longstanding position that the public interest standard authorizes the fairness doctrine. . . . The words employed by Congress also demonstrate that the obligation recognized and preserved was an administrative construction, not a binding statutory directive.[29]

At this point, the FCC could have avoided the constitutional question by simply deciding that the Fairness Doctrine was no longer in the public interest, but it chose a different approach. It reversed its decision in *Meredith* and declared its belief that the Fairness Doctrine was not in the public interest and was unconstitutional.

The Syracuse Peace Council appealed the Commission's decision. In *Syracuse Peace Council v. Federal Communications Commission*, the court of appeals issued an opinion supporting the FCC's refusal to enforce the Fairness Doctrine, but refused to make a determination of the doctrine's constitutionality. Circuit Judge Williams maintained,

☐ Under the "fairness doctrine," the Federal Communications Commission has, as its *1985 Fairness Report* explains, required broadcast media licensees (1) "to provide coverage of vitally important controversial issues of interest in the community served by the licensees," and (2) "to provide a reasonable opportunity for the presentation of contrasting viewpoints on such issues." In adjudication of a complaint against Meredith Corporation, licensee of station WTVH in Syracuse, New York, the Commission concluded that the doctrine did not serve the public interest and was unconstitutional. Accordingly it refused to enforce the doctrine against Meredith. Although the Commission somewhat entangled its public interest and constitutional findings, we find that the Commission's public interest determination was an independent basis for its decision and was supported by the record. We uphold that determination without reaching the constitutional issue.[30]

Following the court of appeals decision in *Syracuse Peace Council*, some members of Congress drafted a bill designed to codify the Fairness Doctrine. The bill, called the Fairness in Broadcasting Act of 1987, was vetoed by President Reagan.

In *Arkansas AFL-CIO v. FCC (1993)*, a three-judge panel of the U.S. Court of Appeals for the Eighth Circuit concluded that the Fairness Doctrine was not codified by the 1959 amendment to the Communications Act, and therefore the FCC was free to declare that the doctrine no longer served the public interest and would no longer be enforced.[31]

Both Congress and various presidential administrations have considered reinstating the Fairness Doctrine. The Personal Attack rules and the Political Editorializing rules were repealed in October 2000 as a result of *Radio Television News Directors Association v. FCC* 229 F.3d 261 (D.C. Cir. 2000).

Reasonable Access to Broadcast Media for Political Candidates

As noted earlier, in *CBS v. Democratic National Committee*, the Supreme Court held that a network policy of refusing to sell time to political groups for the discussion of social and political issues was not a violation of the First Amendment. In 1981, however, the Court added a twist to the matter of access. It might appear that *CBS v. Democratic National*

Committee and *CBS v. FCC* deal with identical issues, and that the Court was inconsistent. In *CBS v. FCC*, the Court was dealing with a statutory right conferred by Section 312(a)(7) of the Communications Act. For the Court to rule against the general network policy that resulted in *CBS v. Democratic National Committee*, it would have required a determination that the First Amendment had been violated.

Enforcement Powers of the Commission

Stations that are found to be in violation of FCC rules or policies may suffer a variety of different punishments. Because the FCC does not monitor programming, nontechnical violations come to its attention via listener and viewer complaints. When a complaint is received, the FCC will ask the broadcaster to respond in writing. The reply is examined. If the FCC is satisfied, the matter might go no further. If the Commission decides to pursue the issue, the broadcaster may be required to rectify the situation in some way. Perhaps an apology to offended parties may be necessary. In more serious cases, the Commission may issue a letter of reprimand to the station. This "wrist slapping" usually does not require payment of a fine, but it serves officially to put the station "on notice" not to repeat the transgression. In still more serious cases, a cease and desist order may be issued. This is a legal notice that requires the licensee to stop a specified activity. Failure to obey such an order carries a fine. The FCC may also fine broadcasters. This is called a forfeiture and may carry a fine of as much as $25,000 per day, up to a maximum of $250,000. In 1990, the FCC fined Infinity Broadcasting $6000 for a shock-jock Howard Stern broadcast transmitted on three Infinity stations. The $250,000 limit applies to a single station. Therefore, if a licensee owns more than one station, multiple fines may be imposed. In 1992, the Commission fined Infinity again, this time a record $600,000 for additional indecent broadcasts on three stations during the Howard Stern Show.

The FCC may consider the past record of licensees at license renewal time and may issue a short-term renewal if it finds a station's performance to be below par. The station is given a period of time to clean up its act, after which time the license may be renewed for the full term or revoked. Attempts to influence the outcome of a pending FCC matter by the president of a Boston television station resulted in several short-term renewals for WHDH-TV in the 1950s and 1960s. In a case that spanned 15 years, the station eventually lost its license.

The "death sentence" for broadcasters is license revocation. This occurs primarily at license renewal. The ultimate penalty is reserved for those who have engaged in the most egregious practices. Lying to the Commission or "lack of candor," failure to observe the Fairness Doctrine, conviction of drug offenses by station owners, and lack of licensee control of station operations have all been reasons for license revocation.

Regulation of Cable Television

The rationale of broadcast regulation rests on the theory of the limited broadcast spectrum. Broadcasters are required to operate in the public interest because they are public trustees of the airwaves. Throughout the 1930s and 1940s, broadcasters and the FCC developed a working relationship with one another. The tensions between the two fostered a certain elasticity as broadcasters tested the limits of the regulatory system. Eventually, the FCC and broadcasters became partners in the regulatory process. The well-being of all parties was intertwined. The economic interests of broadcasters became a concern of the Commission. Put simply: if broadcasting did not exist, neither would the Commission. In the early 1950s, this delicate balance began to shift with the advent of cable television.

Cable television was not originally intended as a means of providing programming to individual households. Coaxial cable was perfected in the 1930s at Bell Labs. "Coax" is capable of delivering a number of different signals within a single wire. Coaxial cable was first used in broadcasting as a means of interconnecting the television networks and their affiliate stations. It was the failure of the FCC to redraw its flawed UHF television allocation scheme of 1952 that led to the use of cable as a means of delivering TV signals to individual homes. In short, the Commission allocated UHF stations to markets too small to support network affiliates. The Commission's goal was to establish a nationwide system of local TV stations. Instead, it created the perfect conditions for an alternative distribution system.

The first cable systems were called community antenna television (or CATV) operations. Early CATV systems developed in mountainous areas of Pennsylvania and Oregon. Their primary purpose was to provide quality television service to areas not served by TV.

In the early 1950s, cable TV was viewed as a temporary solution to the problem of poor television reception. It was assumed that the FCC would allocate more stations to areas that were underserved and reallocate those frequencies unable to support quality operations. By the mid-1950s, it became obvious that this was not to be. As late as 1958, 34 percent of American homes could receive only one television channel.

CATV came to the rescue of both the viewing public and TV broadcasters by using microwaves to link the missing network signals to underserved areas. Broadcasters did not perceive cable as a threat, because CATV expanded the television audience at no cost to the stations or networks. The only FCC interest in cable stemmed from the need for Commission approval of the microwave relay systems used in importing the broadcast signals. This approval was routinely granted, and the FCC stated in 1959 that it had no interest in regulating CATV. It was not until cable systems began competing with over-the-air broadcasters that the FCC changed its mind about regulation.

Eventually, cable systems began to import television signals from distant cities. These signals were often in direct competition with the local television stations. Smaller markets were hurt most by this practice. For example, given a choice of a small, local television station and an imported signal from a station in a larger city, viewers often chose to watch the latter. Of course, this had a detrimental economic impact on the smaller station, and eventually these stations complained to the Commission. After several years of agitation by broadcasters, the FCC decided that it would regulate cable television. The basis for the regulation rested on the premise that the economic impact of cable television on broadcasting may not be in the public interest. Specifically, economic injury to small, local broadcasters did not foster the FCC's policy of localism. Therefore, it was not in the public interest. Of additional concern was the fact that cable operators paid nothing for the programs they carried. The Commission thought that this gave cable operators an unfair economic advantage over broadcasters.

In the mid-1960s, the FCC developed a series of regulations designed to prevent cable television from effectively competing with over-the-air broadcasters. in 1965, the Commission implemented the "must-carry" rule, which required cable systems to carry all local broadcast signals. The FCC also restricted the importation of distant television signals by cable systems. In *United States v. Southwestern Cable Co.*, this regulation was challenged and resulted in a Supreme Court decision to uphold the FCC's authority to regulate cable under the mandate in the Communications Act requiring regulation of all wire and radio communication. The Court also based its decision on the premise that cable systems threatened the growth of local over-the-air television services and therefore could threaten the public interest. FCC regulation would ensure that this did not happen.

The *Southwestern Cable* case established only that the FCC could assert jurisdiction over cable, but it did not outline the limits of this authority. By the late 1960s, the Commission had promulgated rules that required large cable systems to originate local programming. In *United States v. Midwest Video Co.*, the Supreme Court upheld these rules, but noted that the FCC had "strained the outer limits" of its authority to regulate cable. Two years later, the FCC repealed the local origination rule, but issued new rules that required new cable systems to allocate channels for public access. In *United States v. Midwest Video Co.*, the Supreme Court held that the FCC had exceeded its authority by promulgating the access rule. The Court held that

the access rules imposed a common carrier obligation on cable operators—
something that Congress did not intend. Local municipalities were still
allowed to air public access channels as part of the franchising process.[32]

In the late 1970s and early 1980s, the FCC eliminated many of the rules
affecting cable television. The Copyright Act of 1976 provided a means for
compensating broadcasters for carrying cable programming. This act eliminated one of the original bases of regulation. The addition of satellite-
delivered cable programming services in the late 1970s, such as Home Box
Office, reduced the demand for broadcast programming.

The Cable Communications Policy Act of 1984—Congressional Authority to Regulate Cable Television

In late 1984, Congress enacted the Cable Communications
Policy Act of 1984. The act codified many of the cable regulations that had
been developed during the period beginning in the 1960s. The Cable Act
amended the Communications Act of 1934 and formally gave the FCC jurisdiction over cable television. As a result, the FCC no longer had to justify its
regulation of cable television because of cable TV's interface with broadcasting. Significant provisions of the act are presented on the following pages:

Section 521
The purposes of this title are to
1. establish a national policy concerning cable communications;
2. establish franchise procedures and standards which encourage
   the growth and development of cable systems and assure [sic]
   that cable systems are responsive to the needs and interests of
   the local community;
3. establish guidelines for the exercise of Federal, State, and local
   authority with respect to the regulation of cable systems;
4. assure [sic] and encourage that cable communications provide
   and are encouraged to provide the widest possible diversity of
   information sources and services to the public;
5. establish an orderly process for franchise renewal which protects
   cable operators against unfair denials of renewal where the
   operator's past performance and proposal for future performance
   meet the standards established by this title; and
6. promote competition in cable communications and minimize
   unnecessary regulation that would impose an undue economic
   burden on cable systems.[33]

Section 541

. . . (c) Any cable system shall not be subject to regulation as a common carrier or utility by reason of providing any cable service.[34]

Section 559

Whoever transmits over any cable system any matter which is obscene or otherwise unprotected by the Constitution of the United States shall be fined not more than $10,000 or imprisoned not more than two years or both.[35]

Franchises

The Cable Communications Policy Act gives state and local governments the power to award franchises and to determine the qualifications necessary for systems to be awarded local franchises. Section 541 of the act requires cable systems to obtain a franchise. In *City of Los Angeles v. Preferred Communications Inc.*,[36] the Supreme Court ruled that as long as utilities are adequate, a city cannot deny a franchise to more than one cable company. "Adequate" in this case means that rights-of-way are available to support an additional cable system.

Section 622 limits the amount that may be charged for a franchise fee. Section 533 prohibits broadcast and cable cross-ownership in overlapping markets, and ownership by a common carrier of a cable system in its service area. The FCC has been reconsidering this restriction.

Just as broadcasters must obtain renewal of their licenses by the FCC, cable operators are subject to the franchise renewal process by local municipalities. Like broadcasters, cable systems are fearful of nonrenewal. Section 626 of the act requires that a denial of franchise renewal must be based on a finding that the cable operator failed to comply substantially with the franchise agreement. In addition, denial must be predicated on the fact that the cable operator provided inferior service to the community, is legally or technically unqualified, or cannot possibly meet the future needs of the community. Like broadcasters, there is a strong renewal expectancy for existing franchises.

Section 543 provides for the regulation of basic cable rates in the absence of effective competition. Otherwise, cable operators are free to charge whatever the market will bear. This provision has led to charges that cable is a monopoly and should be subjected to more stringent rate regulation.

Programming

Although the Cable Act prohibits the broadcast of obscene programming, the act does not regulate programming services. Unlike over-the-air broadcasters, cable operators are given First Amendment protection for program content. Cable franchises may specify the number and types of channels, and mandate public access, but they may not require specific program services. For example, the franchise may call for an all-news channel but it may not require a cable operator to choose CNN.

Two areas related to programming are the syndicated exclusivity and must-carry rules. The syndicated exclusivity rule, known as the Syndex rule, requires that cable systems "black out" syndicated programs carried on a distant station if the same program (or series) is being carried by a local station. The Syndex rule was originally passed in 1972 and then abolished by the FCC in 1980. The rule was restored in 1990 and is applied to all cable systems with more than 1000 subscribers.[37]

The must-carry rules required cable systems to carry all local television signals. In 1985, a federal court found the rules, as written, to be a violation of cable operators' First Amendment right of editorial discretion.[38] Must-carry was reinstated in 1993 with the passage of the Cable Consumer Protection Act of 1992. The Cable Consumer Protection Act will be discussed later in this book.

Deregulation and Reregulation of Broadcasting and Cable Television

The Communications Act of 1934 was a product of New Deal legislation and of the social forces of the Great Depression. The mid-1970s saw a change in social attitudes toward the role of government as it affected our nation. Between 1934 and 1975, the FCC had steadily promulgated more regulations that affected broadcasters. Many of these regulations resulted in a great deal of paperwork and were only marginally—if at all—effective. Deregulation began as early as 1972 under FCC Chairman Richard Wiley. Wiley called his policy "reregulation" and planned to reregulate the industry by eliminating burdensome administrative procedures.[39]

During the Carter administration, FCC chairman Charles Ferris made deregulation the official policy. It was under his chairmanship that radio was deregulated and the Commission began to deregulate television.[40]

During the Reagan administration and under the FCC chairmanship of Mark Fowler, the Commission began to dismantle much of the monitoring and enforcement structure that had evolved over the years. Fowler's policy of "unregulation" made good on President Reagan's pledge to "get government off the backs of the people," or in this case, off the backs of the broadcasters. The only area of broadcast regulation essentially untouched was the public interest responsibility guaranteed by the Communications Act, although it came under much reinterpretation.

The deregulators preferred to allow the marketplace to satisfy most regulatory goals. Many minor "underbrush" regulations were eliminated in the

1970s, and major rules (e.g., formal community ascertainment and the Fairness Doctrine) fell out of use during the 1980s.

The FCC began deregulating radio in 1981. First the Commission eliminated rules that required formal ascertainment of community needs. No longer were radio stations required to survey the general public and community leaders in their city of license and generate programming that met community needs. Radio was only required to have general knowledge of these needs. The FCC also eliminated the requirement to keep program logs, guidelines for nonentertainment programming, and guidelines for the amount of commercial time. Deregulation of television and noncommercial broadcasting followed in 1984.

The deregulatory trend produced major changes in the rules governing radio, broadcast television, and cable television. The FCC increased the term of a license from three to seven years for radio and from three to five years for television (1981). The Commission increased the number of stations that one person or group could own from 21 to 36 stations (1985) and dropped the requirement that they must be held for at least three years (1982). The Commission reversed its stance on the long-cherished Fairness Doctrine (1985) and virtually dropped most of its cable rules, including the must-carry rules (1985 to 1987), after the rules were twice declared unconstitutional. The FCC even relinquished leadership in the area of technical standards when it eliminated the classes of engineering licenses (1981), relaxed station engineering requirements and failed to specify a standard for AM stereo (1982), deferring to marketplace forces.

This list of deregulations is by no means exhaustive, but by 1987 there was evidence that the pendulum was beginning to swing back. Although the FCC had never intended to eliminate all regulation of broadcast and cable, in theory it hoped to eliminate those regulations that affected how broadcasters conducted their business. Rules affecting program types and content were primary targets. Rules designed to preserve competition in the marketplace should, ideally, be left in place.

Unfortunately, this theoretical model did not hold up well in practice. As the 1980s drew to a close, the Commission, responding again to public pressure, undertook a series of attempts at reregulating program content and types. The FCC had moved away from its policy of "channeling" indecent programming and by early 1990 had proposed a 24-hour ban on indecent programs. In October 1990, Congress passed a bill that required television stations to serve the "educational and informational needs of children" and placed limits on the length and types of advertisements that could be used during these programs. In 1991, FCC Chairman Alfred Sikes called for an "attic-to-basement" review of broadcast regulations. The goal of this review was to study the continued need for certain regulations in today's multichannel video environment. Amid concerns over the shrinking audience of broadcast television, rising cable rates, and poor service to cable subscribers, Congress overrode a Presidential veto and reregulated cable TV with passage of the Cable Consumer Protection Act of 1992.

When Reed Hundt assumed the Chairmanship of the FCC, he further distanced himself from Reagan-era regulators who saw television as "just another appliance" while downplaying the medium's public responsibility. In a twist on former FCC Chair Mark Fowler's observation that "television is just a toaster with pictures," Hundt said that "TV is not a toaster," and he reaffirmed the broadcaster's role as public trustee. He also dismissed arguments that further deregulation is needed if broadcasters are to compete on the information highway.[41]

Under the chairmanship of Michael Powell, the FCC has continued to take a marketplace view of regulation. The Commission has generally been supportive of mergers between large media corporations, has continued to enforce broadcast indecency rules, and has guided the transition to digital television with a more *laissez faire* policy than that of previous Chairman, Willian Kennard.

After two and one-half decades of deregulation, there really have been very few substantial modifications to the legal obligations facing broadcast licensees. The Telecommunications Act of 1996 relaxed cross-ownership and other business regulations that prohibited broadcasters, cable, and telephone companies from engaging in similar activities. However, the basic structure of the public interest standard—with all its penumbra—remains intact.

Summary

The rationale for the regulation of broadcasting is based on the notion of spectrum scarcity. Broadcasters are licensed to serve the public interest as public trustees. For this reason, broadcasters are treated differently under the First Amendment than publishers or cable operators.

In the 1920s, the secretary of commerce acted as a "traffic cop of the air" to sort out growing technical interference between radio stations. In 1927, Congress passed the Radio Act, which created the Federal Radio Commission. The FRC was supplanted in 1934 when passage of the Communications Act created the Federal Communications Commission. Both agencies were charged with regulating broadcasting and ensuring that the public interest standard was met. In the 1960s, the Supreme Court held that the Communications Act gave the FCC jurisdiction over cable television.

Deregulation of broadcasting began in the late 1970s and continued throughout the 1980s. Cable television was reregulated in 1992. In 1996 Congress passed the Telecommunications Act. This legislation relaxed many of the barriers and paved the way for broadcasters, cable, and telephone companies to provide similar competing services. Although many rules and regulations were removed or modified, the public-interest standard mandated by Congress in the Communications Act of 1934 remains in effect for broadcasters today.

Notes/References

1. Erwin G. Krasnow and Lawrence D. Longley, *The Politics of Broadcast Regulation*, 2nd ed. (New York: St. Martin's Press, 1978), 9.
2. *United States v. Zenith Radio Corp. et al.*, 12 F.2d 614 (N.D. Ill., 1926).
3. Don R. Le Duc, *Beyond Broadcasting: Patterns in Policy and Law* (New York: Longman, 1987), 10.
4. 47, U.S.C.A., title III, section 301.
5. Ibid., section 302.
6. Ibid., section 303.
7. Section 1304 pertains to the broadcast of lottery information. Section 1343 prohibits fraud by wire, radio, or television. Section 1464 prohibits broadcasting obscene, indecent, or profane language.
8. This section was part of a 1959 amendment to the Communications Act and served as the basis of the Fairness Doctrine. The Doctrine was repealed by the FCC in 1987, but remains a "live" issue to many in Congress.
9. 47 U.S.C.A. Section 315(c). See R.R.2d 397 (1988) for additional information.
10. 47 CFR Section 73.1940.
11. 47 CFR Section 73.19404(d).
12. Ibid. 4(e)(f).
13. Joe Flint, "FCC Drifts Toward Safe Harbor for Abortion Ads," *Broadcasting* (November 9, 1992): 48. See *Gillett Communications of Atlanta Inc. (WAGA TVS) v. Becker* 21 Med. L. Rptr. 702 Index Digest (DC NGa., 1992).
14. Christopher Stern, "Antiabortion Ads Resurface at FCC," *Broadcasting & Cable* (April 18, 1994): 36.
15. "FCC Allows Movement of Antiabortion Ads," *Broadcasting & Cable* (December 5, 1994): 62.
16. Codification of Commission's Political Programming Policies, 7 FCCRcd. 4611, 70 R.R.2d 1331 (1992).
17. *Branch v. Federal Communications Commission*, 824 F.2d 37, 63 R.R.2d 826, 14 Med.L.Rptr. 1465 (1987).

18. For a detailed discussion of nonfederal candidate obligation see *NAB Legal Guide*, 56–57.
19. *CBS Inc. v. FCC*, 453 U.S. 367 (1981).
20. 18 U.S.C., 1464.
21. *Trinity Methodist Church, South v. Federal Radio Commission*, 62 F.2d 850 (D.C. Cir.Ct., 1932), cert. denied 288 U.S. 599 (1933).
22. *National Broadcasting Co., Inc., et al. v. United States et al.*, 319 U.S. 190 (1943).
23. In Re Application of Great Lakes Broadcasting Co., FRC Docket 4900, 3 F.R.C.Ann.Rep. 32 (1929).
24. *In the Matter of Editorializing by Broadcast Licensees*, 13 FCC 1246 (1949) at 21.
25. *Applicability of the Fairness Doctrine in the Handling of Controversial Issues of Public Importance*, 29 Fed.Reg. 1041 July 25, 1964.
26. *Red Lion Broadcasting Co., Inc., et al. v. FCC et al.*, 395 U.S. 367 (1969).
27. Inquiry into Section 73.1910 of the Commission's Rules and Regulations Concerning the General Fairness Obligations of Broadcast Licensees, 102 F.C.C.2d 143, 58 R.R.2d 1137 (1985).
28. *Meredith Corp. v. Federal Communications Commission* (DC CA, 1987) 13 Med.L.Rptr. 1993.
29. *Telecommunications Research and Action Center v. Federal Communications Commission*, 801 F.2d 501, 61 R.R.2d 330, 13 Med.L.Rptr. 1881, rehearing denied 806 F.2d 1115,61 R.R.2 1342, 13 Med.L.Rptr. 1896 (D.C.Cir. 1986), certiorari denied 482 U.S. 919 (1987).
30. *Syracuse Peace Council v. Federal Communications Commission* (DC CA, 1989) 16 Med.L.Rptr. 1225, cert. denied Jan. 8, 1990.
31. *Arkansas AFL-CIO v. FCC* (8th Cir.CA, 1993) 22 Med.L.Rptr. 1001.
32. 440 U.S. 689 (1979).
33. 47 U.S.C.A., Title VI, 521.
34. Ibid., 541.
35. Ibid., 559.
36. 476 U.S. 488 (1986).
37. C.F.R. 47 Parts 76.151 through 76.163.
38. *Quincy Cable TV v. FCC*, 768 F.2d 1434, 58 RR2d 977 (DC Cir. 1985).
39. "Making Life a Bit Easier; Reregulation Gets Under Way," *Broadcasting* (November 6,1972): 19.
40. "The Laissez Faire Legacy of Charles Ferris," *Broadcasting* (January 19, 1981): 37.
41. Harry A. Jessell, "FCC's New Chairman Speaks Out," *Broadcasting & Cable* (November 29, 1993): 6, 101.

Cases

Adrian Weiss, 58 F.C.C.2d 342, 36 R.R.2d 292 (1976).

American Civil Liberties Union v. Reno, 1996 U.S. Dist. LEXIS, 1617.

Arkansas AFL-CIO v. FCC (8th Cir.CA, 1993) 22 Med.L.Rptr. 1001.

Banzhaf v. Federal Communications Commission, 405 F.2d 1082, 14 R.R.2d 2061 (D.C.Cir., 1968) 1 Med.L.Rptr. 2037, cert. denied 396 U.S. 842 (1969)

Branch v. Federal Communications Commission, 824 F.2d 37, 63 R.R.2d 826,14 Med.L.Rptr. 1465 (1987)

Brandywine-Main Line Radio Inc. v. Federal Communications Commission, 473 F.2d 16, 25 R.R.2d 2010 (DC Cir., 1972) 1 Med.L.Rptr. 2067, cert. denied 412 U.S. 922 (1973).

CBS v. Democratic National Committee, 412 U.S. 94 (1973).

CBS Inc. v. FCC, 453, U.S. 367 (1981).

City of Los Angeles v. Preferred Communications Inc., 476 U.S.488 (1986).

Farmers Educational Cooperative Union v. WDAY Inc., 360 U.S. 525 (1959).

Friends of the Earth v. Federal Communications Commission, 449 F.2d 1164, 22 R.R.2d 2145 (DC Cir., 1971).

Gillett Communications of Atlanta Inc. (WAGA-TV5) v. Becker 21 (DC N.Ga), Med.L.Rptr 702 1992.

Hoover v. Intercity Radio Co. Inc., 286 F. 1003 (DC Cir., 1923).

In Re-Application of Great Lakes Broadcasting Co., FRC Docket 4900, 3 F.R.C.Ann.Rep. 32 (1929).

In the Matter of Editorializing by Broadcast Licensees, 13 F.C.C. 1246 (1949).

In the Matter of the Mayflower Broadcasting and the Yankee Network Inc. (WAAB), 8 F.C.C. 333 (1941).

KFKB Broadcasting v. Federal Radio Commission, 47 F.2d 670 (DC Cir., 1931).

Meredith Corp. v. Federal Communications Commission (DC CA, 1987) 13 Med.L.Rptr. 1993

National Broadcasting Co., Inc. et al. v. United States et al., 319 U.S. 190 (1943).

Nicholas Zapple, 23 F.C.C.2d 707, 19 R.R.2d 421 (1970).

Public Interest Research Group v. Federal Communications Commission, 522 F.2d 1060, 34 R.R.2d 1375 (1st Cir., 1975), cert. denied 424 U.S. 965 (1976).

Radio Television News Directors Association v. FCC 229 F.3d 261 (D.C. Cir. 2000).

Red Lion Broadcasting Co., Inc., et al. v. FCC et al., 395 U.S. 367 (1969).

Reno v. American Civil Liberties Union, 117 S.Ct. 2329, 138 L.Ed.2d 874 (1997).

Syracuse Peace Council v. Federal Communications Commission (DC CA, 1989) 16 Med.L.Rptr. 1225, cert. denied Jan. 8, 1990.

Telecommunications Research and Action Center v. Federal Communications Commission, 801 F.2d 501, 61 R.R.2d 330, 13 Med.L.Rptr. 1881, rehearing denied 806 F.2d 1115, 61 R.R.2d 1342, (DC Cir., 1986)13 Med.L.Rptr. 1896, cert. denied 482 U.S. 919 (1987).

Trinity Methodist Church, South v. Federal Radio Commission, 62 F.2d 850 (DC Cir.Ct., 1932), cert. denied 288 U.S. 599 (1933).

United Church of Christ v. FCC (DC Cir., 1978) 4 Med.L.Rptr 1410, 62.

United States v. Midwest Video Corp., 406 U.S. 649 (1972).

United States v. Southwestern Cable Co., 392 U.S. 157 (1968) United States v. Zenith Radio Corp. et al., 12 F.2d 614 (N.D. Ill., 1926).

4

□ □ □
□ □ □
□ □ □

The Rationale of Cable and Satellite (DSS) Television Regulation

The FCC's authority for jurisdiction over cable television originally stemmed from cable's retransmission of over-the-air broadcast signals. In the mid-1950s, broadcasters concerned with potential harm to over-the-air TV asked the FCC to regulate cable as a common carrier. In *Frontier Broadcasting v. Collier*, the FCC held that cable was not a common carrier and therefore was outside the Commission's jurisdiction. However, by the early 1960s the Commission changed its mind and indicated concern with the potential economic injury to broadcasters posed by cable television. This concern was the impetus to regulation. In 1965, the FCC promulgated rules regulating cable TV. The original rules required cable systems to carry all television stations that placed a grade B signal over a community (as defined by FCC Rules, CFR 47 Vol 4 Part 73 (E)). The rules also prohibited importation of a distant signal if the same program was available at the same time on a local channel. Finally, the FCC required cablecasters who wished to import a distant signal into one of the top 100 markets to show that the importation would serve the public interest. In *United States v. Southwestern Cable Co.*, the Supreme Court upheld the Commission's rules and its authority to regulate cable. The Court noted that the Commission's authority emanated from Section 152 of the Communications Act, which empowers the FCC to regulate all interstate communication by wire or radio.

Protecting Broadcasters: The 1970s

After *Southwestern*, the FCC placed a freeze on the importation of distant signals by cable companies. The freeze was instituted to allow the Commission time to develop new cable rules, which culminated in a *Notice of Proposed Rule Making* and *Notice of Inquiry*.

During the 1970s, the FCC developed a number of rules regulating cable. Again, the underlying premise of most of the rules was the protection of broadcasters. For example, the FCC established franchising standards and required systems in major television markets to have a minimum of 20 channels, two-way capability, public access channels, and program origination. In 1975, the FCC adopted anti-siphoning rules designed to keep cable from taking sports and movie programming away from broadcasters. In *Home Box Office Inc. v. FCC (1977)*, the court ruled that the FCC had exceeded its authority and the anti-siphoning rules were repealed. This decision paved the way for the growth of cable movie channels, which spearheaded cable's growth in the 1980s.

In 1977, the FCC began to relax cable regulations. In a report called *Economic Relationship Between TV Broadcasting and CATV*, the FCC found that deregulation of cable would have no serious economic effect on broadcasting.

Cable in the 1980s: A Period of Growth and Deregulation

In the 1980s, cable was substantially deregulated, which allowed the medium to enjoy tremendous growth. Also during this decade, Congress gave the FCC specific authority to regulate cable television. The 1984 Cable Communications Policy Act established a national policy for cable television.

As the decade closed and cable threatened to unseat traditional broadcasting in the United States, many argued for reregulation of cable. As in the past, the economic impact on broadcasters provided a major impetus for cable regulation. Critics charged that cable systems had become unresponsive to the public and enjoyed monopolies, charging outrageous rates for inferior services. Broadcasters argued for a "level playing field," which would allow them to compete more effectively with cable. Broadcasters watched their shares of the viewing audience dwindle from 90 percent to slightly under 60 percent between 1970 and 1991. In July 1991, the FCC Office of Plans and Policy (OPP) issued a report predicting that increased cable penetration throughout the decade would lead to the demise of all but the healthiest broadcast stations located in the larger markets. In response to the report, FCC Chairman Alfred Sikes called for further relaxation of regulations restraining broadcast stations economically. Sikes told the magazine *Broadcasting*, "The transmission medium that had been dominant is now secondary. Broadcasting has been eclipsed by cable."[1]

The cable industry, on the other hand, worried about a different kind of threat—the entry of telephone companies (telcos) into the video delivery business. Cable feared that if telcos offered a "video dial tone" on fiber optic cable, with the potential of 500 channels in a true common carrier environment, cable television would suffer the same economic woes that they had inflicted on broadcasters. By the end of the 1980s neither prediction proved completely accurate, however the audience for broadcast network television continued to decline, while multichannel services continued to gain audience share and penetration.

It is within this framework that the regulation and proposed reregulation of cable television developed during the 1990s. New communications technologies threaten to alter the landscape drastically in the coming years. Digital television (DTV) and its component, high-definition television (HDTV); direct broadcast satellites (DBS); telco fiber optics; digital video disks (DVD); the Internet; and other developments must be factored into the regulatory equation. When these technologies clash with the archaic regulatory machinery of the FCC, it is certain that an interesting—if not always equitable—result will occur. Let us now turn to the issues and policy questions influencing the regulation of cable television.

Franchising and Overbuilding

The 1984 Cable Communications Policy Act established local franchising procedures. Because local governments control the rights-of-way and utility poles, local franchise authorities are usually municipalities or state agencies. The franchise authority grants a cable company use of the "rights of way" for a specific period of time, provided certain conditions are met. The franchise agreement will specify the number of channels to be provided by the cable operator, including any local access channels.

In the early 1980s, competition for cable franchises was fierce. Cable companies often made grandiose promises to municipalities to obtain the exclusive franchise. Assurances of numerous access channels, two-way communications, rapid wiring of the area, and other public service activities were made. Unfortunately, once the franchise was granted, many cable companies forgot their promises.

The process of choosing between applicants for a franchise triggers First Amendment issues. By selecting one applicant over another, the franchise authority effectively denies the community the programming offered by the rejected applicant. In *Group W Cable Inc. v. Santa Cruz*, the District Court for the District of Northern California ruled that if exclusive franchises are granted, the franchising authority must demonstrate that cable has some unique characteristic that justifies some exception to the rule prohibiting government intrusion into the functioning of the media. The city of Santa Cruz violated the First Amendment because it failed to show that existing physical structures could not accommodate all cable operators who sought access. The issue raised is that of overbuilding, that is, allowing a second cable company (or more) to serve an area already served by cable.

The clash between the exclusive awarding of franchises and the First Amendment reached the Supreme Court when Preferred Communications sued the city of Los Angeles.

City of Los Angeles et al. v. Preferred Communications Inc. (1986)

Justice Rehnquist delivered the opinion of the Court.

☐ Respondent Preferred Communications, Inc. sued petitioners City of Los Angeles (City) and the Department of Water and Power (DWP) in the United States District Court for the Central District of California. The complaint alleged a violation of the respondent's rights under the First and Fourteenth Amendments, and under §§ 1 and 2 of the Sherman Act, by reason of the City's refusal to grant respondent a cable television franchise and of DWP's refusal to grant access to DWP's poles or underground conduits used for power lines. The District Court dismissed the complaint for failure to state a claim upon which relief could be granted. The Court of Appeals for the Ninth Circuit affirmed with respect to the Sherman Act, but reversed as to the First Amendment claim. . . . We granted certiorari with respect to the latter issue. . . .

Respondent asked Pacific Telephone and Telegraph (PT&T) and DWP for permission to lease space on their utility poles in order to provide cable television service in the south central area of Los Angeles. . . . These utilities responded that they would not lease space unless respondent first obtained a cable television franchise from the City. . . . Respondent asked the City for a franchise, but the City refused to grant it one stating that respondent had failed to participate in an auction that was to award a single franchise in the area. . . . The complaint further alleged that cable operators are First Amendment speakers . . . that there is sufficient excess physical capacity and economic demand in the south central area of Los Angeles to accommodate more than one cable company . . . and that the City's auction process allowed it to discriminate among franchise applicants based on which one it deemed to be the "best." Based on these and other factual allegations, the complaint alleged that the City and DWP had violated the Free Speech Clause of the First Amendment, as made applicable to the States by the Fourteenth Amendment. . . .

The City did not deny that there was excess physical capacity to accommodate more than one cable television system. But it argued that the physical scarcity of available space on public utility structures, the limits of economic demand for the cable medium, and the practical and esthetic disruptive effect that installing and maintaining a cable system has on the public right-of-way justified its decision to restrict access to its facilities to a single cable television company. . . .

The Court of Appeals for the Ninth Circuit . . . upheld the conclusion that petitioners were immune from liability under federal antitrust laws. . . . But it reversed the District Court's dismissal of the First Amendment claim, and remanded for further proceedings. . . . It held that, taking the allegations in the complaint as true. . . . the City violated the First Amendment by refusing to issue a franchise to more than one cable company when there was sufficient excess physical and economic capacity to accommodate more than one. . . . The Court of Appeals expressed the view that the facts alleged in the complaint brought respondent into the ambit of cases such as *Miami Herald Publishing Co. v. Tornillo, 418 U.S. 241 (1974)*, rather than of cases such as *Red Lion Broadcasting Co. v. FCC, 395 U.S. 367 (1969)* . . .

. . . We are unwilling to decide the legal questions posed by the parties without a more thoroughly developed record of proceedings in which the parties have an opportunity to prove those disputed factual assertions upon which they rely.

Respondent alleges:

"The business of cable television, like that of newspapers and magazines, is to provide its subscribers with a mixture of news, information and entertainment. As do newspapers, cable television companies use a portion of their available space to reprint (or retransmit) the communications of others, while at the same time providing some original content." . . .

We affirm the judgment of the Court of Appeals reversing the dismissal of respondent's complaint by the District Court, and remand the case to the District Court so that petitioners may file an answer and the material factual disputes between the parties may be resolved.

Preferred essentially says that provided utilities are adequate, a city cannot arbitrarily deny a franchise to more than one cable company. The Supreme Court did not definitively answer the question of overbuilding. If evidence can be presented that shows that a cable company is a natural monopoly in a given market, permission to overbuild can be denied, as evidenced in *Central Telecommunications v. TCI Cablevision, Inc.* For a natural monopoly to occur, it must be demonstrated that no willing competitors exist. The Supreme Court has refused to hear *Preferred.*

Cable in the 1990s: The Bloom Is Off the Rose

The growth of cable television in the 1980s was largely precipitated by deregulation. Rising rates, a record of poor service, and allegations of broken promises by franchise holders, however, followed this growth. Public outcry led Congress to consider reregulating the industry.

The Cable Consumer Protection and Competition Act of 1992

Cable television was significantly reregulated in 1992 with the passage of the Cable Consumer Protection Act. The act was the result of several concerns about the cable industry expressed by Congress resulting from cable's deregulation in the 1980s. Among the concerns of Congress was the fact that between 1986 and 1992, monthly rates for the lowest priced basic cable service had increased by 40 percent. The average monthly cable rate had increased almost 3 times as much as the Consumer Price Index.[2]

In addition, Congress found that most cable systems had no local competition, and that the cable industry had become vertically integrated; that is, cable operators and cable programmers often had common ownership. Congress also noted a shift in market share from broadcast television to cable television services. Lawmakers once again viewed the potential economic harm of broadcasting by cable as an issue worthy of attention. As before, this issue manifested itself as a requirement that cable systems carry local broadcast signals.

The Cable Consumer Protection and Competition Act was passed over Presidential veto and went into effect on October 5, 1992. During the next 12 months, the FCC was charged with making rules enforcing the act. The courts struck down some provisions, such as one championed by North Carolina Senator Jesse Helms prohibiting "indecent" cablecasts. However, the heart of the act was upheld by a U.S. District Court.[3] The must-carry provision was also challenged and will be discussed later in this chapter.

Implementing the 1992 Cable Act

Essentially, the 1992 Cable Act modifies some of the provisions of the 1984 Cable Communications Policy Act. It also establishes new regulations. The result is an amendment of the Communication Act of 1934. The remainder of this chapter discusses some of the more important cable regulations resulting from the combination of the 1984 and 1992 Acts.

Signal Carriage Rules: Must-Carry and Retransmission Consent

The Must-Carry Rules

As noted in Chapter 3, "The Rationale of Broadcast Regulation," the FCC first promulgated must-carry rules for cable in 1965. The rules required cable systems to carry the signals of all local television stations. The intent of the rules was to ensure that "free TV" was not undermined by cable.

In the early development of cable, the must-carry rules benefited both broadcasters and cablecasters. UHF broadcasters in particular reaped positive benefits. Carriage of their signals on cable helped them overcome some of the transmission and channel-positioning problems that had plagued UHF in an effort to compete with VHF signals. Cablecasters benefited from the must-carry rules in that they were given a free source of quality programming, much of it from the major networks. This lent legitimacy to the enterprise.

As cable penetration increased and more viable sources of programming became available to cable systems, must-carry rules became more of a burden to cable operators. Many felt that they should not be forced to tie up channels with the signals of marginal local stations when more lucrative choices were available. In 1980, Turner Broadcasting System filed a petition with the FCC asking that the agency repeal the must-carry rules. The Turner Petition argued that the rules violated the First and Fifth Amendment rights of cable operators and programmers. In *Turner Broadcasting System, Inc. v. FCC (1983)*, the FCC rejected Turner's argument and the rules remained.

In 1980, Quincy Cable TV dropped, without FCC approval, two signals it carried under the must-carry rules. Quincy's rationale for dropping the channels was that the stations did not carry programming of interest to the community. Quincy replaced the dropped channels with stations it believed to be of more interest to the community. The FCC fined Quincy Cable $5000 for the rule infraction.

Quincy Cable and the Turner Broadcasting System appealed their cases to the U.S. Court of Appeals for the District of Columbia. In *Quincy Cable TV, Inc. v. FCC*, the court found the must-carry rules, as drafted, to be in violation of the First Amendment and outside the scope of the FCC's regulatory authority.

Quincy Cable TV, Inc. v. FCC (1985)

☐   . . . Almost from the beginning, the must-carry rules were a centerpiece of the FCC's efforts to actively oversee the growth of cable television. . . .

Then, as now, the applicability of the rules varied according to such factors as the quality of the broadcast signal available in the community. In general, however, the rules required cable operators, upon request, to carry any broadcast signal considered local under the Commission's complex formula. . . .

. . . Although the economic analysis initially advanced in support of the must-carry rules was somewhat complicated, the Commission's general objective was straightforward: to assure [sic] that the advent of cable technology did not undermine the financial viability of free, community oriented television.

. . . At the time of the initial promulgation of the rules, the Commission acknowledged that it had insufficient data to "predict with reliability" the extent of the risk posed by cable. *First Report and Order, 38 FCC at 711.* See also *Second Report and Order, 2 FCC 2d at 744–745.*

. . . By forcing cable systems to carry local and significantly viewed broadcast signals, the Commission sought to channel the growth of cable in a manner consistent with the public's interest in the preservation of local broadcasting.

. . . On several occasions, the Supreme Court has addressed questions concerning the breadth of the FCC's jurisdiction over cable television. See *United States v. Southwestern Cable, 392 U.S. at 178.* . . . However in marked contrast to the extensive First Amendment jurisprudence developed in the context of the broadcast media . . . the Court has never confronted a challenge to the constitutional validity of the must-carry rules or any other regulation affecting cable television. . . .

In the lower federal courts, questions concerning the constitutionality of various cable regulations arose almost from the first moment the Commission asserted its regulatory jurisdiction over the industry.

. . . The most common approach was simply to treat cable and broadcast television as indistinguishable for purposes of First Amendment analysis. Because it was well established that broadcast media could be subject to regulation far more intrusive than the First Amendment would tolerate in other contexts, it naturally followed for these courts that cable regulation, a variant on the same theme, should be subject to no more exacting scrutiny. . . . Other courts undertook a somewhat more discriminating analysis. They upheld the regulations only after concluding that the restraint on speech was no greater than was reasonably required to serve the important interest of preserving local broadcasting. . . .

In recent years, the lower federal courts have subjected FCC regulation of cable television to a far more rigorous constitutional analysis. It is now clearly established, for example, that cable operators engage in conduct protected by the First Amendment.

. . . [I]n *Home Box Office* this court noted that earlier cases that had considered the intersection of the First Amendment and cable television regulations had incorrectly relied on Supreme Court precedent developed in the context of regulation of the broadcast media. . . .

At issue in *Home Box Office* were a number of FCC regulations limiting the programming fare a cablecaster . . . could offer its subscribers. The Commission defended the rules by suggesting that they were necessary to assure [sic] that the various forms of pay television, including cable, not degrade the quality of programming on conventional broadcast television. As in the present controversy, the Commission suggested that the competitive injury to broadcasters would be felt most acutely by those who could not afford the more expensive video services.

The court rejected the FCC's argument and sustained the First Amendment challenge. Concluding that the regulation should be treated as an incidental burden on speech, the court applied the test announced by the Supreme Court in *United States v O'Brien, 391 U.S. 367, 377 (1968)*. Thus the regulations would be valid only if they served a substantial governmental interest and were no more intrusive than necessary to serve that interest. . . .

. . . We begin by evaluating whether First Amendment principles governing regulation of the broadcast media should also apply to the regulation of cable television. Concluding that cable television warrants a standard of review distinct from that applied to broadcasters, we next consider whether the must-carry rules merit treatment as an "incidental" burden on speech and therefore warrant analysis under the balancing test set out in *United States v O'Brien, supra, 367 U.S. at 199*. Although our review leaves us with serious doubts about the appropriateness of invoking O'Brien's interest-balancing formulation, we conclude that the rules so clearly fall under that standard that we need not resolve whether they warrant a more exacting scrutiny.

. . . In short, our examination of the purposes that underlie the must-carry rules, the nature and degree of the intrusions they effect, and prior judicial treatment of analogous regulations leaves us with serious doubts about the propriety of applying the standard of review reserved for incidental burdens on speech. Although the goal of the rules preserving local broadcasting can be viewed as unrelated to the suppression or protection of any particular set of ideas, the rules nonetheless profoundly affect values that lie near the heart of the First Amendment. They favor one group of speakers over another. They severely impinge on editorial discretion. And, most importantly, if a system's channel capacity is substantially or completely occupied by mandatory signals, the rules prevent cable programmers from reaching their intended audience even if that result directly contravenes the preference of cable subscribers.

. . . Regulation of emerging video technologies requires a delicate balancing of competing interests. . . .

When the Commission strikes this balance in favor of regulations that impinge on rights protected by the First Amendment, it assumes a heavy burden of justification . . .

After extensive examination of the purposes and effects of the must-carry rules, we have concluded that the Commission has failed to carry this heavy burden. . . .

We stress that we have not found it necessary to decide whether any version of the mandatory carriage rules would contravene the First Amendment. We hold only that in their current form they can no longer stand.

The Interim Must-Carry Rules of 1987

The FCC did not wait long before promulgating new must-carry rules. In 1987, the Commission developed rules that were the product of a compromise between broadcasters and cablecasters. Small cable systems were exempt from the new rules, while larger systems were granted more leeway in determining which stations they would be required to carry. Only those broadcast stations within 50 miles of a cable system and capable of delivering a high-quality signal to the cable system would be considered for carriage. In addition, commercial stations were required to demonstrate scant viewership if they wanted carriage. Cable systems were not required to carry stations that duplicated programming, such as network affiliates.

To ensure that viewers had easier access to the broadcast signals not carried by cable systems, the FCC required cable companies to sell and install A/B switches in subscriber's homes. An A/B switch enabled subscribers to switch between cable and off-air signals.

Finally, the new rules also required cable systems to carry at least one public television station, regardless of distance or signal quality.

The must-carry rules and the A/B box requirement were to expire after five years. This provision assumed that five years was sufficient time for sub-scribers to be properly "educated" in the method of switching between cable and over-the-air broadcasting. The interim must-carry rules were challenged based on the First Amendment and *O'Brien*. In 1987, the District of Colum-bia court of appeals struck down the rules in *Century Communications Corp. v. FCC*. The Supreme Court refused to review the case.

Century Communications Corp. v. FCC (1988)

☐ . . . In the aftermath of Quincy cable TV, the FCC immediately suspended enforcement of the must-carry rules. Four months later, it announced its intention to undertake rule-making proceedings . . . and eventually, in November 1986, 16 months after Quincy had been handed down, the agency released a new, more limited set of must-carry rules designed to accommodate Quincy Cable TV's concerns . . .

The most salient feature of the new rules was that the Commission substantially altered its stated justification for imposing must-carry rules at all. No longer did the Commission argue, as it had prior to the Quincy Cable TV decision, that the rules were needed for the indefinite future to ensure the viewer access to local broadcast stations. Rather, the Commission now argued that must-carry rules were needed to guarantee such access during a shorter-term transition period during which viewers could become accustomed to an existing and inexpensive but largely unknown piece of equipment known as the "input-selector device."

Such devices, if hooked up to a television, allow viewers at any given time to select, simply by flicking a switch, between shows offered by their cable system and broadcast television shows offered off-the-air. These devices, the most common of which is known in the cable industry as an "A/B switch" are about the size of a standard lightswitch, and work by being hooked up to a roof-top, attic or television-top antenna. . . .

The Commission estimated that it would take approximately five years for the public to become acclimated to the existence of these switches, and accordingly, its interim rules should be in place for that same five years. . . .

The FCC, however, adduces scant evidence for its judgement of a widespread "misperception" among cable subscribers that the only means of access to off-the-air signals is through cable service. It puts forth no attitudinal surveys, or polls, suggesting the likely pace of consumer adaptation to the A/B switch technology. . . .

Additionally, we are skeptical and the FCC's report says nothing to relieve this skepticism that any consumer education campaign will have much impact so long as viewers can continue to rely on must-carry to get their fix of local broadcasts. . . .

Our decision is a narrow one. We hold simply that, in the absence of record evidence in support of its policy, the FCC's reimposition of must-carry rules on a five-year basis neither clearly furthers a substantial governmental interest nor is of brief enough duration to be considered narrowly tailored so as to satisfy the O'Brien test for incidental restrictions on speech. . . . Accordingly, we have no choice but to strike down this latest embodiment of must-carry.

The court did not say that must-carry was, in itself, an unconstitutional concept. It merely found that the FCC had not justified sufficiently the reason for implementing the rules. The FCC began, at the request of

Congress, to collect data useful in determining the impact of the demise of must-carry rules on broadcasters.

Must-carry was revived in the 1992 Act and, as could have been expected, it remained one of the most controversial components of the legislation. This time must-carry was implemented with a twist—an option available only to commercial broadcasters called retransmission consent. When the law took effect on October 5, 1993, broadcasters had the option of exercising must-carry rights or opting for retransmission consent. The latter prohibits cable systems from carrying the signals of broadcast stations without their permission.

Retransmission Consent

Retransmission consent addresses one of broadcasters' earliest concerns over cable carriage of their signals—that of compensation for use of a valuable product. After all, the argument goes, cable companies pay a fee for cable networks such as CNN, Discovery, USA, and MTV, but they transmit the most watched networks such as NBC, ABC, and CBS for free through the carriage of local affiliates. Broadcasters felt that they were not being compensated for their product. Cable systems argued that being on the cable gave broadcasters a larger audience and a cleaner signal—viewers did not have to adjust an antenna every time they changed channels.

The 1992 Cable Act allowed broadcasters to choose between must-carry and retransmission consent. If the broadcaster opted for must-carry, most cable systems were simply required to carry the local station on the cable system's basic tier. If the broadcaster opted for retransmission consent, the broadcaster and cable operator would have to negotiate terms under which the cable system would be allowed to carry the broadcaster's signal. Terms could include monetary payment to the broadcaster in return for carriage rights, or another arrangement under which rights would be granted.

If no agreement could be reached, the cable company could not carry the broadcast signal. As the law was about to go into effect in 1993, cable companies and broadcasters squared off against one another. Cable systems vowed that they would not pay for "free TV." Local broadcasters banded together in public relations campaigns to fight the "cable monopoly." Sales of antennas and A/B switches were brisk. But by October 5, 1993, when push came to shove, most broadcasters and cable systems had reached agreements whereby local stations remained on the cable. Retransmission consent agreements included some monetary payments, but many involved cooperative arrangements between local broadcasters and local cable systems. For example, in Indianapolis the NBC affiliate negotiated carriage of its low-power TV station in lieu of cash. The ABC affiliate negotiated local news cut-ins throughout the CNN day—thereby promoting its news department. The CBS affiliate obtained a cable weather channel. One independent station was briefly removed from cable until an agreement could be reached.

When the dust cleared, retransmission consent appeared to be working and was less controversial than its counterpart, must-carry. Turner Broadcasting System again challenged the signal carriage requirement of the 1992 Cable Act as a violation of cable's First Amendment rights. The Justice Department argued that the signal carriage rules were not First Amendment violations, but necessary economic regulation of a monopoly—cable—that was needed to preserve free over-the-air television broadcasting. Retransmission consent emerged early as constitutional, but must-carry was bound for another journey through the court system. The *Turner* cases discussed next provide useful background about the controversy of must-carry and summarizes the current must-carry rules as promulgated by the FCC as a result of the 1992 Cable Act.

In *Turner Broadcasting System v. FCC (1994)*, the Supreme Court did not find must-carry unconstitutional, but asked the lower court to support more adequately its conclusion that the future of over-the-air broadcasting is threatened by cable in the absence of regulation. In 1997 the case, once again, was heard by the Supreme Court. In a 5-4 decision the High Court upheld must carry. The court found the rules to be content neutral and therefore not a violation of cable television's first amendment rights.

Turner Broadcasting System, Inc. v. Federal Communications Commission, 520 U.S. 180 (1997)
SUPREME COURT OF THE UNITED STATES
Syllabus

☐ . . . Appeal from the United States District Court for the District of Columbia

 . . . Sections 4 and 5 of the Cable Television Consumer Protection and Competition Act of 1992 (Cable Act) require cable television systems to dedicate some of their channels to local broadcast television stations. In *Turner Broadcasting System, Inc. v. FCC, 512 U.S. 622 (Turner)*, this Court held these so called "must carry" provisions to be subject to intermediate First Amendment scrutiny under *United States v. O'Brien*, 391 U.S. 367, 377, whereby a content neutral regulation will be sustained if it advances important governmental interests unrelated to the suppression of free speech and does not burden substantially more speech than necessary to further those interests. However, because a plurality considered the record as then developed insufficient to determine whether the provisions would in fact alleviate real harms in a direct and material way and would not burden substantially more speech than necessary, the Court remanded the case. After 18 months of additional fact finding, the District Court granted summary judgment for the Government and other appellees, concluding that the expanded record contained substantial evidence supporting Congress' predictive judgment that the must carry provisions further important governmental interests in preserving cable carriage of local broadcast stations, and that the provisions are narrowly tailored to promote those interests. This direct appeal followed.

Held: The judgment is affirmed.

910 F. Supp. 734, affirmed.

Justice Kennedy delivered the opinion of the Court with respect to all but a portion of Part II-A-1, concluding that the must carry provisions are consistent with the First Amendment:

1. The record as it now stands supports Congress' predictive judgment that the must carry provisions further important governmental interests . . .

    (a) This Court decided in *Turner*, 512 U. S., at 662, and now reaffirms, that must carry was designed to serve three interrelated, important governmental interests: (1) preserving the benefits of free, over the air local broadcast television, (2) promoting the widespread dissemination of information from a multiplicity of sources, and (3) promoting fair competition in the television programming market. Protecting noncable households from loss of regular broadcasting service due to competition from cable systems is important because 40 percent of American households still rely on over the air signals for television programming. See, e.g., id., at 663. Moreover, there is a corresponding governmental purpose of the highest order in ensuring public access to a multiplicity of information sources, ibid., and the Government has an interest in eliminating restraints on fair competition even when the regulated parties are engaged in protected expressive activity, ibid. The parties' attempts to recast these interests in forms more readily proved—i.e., the Government's claim that the loss of even a few broadcast stations is critically important and appellants' assertions that Congress' interest in preserving broadcasting is not implicated absent a showing that the entire industry would fail, and that its interest in assuring a multiplicity of information sources extends only as far as preserving a minimum amount of broadcast service—are inconsistent with Congress' stated interests in enacting must carry. . . .

    (b) Even in the realm of First Amendment questions where Congress must base its conclusions upon substantial evidence, courts must accord deference to its findings as to the harm to be avoided and to the remedial measures adopted for that end, lest the traditional legislative authority to make predictive judgments when enacting nationwide regulatory policy be infringed. See, e.g., *Turner, 512 U. S., at 665* (plurality opinion). The courts' sole obligation is to assure that, in formulating its judgments, Congress has drawn reasonable inferences based on substantial evidence. Id., at 666. Pp. 11–13.

(c) The must carry provisions serve important governmental interests "in a direct and effective way." *Ward v. Rock Against Racism, 491 U.S. 781, 800.* Congress could reasonably conclude from the substantial body of evidence before it that attaining cable carriage would be of increasing importance to ensuring broadcasters' economic viability, and that, absent legislative action, the free local off air broadcast system was endangered. Such evidence amply indicated that: a broadcast station's viability depends to a material extent on its ability to secure cable carriage and thereby to increase its audience size and revenues; broadcast stations had fallen into bankruptcy, curtailed their operations, and suffered serious reductions in operating revenues as a result of adverse carriage decisions by cable systems; stations without carriage encountered severe difficulties obtaining financing for operations; and the potentially adverse impact of losing carriage was increasing as the growth of "clustering"—i.e., the acquisition of as many cable systems in a given market as possible—gave multiple system operators centralized control over more local markets. The reasonableness of the congressional judgment is confirmed by evidence assembled on remand that clearly establishes the importance of cable to broadcast stations and suggests that expansion in the cable industry was harming broadcasting. Although the record also contains evidence to support a contrary conclusion, the question is not whether Congress was correct as an objective matter, but whether the legislative conclusion was reasonable and supported by substantial evidence. *Turner, supra, at 665–666.* Where, as here, that standard is satisfied, summary judgment is appropriate regardless of whether the evidence is in conflict. . . .

2. The must carry provisions do not burden substantially more speech than is necessary to further the governmental interests they promote. See *e.g., Turner, supra, at 662.* Appellants say must carry's burden is great, but significant evidence adduced on remand indicates the vast majority of cable operators have not been affected in a significant manner. This includes evidence that: such operators have satisfied their must carry obligations 87 percent of the time using previously

unused channel capacity; 94.5 percent of the cable systems nationwide have not had to drop any programming; the remaining 5.5 percent have had to drop an average of only 1.22 services from their programming; operators nationwide carry 99.8 percent of the programming they carried before must carry; and broadcast stations gained carriage on only 5880 cable channels as a result of must carry. The burden imposed by must carry is congruent to the benefits it affords because, as appellants concede, most of those 5880 stations would be dropped in its absence. Must carry therefore is narrowly tailored to preserve a multiplicity of broadcast stations for the 40 percent of American households without cable . . . The possibilities that must carry will prohibit dropping a broadcaster even if the cable operator has no anticompetitive motives or if the broadcaster would survive without cable access are not so prevalent that they render must carry substantially overbroad. This Court's precedents establish that it will not invalidate the preferred remedial scheme merely because some alternative solution is marginally less intrusive on a speaker's First Amendment interests. In any event, a careful examination of each of appellants' suggestions—a more limited set of must carry obligations modeled on those earlier used by the Federal Communications Commission; use of so called A/B switches, giving consumers a choice of both cable and broadcast signals; a leased access regime requiring cable operators to set aside channels for both broadcasters and cable programmers to use at a regulated price; subsidies for broadcasters; and a system of antitrust enforcement or an administrative complaint procedure—reveals that none of them is an adequate alternative to must carry for achieving the Government's aims. Because it has received only the most glancing attention from the District Court and the parties, prudence dictates that this Court not reach appellants' challenge to the Cable Act provision requiring carriage of low power stations in certain circumstances. . . .

☐ Justice Kennedy, joined by The Chief Justice, Justice Stevens, and Justice Souter, and by Justice Breyer in part, concluded . . . that the expanded record contains substantial evidence to support Congress' conclusion that enactment of must carry was justified by a real threat to local broadcasting's economic health. The harm Congress feared was that broadcast stations dropped or denied cable carriage would be at a serious risk of financial difficulty, see *Turner, 512 U. S., at 667,* and would deteriorate to a substantial degree or fail altogether. . . . The evidence before Congress, as supplemented on remand, indicated, *inter alia*, that: cable operators had considerable and growing market power over local video programming markets in 1992; the industry's expanding horizontal and vertical integration would give cable operators increasing ability and incentive to drop, or reposition to less viewed channels, independent local broadcast stations, which competed with the operators for audiences and advertisers; significant numbers of local broadcasters had already been dropped; and, absent must carry, additional stations would be deleted, repositioned, or not carried in an attempt to capture their local advertising revenues to offset waning cable subscription growth. The reasonableness of Congress' predictive judgment is also supported by additional evidence, developed on remand, indicating that the percentage of local broadcasters not carried on the typical cable system is increasing, and that the growth of cable systems' market power has proceeded apace, better enabling them to sell their own reach to potential advertisers, and to deny broadcast competitors access to all or substantially all the cable homes in a market area . . .

Must Carry and Digital TV

The issue of whether cable systems will be required to carry the digital signals of broadcasters became a contentious issue. The National Association of Broadcasters argued that must carry for DTV was required to ensure the survival of the service. The National Cable Television Association contended that extension of must carry to include DTV violates cable's first amendment rights—essentially the same argument used in *Turner*.[4]

The issue was complicated by the fact that each digital television broadcaster has at least four program streams instead of one. Was cable expected to carry all four channels? If cable was not expected to carry all, how many were they to carry, and which ones? Finally, would the FCC extend the must-carry rules to digital, and if so would the rules withstand constitutional scrutiny yet another time?

In January of 2001 the FCC issued rules designed to address the question of cable carriage of digital broadcast television signals. See *Report and Order* and *Further Notice of Proposed Rule Making (FCC 01-22* at http://fcc.gov). The Commission summary of the rules is as follows:

Retransmission Consent

- A commercial television station, broadcasting in both formats during the transition period, may choose must carry or retransmission consent for its analog signal and retransmission consent for its digital signal. A DTV-only commercial television station may elect either retransmission consent or must carry.

- A DTV-only noncommercial station is also entitled to must carry. Although a noncommercial television station does not have retransmission consent rights under Section 325 of the Act, it may nevertheless enter into digital carriage agreements with cable operators and other Multichannel Video Program Distributors (MVPDs).
- A DTV-only television station may make its retransmission consent or must-carry election any time between 60 days prior to commencing service and 30 days after commencing service. If must carry is chosen, the cable operator must commence carriage 90 days after the election is made.
- A television station electing retransmission consent may negotiate with a cable operator for partial carriage of its digital television signal.
- The current prohibition on exclusive retransmission consent agreements encompasses a television station's analog and digital signals. This prohibition expires on January 1, 2006.
- For the time being, a television station may tie the carriage of its digital signal with the carriage of the analog signal as a retransmission consent condition. The Commission will monitor the marketplace for potential abuses.

Channel Capacity

- The *Report and Order* revises the method of calculating a cable system's channel capacity to account for changes in digital technology. To determine whether the one-third statutory cap for the carriage of commercial television station signals has been met, a cable operator shall take the total usable activated channel capacity of the system in megahertz and divide it by three.
- The current statutory definitions of "usable activated channels" and "activated channels" will continue to apply in determining channel capacity in the digital context.
- A cable operator may choose which additional television station signals to carry if the one-third statutory cap is met. Digital television signals carried under retransmission consent count toward the cap.
- The current statutory framework for determining the carriage requirement for noncommercial educational television stations will continue to apply in the digital context.

Signal Quality

- The *Report and Order* finds that the signal strength level necessary to provide a good quality digital signal at a cable system's principal headend is –61 dBm.

Content of Signals Subject to Mandatory Carriage

- *Primary Video.* The *Report and Order* finds that the "primary video" entitled to mandatory carriage includes a single programming stream and other program-related content. The television station chooses which one of its unrelated multiplexed signals gets carried under the Act. The *Further Notice* seeks comment on how to define "program-related" in the context of primary video.
- *Ancillary or Supplementary Services.* The *Report and Order* finds that a cable operator is not required to carry ancillary or supplementary services transmitted on a digital television signal.
- *Program-Related.* A cable operator would be required to carry the following material carried on a digital television signal because it could be considered program-related under the *WGN* factors: (1) closed captioning, (2) V-chip data, (3) Nielsen ratings data, and (4) channel mapping and tuning protocols ("PSIP").
- *Not Program-Related.* A cable operator would not be required to carry Internet and e-commerce services provided by a digital television station if such services are not related to the primary video television signal carried by the cable operator.
- *Electronic Program Guides (EPGs).* Whether a cable operator would be required to carry electronic program guides is subject to a fact-based program-related analysis.

Substantial Duplication

- The *Report and Order* defers further interpretation of "substantial duplication" in the digital context until the Commission decides the dual carriage matter. In the meantime, the current duplication definitions apply.

Material Degradation

- The *Report and Order* finds that a cable operator would not necessarily be materially degrading a digital television signal if it carries less than the full 19.4 mbps transmitted by a broadcaster.
- The *Report and Order* finds that a cable operator may not carry a digital television signal in a lesser format or lower resolution than that afforded to a nonbroadcast digital programmer carried on the cable system. However, a digital-only television station may demand that a cable operator carry its digital signal in an analog format without the prohibition against material degradation being violated. If a television

station chooses to be carried in this manner, it is treated in the same manner as an analog signal.

- Cable operators are permitted to remodulate digital broadcast signals from 8 VSB to 64 or 256 QAM. Cable operators are not required to pass-through 8 VSB.

Set-Top Box Availability

- The *Report and Order* finds that a cable operator is not required under the Act to provide subscribers with a set-top box capable of processing digital television signals for display on analog sets.

Channel Location

- The *Report and Order* finds that there is no need to implement channel positioning requirements for digital television signals like those that exist for analog signals.
- The *Report and Order* finds that channel mapping protocols contained in the PSIP data stream adequately address a television station's channel positioning concerns.

Market Modifications

- The *Report and Order* finds that Nielsen's market designations and assignments are applicable to analog and digital television stations.
- The statutory market modification factors, the current process for requesting market modifications, and the evidence needed to support such petitions, apply to both analog and digital television stations during the transition period.

Digital Signal Carriage on PEG Channels

- The *Report and Order* finds that the carriage of NCE and LPTV digital signals on unused public, educational, and governmental access channels, with the permission of the local franchising authority, is consistent with the Act.

Complaints and Enforcement

- The *Report and Order* finds that the current procedures for filing must-carry complaints should be used for digital carriage complaints.

Subscriber Notification

- The *Report and Order* finds that a cable operator must notify its subscribers whenever a digital television signal is added to the cable system channel line-up.

Program Exclusivity

- The *Report and Order* finds that there is an inadequate record in this proceeding to institute a change or repeal of the network nonduplication, syndicated exclusivity, and sports blackout rules.

Tiers and Rates

- The *Report and Order* finds that digital television signals must be available to subscribers on a basic service tier. The *Further Notice* seeks comment on voluntary carriage of digital signals on a tier other than the basic tier.
- The *Report and Order* finds that there may be some cable systems undertaking significant system upgrades, a part of which will include a digital build-out. For these systems, the *Report and Order* finds that a Form 1235 upgrade rate adjustment would provide an appropriate incentive for a cable operator to upgrade its system and carry digital television signals.

Cable Leased Access

The 1984 Cable Act did not mandate that local franchises set aside channels for public, educational, and government (PEG) access. The act did mandate that systems with more than 35 channels provide commercial, leased access channels. Systems having 36 to 54 channels must set aside 10 percent of their activated channels for commercial leased access. Stations with more than 54 channels must set aside 15 percent of active channels for commercial leased access. In calculating the number of active channels, the cable company cannot deduct retransmitted over-the-air channels. The statute provides a deduction for the number of channels the federal law requires systems to carry. Cable operators are relieved of any liability for libel and other content-related suits filed as a result of material transmitted on a leased access channel. Liability is assumed by the program producer. The cable operator may prohibit the transmission of potentially obscene or indecent programming. Prior to the 1992 Act, cable systems were free to establish leased access rates; however, guidelines for commercial leased access rates are now established by the FCC (47 CFR 76.970).

Public, Educational, and Government Channels

The local franchising authority is empowered by Section 531(a) of the Cable Act to establish PEG channel access. PEG channels are noncommercial in nature and vary in number and form according to the requirements stipulated by the franchise agreement. It must be remembered that cable stations are not required by the act to provide PEG channels. Cable stations are required to provide leased access channels. However, the local community may require PEG channels before a franchise will be awarded.

Federal, State, and Local Relationships

Rate Regulation

The 1992 Cable Act gave the FCC authority to regulate cable system rates in the absence of "effective competition." The 1996 Telecommunications Act allowed the FCC to review consumer complaints about cable rates until March 1999 when this provision expired.

Technical Standards

Cable systems are required to deliver an acceptable signal to the homes of subscribers. Technical standards are regulated by the FCC and may be found in CFR, Subpart K, Section 76.601 to Section 76.619. Federal guidelines supersede local franchising authority in this area. The Supreme Court upheld FCC authority in this area in *New York City v. FCC*. The Court ruled that the Cable Act implied preemption of state and local technical standards by the Commission.

Program Exclusivity

The program exclusivity rules became effective on January 1, 1990. These rules are the syndicated exclusivity (Syndex) and network nonduplication rules. Recall that the Commission abolished similar rules in 1980 as part of the deregulation of cable (see Chapter 3, "The Rationale of Broadcast Regulation"). In *United Video Inc. v. FCC (1989)*, the court ruled that the program exclusivity rules did not violate the First Amendment. The court based the decision on the assumption that no First Amendment right exists to make use of others' copyrighted programs.

Syndicated Exclusivity Rules (Syndex)

The Syndex rules protect local broadcasters from distant signal importation of syndicated programs that are broadcast locally. In other words, if a local station buys the rights to a syndicated program such as *Oprah*, a cable system may be prohibited from importing *Oprah* from a station outside the market. If *Oprah* has been purchased on a market-exclusive basis, the local station can require the local cable company to refrain from transmitting the signal of the distant station at times when that station broadcasts *Oprah*, as stipulated in CFR, Sections 76.151–76.163. The geographic area protected by Syndex is dependent on the terms negotiated between the program supplier and the program purchaser. The contract must contain specific language invoking Syndex. The FCC requires the following language:

> [T]he licensee (or substitute name) shall, by the terms of this contract, be entitled to invoke the protection against duplication of programming imported under the Compulsory Copyright License, as provided in § 76.151 of the FCC rules ("or as provided in the FCC's syndicated exclusivity rules").

Network Nonduplication Rules

Section 76.92 of the FCC rules allows networks and affiliates to enter into agreements that prohibit cable systems from duplicating network signals in a single market. The nonduplication rule applies to stations within 35 miles of a cable system in the top 100 markets and within 55 miles of a cable system in markets 101 and above.

Broadcasters who wish to invoke the nonduplication rules must notify the cable system of their intent to do so within 60 days of signing a nonduplication contract with a network. No specific language (like that required to invoke Syndex) is required in the contract.

Copyright and Cable

In *Fortnightly Corp. v. United Artists Television Inc. (1968)*, the Supreme Court ruled that cable systems could retransmit the signals of local broadcast stations without incurring liability under the Copyright Act of 1909. Six years later, in *Teleprompter Corp. v. CBS*, the Court extended the same protection for the retransmission of distant signals. The rationale for the Court's decision in both cases was that cable retransmission was not a "performance" of a copyrighted work and therefore not subject to liability under the Copyright Act.

Broadcasters and program producers felt that this interpretation of the law was inequitable, and when Congress began a revision of the Copyright Act, they argued that cable ought to pay copyright owners for retransmission. Congress believed it impractical for each cable system to negotiate directly with copyright owners to obtain retransmission rights, so it created a compulsory license for cable television.

The compulsory license originally provided for semiannual royalty payments by cable operators to the Copyright Royalty Tribunal (CRT), which was created as part of the 1976 Copyright Act. In 1993, President Clinton signed into law the Copyright Royalty Tribunal Reform Act, which abolished the CRT. The CRT was replaced by ad hoc arbitration panels convened by the Librarian of Congress. The Librarian of Congress adopted the rules and regulations of the CRT.[5]

Every six months, cable operators must provide the Copyright Office with information about retransmitted broadcast signals, the system's gross subscriber receipts, and receipts from secondary retransmission of local and distant broadcast signals. Royalty payments are established in the Copyright Act of 1976 and may be adjusted from time to time by the Copyright Office.

The compulsory license has many critics. Broadcasters, copyright owners, cablecasters, and members of Congress have called for its repeal. The critics charge that copyright owners are not being compensated fairly and that the compulsory license does not accomplish what it is supposed to do.

Indecency and Cable

The Cable Act prohibits the transmission of obscene material by cable systems. Section 559 provides for a $10,000 fine, or two years imprisonment, or both, for transmission of material "unprotected by the Constitution." Indecency has constitutional protection and is, therefore, not prohibited by the Cable Act. The courts have struck down local ordinances designed to prohibit indecency on cable.

The City of Miami passed an ordinance prohibiting the transmission of obscene and indecent material on cable systems. The ordinance was not challenged on its definition of "obscene," nor on the right to prohibit such material. The ordinance was challenged on First Amendment grounds. It was argued that because "indecent" material is not void of First Amendment protection, it cannot be completely prohibited.

In deciding *Cruz v. Ferre (1985)*, the U.S. Court of Appeals for the Eleventh Circuit distinguished between cable and broadcasting. The court noted that though broadcast signals are pervasive and may "intrude" on the privacy of the home, cable is invited in.

☐ The Cablevision subscriber must affirmatively elect to have cable service come into his home. Additionally, the subscriber must make the additional affirmative decision whether to purchase any "extra" programming services, such as HBO . . .

However noble may have been the city's intentions, we are constrained to recognize the limitations imposed by the Constitution and the opinions of the Supreme Court. The city's attempt through the challenged ordinance to regulate indecency on its cable television system exceeds these limitations.[6]

In *Jones v. Wilkinson (1986)*, the U.S. Court of Appeals for the Tenth Circuit struck down the Utah Cable Television Programming Decency Act. The act authorized nuisance actions against Utah cable systems that transmitted indecent programming. The court ruled that the Utah statute was preempted by the Cable Communications Policy Act, which limits state authority over cable program content to the prosecution of obscenity and material not protected by the Constitution.

In *Playboy Entertainment Group v. U.S. (1996)*, a three-judge district court upheld provisions of the Telecommunications Act of 1996 that require cable operators to scramble audio and video portions of sexually explicit programs. The Playboy Entertainment Group had sought an injunction against enforcement of the provisions on grounds that sections 505 and 506 of the Telecommunications Act violated their First Amendment rights. The court required Playboy to completely block adult-oriented programming during times that children are likely to be in the audience. Since current scrambling technology sometimes allows viewers to get a glimpse of scenes or hear audio, Playboy could not transmit a signal at all during the day. This case was overturned in 1998 when a federal district court in Delaware held that as long as Playboy made a good faith effort to scramble the signal for nonsubscribing homes, they satisfied sections 505 and 506 of the Telecommunications Act.[7] That ruling was upheld by the Supreme Court.

United States v. Playboy Entertainment Group, Inc. (2000) 529 U.S. 803

☐ Playboy Entertainment Group owns and prepares programs for adult television networks, including Playboy Television and Spice. Playboy transmits its programming to cable television operators, who retransmit it to their subscribers, either through monthly subscriptions to premium channels or on a so-called "pay-per-view" basis. Cable operators transmit Playboy's signal, like other premium channel signals, in scrambled form. The operators then provide paying subscribers with an "addressable converter," a box placed on the home television set. The converter permits the viewer to see and hear the descrambled signal. It is conceded that almost all of Playboy's programming consists of sexually explicit material as defined by the statute.

The statute was enacted because not all scrambling technology is perfect. Analog cable television systems may use either "RF" or "baseband" scrambling systems, which may not prevent signal bleed, so discernible pictures may appear from time to time on the scrambled screen. Furthermore, the listener might hear the audio portion of the program.

These imperfections are not inevitable. The problem is that at present it appears not to be economical to convert simpler RF or baseband scrambling systems to alternative scrambling technologies on a systemwide scale. Digital technology may one day provide another solution, as it presents no bleed problem at all. Indeed, digital systems are projected to become the technology of choice, which would eliminate the signal bleed problem. Digital technology is not yet in widespread use, however. With imperfect scrambling, viewers who have not paid to receive Playboy's channels may happen across discernible images of a sexually explicit nature. How many viewers, how discernible the scene or sound, and how often this may occur are at issue in this case.

Section 505 was enacted to address the signal bleed phenomenon. As noted, the statute and its implementing regulations require cable operators either to scramble a sexually explicit channel in full or to limit the channel's programming to the hours between 10 P.M. and 6 A.M. 47 U.S.C. § 561 (1994 ed., Supp. III); 47 CFR § 76.227 (1999). Section 505 was added by floor amendment, without significant debate, to the Telecommunications Act of 1996 (Act), a major legislative effort designed "to reduce regulation and encourage 'the rapid deployment of new telecommunications technologies.'" *Reno v. American Civil Liberties Union*, 521 U.S. 844, 857, 117 S. Ct. 2329, 138 L. Ed. 2d 874 (1997) (quoting 110 Stat. 56). "The Act includes seven Titles, six of which are the product of extensive committee hearings and the subject of discussion in Reports prepared by Committees of the Senate and the House of Representatives." *Reno, supra*, at 858. Section 505 is found in Title V of the Act, which is itself known as the Communications Decency Act of 1996 (CDA). 110 Stat. 133. Section 505 was to become effective on March 9, 1996, 30 days after the Act was signed by the President. Note following 47 U.S.C. § 561 (1994 ed., Supp. III).

On March 7, 1996, Playboy obtained a temporary restraining order (TRO) enjoining the enforcement of § 505. 918 F. Supp. 813 (Del.), and brought this suit in a three-judge District Court pursuant to § 561 of the Act, 110 Stat. 142, note following 47 U.S.C. § 223 (1994 ed., Supp. III).

Playboy sought a declaration that § 505 violates the Constitution and an injunction prohibiting the law's enforcement. The District Court denied Playboy a preliminary injunction, 945 F. Supp. 772 (Del. 1996), and we summarily affirmed, 520 U.S. 1141 (1997). The TRO was lifted, and the Federal Communications Commission announced it would begin enforcing § 505 on May 18, 1997. *In re Implementation of Section 505 of the Telecommunications Act of 1996*, 12 FCC Rcd 5212, 5214 (1997).

When the statute became operative, most cable operators had "no practical choice but to curtail [the targeted] programming during the [regulated] sixteen hours or risk the penalties imposed . . . if any audio or video signal bleed occurred during [those] times." The majority of operators—"in one survey, 69%"—complied with § 505 by time channeling the targeted programmers. *Ibid*. Since "30 to 50% of all adult programming is viewed by households prior to 10 P.M.," the result was a significant restriction of communication, with a corresponding reduction in Playboy's revenues.

In March 1998, the District Court held a full trial and concluded that § 505 violates the First Amendment. The District Court observed that § 505 imposed a content-based restriction on speech. It agreed that the interests the statute advanced were compelling but concluded the Government might further those interests in less restrictive ways. One plausible, less restrictive alternative could be found in another section of the Act: § 504, which requires a cable operator, "upon request by a cable service subscriber . . . without charge, [to] scramble or otherwise fully block" any channel the subscriber does not wish to receive . . . As long as subscribers knew about this opportunity, the court reasoned, § 504 would provide as much protection against unwanted programming as would § 505 . . . At the same time, § 504 was content neutral and would be less restrictive of Playboy's First Amendment rights. *Ibid*.

The court described what "adequate notice" would include, suggesting

> "[operators] should communicate to their subscribers the information that certain channels broadcast sexually-oriented programming; that signal bleed . . . may appear; that children may view signal bleed without their parents' knowledge or permission; that channel blocking devices . . . are available free of charge . . . ; and that a request for a free device . . . can be made by a telephone call to the [operator]." . . .

☐ The means of providing this notice could include

> "inserts in monthly billing statements, barker channels (preview channels of programming coming up on Pay-Per-View), . . . and on-air

advertisement on channels other than the one broadcasting the sexually explicit programming." *Ibid.*

☐ *The court added that this notice could be "conveyed on a regular basis, at reasonable intervals," and could include notice of changes in channel alignments.*

The District Court concluded that § 504 so supplemented would be an effective, less restrictive alternative to § 505, and consequently declared § 505 unconstitutional and enjoined its enforcement . . . The court also required Playboy to insist on these notice provisions in its contracts with cable operators. *Ibid.*

The United States filed a direct appeal in this Court pursuant to § 561. The District Court thereafter dismissed for . . . lack of jurisdiction two post-trial motions filed by the Government . . . We noted probable jurisdiction, 527 U.S. 1021 (1999), and now affirm.

II

☐ Two essential points should be understood concerning the speech at issue here. First, we shall assume that many adults themselves would find the material highly offensive; and when we consider the further circumstance that the material comes unwanted into homes where children might see or hear it against parental wishes or consent, there are legitimate reasons for regulating it. Second, all parties bring the case to us on the premise that Playboy's programming has First Amendment protection. As this case has been litigated, it is not alleged to be obscene; adults have a constitutional right to view it; the Government disclaims any interest in preventing children from seeing or hearing it with the consent of their parents; and Playboy has concomitant rights under the First Amendment to transmit it. These points are undisputed.

The speech in question is defined by its content; and the statute which seeks to restrict it is content based. Section 505 applies only to channels primarily dedicated to "sexually explicit adult programming or other programming that is indecent." The statute is unconcerned with signal bleed from any other channels. See 945 F. Supp. at 785 ("[Section 505] does not apply when signal bleed occurs on other premium channel networks, like HBO or the Disney Channel"). The overriding justification for the regulation is concern for the effect of the subject matter on young viewers. Section 505 is not " 'justified without reference to the content of the regulated speech.' " *Ward v. Rock Against Racism*, 491 U.S. 781, 791, 105 L. Ed. 2d 661, 109 S. Ct. 2746 (1989) (quoting *Clark v. Community for Creative Non-Violence*, 468 U.S. 288, 293, 82 L. Ed. 2d 221, 104 S. Ct. 3065 (1984) (emphasis deleted)). It "focuses *only* on the content of the speech

and the direct impact that speech has on its listeners." *Boos v. Barry*, 485
U.S. 312, 321, 99 L. Ed. 2d 333, 108 S. Ct. 1157 (1988) (opinion of
O'CONNOR, J.). This is the essence of content-based regulation.

Not only does § 505 single out particular programming content for
regulation, it also singles out particular programmers. The speech in
question was not thought by Congress to be so harmful that all channels
were subject to restriction. Instead, the statutory disability applies only to
channels "primarily dedicated to sexually-oriented programming." 47
U.S.C. § 561(a) (1994 ed., Supp. III). One sponsor of the measure even
identified appellee by name. See 141 Cong. Rec. 15587 (1995) (statement
of Sen. Feinstein) (noting the statute would apply to channels "such as
the Playboy and Spice channels"). Laws designed or intended to suppress
or restrict the expression of specific speakers contradict basic First
Amendment principles. Section 505 limited Playboy's market as a penalty
for its programming choice, though other channels capable of . . .
transmitting like material are altogether exempt.

The effect of the federal statute on the protected speech is now
apparent. It is evident that the only reasonable way for a substantial
number of cable operators to comply with the letter of § 505 is to time
channel, which silences the protected . . . speech for two-thirds of the day
in every home in a cable service area, regardless of the presence or likely
presence of children or of the wishes of the viewers. According to the
District Court, "30 to 50% of all adult programming is viewed by
households prior to 10 P.M.," when the safe-harbor period begins. . . . To
prohibit this much speech is a significant restriction of communication
between speakers and willing adult listeners, communication which
enjoys First Amendment protection. It is of no moment that the statute
does not impose a complete prohibition. The distinction between laws
burdening and laws banning speech is but a matter of degree. The
Government's content-based burdens must satisfy the same rigorous
scrutiny as its content-based bans.

Since § 505 is a content-based speech restriction, it can stand only if it
satisfies strict scrutiny. *Sable Communications of Cal., Inc. v. FCC*, 492 U.S.
115, 126, 106 L. Ed. 2d 93, 109 S. Ct. 2829 (1989). If a statute regulates
speech based on its content, it must be narrowly tailored to promote a
compelling Government interest. *Ibid.* If a less restrictive alternative
would serve the Government's purpose, the legislature must use that
alternative. *Reno*, 521 U.S. at 874 ("[The CDA's Internet indecency
provisions'] burden on adult speech is unacceptable if less restrictive
alternatives would be at least as effective in achieving the legitimate
purpose that the statute was enacted to serve"); Sable *Communications*,
supra, at 126 ("The Government may . . . regulate the content of

constitutionally protected speech in order to promote a compelling interest if it chooses the least restrictive means to further the articulated interest"). To do otherwise would be to restrict speech without an adequate justification, a course the First Amendment does not permit.

Our precedents teach these principles. Where the designed benefit of a content-based speech restriction is to shield the sensibilities of listeners, the general rule is that the right of expression prevails, even where no less restrictive alternative exists. We are expected to protect our own sensibilities "simply by averting [our] eyes." *Cohen v. California*, 403 U.S. 15, 21, 29 L. Ed. 2d 284, 91 S. Ct. 1780 (1971); accord, *Erznoznik v. Jacksonville*, 422 U.S. 205, 210–211, 45 L. Ed. 2d 125, 95 S. Ct. 2268 (1975). Here, of course, we consider images transmitted to some homes where they are not wanted and where parents often are not present to give immediate guidance. Cable television, like broadcast media, presents unique problems, which inform our assessment of the interests at stake, and which may justify restrictions that would be unacceptable in other contexts. See *Denver Area Ed. Telecommunications Consortium, Inc. v. FCC*, 518 U.S. 727, 744, 135 L. Ed. 2d 888, 116 S. Ct. 2374 (1996) (plurality opinion); 518 U.S. at 804–805 (KENNEDY, J., concurring in part, concurring in judgment in part, and dissenting in part); *FCC v. Pacifica Foundation*, 438 U.S. 726, 57 L. Ed. 2d 1073, 98 S. Ct. 3026 (1978). No one suggests the Government must be indifferent to unwanted, indecent speech that comes into the home without parental consent. The speech here, all agree, is protected speech; and the question is what standard the Government must meet in order to restrict it. As we consider a content-based regulation, the answer should be clear: The standard is strict scrutiny. This case involves speech alone; and even where speech is indecent and enters the home, the objective of shielding children does not suffice to support a blanket ban if the protection can be [ ] accomplished by a less restrictive alternative.

. . . There is, moreover, a key difference between cable television and the broadcasting media, which is the point on which this case turns: Cable systems have the capacity to block unwanted channels on a household-by-household basis. The option to block reduces the likelihood, so concerning to the Court in *Pacifica*, *supra* at 744, that traditional First Amendment scrutiny would deprive the Government of all authority to address this sort of problem. The corollary, of course, is that targeted blocking enables the Government to support parental authority without affecting the First Amendment interests of speakers and willing listeners—listeners for whom, if the speech is unpopular or indecent, the privacy of their own homes may be the optimal place of receipt. Simply put, targeted blocking is less restrictive than banning, and the

Government cannot ban speech if targeted blocking is a feasible and effective means of furthering its compelling interests. This is not to say that the absence of an effective blocking mechanism will in all cases suffice to support a law restricting the speech in question; but if a less restrictive means is available for the Government to achieve its goals, the Government must use it.

. . . When a plausible, less restrictive alternative is offered to a content-based speech restriction, it is the Government's obligation to prove that the alternative will be ineffective to achieve its goals. The Government has not met that burden here. In support of its position, the Government cites empirical evidence showing that § 504, as promulgated and implemented before trial, generated few requests for household-by-household blocking. Between March 1996 and May 1997, while the Government was enjoined from enforcing § 505, § 504 remained in operation. A survey of cable operators determined that fewer than 0.5% of cable subscribers requested full blocking during that time. The uncomfortable fact is that § 504 was the sole blocking regulation in effect for over a year; and the public greeted it with a collective yawn.

. . . It is rare that a regulation restricting speech because of its content will ever be permissible. Indeed, were we to give the Government the benefit of the doubt when it attempted to restrict speech, we would risk leaving regulations in place that sought to shape our unique personalities or to silence dissenting ideas. When First Amendment compliance is the point to be proved, the risk of non-persuasion—operative in all trials— must rest with the Government . . . not with the citizen.

With this burden in mind, the District Court explored three explanations for the lack of individual blocking requests. First, individual blocking might not be an effective alternative, due to technological or other limitations. Second, although an adequately advertised blocking provision might have been effective, § 504 as written did not require sufficient notice to make it so. Third, the actual signal bleed problem might be far less of a concern than the Government at first had supposed.

To sustain its statute, the Government was required to show that the first was the right answer. According to the District Court, however, the first and third possibilities were "equally consistent" with the record before it. *Ibid.* As for the second, the record was "not clear" as to whether enough notice had been issued to give § 504 a fighting chance. *Ibid.* The case, then, was at best a draw. Unless the District Court's findings are clearly erroneous, the tie goes to free expression.

The District Court began with the problem of signal bleed itself, concluding "the Government has not convinced us that [signal bleed] is a pervasive problem." The District Court's thorough discussion exposes a central weakness in the Government's proof: There is little hard evidence of how widespread or how serious the problem of signal bleed is. Indeed, there is no proof as to how likely any child is to view a discernible explicit image, and no proof of the duration of the bleed or the quality of the pictures or sound. To say that millions of children are subject to a risk of viewing signal bleed is one thing; to avoid articulating the true nature and extent of the risk is quite another. Under § 505, sanctionable signal bleed can include instances as fleeting as an image appearing on a screen for just a few seconds. The First Amendment requires a more careful assessment and characterization of an evil in order to justify a regulation as sweeping as this. Although the parties have taken the additional step of lodging with the Court an assortment of videotapes, some of which show quite explicit bleeding and some of which show television static or snow, there is no attempt at explanation or context; there is no discussion, for instance, of the extent to which any particular tape is representative of what appears on screens nationwide.

The Government relied at trial on anecdotal evidence to support its regulation, which the District Court summarized as follows:

> "The Government presented evidence of two city councillors, eighteen individuals, one United States Senator, and the officials of one city who complained either to their [cable operator], to their local Congressman, or to the FCC about viewing signal bleed on television. In each instance, the local [cable operator] offered to, or did in fact, rectify the situation for free (with the exception of 1 individual), with varying degrees of rapidity. Included in the complaints was the additional concern that other parents might not be aware that their children are exposed to this problem. In addition, the Government presented evidence of a child exposed to signal bleed at a friend's house. Cindy Omlin set the lockout feature on her remote control to prevent her child from tuning to adult channels, but her eleven year old son was nevertheless exposed to signal bleed when he attended a slumber party at a friend's house.
>
> "The Government has presented evidence of only a handful of isolated incidents over the 16 years since 1982 when Playboy started broadcasting. The Government has not presented any survey-type evidence on the magnitude of the 'problem.'"

☐ Spurred by the District Court's express request for more specific evidence of the problem, . . . the Government also presented an expert's spreadsheet estimate that 39 million homes with 29.5 million children had the potential to be exposed to signal bleed, 30 F. Supp. 2d at 708–709. The Government made no attempt to confirm the accuracy of its estimate through surveys or other field tests, however. Accordingly, the District Court discounted the figures and made this finding: "The Government presented no evidence on the number of households actually exposed to signal bleed and thus has not quantified the actual extent of the problem of signal bleed." The finding is not clearly erroneous; indeed it is all but required.

Once § 505 went into effect, of course, a significant percentage of cable operators felt it necessary to time channel their sexually explicit programmers. This is an indication that scrambling technology is not yet perfected. That is not to say, however, that scrambling is completely ineffective. Different cable systems use different scrambling systems, which vary in their dependability. "The severity of the problem varies from time to time and place to place, depending on the weather, the quality of the equipment, its installation, and maintenance." At even the good end of the spectrum a system might bleed to an extent sufficient to trigger the time-channeling requirement for a cautious cable operator. (The statute requires the signal to be "fully blocked." 47 U.S.C. § 561(a) (1994 ed., Supp. III) (emphasis added).) A rational cable operator, faced with the possibility of sanctions for intermittent bleeding, could well choose to time channel even if the bleeding is too momentary to pose any concern to most households. To affirm that the Government failed to prove the existence of a problem, while at the same time observing that the statute imposes a severe burden on speech, is consistent with the analysis our cases require. Here, there is no probative evidence in the record which differentiates among the extent of bleed at individual households and no evidence which otherwise quantifies the signal bleed problem.

In addition, market-based solutions such as programmable televisions, VCRs, and mapping systems (which display a blue screen when tuned to a scrambled signal) may eliminate signal bleed at the consumer end of the cable. Playboy made the point at trial that the Government's estimate failed to account for these factors. Without some sort of field survey, it is impossible to know how widespread the problem in fact is, and the only indicator in the record is a handful of complaints. *Turner Broadcasting System, Inc. v. FCC*, 520 U.S. 180, 187, 137 L. Ed. 2d 369, 117 S. Ct. 1174 (1997) (reviewing " 'a record of tens of thousands of pages' of evidence" developed through "three years of pre-enactment hearings, . . . as well as additional expert submissions, sworn declarations and testimony, and industry documents" in support of complex must-carry provisions). If the number of children transfixed by even flickering pornographic television images in fact reached into the millions we, like the District Court, would have expected to be directed to more than a handful of complaints.

... Basic speech principles are at stake in this case. When the purpose and design of a statute is to regulate speech by reason of its content, special consideration or latitude is not accorded to the Government merely because the law can somehow be described as a burden rather than outright suppression. We cannot be influenced, moreover, by the perception that the regulation in question is not a major one because the speech is not very important. The history of the law of free expression is one of vindication in cases involving speech that many citizens may find shabby, offensive, or even ugly. It follows that all content-based restrictions on speech must give us more than a moment's pause. If television broadcasts can expose children to the real risk of harmful exposure to indecent materials, even in their own home and without parental consent, there is a problem the Government can address. It must do so, however, in a way consistent with First Amendment principles. Here the Government has not met the burden the First Amendment imposes.

... The Government has failed to show that § 505 is the least restrictive means for addressing a real problem; and the District Court did not err in holding the statute violative of the First Amendment. In light of our ruling, it is unnecessary to address the second question presented: whether the District Court was divested of jurisdiction to consider the Government's postjudgment motions after the Government filed a notice of appeal in this Court. The judgment of the District Court is affirmed.

It is so ordered.

Anti-Siphoning Rules

In the 1970s, the FCC became concerned that cable TV would "siphon" programs from over-the-air TV. Of special concern were the rights to sports and feature films. After running in the theater, many films would find their way, often in edited form, to network television. Cable networks such as Home Box Office would run these films uncut, which provided an attractive alternative for program distributors. The FCC promulgated rules that prohibited cable systems from showing films less than three years old. Cable systems also were barred from devoting more than 90 percent of their schedules to films or sports. In *Home Box Office Inc. v. FCC (1977)*, the court overturned the anti-siphoning rules and held that the rules were outside the FCC's jurisdiction over cable television and a violation of the First Amendment.

The 1992 Cable Act directed the Commission to revisit the issue of sports migration from over-the-air to cable television. In February 1993, the Commission adopted a *Notice of Inquiry* addressing this issue. The NOI rested on the following premises:

Issues regarding the broadcasting of sports events, the "siphoning" or "migration" of sports telecasts from broadcast television to subscription or cable television,[] the "blacking-out" of local broadcasts,[] exclusivity in the distribution of televised sports events,[] and concerns relating to the proper application of the antitrust laws and competition policies relating to sports leagues [] have been matters of public policy concern for a number of years.[8]

Comments to the FCC, however, indicated that more sports may be moving back to broadcast television from cable. Examples include Fox Broadcasting Network's contract for NFL games, and figures from Major League Baseball showing that there are more "free" broadcasts of baseball games on local television than ever before. The Association of Independent Television Stations (INTV) disagreed with the impression that sports are moving back to broadcast television. INTV suggested that broadcasters would air more games if they didn't have to compete with pay cable.[9]

Sports Blackouts

Section 76.67 of the FCC rules prohibits a cable system from carrying a live sporting event if that event is not being broadcast by a station carried on the cable system. To invoke prohibition, the broadcast station must request that the event not be carried on the cable system. If a cable system is required to delete a sports program, it may substitute a program from another television station, rather than simply go to black, as stipulated in FCC Rules, Section 76.67(l)(d).

Rules Common to Broadcasting and Cable

Equal Opportunity Employment

Like broadcasters, cable companies are required to adhere to EEO guidelines. Cable companies must file an annual employment report (FCC Form 395A) on or before May 1st of each year, as stipulated in FCC Rules, Section 76.77(a). The FCC uses Form 395A to determine whether cable systems are in compliance with EEO guidelines. Section 76.77(c) requires that the FCC investigate each cable system at least once every five years.

Records Available for Public Inspection

Cable systems must also make certain records available for public inspection. Annual employment reports and complaint reports filed with the Commission (including exhibits and letters that are part of these reports) must be available for public inspection at each cable office that has five or more full-time employees, as stipulated in Section 76.79(a) (b). These documents must be maintained for five years.

Cablecasts by Candidates for Public Office and Personal Attack Rules

Cablecasters are subjected to the same "equal time" and "lowest unit rate" requirements as broadcasters. The Fairness Doctrine was applied to cable and, like broadcasters, the personal attack rules, political editorializing rule, and Zapple Doctrine are applicable, as stipulated in FCC Rules, Section 76.209.

Satellite Television (DBS) Carriage Obligations

In the late 1990s Direct Broadcast Satellite (DBS) grew steadily and developed as an alternative to cable television for many. Although DBS offered a digital signal and a multichannel service, unlike cable, until 1999 it could not offer subscribers access to local television channels. Passage of the Satellite Home Viewer Improvement Act (SHVIA)[10] allowed DBS operators to retransmit the signals of local broadcaster to their own markets. Before January 1, 2002, channel selection was on a selective basis. The SHVIA stipulated that after that date, carriage of one local station meant that all of the other stations in the market had the option of invoking must-carry or retransmission consent—essentially the same as the rules applied to cable. The "carry one–carry all" rules were challenged by DBS operators, but were upheld by the 4th Circuit Court of Appeals. See *Satellite Broadcasting and Communications Association v. FCC*, 01-1151, 4th Cir, 12/6/01 (available at www.fcc.gov).

Summary

The FCC's authority to regulate cable stems from the Communications Act, which empowers the Commission to regulate all interstate wire and radio communication. The Cable Television Act of 1984 outlines the scope of the Commission's authority over cable. Although cable television was substantially deregulated in the 1980s, the industry was reregulated with the passage of the Cable Consumer Protection and Competition Act of 1992. Although many of the same rules apply to both cable and broadcasting, cable is not subjected to the same public interest standard as are over-the-air broadcasters. The Satellite Home Viewer Improvement Act requires DBS systems that carry one local station to carry all local stations in that market.

Notes/References

1. "Sikes Looks to Strengthen Broadcasters' Hand," *Broadcasting* (July 8, 1991): 23.
2. Cable Consumer Protection Act of 1992, *Conference Report* (September 14, 1992) Sec. 29(a)(1).
3. *Daniels Cablevision Inc. v. United States* (DC DC, 1993) 21 Med.L.Rptr 2225. See also: Harry A Jessell, "Court Upholds Heart of Cable Act," *Broadcasting & Cable* (September 20, 1993): 10.
4. Doug Halonen, "NCTA Vows to Fight Digital Must-Carry," *Electronic Media* (October 19, 1998): 1
5. Copyright Royalty Tribunal Reform Act of 1993, Pub.L.No. 103–198.
6. *Cruz v. Ferre*, U.S. Ct App. 11th Cir., 755 F.2d 1415, 57 R.R. 1452 (1985).
7. Court: Playboy Can Play All Day, *Wired News Report* at www.wired.com/news/print/0,1294,17079,00.html (12/30/98).
8. *Inquiry into Sports Programming Migration*, PR Docket 93-21 (*Notice of Inquiry*, February 3, 1994).
9. Christopher Stern, "Sports Migration: Reversing Field?" *Broadcasting & Cable* (April 18, 1994): 37.
10. Pub. Law 106–113, 113 Stat. 1501, 1501A-526 to 1501A-545 (November 29, 1999).

Cases

Central Telecommunications v. TCI Cablevision, Inc., 800 F.2d 711 (8th Cir., 1986)

Century Communications Corp. v. FCC, 835 F.2d 292 (DC Cir., 1987), cert. denied 108 S.Ct. 2014 (1988)

City of Los Angeles et al. v. Preferred Communications Inc., 476 U.S. 488 (1986)

Cruz v. Ferre, U.S. Ct.App. 11th Cir., 755 F.2d 1415, 57 R.R.1452 (1985)

Daniels Cablevision Inc. v. United States (DC DC,1993) 21 Med.L.Rptr 2225

Economic Relationship between TV Broadcasting and CATV 71 F.C.C.2d 632 (1979)

FCC Redefines Effective Competition for Cable; Seeks Comment on Mandatory Signal Carriage Requirements, MM Docket 90–1, (June 13,1991)

First Report and Order Docket Nos. 14895 and 15253, 38 F.C.C. 683 (1965)

Fortnightly Corp. v. United Artists Television Inc., 392 U.S. 390 (1968)

Frontier Broadcasting v. Collier, 24 F.C.C. 251 (1958)

Group W Cable Inc. v. Santa Cruz, 14 Med.L.Rptr. 1769 (1987)

Home Box Office Inc. v. FCC, 567 F.2d 9, 44–15 (DC Cir., 1977), cert. denied 434 U.S. 829 (1977)

Jones v. Wilkinson, (CA 10, 1986) 13 Med.L.Rptr. 1913

New York City v. FCC, (U.S. Sup.Ct., 1988) 15 Med.L.Rptr. 1542

Notice of Proposed Rule Making and Notice of Inquiry, Docket No.18397, 15 F.C.C. 2d 417, 437–19 (1968)

Playboy Entertainment Group v. U.S., Civ. No. 96–94 (D. Del. Nov. 8, 1996)

Quincy Cable TV Inc. v. FCC, U.S. Ct.App. DC, 768 F.2d 1434 (1985), cert. denied 476 U.S. 1169 (1986)

Second Report and Order; Docket Nos. 14895, 15233, and 15971, 2 F.C.C.2d 725 (1966)

Teleprompter Corp. v. CBS, 415 U.S. 394 (1974)

Turner Broadcasting System, Inc. v. Federal Communications Commission, 520 U.S. 180 (1997)

United States v. Southwestern Cable Co., 392 U.S. 157 (1968)

United Video Inc. v. FCC, (CA DC, 1989) 17 Med.L.Rptr. 1129

5

The Broadcast Licensing and Cable Franchising Process

In previous chapters we discussed the development of broadcast and cable regulation. We now turn to the pragmatic task of applying those regulations to the daily operation of commercial over-the-air broadcast and cable facilities. We will look at the process of obtaining and renewing a license, but we will not deal with engineering and technical regulations except as they interface with the issues related to licensing broadcast stations. It is essential that students of electronic media law and regulation become familiar with Title 47 of the Code of Federal Regulations as it applies to broadcasting. Rules that affect daily broadcast operation can be found in Title 47. As a student you should also check the Federal Register for *Notices of Proposed Rule Making* and other FCC actions that affect broadcasters and cable operations. You should also regularly check the FCC Web page (http://www.fcc.gov) for information about the latest Commission actions. Finally, a subscription to a commercial service such as *Pike & Fischer's Communication Regulation* is a valuable aid.

The Process of Obtaining a Broadcast License

There are, essentially, two ways by which a broadcast license may be obtained: a license may be sought either for a new facility or for an existing facility. The latter case is certainly the most common. From time to time, however, the FCC allows for the construction of new stations, although this is becoming extremely rare. Recent examples include the expansion of the AM band by 10 kHz, the authorization of low-power television, and the creation of several Docket 80–90 class A FM stations. In any case, potential applicants must show that they are legally, technically, and financially qualified to hold a broadcast license.

Qualifications of Licensees

The Communications Act requires that any grant of a broadcast license must be in the public interest. Section 308(b) also states,

All applications for station licenses, or modifications or renewals thereof, shall set forth such facts as the Commission by regulation may prescribe as to the citizenship, character, and financial, technical and other qualifications of the applicant to operate the station . . .[1]

The basic qualifications for broadcast ownership are grouped into five categories: legal, technical, financial, character, and adherence to EEO (Equal Employment Opportunity) practices.

Legal Qualifications

Section 310 of the Communications Act requires that holders of broadcast licenses be U.S. citizens. Section 313 prohibits the granting of a license to any applicant whose license has previously been revoked for an antitrust violation. Section 312 applies to holders of construction permits (CP) and licenses and provides for administrative sanctions against those who violate FCC rules or the U.S. Criminal Code. The U.S. Criminal Code prohibits the broadcast of obscene materials and certain lottery information. Violations of FCC rules or failure to meet the standards set forth in the Communications Act render an applicant legally unqualified to hold a broadcast license. This means that a license may be initially denied, not renewed, or revoked.

Technical Qualifications

Potential broadcast licensees must comply with a myriad of technical requirements developed by the Commission. These requirements are designed to minimize interference between stations and increase the operating efficiency of all stations. The technical qualifications also ensure that a certain quality of service is available to the population. Potential broadcast licensees must assure the FCC that audio and video quality, coverage area, and tower and transmission systems all meet Commission standards.

Financial Qualifications

The FCC requires that new broadcast license applicants have enough funds to operate the proposed station for three months without advertising revenue. This is to ensure that the station has adequate time to take root in the community and serve the public interest. This rule also discourages quick turnaround in the sale of broadcast properties.

Character Qualifications

For many years, character issues played a very important role in determining the fitness of broadcast applicants. Then, in keeping with the deregulatory trend of the 1970s and 1980s, the Commission eliminated many of the criteria it previously mandated. In 1986, the FCC redefined its interest in character to take into account misconduct involving violations of FCC rules or the Communications Act, misrepresentations or "lack of candor" (i.e., lying) before the Commission, and fraudulent programming.[2] In 1990, the FCC reconsidered its policy and expanded its character inquiry to include any felony conviction involving an owner or manager. This policy reversal came after the Commission was criticized for renewing the license of WKSP-AM in Kingtree, South Carolina, whose owner had received a drug conviction. In January 1991, FCC Administrative Law Judge Joseph Chachkin revoked WSKP's license, citing the station owner's 1987 drug-trafficking conviction. The Commission also considers licensee convictions for antitrust or anticompetitive activity concerning any area of mass communication.

Equal Employment Opportunity

The FCC requires broadcast licensees to afford equal employment opportunity to all qualified persons and refrain from discrimination on the basis of race, color, religion, national origin, or gender. Stations planning to employ five or more full-time employees must establish a program designed to ensure equal employment opportunity for women and minority groups. The Commission defines minority groups as Blacks not of Hispanic origin, Asians or Pacific Islanders, Native Americans, Alaskan natives, and Hispanics. If minority group representation in the available labor force is less than 5 percent, a program for minorities is not required. Because women always comprise a significant portion of the available workforce, a program for women is required unless the station employs fewer than five full-time employees.

Other Considerations

The FCC also attempts to determine how the grant of a broadcast license to an applicant will serve the public interest. Indeed, the Commission must decide whether the public interest might be better served if the channel were left vacant.

Diversification of Media

Since the 1930s, the FCC has developed various rules designed to limit the concentration of control over media programming. These include the multiple ownership rules, the duopoly rule, and the cross-ownership rules. The Commission has also addressed the issue of diversity indirectly, by attempts to limit or otherwise control the concentration of media ownership.

The effectiveness of the FCC's Diversification of Media policy has waxed and waned over the years, yet it remains an important component in the regulatory framework.

Multiple Ownership Rules

In the case of new applicants, the FCC will consider whether a grant of the license will violate the multiple ownership rules, as stipulated in 47 CFR 73.3555(d)(1)(i) and 76.501 as applied to cable systems.

The number of stations that can be owned by a single group or individual has steadily increased over the years. In 1953, the FCC limited ownership of stations to seven AM, seven FM, and seven television stations, two of which had to be UHF. When Storer Broadcasting applied for a sixth VHF station, the Commission dismissed the application. In *United States v. Storer Broadcasting Co.*, the Supreme Court upheld the FCC's authority to set limits on the number of stations any one individual or group could own. The "rule of sevens" remained in effect until 1985, when it was revised in Multiple Ownership (12-12-12 Reconsideration) to permit ownership of 12 AM, 12 FM, and 12 TV stations. In 1992, the radio portion of the rule was revised again to permit national ownership of 18 AM and 18 FM stations. In September 1994, the national cap was raised to 20 AM stations and 20 FM stations. Under these rules, no party could own more than 12 television stations. No group-owned television stations could reach more than 25 percent of the television households in the country. UHF stations are assessed at 50 percent of their market's television households to encourage purchases of these facilities.

The Telecommunications Act of 1996 modified the multiple ownership rules for television once again. According to 47 C.F.R.§73.3555(e), one entity may own an unlimited number of television stations, provided that the total audience reach of those stations does not exceed 35 percent of the U.S. population. Fox Television Stations Inc. challenged the 35 percent cap, and the Court of Appeals for the District of Columbia ordered the FCC to justify the ownership cap, or repeal the rule. (See *Fox Television Stations Inc. v. Federal Communications Commission* (2002 U.S. App. LEXIS 2575)).

The FCC will also waive the "one-to-a-customer" rule in the top 50 markets. This means that broadcasters may own more than one television station in a single market and may own a radio station and television station in the same market.[3]

The FCC's Television Duopoly Rule prohibited ownership of more than one TV station in the same market. The FCC began to liberalize this rule for radio in 1989, and in 1999 began waiving the rule in markets with at least eight independent owners. Waivers may also be granted when one of the two stations has very low ratings, is in poor financial condition, or is unable to obtain a fair price from out-of-market buyers.

National and Local Radio Ownership Rules

The national ownership limits for radio were repealed in Section 202 of the 1996 Telecommunications Act. The new rules allow one owner to own an unlimited number of radio stations nationwide. The act also repeals the Duopoly rule for radio. The number of stations that a single owner may operate in one market now depends on the total number of stations in that market. The scale is as follows:

Market	One owner may operate
Markets with 45 or more stations	8 stations (no more than 5 of same class)
Markets with 30–44 stations	7 stations (no more than 4 of same class)
Markets with 15–29 stations	6 stations (no more than 4 of same class)
Markets with 14 or fewer stations	5 stations (no more than 3 of same class)

Cross-Ownership Rules

Since 1975, the FCC has prohibited common ownership of broadcast stations and daily newspapers. This policy is designed to foster diversification of media voices. The rationale behind this policy is based on the theoretical assumption that media audiences will be exposed to more than one opinion on issues of public importance. This policy was upheld in *FCC v. National Citizen's Committee for Broadcasting.*[4]

When the Commission enacted the newspaper-broadcast cross-ownership rule in Second Report and Order, it allowed many existing newspaper-broadcast corporations' cross-ownerships to continue until the corporation sold the broadcast station.

As in the case of *Policy Research Group v. FCC*, when a transfer of a license results in a violation of the cross-ownership rules, the FCC often grants a temporary waiver, giving the new licensee two years in which to divest the property.

The 1996 Telecommunications Act repeals the network-cable cross-ownership rules. It also allows cross-ownership of Multichannel Multipoint Distribution Services (MMDS) and cable systems within the same area when cable faces effective competition.

The Cable/Broadcast Cross-Ownership rule prohibited a cable television system from carrying the signal of any television broadcast station if the system owned a broadcast station in the same local market. (See 47 C.F.R.§76.501(a)). In *Fox Television Stations Inc. v. Federal Communications Commission* (2002 U.S. App. LEXIS 2575), this rule was struck down. As noted above, in this same case, the court ordered the FCC to justify its 35 percent ownership cap as well.

The Application Process

The FCC is a bureaucracy and by nature is dependent on procedure. It is imperative that anyone dealing with the Commission file the proper forms. Current FCC forms may be obtained online at http://www.fcc.gov/formpage.html. The forms should be up-to-date and filled in completely. Blanks or partially answered questions can lead to long delays in the processing of an application. Filing an obsolete or improper form can result in the entire application being returned to the applicant.

Authority to Construct or Make Changes in an Existing Station

When applying for a new station, applicants file the proper forms with the Mass Media Bureau requesting authority to construct a new broadcast station or to make changes in an existing facility. Applicants ask the Commission to grant a construction permit (CP) to build or modify a facility.

The FCC requires applicants to provide information designed to determine the applicant's qualifications to hold a broadcast license. The form asks for information about citizenship, character, financial status, other media interests, and sources of capital. Applicants are also required to submit information about the proposed programming of the station and address how that programming will serve the community of license. The form also requires applicants to submit an elaborate engineering study including estimated coverage area, height of the tower, and coordinates of the antenna. Stations having more than five full-time employees are required to submit a detailed EEO plan.

If a CP is granted, the operator of a television station has two years in which to complete construction (a radio station has 18 months) or risk forfeiture. Stations may file for an extension of the CP.

Upon completion of construction, the applicant must apply for a license. Assuming that there are no extenuating circumstances, the license is routinely granted by the Commission.

Buying or Selling a Station

Buyers of broadcast properties must receive FCC approval before the sale can be closed. The proper forms must be filed with the Commission at least 45 days before the proposed sale.

Sellers of broadcast properties are required to publish notice of the proposed sale in local newspapers and broadcast a notice over the station per 47 CFR 73.3580(d)(3). Low-power television stations and FM translator stations are exempt from this requirement.

The Licensing Process

In routine situations, the staff of the Mass Media Bureau handles the licensing process. Section 73.3591 of the FCC Rules provides,

> In the case of any application for an instrument of authorization, other than a license pursuant to a construction permit, the FCC will make the grant if it finds (on the basis of the application, the pleadings filed or other matters which it may officially notice) that the application presents no substantial and material question of fact and meets the following requirements:
>
> 1. There is not pending a mutually exclusive application filed in accordance with paragraph (b) of this section;
> 2. The applicant is legally, technically, financially, and otherwise qualified;
> 3. The applicant is not in violation of provisions of law or the FCC rules, or established policies of the FCC; and
> 4. A grant of the application would otherwise serve the public interest, convenience and necessity.[5]

In other words, if there is no one else applying for the same frequency, and the applicant meets basic qualifications and can reasonably establish that the public interest will be served, the license will be granted. Of course, if the Commission cannot act on an application because it does not meet the stipulated requirements, the FCC may designate a hearing. The hearing is conducted by an administrative law judge (ALJ). This individual functions very much like a regular court judge, but there is no jury present at the hearing and the issues of the case are determined by the FCC.

Hearings

A hearing will be conducted if two or more parties file for use of the same or interfering frequencies. The criteria that the Commission has established for choosing between applicants in comparative hearings is outlined in a 1992 Policy Statement. See *In Re: Reexamination of the Policy Statement on Comparative Broadcast Hearings (Docket No. 92–52, April 10, 1992)*.

Procedures If an Application Is Designated for a Hearing

In accordance with FCC Title 47 CFR 73.3593, if an application is designated for a hearing, the Commission must "notify the applicant and all known parties in the interest of such action and the grounds and reasons therefore." The applicant must give public notice of the hearing by publishing such notice in a local newspaper and broadcasting it, if possible, per 47 CFR 73.3594(a). Notice must be given at least twice a week for two consecutive weeks within the three-week period immediately following the release of the FCC's order of a hearing. The notice must specify the time and commencement of the hearing and must appear in a general circulation paper published in the community in which the station is proposed.

If the application designated for a hearing involves the change in location of a station, the notice must be given in both the present and proposed communities of license, per 73.3594(3).

If an existing station seeks license modification, renewal, assignment, or transfer, and the application is designated for a hearing, the station must broadcast notice over its own facilities per 73.3594(3)(b). This requirement does not apply to international broadcast, low-power TV, TV translator, FM translator, or FM booster stations.

If the station is the only operating station in its broadcast community, or if it is a noncommercial educational station, it is exempt from the requirement to publish hearing information in a local newspaper. Broadcasting the information is usually sufficient. Noncommercial educational stations not on the air during the period in question must still publish the notice, per 47 CFR 73.3594(4)(c).

"Standing" before the Commission

Outside parties have a right to participate in the licensing process and are afforded "standing" before the FCC or the ALJ during a hearing. Originally, other broadcasters could object to the granting of a license on grounds of economic injury, as provided for in the Carroll Doctrine.

In 1988, however, the FCC eliminated the Carroll Doctrine. Instead, it proposed a three-part test to determine when economic injury may be considered in granting a new license. The FCC required hard evidence that such a grant would have a detrimental effect on the service to the public. It also required challengers to address whether the revenue potential of the market was so small that an existing station would lose significant income, whether that loss of income would force the existing station to curtail public service programming, and whether this loss of programming would be offset by non-network programming to be offered by the new station. Stations opposing grants on economic grounds must address all three items.

In 1966, citizens groups were given official standing in broadcast proceedings. Though citizens' groups are most active in license renewal situations, they also may provide input during initial licensing. Matters of character, financial stability, and proposed program service are areas that citizens' groups may address. Citizens' groups and broadcasters may enter into agreements specifying how the broadcaster will serve the community during the license period. The FCC will consider these agreements at renewal time.

The License Renewal Process

Under the 1996 Telecommunications Act, the term of both radio and television licenses has been extended to eight years (Section 203). The act also provides that competing applications will not be accepted unless the Commission has determined that a station has not met the standards for license renewal (Section 204).

Before the deregulation of the 1980s, the paperwork associated with license renewal was substantial. Not only were stations required to fill out a lengthy form, but at varying times in history broadcasters were required to submit a "composite week" of program logs to the Commission; in addition, results of formal community ascertainment-of-needs studies were to be placed in their public files. Stations were measured against the yardstick of "promise versus performance": Did you program what you said you would when you applied for the license?

Stations are no longer required to keep program logs, and deregulation has eliminated much of the paperwork to be submitted to the Commission during the renewal period. The "promise versus performance" policy was deleted in 1983, but broadcasters still must serve the communities in which they are licensed.

In the year of license renewal, commercial broadcasters receive Form 303-S from the FCC (see Appendix 2). For most stations, this is the extent of their contact with the FCC during renewal. For approximately 4 percent of the stations up for renewal, a random visit by an inspector from the Enforcement Bureau may occur. The inspector checks to be sure the public inspection file is in order and that the station is in compliance with technical standards.

The Public Inspection File

The license renewal form requires broadcasters to ensure that the public file is complete. Therefore, before completing the renewal application, licensees must be sure that the file contains all the necessary materials. Rule 4773.3536 outlines the materials to be included in the public file for commercial stations and 4773.3527 lists the requirements for noncommercial stations. Essentially, the public file must contain the following:

- Materials pertaining to applications and forms filed with the Commission must be included in the public file. This includes applications for CPs, license renewal, transfer of license, and lists of anyone who filed a "petition to deny" against any of these applications. All related supporting documents must also be in the file.

- All ownership materials, including the Annual Ownership Report (Form 323) and management agreements with nonemployees and employees (if the agreement involves profit sharing), must be in the public file.
- Annual employment reports (Forms 395 or 395-B) must be in the public file.
- A quarterly issues/programs list must be included. The list should include the issues examined and a narrative that explains how each issue was addressed by the station. The list must include the time, date, and length of each broadcast, as well as the title and program type (documentary, news, interview, etc.).
- Agreements between citizens groups and the station must be placed in the public file.

Television stations must place national network agreements in the public file, as well as children's TV programming records and children's TV commercial limits records. Commercial stations must also file FCC Form 398, Children's Television Programming Report, with the FCC. This can be done via the Internet or electronically on disk. These materials must be retained for a period of seven years. Other materials kept in the file (such as the following) must be retained for varying periods of time:

- Requests for air time by political candidates and disposition of the request, including charges, must be in the file.
- Any free time given within 72 hours of the election must be part of the file. A list of the chief executive officers of any organization that sponsors or provides free information for political programs dealing with controversial issues of public importance must be in the public file.

These last three items must be retained for a period of two to three years. Requests for time by political candidates must be updated daily.

- Letters received from members of the public must be retained for three years.
- *The Public and Broadcasting*, a 1974 procedure manual, is no longer required to be in the file.
- Noncommercial stations must also place in the file a list of donors supporting specific programs aired on the station.

The public file must be located at the main studio location or other location accessible to the general public. Individuals must be allowed access to the file during normal business hours. A station must make copies of documents in the public file but may charge a "reasonable fee" for making copies to anyone requesting copies.

The Postcard Renewal Form

The Commission sends a postcard-sized license renewal form to a station approximately seven months before the expiration of its license. During this period, the station ensures that the public file is in order and gathers information that will be a part of the renewal application.

Pre-filing and Post-filing Announcements

At each license renewal, the licensee must broadcast an announcement over the air that informs the public that the license is up for renewal. The station must also invite comments from the public in pre-filing and post-filing announcements (see Figures 5.1 and 5.2). Because citizens' groups have legal standing before the FCC in license renewal matters, this call for comments is extremely important. FCC rules require that these announcements begin two months before the station files for renewal and continue for three months after the application has been filed, per 73.3580(d)(4).

Stations must file for renewal four months before the expiration date of the license. Therefore, the first pre-filing announcement must be broadcast six months before the license expires. Both pre-filing and post-filing announcements must be broadcast on the first and sixteenth days of the month. Commercial radio stations must make two pre-filing and three post-filing announcements between 7:00 and 9:00 A.M. or between 4:00 and

On [date of last renewal grant] [station call letters] was granted a license by the Federal Communications Commission to serve the public interest as a trustee until [expiration date]. Our license will expire on [date]. We must file an application for renewal with the FCC on or before [first day of fourth full calendar month prior to expiration date]. When filed, a copy of this application will be available for public inspection during our regular business hours. It contains information concerning this station's performance during the last [period of time covered by the application].

Individuals who wish to advise the FCC of facts relating to our renewal application and to whether this station has operated in the public interest should file comments and petitions with the FCC by [first day of last full calendar month prior to the month of expiration].

Further information concerning the FCC's broadcast license renewal process is available at [address of location of the station's public inspection file] or may be obtained from the FCC, Washington, D.C. 20554.

Figure 5.1 Text of pre-filing announcement.

On [date of last renewal grant] [station call letters] was granted a license by the Federal Communications Commission to serve the public interest as a public trustee until [expiration date]. Our license will expire on [date]. We have filed an application for license renewal with the FCC.

A copy of this application is available for public inspection during our regular business hours. It contains information concerning this station's performance during the last [period of time covered by application].

Individuals who wish to advise the FCC of facts relating to our renewal application and to whether this station has operated in the public interest should file comments and petitions with the FCC by [first day of last full calendar month prior to the month of expiration].

Further information concerning the FCC's broadcast license renewal process is available at [address of location of the station's public inspection file] or may be obtained from the FCC, Washington, D.C. 20554.

Figure 5.2 Text of post-filing announcement.

6:00 P.M. If a station is not on the air during these times, the announcement must be made during the first two hours of operation. Noncommercial radio stations must adhere to the same guidelines, but are not required to broadcast an announcement in any month that it does not regularly operate, per 73.3580(A).

Commercial television stations must broadcast at least two of the pre-filing and three of the post-filing announcements between 6:00 and 11:00 P.M. Eastern and Pacific time (between 5:00 and 10:00 P.M. Central and Mountain time). They must also use visuals with the licensee's and the FCC's addresses when the announcement is being presented verbally by an announcer. If an emergency precludes the airing of an announcement at its scheduled time, stations must broadcast the announcement on the day after the emergency has ended, at the time the announcement originally would have been broadcast.

Within seven days after fulfilling the obligation to broadcast these announcements, stations must place a certificate of compliance in the public file. This document indicates the dates and times of each announcement, the text, and any variations from the prescribed FCC schedule.

After the Renewal Application Is Filed

After the renewal application is filed, the Commission staff reviews the applicant's record of compliance with FCC regulations and the Communications Act. It is at this point that members of the public can file a petition to deny. Competitors may also file a competing application. The petition to deny asks the FCC to deny license renewal on grounds that the applicant has not met its public interest responsibilities. A competing application most often alleges that the applicant failed to meet certain licensee obligations and that a competing applicant promises to do a better job than the current licensee in meeting these obligations. As noted above, the Telecommunications Act limits the FCC's acceptance of competing applications to those situations where the Commission has already determined that a station has not met the standards for license renewal.

Comparative Proceedings and Renewal Expectancy

Although the 1996 Telecommunications Act makes comparative hearings an unlikely surprise to broadcasters today, such was not always the case.[6] In the 1960s and 1970s broadcasters faced the threat of hostile challenges to their licenses. Cases such as *Greater Boston Television Corp. v. FCC*, and *RKO General* made the threat of comparative hearings during license renewal very real. RKO General Corporation was found an unfit licensee and lost all of its television and radio licenses.

Section 204 of the Telecommunications Act of 1996 changed all that. The Telecommunications Act now makes license renewal automatic, in the absence of specific findings by the FCC that a station has not operated in the public interest.

Program Format and Renewal Questions

The FCC has been confronted with a variety of petitions requesting that license renewals and transfers be denied on grounds that the station has changed format and no longer serves the audience it once did, such as *Citizens Committee to Preserve Voice of the Arts in Atlanta v. FCC*, *Citizens for Jazz on WRVR, Inc. v. FCC*, and *Citizens Committee to Save WEFM v. FCC*.

In *Citizens Committee to Save WEFM-FM v. FCC*, the court gave the Commission authority to consider a station's format in deciding whether license renewal or transfer would be in the public interest. In this case, the Commission decided that the format change issue should not be considered. The issue later reappeared and ultimately found its way to the Supreme Court. The High Court upheld the FCC policy that did not take format changes into consideration when ruling on an application for license renewal or transfer.[7]

Equal Employment Opportunity (EEO) Practices and Renewal

73.2080 Equal employment opportunities.

(a) General EEO policy. Equal opportunity in employment shall be afforded by all licensees or permittees of commercially or noncommercially operated AM, FM, TV or international broadcast stations (as defined in this part) to all qualified persons, and no person shall be discriminated against in employment by such stations because of race, color, religion, national origin or sex.

(b) EEO program. Each broadcast station shall establish, maintain, and carry out a positive continuing program of specific practices designed to ensure equal opportunity in every aspect of station employment policy and practice.

(c) EEO program requirements. A broadcast station's equal employment opportunity program should reasonably address itself to the specific areas set forth below, to the extent possible, and to the extent that they are appropriate in terms of the station's size, location, etc.

. . . (iii) Seeking the cooperation of labor unions, if represented at the station, in the implementation of its EEO program and the inclusion of nondiscrimination provisions in union contracts; . . .

(d) Mid-term review for television broadcast stations. The Commission will conduct a mid-term review of the employment practices of each broadcast television station at two and one half years following the station's most recent license expiration date as specified in §73.1020 of this part. The Commission will use the employment profile information provided on the first two Form 395-B reports submitted following such license expiration date to determine whether television station's employment profiles as compared to the applicable labor force data, are in compliance with the Commission's processing criteria. Television broadcast stations whose employment profiles fall below the processing criteria will receive a letter noting any necessary improvements identified as a result of the review.

The FCC concluded that discrimination on the basis of race, gender, color, religion, or national origin by broadcast stations is not in the public interest. Therefore, applicants for license renewal having five or more full-time employees must complete Form 396-A, an Equal Employment Opportunity Program, with the license renewal form (see Appendix 2). In addition, all stations are required to file an Annual Employment Report (Form 395-B) by May 31st of each year. Stations having fewer than five full-time employees do not complete the entire form. The Annual Employment Report provides the FCC with a profile of the station staff and is useful in determining EEO compliance.

The Commission periodically reviews broadcasters' EEO materials and reviews the entire record at the time of license renewal. If the FCC finds that a station's records are below par, action may be taken in the form of forfeitures, short-term renewals, or nonrenewal. The early 1990s saw the Commission cracking down on EEO violations. In February 1991, WWGS and WCUP-FM in Tipton, Georgia, were granted short-term renewals and fined $10,000 for EEO violations. An investigation by the FCC did not reveal evidence of discrimination that required a hearing, but the Commission did find a record of inadequate EEO efforts. Although the stations did attract and hire a few minority employees during the license term, the licensee's overall effects in minority recruitment were inadequate.[8]

In 1994, the FCC issued a Policy Statement clarifying its EEO policies and abolished new forfeiture structure for stations violating EEO rules.[9] Under this structure, the base forfeiture for EEO violations is $12,500. The mission stepped up enforcement following the issuance of the Policy Statement. Several short-term renewals and forfeitures were issued to stations in Nevada, Nebraska, Utah, California, and New York. Forfeitures ranged from $18,000 to $25,000. One cable system was fined $121,500 for EEO violations.[10]

In *Lutheran Church–Missouri Synod v. Federal Communications Commission* (DC Cir No. 97–1116 April 14, 1998) the FCC's EEO policy was declared unconstitutional as a means of ensuring diversity in broadcast programming. The FCC has appealed the decision and proposed new EEO rules designed to replace those held unconstitutional. For a second time, the Commission's EEO rules could not pass constitutional muster. In *DC/MD/DE Broadcasters Association v. FCC* (DC Cir No. 00-1094 June 19, 2001) the D.C. Circuit Court of Appeals struck down a portion of the outreach requirements of the broadcast EEO rule adopted in 2000 (see *FCC 00–20, January 20, 2000*, available at www.fcc.gov). The 2000 EEO rule provided two recruitment options, which were referred to as "Option A" and "Option B." The Court found no problem with Option A. However, it found that Option B was unconstitutional. Even though the Court found only Option B unconstitutional, it vacated the Commission's EEO rules. The Court concluded that the two options could not be readily severed.

In December 2001, the FCC proposed new rules designed to address the court's concerns. The proposed new rules would require broadcast licensees to widely disseminate information about job openings to all segments of the community to make sure that all qualified applicants have sufficient opportunity to compete for jobs in the broadcast industry. The Commission also proposed similar EEO rules that would apply to cable entities. The rules would require broadcasters and cablecasters to recruit for every full-time vacancy in a manner designed to achieve broad outreach. The proposed rules would require two other recruitment measures: (1) sending job vacancy announcements to recruitment organizations that request them; and (2) selecting from a menu of nonvacancy-specific outreach approaches, such as job fairs, internship programs, and interaction with educational and community groups.

Digital Television Licensing

Television stations in the top ten markets were required to begin digital television broadcasting by May 1999, although some began the service in November of 1998 to stimulate sales of new digital television sets during the Christmas buying season. All existing television stations will be required to transmit both a digital and analog signal by 2003. Existing commercial stations have been assigned a digital channel and must have applied for a digital license by 1999 or face losing that channel. When digital set penetration reaches 85 percent of the television viewing public, stations will be required to surrender their analog channel and broadcast digital only.[11]

Rules Applied to Noncommercial Educational (NCE) Stations

Many of the rules that apply to commercial stations apply to NCE stations. Political broadcasting rules (Section 315), requirements for maintaining the public file, and quarterly program lists are examples of similarly applied rules, although the "lowest unit rate" is inapplicable. NCE broadcasters also file slightly different forms with the FCC and are usually exempt from filing fees. NCE broadcasters are also given wider latitude in pre-filing and post-filing announcements during license renewal. The FCC recognizes that some NCE stations may have limited broadcast schedules, so the stations are not required to broadcast an announcement at any time they are not regularly on the air. The FCC has reserved the FM frequencies between 88 and 92 solely for noncommercial use. Similarly, the Commission requires that direct broadcast satellite companies set aside 4 percent of their channels for noncommercial educational programming.

Licensing Requirements

NCE stations may be licensed to nonprofit educational organizations. The term *educational organization* has been interpreted loosely by the Commission so that, essentially, four classes of licensees have developed over the years:

1. educational institutions such as colleges, universities, and high schools;

2. nonprofit educational organizations qualifying for tax exemption under IRS Code Section 501(e)(3) (many of which operate public radio and television stations as "community licensees");
3. municipal corporations independent of an educational institution; and
4. state public broadcasting authorities.

State public broadcasting agencies commonly operate one major production center and provide service statewide with a series of repeater stations. Kentucky, Alabama, Arkansas, and Mississippi operate in this fashion. Religious organizations may operate NCE stations but only to the extent that the operation of the station is for educational, rather than religious, purposes.

The FCC has also authorized a low-power noncommercial radio service. These 10- to 100-watt stations are expected to provide community-oriented radio services. For more information, see FCC 00–19 (January 20, 2000, available at www.fcc.gov).

Noncommercial Program Service

NCE stations are required to furnish a nonprofit and noncommercial broadcast service. While NCE stations may not broadcast any promotional announcements on behalf of a commercial entity, acknowledgments of contributions may be made. These acknowledgments may not interrupt regular programming.

In the Second Report and Order, the FCC relaxed certain restrictions on fundraising and language permitted in acknowledging donations. The Commission amended Section 73.503 (for NCE radio) and Section 73.621 (as applied to NCE TV) of the FCC rules to allow public broadcasters to air promotional announcements when they are in the public interest and when no consideration for airing the announcements is received. The FCC defined consideration as "anything of value given in exchange for something else of value."[12] The FCC also eliminated the name-only requirement for donor announcements and allows stations to broadcast informational messages, including the donor's name, logo, location, and product lines. These announcements may not contain value judgments about the donor's product or service (e.g., "best hamburgers in town" or "friendliest service" would not be allowed).

The Second Report reflected the FCC's desire to balance the financial needs of NCE stations against the obligation to provide a noncommercial broadcast service. The Second Report suggests eliminating time and frequency restrictions on donor announcements, but in 1982 the FCC reconsidered this measure. In a Memorandum Opinion and Order (1982), the FCC stated,

To recapitulate, public broadcasters may broadcast: (1) donor acknowledgements which inform but do not promote (i.e., the donor's logogram, may include a general description of product lines or services, as well as the donor's location); (2) announcements which promote the goods, services or activities of profit entities deemed in the public interest for which no consideration is received; and (3) announcements which promote the goods, services or activities of nonprofit organizations, whether or not consideration is received. However, public broadcasters may not schedule announcements so as to interrupt regular programming.

Digital Television Ancillary Services

The FCC amended sections 73.642 and 73.644 in 2001 to allow noncommercial television stations to offer commercial subscription services on their excess digital capacity.

Examples of the kinds of services that NCE stations can offer as ancillary or supplementary in the digital TV signal include, computer software distribution, data transmissions, teletext, interactive materials, aural messages, paging services, audio signals, and subscription video. The FCC said that by allowing NCE stations to offer subscription services on their excess digital capacity the goal of providing NCE licensees with flexibility in the use of their digital spectrum is met. (See *In Re: Ancillary or Supplementary Use of Digital Television Capacity by Noncommercial Licensees* (October 17, 2001) FCC 01–06, available at www.fcc.gov.)

Acceptance of Underwriting

A First Amendment issue over public broadcasting's right to refuse underwriting support arose when the Ku Klux Klan sought to underwrite programming on a state university licensed public radio station. The head of the Missouri KKK charged that KWMU and the University of Missouri St. Louis violated the Klan's First Amendment right of free speech in a public forum when the station would not allow the KKK to underwrite NPR's *All Things Considered*. In *Knights of the Ku Klux Klan, Realm of Missouri and Michael Cuffley v. Patricia Bennett (KWMU) (1998)*, a U.S. District Court rejected the Klan's contention that underwriting is a governmentally designated public forum for speech. The court also upheld KWMU's right to reject underwriting when that underwriting message might result in station loss of revenue if read on the air. In this case the University had received an $8.9 million donation from an African-American donor who had worked to overcome racial prejudice. The University convinced the court that this revenue and other support, as well as the minority student population of the university, would be negatively affected if the Klan message was accepted.[13] The decision was upheld in *Knights of the Ku Klux Klan v. Curators of the University of Missouri 203 F.3d 1085 (8th Cir. 2000)*

Editorializing

Originally, noncommercial educational broadcasters were prohibited by Section 399 of the Communications Act from editorializing. The rationale was that, as an educational service, they should not espouse any one particular point of view. Additionally, a statutory ban made it easier for stations to resist suggestions by donors that they favor an issue in exchange for a contribution.

In 1984, the Supreme Court found that the ban on editorializing violated the First Amendment. In *FCC v. League of Women Voters of California (1984)*, the Court allowed noncommercial stations to air editorials but refused to allow stations to support or oppose candidates for political office.

Cable Franchising

The FCC does not issue a license to cable systems. Instead, cable franchises are awarded by local municipalities. The Commission does, however, require that cable systems adhere to certain obligations. All FCC rules applied to cable television can be found in Title 47, Section 76 of the Code of Federal Regulations.[14] If a cable system does not adhere to these rules, the franchise authority may not renew the franchise or may be able to impose sanctions within the scope of the franchise agreement. The following are a few examples of FCC rules affecting cables systems relationships with the public and the municipality that awards the franchise.

Record-Keeping Obligations

Section 76.305 requires cable systems to maintain a public inspection file, as noted below:

(a) Records to be maintained. The operator of every cable television system having 1000 or more subscribers shall maintain for public inspection a file containing a copy of all records which are required to be kept by §76.207 (political file); §76.221(f) (sponsorship identifications); §76.79 (EEO records available for public inspection); §76.225(c) (commercial records for children's programming); §76.601(c) (proof-of-performance test data); §76.601(e) (signal leakage logs and repair records); and §76.701(h) (records for leased access).

(1) A record shall be kept of each test and activation of the Emergency Alert System (EAS) procedures pursuant to the requirement of Part 11 of this chapter and the EAS Operating Handbook. These records shall be kept for three years.

(b) Location of records. The public inspection file shall be maintained at the office which the system operator maintains for the ordinary collection of subscriber charges, resolution of subscriber complaints, and other business or at any accessible place in the community served by the system unit(s) (such as a public registry for documents or an attorney's office). The public inspection file shall be available for public inspection at any time during regular business hours.

Customer Service Obligations of Cable System Operators

Concerns over poor customer service on the part of cable systems prompted the FCC to enact rules that allow the local franchise authority to regulate cable system behavior in this area. Section 76.309 establishes the minimal behavior expected of cable systems. Franchise authorities are free to establish rules that exceed these standards.

(a) A cable franchise authority may enforce the customer service standards set forth in paragraph (c) of this section against cable operators. The franchise authority must provide affected cable operators ninety (90) days written notice of its intent to enforce the standards.

(b) Nothing in this rule should be construed to prevent or prohibit:

(1) A franchising authority and a cable operator from agreeing to customer service requirements that exceed the standards set forth in paragraph (c) of this section;

(2) A franchising authority from enforcing, through the end of the franchise term, pre-existing customer service requirements that exceed the standards set forth in paragraph (c) of this section and are contained in current franchise agreements;

(3) Any State or any franchising authority from enacting or enforcing any consumer protection law, to the extent not specifically preempted herein; or

(4) The establishment or enforcement of any State or municipal law or regulation concerning customer service that imposes customer service requirements that exceed, or address

matters not addressed by the standards set forth in paragraph (c) of this section.

(c) Effective July 1, 1993, a cable operator shall be subject to the following customer service standards:

  (1) Cable system office hours and telephone availability—

    (i) The cable operator will maintain a local, toll-free or collect call telephone access line which will be available to its subscribers 24 hours a day, seven days a week.

      (A) Trained company representatives will be available to respond to customer telephone inquiries during normal business hours.

      (B) After normal business hours, the access line may be answered by a service or an automated response system, including an answering machine. Inquiries received after normal business hours must be responded to by a trained company representative on the next business day.

    (ii) Under normal operating conditions, telephone answer time by a customer representative, including wait time, shall not exceed thirty (30) seconds when the connection is made. If the call needs to be transferred, transfer time shall not exceed thirty (30) seconds. These standards shall be met no less than ninety (90) percent of the time under normal operating conditions, measured on a quarterly basis.

    (iii) The operator will not be required to acquire equipment or perform surveys to measure compliance with the telephone answering standards above unless an historical record of complaints indicates a clear failure to comply.

    (iv) Under normal operating conditions, the customer will receive a busy signal less than three (3) percent of the time.

    (v) Customer service center and bill payment locations will be open at least during normal business hours and will be conveniently located.

  (2) Installations, outages and service calls. Under normal operating conditions, each of the following four standards will be met no less than ninety-five (95) percent of the time measured on a quarterly basis:

    (i) Standard installations will be performed within seven (7) business days after an order has been placed.

"Standard" installations are those that are located up to 125 feet from the existing distribution system.

(ii) Excluding conditions beyond the control of the operator, the cable operator will begin working on "service interruptions" promptly and in no event later than 24 hours after the interruption becomes known. The cable operator must begin actions to correct other service problems the next business day after notification of the service problem.

(iii) The "appointment window" alternatives for installations, service calls, and other installation activities will be either a specific time or, at maximum, a four-hour time block during normal business hours. (The operator may schedule service calls and other installation activities outside of normal business hours for the express convenience of the customer.)

(iv) An operator may not cancel an appointment with a customer after the close of business on the business day prior to the scheduled appointment.

(v) If a cable operator representative is running late for an appointment with a customer and will not be able to keep the appointment as scheduled, the customer will be contacted. The appointment will be rescheduled, as necessary, at a time which is convenient for the customer.

(3) Communications between cable operators and cable subscribers—

(i) Notifications to subscribers—

(A) The cable operator shall provide written information on each of the following areas at the time of installation of service, at least annually to all subscribers, and at any time upon request:

(1) Products and services offered;

(2) Prices and options for programming services and conditions of subscription to programming and other services;

(3) Installation and service maintenance policies;

(4) Instructions on how to use the cable service;

(5) Channel positions programming carried on the system; and,

(6) Billing and complaint procedures, including the address and telephone number of the local franchise authority's cable office.

    (B) Customers will be notified of any changes in rates, programming services or channel positions as soon as possible in writing. Notice must be given to subscribers a minimum of thirty (30) days in advance of such changes if the change is within the control of the cable operator. In addition, the cable operator shall notify subscribers thirty (30) days in advance of any significant changes in the other information required by paragraph (c)(3)(i)(A) of this section. Notwithstanding any other provision of Part 76, a cable operator shall not be required to provide prior notice of any rate change that is the result of a regulatory fee, franchise fee, or any other fee, tax, assessment, or charge of any kind imposed by any Federal agency, State, or franchising authority on the transaction between the operator and the subscriber.

  (ii) Billing—

    (A) Bills will be clear, concise and understandable. Bills must be fully itemized, with itemizations including, but not limited to, basic and premium service charges and equipment charges. Bills will also clearly delineate all activity during the billing period, including optional charges, rebates and credits.

    (B) In case of a billing dispute, the cable operator must respond to a written complaint from a subscriber within 30 days.

  (iii) Refunds—Refund checks will be issued promptly, but no later than either—

    (A) The customer's next billing cycle following resolution of the request or thirty (30) days, whichever is earlier, or

    (B) The return of the equipment supplied by the cable operator if service is terminated.

  (iv) Credits—Credits for service will be issued no later than the customer's next billing cycle following the determination that a credit is warranted.

(4) Definitions—

  (i) Normal business hours—The term "normal business hours" means those hours during which most similar businesses in the community are open to serve customers. In all cases, "normal business hours" must include some evening hours at least one night per week and/or some weekend hours.

(ii) Normal operating conditions—The term "normal operating conditions" means those service conditions which are within the control of the cable operator. Those conditions which are not within the control of the cable operator include, but are not limited to, natural disasters, civil disturbances, power outages, telephone network outages, and severe or unusual weather conditions. Those conditions which are ordinarily within the control of the cable operator include, but are not limited to, special promotions, pay-per-view events, rate increases, regular peak or seasonal demand periods, and maintenance or upgrade of the cable system.

(iii) Service interruption—The term "service interruption" means the loss of picture or sound on one or more cable channels.

Summary

In order to obtain a broadcast license, applicants must demonstrate that they meet legal, technical, financial, and character qualifications. They must also agree to adhere to EEO guidelines. When determining who will receive a broadcast license, the FCC also considers statements by applicants that detail how they will serve the public interest. Applicants must adhere to multiple and cross-ownership rules. Mutually exclusive applications are designated for a hearing to determine who will be awarded the license.

Broadcast licenses are granted for a limited, renewable term. Both radio and television licenses are issued for eight years. A license may be revoked if licensees violate Commission rules or the terms of the license. Other options available to the FCC when dealing with rule offenders include short-term renewal and nonrenewal of licenses. Lesser offenses may result in fines.

Noncommercial educational broadcasting is the official title of the class of service designated by the FCC to be licensed to nonprofit foundations and educational institutions. Many of the rules and regulations that apply to commercial broadcasters apply to noncommercial stations as well. There are some notable exceptions, however, including a prohibition on the broadcast of commercial advertisements. However, these stations may broadcast underwriting announcements to acknowledge funds raised to support programming. Public radio and television stations are noncommercial educational stations that are qualified to receive funds from the Corporation for Public Broadcasting (CPB).

Cable systems are not licensed by the FCC but are granted franchises by local municipalities. FCC rules do apply to cable systems and may be found in Title 47, Section 76 of the Code of Federal Regulations.

Notes/References

1. 47 U.F.C. Sec. 308(b) (1989).
2. See Character Qualifications in Broadcast Licensing, 102 F.C.C.2d 1179, 59 R.R.2d 801 (1986).
3. Christopher Stern, "FCC Raises Roof on TV Ownership," *Broadcasting & Cable* (December 19, 1994): 6.
4. *FCC v. National Citizens Committee for Broadcasting*, 436 U.S. 775 (1978).
5. 47 CFR., 73.3591.
6. *Central Florida Enterprises, Inc. v. FCC*, U.S. Ct.App. D.C. Cir., 683 F.2d 503, R.R.2d 1045 (1982), cert. denied 460 U.S. 1084 (1983).
7. *Federal Communications Commission v. WNCN Listener's Guild*, 450 U.S. 582 (1981).
8. "EEO Forfeitures and Short Term License Renewals Continue," *Haley, Bader & Potts Information Memorandum* 16 (February 14, 1991): 6.
9. *In The Matter of Standards for Assessing Forfeitures for Violations of the Broadcast EEO Rules*, Policy Statement (FCC 94–27, February 1 1994) Appendix A.
10. FCC Report No. MM827 Mass Media Action (April 28, 1994); FCC Report No. MM823 Mass Media Action (April 28, 1994); FCC Report No. MM822 Mass Media Action (April 28, 1994); "EEO Compliance Guidelines," *Haley, Bader & Potts Information Memorandum* 5 (April 21,1994): 1.
11. See *Fifth Report and Order* on MM Docket No. 87–268 (FCC 97–116, April 23, 1997).
12. *Second Report and Order*, 86 F.C.C.2d 141 (1981) at 142.
13. *Knights of the Ku Klux Klan, Realm of Missouri and Michael Cuffley v. Patricia Bennett (KWMU)*, 1998 U.S.Dist.LEXIS 19473, No. 4:97CV2109 TCM (December 10, 1998).
14. 58 FR 21109, Apr. 19, 1993, as amended at 61 FR 18977, Apr. 30, 1996.

Cases

Bechtel v. Federal Communications Commission, 22 Med.L.Rptr. 1097 (CA, DC, 1993).

Capital Cities/ABC, Inc., 66 R.R.2d 1146 (1989)

Citizens Committee to Preserve Voice of the Arts in Atlanta v. FCC, 141 U.S. Ct.App. DC 109, 436 F.2d 263 (DC Cir., 1970)

Citizens Committee to Save WEFM-FM v. FCC, 165 U.S. App. DC 185, 506 F.2d 246 (DC Cir., 1970)

Citizens Communications Center v. FCC, 447 F.2d 1201 (DC Cir.,1971)

Citizens for Jazz on WRVR, Inc. v. FCC, 755 F.2d 392, 59 R.R.2d 249 (DC Cir.,1985)

Committee to Save WEFM v. FCC, 808 F.2d 113, 61 R.R.2d 1444 (DC Cir.,1986)

Cowles Florida Broadcasting Inc., 60 F.C.C.2d 372, 37 R.R.2d 1487, 1555–56 (1976)

DC/MD/DE Broadcasters Association v. FCC, (DC Cir No. 00-1094 June 19, 2001)

FCC v. League of Women Voters of California, 468 U.S. 364 (1984)

FCC v. National Citizen's Committee for Broadcasting, 436 U.S.775 (1978)

Federal Communications Commission v. WNCN Listener's Guild, 450 U.S. 582 (1981)

Fox Television Stations Inc. v. Federal Communications Commission (2002 U.S. App. LEXIS 2575)

Greater Boston Television Corp. v. FCC, U.S. Ct.App., DC Cir., F.2d 841 (1970), cert. denied 403 U.S. 923 (1971)

In the Matter of WHDH Inc., 16 F.C.C. 1 (1969)

KKK v. Curators of the University of Missouri 203 F.3d 1085 (8th Cir. 2000)

Knights of the Ku Klux Klan, Realm of Missouri and Michael Cuffley v. Patricia Bennett (KWMU), 1998 U.S.Dist.LEXIS 19473, No. 4:97CV2109 TCM (December 10, 1998)

Lutheran Church–Missouri Synod v. Federal Communications Commission (DC Cir No. 97–1116 April 14, 1998)

Multiple Ownership (12–12–12 Reconsideration), 100 F.C.C.2d 74, 75 R.R.2d 967 (1985)

Policy Research Group v. FCC, 807 F.2d 1038, 61 R.R.2d 1450 (DC Cir., 1986)

RKO v. Federal Communications Commission, U.S. Ct.App. DC Cir., 670F.2d215, 50 R.R.2d 821 (1981), cert. denied 457 U.S. 1119 (1982)

United States v. Storer Broadcasting, 351 U.S. 192 (1956)

6

Regulation of Electronic Media Content

Nothing in this Act shall be understood or construed to give the Commission the power of censorship over the radio communications or signals transmitted by any radio station, and no regulation or condition shall be promulgated or fixed by the Commission which shall interfere with the right of free speech by means of radio communication.[1]

Although the Communications Act prohibits outright censorship of broadcast programming by the FCC, this does not mean that broadcasters have escaped Commission action in this area. Throughout the years the Commission has retained varying degrees of interest in the regulation of broadcast programming content. The Commission's concern stemmed from enforcement of the public interest standard. Based on this standard, policies were developed, including localism, network affiliation rules, "promise versus performance," and the Fairness Doctrine. The policy of "promise versus performance" called for the actual programming broadcast to be in line with what was stated on the FCC application. The policy was unevenly enforced and was ultimately eliminated in 1985. The FCC required stations to keep program logs and at one point compelled stations to submit a "composite week" of program logs to the Commission during the license renewal process. One by one, many of these rules and policies disappeared, and Commission program regulation was returned to the original congressional mandate to ensure that stations serve the public interest.

Development of Programming Policy

The Blue Book of 1946 marked the Commission's first serious attempt to regulate program content (see Chapter 3). Policies developed from this document shaped program regulation in various forms until the 1980s.

Ascertainment of Community Needs

Because broadcasters were charged with serving their community of license, it stood to reason that they should be familiar with the problems and needs affecting that community. Indeed, the FCC expected broadcasters to program to those needs. The policy of community ascertainment developed from this expectation. Although community service was always expected, the policy of formal ascertainment for commercial stations was instituted in 1971 in the FCC's *Primer on Ascertainment of Community Problems.* Beginning in 1975, noncommercial stations were required to conduct formal ascertainment.

Formal ascertainment consisted of four major steps. First, broadcasters were required to conduct a survey of the general public in the community of license. The survey was to be designed to allow the broadcaster to determine the major issues and problems facing the community. Second, a survey of community leaders was to be conducted. The FCC provided guidelines that indicated that the leaders must come from such areas as business, education, religion, agriculture, and so on. The bulk of the community leaders survey was to be conducted by station management, not by the clerical staff or an outside firm. Third, the results of the surveys were to be analyzed, and a list of ten major problems facing the community was to be generated. Initially, this list was to be submitted to the FCC, but later the list was to be placed in the station's public file. Fourth, the station was expected to propose and actually broadcast programming designed to meet the needs and problems identified in the ascertainment process.

As one might expect, this process involved considerable personnel hours and paperwork. In 1981, the Commission began reducing the requirements of the formal ascertainment process. The surveys of the general public and community leaders were simplified and stations were required to generate a list of five to ten issues that the station covered during the course of the year. This list was to be kept in the public file. At license renewal time, the FCC retained the right to question stations about the programming aired. By 1984, formal ascertainment had been eliminated. However, as a result of the Federal Communications Commission's deregulation of radio and commercial television, a variation on the scant issues list remained in the form of the quarterly programs-issues list.

The Quarterly Programs-Issues List

When formal ascertainment procedures were eliminated, stations were required to identify five to ten issues of importance to their communities and place this list in the public file. Stations were also expected to provide examples of programming broadcasts that addressed those issues. This policy evolved into the present requirement, which calls for broadcasters to prepare quarterly lists of community issues and to show how those issues were addressed on the air (Figure 6.1). There is no minimum or maximum number of issues to be addressed. However, in *Deregulation of Radio*, the FCC did suggest that stations identifying a minimum of five issues would probably be in compliance with the spirit of the rule.

Each quarterly list must identify the issue and include the program title, a narrative description of the program, the program's length, and time and date of airing. The programming can be almost any kind of non-entertainment program, including public service announcements. The programs need not be locally produced, but they must deal with issues of importance to the local community.

The quarterly lists must be placed in the public inspection file by the tenth of the month following the end of the quarter. In other words, the lists must be in the file by January 10th, April 10th, July 10th, and October 10th of each year. The quarterly reports are extremely important and may be used by the FCC at license renewal to determine whether the station has operated in the public interest.[2] In February 1991, the Commission sanctioned the

While 5 issues are listed in this example, stations should place all issues given significant treatment in their public file.

Issue	Title	Description	Time	Date	Duration
Poor Roads	Five part series following evening newscast	The series documents state of local and state highways and what has been planned to improve them	6:24 PM	M-F 2/1-2/4	Four minutes per segment
	"The Mayor's Hotline"	A call-in program featuring the mayor Viewers discuss the issue with the mayor.	12:30 PM	Friday 2/12	15:00
Aids Awareness	"Healthline"	Doctors and Health officials discuss the issue on camera.	9:30PM	Sunday 3/19	30:00
Military Base Closings locally	"Say Goodnight..."	A documentary on the effects of base closing on the local economy.	7:30 PM	Tuesday 3/22	30:00
Local police community/ relations.	"In-Focus"	A discussion with police and community leaders	10:00AM	Sunday 3/19	30:00
Local economic development	"In Focus"	Conversation with city planners and developers about downtown revitalization project.	10:00AM	Sunday 3/36	30:00

Figure 6.1 Sample quarterly programs-issues list.

Arkansas Educational Television Commission for failure to place a programs-issues list in its public file on a quarterly basis.

Indecent, Suggestive, or Offensive Material

Obscenity versus Indecency

Title 18, Section 1464 of the Federal Criminal Code prohibits broadcasting "obscene, indecent or profane language" and provides punishments of $10,000 in fines, two years imprisonment, or both for violation of the code. Recall that Section 326 of the Communications Act prohibits censorship by the FCC. These contradictory laws do not help to make FCC regulation of obscenity and indecency any less difficult. As the adage goes, one person's pornography is another person's art.

What can be said with certainty is that obscene materials have no First Amendment protection. Obscenity is a legal term applied by a court. For material to be declared obscene, it must meet criteria set forth in *Miller v. California (1973)*. In this case, the Supreme Court developed what has become known as the LAPS test. LAPS is an acronym for literary, artistic, political, or scientific value—the standards that emerged out of Miller for determining obscenity. Under the LAPS test, a work may be judged obscene if the average person, applying contemporary community standards, finds that the work, when taken as a whole, appeals to prurient interest; describes, in a patently offensive way, sexual conduct specifically defined by applicable state law; and lacks serious literary, artistic, political, or scientific value. Needless to say, this test is very difficult to apply.

In *In the Matter of Enforcement of Prohibitions Against Broadcast Obscenity and Indecency*, indecency has been defined by the FCC to include "language that describes, in terms patently offensive as measured by contemporary community standards for the broadcast medium, sexual or excretory activities and organs."[3] Indecency, while not devoid of First Amendment protection, has been determined by the FCC to be unsuitable for the broadcast media. Cable and print media are not subjected to this form of content regulation.

FCC Authority in Regulating Obscene, Indecent, and Offensive Material

Originally, the prohibition against broadcasting obscene, indecent, or profane matter was contained in the Communications Act. In 1948, it was removed from the act and made a part of the U.S. Criminal Code. Sections 312 and 503 of the Communications Act give the FCC the authority to order a broadcaster to cease and desist from broadcasting indecent or obscene material. The Commission may also impose fines of up to $2000 per day per offense, and may revoke or deny renewal of the station's license. These punishments are in addition to the sanctions provided in Section 1464 of the Criminal Code.

Development of FCC Policy

In 1964, the FCC responded during license renewal to complaints received against several stations owned by the Pacifica Foundation in *In re Pacifica Foundation*. The subjects of the complaints included the broadcast of poetry readings by Lawrence Ferlinghetti, a broadcast of Edward Albee's *The Zoo Story*, and a program entitled "Live and Let Live," during which eight homosexuals discussed their attitudes and problems. The Commission upheld the license renewal of the Pacifica stations noting,

> We recognize that as shown by the complaints here, such provocative programming as here involved may offend some listeners. But this does not mean that those offended have the right, through the Commission's licensing power, to rule such programming off the airwaves. Were this the case, only the wholly inoffensive, the bland, could gain access to the radio microphone or camera.[4]

In *Pacifica I (1964)*, the FCC came down squarely on the side of freedom of expression. The remedy for those offended was to turn off the program. Six years later, the Commission took a different view.

In 1970, WUHY-FM, a noncommercial station, broadcast a taped interview with Jerry Garcia, guitarist and singer for the cult rock group, The Grateful Dead. Garcia was joined by an individual known only as "Crazy Max." Garcia discussed music, politics, and philosophy, and presented his opinions on the state of society. Crazy Max warned that computers would soon take over society. Throughout the interview, Garcia used numerous expletives. More specifically, his comments were frequently interspersed with the words "fuck" and "shit" used as adjectives or simply as stand-alone introductions to a phrase.

In response to complaints to the FCC, WUHY argued that the Garcia interview dealt with important topics of the day, and because the program was designed to reach an "underground" audience, Garcia's language was acceptable. The Commission disagreed.

Eastern Educational Radio (WUHY-FM) (1970)

☐   The issue in this case is not whether WUHY-FM may present the views of Mr. Garcia or "Crazy Max" on ecology, society, computers and so on. Clearly that decision is a matter solely within the judgement of the licensee. . . . Further we stress, as we have before, the licensee's right to present provocative or unpopular programming which may offend some listeners . . . Rather the narrow issue is whether the licensee may present previously taped interview or talk shows where the persons intersperse or begin their speech with expressions like, "Shit, man . . . ," "and shit like that," or " 900 fucking times," etc. [I]f WUHY can broadcast an interview with Mr. Garcia where he begins sentences with "Shit, man" or uses "fucking" before word after word, just because he talks that way, so can any other person on radio. Newscasters or disc jockeys could use the same expressions, as could other persons . . . on the grounds that that is the way they talk and it adds flavor and emphasis to their speech. But the consequences of any such widespread practice would be to undermine the usefulness of radio to millions of others. For, these expressions are patently offensive to millions of listeners.[5]

The FCC fined WUHY, a student-run noncommercial station, $100 and told them not to do it again.

In the early 1970s, there developed a radio format that has been dubbed "topless radio." These programs were usually midday, call-in shows targeted to women. The topics discussed were sexual in nature. The host, though tame by today's "shock jock" standards, tended to include sexual innuendoes in his conversations with callers. The FCC ruled in *Sonderling Broadcasting Corp. (WGLD-FM) (1973)* that WGLD-FM in Oak Park, Illinois, had violated both the obscenity and indecency standards of Section 1424. The program in question was the February 23 broadcast of "Femme Forum," the topic of which was oral sex. The FCC stressed that it was not the topic itself that was offensive, but rather the way in which the topic was presented. The FCC objected to the program host's "leering innuendo" when discussing sexual topics. The Commission added that "Gresham's Law" is at work in this case.

If broadcasters can engage in commercial exploitation of obscene or indecent material . . . an increasing number will do so for competitive reasons, with spiraling adverse effects upon millions of listeners.[6]

Sonderling was fined $2000 for the offense.

Channeling Offensive Material

Another theme that reoccurs in the Commission's indecency policy is that of keeping indecent or offensive material away from children who may be in the audience. In *WUHY* and *Sonderling*, the Commission touched on the pervasive nature of broadcast media.

The FCC and others worried that, unlike print (which is selected by the reader), radio and television may intrude uninvited into the home, bringing with it unwanted offensive material, at best. At its worst, it may even be harmful to children in the audience.

Rationalizing this view in light of the First Amendment proved perplexing. After all, unless a broadcast was determined to be obscene under the *Miller* standard, it retained a certain amount of First Amendment protection. Obscenity cases are rare in broadcasting. It is doubtful that *Sonderling* would be declared obscene today. The FCC did find some assistance in dealing with the problem of keeping broadcast indecency away from children in the audience while protecting the First Amendment rights of those wishing to receive such programs. In *Young v. American Mini Theatres Inc. (1976)* the Supreme Court held that cities could zone sexually explicit movie theaters and bookstores and confine them to specific parts of town. Provided an ordinance was carefully drawn, zoning itself would not run afoul of the First Amendment. The FCC used a similar tactic in suggesting that stations "channel" potentially indecent programs to portions of the broadcast day when children were less likely to be in the audience.

FCC v. Pacifica Foundation (1978) [Pacifica II]

This case evolved as a result of the broadcast by noncommercial WBAI, New York, of a 12-minute monologue by humorist George Carlin. The monologue, entitled "Filthy Words," was taken from a Carlin record album. In the monologue, Carlin satirizes the way we use words and how we give them meaning. He includes his version of the "seven words you can never say on TV." The "heavy seven," as he calls them, are *shit, piss, fuck, cunt, cocksucker, motherfucker,* and *tits.* Carlin says in the monologue, "These are the words that will curve your spine, grow hair on your hands and, God help us, bring peace without honor." He then discussed each word individually in a humorous, yet satiric manner. The broadcast was part of an overall program aired on WBAI on the uses of language in society. Other speakers were part of the program, and a warning was broadcast before the Carlin routine aired at around 2:00 P.M.

A man and his young son were driving in their car and inadvertently tuned in to the broadcast. The listener was offended and complained to the FCC. His was the only complaint about the broadcast.

The FCC ruled that Pacifica, the owner of WBAI, was subject to administrative sanction, but imposed no formal sanction. The Commission placed the order in a file in the event other complaints were received.

The FCC cited four reasons for treating broadcasting differently from other media:

1. Access by unsupervised children
2. Because radio receivers are in the home, privacy interests are entitled to extra deference
3. Unconsenting adults may tune in without warning that offensive language is being used

4. Scarcity of spectrum space requires the government to license in the public interest

The Court of Appeals for the District of Columbia overturned the FCC decision, but the Supreme Court upheld the Commission's position and opened the door to the concept of "channeling" broadcast programming.

☐   The Commission characterized the language used in the Carlin monologue as "patently offensive," though not necessarily obscene, and expressed the opinion that it should be regulated by principles analogous to those found in the law of nuisance where the "law generally speaks to channeling behavior more than actually prohibiting it. . . . [T]he concept of 'indecent' is intimately connected with the exposure of children to language that describes, in terms patently offensive as measured by contemporary community standards for the broadcast medium, sexual or excretory activities and organs at times of the day when there is reasonable risk that children may be in the audience."

   . . . It is appropriate . . . to emphasize the narrowness of our holding. This case does not involve a two-way radio conversation between a cab driver and a dispatcher, or a telecast of an Elizabethan comedy. We have not decided that an occasional expletive in either setting would justify any sanction or, indeed, that this broadcast would justify criminal prosecution. The Commission's decision rested entirely on a nuisance rationale under which context is all important. . . . The time of day was emphasized by the Commission. The content of the program in which the language is used will also affect the composition of the audience, . . . and differences between radio, television and perhaps closed-circuit transmissions may also be relevant. As Mr. Justice Sutherland wrote, a "nuisance may merely be the right thing in the wrong place like a pig in the parlor instead of the barnyard." We simply hold that when the Commission finds that a pig has entered the parlor, the exercise of its regulatory power does not depend on proof that the pig is obscene.[7]

Keep in mind that Section 326 of the Communications Act prohibits censorship by the FCC. In *Pacifica II*, channeling indecent material does not represent censorship in the eyes of the Supreme Court, since the material may still be broadcast and receives some First Amendment protection.

Commission Policy after Pacifica II

Between 1975 and 1987, the FCC found no other broadcasters guilty of indecent programming. During this time, the FCC tried to assure broadcasters that it would only be concerned with the "seven dirty words" as defined by Carlin and then, only if they were used repeatedly. In 1987, sparked by complaints from the public, the FCC embarked on a new indecency policy.

The 1987 Revised Indecency Standard

In 1987, the Commission took action against three broadcast stations and one amateur radio facility for indecency. The broadcast stations were WYSP-FM in Philadelphia, Pacifica's KPFK-FM in Los Angeles, and the University of California at Santa Barbara's KCSB-FM.

KFPK had broadcast excerpts from the play *Jerker*, which consists of telephone conversations of two homosexuals dying of AIDS. The complaint against the University of California station was based on offensive lyrics in a song by the Pork Dukes called "Making Bacon." The offensive material broadcast on WYSP involved "shock jock" Howard Stern. The Commission noted that Stern's program regularly dwelled on sexual and excretory matters in a way that was patently offensive as measured by contemporary community standards for the broadcast medium.

Because the indecency provisions of Section 1464 had been applied for the first time in many years, all of the above stations escaped with only a warning, but a major Commission policy change began to take shape. In 1987, the FCC issued a document entitled *New Indecency Enforcement Standards to Be Applied to All Broadcast and Amateur Radio Licensees 2 FCC Rcd. 2726 (1987)*.

The revised standard no longer limited itself to Carlin's seven dirty words. The Commission applied the broad definition of indecency as approved by the Supreme Court in *Pacifica II*. Indecency was defined as "language or material that depicts or describes, in terms patently offensive as measured by contemporary community standards for the broadcast medium, sexual or excretory activities or organs."[8]

Responding to pressure from broadcasters and other organizations in November 1987, the Commission created a "safe harbor" between midnight and 6:00 A.M. for the broadcast of programming that might otherwise be banned as indecent. The "safe harbor" was a variation on the "later evening day parts" concept espoused in *Pacifica*. Even during these hours, broadcasters were required to provide a warning that offensive material might be contained in a given program. Under the policy, indecent speech was to be channeled to day parts, when children were not likely to be listening or viewing. In December 1988, the FCC adopted a 24-hour ban on indecent programming shortly after Congress, led by North Carolina Senator Jesse Helms, passed a law requiring the FCC to act. The 24-hour ban was stayed by the Court of Appeals for the District of Columbia in January 1989. In spite of all this activity, only one enforcement action was taken. That action involved a fine against KZKC-TV in Kansas City for a May 26, 1987, prime time broadcast of the movie *Private Lessons*.

Building Support for a Proposed 24-Hour Ban

In 1989, shortly after Alfred Sikes replaced Dennis Patrick as Chairman of the FCC, the Commission stepped up its indecency enforcement again. In August 1989, the FCC initiated action against three more radio stations for airing indecent programs. This time, the action involved "Morning Zoo" personalities at WFBQ in Indianapolis, WLUP in Chicago, and KSJO in San Jose. Chairman Sikes also asked the court of appeals to remand the stay of the 24-hour ban to the FCC so that the Commission could build a record supporting the ban.

In October 1989, the FCC fined WLLZ-FM in Detroit $2000 for the broadcast of an off-color song "Walk with an Erection." The song, a parody of the Bangles hit "Walk Like an Egyptian," contained lyrics like, "He puts *Penthouse* in his desk/He's got big muscles in his wrist/He holds his organ in his fist/He gives his pink dolphin a mighty twist . . . All the girls in the office they say 'Hard-on, hard-on, beg my pardon.'/Walk with an erection."[9]

In the fall of 1989, the FCC asked for comments from broadcasters to assist the agency in building support for the 24-hour ban of indecent programming. Not surprisingly, only one broadcaster, Bonneville International Corporation, submitted comments favorable to the proposal. The opposition to the total ban on indecent programming was led by a group of 17 media organizations, including the National Association of Broadcasters and the three major television networks. The group argued that the FCC's total ban failed to meet the constitutional test of the least restrictive means of advancing a compelling government interest.

In July of 1990, the FCC adopted a report recommending a 24-hour ban on indecent programs. The Commission concluded that prohibition of indecent broadcasts did not violate the First Amendment because it was "narrowly tailored." Chairman Sikes noted that indecent materials were available to those wishing to receive them, through means other than the broadcast medium. The FCC was concerned that the prevalence of children in the broadcast audience made the proposed ban feasible. The Commission concluded that children are in the broadcast audience for both radio and television at all times, both day and night. The FCC also concluded that channeling and technological devices attached to receivers were not effective in protecting these children from exposure to potentially harmful, indecent programming.

The modified enforcement policy provided stations with the opportunity to demonstrate that children are not present in the broadcast audience during the time in which potentially indecent programming is aired. When Infinity Broadcasting was fined $6000 for a December 1988 broadcast of the Howard Stern show, it vowed to fight the sanction. Infinity argued that the results of a Gallup study demonstrated that no children 12 and younger listen to the Stern show on an unsupervised basis.

Still, the FCC pressed for a 24-hour ban on indecency. The proposed ban continued to come under fire from a federal appeals court judge and from the industry.

In April of 1991, the FCC and the U.S. Department of Justice entered a *Memorandum of Understanding* concerning the resolution of complaints about indecent or obscene programming. Under the agreement, the Justice Department and the FCC have independent jurisdiction over complaints involving the broadcast of allegedly obscene or indecent material. The Department of Justice indicated that it would forward all complaints to the FCC for consideration under FCC rules after evaluating each complaint to determine whether criminal action should be taken. The FCC will continue to process any complaints it receives but may refer complaints to the Justice Department for criminal prosecution.

Shortly after this agreement, the FCC took action against KCNA in Cave Junction, Oregon, and WVIC-FM in East Lansing, Michigan. KCNA was fined $4000 for material broadcast in two segments of the "Guy Kemp Morning Show." The material in question included a taped phone argument between Kemp and former KCNA news director Michael Perry. Kemp used the word "fuck" six times, as well as "shit" and "bullshit." The same show featured a caller who twice said "fuck you, motherfucker," "ass wipe," and "dick shit." Kemp also told an off-color joke. Michael Perry filed the complaint with the FCC. The East Lansing station was fined $2000 for a September 1989 portion of the "Michaels in the Morning" show. The issue centered around a news story about a man who lost a testicle in a hot tub drain while on his honeymoon. Callers were asked to provide headlines for the item. Suggestions included "Drain Sucks Off Man" and "Man Falls Victim to Ball Sucker." The FCC found the remarks to be patently offensive.

Although the Court of Appeals ruling in *Action for Children's Television v. FCC*, 21 Med.L.Rptr. 2289 (DC Cir., 1993) questioned the "safe harbor" of midnight to 6:00 A.M., the Commission announced that it would continue to enforce its indecency standard during the 6:00 A.M., to 8:00 P.M., period. In May 1994 the FCC once again issued notices of apparent liability to Infinity Broadcasting Corporation and its subsidiaries. WJFK-AM, Baltimore, WXRK-FM, New York, WYSP-FM, Philadelphia, and WJFK, Manassas, Virgina were all fined $200,000 for broadcasting indecent material during the Howard Stern show. The Commission said that the indecent broadcasts were made between the hours of 6:00 A.M. and 10:00 P.M.—times when there is a "reasonable risk that children will be in the audience."[10]

The 24-Hour Ban Is Struck Down— The Safe Harbor Is Upheld

In *Action for Children's Television v. Federal Communications Commission (CA DC 1995)* the U.S. Court of Appeals for the District of Columbia affirmed the Safe Harbor. The 7–4 decision allowed the FCC to ban indecent programming between 6:00 A.M. and 10:00 P.M. The court also said that the FCC could broaden the ban from 6:00 A.M. until midnight without violating the Constitution.

The 2001 *Indecency Guildelines*

In April 2001, the Commission offered industry guidance on the enforcement of broadcast indecency rules. (See FCC 10–90. Available at www.fcc.gov.) The FCC restated the definition of indecency and attempted to clarify its standards for enforcement. Following is a summary of some issues addressed in the 2001 Guidelines.

Standards for Determining Liability

1. The explicitness or graphic nature of the description or depiction of sexual or excretory organs or activities;
2. Whether the material dwells on or repeats at length descriptions of sexual or excretory organs or activities;
3. Whether the material appears to pander or is used to titillate, or whether the material appears to have been presented for its shock value.

Examples of Indecent Broadcasts Cited by the FCC in the 2001 Clarification

• WYSP(FM), Philadelphia, PA, the Howard Stern Show:

God, my testicles are like down to the floor . . . you could really have a party with these . . . Use them like Bocci balls. (As part of a discussion of lesbians) I mean to go around porking other girls with vibrating rubber products . . . Have you ever had sex with an animal? Well, don't knock it. I was sodomized by Lambchop.

- KSJO(FM), San Jose, CA, Sung to Tune of *Beverly Hillbillies*:

    Come a listen to a story about a man named Boas, a poor politician that barely kept his winky fed, then one day he's poking a chick and up from his pants came a bubbling crude. Winky oil. Honey pot. Jail Bait. . . . So, he loaded up his winky and he did it with Beverly. Big Breasts. Only 15 years old.

- "Even in the cases of double entendre, not only was the language understandable and clearly capable of a specific sexual or excretory meaning but, because of the context, the sexual and excretory import was inescapable" (see *Narragansett Broadcasting Company of California, Inc., KSJO(FM), 1990*).

Examples Not Found Indecent

- WFBQ(FM)/WNDE, Indianapolis, IN
  —"Elvis"

    As you know, you gotta stop the King, but you can't kill him . . . So you talk to Dick Nixon, man you get him on the phone and Dick suggests maybe getting like a mega-Dick to help out, but you know, you remember the time the King ate mega-Dick under the table at a 095 picnic . . .

  —Power! Power! Power! Thrust! Thrust! Thrust!

    First it was Big Foot, the monster car-crunching 4 × 4 pickup truck. Well, move over, Big Foot! Here comes the most massive power-packed monster ever! It's Big Peter! (Laughter) Big Peter with 40,000 Peterbilt horsepower under the hood. It's massive! Big Peter! Formerly the Big Dick's Dog Wiener Mobile. Big Peter features a 75-foot jacked up monster body. See Big Peter crush and enter a Volvo. (Laughter) . . . strapped himself in the cockpit and put Big Peter through its paces. So look out Big Foot! Big Peter is coming! Oh my God! It's coming! Big Peter!" (Laughter)

Why These Were Not Indecent

- WFBQ provided a fuller transcript of the cited "Elvis" excerpt and explained the context in which it was aired, arguing that no sexual meaning was intended and that no such meaning would be reasonably understood from the material taken as a whole.
- WFBQ also explained the regional humor of the Power, Power, Power excerpt and the context in which it was broadcast.

- The FCC also looks to the audibility of the material as aired.
  —If the material is difficult or impossible to understand, it may not be actionably indecent.
  —However, difficulty in understanding part of the material or an attempt to obscure objectionable material may still be actionable.

FCC Guidelines for Filing an Indecency Complaint

In order for a complaint to be considered, it must generally include:

(1) a full or partial tape or transcript or significant excerpts of the program;
(2) the date and time of the broadcast; and
(3) the call sign of the station involved.

If a complaint does not contain this supporting material, or if a broadcast occurred during "safe harbor" hours, or the material does not fall within the subject matter scope of our indecency definition, it is usually dismissed by a letter to the complainant advising of the deficiency.

Indecency and the Internet

It should be noted here that indecency on the Internet is treated differently than broadcasting. In spite of efforts by Congress to apply a broadcasting model of indecency enforcement to the World Wide Web, these have not survived constitutional scrutiny. In *Reno v. American Civil Liberties Union, 520 U.S. 1113 (1997),* the Supreme Court struck down an indecency standard for the Internet. However, the Court did not question the constitutionality of the broadcast indecency standard. The Court noted that special justifications for regulation of the broadcast media may not apply to other media.

Song Lyrics

Concern over the lyrics to popular songs has been a growing issue since the 1950s. The link between broadcasting and the music industry continues to draw broadcasters into the fray. When Elvis Presley first appeared on the *Ed Sullivan Show* in 1956, camera operators were told to refrain from showing Elvis' gyrating hips. A decade later, the Rolling Stones were required to sing "Let's spend some time together" instead of "Let's spend the night together" on another Sullivan show. Jim Morrison and the

Doors were asked to delete the word "higher" from their 1967 hit, "Light My Fire," when they appeared on the program. They didn't and never came back. The Doors were later to become the first rock group to be prosecuted for obscenity, as a result of a concert in Miami.

The controversy over music lyrics has been unabated ever since. Needless to say, the music and performances of today's rap, rock, and alternative acts remain controversial. At the heart of the matter is a balancing of the First Amendment right of free expression against the concern of potentially harmful material being made available to children. In 1992 the state of Washington passed the "Erotic Sound Recordings" statute. Basically, this law banned the sale of "erotic" sound recordings that met the test for obscenity adjusted to apply to minors. The law was struck down in *Soundgarden v. Eikenberry (1994)*. The court found the statute unconstitutional. The law represented a prior restraint on protected speech as applied to adults, and the definition of "erotic" was overbroad. The court said the statute violated due process of law because it imposed criminal penalties for sale of "erotic" music, without clearly defining what is meant by the term.

In the early 1970s, the Commission became concerned with drug-oriented music aired on some radio stations. The Commission issued a notice that required broadcasters to be aware of the content of the music to be aired. Specifically, the FCC suggested that broadcasters could pre-screen material, monitor selections while they are being played, or consider and respond to complaints made by members of the public. In *Yale Broadcasting Co. v. FCC (1973)*, the court ruled that the Commission's order did not violate the First Amendment. The court noted that for a licensee to serve the public interest, it must have knowledge of what it is broadcasting. The order did not prohibit stations from playing drug-oriented material per se, but stations were required to take reasonable measures to be aware that they had done so.

This list of examples is not exhaustive, but it serves to illustrate the symbiotic relationship between popular music and broadcasting. Radio and television programmers strive to provide audiences with the music they want to hear and performances that will garner viewers. Increasingly, however, the music contains lyrics that, though acceptable on records, may skirt the boundaries of indecency for broadcast matter. Indeed, the material of the rap group 2 Live Crew was initially found obscene by a Florida district court. Although eventually overturned, the case is included because it outlines the parameters of the issue facing society.

Skyywalker Records Inc. v. Navarro (1990)

☐ Gonzalez, J.:

This is a case between two ancient enemies: Anything Goes and Enough Already.

Justice Oliver Wendell Holmes, Jr. observed in *Schenck v. United States, 249 U.S. 47 (1919)*, that the First Amendment is not absolute and that it does not permit one to yell "Fire" in a crowded theater. Today, this court decides whether the First Amendment absolutely permits one to yell another "F" word anywhere in the community when combined with graphic sexual descriptions.

Two distinct and narrow issues are presented: whether the recording *As Nasty As They Wanna Be (Nasty)* is legally obscene; and second, whether the actions of the defendant Nicholas Navarro . . . as Sheriff of Broward County Florida, imposed an unconstitutional prior restraint upon the plaintiffs' right to free speech.

The Facts

The recording *As Nasty As They Wanna Be* was released to the public by 2 Live Crew in 1989. To date, public sales have totalled approximately 1.7 million copies. . . . 2 Live Crew has also produced a recording entitled *As Clean As They Wanna Be (Clean)* which has sold approximately 250,000 copies. . . . [I]t apparently contains the same music as *Nasty* but without the explicit sexual lyrics.

In mid-February 1990, the Broward County Sheriff's office began an investigation of the *Nasty* recording. The investigation began in response to complaints by South Florida residents.

Broward County Deputy Sheriff Mark Wichner was assigned to the case. On February 26, 1990, he traveled to Sound Warehouse . . . and purchased the *Nasty* recording. The tape was purchased from an open display rack marked "Rap Music," easily accessible to all of Sound Warehouse's customers regardless of age.

Deputy Wichner listened to the *Nasty* recording, had six of the eighteen songs transcribed, and prepared an affidavit detailing these facts requesting that the Broward County Circuit Court find probable cause that the Nasty recording was legally obscene. . . .

On March 9, Judge Grossman issued an order after reviewing the *Nasty* recording "in its entirety." The judge found probable cause to believe this recording was obscene under section 847.011 of the Florida Statutes. . . .

The Broward County Sheriff's office received and copied the order and distributed it countywide to retail establishments that might be selling the *Nasty* recording. . . .

Thereafter, Deputy Wichner revisited the store where he had purchased the original recording plus another Sound Warehouse and a store called Uncle Sam's Records. On these visits, the deputy wore a jacket marked "Broward County Sheriff" and displayed his badge in plain view. He spoke with a manager in each of the three stores, provided them with a copy of Judge Grossman's order, and told them, in a friendly and conversational tone, that they should refrain from selling the *Nasty* recording. The managers were warned that further sales would result in arrest and if convicted, the penalty for selling to a minor was a felony, and a misdemeanor if sold to an adult. . . .

The Sheriff's office warnings were very effective. Within days, all retail stores in Broward County ceased offering the *Nasty* recording for sale. . . . Some stores continued to sell the clean recording. *Nasty* was no longer sold, even by stores having a policy of specially marking the recording with a warning and of not selling it to minors.

On March 16, 1990, the plaintiffs filed this action in federal district court. On March 27, 1990, Sheriff Nicholas Navarro filed an in rein proceeding in Broward County Circuit Court against the *Nasty* recording seeking a judicial determination that it was obscene under state law.

This is . . . not a case about whether the group 2 Live Crew or any of its music is obscene. The third element of the *Miller Test* focuses upon the social value of the particular work, not its creators. The fact that individuals of whom we approve hold objectionable ideas or that people of whom we do not approve hold worthy ideas does not affect judicial review of the value of the ideas themselves. . . .

Finally, this court's role is not to serve as a censor or an art or music critic. If the *Nasty* recording has serious literary, artistic, political, or scientific value, it is irrelevant that the work is not stylish, tasteful, or even popular.

The plaintiffs themselves testified that neither their music nor their lyrics were created to convey a political message.

The only witness testifying at trial that there was political content in the *Nasty* recording was Carlton Long, who was qualified as an expert on the culture of black Americans. This witness first stated that the recording was political because the 2 Live Crew, as a group of black Americans, used this medium to express themselves. While it is doubtless true that *Nasty* is a product of the group's background, including their heritage as black Americans, this fact does not convert whatever they say, or sing, into political speech. . . .

In terms of science, Professor Long also suggested that there is cultural content in 2 Live Crew's recording which rises to the level of serious sociological value. According to this witness, white Americans "hear" the Nasty recording in a different way than black Americans because of their frames of reference. Long identifies three cultural devices evident in the work here: "call and response," "doing the dozens," and "boasting." The court finds none of these arguments persuasive.

The only examples of "call and response" in the *Nasty* recording are portions where males and females yell in repetitive verse, "Tastes Great Less Filling." The phrases alone have no significant artistic merit nor are they examples of black American culture . . . this is merely a phrase lifted from a beer commercial.

The device of "doing the dozens" is a word game composed of a series of insults escalating in their satirical content. The "boasting" device is a way for persons to overstate their virtues as sexual prowess.

While this court does not doubt that both "boasting" and "doing the dozens " is commonly found in the culture of black Americans, these devices are also found in other cultures. . . .

The plaintiffs stress that the *Nasty* recording has value as comedy and satire. Certainly, people can and do laugh at obscenity. The plaintiffs point to the audience reaction at trial when the subject recording was played in open court. The audience giggled initially, but the court observed that after the initial titillation, all fell silent. . . .

It cannot be reasonably argued that the violence, perversion, abuse of women, graphic depictions of all forms of sexual conduct, and microscopic descriptions of human genitalia contained on this recording are comedic art.

The *Nasty* recording is not comedy, but is first and foremost, music. . . .

. . . Musical works are obscene if they meet the *Miller Test*. . . . The focus of the *Nasty* recording is predominately on the lyrics. . . .

. . . 2 Live Crew has "borrowed" components called "riffs" from other artists. Taking the work in its entirety, the several riffs do not lift *Nasty* to the level of serious artistic work. Once the riffs are removed, all that remains is the rhythm and the explicit sexual lyrics which are without any redeeming social value.

Obscenity is not a required element for socially valuable "rap" or "hip-hop" music. 2 Live Crew proved this point by its creation of the Clean recording. . . .

. . . The recording *As Nasty As They Wanna Be*, taken as a whole, is legally obscene.[11]

The court also found the actions of the Broward County Sheriff's Department in threatening retail stores with arrest for selling the *Nasty* recording before the judgment to be an unconstitutional prior restraint. The court issued a permanent injunction against Sheriff Navarro and his agents, prohibiting future such action.

On appeal, the obscenity decision was reversed. The U.S. Court of Appeals for the 11th Circuit found that not all elements of the *Miller Test* had been met.

Luke Records Inc. v. Navarro (1992)

☐ . . . This case is apparently the first time that a court of appeals has been asked to apply the *Miller Test* to a musical composition, which contains both instrumental music and lyrics. Although we tend to agree with appellants' contention that because music possesses inherent artistic value, no work of music alone may be declared obscene, that issue is not presented in this case. The Sheriff's contention that the work is not protected by the First Amendment is based on the lyrics, not the music. The Sheriff's brief denies any intention to put rap music to the test, but states "it is abundantly obvious that it is only the 'lyrical' content which makes '*As Nasty As They Wanna Be*' obscene." Assuming that music is not simply a sham attempt to protect obscene material, the *Miller Test* should be applied to the lyrics and the music of "*As Nasty As They Wanna Be*" as a whole. A work cannot be held obscene unless each element of the test has been evaluated independently and all three have been met.

. . . There are two problems with this case which make it unusually difficult to review. First, the Sheriff put in no evidence but the tape recording itself. The only evidence concerning the three-part *Miller Test* was put in evidence by the plaintiffs. Second, the case was tried by a judge without a jury, and he relied on his own expertise as to the prurient interest community standard and artistic value prongs of the *Miller Test*.

. . . [I]t can be conceded without deciding that the judge's familiarity with contemporary community standards is sufficient to carry the case as to the first two prongs of the *Miller Test*: prurient interest applying contemporary community standards and patent offensiveness as defined by Florida law. The record is insufficient, however, for this Court to assume the fact finder's artistic or literary knowledge or skills to satisfy the last prong of the *Miller* analysis, which requires determination of whether a work "lacks serious artistic, scientific, literary or political value."

. . . We reject the argument that simply by listening to this musical work, the judge could determine it had no serious artistic value.

The *Real Slim Shady* Case

In an interesting turn of events, the FCC issued and then rescinded a $7000 indecency fine against a Pueblo Colorado radio station for broadcasting rapper Eminem's *The Real Slim Shady.*

In the Matter of File No. EB-00-IH-0228, Citadel Broadcasting Company, Licensee of Station KKMG(FM), Pueblo, Colorado

☐ MEMORANDUM OPINION AND ORDER

Adopted: January 7, 2002 Released: January 8, 2002

By the Chief, Enforcement Bureau:

I. INTRODUCTION

1. In this Order, we rescind the Notice of Apparent Liability ("NAL") in which we found that Citadel Broadcasting Company ("Citadel"), licensee of Station KKMG(FM), Pueblo, Colorado, apparently violated 18 U.S.C. § 1464 and Section 73.3999 of the Commission's rules, 47 C.F.R. § 73.3999, by willfully broadcasting apparently indecent language. Having reviewed Citadel's response and having again reviewed the relevant case law, we disagree with our initial analysis and we now conclude that the material at issue was not patently offensive under contemporary community standards for the broadcast medium. Accordingly, we conclude that the licensee did not violate the applicable statute or our indecency rule, and that no sanction is warranted.

II. BACKGROUND

2. The Commission received a letter dated July 18, 2000, complaining about repeated broadcasts of a song entitled *"The Real Slim Shady"* on Station KKMG(FM). The complaint included lyrics that the complainant contended are offensive. After reviewing the lyrics, Enforcement Bureau ("Bureau") staff issued a letter of inquiry to Citadel, licensee of the station involved. In its response to the staff's inquiry, Citadel claimed that the song version that the station aired was different from the one complained about, and that the station carefully screened the broadcast version to omit any offensive language through the use of a muting device or overdubbed sound effect. In support, Citadel submitted a copy of the "radio edit" version, and argued that the lyrics contained therein are not indecent under the applicable Commission standards.

3. On June 1, 2001, the Bureau issued a Notice of Apparent Liability ("NAL") which rejected Citadel's arguments and found that the "radio edit" version of *"The Real Slim Shady"* apparently violated the Commission's indecency rule. In the NAL, we acknowledged that Citadel attempted to render the song suitable for broadcast through editing, but found that the licensee failed to purge several

apparently indecent references. To redress this apparent rule violation, we concluded that a monetary sanction in the base forfeiture amount of $7000 appeared appropriate.

4. Citadel challenges the NAL's findings, arguing that the version broadcast makes no explicit sexual or excretory references, and is not patently offensive. In this regard, Citadel contends that any of the song's sexual or excretory references cited in the NAL are oblique, and are intended merely to satirize and parody popular culture, and not to titillate, shock, or pander to listeners. In view of this, Citadel asks that the NAL's findings be set aside and that a monetary forfeiture not be imposed.

III. DISCUSSION

5. It is a violation of federal law to broadcast obscene or indecent programming. Specifically, Title 18 of the United States Code, Section 1464 (18 U.S.C. § 1464), prohibits the utterance of "any obscene, indecent or profane language by means of radio communication." Congress has given the Federal Communications Commission the responsibility for administratively enforcing 18 U.S.C. § 1464. In doing so, the Commission may, among other things, impose a monetary forfeiture, pursuant to Section 503(b)(1) of the Communications Act (the "Act"), 47 U.S.C. § 503(b)(1), for broadcast of indecent material in violation of 18 U.S.C. § 1464. Federal courts have upheld Congress's authority to regulate obscene speech and, to a limited extent, indecent speech. Specifically, the U.S. Supreme Court has determined that obscene speech is not entitled to First Amendment protection. Accordingly, Congress may prohibit the broadcast of obscene speech at any time. In contrast, federal courts have held that indecent speech is protected by the First Amendment. Nonetheless, the federal courts consistently have upheld Congress's authority to regulate the broadcast of indecent speech, as well as the Commission's interpretation and implementation of the statute. However, the First Amendment is a critical constitutional limitation that demands we proceed cautiously and with appropriate restraint. Consistent with a subsequent statute and case law, under the Commission's rules, no radio or television licensee shall broadcast obscene material at any time, or broadcast indecent material during the period 6 A.M. through 10 P.M. *See* 47 C.F.R. § 73.3999.

6. In enforcing its indecency rule, the Commission has defined indecent speech as language that first, in context, depicts or describes sexual organs or activities. Second, the broadcast must be "patently offensive as measured by contemporary community

standards for the broadcast medium." *Infinity Broadcasting Corporation of Pennsylvania*, 2 FCC Rcd 2705 (1987) (subsequent history omitted) (*citing Pacifica Foundation*, 56 FCC 2d 94, 98 (1975), *aff'd sub nom. FCC v. Pacifica Foundation*, 438 U.S. 726 (1978)). This definition has been specifically upheld by the federal courts. The Commission's authority to restrict the broadcast of indecent material extends to times when there is a reasonable risk that children may be in the audience. *ACT I, supra*. As noted above, current law holds that such times begin at 6 A.M. and conclude at 10 P.M.

7. The Commission's indecency enforcement is based on complaints from the public. Once a complaint is before the Commission, we evaluate the facts of the particular case and apply the standards developed through Commission case law and upheld by the courts. See *Industry Guidance on the Commission's Case Law Interpreting 18 U.S.C. §1464 and Enforcement Policies Regarding Broadcast Indecency ("Indecency Policy Statement")*, 16 FCC Rcd 7999 at 8015 24 (2001). "Given the sensitive nature of these cases and the critical role of context in an indecency determination, it is important that the Commission be afforded as full a record as possible to evaluate allegations of indecent programming." *Id.* In evaluating the record to determine whether the complained of material is patently offensive, three factors are particularly relevant: (1) the explicitness or graphic nature of the description; (2) whether the material dwells on or repeats at length descriptions of sexual or excretory organs or activities; and (3) whether the material appears to pander or is used to titillate or shock. See *Indecency Policy Statement*, 16 FCC Rcd at 8003

8. In the NAL, we found two passages in the edited version of the song *"The Real Slim Shady"* to be apparently indecent:

> My bum is on your lips
> My bum is on your lips
> And if I'm lucky you might just give it a little kiss
> And that's the message we deliver to little kids
> And expect them not to know what a woman's BLEEP is
> Of course, they're gonna know what intercourse is
> * * * * * *
> It's funny cause at the rate I'm goin'
> When I'm 30 I'll be the only person in the nursing home flirting
> Pinching nurses asses when I'm BLEEP or jerkin'
> Said I'm jerkin' but this whole bag of Viagra isn't workin.'

9. The passages in question, in context, refer to sexual activity. Thus, the material warranted scrutiny. Based on our review of Citadel's response, however, we conclude that the material broadcast was not patently offensive, and thus not actionably indecent.

10. With respect to the first key factor set out in the *Indecency Policy Statement*, we agree with Citadel's contention that the sexual references contained in the song's "radio edit" version are not expressed in terms sufficiently explicit or graphic enough to be found patently offensive. Although the song, as edited, refers to sexual activity, these references are oblique. In this regard, the material is less explicit and graphic than every example of indecent material mentioned in the *Indecency Policy Statement* in connection with this factor.

11. We also agree with Citadel's contention, with respect to the third key factor, that the sexual references contained in the "radio edit" version, in the context presented, do not appear to pander to, or to be used to titillate or shock its audience. Thus, the sexual references do not have the effect of a "verbal shock treatment." *See, e.g., FCC v. Pacifica Foundation*, 438 U.S. 726, 757 (1978)(Powell, J., concurring in part and concurring in the judgment). In this regard, the material is of less concern than all of the examples mentioned in the *Indecency Policy Statement* in connection with this factor.

12. Consequently, based on our review of Citadel's response in light of the applicable case law, we conclude that Citadel did not violate the statute or the Commission's indecency rule through its broadcast of the "radio edit" version of *"The Real Slim Shady."*

IV. ORDERING CLAUSES

13. Accordingly, pursuant to Sections 0.111(a)(7), 0.311 and 1.80(f)(3) of the Commission's rules, 47 C.F.R. §§ 0.111(a)(7), 0.311 and 1.80(f)(3), IT IS ORDERED THAT the Bureau's June 1, 2001, NAL against Citadel Broadcasting Company, licensee of Station KKMG(FM), Pueblo, Colorado, is hereby RESCINDED.

☐ Conclusion that the material here is not indecent.

Audience Harm by Broadcast Programming

One of the earliest concerns over the direct harmful effects of broadcast programming is certainly the 1938 "War of the Worlds" broadcast. Even though Orson Welles and the Mercury Theater actors issued a disclaimer before and during the broadcast, the realistic (for 1938) broadcast format caused many to believe that an invasion from Mars was real. The pervasive nature of the broadcast media makes it impossible to predict accurately how listeners and viewers will interpret messages. Advertisers strive to capture interest and attention. They hope to motivate individuals in the audience to purchase their products. Broadcast news has worked to combine credibility with an attractive format designed to hold the attention of the audience. Sometimes, these factors have unintended effects. Should the broadcaster be held legally responsible when members of the audience misinterpret messages and behave in an antisocial manner? The courts have ruled that broadcasters are rarely liable for such behavior. Only if broadcasters actively encourage harmful behavior are they to be blamed.

In *Weirum v. RKO General (1975)*, the court found that a radio station promotion was responsible for causing a fatal accident. The station promotion offered a cash prize for the first listener to find the location of a disc jockey (DJ), who was driving to various points in a station vehicle. Two teenagers arrived at the correct location, but failed to win the prize because they were not the first on the scene. They followed the DJ to his next location, hoping to be the first to arrive. While speeding to the location on a crowded freeway, they caused a fatal accident. The court held that the station promoted reckless driving by requiring potential winners to hurry to the next location of the DJ.

In most other major cases, the broadcast media fared better. In *Olivia v. NBC (1981)*, the California court of appeals dealt with a made-for-television movie, starring Linda Blair of *The Exorcist*. The program contained a scene depicting a broom handle rape in a state-run girls home. The plaintiff was the victim of a similar crime in real life, said to have been inspired by the movie. The court held that NBC had not met the "incitement" test. At no time did the network overtly suggest to viewers that they "copy" this crime.

In 1982, a segment on the *Tonight Show Starring Johnny Carson* spawned *DeFilippo v. NBC (1982)*. A professional stunt man appeared on the program, explaining how certain apparently dangerous movie stunts were accomplished. Johnny Carson announced that following the commercial break, he would drop through a trap door with a noose around his neck. The man warned the audience that this was a dangerous stunt and not to try it at home. After the commercial break, Carson did the stunt and emerged unscathed. Several hours after the broadcast, the plaintiff's 13-year-old son, Nicky, was found hanging in front of the television set, which was still tuned to WJAR-TV the NBC affiliate. Once again, the court ruled that no incitement had occurred, because no one else emulated the action and the program took action to prevent emulation by warning viewers not to try the stunt.

In *Zamora v. CBS*, a teenager named Ronny Zamora blamed television for having caused him to commit murder. Zamora claimed that TV incited him to duplicate atrocities he saw in TV programs. The district court did not buy the argument. Similar rulings were reached in cases involving suicides and heavy metal music. In *McCollum v. CBS Inc. (1988)*, the California Court of Appeals for the Second District held that the death of a 19-year-old who repeatedly listened to Ozzy Osbourne albums before taking his own life was not caused by the records. The boy had a history of alcohol abuse and other emotional problems. Even though the content of the songs on the Osbourne records emphasized death, suicide, and other antisocial activities, the Court held that incitement was not present.

In a comparable case, *Vance v. Judas Priest (1990)*, a Nevada district court held that subliminal messages and "back-mastered" lyrics on the album *Stained Class*, urging "do it," did not incite two teenaged boys to shoot themselves. The court did note that subliminal messages, because they cannot be detected by the listener, have no First Amendment protection. The Nevada district court based the decision on the assumption that subliminal speech does not advance any purposes of free speech, there is a First Amendment right to be free from unwanted speech, and the listener's right of privacy outweighs the speaker's right of free speech. When a person is exposed to subliminal messages, that person is deprived of the constitutional right to choose which speech to listen to. The court added that hidden messages also violate the right to privacy.

Contests and Promotions

Broadcast stations regularly run contests to boost audiences. Station-sponsored contests are legal, as long as they are not fraudulent, are not broadcast only during ratings periods, and do not disturb the public safety.

Section 73.1216 of the FCC rules also regulates contests:

A licensee that broadcasts or advertises information about a contest it conducts shall fully and accurately disclose the material terms of the contest, and shall conduct the contest substantially as announced or advertised. No contest description shall be false, misleading or deceptive with respect to any material term. For the purpose of this rule:

(a) A contest is a scheme in which a prize is offered or awarded, based upon chance, diligence, knowledge or skill, to members of the public.

(b) Material terms include those factors which define the operation of the contest and which affect participation therein. Although the material terms may vary widely depending upon the exact nature of the contest, they will generally include: how to enter or participate; eligibility restrictions; entry deadline dates; whether prizes can be won; when prizes can be won; the extent, nature and value of the prizes; basis for valuation of the prizes; time and means of selection of winners; and/or tie breaking procedures.[12]

Stations also schedule stunts and promotional events as audience-building and -retaining devices. Though the FCC is lenient in allowing most stunts and promotions, stations should exercise care when these activities might cause adverse community action or result in public injury.

Hoaxes

A St. Louis radio station's promotional stunt that broadcast a false nuclear attack netted the licensee a $25,000 fine as a result. On January 29, 1991, KSHE-FM aired a phony announcement that the United States had come under nuclear attack. The broadcast was complete with the Emergency Broadcasting System (EBS) tone and sound effects of exploding bombs. The broadcast occurred in the midst of the Gulf War. The stunt evoked more than 100 calls to the station and complaints were filed to the FCC. KSHE's morning personality John Ulet said he initiated the false broadcast to demonstrate the seriousness of nuclear war.

The KSHE decision crossed the line into what FCC Mass Media Bureau and Enforcement Division Chief Chuck Kelly called a "War of the Worlds" situation. NAB Deputy General Counsel Barry Umansky noted,

A station is responsible for all its on-air programming. . . . At license renewal time, if there were to be a finding that the station's programming led to injuries or some development where the station was sued, it would constitute a major black mark against the station.[13]

In April 1991, the FCC began investigating KROQ-FM, Pasadena-Los Angeles, for the broadcast of a false murder confession on the station's morning drive-time show. The morning team at the Infinity station, Kevin Ryder and Gene (Bean) Baxter, had developed a bit called "Confess Your Crime." Listeners were encouraged to call the program and reveal personal "crimes" on the air. One of the callers claimed to have killed his girlfriend. The story was picked up by TV's "Unsolved Mysteries," which aired a segment on October 19, 1990.

The "confessed killer" was actually Doug Roberts, another DJ friend of Ryder and Baxter working in Arizona. The hoax began to unravel after Roberts came to work for KROQ and the similarity between Roberts' voice and the "killer" was noticed. When Infinity began an internal investigation, the DJs admitted the hoax. Infinity suspended the DJs involved and KROQ-FM broadcast several apologies. The station also cooperated with police and made an offer of restitution. The FCC sent Infinity a letter to determine whether the company acted "responsibly and effectively" once it learned that the broadcast was a hoax.

In 1992 the FCC enacted a rule prohibiting the broadcast of hoaxes that may be harmful to the public.

Violence on Television

Concern over violence in television programming is as old as the medium itself. In the 1950s and 1960s, the small screen was the home of numerous westerns and private detective programs. Each of these genres naturally lent themselves to gunplay, fistfights, and other violent acts. Although every western had to have a gunfight, the networks and the National Association of Broadcasters had established a set of standards designed to guide portrayals of violent acts. Broadcasters believed that self-regulation of content was the best way to avoid government regulation. The NAB Television Code set the following standards for portrayals of television violence:

Violence, physical or psychological, may only be projected in responsibly handled contexts, not used exploitatively. Programs involving violence should present the consequences of it to its victims and perpetrators.

Presentation of the details of violence should avoid the excessive, the gratuitous and the instructional.

The use of violence for its own sake and the detailed dwelling upon brutality or physical agony, by sight or by sound, are not permissable.[14]

In 1982, the NAB Codes were dropped as a result of a consent decree in which the Justice Department found the codes to be a violation of antitrust law. By the late 1980s, public concern over violence in television programs spurred Congress to pass the Television Violence Act of 1989. The act granted a three-year exemption from antitrust laws allowing the broadcast and cable industries to develop voluntary guidelines to control televised violence. In December 1992, ABC, CBS, and NBC adopted broadly worded standards, similar in scope to the old NAB Code.[15] The Television Violence Act expired at the end of 1993; however, Congress and media watchdog groups continued to express concern over violent media contact. In February 1994, the broadcast and cable industry agreed to independent monitoring of their programming for violent content.[16]

The Federal Government Steps In

The Telecommunications Act of 1996 contains provisions addressing violent and other potentially offensive content on television. The act provided for establishment of an advisory committee composed of parents, television broadcasters, television programming producers, cable operators, appropriate public interest groups and other interested individuals from the private sector (see Section 551(b) (2) of the Telecommunications Act of 1996). This group was charged with developing ratings for violent and sexually explicit programming that may be broadcast. A panel headed by Motion Pictures Association president, Jack Valenti, developed a ratings code in early 1997. This code generated much controversy within the broadcast industry and did not achieve universal acceptance.

The V-Chip

The Telecommunications Act also directed the FCC to require manufacturers of television sets, with screens larger than 13 inches, to be equipped with V-chip technology. The V-chip enables viewers to electronically screen out programming that they deem objectionable due to violent or sexual content. Screening is based on the ratings system noted above.

Children's Television Programming

In the early days of television, local children's programs became a staple of the broadcast day. Indeed, the FCC expected broadcasters to program to the needs and interests of children, as stipulated in *Report and Statement of Policy re: Commission en banc Programming Inquiry*. Gradually, economic changes in the industry forced the demise of local children's programs and the task of children's programming fell to the networks. What emerged was a block of animated, made-for-TV series that aired primarily on Saturday mornings. Responding to pressure from such groups as Action for Children's Television, in 1974 the FCC issued a policy statement as a result of *Children's Television Report and Policy Statement*, urging broadcasters to increase the amount of children's programming offered and to schedule it throughout the week. The FCC also suggested that this programming contain informational and educational material, in addition to pure entertainment. The Commission also expressed concern over the commercial practices used in existing programs. Of special concern was the concept of "host selling," whereby the cartoon character appears in commercials during the program.

In 1979, the Commission examined the effect of the 1974 Policy Statement and concluded in *Children's Television Programming and Advertising
Practices (1979)* that the policy had little effect on children's programming
in most areas. However, the FCC did not act until 1984. Then, the FCC,
in keeping with the deregulatory spirit of the Reagan years, abandoned the
1974 Policy Statement, preferring to allow the marketplace to respond to
children's needs. The Commission no longer expected broadcast stations to
provide any children's programming. The FCC noted in *Children's Television
Programming and Advertising Practices (1984)* that the emergence of new
technologies (VCRs and cable television) also would help meet the programming needs of children. In *Action for Children's Television v. FCC (1985)*, the
Commission policy was upheld. Two years later, in *Action for Children's
Television v. FCC (1987)*, the court concluded that the FCC had failed
sufficiently to justify its deregulatory approach in regard to commercial practices in children's television programs. The court remanded the case to the
Commission for further study. It is at this point that the FCC considered creating new rules for children's TV.[17]

After three years and a veto by outgoing President Reagan, Congress
finally passed the Children's Television Act of 1990. The Commission
adopted rules implementing the act in April 1991, and the rules went into
effect on January 1, 1992.

The 1991 Children's Television Rules

The 1991 Children's Television Rules limit commercial time
in children's programming to 10.5 minutes per hour on weekends and 12
minutes per hour on weekdays. These rules apply to programs originally produced and broadcast primarily for persons 12 years of age and younger. The
rules also apply to cable television.

Commercial television stations are required to air some programming
that meets the educational and informational needs of children. The Commission defines educational and informational programming as "furthering
the positive development of the child in any respect, including the child's
cognitive/intellectual or emotional/social needs."[18] The Commission
requires licensees to place in their public files a summary of programming,
nonbroadcast efforts, and other ways in which the educational and informational needs of children have been served.

The FCC also prohibits program-length commercials in children's programs. The Commission defined program-length commercials as "associated
with a product, in which commercials for that product are aired."[19]

The issue of children's television remains an important concern at the
FCC. In 1996 the White House lobbied broadcasters to be more responsive to

the educational needs of children. Toward that end, the FCC voted to tighten the definition of children's educational programming. The Commission also voted to require over-the-air broadcasters (not cable systems) to devote three hours per week to programming meeting the educational and informational needs of children 16 years of age and younger. The new Children's Television rules went into effect September 1, 1997.

Essentially, television broadcasters must air three weekly hours of core children's programming to be considered for expedited license renewal. Broadcasters may choose to air less than three hours of core programming, provided they make up the difference with short-form programs, specials or public service announcements. Broadcasters are required to note, both at the beginning of the program and in program guide services (like *TV Guide* or newspaper listings), those programs considered "core" and the target age group of each program. This requirement went into effect January 2, 1997.

Information on programming and efforts designed to serve the educational and informational needs of children must be kept in the station's public inspection file. Commercial stations must file Form 398 electronically with the FCC each quarter.[20] Broadcasters who do not meet the three-hour-a-week minimum will be required to justify why their license should be renewed to the FCC.

Lotteries

Section 73.1211 of the FCC rules prohibits the broadcast of most lottery information. Exceptions include state lotteries;[21] certain fishing contests when all receipts defray the actual costs of operation;[22] certain gaming conducted by Indian Tribes;[23] lotteries conducted by certain "not-for-profit" organizations;[24] and contests conducted by a commercial organization as promotional activities that are clearly occasional and incidental to the primary business of that organization.[25]

The Elements of a Lottery

The elements of a lottery are chance, consideration, and prize. Unless all three of these elements are present, there is no lottery.

Chance

The element of chance is present if no skill is required to win a prize or other consideration. Spinning a wheel, drawing numbers or names from a jar, random numbers generated by a computer, or being the third caller to a radio station are all elements of chance. Guessing the number of beans in a jar is also chance, because there is no skill involved in deriving the answer.

Chance may also be present in a contest that initially involves skill. For example, suppose a station contest required a listener to name the number-one CD for the week of January 18, 1999. If two listeners called with the right answer (DMX, "Flesh of My Flesh—Blood of My"), the tie must be broken by another means involving skill. The station could not simply flip a coin to decide the winner.

Consideration

Consideration means exchanging something of value to win a prize or participate in a game, contest, or other promotional arrangement. Examples of consideration include the payment of an entry fee, a required purchase, a test drive to enter a contest (which is a consideration because time and effort are required to win the prize), or receiving a discount after purchase.

Requiring an individual to be present to win is not consideration, nor is requiring listeners to call the station after hearing their name broadcast over the air. Age and eligibility requirements also are not consideration. It must also be remembered that consideration must flow to the promoter and co-promoters.

In *Greater Indianapolis Broadcasting Co. Inc. (WXLW)*, the Commission held that a radio station–sponsored golf contest in which the winner was determined by a random drawing of score cards was not a lottery. Entrants paid a greens fee to play a round of golf, but they paid no money to place their score card in the drawing. The money to play the round of golf did not go to WXLW, nor was the golf course a cosponsor of the contest. Had this been the case, the event would have been a lottery.

Prize

A prize is anything of value offered to a contestant. It can be in the form of goods, money, services, discounts, or refunds. In short, it can be worth a million dollars or one penny. The prize is the primary element in a lottery, for without a prize, a lottery does not exist.

State-Sanctioned Lotteries

Broadcasters may advertise state-sanctioned lotteries, provided that they are licensed to markets within states operating those lotteries. If a state does not have a state-sanctioned lottery, stations licensed to markets within that state may not advertise any other state's lottery. The prohibition against lottery ads in states without lotteries was upheld by the Supreme Court in *United States v. Edge Broadcasting 509 U.S. 418 (1993).*

If a state has a sanctioned lottery, stations licensed to markets within that state may advertise adjacent state's sanctioned lotteries. The same applies to live lottery drawings.

Fishing Contests

If a station conducts a fishing contest in which the funds are "self-liquidating" it is exempted from the prohibition on broadcasting lotteries (18 U.S.C. 1305 [1982]). This means that all money received by the station from the contest must be used to pay expenses of running the contest and may not be used for any other collateral purpose. No personal gain by the station or establishment of a charitable fund from the contest proceeds is permitted.

Gaming on Indian Lands

In 1989, the FCC amended its lottery rules to permit broadcast of lottery information about games conducted on Indian lands. This modification came in response to the Indian Gaming Regulatory Act. To qualify for this exemption, the game must be operated by an Indian tribe or be allowed under a "grandfather" clause in specific Federal law, and it must be legal in the state in which it is held. For games where players bet against the "house," the tribe and state must have reached an agreement approved by the federal government permitting and specifying the requirements of such an agreement.

Sanctions and Broadcasters' Responsibility

If radio or television stations broadcast a lottery, they may face a fine or other difficulty at license renewal time. Broadcasters cannot escape penalty by claiming that they didn't know that a commercial, promotion, or other program actually constituted a lottery. Stations must exercise diligence in identifying a potential lottery.

Summary

Section 326 of the Communications Act prohibits FCC censorship of broadcast programming. The Commission may set guidelines affecting programs that are broadcast to ensure that stations are operating in the public interest. The political broadcasting rules in Section 315 of the

Communications Act are one example of this kind of regulation. Channeling of certain kinds of programs, such as those considered indecent, is another means of program content regulation without direct FCC censorship.

Concern over failure of television programs to meet the educational and information needs of children led to passage of the Children's Television Act of 1990. Broadcasters are required to telecast three hours of children's programming each week.

Broadcast stations are prohibited from advertising or promoting lotteries. Exceptions to this rule include the broadcast of state-run lotteries, certain fishing contests, and gaming on Indian lands. Stations licensed to markets within a state sponsoring such a lottery may broadcast that lottery information. In states where there is a state-sanctioned lottery, broadcasters may transmit information about state-sanctioned lotteries in adjacent states.

Notes/References

1. 47 U.S.C. Sec. 326 (1989).
2. See *Programming Information in Broadcast Applications*, 65 R.R.2d 397 (1988) for additional information.
3. *In the Matter of Enforcement of Prohibitions Against Broadcast Obscenity and Indecency*, 18 U.S.C. 1464, Order FCC 88-416 (Dec. 19, 1988), 53 (249) FR. 52425 (Dec. 28, 1988).
4. *In re Pacifica Foundation*, 36 FCC 147 (January 22, 1964).
5. *Eastern Educational Radio (WUHY-FM)* 24 F.C.C.2d 408 (1970).
6. *Sonderling Broadcasting Corp. (WGLD-FM)*, 27 R.R.2d 285 (FCC 1973). (October 9, 1989), 41.
7. *FCC v. Pacifica Foundation*, 438 U.S. 726 (1978).
8. Ibid.
9. "FCC Fines Detroit Station for Indecency," *Broadcasting* (October 9, 1989): 41.
10. "FCC Issues NALS for $200,000 to Infinity Licensees for Broadcast of Indecent Material During the Howard Stern Show," Report No. MM-829 (May 20, 1994).
11. *Skyywalker Records Inc. v Navarro*, 17 Med.L.Rptr. 2073 (DC So.Fla., 1990).
12. 47 CF4, Section 73.1216.
13. "Station Stunts Tread Fine Line of Humor and Hoax," *Broadcasting* (April 8, 1991): 55.
14. Frank J. Kahn, ed., "NAB Television Code," in *Documents of American Broadcasting*, 2nd ed. (New York: Appleton Century Crofts, 1973), 342–43.

15. Randy Sukow, "Nets Adopt Violence Code," Broadcasting (Dec. 14, 1992) p. 9.

16. Doug Halonen, "TV Industry Creates Own Violence Plan," *Electronic Media* (February 7, 1994): 32.

17. See *Revision of Programming and Commercialization Policies, Ascertainment Requirements, and Program Log Requirements for Commercial Television Stations,* MM Docket No. 83-670 and *Further Notice of Proposed Rule Making/Notice of Inquiry,* FCC 87-338, R.R.2d, Current Service, 53:365 (1987).

18. Public Law No. 101–437 (October 18, 1990).

19. "New Children's Television Rules Adopted," *Pike & Fischer's Broadcast Rules,* Service No. 27 (March/April, 1991): 2.

20. 47 CFR 73.658.

21. This provision went into effect May 7, 1990, as a result of the Charity Games Advertising Clarification Act of 1988. See 18 USC § 1307(a); 102 Stat. 3205.

22. See USC § 1305.

23. See Indian Gaming Regulatory Act, 25 USC § et. seq.

24. See 18 USC § 1307; 102 Stat 3205. "Not-for-profit" organizations are defined as those that qualify as tax-exempt under Section 501 of the Internal Revenue Code of 1986.

25. See 18 USC § 1307(a); 102 Stat 3205.

Cases

Action for Children's Television v. FCC, 244 U.S. App. D.C. 190; 756 F.2d 899 (1985)

Action for Children's Television v. FCC, 261 U.S. App. D.C. 253; 821 F.2d 741 (1987)

Action for Children's Television v. FCC, 852 F.2d 1332 [15 Med.L.Rptr. 1907] (DC Cir., 1988) ("ACT I")

Action for Children's Television v. FCC, 932 F.2d 1504 [18 Med.L.Rptr. 2153] (DC Cir., 1991), cert. denied, 112 S.Ct. 1281 (1992) ("ACT II")

Action for Children's Television v. FCC, 21 Med.L.Rptr. 2289 (DC Cir., 1993)

Broadcast of Station Contests, 37 R.R.2d 260 (FCC, 1976)

CBS v. FCC, 453 U.S. 367 (1981)

Children's Television Programming and Advertising Practices, 75 F.C.C.2d 138 (1979)

Children's Television Programming and Advertising Practices, 96 F.C.C.2d 634 (1984)

Children's Television Report and Policy Statement, 50 F.C.C.2d 1 (1974)

Competition and Responsibility in Network Television Broadcasting, 23 F.C.C.2d 382 (1970)

DeFilippo v. NBC, (CA, RI) 8 Med.L.Rptr. 1872 (1982)

Deregulation of Commercial Television, 98 F.C.C.2d 1076, 56 R.R.2d 1005 (1984), 60 R.R.2d 526 (1986)

Deregulation of Radio, 104 F.C.C.2d. 505, note 8 (1986)

Eastern Educational Radio (WUHY-FM), 24 F.C.C.2d 408, 18 R.R.2d 860 (1970)

FCC Sanctions Noncommercial Licensee for Failure to Prepare and Maintain Issues/Programs List in Public File; Haley, Bader & Potts Information Memorandum 21:1 (February 28, 1991)

FCC v. Pacifica Foundation, 438 U.S. 726 (1978)

Federal Communications Commission, Deregulation of Radio, 84 F.C.C.2d 968, 49 R.R.2d 1 (effective April 3, 1981), 53 R.R.2d 805, 53 R.R.2d 1371, affirmed 706 F.2d 1224, 53 R.R.2d 1501, 707 F.2d 1413, 53 R.R.2d 1371, 719 F.2d 407, 54 R.R.2d 811, 1151 (DC Cir., 1983)

Greater Indianapolis Broadcasting Co. Inc. (WXLW), 44 F.C.C.2d 37 (1973)

Henry Geller et. al., F.C.C.2d 1236, 54 R.R.2d 1246 (1983)

In re Pacifica Foundation, 36 F.C.C. 147 (January 22, 1964)

In the Matter of Enforcement of Prohibitions Against Broadcast Obscenity and Indecency, 18 U.S.C. 1464, Order FCC 88-416 (Dec. 19, 1988), 53 (249) F.R. 52425 (Dec. 28, 1988)

Infinity Broadcasting Corps of Pennsylvania, 2 F.C.C.Red. 2705, 62 R.R.2d 1202 (1987)

Luke Records Inc. v. Navarro, (CA 11 Cir., 1992) 20 Med.L.Rptr. 1114

McCollum v. CBS Inc., (CA Cal. 2 Cir., 1988) 15 Med.L.Rptr. 2001

Miller v. California, 413 U.S. 15 (1973)

Narragansett Broadcasting Company of California, Inc. KSJO(FM) (1990)

National Association of Independent Television Producers and Distributors v. F.C.C., 502 F.2d 249 (2d Cir., 1974), 50 F.C.C.2d at 852

Olivia v. NBC, 7 Med.L.Rptr. 2359 (1981)

Pacifica Foundation Inc., 2 F.C.C.Rcd. 2698, 62 R.R.2d 1191 (1987)

Primer on Ascertainment of Community Problems (1971); revised, 74 F.C.C. 942, 39 F.R. 32288 (1974)

The Regents of the University of California, 2 F.C.C.Rcd. 2703, 62 R.R.2d 1199 (1987)

Reno v. American Civil Libertres Union, 520 U.S. 1113 (1997)

Report and Statement of Policy re: Commission en banc Programming Inquiry, 25 F.R. 7291 (July 29, 1960)

Sable Communications v. FCC, (CA DC, 1989) 16 Med.L.Rptr. 1961

Schurz Communications v. FCC, 982 F.2d 1043 (7th Cir. 1992)

Skyywalker Records Inc. v. Navarro, (DC So.Fla., 1990) 17 Med.L.Rptr. 2073

Sonderling Broadcasting Corp. (WGLD-FM), 27 R.R.2d 285 (FCC, 1973)

Soundgarden v. Eikenberry, 123 Wash.2d 750, 871 P.2d 1050, 1994

United Church of Christ v. FCC, (DC Cir., 1978) 4 Med.L.Rptr. 1410

United States v. Edge Broadcasting, 509 U.S. 418 (1993).

Vance v. Judas Priest, (DC 2 Nev., 1990) 15 Med.L.Rptr. 2010

Weirum v. RKO General, 15 Cal.3d 40 (1975)

Yale Broadcasting Co. v. FCC, U.S. Ct.App. DC, 478 F.2d 594 (1973), cert. denied 414 U.S. 914 (1973)

Zamora v. CBS, (DC Fla., 1979) 5 Med.L.Rptr. 2109

7

Regulation of Commercial Practices

The Development of Commercial Regulation

The regulation of commercial content in the United States emerged early in the twentieth century as a result of excesses spawned by laissez faire capitalism. Muckraking journalists fueled the passage of regulations such as the Pure Food and Drug Act of 1906, which prohibited misrepresentation of cures and required that all ingredients be identified on the product label.

The Federal Trade Commission

Congressional concern over enforcement of the Sherman Antitrust Act and the Clayton Act led to the 1914 Federal Trade Commission Act. This act created the FTC, an independent regulatory agency originally charged with regulating unfair competition. In *FTC v. Winstead Hosiery Co.*, the Supreme Court upheld the FTC's authority to regulate exaggerated advertising claims. In 1938, the Wheeler-Lea amendment to the FTC Act expanded the FTC's power to include the regulation of false and deceptive advertising. Congress also allowed the FTC to issue cease and desist orders and levy fines for violation of those orders. The Wheeler-Lea amendment was passed as a result of *FTC v. Raladam Co.*, in which the Supreme Court ruled that the Commission could not ban false advertising unless it could be shown that it was a form of "unfair competition." In 1975, Congress passed the Magnuson-Moss Act, which gave the FTC authority over local as well as national advertising.

The FTC is organized very much like the FCC. It has five commissioners who are appointed by the president. No more than three commissioners may belong to the same political party. The FTC has three bureaus: the Bureau of

Consumer Protection, the Bureau of Competition, and the Bureau of Economics. The Bureau of Consumer Protection is most concerned with advertising, and it is through this bureau that investigations are initiated. You may learn more about the Federal Trade Commission by visiting its Website at http://www.ftc.gov.

In spite of legislation giving the FTC enforcement powers, the agency was viewed as a paper tiger until the consumer movements of the 1960s and 1970s. At one point in the late 1970s, under the chairmanship of Michael Pertschuk, the FTC became so active in the area of children's television advertising that Congress threatened to cut off funding, because many powerful advertisers with friends in Congress felt threatened by FTC actions. In the 1980s, the FTC's power declined as the Reagan administration drastically reduced the agency's budget for regulating deceptive advertising. In the early 1990s, the FTC stepped up enforcement practices. Of special interest to the FTC were issues of competition in cable television, children's advertising, and program-length commercials often dubbed "infomercials."

In 2000 the FTC issued a report titled "Marketing Violent Entertainment to Children: A Review of Self-Regulation and Industry Practices in the Motion Picture, Music Recording and Electronic Game Industries." The report found that although the entertainment industry has taken steps to identify content that may not be appropriate for children, the companies in those industries still routinely targeted children under 17 in their marketing of products, in violation of their own ratings systems. The FTC found evidence of marketing and media plans that expressly targeted children under 17. The report also published an FTC survey indicating that children under 17 are frequently able to buy tickets to R-rated movies without parental accompaniment and to purchase music recordings and electronic games with parental advisory labels or restricted to an older audience.

In response to these findings, the Commission recommended additional action by the industry to enhance their self-regulatory efforts. The Report is available online at http://www.ftc.gov or from the FTC's Consumer Response Center, Room 130, 600 Pennsylvania Avenue, N.W., Washington, D.C. 20580.

Enforcement Powers of the FTC

Consent Decrees

If the FTC determines that certain advertising is deceptive, it notifies the offender and asks that a consent decree be signed. In signing a consent decree, the advertiser agrees that it will stop the deceptive ads but admits no guilt. Failure to adhere to the consent decree may result in a $10,000-a-day fine for the offender.

Cease and Desist Orders

If an advertiser chooses not to sign a consent decree, the FTC may issue a cease and desist order. The cease and desist order is heard by an Administrative Law Judge (ALJ) before becoming final. Advertisers may appeal the order to the FTC and then to a federal appellate court. Acting on a cease and desist order can be a time-consuming process. For example, the FTC began a proceeding against the makers of Carter's Little Liver Pills in 1943. The complaint revolved around the use of the word "liver." The pills in question are a laxative and have nothing to do with the liver. *Carter Products Inc. v. FTC* was finally resolved in 1959, with the agreement to remove the word "liver" from the product title.

Corrective Advertising

If the FTC determines that an advertisement has created a false impression in the minds of the public, it may require corrective advertising. In 1971, the FTC required the makers of Profile Bread to issue corrective ads to change public misconception that the bread was lower in calories than other breads. In reality, the slices of Profile were smaller, but contained the same number of calories based on overall weight.

In 1975, in *Warner-Lambert Co. v. Federal Trade Commission*, the FTC required Warner-Lambert, the makers of Listerine, to include a statement in their advertising that corrected the misconception that Listerine prevented colds or lessened the severity of sore throats. Warner-Lambert was required to run the corrective statement until the company had spent $10 million on ads. This was roughly the amount spent on creating the false impression.

Advertising and the First Amendment

Until the mid-1970s, commercial speech was not protected by the First Amendment. In fact, the Commercial Speech Doctrine that emerged from the Supreme Court in 1942, in *Valentine v. Chrestensen*, stated that speech promoting goods and services is less deserving of constitutional protection than speech promoting other ideas.

Valentine v. Chrestensen 316 U.S. 52 (1942)

☐ The respondent, a citizen of Florida, owns a former United States Navy submarine which he exhibits for profit. In 1940 he brought it to New York City and moored it at a State pier in the East River. He prepared and printed a handbill advertising the boat and soliciting visitors for a stated admission fee. On his attempting to distribute the bill in the city streets, he was advised by the petitioner, as Police Commissioner, that this activity would violate § 318 of the Sanitary Code, which forbids distribution in the streets of commercial and business advertising matter, but was told that he might freely distribute handbills solely devoted to "information or a public protest."

. . . Respondent thereupon prepared and showed to the petitioner, in proof form, a double-faced handbill. On one side was a revision of the original, altered by the removal of the statement as to admission fee but consisting only of commercial advertising. On the other side was a protest against the action of the City Dock Department in refusing the respondent wharfage facilities at a city pier for the exhibition of his submarine, but no commercial advertising. The Police Department advised that distribution of a bill containing only the protest would not violate § 318, and would not be restrained, but that distribution of the double-faced bill was prohibited. The respondent, nevertheless, proceeded with the printing of his proposed bill and started to distribute it. He was restrained by the police.

. . . Respondent then brought this suit to enjoin the petitioner from interfering with the distribution. In his complaint he alleged diversity of citizenship; an amount in controversy in excess of $3000; the acts and threats of the petitioner under the purported authority of § 318; asserted a consequent violation of § 1 of the Fourteenth Amendment of the Constitution; and prayed an injunction. The District Court granted an interlocutory injunction, n2 and after trial on a stipulation from which the facts appear as above recited, granted a permanent injunction. The Circuit Court of Appeals, by a divided court, affirmed. The question is whether the application of the ordinance to the respondent's activity was, in the circumstances, an unconstitutional abridgement of the freedom of the press and of speech.

. . . (1) This court has unequivocally held that the streets are proper places for the exercise of the freedom of communicating information and disseminating opinion and that, though the states and municipalities may appropriately regulate the privilege in the public interest, they may not unduly burden or proscribe its employment in these public thoroughfares. We are equally clear that the Constitution imposes no such restraint on government as respects purely commercial advertising. Whether, and to what extent, one may promote or pursue a gainful occupation in the streets, to what extent such activity shall be adjudged a derogation of the public right of user, are matters for legislative judgment. The question is not whether the legislative body may interfere with the harmless pursuit of a lawful business, but whether it must permit such pursuit by what it deems an undesirable invasion of, or interference with, the full and free use of the highways by the people in fulfillment of the public use to which streets are dedicated. If the respondent was attempting to use the streets of New York by distributing commercial advertising, the prohibition of the code provision was lawfully invoked against his conduct.

(2) The respondent contends that, in truth, he was engaged in the dissemination of matter proper for public information, none the less so because there was inextricably attached to the medium of such dissemination commercial advertising matter. The court below appears to have taken this view, since it adverts to the difficulty of apportioning, in a given case, the contents of the communication as between what is of public interest and what is for private profit. We need not indulge nice appraisal based upon subtle distinctions in the present instance nor assume possible cases not now presented. It is enough for the present purpose that the stipulated facts justify the conclusion that the affixing of the protest against official conduct to the advertising circular was with the intent, and for the purpose, of evading the prohibition of the ordinance. If that evasion were successful, every merchant who desires to broadcast advertising leaflets in the streets need only append a civic appeal, or a moral platitude, to achieve immunity from the law's command.

The decree is *Reversed*.

The Commercial Speech Doctrine rested on the premise that advertising served no important social function. Advertising was viewed as self-serving, with little or no benefit transferred to the receiver of such communication. This assumption began to change in 1975. In *Bigelow v. Virginia*, the Supreme Court held that an advertisement in a Virginia newspaper for a New York abortion referral service was protected by the First Amendment. Abortions were legal in New York but illegal in Virginia. The Court found that Virginians had a First Amendment right to receive information about a legal service. Additionally, the state of Virginia was not able to demonstrate sufficient reason for prohibiting the ad.

The Commercial Speech Doctrine fell the following year in *Virginia State Bd. of Pharmacy v. Virginia Citizens Consumer Council Inc. (1976)*. The Supreme Court struck down a Virginia statute prohibiting the advertising of prescription drug prices.[1]

Virginia State Board of Pharmacy v. Virginia Citizens Consumer Council, Inc., 425 U.S. 748 (1976)

☐ Here, in contrast, the question whether there is a First Amendment exception for "commercial speech" is squarely before us. Our pharmacist does not wish to editorialize on any subject, cultural, philosophical, or political. He does not wish to report any particularly newsworthy fact, or to make generalized observations even about commercial matters. The "idea" he wishes to communicate is simply this: "I will sell you the X prescription drug at the Y price." Our question, then, is whether this communication is wholly outside the protection of the First Amendment.

V

☐ We begin with several propositions that already are settled or beyond serious dispute. It is clear, for example, that speech does not lose its First Amendment protection because money is spent to project it, as in a paid advertisement of one form or another. . . . Speech likewise is protected even though it is carried in a form that is "sold" for profit, *Smith v. California*, 361 U.S. 147, 150 (1959) (books); *Joseph Burstyn, Inc. v. Wilson*, 343 U.S. 495 , 501 (1952) (motion pictures); *Murdock v. Pennsylvania*, 319 U.S. at 111 (religious literature), and even though it may involve a solicitation to purchase or otherwise pay or contribute money. *New York Times Co. v. Sullivan, supra; NAACP v. Button*, 371 U.S. 415 , 429 (1963); *Jamison v. Texas*, 318 U.S. at 417; *Cantwell v. Connecticut*, 310 U.S. 296, 306–307 (1940).

If there is a kind of commercial speech that lacks all First Amendment protection, therefore, it must be distinguished by its content. Yet the speech whose content deprives it of protection cannot simply be speech on a commercial subject. No one would contend that our pharmacist may be prevented from being heard on . . . the subject of whether, in general, pharmaceutical prices should be regulated, or their advertisement forbidden. Nor can it be dispositive that a commercial advertisement is noneditorial, and merely reports a fact. Purely factual matter of public interest may claim protection. *Bigelow v. Virginia*, 421 U.S. at 822; *Thornhill v. Alabama*, 310 U.S. 88, 102 (1940).

Our question is whether speech which does "no more than propose a commercial transaction," . . . and from " 'truth, science, morality, and arts in general, in its diffusion of liberal sentiments on the administration of Government,' " . . . [T]hat it lacks all protection. Our answer is that it is not. [Emphasis added.]

Focusing first on the individual parties to the transaction that is proposed in the commercial advertisement, we may assume that the advertiser's interest is a purely economic one. That hardly disqualifies him from protection under the First Amendment. The interests of the contestants in a labor dispute are primarily economic, but it has long been settled that both the employee and the employer are protected by the First Amendment when they express themselves on the merits of the dispute in order to influence its outcome. . . . We know of no requirement that, in order to avail themselves of First Amendment protection, the parties to a labor dispute need address themselves to the merits of unionism in general . . . or to any subject beyond their immediate dispute.

As to the particular consumer's interest in the free flow of commercial information, that interest may be as keen, if not keener by far, than his interest in the day's most urgent political debate. Appellees' case in this respect is a convincing one. Those whom the suppression of prescription drug price information hits the hardest are the poor, the sick, and particularly the aged. A disproportionate amount of their income tends to be spent on prescription drugs; yet they are the least able to learn, by shopping from pharmacist to pharmacist, where their scarce dollars are best spent. . . . When drug prices vary as strikingly as they do, information as to who is charging what becomes more than a convenience. It could mean the alleviation of physical pain or the enjoyment of basic necessities.

Generalizing, society also may have a strong interest in the free flow of commercial information. Even an individual advertisement, though entirely "commercial," may be of general public interest. The facts of decided cases furnish illustrations: advertisements stating that referral services for legal abortions are available, *Bigelow v. Virginia, supra;* that a manufacturer of artificial furs promotes his product as an alternative to the extinction by his competitors of fur-bearing mammals, *see Fur Information & Fashion Council, Inc. v. E. F. Timme & Son*, 364 F.Supp. 16 (SDNY 1973); and that a domestic producer advertises his product as an alternative to imports that tend to deprive American residents of their jobs, *cf. Chicago Joint Board v. Chicago Tribune Co.*, 435 F.2d 470 (CA7 1970), *cert. denied*, 402 U.S. 973 (1971). Obviously, not all commercial messages contain the same or even a very great public interest element. There are few to which such an element, however, could not be added. Our pharmacist, for example, could cast himself as a commentator on store-to-store disparities in drug prices, giving his own and those of a competitor as proof. We see little point in requiring him to do so, and little difference if he does not.

Moreover, there is another consideration that suggests that no line between publicly "interesting" or "important" commercial advertising and the opposite kind could ever be drawn. *Advertising, however tasteless and excessive it sometimes may seem, is nonetheless dissemination of information as to who is producing and selling what product, for what reason, and at what price. So long as we preserve a predominantly free enterprise economy, the allocation of our resources in large measure will be made through numerous private economic decisions. It is a matter of public interest that those decisions, in the aggregate, be intelligent and well informed. To this end, the free flow of commercial information is indispensable. . . .* [Emphasis added.] And if it is indispensable to the proper allocation of resources in a free enterprise system, it is also indispensable to the formation of intelligent opinions as to how that system ought to be regulated or altered. Therefore, even if the First Amendment were thought to be primarily an instrument to enlighten public decision making in a democracy, we could not say that the free flow of information does not serve that goal . . .

. . . The challenge now made, however, is based on the First Amendment. This casts the Board's justifications in a different light, for on close inspection it is seen that the State's protectiveness of its citizens rests in large measure on the advantages of their being kept in ignorance. The advertising ban does not directly affect professional standards one way or the other. It affects them only through the reactions it is assumed people will have to the free flow of drug price information. There is no claim that the advertising ban in any way prevents the cutting of corners by the pharmacist who is so inclined. That pharmacist is likely to cut corners in any event. The only effect the advertising ban has on him is to insulate him from price competition and to open the way for him to make a substantial, and perhaps even excessive, profit in addition to providing an inferior service. The more painstaking pharmacist is also protected but, again, it is a protection based in large part on public ignorance. . . .

It appears to be feared that if the pharmacist who wishes to provide low cost, and assertedly low quality, services is permitted to advertise, he will be taken up on his offer by too many unwitting customers. They will choose the low-cost, low-quality service and drive the "professional" pharmacist out of business. They will respond only to costly and excessive advertising, and end up paying the price. They will go from one pharmacist to another, following the discount, and destroy the pharmacist-customer relationship. They will lose respect for the profession because it advertises. All this is not in their best interests, and all this can be avoided if they are not permitted to know who is charging what.

There is, of course, an alternative to this highly paternalistic approach. That alternative is to assume that this information is not in itself harmful, that people will perceive their own best interests if only they are well enough informed, and that the best means to that end is to open the channels of communication, rather than to close them. If they are truly open, nothing prevents the "professional" pharmacist from marketing his own assertedly superior product, and contrasting it with that of the low-cost, high-volume prescription drug retailer. But the choice among these alternative approaches is not ours to make, or the Virginia General Assembly's. It is precisely this kind of choice, between the dangers of suppressing information, and the dangers of its misuse if it is freely available, that the First Amendment makes for us. Virginia is free to require whatever professional standards it wishes of its pharmacists; it may subsidize them or protect them from competition in other ways. . . . But it may not do so by keeping the public in ignorance of the entirely lawful terms that competing pharmacists are offering. In this sense, the justifications Virginia has offered for suppressing the flow of prescription drug price information, far from persuading us that the flow is not protected by the First Amendment, have reinforced our view that it is. We so hold.

VI

☐ In concluding that commercial speech, like other varieties, is protected, we of course do not hold that it can never be regulated in any way. Some forms of commercial speech regulation are surely permissible. We mention a few only to make clear that they are not before us and therefore are not foreclosed by this case.

There is no claim, for example, that the prohibition on prescription drug price advertising is a mere time, place, and manner restriction. We have often approved restrictions of that kind provided that they are justified without reference to the content of the regulated speech, that they serve a significant governmental interest, and that, in so doing, they leave open ample alternative channels for communication of the information. . . . Nor is there any claim that prescription drug price advertisements are forbidden because they are false or misleading in any way. Untruthful speech, commercial or otherwise, has never been protected for its own sale. . . . Also, there is no claim that the transactions proposed in the forbidden advertisements are themselves illegal in any way. . . .

The basis of the *Virginia Pharmacy* decision, like that of *Bigelow,* was the public's right to receive information about a service. The Court added that this decision did not mean commercial speech could not be regulated. The ruling left room for governments to draft carefully constructed commercial speech regulations designed to deal with specific problems and concerns associated with advertising. For example, false and misleading ads and advertisements for illegal products might easily be regulated.

The revised Commercial Speech Doctrine was clarified in *Central Hudson Gas & Electric Corp. v. Public Service Commission (1980).*

Central Hudson Gas & Electric Corp. v. Public Service Commission of New York. 447 U.S. 557 (1980)

☐   ... This case presents the question whether a regulation of the Public Service Commission of the State of New York violates the First and Fourteenth Amendments because it completely bans promotional advertising by an electrical utility.

I

☐   In December 1973, the Commission, appellee here, ordered electric utilities in New York State to cease all advertising that "[promotes] the use of electricity." ... The order was based on the Commission's finding that "the interconnected utility system in New York State does not have sufficient fuel stocks or sources of supply to continue furnishing all customer demands for the 1973–1974 winter."

Three years later, when the fuel shortage had eased, the Commission requested comments from the public on its proposal to continue the ban on promotional advertising. Central Hudson Gas & Electric Corp., the appellant in this case, opposed the ban on First Amendment grounds. After reviewing the public comments, the Commission extended the prohibition in a Policy Statement issued on February 25, 1977.

The Policy Statement divided advertising expenses "into two broad categories: promotional—advertising intended to stimulate the purchase of utility services—and institutional and informational, a broad category inclusive of all advertising not clearly intended to promote sales." ... [The Policy Statment] declared all promotional advertising contrary to the national policy of conserving energy. It acknowledged that the ban is not a perfect vehicle for conserving energy. For example, the Commission's order prohibits promotional advertising to develop consumption during periods when demand for electricity is low. By limiting growth in "off-peak" consumption, the ban limits the "beneficial side effects" of such growth in terms of more efficient use of existing powerplants. And since oil dealers are not under the Commission's jurisdiction and thus remain free to advertise, it was recognized that the ban can achieve only "piecemeal conservationism." Still, the Commission adopted the restriction because it was deemed likely to "result in some dampening of unnecessary growth" in energy consumption. The Commission's order explicitly permitted "informational" advertising designed to encourage "*shifts* of consumption" from peak demand times to periods of low electricity demand. [Emphasis in original.] Informational advertising would not seek to increase aggregate consumption, but would invite a leveling of demand throughout any given 24-hour period. The agency offered to review "specific proposals by the companies for specifically described [advertising] programs that meet these criteria."

When it rejected requests for rehearing on the Policy Statement, the Commission supplemented its rationale for the advertising ban. The agency observed that additional electricity probably would be more expensive to produce than existing output. Because electricity rates in New York were not then based on marginal cost, the Commission feared that additional power would be priced below the actual cost of generation. The additional electricity would be subsidized by all consumers through generally higher rates. The state agency also thought that promotional advertising would give "misleading signals" to the public by appearing to encourage energy consumption at a time when conservation is needed. Appellant challenged the order in state court, arguing that the Commission had restrained commercial speech in violation of the First and Fourteenth Amendments. The Commission's order was upheld by the trial court and at the intermediate appellate level. The New York Court of Appeals affirmed. It found little value to advertising in "the noncompetitive market in which electric corporations operate." *Consolidated Edison Co. v. Public Service Comm'n*, 47 N.Y. 2d 94, 110, 390 N. E. 2d 749, 757 (1979). Since consumers "have no choice regarding the source of their electric power," the court denied that "promotional advertising of electricity might contribute to society's interest in 'informed and reliable' economic decisionmaking." The court also observed that by encouraging consumption, promotional advertising would only exacerbate the current energy situation. *The court concluded that the governmental interest in the prohibition outweighed the limited constitutional value of the commercial speech at issue. We noted probable jurisdiction . . . and now reverse.* [Emphasis added]

In *Central Hudson*, the Supreme Court developed a four-part test to help determine whether a particular commercial expression is protected by the First Amendment. For commercial speech to be protected it must meet the following criteria of the *Central Hudson Test*:

- It must concern lawful activity and cannot be misleading.
- The asserted government interest in regulating the speech must be substantial.
- Regulation of the commercial speech must further the government's goals.
- If the first three parts of the test are met, the proposed regulation must not be more extensive than necessary to further the government's interest.

Sponsor Identification

Section 317 of the Communications Act and Section 73.1212 of the FCC Rules requires that stations must identify who sponsored a given program. The rule applies at any time that a station receives money, services, or other valuable consideration in exchange for an announcement or a program.

Children's TV Advertising

Time Standards

In the 1980s the deregulation of television by the FCC included the elimination of commercial time guidelines for children's television programs. Action for Children's Television (ACT) appealed this decision and in *Action for Children's Television v. FCC (1987)*, the court of appeals remanded the case to the FCC for further consideration of the issue. In 1987, the FCC issued a *Further Notice of Proposed Rule Making*, requesting comments from the public to assist the agency in developing a children's television commercial policy.[2] Specifically, the Commission sought to determine whether market forces were sufficient to regulate commercial time in children's television programming or whether additional government regulation was required.

In July 1990, the Senate passed a children's television bill that provided for commercial time limits during programs primarily aimed at children. The bill limited commercial time during children's programs to 10.5 minutes on weekends and 12 minutes on weekdays. The House accepted these guidelines in a compromise bill that was passed on October 2, 1990. The bill became law on October 17, 1990, without the signature of President Bush. The House legislation removed a Senate provision requiring a national endowment to support public broadcasting. The commercial time limits apply in programs directed primarily to children 12 years of age and younger. The rules apply to over-the-air and cable programs, but not to low-power television stations.

Program-Length Commercials

The FCC has defined program-length commercials as programs associated with a product in which commercials for that product are aired.[3] ACT filed a complaint with the FCC in 1983 alleging that programs such as *He Man*, *Thunder Cats*, and *Masters of the Universe* violated FCC policies against directing program-length commercials to children. ACT argued that these animated programs promoted products or services under the guise of entertainment. The characters in the programs were marketed as plastic toys that are available to children. ACT contended that these programs should have been logged as commercial time.

In *Action for Children's Television (1985)*, the FCC dismissed ACT's complaint, noting that there was no evidence that program-length commercials were harmful to children in the audience and that there was no evidence in this case showing an intermingling of commercial and program material. The Commission ruling was appealed by the National Association for Better Broadcasting (NABB) in 1985, in *National Association for Better Broadcasting v. FCC.* The court of appeals reversed and remanded *NABB v. FCC* to the FCC. The Commission denied NABB's complaint on grounds that the programs in question were bartered and thereby did not trigger the sponsorship identification requirements.

ACT remains concerned over the FCC's definition of program-length commercials. In 1986, ACT requested the Commission to require programs depicting products as toys to carry announcements that the program material is designed to promote the sale of the product in the story. The following year, ACT filed another petition asking the FCC to rule that children's programs that carry an inaudible signal that interacts with certain toys was in violation of the public interest. The FCC did not act specifically on these recommendations, but included a prohibition against program-length commercials in the 1991 children's television rules.

ACT filed a petition with the FCC in May 1991, contending that the Commission erred in failing to define program-length commercials in terms of the public interest. ACT noted that the FCC definition is currently limited to shows associated with a product in which commercials for that product are aired. ACT argued that this definition failed to address public interest issues and that Commission action was arbitrary and unlawful.

Home Shopping Channels

During the late 1980s and early 1990s, a number of television channels dedicated solely to "home shopping" developed. Essentially, these channels are one continuous commercial for various products that can be ordered by viewers from home via the telephone. Though most home shopping channels (e.g., The Home Shopping Network and QVC) originated on cable, some broadcast stations began devoting their schedules to home shopping. In 1993, the FCC held that the home shopping format served the public interest, paving the way for more over-the-air stations to adopt the format.[4] In a related matter, the Commission held that home shopping broadcast stations qualify for must-carry stipulations under the 1992 Cable Consumer Protection Act.

Liquor and Wine Ads on Radio, TV, and Cable

There is no federal prohibition against advertising legal alcoholic beverages on radio, television, or cable. Traditionally, broadcasters have exercised self-restraint in accepting alcoholic beverage ads. Until 1996 broadcasters generally refused advertisements for hard liquor and refrained from showing individuals engaged in excessive consumption. Since 1996 hundreds of local broadcast television and radio stations and cable systems have accepted hard liquor advertisements. Cable networks have also accepted these advertisements.

In 2001 NBC became the first of the major broadcast networks to accept hard liquor ads. The network developed guidelines that the distilled spirits manufacturers must adhere to before a hard liquor ad will be accepted by the network. The guidelines stipulated that the advertiser must commit to a four-month on-air social responsibility campaign. After that, 20 percent of time bought must be devoted to social-responsibility themes. Other guidelines include:

- No liquor ads before 9:00 P.M.
- 85 percent of audience exposed to ad must be over 21 years of age
- Actors in commercials must be at least 30 years old
- No current athletes can endorse the product
- No celebrities appealing to young people may endorse
- Ads can't imply that liquor reduces stress or improves sexual prowess

States, on the other hand, may restrict alcoholic beverage advertising in over-the-air broadcast media. However, states may not prohibit cable systems from retransmitting out-of-state signals that contain alcoholic beverage commercials. When Oklahoma attempted to apply its statewide ban on alcoholic beverage advertising to signals imported by cable systems, the Supreme Court ruled in *Capital Cities v. Crisp* that authority over out-of-state signals was part of FCC jurisdiction and therefore subject to federal law.[5]

Nor is hard liquor immune from possible action by the federal government. As far back as 1985, the Senate conducted hearings that considered legislative restrictions on beer and wine advertising on radio and television. The Senate Subcommittee sought evidence to determine whether advertising caused nondrinkers to become drinkers and whether ads caused drinkers to increase consumption. The results were inconclusive. In May 1985, the House Subcommittee on Telecommunications, Consumer Protection, and Finance addressed the relationship between beer and wine ads, and abuse of those products. Again, no conclusive evidence was produced and eventually congressional interest in the topic waned. In 1997 the FCC considered a

Notice of Inquiry on the subject of liquor advertising, but no action was taken. Periodically, however, Congress shows renewed interest in revisiting this topic.

Cigarette and Tobacco Products Advertising

The congressional ban on cigarette and smokeless tobacco products advertising on broadcast and cable originated from the Fairness Doctrine. In the mid-1960s, with mounting evidence that indicated that cigarette smoking was a health hazard, individuals became increasingly concerned over the plethora of ads for cigarettes on television. Indeed, cigarettes had been a major sponsor of network programs since the early days of the *Camel News Caravan with John Cameron Swayze*. Even the animated *Flintstones* were sponsored by Winston cigarettes. Television personalities like Edward R. Murrow, Jack Paar, and Andy Griffith smoked during the course of their programs. Cigarettes were touted as "refreshing."

Applying the Fairness Doctrine to Advertising Cigarettes

In December 1966, an attorney named John Banzhaf asked WCBS-TV in New York for reply time to respond to cigarette commercials. He based his request on the Fairness Doctrine. His rationale was that smoking cigarettes poses a potential health hazard. Therefore, he argued, the discussion of cigarette smoking fell into the category of a "controversial issue of public importance," triggering the Fairness Doctrine. There was precedence in FCC case law in the Petition of Sam Morris, which extended the concept of "fairness" to advertising.

When WCBS-TV refused to allow Banzhaf time to rebut the cigarette ads it had broadcast, Banzhaf filed a complaint with the FCC. In WCBS-TV, the Commission ordered WCBS-TV to grant reply time. The decision was upheld by the U.S. court of appeals in *Banzhaf v. FCC*. The *Banzhaf* decision attempted to limit the application of the Fairness Doctrine to cigarette advertising only. The court of appeals held that cigarette ads had to be counterbalanced by expression devoted to pointing out the hazards of cigarette smoking.

Although *Banzhaf* tried to limit the application of the Fairness Doctrine to advertising, the cat had been let out of the bag. In *Friends of the Earth v. FCC*, a citizens group argued that free time should be made available to anti-pollution groups wishing to respond to automobile advertisements. The rationale behind their argument was that cars pollute the air—a controversial issue of public importance. The FCC refused to order counter ads in this case, but the court of appeals reversed the Commission ruling.

As a result of the *Friends of the Earth* case, the FCC issued the *1974 Fairness Report*.[6] In this report, the FCC states that product commercials do not trigger the "controversial issue of public importance" test required to induce a Fairness Doctrine complaint. In short, the Commission developed a new policy that refused to apply the Fairness Doctrine to product advertising. Fairness still applied to editorial advertising.

The Congressional Ban of Cigarette and Smokeless Tobacco Ads

Congress passed the Federal Cigarette Labeling and Advertising Act in 1965. The act required cigarette packages and advertisements to display the statement "Caution: Cigarette Smoking May Be Hazardous to Your Health." In 1969, the Public Health Cigarette Smoking Act was enacted. This legislation beefed up the warning required on cigarette packages and ads to "Warning: Excessive Cigarette Smoking Is Dangerous to Your Health." The act also banned cigarette advertising from the airwaves after January 1, 1971. In 1986, the Comprehensive Smokeless Tobacco Health Education Act extended the broadcast and cable advertising ban to smokeless tobacco products such as snuff and chewing tobacco.

Self-Regulation

Broadcasters and cablecasters exercise self-regulation in the area of advertising. The networks, Multiple System Owners (MSOs), and individual stations and franchises have adopted standards for acceptable advertising. All must be within the bounds of the law, but some are more restrictive than others. Through self-regulation, the industry hopes to stave off additional regulation by Congress through the FCC. This regulation is usually the result of a widespread public outcry that manifests itself in the form of pressure on Congress. Congress, in turn, pressures the FCC. Examples of regulatory measures, both successful and unsuccessful, include the Children's Television Act, the failed 24-hour ban on indecency, and the reregulation cable television.

The National Association of Broadcasters (NAB) developed advertising codes for radio advertising in 1929 and for television advertising in 1952. The codes were voluntary guidelines set up to ward off government regulation. The NAB codes suggested that radio stations broadcast no more than 18 minutes of commercial time per hour and that television stations limit commercials to 14 minutes per hour.

In 1979, the Justice Department brought suit against the Television Code, alleging that the code violated antitrust laws. Television stations were suspected of artificially limiting advertising and depriving advertisers of the benefits of open competition. In 1982, the NAB voluntarily dissolved the radio and television codes.

Summary

The FTC is empowered to regulate false and misleading advertising. Though the FTC may order a broadcaster to stop airing an ad that is deemed deceptive, the FTC cannot revoke a broadcast license. Advertising receives some protection under the First Amendment, although that protection is limited.

One of the FCC's major concerns is the advertising in children's television programs. The Commission limits the amount of commercial time in children's programs and prohibits host selling.

Cigarettes and smokeless tobacco product advertisements are the only legal products specifically banned from the airwaves by Congress. Liquor and wine ads and other personal products must adhere to broadcaster imposed standards designed to stave off regulation by outside authorities like state and federal agencies.

Suggested Links

Federal Trade Commission, http://www.ftc.gov

FTC Report on marketing violent entertainment to children, http://www.ftc.gov/opa/2000/09/youthviol.htm

FCC Staff Report on children's educational programming, http://www.fcc.gov/mmb/prd/cetv/

FCC material on "Complaints about Broadcast Advertising," http://www.fcc.gov/cib/consumerfacts/advertising.html

FCC Chairman Hundt's statement on proposed Notice of Inquiry (NOI) on liquor advertising, http://ftp.fcc.gov/Bureaus/Miscellaneous/News_Releases/1997/nrmc7032.html

Notes/References

1. *Virginia State Bd. of Pharmacy v. Virginia Citizens Consumer Council Inc.*, 425 U.S. 748 (1976).
2. See *Further Notice of Proposed Rule Making/Notice of Inquiry*, MM Docket No. 83-670, F.C.C. 87-338, 2 F.C.C.Red. 6822 (1987).

3. MM Docket 90-570, FCC 90-373.
4. 8 F.C.C. Red. 5321.
5. Steve McClellan, "NBC Tiptoes off the Wagon," *Broadcasting & Cable* (December 17, 2001).
6. See *In the Matter of the Handling of Public Issues Under the Fairness Doctrine* and the *Public Interest Standards of the Communications Act*, 48 F.C.C.2d 1 (1974).

Cases

Action for Children's Television, 58 R.R.2d 61(1985)
Action for Children's Television v. FCC, 821 F.2d 741 (DC Cir., 1987)
Banzhaf v. FCC, 405 F.2d 1082 (DC Cir., 1968)
Bigelow v. Virginia, 421 U.S. 809 (1975)
Capital Cities Cable v. Crisp, (U.S. Sup.Ct., 1984) 10 Med.L.Rprt. 1873
Carter Products Inc. v. FTC, 268 F.2d 461 (9th Cir., 1959), cert. denied 361 U.S. 884 (1959)
Central Hudson Gas & Electric Corp. v. Public Service Commission, 447 U.S. 557 (1980)
Friends of the Earth v. FCC, 449 F.2d 1164 (DC Cir., 1971)
FTC v. Raladam Co., 283 U.S. 643 (1931)
FTC v. Winsted Hosiery Co., 258 U.S. 483 (1922)
National Association for Better Broadcasting v. FCC, 830 F.2d 270 (DC Cir., 1986)
National Association for Better Broadcasting v. FCC, U.S. Court of Appeals, DC, Court Case No. 89-1462 (1989)
Petition of Sam Morris, 11 F.C.C. 197 (1946)
Valentine v. Chrestensen, 316 U.S. 52 (1942)
Virginia State Bd. of Pharmacy v. Virginia Citizens Consumer Council Inc., 425 U.S. 748 (1976)
Warner-Lambert Co. v. Federal Trade Commission, 562 F.2d. 749 (DC Cir., 1977), cert. denied 435 U.S. 958 (1978)
WCBS-TV, 8 F.C.C.2d 381 (1967), 9 F.C.C.2d 921 (1967)

8

□ □ □
□ □ □
□ □ □

Copyright, Music Licensing, and Trademark

Copyright

The first federal Copyright Act was adopted in 1790. The original act protected books and maps from unauthorized use for a 14-year renewable term. In 1802, protection for prints was added to the act. Musical compositions received protection in 1831. Photographs became copyrightable in 1865, and paintings became copyrightable in 1870. It was not until 1978 that sound and video recordings could be copyrighted.

The basic copyright statute was revised twice in this century to accommodate the emergence of new technologies. As a result, many creative works are still protected under the 1909 Copyright Act, while those works registered after January 1, 1978 are protected under the Copyright Act of 1976. The 1976 act preempted all state copyright laws.

The Scope of Copyright Protection

The Copyright Act is found in title 17 of the U.S. Code. Copyright provides protection from unauthorized use of original works of authorship, including literary, dramatic, musical, artistic, and certain other intellectual works. The 1976 act provides protection for published and unpublished works. Section 106 of the Copyright Act gives the owner of a copyright the exclusive right

(1) To reproduce the work in copies or phonorecords;
(2) To prepare derivative works based on the original;
(3) To distribute copies or phonorecords of the work to the public by sale or other transfer of ownership, or by rental, lease, or lending;
(4) To perform the copyrighted work publicly, in the case of literary, musical, dramatic and choreographic works, pantomimes, and motion pictures and other audiovisual works; and

(5) To display the copyrighted work publicly, in the case of literary, musical, dramatic and choreographic works, pantomimes, and pictorial, graphic or sculptural works, including the individual images of a motion picture or other audiovisual work.[1]

A copyright protects the expression of ideas, not the ideas themselves. The historical fact that someone died is not copyrightable, but a particular version of the death is copyrightable. When a television news program copyrights video of a news event, it does not claim rights to the event itself, only to its particular expression of the event. News departments may not keep competitors from covering a news event by copyrighting it, but the competitors must shoot their own video or obtain their own audio.

In *Hoeling v. Universal Studios (1980)*, the U.S. Court of Appeals for the Second Circuit dealt with the concept of separating an idea from the expression of that idea.

In 1937, the German dirigible Hindenberg exploded just before landing at Lakehurst, New Jersey, killing 36 people. The airship had just completed a trip across the Atlantic. The official explanation for the tragedy was that static electricity had ignited the highly flammable hydrogen gas used to provide the airship's buoyancy.

A. A. Hoeling, after years of research, came to a different conclusion. In 1962, he wrote a book espousing his thesis that the Hindenberg was destroyed by a bomb planted by one of the ship's riggers before it left Germany. The bomb was timed to explode after the ship had landed, but a thunderstorm delayed the landing and the bomb exploded while the ship was still airborne.

In 1972, Michael Mooney wrote a work of fiction entitled *The Hindenberg*. Mooney's book was built around Hoeling's thesis. Universal Studios bought the rights to Mooney's book and a motion picture of the same name was released in 1975. Hoeling sued Universal Studios for copyright infringement, arguing that his thesis was copyrighted in his 1962 book.

The court held that Hoeling's thesis was not subject to copyright protection. The theory of the bombing was viewed as "historical fact." The court ruled that facts are not copyrightable—only the expression of the facts is copyrightable. Therefore, a verbatim copying of Hoeling's book would have resulted in copyright infringement, which did not extend to a new expression of the facts as found in the Mooney book and subsequent movie.

Works That Can Be Copyrighted

Copyright protection exists for original works of authorship as soon as they become fixed in a tangible form of expression. This includes works that are perceived by means of a machine, such as videotape or audio-tape. Copyrightable works include the following:

- Literary works, including compilations and computer programs
- Musical works, including accompanying words
- Dramatic works, including accompanying music
- Pantomimes and choreographic works
- Pictorial, graphic, and sculptural works, including maps and blueprints
- Motion pictures and other audiovisual works
- Sound recordings
- Computer programs

Materials That May Not Be Copyrighted

Any work that is not in a fixed, tangible form and is not an original expression of an idea cannot be copyrighted. Ideas, procedures, methods, concepts, or processes in themselves may not be copyrighted. If a work consists entirely of information that is common property with no original authorship, it may not be copyrighted. Examples include calendars, rulers, or lists and tables taken from public documents or other common sources.

In *WCVB-TV v. Boston Athletic Association*, the appellate court upheld a lower court ruling that allowed Boston's WCVB Channel 5 to televise the Boston Marathon even though race officials asserted that another local television station was licensed to cover the event. Race promoters argued that the use of the words "Boston Marathon" by Channel 5 constituted a trademark infringement and coverage of the event was a copyright violation.

The appellate court ruled that there was no evidence to suggest that use of the words "Boston Marathon" by Channel 5 suggested official sponsorship of the event. Indeed, the station had broadcast a disclaimer noting that it was not the official sponsor. The court could find no evidence suggesting that Channel 5 might profit from viewers who wrongly believed that the Boston Marathon Association had authorized the broadcasts. No trademark or copyright violations occurred. The words "Boston Marathon" describe the event and are not protected.

The concept of "original authorship" served as the basis of the decision in *Production Contractors v. WGN Continental Broadcasting Co.*, which involved the telecasting of a public event. When WGN-TV announced its intentions to televise the 1985 Chicago Christmas parade, Production Contractors, the parade's organizer, sought to prohibit WGN from doing so. Although the parade was a public event, Production Contractors had granted exclusive rights to WLS-TV and ABC. The U.S. District Court for the

Northern District of Illinois ruled that the parade was not a work of authorship and not entitled to copyright protection. WLS could not prevent WGN from televising the parade, provided WGN used its own equipment, camera operators, and directors. In so doing, WGN would create its own "authorship." Both WLS and WGN could create copyrightable versions of the event.

Other noncopyrightable material includes titles, names, short phrases, symbols, or designs. These may be registered as trademarks, which are discussed later in this chapter.

Obtaining a Copyright

It should be emphasized that a work is protected by copyright from the moment it is fixed in a tangible form—either as a written copy or other media, such as audiotape or videotape. Authors are not required to register their work with the Copyright Office to obtain protection; however, there are advantages to doing so. A major advantage is that registration allows the copyright owner to collect statutory damages and attorney's fees in cases of infringement. Registration also makes prosecution of infringement easier, because a public record of the copyright has been established and serves as *prima facie* evidence in court.

To register a work, the author must complete the proper application form. If a work has been published, two copies must be included. If the work is unpublished, one copy of the work is required. The author must then submit the application, copies of the work, and a filing fee to the Register of Copyrights, Library of Congress, Washington, D.C. 20559. It is important to submit all materials in one envelope. Copyrights may also be filed online. Information on this procedure and copyright forms may be obtained from the Copyright Office Website, http://www.loc.gov/copyright.

Duration of a Copyright

Under the 1909 Copyright Act, copyright duration was 28 years, with a provision for one renewal for another 28 years—a total of 56 years. After that time, works fell into the public domain. This means that they are no longer protected by copyright and may be freely used. Users of public domain works are free to copyright their own arrangements, adaptations, or translations of those works. The 1976 Copyright Act extended to 75 years the protection of works covered under the 1909 act.

In 1998 Congress passed the Sonny Bono Copyright Term Extension Act. This legislation extended protection for works created before January 1, 1978 to 95 years from the date that the copyright was secured.[2]

The Sonny Bono Copyright Extension Act also extended the term of works created after January 1, 1978, from the life of the author plus 50 years to life of the author plus 70 years.[3] Seventy years after the author's death, the work becomes part of the public domain. Copyrights are assignable and may be willed to the heirs of the author for the remainder of the copyright period.

In February 2002, the Supreme Court agreed to hear a challenge to the Bono Act. The operator of a Website that posts public domain literary works on the World Wide Web challenged the constitutionality of the Act on grounds that it unconstitutionally confers copyright protection retroactively and that the extended copyright terms are unreasonably long. The District Court dismissed the claim and the Court of Appeals affirmed. The Supreme Court agreed to hear the case. (See *Eldred v. Reno*, 74 F.Supp.2d (D.D.C. 1999); *Eldred v. Reno*, 239 F.3d (D.C.Cir. 2001); *Eldred v. Ashcroft*, 255 F.3d 849 (D.C.Cir. 2001), cert.granted (U.S. Oct. 11, 2001).)

Work for Hire

Section 101 of the Copyright Act defines a "work made for hire" as:

(1) A work prepared by an employee within the scope of his or her employment; or

(2) A specifically ordered or commissioned work in one of nine specified categories, *provided there is a written agreement signed by the parties specifying that the work shall be considered one made for hire* [emphasis added]. These categories are: as contribution to a collective work, as part of a motion picture or other audiovisual work, as a transition, as supplementary work, as a compilation, as an instructional text, as a test, as answer material for a test, or as an atlas.

Many works produced by the electronic media are works for hire (i.e., the work is prepared as part of an employee's job or as an independent contractor conducting work on behalf of an organization). Either way, the primary author or authors do not retain the sole rights to the work. Instead, ownership is retained by another individual or organization. When an evening television newscast is copyrighted, the rights are retained by the television station owner, not by the anchor or producer. The duration of copyright for works for hire is 95 years after publication or 120 years after creation, whichever occurs first.[4]

In *Baltimore Orioles v. Major League Baseball Players*, the Major League Baseball Players Association argued that the players, not the franchise holder, owned the rights to telecasts of games in which they appeared. The U.S.

Court of Appeals for the Seventh Circuit held that the telecast of major league games consisted of performance by employees acting within the scope of their employment. Therefore, the telecasts were works for hire and the ball players had no ownership rights to the broadcasts.

Notice of Copyright

Copyright notice is not required to protect a work from infringement. Prior to 1989 and the United States accession to the Berne Convention Implementation Act of 1988, formal notice was required to protect published works. Since 1989, the primary significance of copyright notice is protection against a defense of innocent infringement. Even in this case, the burden of proof remains on the infringer.

Formal copyright notice may still protect published works created before 1989. The copyright protection afforded these works can be lost if notice was omitted and not remedied within five years of publication. As noted earlier in this chapter, notice and registration are required to obtain certain statutory damages and attorney's fees.

The Copyright Act, as amended by the Berne Convention Implementation Act of 1988, requires that two copies of a work published in the United States be deposited, with or without copyright notice, in the Copyright Office within three months of publication. The work need not be registered. The Copyright Office may request that works be deposited. Failure to comply may result in a fine of not more than $250 per work, payment to the Library of Congress of the total retail price of copies requested, and an additional fine of $2500 for willful or repeated failure to comply.

Elements of Copyright Notice

The traditional copyright notice contains three elements. The Copyright Office suggests that the elements appear together on the protected copies. Copyright notice consists of

- The symbol ©, the word "Copyright," or the abbreviation "Copr."
- The year of first publication
- The name or owner of the copyright

An example of copyright notice is © 1999 Jane Doe.

The copyright notice for records of a sound recording is somewhat different. Records, tapes, or compact disks contain the symbol ℗ in place of the symbol ©. An example of copyright notice on a record is ℗ 1999 ABC Records Inc. This denotes that the mechanical right is protected.

Fair Use

The concept of fair use places limitations on the exclusive rights of the copyright holder. Fair use is usually applied in matters involving educational materials, literary or social criticism, parody, and First Amendment activities. The rights of the copyright holder are balanced against other interests in determining the level of protection afforded by the Copyright Act. The courts have identified four areas that are considered before copyrighted material may be used without securing the permission of the copyright holder:

- The purpose and character of the use, including whether such use is of a commercial nature or is for nonprofit educational purposes;
- The nature of the copyrighted work;
- The amount and substantiality of the portion used in relation to the copyrighted work as a whole; and
- The effect of the use upon the potential market for or value of the copyrighted work.[5]

It should be noted that there is no limit set on what percentage of use of material constitutes a violation of the Fair Use Doctrine. The use of even a few words may constitute copyright infringement if that use adversely affects the economic value of the original work, as evidenced in *Meerpol v. Nizer.* This case held that the publication of portions of 28 copyrighted letters written by convicted spies, Ethel and Julius Rosenberg, constituted infringement. This, in spite of the fact that the Rosenbergs had been executed and the letters had been out of print for more than 20 years. The U.S. Court of Appeals based its decision on the potential economic impact that unauthorized publication of the letters may have on their future use by the copyright owners—the sons of Julius and Ethel Rosenberg. Even paraphrasing copyrighted material can be considered infringement, as evidenced in *Salinger v. Random House Inc.*

The home videotaping of broadcast television programs was deemed to be fair use by the Supreme Court. In *Sony Corp. v. Universal Studios Inc. (1984),* the Court held that noncommercial in-home use of videotaped programs was not copyright infringement. This case has been referred to as the Betamax case, so named because of Sony's tape format at the time. Two critical findings resulted from this ruling: Most copyright holders of broadcast programming would not object to "time shifting" (i.e., recording a program for viewing at another time), and time shifting has no direct harm on the market.

The decision in the *Betamax* case opened the door to legal home video-taping of broadcast programs and spurred the purchase of home videotape recorders in the 1980s.

When a television news clipping service videotaped copyrighted television newscasts and sold them to clients who were featured in the newscasts, the District Court for Northern Georgia found that the practice was not fair use, in *Pacific & Southern Co. v. Duncan*.

When Evangelist Jerry Falwell distributed copies of a parody of him published by *Hustler* magazine to raise money to rebut the parody's attack on him, a different decision was reached. In *Hustler v. Moral Majority*, the U.S. Court of Appeals for the Ninth Circuit held that Falwell's copying of the copyrighted parody did not interfere with the magazine's potential sales or the parody's marketability.

In *Tin Pan Apple v. Miller Brewing (1990)*, the U.S. District Court for the Southern District of New York ruled that a parody of the rap group The Fat Boys by comedian Joe Piscapo as part of a beer commercial violated copyright law. The parody, said the court, did not build on the original and was used solely to promote a commercial product. Therefore, the Fat Boys rights of publicity were violated.

When *The Nation* magazine published excerpts from Gerald Ford's unpublished manuscript without permission, the Supreme Court ruled that the publication violated the doctrine of fair use.

Harper & Row Publishers Inc. v. Nation Enterprise (1985)

☐   Justice O'Connor delivered the opinion of the Court.

This case requires us to consider to what extent the "fair use" provision of the copyright Revision Act of 1976, 17 U.S.C. § 107 (hereinafter the Copyright Act), sanctions from a public figure's unpublished manuscript. In March 1979, an undisclosed source provided *The Nation* magazine with the unpublished manuscript of "A Time to Heal: The Autobiography of Gerald R. Ford." Working directly from the purloined manuscript, an editor of *The Nation* produced a short piece entitled "The Ford Memoirs—Behind the Nixon Pardon." The piece was timed to "scoop" an article scheduled shortly to appear in *Time* magazine. *Time* had agreed to purchase the exclusive right to print prepublication excerpts from the copyright holders, Harper & Row Publishers, Inc. . . . and *Reader's Digest*.

. . . As a result of The *Nation* article, *Time* canceled its agreement. Petitioners brought a successful copyright action against *The Nation*. On appeal, the Second Circuit reversed the lower court's finding of infringement, holding that *The Nation*'s act was sanctioned as a "fair use" of the copyrighted material. We granted certiorari . . . and we now reverse.

. . . Fair use was traditionally defined as "a privilege in others than the owner of the copyright to use the copyrighted material in a reasonable manner without his consent." . . .

. . . Respondents, however, contend that First Amendment values require a different rule under the circumstances of this case. . . . Respondents advance the substantial public import of the subject matter of the Ford memoirs as grounds for excusing a use that would ordinarily not pass muster as a fair use—the piracy of verbatim quotations for the purpose of "scooping" the authorized first serialization. Respondents argue that the public's interest in learning this news as fast as possible outweighs the right of the author to control its first publication.

The Second Circuit noted, correctly, that copyright's idea/expression dichotomy "strike[s] a definitional balance between the First Amendment and the Copyright Act by permitting free communication of facts while still protecting an author's expression." . . .

. . . As this Court long ago observed: "[T]he news element—the information respecting current events contained in the literary production—is not the creation of the writer, but is a report of matters that ordinarily are publici juris; it is the history of the day." *International News Service v. Associated Press*, 248 U.S. 215, 234 (1918). But copyright assures those who write and publish factual narratives such as "A Time to Heal" that they may at least enjoy the right to market the original expression contained therein as just compensation for their investment. Cf. *Zacchini v. Scripps-Howard Broadcasting Co.*, 433 U.S. 562, 575 (1977).

. . . The promise of copyright would be an empty one if it could be avoided merely by dubbing the infringement a fair use "news report" of the book. . . .

. . . Nor do respondents assert any actual necessity for circumventing the copyright scheme with respect to the types of works and users at issue here. . . .

In our haste to disseminate news, it should not be forgotten that the Framers intended copyright itself to be the engine of free expression. By establishing a marketable right to the use of one's expression, copyright supplies the economic incentive to create and disseminate ideas. . . .

The four factors identified by Congress as especially relevant in determining whether the use was fair are: (1) the purpose and character of the use; (2) the nature of the copyrighted work; (3) the substantiality of the portion used in relation to the copyrighted work as a whole; (4) the effect on the potential market for or value of the copyrighted work. We address each one separately.

Purpose of the Use. The Second Circuit correctly identified news reporting as the general purpose of *The Nation*'s use. News reporting is one of the examples enumerated in § 107 to "give some idea of the sort of activities the courts might regard as fair use under the circumstances." . . .

The Nation has every right to seek to be the first to publish information. But *The Nation* went beyond simply reporting uncopyrightable information and actively sought to exploit the headline value of its infringement, making a "news event" out of its unauthorized first publication of a noted figure's copyrighted expression.

The fact that a publication was commercial as opposed to nonprofit is a separate factor that tends to weigh against a finding of fair use. . . .

Nature of the Copyrighted Work. Second, the Act directs attention to the nature of the copyrighted work. "A Time to Heal" may be characterized as an unpublished historical narrative or autobiography. The law generally recognizes a greater need to disseminate factual works than works of fiction or fantasy. . . .

In the case of Mr. Ford's manuscript, the copyrightholder's interest in confidentiality is irrefutable; the copyrightholders had entered into a contractual undertaking to "keep the manuscript confidential" and required that all those to whom the manuscript was shown also "sign an agreement to keep the manuscript confidential." A use that so clearly infringes on the copyrightholder's interests in confidentiality and creative control is difficult to characterize as "fair."

Amount and Substantiality of the Portion Used. . . . In absolute terms, the words actually quoted were an insubstantial portion of "A Time to Heal." The district court, however, found that "[*T*]*he Nation* took what was essentially the heart of the book." . . .

As the statutory language indicates, a taking may not be excused merely because it is insubstantial with respect to the infringing work. As Judge Learned Hand cogently remarked, "[N]o plagiarist can excuse the wrong by showing how much of his work he did not pirate." . . .

Effect on the Market. . . . The trial court found not merely a potential but an actual effect on the market. *Time*'s cancellation of its projected serialization and its refusal to pay the $12,500 were the direct effect of the infringement. . . . Rarely will a case of copyright infringement present such clear-cut evidence of actual damage. . . .

The Nation conceded that its verbatim copying of some 300 words of direct quotation from the Ford manuscript would constitute an infringement unless excused as a fair use. Because we find that *The Nation*'s use of these verbatim excerpts from the unpublished manuscript was not a fair use, the judgment of the Court of Appeals is reversed and remanded for further proceedings consistent with this opinion.

News and Copyright

Although the facts of news may not be copyrighted, the expression of those facts arc protected. It is copyright infringement to read a newspaper or other print media story over the electronic media, verbatim or rewritten, without permission. Using a competitor, such as a newspaper, as a source of tips is acceptable, provided the user generates an original expression of the events. This means calling or otherwise following up the story and presenting an original interpretation.

In cases of exclusive interviews, both the publisher and the subject of the interview may have remedy. In *Cher v. Forum International Ltd.*, entertainer Cher successfully sued *Forum* magazine for the unauthorized use of an interview with a freelance writer originally intended for *Us* magazine.

Parody or "Sound-Alike" Recordings

Permission must be obtained for parody recordings that alter the words or other elements of a song. "Weird Al" Jankovich's parodies of Michael Jackson and other pop artists of the 1980s were done with such permission.

Sound-alikes are popular as commercial jingles. Advertisers often like to employ musicians to imitate well-known performers in spots (because the public often identifies with a "sound" or recent hit) without the cost of hiring the original artist. This practice has been common for a number of years with few successful suits brought against the imitators. In 1988, however, singer Bette Midler brought a successful suit against Ford Motor Company for the imitation of her 1970s hit "Do You Wanna Dance." In *Midler v. Ford Motor Company*, the U.S. Court of Appeals for the Ninth Circuit held that the commercial sounded so much like Midler that the average listener might believe it to be she. Therefore, the court ruled that Ford's commercial violated the singer's right of publicity and artistic persona.

The issue of parody and copyright reached the Supreme Court when 2 Live Crew recorded a version of Roy Orbison's "Pretty Woman" on the *As Clean As They Wanna Be (Clean)* CD. The Supreme Court found that copyright infringement had not taken place. The case makes interesting reading, and the lyrics for the original and parodied versions are included in appendixes to the decision.

**Luther R. Campbell aka Luke Skyywalker, et al.,
Petitioners v. Acuff-Rose Music, Inc.**
ON WRIT OF CERTIORARI TO THE UNITED STATES COURT OF APPEALS FOR THE SIXTH CIRCUIT [MARCH 7, 1994]

☐   Justice Souter delivered the opinion of the Court. We are called upon to decide whether 2 Live Crew's commercial parody of Roy Orbison's song, "Oh, Pretty Woman," may be a fair use within the meaning of the Copyright Act of 1976, 17 U.S.C. 107 (1988 ed. and Supp. IV). Although the District Court granted summary judgment for 2 Live Crew, the Court of Appeals reversed, holding the defense of fair use barred by the song's commercial character and excessive borrowing. Because we hold that a parody's commercial character is only one element to be weighed in a fair use enquiry, and that insufficient consideration was given to the nature of parody in weighing the degree of copying, we reverse and remand.

In 1964, Roy Orbison and William Does wrote a rock ballad called "Oh, Pretty Woman" and assigned their rights in it to respondent Acuff-Rose Music, Inc.[ ] Acuff-Rose registered the song for copyright protection. Petitioners Luther R. Campbell, Christopher Wongwon, Mark Ross, and David Hobbs, are collectively known as 2 Live Crew, a popular rap music group. In 1989, Campbell wrote a song entitled "Pretty Woman," which he later described in an affidavit as intended, "through comical lyrics, to satirize the original work . . . [ ] On July 5, 1989, 2 Live Crew's manager informed Acuff-Rose that 2 Live Crew had written a parody of "Oh, Pretty Woman," that they would afford all credit for ownership and authorship of the original song to Acuff-Rose, Dees, and Orbison, and that they were willing to pay a fee for the use they wished to make of it. Enclosed with the letter were a copy of the lyrics and a recording of 2 Live Crew's song. [ ] Acuff-Rose's agent refused permission, stating that "I am aware of the success enjoyed by 'The 2 Live Crews', but I must inform you that we cannot permit the use of a parody of 'Oh, Pretty Woman.' "[ ] Nonetheless, in June or July 1989, 2 Live Crew released records, cassette tapes, and compact discs of "Pretty Woman" in a collection of songs entitled "As Clean As They Wanna Be." The albums and compact discs identify the authors of "Pretty Woman" as Orbison and Dees and its publisher as Acuff-Rose.

Almost a year later, after nearly a quarter of a million copies of the recording had been sold, Acuff-Rose sued 2 Live Crew and its record company, Luke Skyywalker Records, for copyright infringement. The District Court granted summary judgment for 2 Live Crew, reasoning that the commercial purpose of 2 Live Crew's song was no bar to fair use; that 2 Live Crew's version was a parody, which "quickly degenerates into a play on words, substituting predictable lyrics with shocking ones" to show "how bland and banal the Orbison song" is; that 2 Live Crew had taken no more than was necessary to "conjure up" the original to parody it; and that it was "extremely unlikely that 2 Live Crew's song could adversely affect the market for the original."[ ] The District Court weighed these factors and held that 2 Live Crew's song made fair use of Orbison's original.[ ]

The Court of Appeals for the Sixth Circuit reversed and remanded. 972 F.2d 1429, 1439 (1992). Although it assumed for the purpose of its opinion that 2 Live Crew's song was a parody of the Orbison original, the Court of Appeals thought the District Court had put too little emphasis on the fact that "every commercial use is presumptively . . . unfair," *Sony Corp. of America v. Universal City Studios, Inc.*, 464 U.S. 417, 451 (1984), and it held that "the admittedly commercial nature" of the parody "requires the conclusion" that the first of four factors relevant under the statute weighs against a finding of fair use.[ ] Next, the Court of Appeals determined that, by "taking the heart of the original and making it the heart of a new work," 2 Live Crew had, qualitatively, taken too much.[ ] Finally, after noting that the effect on the potential market for the original (and the market for derivative works) is "undoubtedly the single most important element of fair use," *Harper & Row, Publishers, Inc. v. Nation Enterprises*, 471 U.S. 539, 566 (1985), the Court of Appeals faulted the District Court for "refus[ing] to indulge the presumption" that "harm for purposes of the fair use analysis has been established by the presumption attaching to commercial uses."[ ] In sum, the court concluded that its "blatantly commercial purpose prevents this parody from being a fair use."[ ]

We granted certiorari, 507 U.S. __ (1993), to determine whether 2 Live Crew's commercial parody could be a fair use.

II

☐ It is uncontested here that 2 Live Crew's song would be an infringement of Acuff-Rose's rights in "Oh, Pretty Woman," under the Copyright Act of 1976, 17 U.S.C. 106 (1988 ed. and Supp. IV), but for a finding of fair use through parody. From the infancy of copyright protection, some opportunity for fair use of copyrighted materials has been thought necessary to fulfill copyright's very purpose, "[t]o promote the Progress of Science and useful Arts" . . . U.S. Const., Art. I, 8, cl. 8. For as Justice Story explained, "[i]n truth, in literature, in science and in art, there are, and can be, few, if any, things which in an abstract sense, are strictly new and original throughout. Every book in literature, science and art, borrows, and must necessarily borrow, and use much which was well known and used before." *Emerson v Davies, 8 F. Cas. 615, 619 (No. 4,436) (CCD Mass. 1845)*. Similarly, Lord Ellenborough expressed the inherent tension in the need simultaneously to protect copyrighted material and to allow others to build upon it when he wrote, "while I shall think myself bound to secure every man in the enjoyment of his copyright, one must not put manacles upon science." *Carey v Kearsley, 4 Esp. 168, 170, 170 Eng. Rep. 679, 681 (K.B. 1803).* In copyright cases brought under the Statute of Anne of 1710, English courts held that in some instances "fair abridgements" would not infringe an author's rights,[ ] and although the First Congress enacted our initial copyright statute, Act of May 31, 1790, 1 Stat. 124. without any explicit reference to "fair use," as it later came to be known, the doctrine was recognized by the American courts nonetheless. . . .

A

☐ The first factor in a fair use enquiry is "the purpose and character of the use, including whether such use is of a commercial nature or is for nonprofit educational purposes." 107(1) . . .

This Court has only once before even considered whether parody may be fair use, and that time issued no opinion because of the Court's equal division. *Benny v. Loew's Inc., 239 F.2d 532 (CA9 1956), aff'd sub nom. Columbia Broadcasting System, Inc. v. Loew's Inc., 356 U.S. 43 (1958).* Suffice it to say now that parody has an obvious claim to transformative value, as Acuff-Rose itself does not deny. Like less ostensibly humorous forms of criticism, it can provide social benefit, by shedding light on an earlier work, and, in the process, creating a new one. We thus line up with the courts that have held that parody, like other comment or criticism, may claim fair use under 107 . . .

The fact that parody can claim legitimacy for some appropriation does not, of course, tell either parodist or judge much about where to draw the line. Like a book review quoting the copyrighted material criticized, parody may or may not be fair use, and petitioner's suggestion that any parodic use is presumptively fair has no more justification in law or fact than the equally hopeful claim that any use for news reporting should be presumed fair, *see Harper & Row, 471 U.S., at 561.* The Act has no hint of an evidentiary preference for parodists over their victims, and no workable presumption for parody could take account of the fact that parody often shades into satire when society is lampooned through its creative artifacts, or that a work may contain both parodic and nonparodic elements. Accordingly, parody, like any other use, has to work its way through the relevant factors, and be judged case by case, in light of the ends of the copyright law. . . .

While we might not assign a high rank to the parodic element here, we think it fair to say that 2 Live Crew's song reasonably could be perceived as commenting on the original or criticizing it, to some degree. 2 Live Crew juxtaposes the romantic musings of a man whose fantasy comes true, with degrading taunts, a bawdy demand for sex, and a sigh of relief from paternal responsibility. The later words can be taken as a comment on the naivete of the original of an earlier day, as a rejection of its sentiment that ignores the ugliness of street life and the debasement that it signifies. It is this joinder of reference and ridicule that marks off the author's choice of parody from the other types of comment and criticism that traditionally have had a claim to fair use protection as transformative works . . .

B

☐ The second statutory factor, "the nature of the copyrighted work," 107(2), draws on Justice Story's expression, the "value of the materials used." *Folsom v. Marsh, 9 F. Cas.,* at *348.* This factor calls for recognition that some works are closer to the core of intended copyright protection than others, with the consequence that fair use is more difficult to establish when the former works are copied. . . . We agree with both the District Court and the Court of Appeals that the Orbison original's creative expression for public dissemination falls within the core of the copyright's protective purposes. *754 F.Supp.,* at *1155–1156; 972 F.2d. at 1437.* This fact, however, is not much help in this case, or ever likely to help much in separating the fair use sheep from the infringing goats in a parody case, since parodies almost invariably copy publicly known, expressive works.

C

☐ The third factor asks whether "the amount and substantiality of the portion used in relation to the copyrighted work as a whole . . . are reasonable in relation to the purpose of the copying. Here, attention turns to the persuasiveness of a parodist's justification for the particular copying done, and the enquiry will harken back to the first of the statutory factors, for, as in prior cases, we recognize that the extent of permissible copying varies with the purpose and character of the use . . .

In *Harper & Row,* for example, *The Nation* had taken only some 300 words out of President Ford's memoirs, but we signalled the significance of the quotations in finding them to amount to "the heart of the book," the part most likely to be newsworthy and important in licensing serialization. 471 U.S., at 564–566. 568 (internal quotation marks omitted). We also agree with the Court of Appeals that whether a substantial portion of the infringing work was copied verbatim from the copyrighted work is a relevant question. . . .

Where we part company with the court below is in applying these guides to parody, and in particular to parody in the song before us. Parody presents a difficult case. Parody's humor, or in any event its comment, necessarily springs from recognizable allusion to its object through distorted imitation. Its art lies in the tension between a known original and its parodic twin. When parody takes aim at a particular original work, the parody must be able to "conjure up" at least enough of that original to make the object of its critical wit recognizable . . . It is true, of course, that 2 Live Crew copied the characteristic opening bass riff (or musical phrase) of the original, and true that the words of the first line copy the Orbison lyrics. But if quotation of the opening riff and the first line may be said to go to the "heart" of the original, the heart is also what most readily conjures up the song for parody, and it is the heart at which parody takes aim. . . . If 2 Live Crew had copied a significantly less memorable part of the original, it is difficult to see bow its parodic character would have come through.[ ]

This is not, of course, to say that anyone who calls himself a parodist can skim the cream and get away scot free . . . It is significant that 2 Live Crew not only copied the first line of the original, but thereafter departed markedly from the Orbison lyrics for its own ends. 2 Live Crew not only copied the bass riff and repeated it, but also produced otherwise distinctive sounds, interposing "scraper" noise, overlaying the music with solos in different keys, and altering the drum beat . . .

D

☐ The fourth fair use factor is "the effect of the use upon the potential market for or value of the copyrighted work." 107(4) . . . The court reasoned that because "the use of the copyrighted work is wholly commercial, . . . we presume a likelihood of future harm to Acuff-Rose exists." . . . In so doing, the court resolved the fourth factor against 2 Live Crew, just as it had the first, by applying a presumption about the effect of commercial use, a presumption which as applied here we hold to be error. . . .

We do not, of course, suggest that a parody may not harm the market at all, but when a lethal parody, like a scathing theater review, kills demand for the original, it does not produce a harm cognizable under the Copyright Act. Because "parody may quite legitimately aim at garroting the original, destroying it commercially as well as artistically,"[ ] the role of the courts is to distinguish between "[b]iting criticism [that merely] suppresses demand [and] copyright infringement[, which] usurps it. . . .''

Although 2 Live Crew submitted uncontroverted affidavits on the question of market harm to the original, neither they, nor Acuff-Rose, introduced evidence or affidavits addressing the likely effect of 2 Live Crew's parodic rap song on the market for a non-parody, rap version of "Oh, Pretty Woman." And while Acuff-Rose would have us find evidence of a rap market in the very facts that 2 Live Crew recorded a rap parody of

"Oh, Pretty Woman" and another rap group sought a license to record a rap derivative, there was no evidence that a potential rap market was harmed in any way by 2 Live Crew's parody, rap version. The fact that 2 Live Crew's parody sold as part of a collection of rap songs says very little about the parody's effect on a market for a rap version of the original, either of the music alone or of the music with its lyrics.

III

☐ It was error for the Court of Appeals to conclude that the commercial nature of 2 Live Crew's parody of "Oh, Pretty Woman" rendered it presumptively unfair. No such evidentiary presumption is available to address either the first factor, the character and purpose of the use, or the fourth, market harm, in determining whether a transformative use, such as parody, is a fair one. The court also erred in holding that 2 Live Crew had necessarily copied excessively from the Orbison original, considering the parodic purpose of the use. We therefore reverse the judgment of the Court of Appeals and remand for further proceedings consistent with this opinion.

It is so ordered.

Appendix A

☐ "Oh, Pretty Woman" by Roy Orbison and William Dees

Pretty Woman, walking down the street.
Pretty Woman, the kind I like to meet,
Pretty Woman, I don't believe you, you're not the truth.
No one could look as good as you
Mercy
Pretty Woman, won't you pardon me,
Pretty Woman, I couldn't help but see,
Pretty Woman, that you look lovely as can be
Are you lonely just like me?
Pretty Woman, stop a while,
Pretty Woman, talk a while,
Pretty Woman, give your smile to me
Pretty Woman, yeah, yeah, yeah
Pretty Woman, look my way,
Pretty Woman, say you'll stay with me
'Cause I need you, I'll treat you right
Come to me baby, Be mine tonight
Pretty Woman, don't walk on by,
Pretty Woman, don't make me cry,
Pretty Woman, don't walk away,
Hey, O.K.

If that's the way it must be, O.K.
I guess I'll go on home, it's late
There'll be tomorrow night, but wait!
What do I see
Is she walking back to me?
Yeah, she's walking back to me!
Oh, Pretty Woman.

Appendix B

☐   "Pretty Woman" as Recorded by 2 Live Crew

Pretty woman walkin' down the street
Pretty woman girl you look so sweet
Pretty woman you bring me down to that knee
Pretty woman you make me wanna beg please
Oh, pretty woman
Big hairy woman you need to shave that stuff
Big hairy woman you know I bet it's tough
Big hairy woman all that hair it ain't legit
'Cause you look like 'Cousin It'
Big hairy woman
Bald headed woman girl your hair won't grow
Bald headed woman you got a teeny weeny afro
Bald headed woman you know your hair could look nice
Bald headed woman first you got to roll it with rice
Bald headed woman here, let me get this hunk of biz for ya
Ya know what I'm saying you look better than rice a roni
Oh bald headed woman
Big hairy woman come on in
And don't forget your bald headed friend
Hey pretty woman let the boys
Jump in
Two timin' woman girl you know you ain't right
Two timin' woman you's out with my boy last night
Two timin' woman that takes a load off my mind
Two timin' woman now I know the baby ain't mine
Oh, two timin' woman
Oh pretty woman

Music Rights

The electronic media are required to pay copyright holders for the music used in programming, continuity, and commercials. As discussed in Chapter 5, cable television pays royalties under a compulsory license to the Copyright Office for the programs it transmits. Broadcasters and cable operators also pay a license fee to the three major music performing rights organizations—American Society of Composers, Authors, and Publishers (ASCAP); Broadcast Music Incorporated (BMI); and Society of European Stage Actors and Composers (SESAC). Electronic media organizations wishing to use music as part of their programming usually enter into an agreement for performance rights with these organizations. The fee paid is based on the market size of the medium and the amount of music used.

Performance, Synchronization, and Mechanical Rights

It is important to realize that any transmission of copyrighted music requires a license from a performing rights organization. If music will be used as part of a commercial, or in conjunction with film or videotape, additional rights must be secured. Synchronization rights must be secured for jingles and commercial uses of music, or when music is integrated with video or film. Mechanical rights must be secured if the product is to be duplicated and distributed as a recording or tape. Synchronization and mechanical rights may be obtained by contacting the Harry Fox Agency, 711 Third Avenue, New York, NY 10017. General information on obtaining a license from the Harry Fox Agency is available on the Web at http://www.mnpa.org/hfa/hfafaq.html.

Limits of the License

A performance license from ASCAP, BMI, or SESAC is generally granted with limited conditions. For example, a radio station's performing rights agreement applies only to music broadcast on the air. It does not cover uses such as "music on hold," when callers to the station hear the broadcast signal when their call is placed on hold. A separate license is required for this and other uses, such as DJ dance appearances and external promotions.

Another area that has generated attention is that of "storecasting." Until passage of the Fairness in Music Licensing Act of 1998, radio stations did not have the authority to grant permission to a retail establishment (or any other public venue) allowing broadcast of the station's signal, including music played, on the premises. With the passage of this legislation, retail establishments of less than 2000 square feet and food service or drinking establishments of not more than 3750 square feet, are permitted to play a nondramatic musical work being broadcast to the general public on their premises. This means a store or restaurant is free to play a radio or set up a television set, provided the devices are tuned to a broadcast, cable, or satellite service available to the general public. The act limits the number of speakers or monitors that may be located in any room and the size of any video screen to not more than 55 inches.[6] Music or video that is played from any other medium is subject to licensing.

Copyright and Digital Music

With the continued refinement of computer technology and the development of MP3 technology, new concerns over the distribution of copyrighted music via the Internet surfaced in late 1999. One of the early digital music services was Napster, and the events surrounding the growth and demise of this Internet song-swapping service laid the framework for a copyright battle that pitted digital audio technology against the limitations of the Copyright Act and the major record labels.

A&M Records Inc. et al. v. Napster Inc. No. 00-16401 DC No.CV-99-05183-MHP (February 12, 2001)

A&M Records et al. claim that Napster users engage in "wholesale reproduction and distribution of copyrighted work." Therefore, they are guilty of "direct infringement" under U.S. Copyright law. In order to prove direct infringement, A&M must show:

1. That it has ownership of the copyrighted material in question
2. That Napster violated at least one exclusive right granted to A&M

The District Court held that Napster did infringe directly by making it possible for users to download and upload copyrighted music. The District Court found that Napster infringed on two of A&M et al.'s rights:

1. Reproduction of copyrighted material (downloads)
2. Distribution of copyrighted material (uploads)

Napster's defense against these charges was fair use. The court disagreed.

The Fair Use Argument

The Nature of the Work—This focuses on whether the new work merely replaces the original creation or adds a "further purpose" or different character to the work. It asks whether the work is "transformative." The court held that Napster only replaces the original and therefore fails this part of the Fair Use test.

Noncommercial or Commercial—The court says Napster is a commercial use of copyrighted material. Napster users get for free something that they would otherwise have to purchase. Trading infringing copies for other items (i.e., other infringing copies) is a financially motivated transaction. Napster fails this aspect of the Fair Use Test.

Nature of the Use—Because music is a creative activity, it is less likely to be viewed as Fair Use than a fact-based work.

Portion Used—Although permitted Fair Use might include an entire work, the court says "copying an entire work militates against a finding of fair use." Napster fails this test.

Effect on Market—When properly applied, Fair Use does not materially impair the marketability of a copyrighted work. The District Court found that Napster harmed the market as follows:

1. It reduces sales of CD's among college students.
2. It raises barriers to the record companies entry to the digital downloading market.

In reaching this conclusion, the Court cited three studies: the Jay Report, the Fine Report, and the Teece Report. Dr. Deborah Jay sampled college students' music buying habits and found evidence of lost CD sales because of students' use of Napster. Michael Fine, CEO of SoundScan, noted a loss in "album sales" as a result of online file sharing. Finally, David Teece, an expert witness for the record companies, filed a report stating that the companies were likely to suffer harm in their existing and planned businesses because of Napster.

Napster asked the Court to consider testimony from their expert witness, Dr. Peter Fader. Fader had concluded that Napster was beneficial to the music industry because sharing MP3 files "stimulates more CD sales than it displaces." The District Court discounted Fader's testimony because of concerns over his methodology and the administration of his survey.

The Court did cite the Jay, Fine, and Teece Reports as providing data used in reaching the final decision against Napster:

> Having digital downloads available for free on the Napster system
> necessarily harms the copyright holders' attempts to charge for the
> same downloads. Judge Patel did not abuse her discretion in reaching
> the above fair use conclusions, nor were the findings of fact with respect
> to fair use considerations clearly erroneous.

Sampling and Space Shifting as Fair Use

Napster also contends that space shifting is a fair use. The Court disagreed:

☐ Space-shifting occurs when a Napster user downloads MP3 music files in order to listen to music he already owns on audio CD. Napster asserts that we have already held that space-shifting of musical compositions and sound recordings is a fair use. See *Recording Indus. Ass'n of Am. v. Diamond Multimedia Sys., Inc.,* 180 F.3d 1072, 1079 (9th Cir. 1999) ("Rio [a portable MP3 player] merely makes copies in order to render portable, or 'space-shift,' those files that already reside on a user's hard drive. . . . Such copying is a paradigmatic noncommercial personal use."). See also generally *Sony,* 464 U.S. at 423 (holding that "time-shifting," where a video tape recorder owner records a television show for later viewing, is a fair use).

We conclude that the district court did not err when it refused to apply the "shifting" analyses of Sony and Diamond. Both Diamond and Sony are inapposite because the methods of shifting in these cases did not also simultaneously involve distribution of the copyrighted material to the general public; the time or space-shifting of copyrighted material exposed the material only to the original user. In Diamond, for example, the copyrighted music was transferred from the user's computer hard drive to the user's portable MP3 player. So too Sony, where "the majority of VCR purchasers . . . did not distribute taped television broadcasts, but merely enjoyed them at home." Conversely, it is obvious that once a user lists a copy of music he already owns on the Napster system in order to access the music from another location, the song becomes "available to millions of other individuals," not just the original CD owner.

The final Fair Use claim made by Napster was "permissive reproduction." The Court saw this as a "non-infringing" use and did not seek to enjoin that activity.

Record Companies Claims

The record companies made several claims against Napster. They are as follows:

Contributory Copyright Infringement—One who knowingly causes or contributes to the infringing conduct of another is guilty of this charge. The Court found that Napster fit this category:

☐ It is apparent from the record that Napster has knowledge, both actual and constructive. The district court found actual knowledge because: (1) a document authored by Napster co-founder Sean Parker mentioned "the need to remain ignorant of users' real names and IP addresses 'since they are exchanging pirated music' "; and (2) the Recording Industry Association of America ("RIAA") informed Napster of more than 12,000 infringing files, some of which are still available. 114 F. Supp. 2d at 918.

The district court found constructive knowledge because: (a) Napster executives have recording industry experience; (b) they have enforced intellectual property rights in other instances; (c) Napster executives have downloaded copyrighted songs from the system; and (d) they have promoted the site with "screen shots listing infringing files." Id. at 919. of direct infringement. Napster claims that it is nevertheless protected from contributory liability by the teaching of Sony Corp. v. Universal City Studios, Inc., 464 U.S. 417 (1984). We disagree. We observe that Napster's actual, specific knowledge of direct infringement renders Sony's holding of limited assistance to Napster.

. . . The court determined that for the operator to have sufficient knowledge, the copyright holder must "provide the necessary documentation to show there is likely infringement."

. . . The record supports the district court's finding that Napster has actual knowledge that specific infringing material is available using its system, that it could block access to the system by suppliers of the infringing material, and that it failed to remove the material.

. . . Under the facts as found by the district court, Napster materially contributes to the infringing activity . . . [T]he district court concluded that "[w]ithout the support services defendant provides, Napster users could not find and download the music they want with the ease of which defendant boasts." ("Napster is an integrated service designed to enable users to locate and download MP3 music files.") We agree that Napster provides "the site and facilities" for direct infringement. See Fonovisa, 76 F.3d at 264; cf. Netcom, 907 F. Supp. at 1372 ("Netcom will be liable for contributory infringement since its failure to cancel [a user's] infringing message and thereby stop an infringing copy from being distributed worldwide constitutes substantial participation.") The district court correctly applied the reasoning in Fonovisa, and properly found that Napster materially contributes to direct infringement.

We affirm the district court's conclusion that plaintiffs have demonstrated a likelihood of success on the merits of the contributory copyright infringement claim.

Vicarious Infringement—This violation occurs when one who has the right and ability to supervise an infringing activity and a financial interest in that activity refuses to do so. Financial benefit exists where the availability of the infringing material acts as a "draw" for the customers. The court noted that Napster's future revenue is directly dependent on "increases in userbase." Therefore, there is a financial interest in signing up subscribers who are "infringers."

The District Court also determined that Napster had a "right and ability" to supervise the conduct of its users. The Circuit Court agreed in part, but cited the limitations of Napster's system as making control difficult:

☐ . . . Napster's reserved "right and ability" to police is cabined by the system's current architecture. As shown by the record, the Napster system does not "read" the content of indexed files, other than to check that they are in the proper MP3 format.

Napster, however, has the ability to locate infringing material listed on its search indices, and the right to terminate users' access to the system. The file name indices, therefore, are within the "premises" that Napster has the ability to police. We recognize that the files are user-named and may not match copyrighted material exactly (for example, the artist or song could be spelled wrong). For Napster to function effectively, however, file names must reasonably or roughly correspond to the material contained in the files, otherwise no user could ever locate any desired music. As a practical matter, Napster, its users and the record company plaintiffs have equal access to infringing material by employing Napster's "search function."

Our review of the record requires us to accept the district court's conclusion that plaintiffs have demonstrated a likelihood of success on the merits of the vicarious copyright infringement claim. Napster's failure to police the system's "premises," combined with a showing that Napster financially benefits from the continuing availability of infringing files on its system, leads to the imposition of vicarious liability.

Despite these limitations, the court held that Napster has a duty to "police the system's premises." This failure, along with Napster's financial interest in continuing to make infringing files available to users, served as the basis for the Court's finding for vicarious liability against Napster.

Napster's Other Defenses against the Injunction

Napster argued that the Audio Home Recording Act of 1992 and Section 512 of the Digital Millennium Copyright Act (DMCA) afforded protection for the service. The Court rejected both defenses. Below is the rationale for how both defenses were addressed.

Audio Home Recording Act of 1992—The Audio Home Recording Act of 1992 allows the noncommercial distribution of digital audio recordings. Napster argued that MP3 falls into this category. The Court rejected this contention on grounds that audio home recording does not cover downloading

MP3 files from computer hard drives. The Copyright Office filed *amicus curiae* brief in the Napster case noting:

☐ Napster asserts that Section 1008 of the Audio Home Recording Act provides its users with immunity from liability for copyright infringement and, in so doing, relieves Napster itself from any derivative liability for contributory or vicarious infringement. The district court was correct to reject that defense. Napster's invocation of Section 1008 is flatly inconsistent with the terms of the statute and the legislative policies that underlie the AHRA. Accordingly, if Napster is otherwise liable under the copyright laws, Section 1008 does not relieve Napster of liability. . . .

Napster's Users Are Not Making "Digital Musical Recordings" or "Analog Musical Recordings"

☐ Section 1008 protects the noncommercial consumer use of digital and analog recording devices and media for making "digital musical recordings or analog musical recordings." 17 U.S.C. § 1008. Even if Napster's users were using the specified devices or media, they are not making "digital musical recordings" or "analog musical recordings." Their activities fall outside the scope of Section 1008 for that reason as well.

The Act defines a "digital musical recording" as "a material object . . . in which are fixed, in a digital recording format, *only* sounds, and material, statements, or instructions incidental to those fixed sounds, if any. . . ." 17 U.S.C. § 1001(5)(A)(i) (emphasis added). The definition goes on to exclude, among other things, "a material object . . . in which one or more computer programs are fixed. . . ." *Id.* § 1001(5)(B)(ii).

Napster's users copy music files to their computers' hard drives. Hard drives store data of all kinds, from word processing files to multimedia files, and they ordinarily store computer programs as well. As a result, hard drives fall outside the statutory definition of "digital musical recording" in two respects: first, they are not objects in which "only sounds" are "fixed," and second, they are objects in which "one or more computer programs are fixed." See *Diamond Multimedia*, 180 F.3d at 1076 ("a hard drive is a material object in which one or more programs are fixed; thus, a hard drive is excluded from the definition of digital musical recordings").

Unlike "digital musical recording," "analog musical recording" is not a defined term under the Act. However, just as a computer's hard drive cannot be an "analog recording medium" (see p. 15 *supra*), neither can it be (or be used to store) an "analog musical recording," because hard drives store data in digital rather than analog form. Thus, Napster's users cannot be claimed to be making either "digital musical recordings" or "analog musical recordings"—and if a consumer is not making a digital or analog musical recording, the terms of Section 1008 do not provide him with any immunity.

. . . Section 1008 Provides Immunity Only for Noncommercial Copying, Not for Public Distribution

The Copyright Act grants the owner of a copyright a number of distinct legal rights. See 17 U.S.C. § 106(1)–(5). The most widely known right is the right of *reproduction*—the "exclusive right . . . to reproduce the copyrighted work in copies or phonorecords." *Id.* § 106(1). However, the Copyright Act also grants the copyright holder a separate and distinct right of *public distribution*—the "exclusive right . . . to distribute copies or phonorecords of the copyrighted work to the public by sale or other transfer of ownership, or by rental, lease, or lending." *Id.* § 106(3).

The plaintiffs assert not only infringements on the right of reproduction, but also infringements on the right of public distribution. In the proceedings below, Napster stated that it has at least 20 million users, all of whom are able to use Napster's service to access and download music files containing copyrighted sound recordings. When a Napster user makes the music files on his or her hard drive available for downloading by other Napster users, he or she is distributing the files to the public at large. *Cf. Michaels v. Internet Entertainment Group, Inc.*, 5 F. Supp. 2d 823, 830–31 (C.D. Cal. 1998); *Playboy Enterprises, Inc. v. Webbworld, Inc.*, 991 F. Supp. 543, 551 (N.D. Tex. 1997), *aff'd mem.*, 168 F.3d 486 (5th Cir. 1999); *Marobie-Fl, Inc. v. Nat'l Ass'n of Fire and Equip. Distributors and Northwest Nexus, Inc.*, 983 F.Supp. 1167, 1173 (N.D. Ill. 1997).

To the extent that Napster users are engaged in the distribution of copyrighted works to the public at large, such activity falls outside the scope of Section 1008. The language of Section 1008 is directed at uses that infringe on the right of reproduction, not at uses that infringe on the right of public distribution. By its terms, Section 1008 only bars infringement actions "based on the noncommercial use" of the specified products "for making digital musical recordings or analog musical recordings"—in other words, for making copies of the music. Section 1008 makes no reference, and provides no possible defense, to infringement claims based on the public distribution of copied works. Thus, even if it were proper to treat the use of Napster's service for the public dissemination of copyrighted music as a "noncommercial" consumer use, which is far from clear, it is not the use at which the terms of Section 1008 are directed—the "making [of] digital musical recordings or analog musical recordings."

4. Section 1008 Does Not Transform Infringing Consumer Uses Into NonInfringing Ones

As the foregoing discussion shows, the language of Section 1008 cannot be read to encompass the activities of Napster's users. But even if Section 1008 did apply to Napster's users, it would not provide Napster itself with a defense to liability for contributory or vicarious infringement. That is because the terms of Section 1008 address only whether consumers can be *sued* for infringement; nothing in Section 1008 addresses or changes whether they are *engaged* in infringement.

Digital Millennium Copyright Act § 512—This section provides a "safe harbor" for Internet Service Providers (ISP) from infringement suits, provided that the ISP lacks "requisite knowledge" of infringing activity. The District Court was not persuaded by Napster's argument, however it left the matter to be settled at trial.

☐   "Napster also interposes a statutory limitation on liability by asserting the protections of the "safe harbor" from copyright infringement suits for "Internet service providers" contained in the Digital Millennium Copyright Act, 17 U.S.C. § 512. See Napster, 114 F. Supp. 2d at 919 n.24. The district court did not give this statutory limitation any weight favoring a denial of temporary injunctive relief. The court concluded that Napster "has failed to persuade this court that subsection 512(d) shelters contributory infringers." Id.

We need not accept a blanket conclusion that § 512 of the Digital Millennium Copyright Act will never protect secondary infringers. See S. Rep. 105–190, at 40 (1998) ("The limitations in subsections (a) through (d) protect qualifying service providers from liability for all monetary relief for direct, vicarious, and contributory infringement."), reprinted in Melville B. Nimmer & David Nimmer, *Nimmer on Copyright: Congressional Committee Reports on the Digital Millennium Copyright Act and Concurrent Amendments* (2000); see also Charles S. Wright, *Actual versus Legal Control: Reading Vicarious Liability for Copyright Infringement into the Digital Millennium Copyright Act of 1998*, 75 Wash. L. Rev. 1005, 1028–31 (July 2000) ("[T]he committee reports leave no doubt that Congress intended to provide some relief from vicarious liability").

We do not agree that Napster's potential liability for contributory and vicarious infringement renders the Digital Millennium Copyright Act inapplicable per se. We instead recognize that this issue will be more fully developed at trial.

Section 512 provides limitations on liability for copyright infringement based on four categories:

1. Transitory communications
2. System caching
3. Storage of information on systems or networks at the direction of users
4. Information location tools

Each limitation bans monetary damages and restricts injunctive relief [§ 512 (j)]. If a service provider does not qualify for any of the limitations in § 512, the service is not necessarily liable for copyright infringement. The copyright owner must demonstrate that the provider has infringed. Napster may also avail itself of any other defenses, like fair use. [§ 512(h)]

§ 512© of the DMCA limits the liability of service providers for infringing material as long as:

1. The provider does not have a requisite level of knowledge of the infringing activity as follows:
2. If the provider has the right and ability to control the infringing activity it must not receive a financial benefit directly from the infringing activity.
3. When properly notified of infringing activity the provider must take down or block access to the channel.

All of these are key elements in the Napster decision. Additionally, the record companies raised the following questions relevant to the DMCA and Napster:

☐ (1) whether Napster is an Internet service provider as defined by 17 U.S.C. § 512(d); (2) whether copyright owners must give a service provider "official" notice of infringing activity in order for it to have knowledge or awareness of infringing activity on its system; and (3) whether Napster complies with § 512(i), which requires a service provider to timely establish a detailed copyright compliance policy. See *A&M Records, Inc. v. Napster, Inc.*, No. 99-05183, 2000 WL 573136 (N.D. Cal. May 12, 2000) (denying summary judgment to Napster under a different subsection of the Digital Millennium Copyright Act, § 512(a)).

The district court considered ample evidence to support its determination that the balance of hardships tips in plaintiffs' favor: Any destruction of Napster, Inc. by a preliminary injunction is speculative compared to the statistical evidence of massive, unauthorized downloading and uploading of plaintiffs' copyrighted works—as many as 10,000 files per second by defendant's own admission. The court has every reason to believe that, without a preliminary injunction, these numbers will mushroom as Napster users, and newcomers attracted by the publicity, scramble to obtain as much free music as possible before trial.

Napster argued that it never "knowingly provided customers with technology designed to copy and distribute MP3 files over the Internet, and as a result, waived any legal authority to exercise control as required in § 512(c)." Incredibly, Napster further blamed the record companies for "creating the monster that is now devouring their intellectual property rights." The Court of Appeals disagreed. Napster further argued:

☐   ... [T]hat plaintiffs granted the company an implied license by encouraging MP3 file exchange over the Internet. Courts have found implied licenses only in "narrow" circumstances where one party "created a work at [the other's] request and handed it over, intending that [the other] copy and distribute it." *SmithKline Beecham Consumer Healthcare, L.P. v. Watson Pharms., Inc., 211 F.3d 21, 25 (2d Cir. 2000)* (quoting *Effects Assocs., Inc. v. Cohen, 908 F.2d 555, 558 (9th Cir. 1990)), cert. denied, 121 S. Ct. 173 (2000)*. The district court observed that no evidence exists to support this defense: "indeed, the RIAA gave defendant express notice that it objected to the availability of its members' copyrighted music on Napster." *Napster, 114 F. Supp. 2d at 924–25*. The record supports this conclusion.

Misuse of Copyright Monopoly

Finally, Napster argued that the record companies "misused" their copyright authority by seeking protection beyond the bounds intended by the Copyright Act. Napster contended that online music distribution was not within the "copyright monopoly." The courts disagreed:

☐   The defense of copyright misuse forbids a copyright holder from "secur[ing] an exclusive right or limited monopoly not granted by the Copyright Office." *Lasercomb Am., Inc. v. Reynolds, 911 F.2d 970, 977–79 (4th Cir. 1990)*, quoted in *Practice Mgmt. Info. Corp. v. American Med. Ass'n, 121 F.3d 516, 520 (9th Cir.)*, amended by *133 F.3d 1140 (9th Cir. 1997)*. Napster alleges that online distribution is not within the copyright monopoly. According to Napster, plaintiffs have colluded to "use their copyrights to extend their control to online distributions."
      We find no error in the district court's preliminary rejection of this affirmative defense. The misuse defense prevents copyright holders from leveraging their limited monopoly to allow them control of areas outside the monopoly. See *Lasercomb, 911 F.2d 970 at 976–77*; see also *Religious Tech. Ctr. v. Lerma, No. 95-1107A, 1996 WL 633131, at *11 (E.D. Va. Oct. 4,*

1996) (listing circumstances which indicate improper leverage). The district court correctly stated that "most of the cases" that recognize the affirmative defense of copyright misuse involve unduly restrictive licensing schemes. See *Napster*, 114 F. Supp. 2d at 923; see also *Lasercomb*, 911 F.2d at 973 (stating that "a misuse of copyright defense is inherent in the law of copyright"). We have also suggested, however, that a unilateral refusal to license a copyright may constitute wrongful exclusionary conduct giving rise to a claim of misuse, but assume that the "desire to exclude others . . . is a presumptively valid business justification for any immediate harm to consumers." See *Image Tech. Servs. v. Eastman Kodak Co., 125 F.3d 1195, 1218 (9th Cir. 1997).* But see *Intergraph Corp. v. Intel Corp., 195 F.3d 1346, 1362 (Fed. Cir. 1999)* ("[M]arket power does not 'impose on the intellectual property owner an obligation to license the use of that property to others.'" (quoting United States Dep't of Justice & Fed. Trade Comm'n, Antitrust Guidelines for the Licensing of Intellectual Property 4 (1995)). There is no evidence here that plaintiffs seek to control areas outside of their grant of monopoly. Rather, plaintiffs seek to control reproduction and distribution of their copyrighted works, exclusive rights of copyright holders. 17 U.S.C. § 106; see also, e.g., *UMG Recordings*, 92 F. Supp. 2d at 351 ("A [copyright holder's] 'exclusive' rights, derived from the Constitution and the Copyright Act, include the right, within broad limits, to curb the development of such a derivative market by refusing to license a copyrighted work or by doing so only on terms the copyright owner finds acceptable."). That the copyrighted works are transmitted in another medium—MP3 format rather than audio CD—has no bearing on our analysis. See id. at 351 (finding that reproduction of audio CD into MP3 format does not "transform" the work).

The Decision

The Ninth Circuit Court of Appeals modified the injunction issued by the District Court.

☐ The district court correctly recognized that a preliminary injunction against Napster's participation in copyright infringement is not only warranted but required. We believe, however, that the scope of the injunction needs modification in light of our opinion. Specifically, we reiterate that contributory liability may potentially be imposed only to the extent that Napster: (1) receives reasonable knowledge of specific infringing files with copyrighted musical compositions and sound recordings; (2) knows or should know that such files are available on the Napster system; and (3) fails to act to prevent viral distribution of the works. See *Netcom*, 907 F. Supp. at 1374–75. *The mere existence of the Napster system, absent actual notice and Napster's demonstrated failure to remove the offending material, is insufficient to impose contributory liability.* [Emphasis added.] See *Sony*, 464 U.S. at 442–43.

Conversely, Napster may be vicariously liable when it fails to affirmatively use its ability to patrol its system and preclude access to potentially infringing files listed in its search index. Napster has both the ability to use its search function to identify infringing musical recordings and the right to bar participation of users who engage in the transmission of infringing files.

The preliminary injunction which we stayed is overbroad because it places on Napster the entire burden of ensuring that no "copying, downloading, uploading, transmitting, or distributing" of plaintiffs' works occur on the system. As stated, we place the burden on plaintiffs to provide notice to Napster of copyrighted works and files containing such works available on the Napster system before Napster has the duty to disable access to the offending content. Napster, however, also bears the burden of policing the system within the limits of the system. Here, we recognize that this is not an exact science in that the files are user named. In crafting the injunction on remand, the district court should recognize that Napster's system does not currently appear to allow Napster access to users' MP3 files.

Based on our decision to remand, Napster's additional arguments on appeal going to the scope of the injunction need not be addressed.

Lastly, the Court put to rest any First Amendment claims raised by Napster in this case. Napster had asserted two First Amendment issues:

1. The right to publish a "directory," that is a search index, and
2. Napster user's right to exchange information.

The Court rejected Napster's First Amendment claims on the grounds that the Fair Use Doctrine allays all First Amendment claims in copyright, and since Napster was not a "fair user," it could not claim First Amendment privilege.

☐ We, however, briefly address Napster's First Amendment argument so that it is not reasserted on remand. Napster contends that the present injunction violates the First Amendment because it is broader than necessary. The company asserts two distinct free speech rights: (1) its right to publish a "directory" (here, the search index), and (2) its users' right to exchange information. We note that First Amendment concerns in copyright are allayed by the presence of the fair use doctrine. See 17 U.S.C. § 107; see generally *Nihon Keizai Shimbun v. Comline Business Data,*

Inc., 166 F.3d 65, 74 (2d Cir. 1999); *Netcom*, 923 F. Supp. at 1258 (stating that the Copyright Act balances First Amendment concerns with the rights of copyright holders). There was a preliminary determination here that Napster users are not fair users. Uses of copyrighted material that are not fair uses are rightfully enjoined. See *Dr. Seuss Enters. v. Penguin Books USA, Inc.*, 109 F.3d 1394, 1403 (9th Cir. 1997) (rejecting defendants' claim that injunction would constitute a prior restraint in violation of the First Amendment).

Events after the Court of Appeals Ruling

As might have been expected, Napster reacted to the Court of Appeals decision by mounting a public relations campaign that included urging subscribers to "contact their representatives to let Congress know how much Napster means to them." Napster promised to do whatever it could to "work within the limits of the injunction to continue to provide the more than 50-million Napster community members access to music." Napster also continued discussions with the record companies, offering Sony, Warner, BMG, EMI, and Universal $150 million annually for five years and $50 million to independent labels if they would settle the suit. This public relations move was timed to coincide with the Grammy Awards. The record companies declined the offer.

In late February 2001, following the industry rebuff, Napster asked for a full hearing by the 25 justices of the Ninth Circuit. Napster contended that it did not get a fair hearing by the three-judge-panel, especially on the issue of "safe harbor" under § 512 of the Digital Millennium Copyright Act. The request, of course, went unheeded.

On March 6, Judge Patel asked the record companies to provide Napster with a list of copyrighted songs to remove from its service. Upon receipt of that list, Napster was given seventy-two hours to remove the offending material. Anticipating court action, Napster began removing songs on the weekend of March 3, but software and file identification problems slowed the process. Napster shut down in the Summer of 2001, with plans to re-emerge as a subscription-only service.

Conclusion

As a result of *Napster*, the courts and the Congress will be required to develop policy addressing the shortcomings of the Digital Millennium Copyright Act. As a result of *Napster*, the courts and U.S. Copyright Office have already reached conclusions on the applicability of the Online Recording Act of 1992 and Fair Use as applied to an online service provider.

Regardless of whether these conclusions stand the test of time, the *Napster* cases provided the fodder that led to the necessary examination of how current law applies to new technologies and services.

Streaming Music on the Web

In December 2000, the Copyright Office began requiring Internet radio stations to pay mechanical royalties to record companies for music that the stations stream over the Web; record companies often protect their mechanical rights by marking music CDs with the letter "P" in a circle Ⓟ. Broadcasters challenged the requirement. In *Bonneville International Corporation, et al., v. Register of Copyrights* (DC E.Pa. No. 01-0408, August 1, 2001), the decision of the Copyright Office was upheld. This fee is different from the fee paid to the performing rights societies; it is paid directly to the record companies.

The *Bonneville* ruling also applies to Web-only "radio" broadcasters, however the formula for determining the amount of royalties due will likely differ from that of licensed AM or FM stations that stream Web audio. In February 2002, the Copyright Office proposed royalty rates for Internet transmissions of AM/FM radio broadcasts and for Internet-only transmissions. The proposed rate for an Internet-only station was $0.14 per song per performance per listener. In addition, a minimum fee of $500 per year was proposed for each licensee. In May 2002, the Register of Copyrights rejected this proposal. Current royalty rates are available online from the U.S. Copyright Office Website (http://www.loc.gov/copyright/carp/webcasting_rates.html).

Trademark and Service Mark

A trademark protects identifying symbols, words, or names associated with intellectual property. The legislation governing trademarks is the Federal Trademark Act of 1946, also known as the Lanham Act. Trademarks are registered with the United States Patent and Trademark Office. The notice that an intellectual property is protected by trademark is ® or ™.

To obtain a trademark registration, an application must be filed with the United States Patent and Trademark Office in Washington, DC. There is a filing fee for each trademark application. The applicant must state that there is a bona fide intention to use the mark in commerce or that the mark is already in use. Commercial trademark search firms may be engaged to assist applicants with determining whether a proposed trademark is already in use. Trademarks must be renewed every ten years.

Eligibility for Trademark Protection

Letters, groups of letters, graphics, type styles, characters, and names are all eligible for trademark (or service mark) protection. The Trademark Law Revision Act of 1988 made it easier for broadcasters to protect call letters and identifying slogans. Prior to 1983, the FCC mitigated disputes over such matters, but deregulation ended FCC intervention. Service marks include broadcast station call letters and identifying symbols and phrases. For example, "Q-95," "X-103," "The Fox," or "The Bear" may be registered within the geographic area served by the station. The same moniker may be trademarked by another station outside the geographic area. However, under a 1989 amendment to the Trademark Law, the mark may be registered for nationwide protection. Because frequencies are generic, they may not be protected. Phrases like "FM 95" or "AM 1230" could not be registered.

Distinctive names may be registered with the Trademark Office. "Billy Joel," "Chicago" (the pop group), and "Johnny Carson" are all registered trademarks.

A trademark must be distinctive to be registered. This means that generic terms may not be trademarked. "Poison" cannot be registered as a trademark for an insecticide product. However, a manufacturer of perfume can register "Poison" as a trademark; because there is no confusion as to the differences between the general term and the specific fragrance, this is permissible.

Protecting the Mark

Trademark and service mark owners may lose their protection if the trademark becomes generic. Such terms as aspirin and cellophane were once trademarks for a painkiller and a plastic material, respectively. Both fell into common usage as descriptive of all products similar to the original product. Companies such as Xerox and Coca-Cola go to great lengths to protect their trademarks. Xerox, for example, constantly reminds broadcasters that not all copies are Xerox copies and that Xerox is not a verb.

Offensive or immoral symbols may not be trademarked. The Trademark Office judges marks on their "primary meaning." If the primary meaning is judged offensive, a trademark cannot be registered. One can only imagine the extent to which would-be trademark holders have pushed this prohibition. A chicken restaurant submitted one particularly interesting phrase denied by the Trademark Office. The restaurant wanted to trademark the phrase, "Only a breast in the mouth is better than a leg in the hand."

Commercial Exploitation

The First Amendment protects noncommercial uses of trademarks when trademark uses are for purposes of editorial or artistic expression, as ruled in *L.L. Bean Inc. v. Drake Publishers Inc.* The Maine mail-order house objected to a parody of its catalog entitled the *L.L. Bean's-Back-to-School-Sex-Catalog* on grounds that the parody damaged its good name. The court ruled, however, that the parody was protected expression.

Moviemaker George Lucas objected to the use of his trademark "Star Wars" when describing the Reagan administration's space-based Strategic Defense Initiative. In *Lucasfilm Ltd. v. High Frontier*, the U.S. District Court for the District of Columbia rejected his claim of trademark infringement because the alleged use was noncommercial.

In cases where commercial exploitation has occurred, the courts have ruled against those who appropriate the reputations and styles of celebrities. For example, singer Tom Waits brought a successful trademark suit against Frito-Lay for misappropriation of his distinctive singing style in a snack food commercial. Waits contended that Frito-Lay had wrongfully used his professional trademark, his unique voice, and in so doing would injure him professionally. He was awarded $2.6 million in compensatory damages, punitive damages, and attorney's fees.

Finally, Apple Corps Limited, owner of trade names and trademarks of the Beatles music group, brought successful suit against a group performing as "1964 as The Beatles." The group's objective was to look and sound as much like the Beatles as possible, even referring to themselves as "John," "Paul," "George," and "Ringo" on stage. A U.S. District Court found the impersonation to be a violation of Tennessee's Personal Rights Protection Act and the Lanham Act. The defendants were permanently enjoined from (1) using the names "John," "Paul," "George," and "Ringo" in advertising or promoting their performances; (2) using any likeness of the group The Beatles, or any individual members thereof in promoting the defendant's performances; and (3) using the name "The Beatles" in promoting performances or products. The group could no longer call themselves "1964 as The Beatles."[7]

Copyright and the Internet

The proliferation and easy availability of material on the Internet has given rise to new issues surrounding copyright liability and the protection of original work. Although this is a developing area, there has been legislation and a good deal of case law addressing these issues. Indeed, case law has served as much of the impetus behind passage of the Online

Copyright Infringement Liability Act, enacted in October 1998. This act addresses the copyright liability of online service providers. The Online Copyright Infringement Liability Act essentially grants copyright immunity to service providers who exercise no editorial control over material available on individual sites carried on their service. It also exempts service providers from copyright liability during transmission, storage, "good faith" downloads, and posting of hyperlinks by those using their service.[8] Limitations on liability only apply if the service provider has designated an agent to receive notifications of claimed infringement by providing contact information for that agent to the Copyright Office and through the service provider's publicly accessible Website.[9]

Copyright Liability for Web Publishers

Although content providers are afforded some immunity under copyright law, authors of Web pages are treated differently. Generally, copyright law is applied to Web content in much the same way that it is applied to other publications and electronic transcriptions. A Web page is treated like a magazine or a CD, and copyright law protects original content. The ease with which material may be posted on a page, however, makes Internet publishing particularly susceptible to unauthorized use of copyrighted material. Taking pictures, graphics, text, video, or audio from another Web page and including them in your page is likely to violate copyright law. Web authors are advised to obtain permission before using such material. Similarly, using copyrighted or trademarked material from any source on your Web page should not be done without first obtaining permission from the owner of that material.

In *Playboy Enterprises Inc. v. Frena*, 839 F.Supp. 1552 (1993), the operator of an Internet subscription bulletin board service was guilty of copyright infringement when it downloaded photographs from *Playboy* magazine.

Simply creating a link to another page is a somewhat different situation. While "netiquette" dictates that you should seek permission before linking your site to someone else's, it is not illegal to do so. By placing a page on the Web, permission to access that page is implied. If another site provides a link to your Website, and you object to that linkage, there is little remedy save for your requesting that the link be removed.

Trademark and the Internet: Domain Names

The registration of domain names on the Internet has become a growing area of concern when those names are potential trademarks. Domain names (e.g., "mtv.com" or "burgerking.com") were originally registered by Network Solutions, Inc. (NSI) of Herndon, Virginia. Domain names were assigned on a first-come-first served basis.[10] This policy resulted in individuals registering domain names closely related to that of a business, in hopes of extorting money from the company as it seeks to obtain the domain name, a process called "cybersquatting." For example, an individual registered the domain name "mcdonalds.com" and was able to obtain a $3500 "ransom" from the fast food giant in exchange for relinquishing the name. The $3500 was in the form of a donation enabling a New York City school to obtain Internet access.[11]

In 1999 NSI's sole control of domain registration ended. That same year Congress passed the Anticybersquatting Piracy Act, 15 U.S.C. § 1125(d), which allowed plaintiffs to sue cybersquatters who register a name confusingly close to a registered trademark.

In an early test of the 1999 Anticybersquatting Consumer Protection Act (ACPA), Volkswagen challenged Virtual Works, Inc.'s use of the domain name "vw.net." Volkswagen argued that Virtual Works registered "vw.net" with the purpose of one day selling it to Volkswagen. The district court agreed, holding that Virtual Works had a bad faith intent to profit from the vw.net domain name and that its use of vw.net diluted and infringed upon the VW mark. (See *Virtual Works, Inc. v. Network Solutions, Inc.*, 106 F. Supp.2d 845 (E.D. Va. 2000).) The 4th Circuit Court of Appeals upheld the decision (see 00-1356).

First Amendment Issues

It has been a practice to refuse licensing domain names that are profane, vulgar, or otherwise offensive. This practice was challenged in *Seven Words LLC v. Network Solutions* (No. 99-56909, 9th Cir. 2001) and *Name.Space, Inc. v. Network Solutions Inc.* (No. 99-6080, 2nd Circuit 2000). The courts held that NSI did not violate the First Amendment when it refused to register a "vulgar" domain name.

Summary

The Copyright Act is found in Title 17 of the U.S. Code. A copyright provides protection from unauthorized use of original works of authorship, including literary, dramatic, musical, artistic, and certain other intellectual works.

The electronic media are required to pay copyright holders for the music used in programming, continuity, and commercials. Cable television pays royalties under a compulsory license to the Copyright Royalty Tribunal

(CRT) for the programs it transmits. Broadcasters and cable operators also pay a license fee to the three major music performing rights organizations—ASCAP, BMI, and SESAC. The Copyright Office requires Internet broadcasters to pay royalties to record companies for music streamed on the Web.

A trademark protects identifying symbols, words, or names associated with intellectual property. The legislation governing trademarks is the Federal Trademark Act of 1946, also known as the Lanham Act. Trademarks are registered with the United States Patent and Trademark Office.

Material posted on Internet Web pages is protected by copyright. Web authors are advised to obtain permission before using such material. Similarly, using copyrighted or trademarked material on your Web page from any source should not be done without first obtaining permission from the owner of that material.

The registration of domain names on the Internet is an area of recent controversy as applied to trademark law. The Anticybersquatting Piracy Act provides remedy for victims of cybersquatting.

Notes/References

1. *Copyright Basics*, Circular 1 (Washington, D.C.: Copyright Office, Library of Congress, 1987), 3.
2. S.505, Sonny Bono Copyright Term Extension Act, Sec 102 (B. Enacted October 27, 1998).
3. Ibid., (b) (1).
4. Ibid., (b)(3)(A) (B).
5. *Harper & Row Publishers, Inc. v. Nation Enterprises*, 471 U.S. 539 (1985).
6. S.505, Fairness in Music Licensing Act of 1998, Sec.202. Enacted October 27, 1998.
7. *Apple Corp Limited v. A.D.P.R. Inc.* (DC Mid.Tenn., 1993) 22 Med.L.Rptr at 1567.
8. Digital Millenium Copyright Act, Title II "Online Copyright Infringement Liability Limitation," Sec. 202 available at http://www.loc.gov/copyright (November, 19, 1998); see also 17 U.S.C. 512 (c).
9. "Designation of Agent to Receive Notification of Claimed Infringement," *Federal Register* Vol. 63:212 (November 3, 1998): 59234.
10. Andre Brunel, "Trademark Protection for Internet Domain Names," in *The Internet and Business: A Lawyer's Guide to Emerging Legal Issues* (Fairfax VA: Computer Law Association 1996, http://www.cla.org/RuhBook/chp3.htm, Feb.17, 1999), 2.
11. Ibid., 1.

Cases

A&M Records Inc. et al. v. Napster Inc. No. 00-16401 DC No.CV-99-05183-MHP (February 12, 2001)

Apple Corp Limited v. A.D.P.R. Inc. (DC Mid.Tenn., 1993) 22 Med.L.Rptr 1562

Baltimore Orioles v. Major League Baseball Players (CA 7, 1986) 13 Med.L.Rptr. 1625

Bonneville International Corporation et al. v. Register of Copyrights, DC E.Pa. No. 01-0408 (August 1, 2001)

Cher v. Forum International, Ltd., 692 F.2d 634 (9th Cir., 1982)

Eldred v. Ashcroft, 255 F.3d 849 (D.C.Cir.2001), cert.granted (U.S. Oct. 11, 2001).

Eldred v. Reno, 74 F.Supp.2d (D.D.C. 1999)

Eldred v. Reno, 239 F.3d (D.C.Cir.2001)

Harper & Row Publishers, Inc. v. Nation Enterprises, 471 U.S. 539 (1985)

Hoeling v. Universal Studios, 618 F.2d 972 (2nd Cir., 1980), cert. denied 499 U.S. 841 (1980)

Hustler v. Moral Majority (CA 9, 1986) 13 Med.L.Rptr. 1151

L.L. Bean Inc. v. Drake Publishers Inc. (CA 1, 1987) 13 Med.L.Rptr. 2009

Lucasfilm Ltd. v. High Frontier, 622 F.Supp 931 (DC DC, 1985)

Meerpol v. Nizer, 560 F.2d 1061 (2d Cir., 1977) 2 Med.L.Rptr. 2269, Cert. denied 434 U.S. 1013 (1978)

Midler v. Ford Motor Company, 849 F.2d 460 (9th Cir., 1988)

Name.Space, Inc. v. Network Solutions Inc. (No. 99-6080, 2nd Circuit 2000)

Pacific & Southern Co. v. Duncan (DC N.Ga., 1985) 12 Med.L.Rptr. 1221

Playboy Enterprises Inc. v. Frena, 839 F.Supp. 1552 (1993)

Production Contractors v. WGN Continental Broadcasting Co. (ND. Ill., 1985) 12 Med.L.Rptr. 1708

Salinger v. Random House Inc., 811 F.2d 90 (2d Cir., 1987) 13 Med.L.Rptr. 1954

Seven Words LLC v. Network Solutions (No. 99-56909, 9th Cir. 2001)

Sony Corp. v. Universal Studios Inc., 464 U.S. 417 (1984)

Tin Pan Apple v. Miller Brewing (DC So.NY, 1990) 17 Med.L.Rptr. 2273

Virtual Works, Inc. v. Network Solutions, Inc., 106 F. Supp.2d 845 (E.D. Va. 2000)

Waits v. Frito-Lay Inc. (CA 9,1992) 20 Med.L.Rptr. 1585

WCVB-TV v. Boston Athletic Association (CA 1, 1991) 18 Med.L.Rptr. 1710

9

□ □ □
□ □ □
□ □ □

Privacy and the
Electronic Media

Defamation changes the way society feels about an individual. Invasions of privacy change the way individuals feel about themselves. Today, invasion of privacy suits may be based on personal humiliation, shame, suffering, or emotional distress. Though defamation involves the communication of a falsehood, invasions of privacy may involve the publication of true but embarrassing facts. Other invasions of privacy include appropriation of a person's likeness for commercial gain, intrusion by cameras or other devices into the privacy of one's home or office, and the publication of material that places one in a "false light"—that is, appearing to do something that is embarrassing or socially unacceptable. False light is closest to defamation and is sometimes prosecuted as libel.

Most invasion of privacy suits against the media result from individuals who are caught up in newsworthy situations and object to the way their involvement in the event has been communicated by the media. In a majority of cases, responsible journalists prevail over individuals in court. When the news media cover a newsworthy event, most of the restraints placed on them are in the form of professional ethics rather than law. Though it may be revolting to see local TV news close-ups of persons mangled in an auto accident, nothing but good taste prevents a station from broadcasting such a scene. The only recourse is that if enough viewers object to this kind of news coverage, ratings will decline, thereby forcing an editorial policy change by management in the never-ending pursuit of viewers and advertising dollars.

Also of concern over the past two decades has been the protection from surveillance by government and other components of society. Advances in technology have allowed myriad users access to information about individuals. Organizations ranging from businesses to law enforcement agencies can easily retrieve information about a person's finances, legal and medical history, arrest records, sites visited on the Internet, and recent purchases, to name a few. Needless to say, many people are concerned about who is granted access to such information, how it can be used, and for what purposes. The Federal Privacy Act of 1974 was passed to deal with some of these issues. The Privacy Act defines how individuals are protected from government invasions of privacy and is discussed later in this chapter. The Electronic Communications Privacy Act of 1986 provides additional protection for electronic transmissions from third-party monitoring and interference.

Protection from privacy invasions by individuals and the news media developed in a way quite different from that of protection from government snooping.

The Development of Privacy Law

Although the concept of libel has its roots in English common law of the Middle Ages, the law of privacy is a nineteenth-century American development. Before 1890, no American court had recognized a right of privacy. One hundred years later, some right of privacy was recognized in almost all jurisdictions. To this day, the extent of our personal rights of privacy are not clearly delineated and remain somewhat controversial.

Although there were a few early nineteenth-century cases based on the nonexistent right to privacy, it was not until 1888 that Judge Cooley defined privacy as "the right to be let alone."[1] In 1890, an article entitled "The Right of Privacy" by Samuel D. Warren and future Supreme Court Justice Louis Brandeis was published in the *Harvard Law Review*. Although there is little evidence to support the assertion, the two Boston lawyers claim inspiration for the article from gossip in the press about the social affairs of the wealthy Warren family. Warren and Brandeis argued that the growing excesses of the press required the courts to consider granting private individuals protection against the hounding media.[2] In essence, "The Right of Privacy" attempted to establish a common law right of privacy using property rights, defamation, and breach of confidence as its basis. The authors argued that property owners should be allowed to apply the same right of protection of their houses and lands from trespass to the protection of their private lives. Warren and Brandeis wrote,

> Instantaneous photographs and newspaper enterprise have invaded the sacred precincts of private and domestic life and numerous mechanical devices threaten to make good the prediction that "what is whispered in the closet shall be proclaimed from the house-tops."
> . . . Gossip is no longer the resource of the idle and vicious, but has become a trade, which is pursued with industry as well as effrontery. . . .
> The intensity and complexity of life attendant upon an advancing civilization have rendered necessary some retreat from the world, and

man, under the refining influence of culture, has become more sensitive to publicity, so that solitude and privacy have become more essential to the individual; but modern enterprise and invention have, through invasions of his privacy, subjected him to mental pain and distress, far greater than could be inflicted by mere bodily injury.[3]

Although Brandeis and Warren protested the excesses of the press, they offered no specific evidence to support their claim. Nor did they deal with the problems that inevitably would result when this new privacy right came into conflict with the First Amendment right of a free press. Brandeis' biographer, Lewis Paper, summarizes the impact of the article:

> None of these defects seemed to matter much to readers. The reaction to the article was nothing short of incredible, lawyers read it, and courts relied on it—all to the seeming end of creating a new right to privacy. Twenty-six years after its publication, Dean Roscoe Pound of the Harvard Law School observed that the article "did nothing less than to add a chapter to our law." Subsequent scholars were just as impressed. One commentator referred to it as "the outstanding example of the influence of legal periodicals upon the American law." Another writer said that the article was "perhaps the most influential law journal piece ever published." In some sense all of this praise was justified. After all, concerns for privacy in part motivated the American Revolution, and there could be no doubt that protection of privacy was a central concern of the populace.[4]

Despite this critical acclaim, there was no great rush to enact privacy statutes across the country. In fact, the first major test of the theory in 1902 resulted in a New York appellate court ruling that found no common law right of privacy. Ironically, it was this ruling that gave New York the first statutory right of privacy in the United States.

In *Roberson v. Rochester Folding Box Co. (1902)*, a flour company lithographed a picture of a young woman—without her consent—on boxes of its brand of flour. She objected to the appearance of her likeness on flour boxes, noting that it violated her right of privacy. Although the lower courts in that state had earlier relied on the Warren and Brandeis article in upholding a right to privacy, the New York court of appeals rejected her claim.

Although this was what we now would call an "appropriation" case, and unrelated to the kind of privacy Warren and Brandeis outlined, Roberson generated enough controversy to prompt the New York legislature to act. *Manola v. Stevens* was the first case to allow recovery on the basis of a privacy claim. It enjoined an individual from publishing a photograph snapped from a box in the theater and picturing an actress "scandalously" attired in tights. In 1903, New York passed Section 50 of the state Civil Rights Law, making it unlawful to use people's names or likenesses for trade purposes without their consent.

Two years later, a Georgia court became the first to recognize a common law right to privacy. *Pavesich v. New England Life Insurance Co. (1905)* was similar to the *Roberson* case. A newspaper ad for the insurance company contained an unauthorized photograph of the plaintiff. The ad also attributed statements to him that urged the purchase of life insurance from the company. The Georgia Supreme Court ruled in favor of Pavesich and established that a common law right of privacy existed in that state.

It was not until the 1930s that there emerged in the states a pattern that favored the general recognition of a right to privacy. In 1965, the Supreme Court recognized a penumbral right to privacy in the First, Third, Fourth, and Ninth Amendments to the Constitution. In *Griswold v. Connecticut (1965)*, the Court struck down a state law making the use of contraceptives—even by married couples—a crime and upheld the right of Planned Parenthood to publish advice on their use. Justice Douglas wrote,

☐ [S]pecific guarantees in the Bill of Rights have penumbras, formed by emanations from those guarantees that help give them life and substance. Various guarantees create zones of privacy. The right of association contained in the First Amendment is one. . . . The Third Amendment in its prohibition against the quartering of soldiers . . . is another facet of that privacy. The Fourth Amendment explicitly affirms the "right of people to be secure in their persons, houses, papers, and effects, against unreasonable searches and seizures." The Fifth Amendment in its Self Incrimination Clause enables the citizen to create a zone of privacy which government may not force him to surrender to his detriment. The Ninth Amendment provides: "The enumeration in the Constitution, of certain rights, shall not be construed to deny or disparage others retained by the people."[5]

Although Douglas' opinion specifically addressed privacy invasions by the state, subsequent court decisions, including *Roe v. Wade (1973)*, which legalized abortions, recognized a right of personal privacy.

Today, most states recognize some common law or statutory right of privacy. Some states recognize very limited privacy rights, and there is no universal agreement in recognizing the categories of these rights.

Categories of Invasion of Privacy

Most jurisdictions recognize some or all of the four categories of privacy invasion originally developed by Dean William Prosser. Prosser was an expert on tort law and, through his studies, he organized the subject of invasions of privacy into four areas: appropriation, intrusion, embarrassing facts, and false light. You should check your state laws to determine which of these categories are recognized in your state.

Appropriation

Appropriation involves the use of a person's name or likeness for commercial gain. This form of the tort is the earliest to be recognized and has its roots in the *Roberson* case. The first privacy statute in New York was designed to deal with appropriation, as was the first common law decision in Georgia, as previously discussed.

Illegal appropriation occurs when consent is not obtained before using someone's name, picture, or likeness to advertise a product, to accompany an article sold, or to add "luster" to a company name. Courts have held, however, that the incidental use of a person's name or picture in a book, film, magazine, or other medium is not an invasion of privacy. If a name or likeness is not published for commercial gain, it cannot be appropriation. Therefore, the primary defenses against a claim of misappropriation are newsworthiness and consent. A signed release that shows that a person agreed to allow publication of his or her likeness for commercial gain will defeat a claim, provided that the publication has not been altered beyond the terms of the agreement.

Examples of the application of the law of appropriation include a television station's use of a photograph taken while the plaintiff was receiving emergency medical treatment (*Anderson v. Fisher Broadcasting Companies*). The photo was later used in an advertisement for the station's special news report. Although the plaintiff objected to the use of the picture, it was judged newsworthy by an Oregon court of appeals, hence, no misappropriation occurred. Similarly, in *Lawrence v. A. S. Abell Co.*, republication of a front-page photograph by *The Baltimore Evening Sun* of two children attending a festival in the city as part of the paper's advertising campaign was found not to be illegal appropriation. Finally, the players on the Baltimore Orioles baseball team could not prevent team owners from using portions of videotaped games in which they appeared. In *Baltimore Orioles v. Major League Baseball Players*, the Seventh Circuit Court ruled that the performances were "owned" by the teams—not the players—and that, essentially, consent had been given.

Right of Publicity

More recently, concern over what has come to be called the "right of publicity" has emerged. Most cases in this category involve entertainers, sports figures, and other well-known personalities whose actual names or likenesses, or that of characters they have created, are used to promote a product or other commercial gain.

When *Forum* magazine, a *Penthouse* magazine affiliate, borrowed from an exclusive interview with singer-entertainer Cher portions that were originally published in *Us* magazine and implied that Cher had also spoken with *Forum* reporters, a California court ruled that the singer's right of publicity had been misappropriated. In *Cher v. Forum International (1982)*, the court noted that a celebrity retains the right to control the publicity and establish conditions for the use of her or his name or likeness when she or he chooses voluntarily to give an "exclusive interview" to a particular publication.[6]

Similarly, in *Eastwood v. Superior Court*, actor Clint Eastwood had cause for action when a newspaper used without consent his name and photograph in the paper and in television ads that promoted a nondefamatory but nevertheless false article about the actor.

Author Jackie Collins' right of publicity was violated when *Adelina* magazine published her name on its cover under the heading "In the Nude from the Playmen Archives." Although the nude picture was not really Collins, in *Lerman v. Chuckleberry* the court ruled that the magazine had used Collins' name solely for the purpose of enhancing the sale of magazines, rather than for the purpose of informing the public about a newsworthy event.

In *Brinkley v. Casablancas*, model Christie Brinkley successfully sued for misappropriation of her right of publicity when an unauthorized pinup poster of her likeness was distributed in 1980. In *Onassis v. Christian Dior*, Jackie Onassis was successful in her claim against Christian Dior's advertising series that used a model who strongly resembled the former first lady to sell their line of clothing. Citing *Negri v. Schering*—in which silent film star Pola Negri objected to the publication of a scene from one of her movies so captioned as to appear that she endorsed use of the antihistamine drug Polaramine—the Supreme Court of New York noted that

☐   if a picture is a clear and identifiable likeness of a living person, he or she is entitled to recover damages suffered by reason of such use.[7]

Game show hostess Vanna White brought suit against Samsung Electronics for an advertisement featuring a robot posed next to a game board reminiscent of that used in *Wheel of Fortune*. The robot was dressed in a gown, wig, and jewelry resembling White's appearance on the game show. The U.S. Court of Appeals for the Ninth Circuit held that "right of publicity" includes the "identity" of an individual, as well as the "name or likeness."[8]

In one of the first right of publicity cases involving the Internet, actress Alyssa Milano was awarded a $230,000 judgement in a suit against an Internet provider that published nude photographs of her without her permission.

Milano is best known for her role in the 1980s sitcom *Who's the Boss*, but she also appeared on the television show *Melrose Place* and in several movies.[9]

To date, only one appropriation case has reached the U.S. Supreme Court. It involved Hugo Zacchini, known as the "Human Cannonball," and a Cleveland Ohio television station.

Zacchini v. Scripps-Howard (1977)

Hugo Zacchini made his living by performing an act that consisted of shooting himself from a cannon into a net some 200 feet away. The entire act lasted about 15 seconds. Zacchini was performing the act at a county fair in Ohio. WEWS-TV asked to film Zacchini's act as part of a news story about the county fair. Zacchini refused to grant the station permission to film the act.

The next day, acting on instructions from his employer, a reporter from WEWS came to the fair and filmed Zacchini's act in its entirety. The 15-second act was subsequently broadcast on the WEWS evening news.

Zacchini sued WEWS on grounds that his personal property had been appropriated without his consent. He contended that if people could watch his act for free on television, they would not pay to see the act live at the fair. WEWS contended that the filming of the act depicted a newsworthy event of public interest and that commercial exploitation of Zacchini's personal property had not occurred.

The trial court ruled in favor of the television station, an appellate court reversed in favor of Zacchini, and the Ohio Supreme Court reversed again and found in favor of WEWS. The U.S. Supreme Court reversed again and Zacchini ultimately won the case. Justice White delivered the opinion of the Court.

☐ The Ohio Supreme Court held that respondent is constitutionally privileged to include in its newscasts matters of public interest that would otherwise be protected by the right of publicity, absent an intent to injure or to appropriate for some nonprivileged purpose. If under this standard respondent had merely reported that petitioner was performing at the fair and described or commented on his act, with or without showing his picture on television, we would have a very different case. But petitioner is not contending that his appearance at the fair and his performance could not be reported by the press as newsworthy items. His complaint is that respondent filmed his entire act and displayed that film on television for the public to see and enjoy. This, he claimed, was an appropriation of his professional property. . . .

The broadcast of a film of petitioner's entire act poses a substantial threat to the economic value of that performance. As the Ohio court recognized, this act is the product of petitioner's own talents and energy, the end result of much time, effort and expense. Much of its economic value lies in the "right of exclusive control over the publicity given to his performance"; if the public can see the act for free on television, they will be less willing to pay to see it at the fair. The effect of a public broadcast of the performance is similar to preventing petitioner from charging an admission fee. . . . "No social purpose is served by having the defendant get for free some aspect of the plaintiff that would have market value and for which he would normally pay." Kalven, "Privacy in Tort Law—Were Warren and Brandeis Wrong?" 31 *Law and Contemporary Problems* 326, 331 (1966). Moreover, the broadcast of petitioner's entire performance, unlike the unauthorized use of another's name for purposes of trade or the incidental use of a name or picture by the press, goes to the heart of petitioner's ability to earn a living as an entertainer. Thus in this case, Ohio has recognized what may be the strongest case for a "right of publicity"—involving not the appropriation of an entertainer's reputation to enhance the attractiveness of a commercial product, but the appropriation of the very activity by which the entertainer acquired his reputation in the first place.[10]

Descendibility

Although the appropriation of the entire act of a performer is unlikely and limits the impact of Zacchini, a related issue gained momentum in the 1980s. The issue was the question of descendibility, which means that the right of publicity can be retained even after the death of an individual. Although recent decisions have upheld this right, this was not always the case. In 1979 in *Lugosi v. Universal Pictures*, the California Supreme Court held that the heirs of Bela Lugosi, Hollywood's original Count Dracula, did not have exclusive rights to exploit his name and likeness for those commercial situations not exploited by him during his lifetime.

Much litigation on the question of descendibility followed the death of Elvis Presley and, consequently, forced Tennessee to deal with the issue before other jurisdictions. Questions ranging from the legality of marketing Elvis memorabilia to the performances of Elvis impersonators eventually found their way into courtrooms. In *Memphis Development Foundation v. Factors Etc. Inc. (1980)*, the sixth circuit reversed a trial court decision protecting exclusive exploitation of Elvis Presley's likeness, noting that the right of publicity terminates at death.

The following year, the state of Tennessee recognized a right of descendibility in *Commerce Union Bank v. Coors*. In this case, deceased bluegrass singer Lester Flatt's likeness was used in a Coors beer advertisement. Tennessee now assigns the right of publicity to the heirs of the deceased. In 1987, the Sixth Circuit adopted Tennessee's recognition of descendibility when it ruled that celebrities' right of publicity is descendible under the common law of Tennessee.

Several other states now recognize descendibility. Some states automatically assign a public figure's right of publicity to that person's heirs for a period of 50 years from the date of death. Among these states are Kentucky, California, Florida, Virginia, Nebraska, Oklahoma, and Utah. In *Marx Productions v. Day and Night Co.*, it was ruled that a Marx Brothers imitation violates the common law right of publicity to that which they exploited during their lifetimes.

Litigation in this area remains dynamic. It must be remembered that descendibility is by no means a universally recognized concept. Some states still contend that right of publicity terminates at death, others limit the right to those activities exploited by the deceased before death.

Intrusion

This form of privacy invasion involves an unreasonable intrusion by an individual on the seclusion or personal affairs of another. While the Fourth Amendment protects Americans from unreasonable searches and seizures by government, tort law protects us from one another. Civil intrusion occurs most often in the course of news gathering and, although linked to trespass, can take place without physically invading someone else's property. Examples of intrusion consist of unreasonable searches; eavesdropping on conversations; surveillance by cameras, telescopes, or other devices; telephone harassment; peering into windows; and wiretapping. The latter is prohibited by federal law. To be considered intrusion, the act clearly must encompass prying into matters that are of no public concern, and such prying must be judged offensive by a reasonable person.

It is not intrusion to watch, follow, photograph, or attempt to communicate with someone on a public street or other public place. As ruled in *Mark v. Seattle Times*, a television station did not intrude when it broadcast video showing the interior of a pharmacy taken from outside the building as part of a piece on Medicare fraud. Additionally, in *Wehling v. CBS*, a television broadcast showing a private residence—but no more than what could be seen from a public street—was not intrusion.

It is not an invasion of privacy when police or other officials, acting within the scope of their authority, ask for fingerprints, photographs, or other information in the course of their duties. News reports, photographs, or videotapes of individuals caught up in newsworthy events are generally not treated as intrusion. When a newspaper reported from a murdered girl's private diary information that had been obtained from police, the girl's family sued for intrusion. In *Andren v. Knight-Ridder*, a Michigan district court ruled that no intrusion had taken place because the topic was newsworthy.

It is safe to say that it is very difficult to bring a successful intrusion suit against the news media during the course of normal events. Red-flag areas are those situations that take place on private property or involve news personnel in criminal activities such as trespass, breaking and entering, illegal wiretapping, or misrepresentation of facts to gain entry to a private locale. For example, CBS News, uninvited and with cameras rolling, entered an expensive French restaurant in New York City. The network was working a story on city health code violations. The restaurant asked CBS to leave. When they didn't, the restaurant ejected the news crew and filed suit. In *Le Mistral, Inc. v. CBS*, CBS lost a judgment amounting to $250,000 in punitive and $1200 in compensatory damages for intrusion and trespass. The trial judge noted that the right to gather news does not include the right to break and enter or trespass.

In *Huskey v. NBC*, an Illinois court found cause for intrusion when an NBC television camera crew filmed an inmate at Marion Penitentiary without his consent. The inmate was stripped to the waist in gym shorts and engaged in "private activities" in the prison's exercise cage.

Defenses

The primary defenses against a claim of intrusion are newsworthiness and consent. However, unlike the other forms of privacy invasion, actual publication of information gained from intrusion is immaterial. The damage occurs at the information-gathering stage.

Sometimes, what would normally be considered trespass is legal when done in the course of following a breaking news story, particularly when reporters are accompanying or working with law enforcement officials. It was not intrusion when journalists accompanied Florida officials onto private property that was the scene of a fatal fire. A 17-year-old girl had been burned to death. In what has come to be known as the "Silhouette of Death" case, the girl's mother first learned of her daughter's death by reading about the tragedy in a newspaper account that included a photograph taken by a news photographer in the girl's bedroom. A silhouette of the girl's body had been formed on the floor where she was burned to death. In *Florida Publishing Co. v. Fletcher*, the Florida Supreme Court ruled that although the photograph's inclusion was ethically questionable, no intrusion had occurred because the fire marshall had asked the news photographer to take the picture as part of the official investigation. The photograph was technically part of the public record. Recognition of this privilege differs from state to state and caution must be exercised.

In 1971, a *Life* magazine reporter gained access to the home of a former plumber named A. A. Dietemann who claimed to have special healing abilities. The reporter pretended to be a friend of a woman who had gone to Dietemann for an examination of feigned breast cancer. The woman had been planted by police and health department officials who were investigating complaints that Dietemann was practicing medicine without a license. The reporter took pictures inside Dietemann's home and relayed tape recordings of the diagnosis and treatment to police waiting outside. Dietemann was arrested for quackery, and *Life* published a story on the episode. Dietemann sued for invasion of privacy, contending that the hidden camera constituted intrusion, and won the case. In *Dietemann v. Time Inc. (1971)*, Ninth Circuit Court Judge Shirley Hufstedler noted,

☐ Plaintiff's den was a sphere from which he could reasonably expect to exclude eavesdropping newsmen. He invited two of the defendant's employees to the den. One who invites another into his home or office takes a risk that the visitor may not be what he seems, and that the visitor may repeat all he hears and observes when he leaves. But he does not and should not be required to take the risk that what is heard and seen will be transmitted by photograph or recording, or in our modern world, in full living color and hi-fi to the public at large or to any segment of it that the visitor may select.[11]

The ruling in *Dietemann* is a narrow one. Later rulings suggest that had the police been acting directly in the line of duty and had the photographer not been in a private home, the outcome might have been different. For example, when a TV investigative reporter gained access to an alcoholic treatment center by posing as an alcoholic, a Missouri court ruled in *WCH of Waverly v. Meredith Co.* that no intrusion occurred. The reporter was subject to state action for fraud and to prosecution under the federal eavesdropping statute.

Convicted murderer David Berkowitz, suspected of being New York City's "Son of Sam" serial killer, objected to reporters entering his apartment after his arrest. In *People v. Berliner*, a New York City court said reporters were not guilty of criminal trespass because only Berkowitz (who would have to have been in the apartment) or the apartment owner could have withheld consent to enter the apartment. However, police could have excluded reporters from the premises while a search was being conducted.

In 1981 in *Anderson v. WROC-TV*, another New York court ruled against a television station reporter who accompanied a Rochester Humane Society official into the home of an individual suspected of mistreating animals. The court said that public officials had no right to invite others, including journalists, to accompany them onto private property during the performance of their duties. Reporters are advised to use caution and to be familiar with practices accepted in their state regarding accompanying officials onto private property.

Generally speaking, the media will lose an intrusion case when it can be demonstrated that they have gone out of their way and harassed newsworthy people. Freelance photographer Ron Galella did just that in his attempts to photograph former first lady Jacqueline Kennedy Onassis. Galella made the bulk of his living photographing Mrs. Onassis, who objected to his continual pursuit of her. In search of a photo, he was known to go to any extremes, including shadowing Mrs. Onassis and her children, jumping into their path and taking a picture, using telephoto lenses to snap pictures on private property, and reputedly romancing the Onassis housekeeper so as to gain access to their home. Having lost a husband and brother-in-law to assassins' bullets, Mrs. Onassis found Galella's erratic behavior and surveillance of her family disturbing. In *Galella v. Onassis*, the former first lady persuaded a New York district court to enjoin Galella's incessant behavior. Although a judge ordered Galella to remain at least 300 feet from the Onassis and Kennedy homes, 150 feet from Mrs. Onassis, and 225 feet from her children, an appellate court reduced the distances to 25 and 30 feet, respectively. Galella continued his pursuit of Mrs. Onassis. In 1982, however, the original New York court found Galella in contempt of its order and fined him $10,000. Galella also promised never to take another picture of Onassis.

Taping Telephone Calls and Third-Party Monitoring

Under provisions of the Electronic Communications Privacy Act of 1986, federal and state law prohibits the surreptitious recording of telephone and other conversations between individuals. Included are wire and wireless telephone conversations, electronic mail, satellite transmissions, and computer data. By virtue of the Omnibus Crime Control and Safe Streets Act of 1968, bugging, wiretapping, and other third-party monitoring are also prohibited.

One-sided recording of telephone calls is a separate issue. In many states, it is legal for an individual to record his or her personal telephone calls without informing the other party that the conversation is being recorded. Reporters in Indiana, for example, may record all telephone interviews without violating the law. Broadcasting these recordings is another matter. Though state law governs single-party recording, the FCC requires broadcasters to inform persons that their call will be broadcast. Similarly, if the phone call is to be broadcast live, the FCC requires broadcasters to inform callers that they are "on the air," thereby allowing them to terminate the call if they object to the broadcast.

Stolen or Illegally Obtained Materials

Sometimes, newsworthy material comes to the attention of journalists as a result of trespass or theft by a third parry. If journalists publish stolen information, are they liable for intrusion? Case law would indicate that, for the most part, they are not. Both major cases in this area involved national columnist Drew Pearson and his young assistant, Jack Anderson.

In *Liberty Lobby v. Pearson (1968)*, the U.S. Court of Appeals for the District of Columbia ruled that unless the Liberty Lobby could show that Pearson or Anderson had actually stolen the documents in question, they could not successfully sue. Additionally, then Circuit Judge Warren Burger ruled that if the publication of documents is found to be in the public interest, journalists will prevail.

A year later, in *Pearson v. Dodd (1969)*, Senator Thomas Dodd brought suit against Pearson and Anderson. The senator alleged that the journalists had received copies of private memoranda from disgruntled staff members relating to Dodd's misappropriation of campaign funds. Although Pearson and Anderson had not physically intruded into the senator's files, Dodd claimed that because the journalists knew that the material was stolen, they should be held liable for conversion (i.e., the unauthorized use of someone else's property). The court ruled that no conversion had occurred because the files themselves were not taken. Pearson had received photocopies and the originals remained in place.

Although newsworthiness is a sturdy defense in cases such as these, journalists must be careful not to run afoul of state and local laws that may have consequences that result from the publication of stolen material. When the *Los Angeles Free Press* published a stolen list containing names, addresses, and phone numbers of undercover narcotics agents under the heading "Know Your Local Narc," the paper's publisher was indicted for violation of California's penal code. The code makes it a crime to receive stolen property. In *People v. Kunkin (1972)*, the publisher was convicted by a trial court and the conviction was upheld by the California court of appeals. The California Supreme Court reversed the conviction on a technicality. There was reason to doubt that the reporters who had obtained the list knew that it was stolen.

Embarrassing Facts

Sometimes an invasion of privacy action can be brought against the media for the publication of truthful, nondefamatory facts that are embarrassing to an identified individual. Generally these facts must be communicated to a widespread public, be private in nature (rather than newsworthy), and be highly offensive and objectionable to a reasonable person.

The major case dealing with public disclosure of embarrassing facts involved a child prodigy named William James Sidis. Sidis graduated from Harvard in 1910 with a degree in mathematics. Because he was 16 years old at the time of graduation, he naturally received a great deal of media attention. Predictions about his future contributions to society appeared in the news media. In reality, however, Sidis was to become a recluse and certainly did not meet the expectations of one so intellectually endowed. In 1937, the *New Yorker* magazine published an article entitled "Where Are They Now?" which exposed personal facts about Sidis' uneventful life. Although the tone of the article was sympathetic, Sidis filed suit, noting that detailing his unsuccessful life was an invasion of privacy.

In *Sidis v. F-R Publishing Corporation (1940)*, the court ruled in favor of the magazine, noting that Sidis was a public figure—even though 20 years had passed since he had first received media attention. The story, said the court, had legitimate news interest. Finally, the court postulated what has come to be known as "the rule of Sidis." This standard has been used to measure the legitimacy of embarrassing facts claims ever since. Circuit Judge Clark wrote:

☐   . . . Everyone will agree that at some point the public interest in obtaining information becomes dominant over the individual's desire for privacy. Warren and Brandeis were willing to lift the veil somewhat in the case of public officers. We would go further, though we are not yet prepared to say how far. At least we would permit limited scrutiny of the "private" life of any person who has achieved or has had thrust upon him, the questionable and indefinable status of a "public figure."

. . . We express no comment on whether or not the newsworthiness of the matter printed will always constitute a complete defense. Revelations may be so intimate and so unwarranted in view of the victim's position as to outrage the community's notions of decency. But when focused upon public characters, truthful comments upon dress, speech, habits and the ordinary aspects of personality will usually not transgress this line. Regrettably or not, the misfortunes and frailties of neighbors and "public figures" are subjects of considerable interest and discussion to the rest of the population. And when such are the mores of the community, it would be unwise for a court to bar their expression in the newspapers, books, and magazines of the day.[12]

Newsworthiness

It should be noted that "newsworthiness" is a strong defense in these kinds of cases, and it is difficult to bring a successful embarrassing-facts case against the news media. The rule of Sidis must be shown to have been exceeded before a claim of newsworthiness can be defeated. It is safe to say that embarrassing-facts cases cannot be successfully brought by persons (including innocent bystanders) caught up in newsworthy events. Although it may be embarrassing to be arrested, it is not an invasion of privacy for the local news to report the arrest. This is true even if the arrest is based on mistaken identity.

When a temporarily deranged man in Idaho ran nude out of his house brandishing a shotgun, a local television station filmed the event. On regaining his senses, the man filed an embarrassing facts privacy suit against the TV station. He claimed that the station could have edited the film so that he was not pictured nude. Although he won the initial judgment, in *Taylor v. KTVB, Inc.*, the Idaho Supreme Court ordered a new trial because the event was newsworthy.

When Oliver "Bill" Sipple, a veteran confined to a wheelchair, grabbed would-be presidential assassin Sarah Jane Moore's arm as she fired a shot at Gerald Ford, he was hailed a hero. Sipple was also a homosexual, a fact disclosed to the news media by members of San Francisco's gay community. The disclosure was not meant to be defamatory but rather to show that gays could be positive forces in society. In any case, Sipple had not volunteered the information about his sexual preference and filed suit. In *Sipple v. Chronicle Publishing Co.*, the court ruled that disclosure of the fact that one is homosexual is not an invasion of privacy, especially when it is part of a newsworthy story such as an attempted assassination of a president.

Consent

Another defense is consent. Provided an individual has granted permission for information to be published, there can be no cause for action. When *Sports Illustrated* published an interview with a rather eccentric body-surfer named Mike Virgil, he brought suit against the magazine because he was embarrassed by statements and actions attributed to him. Virgil told *Sports Illustrated* that he sometimes dove head first down flights of stairs to "impress girls," intentionally injured himself working construction so as to collect unemployment compensation, and ate spiders and other insects. The thrust of the article was that bodysurfing is a particularly rugged sport and requires a special individual to be successful at it. In *Virgil v. Time Inc.*, the Ninth Circuit Court ruled that although these things may now embarrass Virgil, they were relevant to the story, and he had given consent to *Sports Illustrated* by granting the interview and making these statements. The rule of Sidis had not been breached.

How far can the press go before the rule of Sidis is breached? In 1964, in *Daily Times Democrat v. Graham*, Flora Bell Graham won a $4000 judgment against the Culiman County, Alabama *Daily Times Democrat*. The paper had published a picture of Graham taken as she emerged from a Fun House at a county fair. The 44-year-old housewife's skirt had been blown over her head by air jets, exposing her legs and underpants. Although the picture had been taken in a public place, the Alabama Supreme Court found the picture offensive to modesty and decency because it revealed private information in which the public had no legitimate interest.

Certainly *Time* magazine crossed the line when it photographed hospital patient Dorothy Barber against her will. Barber had a rare disease that caused her to lose weight even though she ate a great deal of food. *Time* referred to Barber as "the starving glutton" and "Insatiable Eater Barber" who "eats for ten." In *Barber v. Time* Inc., the Missouri Supreme Court found the story to be an invasion of privacy and noted that privacy rights include the receipt of medical treatment without "personal publicity."

Similarly, the Dow Chemical company lost an invasion of privacy suit in *Lambert v. Dow Chemical Co.* when, as part of the company's on-the-job safety program, it exhibited pictures of an employee injured in an industrial accident. The court ruled that pictures taken during the employee's surgery and used without his permission embarrassed and humiliated him.

Stories dealing with matters of public concern are generally not subject to successful invasion-of-privacy claims. When the *Washington Post* printed an article about heroin addiction and included the photograph of Monica Little, who had been interviewed as part of the story, she sued for privacy invasion. Little contended that although she had agreed to be interviewed, she had used a false name and her family did not know that she was an addict. The use of a photograph had damaged her anonymity. She claimed that the Post had intentionally caused her emotional distress.

In *Little v. Washington Post*, the U.S. District Court for the District of Columbia ruled against Little, stating that the public interest supports dissemination of accurate information about the risk of drugs and drug addiction, and that she waived her privacy rights when she agreed to the interview. In short, the *Post* did not go beyond the limits of her consent.

The Public Record

The courts have ruled that if the news media exceed the limits outlined in the rule of Sidis, successful invasion-of-privacy suits may be brought. In the only embarrassing-facts case to reach the Supreme Court, however, the media found protection even when publication might "outrage the community's notions of decency." When newsworthy private facts are part of the public record, suit cannot be brought. In 1975 in *Cox Broadcasting Corp. v. Cohn*, some constitutional protection was granted to embarrassing facts found in the open records of court proceedings.

Cox Broadcasting Corp. v. Cohn (1975)

This case resulted from the controversy surrounding the release by Atlanta police of the name of a 17-year-old rape and murder victim. A Georgia statute protected the identity of rape victims, but the girl's name was obtained by WSB-TV from a court clerk as part of an official record of indictment. On April 2, 1972, WSB-TV broadcast a story that identified the girl. Relying on the Georgia statute, the girl's father brought suit against the television station, claiming that his right of privacy had been invaded by the broadcast.

Although the trial court and the Georgia Supreme Court ruled in favor of the plaintiff, the U.S. Supreme Court reversed the decision, finding the Georgia statute to be an unconstitutional limitation on freedom of the press. Essentially, the Court ruled that an accurate account of material obtained from a public record is not actionable as an embarrassing-facts invasion of privacy. Justice White delivered the opinion of the Court:

☐   ... The version of the privacy tort now before us—termed in Georgia "the tort of public disclosure"—is that in which the plaintiff claims the right to be free from unwanted publicity about his private affairs, which although wholly true, would be offensive to a person of ordinary sensibilities. ...
The face-off is apparent, and the appellants urge upon us the broad holding that the press may not be made criminally or civilly liable for publishing information that is neither false nor misleading but absolutely accurate, however damaging it may be to reputation or individual sensibilities.

    ... Rather than address the broader question whether truthful publications may ever be subjected to civil or criminal liability consistently with the First and Fourteenth Amendments, or to put it another way, whether the State may ever define and protect an area of privacy free from unwanted publicity in the press, it is appropriate to focus on the narrower interface between press and privacy that this case represents, namely, whether the State may impose sanctions on the accurate publication of the name of a rape victim obtained from public records—more specifically, from judicial records which are maintained in connection with a public prosecution and which themselves are open to public inspection. We are convinced that the State may not do so.

    ... We are reluctant to embark on a course that would make public records generally available to the media but forbid their publication if offensive to the sensibilities of the supposed reasonable man. Such a rule would make it very difficult for the media to inform citizens about the public business and yet stay within the law. The rule would invite timidity and self-censorship and very likely lead to the suppression of many items that would otherwise be published and that should be made available to the public.[13]

In 1989, the Supreme Court invalidated a Florida law making it a misdemeanor to publish the name of a victim of a sex crime. In *Florida Star v. B.J.F.*, the court reaffirmed that the publication lawfully obtained truthful information that is part of the public record and is protected by the First Amendment.

Journalists must remember that reports from the public record must also be accurate and timely. The *Oakland Tribune* published a story stating that the first female student body president at the College of Alameda, Toni Diaz, had received a sex-change operation. The paper used what it thought were public records to establish that Toni was the former Antony Diaz. In *Diaz v. Oakland Tribune Inc.*, the court ruled that the *Tribune* could not rely on identification records such as drivers' licenses and high school transcripts issued before her operation, because Diaz had legally changed those records. The court also could not see how this story was newsworthy.

False Light

The false-light tort involves the publication of false information that is highly offensive to an ordinary person. False-light invasions of privacy are similar to libel, but the important distinction is that the false light is nondefamatory. Libel actions are instigated to protect persons' reputations (i.e., the way they are viewed by society). False-light privacy actions stem from a person's right to be let alone and is based on the way people view themselves. Emotional distress is often the basis for false-light privacy suits. Unlike libel, false-light invasions of privacy actually may embellish one's reputation. When an unauthorized biography of famous baseball pitcher Warren Spahn portrayed him as a war hero, Spahn was able to bring a successful suit in *Messner Inc. v. Warren E. Spahn*. Even though the material was flattering, the "gross misstatement of fact" portrayed the former pitcher in a false light, thereby causing him emotional distress.

False-light claims often result from dramatizations and fictional accounts of real-life incidents. In 1931, a woman was awarded damages as a result of her portrayal in a 1924 film entitled *The Red Kimono*. Gabrielle Darley Melvin, a former prostitute, was acquitted of murder in 1918 and began a new life. She married and became a respectable housewife. Her new family was unaware of her sordid past, until she was identified in the motion picture. Although it is questionable whether a court would reach the same decision today (her past is part of the public record), in *Melvin v. Reid*, Melvin won the case on appropriation grounds and "willful and wanton disregard of that charity which should actuate us in our social intercourse."[14]

The first false-light case to reach the U.S. Supreme Court began with a drama review in *Life* magazine and ended some 15 years later, when the case was sent back for retrial.

In 1952, James Hill, his wife, and five children were held hostage in their home by three escaped convicts. The family was not harmed during the ordeal, nor were they abused in any way. This situation naturally attracted a great deal of media attention. A novel entitled *Desperate Hours* was eventually written about the episode. To spice up the story, some license was taken by the author. The book included fictionalized violence against the family. So gripping was the story that it was adapted into a Broadway play. Although based on the Hills' story, the play changed the names of the characters, thereby making identification of the actual family difficult. When *Life* magazine reviewed the play, it noted that *Desperate Hours* was based on the Hill family and mirrored their actual experiences. James Hill found this identification offensive, noting that there was little similarity between what had happened to his family and the contents of the drama. The play eventually became a film starring Frederick March as the hero-like father and Humphrey Bogart as the convict leader.

Because Hill was not directly identified in the play, he could not bring suit against the playwright. Because *Life* magazine did identify him as the father in the drama, he filed a false-light suit against the magazine. *Life* contended that the Hill family had been caught up in a public issue and members of the family were, therefore, public figures, even if reluctantly so. Hill argued that by identifying his family as the one in *Desperate Hours*, *Life* had acted with reckless disregard for the truth and therefore had violated the actual malice standard of *New York Times v. Sullivan*.

In *Time Inc. v. Hill*, a jury awarded Hill $30,000 in compensatory damages. The decision was affirmed by the Court of Appeals, but in 1967 the Supreme Court reversed the decision and sent the case back to trial. Justice Brennan delivered the opinion of the Court.

☐ The question in this case is whether appellant, publisher of *Life* magazine, was denied constitutional protections for speech and press by the application by the New York courts of Pts. 5–51 of the New York Civil Rights Law . . . to award appellee damages on allegations that *Life* falsely reported that a new play portrayed an experience suffered by appellee and his family.

. . . [A]lthough the New York statute affords "little protection" to the "privacy" of a newsworthy person, "whether he be such by choice or involuntarily" the statute gives him a right of action when his name, picture, or portrait is the subject of a "fictitious" report or article.

. . . We hold that the constitutional protections for speech and press preclude the application of the New York statute to redress false reports of matters of public interest in the absence of proof that the defendant published the report with knowledge of its falsity or in reckless disregard of the truth.

. . . One need only pick up any newspaper or magazine to comprehend the vast range of published matter which exposes persons to public view, both private citizens and public officials. . . . We create grave risk of serious impairment of the indispensable service of a free press in a free society if we saddle the press with the impossible burden of verifying to a certainty the facts associated in news articles with a person's name, picture or portrait, particularly as related to nondefamatory matter. Even negligence would be a most elusive standard, especially when the content of the speech itself affords no warning of prospective harm to another through falsity. A negligence test would place on the press the intolerable burden of guessing how a jury might assess the reasonableness of steps taken by it to verify the accuracy of every reference to a name, picture or portrait.

. . . But the constitutional guarantees can tolerate sanctions against calculated falsehood without significant impairment of their essential function. We held in *New York Times* that calculated falsehood enjoyed no immunity in the case of alleged defamation of a public official's official conduct. Similarly calculated falsehood should enjoy no immunity in the situation here presented us. . . .

The judgement of the Court of Appeals is set aside and the case is remanded for further proceedings not inconsistent with this opinion.[15]

The Court's decision was based on the opinion that although *Time Inc.* had published a falsehood, it did not exceed the actual malice standard of *New York Times*. The Hills had been in litigation since 1952 and, facing the prospect of beginning the case all over again, decided not to pursue the matter further.

Seven years after *Hill*, the Supreme Court heard another false-light case. This time the Court found that *The Cleveland Plain Dealer* had acted with actual malice when it published a story about Margaret Cantrell. Mrs. Cantrell's husband had been one of 44 persons killed ten days before Christmas in 1967 in the collapse of the Silver Bridge spanning the Ohio River at Point Pleasant, West Virginia. She had been left with little money to care for four children. The story was published in August 1968 as part of a follow-up on the lives of the families involved in the bridge disaster.

In *Cantrell v. Forest City Publishing Co. (1974)*, according to testimony taken in court, the story contained a number of inaccuracies. It implied that reporters had spoken with Mrs. Cantrell in her home and that the home was untidy and her children were poorly clothed. Mrs. Cantrell charged that the story made them the objects of pity and ridicule.

In reality, Mrs. Cantrell had not been present when reporter Joseph Eszterhaus came to call. Eszterhaus spoke with one of her children, while a photographer snapped some pictures. Writing for the Supreme Court, Justice Potter Stewart noted,

☐   There was no dispute during the trial that Eszterhaus . . . must have known that a number of the statements in the feature story were untrue. In particular, his article plainly implied that Mrs. Cantrell had been present during his visit to her home and that Eszterhaus had observed her "wear(ing) the same mask of non-expression she wore at the funeral." These were "calculated falsehoods," and the jury was plainly justified in finding that Eszterhaus had portrayed the Cantrells in a false light through knowing or reckless untruth.[16]

Even unintentional distortion of facts can be dangerous to the media. When a Washington, D.C., television station broadcast a report on the growing herpes epidemic in America, it opened the story with video of pedestrians standing on a street corner. One of the pedestrians, Linda Duncan, happened to turn and face the camera as it zoomed in on the persons standing on the corner. Ms. Duncan's face was clearly recognizable to those who knew her. She filed a false-light claim, charging that reports on the 6:00 P.M. and 11:00 P.M. news implied that she had herpes. The report broadcast at 6:00 P.M. was an on-the-street report, narrated by a reporter on the scene. Even though Ms. Duncan was recognizable, the court ruled that no invasion of privacy had taken place because she was shown on the street with other pedestrians. At 11:00 P.M., however, the report had been edited and the anchorman in the studio read lines over the video shot on the street. With the camera focused on Ms. Duncan, the anchorman said, "[f]or the twenty million Americans who have herpes, it's [a new medical treatment] not a cure . . . " The video concluded as Ms. Duncan turned away from the camera and proceeded down the street. In *Duncan v. WJLA-TV*, the court ruled that the 11:00 P.M. broadcast did cast Ms. Duncan in a false light. The video had been edited so that other pedestrians did not appear in the scene.

False-light problems may also lurk in "ambush" interviews. Arnold Diaz, a reporter for WCBS-TV in New York conducted such an on-the-street interview with Irving Machleder. Diaz implied that Machleder was involved in the illegal dumping of chemical waste in New Jersey. In *Machleder v. Diaz*, a jury found CBS guilty of false-light invasion of privacy and awarded

Machleder $1 million in punitive damages and $250,000 in compensatory damages.

Although the Supreme Court refused to set a "negligence" standard for false-light claims in *Hill* and *Cantrell*, some states, including Texas, have adopted that standard. Journalists are expected to follow accepted practices to ensure that potentially offensive material is true, newsworthy, or has been obtained with the consent of individuals involved.

When LaJuan and Billy Wood went camping in a state park, they went swimming nude. They took several pictures of one another. Upon returning home, the couple had the film developed and stored the nude photos in their dresser drawer. They did not show the photos to anyone else. One day, their neighbor Steve Simpson broke into the Woods' home, stole the photographs, and submitted a nude photo of LaJuan to *Hustler* magazine for publication. Simpson filled out a consent form that provided personal information about LaJuan. Simpson included some true information, such as LaJuan's name and hobbies, but added some false statements, including a fantasy attributed to LaJuan of being "tied down and screwed by two bikers." Simpson's wife forged LaJuan's signature on the consent form and mailed the package to *Hustler*.

The magazine has a policy of calling persons who submit photos, to verify that such persons really wish to have the photos published. The consent form asks that a telephone number be included with all submissions. Simpson did not include a phone number, so the magazine sent a mailgram to the address on the consent form, which was Simpson's. The mailgram asked LaJuan to call the magazine collect. Simpson's wife did just that, pretending to be LaJuan. The *Hustler* representative asked a series of leading "yes" and "no" questions, and terminated the conversation in about two minutes. Assuming (incorrectly) that a magazine representative had spoken with LaJuan, *Hustler* published the photographs in the February 1980 issue of the magazine.

LaJuan and Billy Wood first learned of the publication of the photos when friends began to tease them. LaJuan was mortified and sought psychological counseling. Ultimately, in *Wood v. Hustler*, LaJuan Wood was able to recover $150,000 in damages for false-light invasion of privacy. As a private figure, she needed only to show that *Hustler* was negligent in checking the identity of the person in the photograph.

Protection from Misuse of Personal Data by the Government

The cases and issues discussed thus far have traced the development of the right to privacy concerning individuals—that is, privacy protection from one another and the news media. A separate issue concerns the protection of certain information about individuals by federal and state laws. Though there has been a tendency toward the opening of public records, as in *Cox Broadcasting Corp. v. Cohn,* the Federal Privacy Act of 1974 and accompanying state legislation has excluded some data from public scrutiny.

The Privacy Act of 1974 seeks to protect individuals against the misuse of personal information contained about them in government files. Under the act, a government agency must obtain an individual's permission before divulging the contents of certain files containing information about him or her. Although the Privacy Act regulates what may be divulged about a person, it in no way limits what may be collected about an individual.

There are, of course, exemptions to the Privacy Act. Law enforcement agencies and the CIA have access to all information collected about an individual. There are 11 exemptions or conditions of disclosure built into the act:

1. Officers and employees of the agency maintaining the record may have access to the record in the performance of their duties.
2. Information may be given if disclosure is required by the Freedom of Information Act.
3. Information may be accessed for routine use (i.e., information may be used for the purpose for which it was collected).
4. Information may be divulged for use by the Bureau of the Census.
5. Information may be given to recipients who assure the agency that information will be used for statistical purposes only and that the information will not specifically identify any individuals.
6. If a record has national historical value, it may be given to the National Archives.
7. Information may be provided to law enforcement agencies.
8. Disclosure may be given provided the person requesting information can show that there are "compelling circumstances affecting the health or safety of an individual."
9. Information may be given if requested by Congress.
10. Information may be given to the General Accounting Office.
11. Information may be given pursuant to the order of a court.

Since 1974, several states, including Minnesota, Indiana, California, Arkansas, Kentucky, Ohio, Utah, Connecticut, Virginia, and Massachusetts, have enacted similar privacy protection laws. All allow law enforcement agencies access to information. These state laws are based on the openness of public records.

Privacy and the Electronic Media

Though wiretapping and other uninvited forms of electronic snooping are prohibited by law, some invited technologies may generate privacy concerns.

Hidden Cameras and Microphones

Although federal wiretap law prohibits third-party interception and recording of wired or wireless private conversations where one "expects privacy,"[17] federal law allows a participant in a conversation secretly to tape the conversation.[18] State laws govern the legality of "one-party" audio or video taping. Most states allow surreptitious audio recording; however, California, Delaware, Illinois, Michigan, Pennsylvania, Oregon, New Hampshire, Louisiana, Massachusetts, Maryland, Washington, Florida, and Montana do not. These states require consent of all parties before a conversation may be tape recorded.

Use of hidden video cameras is legal in all states except New Hampshire, Delaware, Georgia, Utah, Alabama, Michigan, and South Dakota. In Massachusetts, it is illegal to audiotape a conversation secretly, but it is legal to videotape the same conversation using a hidden camera.[19]

Protection of Cable Television Subscriber Privacy

The development of cable television brought about concern over how subscriber data could be used. The Cable Act of 1984 first addressed cable subscriber privacy issues, and the 1992 Cable Consumer Protection Act further protected consumers against unauthorized use of personal information gathered by cable operators. Essentially, the Act prohibits cable operators from using any information collected about subscribers without first obtaining the subscriber's written permission.[20]

Online Computer Privacy

The use of computer networks for both commercial and personal services presents additional privacy concerns. Electronic mail (e-mail), bulletin boards, online services, and the World Wide Web are but a few examples. Though wiretap law applies to systems providing some forms of e-mail and other online communications, privacy law and the Internet is a developing area. Case law has established that personal e-mail communications transmitted on computers and systems provided by an individual's employer do not enjoy privacy protection.[21]

Also of concern has been the use of "cookies" by Websites. Cookies are information generated by a Web server and stored on the computer of anyone accessing the Website. Cookies allow user customization of Websites by storing personal information for access by the site. Web search engines and Internet portals like *Yahoo!*, customized news pages, shopping, and travel pages all make extensive use of cookies. Whenever a user calls up a specific Web page, the user's browsing software transmits the cookie, and the personal information it stores, to the Web server. Privacy concerns are triggered because unless a user's Web browser is set to detect an incoming cookie, the user may be unaware that the server has access to personal information stored on the user's computer.

Another privacy issue surrounding the use of the Internet is the transmission of unsolicited messages or "spam." In *Cyber Promotions, Inc. v. America Online Inc. (1996)* a Pennsylvania District Court found that, as a private online company, *America Online* had the right to block unsolicited messages sent via the Internet to its subscribers. Spam, however received renewed attention as courts considered the First Amendment issue raised by blocking unsolicited messages. Although many states have passed laws regulating spam, few have tried to ban it altogether. (See *Missouri ex rel. Nixon v. American Blast Fax, Inc.,* __ F. Supp. 2d __, 2002 U.S. Dist. LEXIS 5707, 2002 WL 508330 (E.D. Mo. Mar. 13, 2002).)

Directly targeting children online for commercial purposes is another concern. The Children's Online Privacy Protection Act of 1998 (15 U.S.C.S. § 6501) makes it illegal for a Website to knowingly collect personal information from or about children who visit the site. Finally, provisions of the controversial USA Patriot Act of 2001, have raised new concerns about the limits of government access to personal Internet activity.[22]

Summary

The concept of personal privacy has its roots in an 1890 law journal article written by Brandeis and Warren. The right of privacy has been divided into four forms: appropriation, intrusion, embarrassing facts, and false light. Privacy invasions generally change the way persons feel about themselves, and defamation is not present. Defenses against invasions of privacy are consent and newsworthiness.

Though the common law in most states recognizes some right of personal privacy, not all four forms of the tort are universally recognized. The common law protects against some privacy invasions by individuals, while the Federal Privacy Act and various state laws protect against misuse of private information by the government.

The Cable Consumer Protection Act of 1992 contains provisions designed to protect the privacy of cable subscribers.

The number of telecommunications offerings has grown so quickly and privacy law as it is applied to new technologies and to the Internet is a rapidly unfolding area. Case law and legislation have begun to address privacy concerns online. As these technologies continue to develop, so will the application of law and regulatory activity.

Notes/References

1. Thomas M. Cooley, *A Treatise on the Law of Torts* (Chicago: Callaghan & Co., 1888), 29.
2. Samuel D. Warren and Louis D. Brandeis, "The Right of Privacy," *Harvard Law Review* 4 (December 15, 1890): 193.
3. Ibid., 195–96.
4. Lewis J. Paper, *Brandeis* (New York: Citadel Press, 1983), 34.
5. *Griswold v. Connecticut*, 381 U.S. 479 (1965).
6. *Cher v. Forum International*, 213 U.S.P.Q. 96, (DC CA, 1982) 7 Med.L.Rptr. 2593.
7. *Onassis v. Christian Dior*, (NY Sup.Ct., 1984) 10 Med.L.Rptr. at 1861.
8. *White v. Samsung Electronics America Inc.*, 989 F.2d 1512, 21 Med.L.Rptr. 1330 (9th Cir.), cert. denied 113 S.Ct. 2443 (1993).
9. Mike Brunker, "Actress Given Six-Figure Award over Nude Photos," MSNBC News, http://www.msnbc.com/news/226315.asp (December 24, 1998).
10. Zacchini v. Scripps-Howard, 433 U.S. 562 (1977).
11. *Dietemann v. Time Inc.*, 449 F.2d 245 (9th Cir., 1971).
12. *Sidis v. F-R Publishing Corporation*, 113 F.2d 806 (1940).
13. *Cox Broadcasting Corp. v. Cohn*, 420 U.S. 469, 95 S.Ct. 1029, 43 L.Ed.2d 328 (1975).
14. *Melvin v. Reid*, 112 Cal.App. 285, 297, p. 91 (1931).
15. *Time Inc. v. Hill*, 385 U.S. 374 (1967).
16. *Cantrell v. Forest City Publishing Co.*, 419 U.S. 245, 95 S.Ct. 465, 42 L.Ed.2d 419 (1974).
17. The "wiretap law" is the Omnibus Crime Control and Safe Streets Act 18 U.S.C.A. §§ 2510–2520. Amended as the "Electronic Communications Privacy Act of 1986."
18. 18 U.S.C. 2511(2)(d).
19. T. Barton Carter, Juliet Lushbough Dee, Martin J. Gaynes, and Harvey L. Zuckman, *Mass Communication Law in a Nutshell*, 4th ed. (St. Paul: West Publishing Co., 1994), 127–28.

20. Section 631. [47 USC Section 551].
21. See *Bourke v. Nissan Motor Corporation (1993)*, unpublished, Cal.App.2nd; http://www.loundy.com/cases/Bourke_v_Nissan.html (December 8, 1998).
22. H.R. 3162, Uniting and Strengthening America by Providing Appropriate Tools Required to Intercept and Obstruct Terrorism (USA PATRIOT ACT) Act of 2001.

Cases

Anderson v. Fisher Broadcasting Companies (OR Ct.App., 1985) 11 Med.L.Rptr. 1839

Anderson v. WROC-TV, 441 N.Y.S.2d 220 (Sup.Ct., 1981)

Andren v. Knight-Ridder, (DC E.Mich, 1984) 10 Med.L.Rptr. 2109

Baltimore Orioles v. Major League Baseball Players, (CA 7, 1986) 13 Med.L.Rptr. 1625

Barber v. Time Inc., 348 Mo. 1199, 159 S.W.2d 291 (1942)

Bourke v. Nissan Motor Corporation, Unpublished Cal.App.2nd(1993); http://www.loundy.com/cases/Bourke_v_Nissan.html (December 8, 1998)

Brinkley v. Casablancas (NY Sup.Ct. App.Div., 1981) 7 Med.L.Rptr.1457

Cantrell v. Forest City Publishing Co., 419 U.S. 245, 95 S.Ct. 465, 42 L.Ed.2d 419 (1974)

Cher v. Forum International, 213 U.S. P.Q. 96, (DC CA, 1982) 7 Med.L.Rptr 2593

Commerce Union Bank v. Coors, (Tenn. Chanc.Ct, 1981) 7 Med.L.Rptr. 2204

Cox Broadcasting Corp. v. Cohn, 420 U.S. 469, 95 S.Ct. 1029, 43 L.Ed.2d 328 (1975)

Cyber Promotions, Inc. v. America Online, Inc. 948 F. Supp. 456 (E.D. Penn. 1996)

Daily Times Democrat v. Graham, 162 So.2d 474 (Ma., 1964)

Diaz v. Oakland Tribune Inc., 188 Cal.Rptr. 762 (Cal. App., 1983)

Dietemann v. Time Inc., 449 F.2d 245 (9th Cir., 1971)

Duncan v. WJLA-TV (DC DC, 1984) 10 Med.L.Rptr. 1395

Eastwood v. Superior Court, (Cal. Ct.App., 1983) 10 Med.L.Rptr. 1073

Florida Publishing Co. v. Fletcher, 340 So.2d 914 (Fla., 1976) cert. denied 431 U.S. 930 (1977)

Florida Star v. B.J.F. 491 U.S. 524 (1989)

Galella v. Onassis, 353 F.Supp. 196 (SD NY, 1972), 533 F.Supp. 1076 (DC NY, 1982), 487 F.2d 986 (CA NY, 1973)

Griswold v. Connecticut, 381 U.S. 479 (1965)

Huskey v. NBC (U.S. DC N.Ill., 1986) 12 Med.L.Rptr. 2105

Lambert v. Dow Chemical Co., 215 So.2d 673 (LA. App., 1968)

Lawrence v. A.S. Abell Co. (MD CA, 1984) 10 Med.L.Rptr. 2001

LeMistral, Inc. v. CBS, 61 A.D.2d. 491, 402 N.Y.S.2d 815 (NY App.Div., 1978)

Lerman v. Chuckleberry (US DC S.NY, 1981) 7 Med.L.Rptr. 2282, 2284

Liberty Lobby v. Pearson, 390 F.2d 489 (DC Cir., 1968)

Little v. Washington Post (DC DC, 1985) 11 Med.L.Rptr. 1428

Lugosi v. Universal Pictures, 25 Cal.3d 813, 603 P.2d 425, 5 Med.L.Rptr. 2185 (1979)

Machleder v. Diaz (U.S. DC So.NY, 1985) 12 Med.L.Rptr. 1193

Manola v. Stevens, N.Y. Sup.Ct. 1890

Mark v. Seattle Times (Wash. Sup.Ct., 1982) 7 Med.L.Rptr. 2209

Marx Production v. Day and Night Co., (DC S.NY, 1981) 7 Med.L.Rptr. 2030

Melvin v. Reid, 112 Cal.App. 285, 297, p. 91 (1931)

Memphis Development Foundation v. Factors Etc. Inc., (6th Cir., 1980) 5 Med.L.Rptr. 2521, cert. denied 449 U.S. 953 (1980)

Messner Inc. v. Warren E. Spahn, 393 U.S. 1046 (1967)

Missouri ex rel. Nixon v. American Blast Fax, Inc., ____ F. Supp. 2d ____, 2002 U.S. Dist. LEXIS 5707, 2002 WL 508330 (E.D. Mo. Mar. 13, 2002)

Negri v. Schering Corp., 333 F.Supp. 101, 105 (1969)

New York Times v. Sullivan, 376 U.S. 279–80 (1964)

Onassis v. Christian Dior, (NY Sup.Ct., 1984) 10 Med.L.Rptr. 1861

Pavesich v. New England Life Insurance Co., 122 Ga. 190, 50 S.F. 68, 69 L.R.A. 101 (1905)

Pearson v. Dodd, 410 F.2d 701 (DC Cir., 1969), cert. denied 395 U.S. 947 (1969)

People v. Berliner (NYC Ct., 1978) 3 Med.L.Rptr. 1942

People v. Kunkin, 100 Cal.Rptr. 845 (1972)

People v. Kunkin, 107 Cal.Rptr. 184 (1973)

Roberson v. Rochester Folding Box Co., 171 NY 538, 64 N.E. 442 (1902)

Roe v. Wade, 410 U.S. 113 (1973)

Sidis v. F-R Publishing Corporation, 113 F.2d 806 (1940)

Sipple v. Chronicle Publishing Co. (CA Ct.App., 1984) 10 Med.L.Rptr. 1690

Taylor v. KTVB, Inc., 96 Idaho 202, 525 P.2d 984 (1974)

Time Inc. v. Hill, 385 U.S. 374 (1967)

Virgil v. Time Inc., 527 F.2d 1122 (9th Cir., 1975)

WCH of Waverly v. Meredith Corp. (DC W.Mo., 1986) 13 Med.L.Rptr. 1648

Wehling v. CBS (CA 5, 1983) 10 Med.L.Rptr. 1125
White v. Samsung Electronics America Inc., 989 F.2d 1512, 21
    Med.L.Rptr. 1330 (9th Cir.), cert. denied 113 S.Ct. 2443 (1993)
Wood v. Hustler (U.S. CA 5, 1984) 10 Med.L.Rptr. 2113
Zacchini v. Scripps-Howard, 433 U.S. 562 (1977)

10

Defamation: Libel and the Media

Libel may be defined generally as a publication or broadcast that is injurious to the reputation of another. Libel includes defamatory material that is expressed in print, pictures, signs, or is broadcast by radio, television, or cable communications media. Gillmor and Barron define libel as "a defamatory, false, malicious, or negligent publication that tends to hold a person up to hatred, contempt, or ridicule, causing him or her to be shunned or avoided."[1] Essentially, libel changes the way an individual is viewed by others. In the United States, there is no single definition of libel, because each state and the District of Columbia define libel for their own jurisdictions. Fortunately, the definitions are similar, which allows for general characteristics of libel to be deduced.

Libel and its spoken counterpart, slander, have roots in English common law. Traditionally, libel involved printing a defamatory statement, while slander was a verbal defamation. Records indicate that slander was recognized as a cause of action as far back as the thirteenth century. Libel was criminal in its origin and has remained a common law crime. Slander could only become a criminal offense when the words amounted to another offense, such as blasphemy or sedition. Defamation was part of England's ecclesiastical law of the Middle Ages and was punishable as a sin until the Protestant reformation. The common law of the Middle Ages provided that

> If one calls a man "wolf" or "hare" one must pay him three shillings, while if one calls a woman "harlot" and can not prove the truth of the charge, one must pay forty-five shillings. . . . the man who falsely called another a "thief" or "manslayer" must pay damages, and, holding his nose with his fingers, must publicly confess himself a liar.[2]

Although the punishment was refined over the centuries, libel became a part of England's statutory law in 1792 with the passage of the Fox Libel Act.

Slander is usually heard by fewer individuals and is more ephemeral in impact, while libel usually commands a wider audience and, because it involves printed or broadcast matter, is usually more permanent. Because libel represents a potentially greater harm to a person's reputation, greater damages are awarded. Although it would seem that defamatory material broadcast on radio or television would be prosecuted as slander, the pervasive nature of the broadcast media, coupled with the fact that most broadcasts are scripted, causes most broadcast defamation to be treated as libel.

An exception to this rule occurred in the case of a San Diego woman mistakenly identified as a prostitute in a 1983 news report by KCST-TV. The California Supreme Court refused to review a Fourth District Court of Appeals ruling ordering KCST to pay Naomi O'Hara $300,000 plus $165,000 in interest as a judgment in her slander case against the station. However, this is not always the case, as evidenced in *Brauer v. Globe Newspaper Co.* An actionable libel may involve only three people—the plaintiff, the defendant, and a witness.

As in England, common law courts in America were concerned with the protection of reputation. Until 1964, all libel cases in the United States were governed by the common law, as applied by the various states. The landmark Supreme Court decision in *New York Times v. Sullivan (1964)* brought libel law under the constitutional umbrella. Since then, the courts have viewed libel as a First Amendment issue that balances the right of free speech against the protection of an individual's or corporation's reputation.

Elements of Actionable Libel

No libel suit can succeed unless a plaintiff can establish that three elements have been met:

- The plaintiff must establish that a false defamatory statement was made by the defendant,
- that the plaintiff is clearly identified as the person defamed, and
- that the defamatory statement was published in some manner.

Defamation

Direct Libel—*per se*

The words in question must be interpreted as damaging to the plaintiff's reputation. Under the common law, libel *per se* (or direct libel) might have included calling someone a "thief" or a "murderer." Libel *per se* survives today. However, the words regarded as libelous need not be specific. The average reader or listener must merely conclude that plaintiffs were engaged in activities that are damaging to their reputations. For example, in

Donaldson v. Washington Post Co., the *Washington Post* was declared guilty of libel when it falsely reported that Michael Donaldson pleaded guilty to a murder charge. When journalist Victor Lasky referred to West Virginia college professor Luella Mundel as a "Communist" in an ABC television broadcast about the McCarthy era of the 1950s, a New York district court ruled in *Lasky v. ABC* that the statement was libelous.

It is defamatory to say that someone is a drunkard, has attempted suicide, is immoral or unchaste, is "queer," is a hypocrite, is a coward, has made improper advances to women, is having "wife trouble," is "unfair" to labor, or has done something dishonorable.

Courts do attempt to separate assertions of fact from statements made in the heat of an argument. Calling someone a "sleaze bag" may not be libel *per se*, because it is difficult to define just what is meant by the term. In *Fleming v. Kane County*, an Illinois court ruled that when a fired employee called his former supervisor a "gutless bastard" and a "black son of a bitch," the terms were not libel *per se*. However, when the former employee called him a "liar," the court found the statement actionable as defamation.

"Alleged" Doesn't Get You Off the Hook

The use of the word "alleged" before a statement accusing someone of a crime or other potentially libelous act does not render the statement nondefamatory. As we shall see later in this chapter, it is not libelous to report accurately that someone has been charged with murder. It is libelous to call someone an "alleged murderer."

Indirect Libels—*per quod*

Libel *per quod* (or indirect libel) is libel that is not evident from the words themselves but is implied. Although libel *per quod* is a common law concept, courts still sometimes distinguish between indirect and direct libel. The working journalist or broadcaster must understand the concept, because the choice of language may invite an unanticipated libel suit. The classic common law example of libel *per quod* would be the newspaper publication that erroneously indicates that a newly married woman has just given birth to a child. Under the common law of libel *per quod*, the woman could sue for damages, provided she could show that her reputation had been harmed by the announcement. These classic cases still occur. When a Charlottesville, Virginia, newspaper identified a married woman (who had filed charges against a man for rape) as "Miss" and then casually mentioned in the same article that she was pregnant, the Virginia Supreme Court agreed, in *Charlottesville Newspapers Inc. v. Debra C. Matthews*, that she had been libeled. The mistake cost *The Daily Progress* $25,000 in damages. In 1961, the *Spokane Chronicle* falsely reported that Phillip Pitts had obtained a divorce in 1961. Pitts married his second wife shortly after actually obtaining the divorce in 1960. In *Pitts v. Spokane Chronicle Co.*, the Washington Supreme Court ruled that Pitts was defamed because the newspaper article made it appear that he was a bigamist.

Indirect libels are seldom easy to identify in reality. They lurk in the interpretation of seemingly innocent words. For example, the word "fix" can have several meanings. When used in the context of "fixing" a court case, the word can take on a defamatory meaning. In *McCall v. Courier Journal*, the word "fix" was associated with a bribery investigation. McCall, an attorney, brought a libel suit against the *Louisville Courier Journal* for implying that he would "fix" a case. When a defamatory meaning is not apparent, the plaintiff has the burden of proving that a defamatory meaning was intended. A statement that someone has burned down their own house is not defamatory per se. However, if it can be shown that the words were understood to mean that he had done so in order to defraud an insurance company, the statement would be defamatory.

In *Tavoulareas v. Washington Post*, the president of Mobil Oil, William Tavoulareas, sued the *Washington Post* for libel as a result of a 1979 article that stated that the oil company president had "set up" his son in a shipping venture. The article was originally found defamatory in 1982 by a trial court because it implied that Tavoulareas had engaged in nepotism, breached his fiduciary duty, and misused corporate assets. A jury awarded Tavoulareas $2 million. In 1983, the presiding judge declared that the article was not libelous because it represented "unbiased investigative journalism." In 1985, a three-judge panel reinstated the jury verdict once again. An appellate court overturned the decision on grounds that the *Washington Post* story was substantially true and was not published with actual malice. In 1987, eight years after the publication of the article, the Supreme Court refused to review the case, allowing the court of appeals decision to stand. Although ultimately the decision was in favor of the media, the cost of defending against such a case can be time-consuming and costly. For this reason, the media will usually try to avoid going to court.

Headlines

Courts have ruled that headlines may be the basis for a libel action, even if the story that follows is not defamatory. A headline must be a "fair index" of an accurate article with which it appears. A headline reading "Records Reveal Gifts to Police Jury Members," followed as it was by references to "gestures of friendship" in a report about the plaintiff's unethical activities, was judged defamatory in *Buratt v. Capital City Press*.

Headlines are supposed to attract a reader's attention. Some newspapers feel the urge to "spice up" an otherwise bland story with tantalizing banners that are not exactly related to the story that follows. Supermarket tabloids are notorious for this practice. Captions such as "Aliens Found in Arizona Desert" are usually followed by stories about a tour bus loaded with German tourists stranded when the bus broke down on the way to Las Vegas. Although sometimes irritating, such mismatched stories do no real harm. There are times, however, when an individual's reputation is at stake. The courts have taken a dim view of misleading headlines because often it is only the headlines that are read.

Broadcasters must use similar caution when it comes to "promos," "bumpers," and "teases" used to build an audience for upcoming newscasts. In addition, the use of "B-roll" or "generic" shots can be sources of trouble. Although, in recent years, most cases of this type have been decided in favor of the media, the cost of defending such suits successfully warrants caution.

Innocent Construction Rule

Some states (e.g., Illinois, Ohio, and Indiana) adhere to the innocent construction rule. This means that if the language is capable of nondefamatory meaning, it should be interpreted that way. In most states, the words must be given their natural meaning and courts are not to seek inferences that may be unintended. Some states require that a jury determine the meaning of language that is susceptible to both defamatory and nondefamatory meanings.

Identification

Plaintiffs must show that defamatory statements refer to them. Anyone exposed to the defamatory material must reasonably infer that it is intended to describe the plaintiff. The identification need not refer to the plaintiff by name. In the landmark case, *New York Times v. Sullivan*, the term "Southern violators" was sufficient identification for L. B. Sullivan to establish identification in his libel suit filed in Alabama against the *New York Times*.

Author Gwen Davis Mitchell lost a libel suit resulting from a work of fiction. Even though the physical characteristics of the character in her novel *Touching* did not resemble the plaintiff, a California court ruled that there were enough other similarities to permit identification and, ultimately, libel.

In *Touching*, Mitchell created a character called Simon Herford. Herford was a psychiatrist who conducted nude therapy sessions. Prior to writing the novel, Mitchell had attended similar sessions under Dr. Bindrim, a psychologist. Mitchell had signed a contract with Bindrim agreeing not to disclose what had taken place in the therapy sessions. Upon publication of the novel,

Bindrim asserted that the character of Simon Herford was identifiable as himself. Bindrim also asserted that the book contained several false statements of fact and that several incidents described in the book were libelous. One such incident depicted an encounter group patient who became so distressed after a weekend of nude therapy that she is killed when she crashes her car. Bindrim also objected to his being depicted as "pressing," "clutching," "ripping" a patient's cheeks, and calling a female patient a "bitch."

Mitchell claimed that the character Herford was not Bindrim. She also claimed that there can be no statement of false fact, because *Touching* is a novel and is not based on fact. In *Bindrim v. Mitchell*, the court ruled in favor of the plaintiff.

☐   . . . In the case at bar the only differences between plaintiff and the Herford character in *Touching* were physical appearance and that Herford was a psychiatrist rather than psychologist. Otherwise, the character Simon Herford was very similar to the actual plaintiff.

. . . Plaintiff was identified as Herford by several witnesses and plaintiff's own tape recordings of the marathon sessions show that the novel was based substantially on plaintiff's conduct in the nude marathon. . . . There is overwhelming evidence that plaintiff and "Herford" were one.

. . . The test is whether a reasonable person, reading the book, would understand that the fictional character therein pictured was, in actual fact, the plaintiff acting as described.[3]

The court went on to say that if only one reader assumed that Bindrim was Herford, that would be sufficient for identification. The false facts, based on real incidents, gave rise to the libel verdict.

Publication

The real harm in libel comes in publication. It is at the time when others are exposed to the defamation that damage to reputation may occur. Publication may be in the form of a magazine or newspaper story, a radio or television broadcast, a posting on the Internet, a handbill distributed on the street, or a memo to a secretary in the office. The publication must also be intended by the defamer. The victim may not publish a private defamatory communication and then sue for libel. Unlike defamation and identification, publication is usually not a contested issue in a libel case. The printed matter or tape containing the alleged defamation is most often the basis on which a libel suit is originally filed. Any repetition or republication of the original defamation is grounds for additional libel action. Many states adhere to the single publication rule, which treats all copies of a single edition or press run of a defamatory statement as one count of libel.

Under the complicity rule, reporters, editors, and publishers are all liable in a defamation suit. This liability is based on the premise that editors and publishers have the responsibility for approving the work of the reporters. Therefore, any published defamatory material should have been checked by them. Some contributing personnel may not be named in the publication process, including technicians and office workers. In 1986 in *Catalfo v. Jensen*, a U.S. district court held that a freelance photographer who was responsible only for the photographs accompanying an allegedly defamatory article was not part of the publishing process. The photographer had no hand in writing or editing the article.

When a communications medium exercises editorial control over material it becomes liable for defamatory statements that it publishes. The editorial practices of online Internet services, like America Online and CompuServe, have raised questions as to their culpability as publishers in defamation matters.

Provided that an online service does not exercise editorial control over content posted by subscribers on the site, the service is not treated as a publisher and is not subject to libel laws. In *Cubby Inc. v. CompuServe Inc. (1991)* the court noted that CompuServe had no editorial system in place and was therefore not liable for statements published on its service by third parties.

If an online service does exercise editorial control over content, it becomes a publisher and thereby is subject to libel law. The online service Prodigy prescreened messages posted on its bulletin boards. When a subscriber posted a defamatory message, the New York Supreme Court determined that the service was guilty of publishing a libelous statement in *Stratton Oakmont, Inc. v. Prodigy Services Co. (1995)*.

Individuals and corporations are still subject to liability for defamatory statements posted or otherwise transmitted online, however it is the service provider that has been afforded immunity.

The Telecommunications Act of 1996 provides additional protection for online providers and users. Section 509 states:

> No provider or user of an interactive computer service shall be treated as the publisher or speaker of any information provided by another information content provider.

Common Law Defenses

Under the common law, once a plaintiff establishes the three elements of an actionable libel (i.e., defamation, identification, and publication), the burden of proof shifts to the defendant. The defamation is assumed to be false unless the defendant can prove otherwise. Therefore, in common law libel cases, the burden of proof is said to be on the defendant. Publishers accused of libel could defend themselves by claiming that the defamatory statement was true, that the defamatory statement was protected by privilege, or that the defamatory statement was a fair comment or criticism of the public performance of an official or entertainer.

Truth

The defendant who pleads truth in a libel case does not have to prove literally every aspect of the charge, but must show that the statement that is charged as defamatory is substantially true. For example, in *Baia v. Jackson Newspapers*, a newspaper article stating that a man had been charged with "pulling off" a bank robbery when, in fact, he had been charged with conspiracy to commit bank robbery, was judged substantially true by a Connecticut court.

When a television station accurately reported as part of an investigative story on auto repair shops, that the Action Repair Company was unwilling to talk and had cancelled interviews, a California court ruled in *Action Repair v. ABC* that the report was true and thus nondefamatory.

A court may determine that alleged defamatory statements are true if a reasonable jury could come to only one conclusion. When *60 Minutes* aired a story that contained the statement "multipiece tire rims kill people," the statement was found to be true in *Redco Corporation v. CBS*, even though no one had died from injuries incurred in accidents involving multipiece rims manufactured by the plaintiff.

Proving truth is not always as simple as it first appears. Reporters are sometimes convinced of the truth of the charges they have made. Circumstantial evidence may be in a defendant's favor. However, convincing a jury is another matter. Sometimes the evidence needed is simply not available. Although truth may be a complete defense, it can be costly and may not be practical.

Privilege

There are two types of privilege—absolute and qualified. Absolute privilege applies to agencies of government, the courts, and government officials when they are conducting official business. One cannot sue for defamatory remarks made as part of an official court proceeding. Similarly, absolute privilege exists for remarks made as part of political campaigns and broadcast on radio and television stations. Stations may not edit remarks, nor may they be sued for broadcasting defamatory material under Section 315 of the Communications Act.

Qualified privilege protects the media in their coverage of public affairs. The underlying rationale is that in a democracy, the public has a right to be informed about public issues. The qualification is that these reports be fair and accurate.

Under the common law, journalists could publish a fair and accurate report of any public or official meeting at any level of government. Information contained in reports or proceedings of these meetings could also be published. Additional protection was afforded under the "actual malice" ruling of *New York Times v. Sullivan* and the "negligence" standard of *Gertz v. Robert Welch Inc. (1974)*.

Information found in public records, such as official arrest reports, court records, and other local or state documents, is protected under the defense of privilege. Although state laws regarding privilege differ, protection is usually afforded for publication of material on which official action has been taken and that contains accurate and current information. The point at which "official action" took place is sometimes questionable. Reporting based only on information gathered from a police scanner would not be privileged information. An arrest that has not formally been entered on the police blotter would not constitute official action and therefore would not be privileged.

The common law standards of "fair and accurate reporting" must also be observed in order for privilege to be an effective defense. When *Playboy* magazine reported the criminal conviction of Thelma Torres, a federal customs inspector, they relied on out-of-date records. During the four months between her initial conviction and the publication of the *Playboy* article, Torres was given a new trial and acquitted. In *Torres v. Playboy*, *Playboy* lost the defenses of both privilege and truth, because the court ruled that the article did not accurately represent Torres' case.

In some states, privilege includes information gathered at all public meetings where public issues are discussed. This would include public meetings of unions, church boards, political parties, and medical or bar associations.

Fair Comment

The defense of fair comment traditionally involved an honest expression of opinion on a matter of public interest. The common law defense has now been incorporated into the constitutional defense outlined in *New York Times v. Sullivan* and by language found in *Gertz v. Welch*. This includes commentary on the conduct of government and public officials and criticisms of various entertainment media, including restaurant reviews, theater, television, sports, and movies. Provided these commentaries limit themselves to opinion and are not published with actual malice (i.e., knowing falsehood or reckless disregard for the truth), they enjoy absolute immunity from libel. In *Gertz v. Welch*, the Supreme Court stated,

☐ Under the First Amendment there is no such thing as a false idea. However pernicious an opinion may seem, we depend for its correction not on . . . judges and juries but on the competition of other ideas.[4]

Other Defenses

Neutral Reportage

Some states recognize the privilege of neutral reportage. This privilege protects all accurate and neutral republications of defamatory statements made by persons involved in public controversies against public figures involved in that controversy. The defense was first articulated in *Edwards v. National Audubon Society (1977)*. Essentially, neutral reportage provides immunity from defamation suits for journalists who believe that they are reporting an accurate account of defamatory remarks or charges against a public figure.

In *Barry v. Time*, the privilege of neutral reportage protected *Time* magazine's accurate account of a basketball player's charge that he had received illegal payments from his coach, even though the player had pleaded guilty to aggravated assault and had failed to pass a lie detector test regarding that assault. Similarly, in *J. V. Peters v. Knight Ridder*, the *Akron Beacon Journal's* accurate report of a statement made by a state attorney regarding the dumping of toxic wastes by J. V. Peters & Company was ruled to be newsworthy and protected as neutral reportage. The report was a statement made by a public person, about a public controversy, and directed at another public person involved in the controversy.

Most states, including New York and Kentucky, do not recognize the privilege of neutral reportage. In *McCall v. Courier Journal*, the Kentucky Supreme Court rejected the privilege defense, noting that the "doctrine has not been approved by the Supreme Court of the United States and has not received approval in other jurisdictions."[5] The U.S. Supreme Court declined to review both *Edwards* and *McCall*, thereby placing the defense of neutral reportage on somewhat uncertain ground.

The Libel-Proof Doctrine—
A Mitigating Factor

Questions of moral character and fidelity may be direct libel, but courts sometimes consider the previous reputation of a plaintiff when determining if suit may be brought. Courts have ruled that the reputations of some individuals render them libel-proof. In *Cardillo v. Doubleday Inc.*, the libel-proof doctrine was established. The Second Circuit Court of Appeals ruled that the reputation of a man convicted on several charges, including conspiracy, could not be further damaged by allegations that he had participated in a robbery and attempted to fix a horse race. Subsequent cases in which plaintiffs' reputations were classified as libel-proof include *Ray v. Time Inc.*, in which the convicted assassin of Dr. Martin Luther King objected to allegations he had been involved in other criminal activity; *Jackson v. Longcape*, in which a convicted murderer objected to a newspaper report that he raped and strangled his victims, when not all were killed in that manner; and *Logan v. District of Columbia*, in which an admitted drug user claimed the media exaggerated the number of times he tested positive for drug use.

In *Schiavone Construction v. Time*, *Time* magazine's publication of a report linking the president of a construction company with organized crime and the disappearance of Jimmy Hoffa was originally found libelous *per se* by a New Jersey district court. Later, the court ruled that because of numerous published reports linking the company to organized crime, and because information had been obtained from FBI files, both the company and its president were libel-proof.

In *Guccione v. Hustler*, when *Hustler* published the false statement that *Penthouse* magazine publisher Bob Guccione "is married and has a live-in girlfriend," a U.S. district court found the statement to be libelous per se, because it implied that Guccione was engaged in an adulterous relationship. The jury awarded Guccione $1.6 million in punitive damages and $1.00 in compensatory damages.

However, the U.S. court of appeals overturned the verdict because of Guccione's long-term relationship with his "girlfriend" prior to and following his divorce. Guccione's reputation thus rendered him libel-proof. Writing for the court, Judge Newman noted that as publisher of *Penthouse*, Guccione often advocated conduct that he now asserted was libelous to him. While statements calling someone an adulterer would generally be libelous *per se*, because the duration of Guccione's adultery had encompassed 13 of the past 17 years, the court concluded that his reputation had not been further damaged by the *Hustler* article.

Like neutral reportage, the libel-proof doctrine is by no means universally accepted. It is not a part of federal constitutional law, and states are free to accept or reject the doctrine.

Damages

Plaintiffs who successfully sue publishers or broadcasters may recover three kinds of damages: compensatory or general damages, special or actual damages, and punitive damages. State laws and the landmark Supreme Court case *Gertz v. Robert Welch Inc.* greatly affect the kinds of damages that may be awarded. Some states allow only actual damages to be collected, and many prohibit punitive damages. The Gertz ruling prohibits punitive damages if actual malice has not been demonstrated by the plaintiff.

Compensatory or general damages are awarded for injury to reputation. These damages are assumed in most libel *per se* cases and are based on humiliation, shame, embarrassment, and emotional distress. A jury may set the amount of the award, which may be reviewed by a judge.

Special or actual damages are meant to compensate for proven monetary loss suffered as a result of a defamatory statement. Kentucky and Indiana allow libel plaintiffs to recover only special or actual damages. In the Kentucky Code, "special damages" are defined as pecuniary (monetary) damages that are suffered by a libel plaintiff in respect to his property, business, trade, profession, or occupation. Plaintiffs may also recover money spent as a result of any defamation.[6] In the Indiana Code, "actual damages" is defined in much the same way. Indiana plaintiffs may recover only damages suffered in respect to character, property, business, trade, profession, or occupation, and no other damages whatever.[7]

Punitive damages are meant to punish a publisher or broadcaster for communicating a defamatory statement. Punitive damage awards are high so as to serve as a deterrent to others who may consider publishing similar material. This tactic, however, raises the issue of prior restraint. Punitive damages are controversial in that publishers may shy away from potentially libelous material for fear of incurring fines that might put them out of business. They may also be a death sentence for small publications. For example, in 1981, a small newspaper in Illinois was nearly put out of business after losing a $9.2 million judgment in *Green v. Alton Telegraph*. The case was settled for $1.4 million and the *Alton Telegraph* managed to borrow just enough money to stay in business. Similarly, in *Pring v. Penthouse*, although the case eventually was reversed, *Penthouse* magazine originally lost a $26 million judgment for publishing a work of fiction entitled (and espousing) "Miss Wyoming's Unique Talents."

In 1986, in *Newton v. NBC*, a jury awarded singer Wayne Newton $19.3 million in punitive damages in his suit against NBC. That figure was reduced to $5.27 million by the court and overturned completely by the Ninth U.S. Circuit Court. The U.S. Supreme Court refused to hear the case in 1991. Newton alleged he was defamed by NBC broadcasts linking him to organized crime.

The trend of reversing large awards continued through the 1990s. In 2000 a $600,000 award was reversed in *Journal Publishing v. McCullough (1999)*.

Retraction Statutes

A number of states have retraction statutes. These laws allow a publisher to mitigate (or lessen) the harm done by a defamatory statement. Most retraction statutes require that a publisher essentially admit that the defamatory statement was false and apologize for that statement. Usually, the retraction must be timely, without comment, and as prominently displayed as the original libelous statement. Burying the retraction with the crossword puzzles, for example, will not suffice. It should be remembered that, in most jurisdictions, a retraction merely mitigates damages and may help to demonstrate a lack of malice. A retraction may result in a disallowance of punitive damages, but special or actual damages may still be awarded. For example, Indiana requires that a plaintiff notify a publisher in writing three days before filing a libel suit, identifying the statements in a given article which are thought to be false and defamatory. The publisher then has three days to print a "full and fair retraction" or face the filing of a suit. Many publishers are reluctant to retract, for to do so is a direct admission of fault and injures their credibility.

States may not force a publisher to retract defamatory statements. Ohio's retraction statutes once required newspapers to print within 48 hours any demanded correction of any false statement, allegation, or rumor. This statute was found to be in violation of the First Amendment. In *Beacon Journal v. Lansdowne*, the Summit County Common Pleas Court of Ohio noted that the Ohio retraction statutes "clearly result in the coerced publication of particular views and thus violate the First Amendment."[8]

Publishing a retraction in and of itself may not be enough to mitigate a charge of actual malice. When a New York newspaper published a defamatory article based on research that did not comply with accepted standards of the newsgathering profession, the court ruled in *Kerwick v. Orange County Publications* that the paper's retraction was not sufficient to establish a lack of actual malice. Conversely, in *Pelzer v. Minneapolis Tribune*, the failure to retract an allegedly libelous statement did not show automatically that the publisher had acted with actual malice.

Statute of Limitations

Libel suits must be filed within a certain period of time. Most states have statutes of limitations of two years, although some require suits to be brought anywhere from one year to as much as three years after a defamatory statement has been published. In all cases, the statute begins running when a publication goes into general circulation for the first time. For newspapers, this usually means the date on the edition containing the alleged defamatory statement. For broadcasters, it means the date of the first broadcast in question. Because magazines often distribute editions months ahead of the date listed on the cover, statutes of limitations are not triggered by that date. Instead, magazines are governed by the date on which substantial distribution occurred.

National publications whose materials are distributed in states with varying statutes of limitations may find that, although the statute has run out in one state, a plaintiff may file suit in another state. In *Keeton v. Hustler*, the Supreme Court ruled that plaintiffs may search for states having lengthy statutes of limitations and bring suits in those states, provided a substantial number of copies of the offending publication are regularly sold and distributed there.

Consent

A minor defense against a libel suit is that of consent. A written statement giving permission to publish a statement (provided that the statement has not been edited so as to change its meaning) may be a complete defense. At other times, consent may serve to mitigate damages and charges of actual malice.

In *Falwell v. Penthouse (1981)*, the Reverend Jerry Falwell sued *Penthouse* magazine for the publication of an accurate account of an interview he had granted to a freelance journalist. Falwell, a public figure and an outspoken critic of magazines like *Penthouse*, granted the interview under conditions given verbally to the author. Essentially, Falwell stated that the interview should be sold to a magazine that was consistent with the image of his ministry. When the interview was published in the March 1981 issue of *Penthouse*, Falwell appeared on the cover of the magazine. That space was usually reserved for scantily clad women. Falwell contended that the reporter had violated his consent and had acted with actual malice by selling the article to a publication embarrassing to Falwell. The court dismissed the suit, noting

☐   . . . The mere fact that the plaintiff may not approve of publications such as *Penthouse*, or may not desire *Penthouse* to discuss his activities or publish his spoken words, does not give rise to an action cognizable under the law. The First Amendment freedoms of speech and press are too precious to be eroded or undermined by the likes and dislikes of persons who invite attention and publicity by their own voluntary actions.[9]

The Constitutional Defense

Before 1964 and the *New York Times* decision, libel suits were a matter of state law. For the most part, states recognized the previously discussed common law defenses. However, they sometimes differed in their application of principles. One such principle involves the criticism of public officials. The constitutional defense extends qualified privilege and bases it on the First Amendment guarantee of freedom of the press, coupled with the Warren Court's belief that our elected officials should expect public criticism of their official conduct. The media are now given wide latitude in reporting on public officials, public figures, and public issues. The constitutional defense recognizes that individual reputations must yield to the greater constitutional right freely to report the news, even if it may be false.

The Burden of Proof

The constitutional defense has superseded the common law defense of fair comment and has shifted the burden of proving truth from the defendant to the plaintiff. Case law since 1964 has established that libel plaintiffs must establish the falsity of a defamatory statement. Public figure plaintiffs must also establish that misstatements of fact were made with actual malice. The Supreme Court defined actual malice in *New York Times v. Sullivan* as a false statement made "with knowledge that it was false or with reckless disregard of whether it was false or not."[10]

The constitutional defense grew out of a case that was representative of the turbulent 1960s. The principals involved were the major leaders of the burgeoning civil rights movement. As the movement altered America's social laws over the next decade, so too would *New York Times v. Sullivan* alter American libel law.

New York Times v. Sullivan (1964)

On March 29, 1960, the *New York Times* published a full-page editorial advertisement under the headline "Heed Their Rising Voices." The advertisement was placed by civil rights activists in the South. They were soliciting funds to aid in the legal defense of Dr. Martin Luther King, Jr. The activists also sought support for what they called "embattled students" and for the voting rights movement in the South. The advertisement follows:

HEED THEIR RISING VOICES
As the whole world knows by now, thousands of Southern Negro
students are engaged in wide-spread non-violent demonstrations in
positive affirmation of the right to live in human dignity as guaranteed
by the U.S. Constitution and the Bill of Rights. In their efforts to uphold

these guarantees, they are being met by an unprecedented wave of terror by those who would deny and negate that document which the whole world looks upon as setting the pattern for modern freedom. . . .

In Orangeburg, South Carolina, when 400 students peacefully sought to buy doughnuts and coffee at lunch counters in the business district they were forcibly ejected, tear gassed, soaked to the skin in freezing weather with fire hoses, arrested en masse and herded into an open barbed-wire stockade to stand for hours in the bitter cold.

In Montgomery, Alabama, after students sang "My Country 'Tis of Thee" on the State Capitol steps their leaders were expelled from school, and truckloads of police armed with shotguns and tear gas ringed the Alabama State College Campus. When the entire student body protested to state authorities by refusing to re-register, their dining hall was padlocked in an attempt to starve them into submission.

In Tallahassee, Atlanta, Nashville, Savannah, Greensboro, Memphis, Richmond, Charlotte, and a host of other cities in the South, young American teenagers, in the face of the entire weight of official state apparatus and police power, have boldly stepped forth as protagonists of democracy. Their courage and amazing restraint have inspired millions and given a new dignity to the cause of freedom.

Small wonder that the Southern violators of the Constitution fear this new, non-violent brand of freedom fighter. . . . even as they fear the upswelling right-to-vote movement. Small wonder that they are determined to destroy the one man who, more than any other, symbolizes the new spirit now sweeping the South—the Rev. Dr. Martin Luther King, Jr., world-famous leader of the Montgomery Bus Protest. . . .

Again and again the Southern violators have answered Dr. King's peaceful protests with intimidation and violence. They have bombed his home, almost killing his wife and child. They have assaulted his person. They have arrested him seven times—for "speeding," "loitering" and similar "offenses." And now they have charged him with "perjury"—a felony under which they could imprison him for ten years. Obviously, their real purpose is to remove him physically as the leader to whom the students—and millions of others—look for guidance and support, and thereby to intimidate all leaders who may rise in the South. . . . The defense of Martin Luther . . . is an integral part of the total struggle for freedom in the South.

Decent-minded Americans cannot help but applaud the creative daring of the students and the quiet heroism of Dr. King. But this is one of those moments in the history of Freedom when men and women of good will must do more than applaud the rising-to-glory of others. . . .

We must heed their rising voices—yes—but we must add our own.

We urge you to join hands with our fellow Americans in the South by supporting, with your dollars, this Combined Appeal for all three needs—the defense of Martin Luther King—the support of the embattled students—and the struggle for the right to vote.[11]

The ad was signed by 64 prominent Americans, including former First Lady Eleanor Roosevelt, journalist Nat Hentoff, and major league baseball's first black player, Jackie Robinson. Also among the signatories were show business personalities such as Marlon Brando, Sammy Davis, Jr., Harry Belafonte, Sidney Poitier, Nat "King" Cole, Diahann Carroll, Hope Lange, Robert Ryan, and Shelley Winters. In addition, 16 southern clergymen were purported to have signed the ad. They included the Reverends Ralph D. Abernathy, Fred L. Shuttlesworth, and Martin Luther King, Sr.

A coupon appeared in the lower right-hand corner of the ad urging readers to "mail this coupon TODAY!" along with a contribution to the Committee to Defend Martin Luther King and The Struggle for Freedom in the South.

L.B. Sullivan, the elected police commissioner of Montgomery, Alabama, objected to several passages contained in the third and fifth paragraphs of the ad. The ad contained several factual errors that related to questionable or illegal activities by the Montgomery police. Although Sullivan was not mentioned by name, he contended that he represented the "police" and was therefore being accused of "ringing the campus" and "starving the students into submission." He also claimed that he was characterized as one of the "Southern violators" being accused of "intimidation and violence," bombing Dr. King's home, and falsely charging King with perjury. Sullivan filed suit against four of the clergymen who had signed the ad and who had been critical of the conduct of the police during civil rights demonstrations in Montgomery. In accordance with Alabama law, Sullivan demanded a retraction from the clergymen and the *New York Times*. The clergymen said that their signatures were unauthorized and took no further part in the case. The *New York Times* could not understand how the ad applied to Sullivan.

Under the common law, the burden of proof was on the *New York Times*, and a trial court in Alabama found portions of the ad libelous *per se*. The court also ruled that Sullivan could be identified as representing the "police" and "Southern violators." The Alabama Supreme Court upheld the trial court's award of $500,000 to Sullivan, and the *New York Times* appealed to the United States Supreme Court. The Supreme Court unanimously reversed the judgment and, in its decision, granted the media greater protection from libel suits filed by public officials. This was done by bringing such suits into the realm of constitutional law. Justice Brennan delivered the opinion of the Court.

☐ We hold that the rule of law applied by the Alabama courts is constitutionally deficient for failure to provide the safeguards for freedom of speech and of the press that are required by the First and Fourteenth Amendments in a libel action brought by a public official against critics of his official conduct. . . .

The general proposition that freedom of expression upon public questions is secured by the First Amendment has long been settled by our decisions. The constitutional safeguard, we have said, "was fashioned to assure [sic] the unfettered interchange of ideas for bringing about political and social changes desired by the people." *Roth v. United States*, 354 U.S. 476 (1957). . . . "It is a prized American privilege to speak one's mind, although not always with perfect good taste, on all public institutions." *Bridges v. California* 314 U.S. 252 (1941). . . .

Thus we consider this case against the background of a profound national commitment to the principle that debate on public issues should be uninhibited, robust, and wide-open, and that it may well include vehement, caustic, and sometimes unpleasantly sharp attacks on government and public officials.

The present advertisement, as an expression of grievance and protest on one of the major public issues of our time, would seem clearly to qualify for constitutional protection. . . .

Authoritative interpretations of the First Amendment guarantees have consistently refused to recognize an exception for any test of truth, whether administered by judges, juries, or administrative officials—and especially not one that puts the burden of providing truth on the speaker. . . .

The constitutional guarantees require, we think, a federal rule that prohibits a public official from recovering damages for a defamatory falsehood relating to his official conduct unless he proves that the statement was made with "actual malice"—that is, with knowledge that it was false or with reckless disregard of whether it was false or not. . . .

We conclude that such a privilege is required by the First and Fourteenth Amendments.

We hold today that the Constitution delimits a state's power to award damages for libel in actions brought by public officials against critics of their official conduct.[12]

Extensions of the Public Official Doctrine

Although the *New York Times* decision sought to limit libel suits brought by public officials against the media, it left uncertainties about who was to be included in the definition of a "public official." Certainly, elected officials were to be included in the definition, but was it to include off-duty police officers, firefighters, and teachers? How were prominent persons who move in and out of government service to be classified? In *New York Times*, the Court also redefined actual malice, moving from its traditional meaning of "evil motive," "spite," or "ill will" to that of "knowing falsehood or reckless disregard for the truth." The standards for determining actual malice, however, were unclear. The Supreme Court would rule on these questions in the decade following *New York Times v. Sullivan*.

In 1967, the Supreme Court combined two libel cases in a decision that extended the Public Official Doctrine to include public figures. Public figures were defined as those individuals not holding public office, but who willingly take part in public affairs. In *Curtis Publishing Co. v. Butts* and *Associated Press v. Walker*, the Court unanimously extended the constitutional defense against libel to include public figures. A divided Court also extended the "actual malice" and "reckless disregard" tests of *New York Times* to public figures. Four justices would have preferred a standard based on "extreme departure from the standards of investigation and reporting ordinarily adhered to by responsible publishers."[13] This standard would be clarified in *Gertz v. Robert Welch Inc.* and would make it easier for plaintiffs successfully to sue the media.

In the *Butts* case, University of Georgia Athletic Director Wally Butts originally sued for $5 million but was awarded $460,000 in damages against the *Saturday Evening Post*, based on an article that charged that Butts and Alabama coach Bear Bryant had conspired to "fix" a football game. The *Post* article, entitled "The Story of a College Football Fix," was based on notes taken by an insurance salesman named George Burnett, who was on probation for writing bad checks. Burnett claimed to have overheard the conspiracy to "fix" the game when he picked up the receiver of a pay telephone and was accidentally cut into the conversation. This somewhat questionable evidence was printed in the article, which compared the Butts-Bryant collusion to the Chicago Black Sox scandal of the 1919 World Series.

In the *Walker* case, retired army General Edwin Walker had secured a $500,000 judgment against the Associated Press, which falsely reported that Walker had "assumed command" of rioters at Mississippi State University who were protesting the admission of the first black student to the school. The Associated Press report stated that Walker personally led a charge against federal marshals and encouraged rioters to use violence. The article also stated that Walker provided technical advice to the rioters on combating the effects of tear gas.

Technically, Walker was a private citizen at the time, but he had enjoyed an illustrious military career before resigning to engage in political activity. Walker had been in command of federal troops during the Little Rock Central

High School desegregation confrontation in 1957. He now spoke out strongly against such federal intervention and had become a political activist. The Supreme Court found that although he was not a public official, Walker certainly was a public figure. The Supreme Court ruled in favor of Butts and against General Walker. Justice Harlan delivered the opinion of the Court.

☐ In *New York Times Co. v. Sullivan*, this Court held that "the constitutional guarantees (of freedom of speech and press) require a federal rule that prohibits a public official from recovering damages for a defamatory falsehood relating to his official conduct unless he proves that the statement was made with 'actual malice'—that is, with knowledge that it was false or with reckless disregard of whether it was false or not." We brought these two cases here to consider the impact of that decision on libel actions instituted by persons who are not public officials, but who are "public figures" and involved in issues in which the public has a justified and important interest.

. . . We consider and would hold that a "public figure" who is not a public official may also recover damages for a defamatory falsehood whose substance makes substantial danger to reputation apparent, on a showing of highly unreasonable conduct constituting an extreme departure from the standards of investigation and reporting ordinarily adhered to by responsible publishers. . . .

. . . The Butts story was in no sense "hot news" and the editors of the magazine recognized the need for a thorough investigation of the serious charges. Elementary precautions were, nevertheless, ignored. The *Saturday Evening Post* knew that Burnett had been placed on probation in connection with bad check charges, but proceeded to publish the story on the basis of his affidavit without substantial independent support. Burnett's notes were not even viewed by any of the magazine's personnel prior to publication. John Carmichael, who was supposed to have been with Burnett when the phone call was overheard, was not interviewed.

. . . In short, the evidence is ample to support a finding of highly unreasonable conduct constituting an extreme departure from the standards of investigation and reporting ordinarily adhered to by responsible publishers.

. . . In contrast to the Butts article, the dispatch which concerns us in Walker was news which required immediate dissemination. The Associated Press received the information from a correspondent who was present at the scene of the events and gave every indication of being trustworthy and competent. His dispatches in this instance, with one minor exception, were internally consistent and would not have seemed unreasonable to one familiar with General Walker's prior publicized statements on the underlying controversy. Considering the necessity for rapid dissemination, nothing in this series of events gives the slightest hint of a severe departure from accepted publishing standards. We therefore conclude that General Walker should not be entitled to damages from the Associated Press.[14]

Expansion of the Public Figure Test

Subsequent cases attempted to define "public officials" and "public figures" for purposes of the constitutional defense against libel. The definitions increasingly became more expansive. The courts included in the definition elected officials, such as mayors and judges, and civil servants. County clerks, police chiefs, and their deputies were defined as public officials. In *Rosenblatt v. Baer*, the Supreme Court defined Public officials as those

☐   government employees who have, or appear to the public to have, substantial responsibility for the conduct of government affairs.[15]

Ultimately, the Supreme Court was to expand the doctrine from applying only to public officials to including public figures, and finally to meaning private individuals caught up in public issues. A plurality of the Supreme Court held in *Rosenbloom v. Metromedia (1971)* that First Amendment protection should be extended to

☐   all discussion and communication involving matters of public or general concern, without regard to whether the persons involved are famous or anonymous.[16]

The Rosenbloom decision stretched the constitutional defense to its limits. For a brief time, the media enjoyed immunity from libel suits involving virtually anyone caught up in a public issue. Three years later, in *Gertz*, the Supreme Court overruled the Public Issues Doctrine as outlined in Rosenbloom.

Gertz v. Robert Welch Inc. (1974)

In 1968, a Chicago police officer named Richard Nuccio shot and killed a youth named Nelson. Nuccio was convicted of second-degree murder. The Nelson family retained attorney Elmer Gertz to represent them in civil litigation against Nuccio.

Robert Welch was the founder of the staunchly anticommunist, ultra-conservative John Birch Society and publisher of *American Opinion*, a monthly magazine espousing the views of the organization. In the early 1960s, *American Opinion* warned of a nationwide conspiracy to discredit local law enforcement agencies and of a movement to create a national police force capable of supporting a Communist dictatorship. As part of this continuing effort to warn the public of this conspiracy, *American Opinion* commissioned an article on the murder trial of Richard Nuccio.

In March 1969, *American Opinion* published an article entitled "Frame-Up: Richard Nuccio and the War on Police." The article asserted that Nuccio's conviction was part of a Communist campaign against the police. Although Gertz took no part in the criminal prosecution of Nuccio, he had been retained by the Nelson family as counsel in the civil proceeding. *American Opinion*, however, portrayed Gertz as an architect of the frame-up. The article stated that Gertz had a criminal record, was an official in several Communist organizations, and had assisted in the planning of the demonstrations during the 1968 Democratic Convention in Chicago. All of these assertions were false, and *American Opinion* made no effort to verify the accuracy of the statements.

When Gertz sued *American Opinion* for libel, the magazine claimed constitutional privilege, asserting that Gertz was a public official or a public figure and that the article concerned an issue of public concern. Although the trial court found in favor of Gertz, a federal district court and an appellate court, in citing Rosenbloom, ruled in favor of *American Opinion*. The Supreme Court overruled the decision and the Public Issues Doctrine. Justice Powell delivered the opinion of the Court.

☐ ... [T]hose classed as public figures have thrust themselves into the forefront of particular public controversies in order to influence the resolution of the issues involved. In either event, they invite attention and comment. ... [T]he communications media are entitled to act on the assumption that public officials and public figures have voluntarily exposed themselves to increased risk of injury from defamatory falsehood concerning them. No such assumption is justified with respect to a private individual. ... [P]rivate individuals are not only more vulnerable to injury than public officials and public figures, they are also more deserving of recovery. For these reasons we conclude that the states should retain substantial latitude in their efforts to enforce a legal remedy of defamatory falsehood injurious to the reputation of a private individual. The extension of the *New York Times* test proposed by the Rosenbloom plurality would abridge this legitimate state interest to a degree that we find unacceptable.

... We hold that, so long as they do not impose liability without fault, the states may define for themselves the appropriate standard of liability for a publisher or broadcaster of defamatory falsehood injurious to a private individual.

. . . Our accommodation of the competing values at stake in defamation suits by private individuals allows the States to impose liability on the publisher or broadcaster of defamatory falsehood on a less demanding showing than that required by *New York Times*.

. . . In some instances an individual may achieve such pervasive fame or notoriety that he becomes a public figure for all purposes and in all contexts. More commonly, an individual voluntarily injects himself or is drawn into a particular public controversy and thereby becomes a public figure for a limited range of issues. In either case such persons assume special prominence in the resolution of public questions.

Petitioner [Gertz] has long been active in community and professional affairs. . . . Although . . . well known in some circles, he had achieved no general fame or notoriety in the community. None of the prospective jurors called at the trial had ever heard of petitioner prior to this litigation . . . Absent clear evidence of general fame or notoriety in the community and pervasive involvement in the affairs of society, an individual should not be deemed a public personality for all aspects of his life.

. . . In this context it is plain that petitioner was not a public figure. . . . He plainly did not thrust himself into the vortex of this public issue, nor did he engage the public's attention in an attempt to influence its outcome.[17]

The Court added that private individuals who establish liability under a less demanding standard than *New York Times* may recover only actual damages.

In *Gertz*, the Court redefined the public figure/public issues standard and lessened the media libel immunity that began with *New York Times* and continually expanded through *Rosenbloom*. The Court also returned to the states the freedom to define the standards of liability for libel when private individuals are involved. The Court suggested that this standard should not require a showing of actual malice, but a less demanding standard. As of this writing, 20 states, the District of Columbia, and Puerto Rico have opted for a negligence standard for private individual libel actions. New York has adopted a gross negligence standard. Simply defined, negligence may result when "due care" is not exercised by publishers or broadcasters. Among the jurisdictions adopting the negligence standard are Arkansas, Arizona, California, District of Columbia, Georgia, Hawaii, Illinois, Kansas, Kentucky, Maryland, Massachusetts, Mississippi, Ohio, Oklahoma, Pennsylvania, Puerto Rico, Tennessee, Texas, Utah, Virginia, West Virginia, and Washington. Alaska, Colorado, Indiana, and Michigan still adhere to the actual malice standard. This concept is discussed further in this chapter.

The State of Libel Since *Gertz*

Public Figures

The definition of a public figure narrowed considerably following the *Gertz* ruling. In 1976, the Supreme Court ruled that Mary Alice Firestone, a society fixture in Palm Beach, Florida, and former wife of tire and rubber heir Russell Firestone, was not a public figure. *Time* magazine had reported inaccurate information about her recent divorce. When she filed a libel suit, *Time* claimed a constitutional defense. In *Time Inc. v. Firestone*, the Supreme Court rejected the defense, stating that involvement in a public trial does not necessarily make one a public figure. It added that the dissolution of a marriage is not a public controversy as defined in *Gertz*.

The impact of *Gertz* was modified further in the 1990 Supreme Court ruling in *Milkovich v. Lorain Journal*. In this case, the Court held that defamatory opinion that is susceptible to being proved true or false is not protected by the First Amendment.

Milkovich v. Lorain Journal (1990)

A high school wrestling team was involved in an altercation during a match. Several people were injured during the fracas. The state athletic commission held a hearing on the matter and took testimony from Coach Milkovich. The day after the hearing, a local newspaper, the *News Herald*, ran an editorial that was critical of Milkovich. The paper stated that Milkovich "had beat the law with a big lie" and that anyone who attended the meet "knows in his heart that [Milkovich] lied at the hearing after giving his solemn oath to tell the truth." Milkovich sued for libel. The paper claimed the statement was protected opinion. Chief Justice Rehnquist wrote,

☐ We are not persuaded that . . . an additional separate constitutional privilege for "opinion" . . . is required to ensure the freedom of expression guaranteed by the First Amendment. The present case then becomes whether or not a reasonable fact finder could conclude that the statements in the . . . column imply that petitioner Milkovich perjured himself in a judicial proceeding. We think this question must he answered in the affirmative. . . .

. . . [W]e also think the connotation that petitioner committed perjury is sufficiently factual to be susceptible of being proved true or false. . . .

. . . The numerous decisions discussed above establishing First Amendment protection for defendants in defamation actions surely demonstrate the Court's recognition of the Amendment's vital guarantee of free and uninhibited discussion of public issues. But there is also another side to the equation; we have regularly acknowledged the "important social values which underlie the law of defamation" and recognize that "society has a pervasive and strong interest in preventing and redressing attacks upon reputation" *Rosenblatt v. Baer*, 383 U.S. 75, 86.51.[18]

Although it was generally more difficult for the media to claim a constitutional defense after *Gertz*, in 1986 the Supreme Court slowed the swing of the pendulum away from the Rosenbloom standard when it decided *Philadelphia Newspapers v. Hepps*. In *Philadelphia Newspapers*, the Court reversed a lower court ruling and required that private figure libel plaintiffs bringing suit against the media for defamatory statements involving matters of public concern, demonstrate the falsity of such statements. Previously, falsity was assumed and the burden of proof fell on the defendant. This decision indicates that Rosenbloom still has some residual impact on post-*Gertz* interpretations.

In *Philadelphia Newspapers v. Hepps (1977)*, the *Philadelphia Inquirer* published a series of articles stating that Maurice Hepps, the owner of a chain of stores called "Thrifty," had connections to organized crime. The articles also alleged that Hepps had used those connections to influence Pennsylvania's government processes. Hepps was a private figure. However, the allegations that he had influenced the Pennsylvania government made the issue one of public concern. The trial court and the Pennsylvania Supreme Court found in favor of Hepps, following the common law assumption that a defamatory statement is assumed to be false unless the plaintiff proves otherwise. The U.S. Supreme Court reversed the decision. Justice O'Connor delivered the opinion of the Court.

☐ Here as in *Gertz*, the plaintiff is a private figure and the newspaper articles are of public concern. In *Gertz*, as in *New York Times*, the common law rule was superceded by a constitutional rule. We believe that the common law's rule on falsity—that the defendant must bear the burden of proving truth—must similarly fall here to a constitutional requirement that the plaintiff bear the burden of showing falsity, as well as fault, before recovering damages. . . .

To ensure that true speech on matters of public concern is not deterred, we hold that the common-law presumption that defamatory speech is false cannot stand when a plaintiff seeks damages against a media defendant for speech of public concern.[19]

The Negligence Standard of Fault

As previously noted, since *Gertz*, most states have opted for a lesser standard of fault for private figures who are objects of a defamatory falsehood. Negligence usually results from failure to exercise normal care in reporting a story (i.e., departing from accepted journalistic procedures), thereby risking the publication of a defamatory falsehood.

A Little Rock, Arkansas television station was guilty of negligence in its reporting of a "robbery/hostage" situation. Interestingly, in *KARK-TV v. Simon*, the Arkansas Supreme Court technically ruled in favor of the TV station, because the trial court had found the station guilty of the more serious charge of actual malice. Although the $12,500 award of compensatory damages was vacated as being excessive, the court did suggest that further proceedings could result in damages against KARK-TV based on a finding of negligence.

At 8:30 P.M. on the evening of August 11, 1982, police were called to the Galleria Shopping Center on Little Rock's west side. They were responding to a report that the Custom Design store was being robbed by two men. At the Galleria, Andre Smith and Barry Simon were handcuffed, searched, and placed in a squad car by police. A reporter for KARK-TV, Carolyn Long, happened to be shopping in the Galleria. From someone who had been listening to a police scanner, she received information that there was a potential robbery situation. Long met a camera crew that had been dispatched to the scene from KARK. She questioned police on the scene and interviewed a clerk at Custom Design. The police provided no information and the store clerk gave vague responses to Long's questions. At approximately 9:00 P.M., police released Smith and Simon and decided that no crime had taken place, nor had any crime been attempted.

On the 10 o'clock news, KARK broadcast the following report:

> Quick action by Little Rock Police tonight stopped a robbery attempt at Custom Design at the Galleria Shopping Center. Details are sketchy; however, it appears two suspects backed their car up to the store in order to rob it. For a time, the two men allegedly held a store clerk hostage. The clerk was shaken, and wasn't sure about exactly what had happened.[20]

Although Simon and Smith were not named in the report, the newscast included scenes of the police putting the two men in a police car. It was broadcast to approximately 82,000 households.

Judge Hays wrote:

☐ ... The court instructed the jury here that the defendant [KARK-TV] was held to the standard of care a reasonably careful person would exercise under circumstances similar to those shown by evidence.

... The reporter could get no information from police officers at the scene nor could the producer of the news get any information verified by police headquarters. The story was written and shown a little over an hour later. We cannot say that a news report with its sources consisting of information from a police scanner, uncorroborated by police on the scene, in conjunction with an eyewitness account by a news reporter who did not know the surrounding circumstances of what she observed, will be found to be due care as a matter of law. We think the issue of negligence was properly submitted to the jury.[21]

Negligence can also result when reporters and editors fail to check facts or misrepresent information that may be part of the public record.

Actual Malice

Under *New York Times*, for public figures to bring a successful libel suit, they must demonstrate that a defamatory falsehood was published with reckless disregard of whether it was false. In *Curtis Publishing v. Butts*, the Supreme Court extended the definition of actual malice to include an extreme departure from normal standards of journalism. The Supreme Court refined the definition of actual malice in *St. Amant v. Thompson*. In that decision, the Court ruled that there must be "sufficient evidence to permit the conclusion that the defendant entertained serious doubts as to the truth of the publication."[22]

In *Herbert v. Lando*, the Supreme Court ruled that a public figure defendant could be questioned as to his state of mind when writing a defamatory article. This, according to six members of the Court, was essential for a plaintiff to establish actual malice. Since *Herbert*, reporters can be asked to identify their sources of information and to produce transcripts of notes and tapes of interviews. Prior to this ruling, it was generally assumed that a reporter's thoughts and opinions on the editorial process were privileged. Since *Herbert*, any information that would enable a plaintiff to establish that a reporter acted with reckless disregard for the truth—thereby establishing actual malice—can now be asked during trial procedures.

In *Bose Corporation v. Consumers Union (1985)*, a trial court found *Consumer Reports* magazine guilty of libeling the Bose Corporation in a 1970 review of the Bose 901 loudspeakers. Because Bose Corporation was found to be a public figure, it had to show that false material in the article was published with actual malice. Based on testimony provided by the author of the article, a trial court found that a false statement was published with reckless disregard of its truth or falsity. The statement in question accused the loudspeakers of producing sound that "wandered about the room." The issue at question was whether the author's word choice accurately described what he heard when listening to the Bose 901 speakers. The court of appeals reversed the trial court's libel verdict on grounds that, based on facts before the court, the statement was not made with actual malice. The Supreme Court affirmed the holding.

This decision is significant in that when media defendants appeal a ruling based on actual malice, the appellate court does not hear testimony. That court does not have the chance to evaluate the demeanor of witnesses. State-of-mind questioning, like that allowed under *Herbert*, is not possible. Justices Rehnquist and O'Connor dissented in *Bose*, noting that the trial court based its original finding of actual malice on the credibility of the defendant's testimony. Rehnquist could not see how the appellate court could rule on actual malice without having the opportunity to hear testimony from the defendant and thereby evaluate his intentions.

Although a newspaper's accurate summary of charges made in a recall petition filed against a Washington state county prosecutor under investigation for racketeering was ruled privileged, the Washington State Supreme Court found that a television report of the same story may have been made with actual malice. In *Herron v. King Broadcasting Co.*, KING-TV reporter Don McGaffin's statement that he would "get" Pierce County Prosecutor Don Herron, the subsequent broadcast of a story riddled with defamatory falsehoods supported by unreliable sources, and the destruction of the tapes of the broadcast after Herron filed a complaint, were enough to warrant a trial based on actual malice.

Entertainer Wayne Newton brought a suit against NBC as a result of a news report linking him to organized crime. A Nevada district court found that the NBC broadcast concerning Newton's purchase of a Las Vegas hotel was defamatory and could be found by a jury to have been made with actual malice. The jury awarded Newton $7.9 million for loss of past income, $1.1 million for loss of future income, $5 million for damages to his reputation, $225,000 for physical and mental suffering, and $5 million in punitive damages—for a total judgment of $22 million. Although the trial judge found some of the jury's damage awards excessive, the court upheld the jury award of $5 million in punitive damages, and established an award of $225,000 to Newton for physical and mental injury, and $50,000 for presumed damage to his reputation. A motion for a new trial was granted on the question of damages only. In January 1989, in *Newton v. NBC*, Newton filed a remittitur of all damages except $225,000 for physical and mental injury, $50,000 as presumed damages for reputation, and $5 million in punitive damages. The judgment was reduced to $5.2 million and, before being overturned in the summer of 1990, was the highest award ever entered in a libel case against a news organization.

Summary Judgment

In some libel suits, after the plaintiff has presented his or her allegations before the court, the defendant may ask for summary judgment. Summary judgment is an immediate ruling by the judge based on the facts before the court. If the judge believes that a jury could not reasonably find in favor of the plaintiff, she or he may grant a summary judgment in favor of the defendant. This means that the case will not go to trial. Since *New York Times*, and the requirement that public figures prove actual malice, many public figure libel suits have been dismissed on a motion for summary judgment. This policy has been encouraged by the Supreme Court. To overcome a motion for summary judgment, a plaintiff may present evidence of facts from which a jury could reasonably infer actual malice and is required to show the existence of actual malice with convincing clarity.

Columnist Jack Anderson published three articles in the October 1981 issue of *The Investigator* magazine about a not-for-profit corporation called the Liberty Lobby. The Liberty Lobby complained that 30 statements in the articles were defamatory. Essentially, *The Investigator* articles characterized the Liberty Lobby as being anti-Semitic, "infiltrated by Nazis," and "a nest of Nazis."

Both Anderson and the Liberty Lobby were limited-purpose public figures, and the constitutional defense was used. In *Liberty Lobby v. Anderson (1986)*, the district court granted the defendant's motion for summary judgment on grounds that the actual malice standard of *New York Times* had not been met. The appellate court reversed, in part noting that 9 of the 30 statements in question were capable of defamatory meaning, and that a jury could reasonably conclude that they were made with actual malice. One year later, the U.S. Supreme Court reversed the appellate court's decision. Interestingly, the appellate court judge who authored the opinion was Antonin Scalia. Scalia was appointed to the Supreme Court in June 1986. In July, the Supreme Court overruled Scalia's interpretation of summary judgment.

Writing for the three-judge court, two years before his appointment to the U.S. Supreme Court, Appellate Court Judge Antonin Scalia authored this opinion on the application of summary judgment:

☐   ... To prevail in a libel trial, not only must the public figure plaintiff prove the existence of actual malice; he must prove it with "convincing clarity." ... The issue we address in this portion of our opinion is whether these requirements of "convincing clarity" ... apply at the summary judgement stage.

... [T]he issue can be framed as follows: whether, in order to deny the defendant's motion for summary judgement, the court must conclude that a reasonable jury not only could (on the basis of the facts taken in the light most favorable to the plaintiff) find that it had been established with "convincing clarity." We conclude that the answer is no. Imposing the increased proof requirement at this stage would change the threshold summary judgement inquiry from a search for a minimum of facts supporting the plaintiff's case to an evaluation of the weight of those facts and (it would seem) of the weight of at least the defendant's uncontroverted facts as well. It would effectively force the plaintiff to try his entire case in pretrial affidavits and depositions—marshalling for the court all the facts supporting his case, and seeking to contest as many of the defendant's facts as possible. . . . In other words, disposing of a sugary judgement motion would rarely be the relatively quick process it is supposed to be.[23]

In July 1986 in *Anderson v. Liberty Lobby,* the Supreme Court struck down this opinion. The Court ruled that in actual malice cases, the plaintiff must establish with convincing clarity that the defendant acted with reckless disregard of the truth or the case will be disposed of with a summary judgment in favor of the defendant. Justice White delivered the opinion of the Court.

☐   . . . [W]here the factual dispute concerns actual malice, clearly a material issue in a *New York Times* case, the appropriate summary judgement question will be whether the evidence in the record could support a reasonable jury finding either that the plaintiff has shown actual malice by clear and convincing evidence or that the plaintiff has not. . . .
      In sum, a court ruling on a motion for summary judgement must be guided by the *New York Times* "clear and convincing" evidentiary standard in determining whether a genuine issue of actual malice exists—that is, whether the evidence presented is such that a reasonable jury might find that actual malice had been shown with convincing clarity. Because the Court of Appeals did not apply the correct standard in reviewing the District Court's grant of summary judgement, we vacate its decision and remand the case for further proceedings consistent with this opinion.[24]

Group Libel

Sometimes the publication of a false, defamatory statement about a group of people may give rise to suits against the media. When a defamatory statement is published about a particular group of people, any one of them may sue for libel, provided they can show that they are readily identified as members of that group and that the defamatory statement applies to them personally. Obviously, the smaller the group, the more likely that individuals can be identified and may sue as a result of a defamatory publication. Generally, groups consisting of more than 25 individuals have some difficulty establishing identity. However, in 1962 in *Fawcett Publications v. Morris* a member of a football team consisting of 60 players brought a successful group libel suit.

In the classic group libel case, *Neiman-Marcus Co. v. Lait*, 9 models and 15 of 25 salesmen employed by the Dallas department store were allowed to bring suit against *U.S.A. Confidential* for calling them prostitutes and homosexuals, respectively. The publication also referred to the 382 Neiman-Marcus saleswomen as prostitutes, but the 30 women who attempted to sue were not able to bring suit, because the group was too large.

Not surprisingly, in *McCullough v. Cities Service (1984)*, the Oklahoma Supreme Court ruled that a doctor of osteopathy could not sue for an allegedly defamatory article on behalf of the 19,686 osteopaths in the United States. The court did, however, attempt to clarify the standards under which group libel suits may be brought. The Oklahoma Supreme Court rejected the notion that a simple numerical limit could determine when a group was too large for a suit to be brought. They noted that although Prosser's Restatement of Torts had set an arbitrary limit of 25, a New York Court had determined that a suit by a member of a group of 53 was legally actionable.

Citing *Brady v. Ottaway Newspapers (1981)*, the Oklahoma Supreme Court outlined the following principles for determining when a group libel action may be actionable:

☐ From the teaching of Brady, we glean the following principles to which we subscribe:

1. The "of and concerning" element in defamation actions requires that the allegedly defamatory comment refer to the plaintiff.

2. Generally an impersonal reproach of an indeterminate class is not actionable. The underlying premise of this principle is that the larger the collectivity named in the libel, the less likely it is that a reader would understand it to refer to a particular individual. The rule was designed to encourage frank discussions of matters of public concern under the First Amendment guarantees. Thus the incidental and occasional injury to the individual resulting from the defamation of large groups is balanced against the public's right to know.

3. In contrast to the treatment of an individual in a large group which has been defamed, an individual belonging to a small group may maintain an action for individual injury resulting from a defamatory comment about the group, by showing that he is a member of the group. Because the group is small and includes few individuals, reference to the

individual plaintiff reasonably follows from the statement and the question of reference is left for the jury.

4. *Size alone is too narrow a focus to determine the issue of individual application in group defamation.* [Emphasis added by the author.]

5. The intensity of suspicion test recognizes that even a general derogatory reference to a group may affect the reputation of every member. In order to determine personal application it requires that a factual inquiry be made to determine the degree that the group accusation focuses on each individual member of the group. The numerical size of the group is a consideration, but is not the only factor to be considered. One element to be considered is the prominence of the individual within the group.[25]

In keeping with these standards, in 1987 the Tenth U.S. Court of Appeals ruled in *Weatherland v. Globe International* that a group of 955 was too large to bring a group libel action. The attempted action stemmed from an article in the *Midnight Globe* entitled "America's Dog 'Death Camps'." The report depicted cruel methods employed by some dog breeders in the raising of puppies. The court ruled that although some breeders may practice these methods, the entire group of breeders was too large to permit individual identification of those engaged in such practices.

Criminal Libel

Thus far we have discussed the civil law of libel. Civil law provides monetary awards for successful plaintiffs. On the other hand, jail sentences are part of the punishment for those who violate criminal law. Many states have criminal libel laws on the books. These laws were designed to punish those who might utter words that provoke riots or otherwise threaten the public order and are rarely enforced today. In fact, rulings based on *New York Times* have made many of these laws unconstitutional.

In some jurisdictions, group libel is part of criminal law. In 1949, Illinois enacted a law that made it a crime to disseminate or publish racist material. The law was not enforced, however, when American Nazis displaying swastikas marched through the predominately Jewish Chicago suburb of Skokie in 1978. It is unlikely that the law would stand today.

In civil libel, a dead person cannot be defamed. No action can be attempted unless the statement in question reflects on those still living, who are in turn defamed. Criminal libel laws, however, often provide for punishment if one defames the memory of one who is dead, and scandalizes or provokes surviving relatives or friends. These laws were based on the theory that riots and other civil disorders can be started by the defamation of a deceased political or social leader. The laws were designed primarily to protect the public order, not the surviving relatives.

Like that of many states, Indiana's criminal libel law had its roots in the nineteenth century and provided for a fine of up to $1000 and six months in jail for the false publication of material that "imputes official dishonesty and corruption in an officer."[26] A northern Indiana newspaper was prosecuted for criminal libel in 1881 for accusing the town's mayor of "rascally conduct." Indiana's law was modified several times before being repealed in 1976.

As was the case in Indiana, some of these state laws have been modified or declared unconstitutional. However, many remain on the books. In a number of states, including Louisiana, the truth of the utterance was of no concern in criminal libel. The rationale was that even a true defamatory statement is capable of disturbing the public order. In the wake of *New York Times*, the Supreme Court ruled this concept to be unconstitutional where public figures are concerned. In *Garrison v. Louisiana*, the Supreme Court stated that

☐ ... only those false statements made with the high degree of awareness of their probable falsity demanded by *New York Times* may be the subject of either civil or criminal actions.[27]

The Garrison decision forced many states to revise their criminal libel laws.

Humor and Fiction

Generally, defamatory remarks published as humor are protected as the expression of opinion. Many such publications lampoon only public figures, and the added protection of *New York Times* allows a wide range of commentary. Editorial cartoons, political satirists, stand-up comics, and other humorists are essentially free to offer their opinions on people and issues facing society. Rhetorical hyperbole is protected as opinion, provided that such language is not a defamatory statement of fact. For example, in *Keller v. Miami Herald*, a federal district court found that a *Miami Herald* editorial cartoon using stereotyped images and caricatures to comment on the character of a person involved with a nursing home was a statement of opinion and not fact. The state of Florida had closed the nursing home for numerous health code violations, and the court ruled that the cartoon was pure opinion, based on publicly available information.

When a television and radio talk show host was lampooned by *Heavy Metal* magazine, the New York Supreme Court found the allegedly defamatory statements to be protected opinion.

Joe Franklin hosted a talk show on New York City broadcast stations WOR-TV and WOR-AM. The television show was syndicated throughout the country on various cable television systems. *Heavy Metal* was a publication owned by National Lampoon Inc., and was self-described as an "adult fantasy magazine." *Heavy Metal* consisted of science fiction and fantasy stories done in cartoon or comic strip form. The magazine also included some textual material, such as book and music reviews.

The November 1984 issue contained a one-page comic strip entitled "HM's Star Dissections," in which the plaintiff was referred to as "The Incredible Shrinking Joe Franklin." In the cartoon that followed, Franklin was caricatured on the set of his TV show. One of the guests on Franklin's program is drawn as saying "Joe, you look good . . . you lose some weight?" The panels that follow show Franklin in various situations, each of which shows him as getting physically smaller, until his head is barely visible above his desk. The final panel depicts a meeting between Franklin and WOR-TV executives in which he is told that he will be "let go."

Franklin found the cartoon to be defamatory. He noted that he was represented as "shrinking in stature" and was told he will be fired, thereby meeting the standards for actionable libel. The New York Supreme Court did not agree.

☐ . . . Where it appears in the context of fiction and deliberate humor which does not purport to relate to actual events, or is obvious satire . . . a statement cannot reasonably be susceptible of libelous meaning. . . .

At worst, the cartoon could be read as the obvious pun: Joe Franklin is shrinking in stature and will be fired. However, even if so read it is not a defamatory statement. Any reader interpreting it as a pun would understand it not as fact but as criticism.[28]

The fact that *Heavy Metal* billed itself as a "fantasy magazine" was important in the decision. Readers expect humor and fantasy when reading publications like *Heavy Metal* and are less likely to interpret material in these publications as fact.

Although sometimes difficult to identify, a defamatory statement of fact would still be actionable libel, especially when a private person is involved. The student newspaper published by the Medical College of Georgia crossed that line when responding to a criticism of its editorial policy.

Brooks v. Stone (1984)

Students at the Medical College of Georgia published the *Cadaver*, a newspaper for medical students. The *Cadaver* can be characterized as an irreverent publication, often satirical and risqué. The editors of the paper published under the pen name of "Bones."

A student nurse, Susan Brooks, wrote a letter to the editors of the *Cadaver*, criticizing the nature and quality of the paper. The editors responded in their usual irreverent style. However, Ms. Brooks found the editors' reply to be defamatory. The following is how Susan Brooks' letter to the editors was published:

GRADUATE NURSING STUDENT COMPLAINS, OR 50
WAYS TO IRRITATE THE EDITORS

Dear Editors

During orientation I caught myself almost wishing things would be the same here at MCG as they were two years ago. Almost everything that is.

This year I hope that the editors of the *Cadaver* have more sense of humor (in a less sick way), have more respect for the students that aren't in the School of Medicine, and that they just have more sense! If things aren't going to change in the Editor's Office, I hope that the nursing students and allied health students won't put up with it. Nursing students, I appeal to you—Write! Add articles, announcements, and letters so that the pages will not be filled up with junk this year. Write—so articles by "Ramondo" won't have to be dug out of the garbage heap again.

Editors—I appeal to you. Make the *Cadaver* a paper everyone can read. There is a difference in humor and trash. If you do—maybe the *Cadaver* will be in the hands of students more—and in the bottom of bird cages less.

Sincerely,

S. Brooks, Graduate Student

The editors of the *Cadaver* published this reply:

Dear Ms. Brooks:

You are obviously a sensitive, caring member of society. We appreciate that, we really do, and certainly with your God given sensitivity, you should try to understand how and why those less fortunate members of our society deviate from acceptable forms of behavior. Take us for example; our style of humor is really out of control. Well, let us give you a little family history and you'll understand.

We have backgrounds different from the rest of you. Our mothers were German Shepherds; our fathers were Camels, so naturally we love to hump bitches in heat. Say, Ms. Brooks, when do you come in season?

Bones

Had "Bones" omitted the last sentence, no libel action would have been possible. However, in *Brooks v. Stone*, the Georgia court of appeals found that

Ms. Brooks had cause for a libel action. They noted that affidavits indicated that readers of the reply understood the editors to be questioning her chastity. The court also said the reply connoted that Ms. Brooks was sexually promiscuous and was one with whom the editors would like to have sex. The court also distinguished between the normal, humorous content of the newspaper and the "letters to the editor" column:

□ (1) A letters-to-the-editor feature customarily serves as a forum for reader opinion, including criticism of the newspaper itself; and (2) the plaintiff obviously was criticizing the nature and quality of the newspaper, and did not launch a personal invective upon the editors.[29]

Liability of Online Services

Defamatory statements posted on the Internet pose questions of liability. Case law has provided some conflicting interpretations, but generally favored limiting the liability of the online service provided that the service does not exercise editorial control over material posted by users. For example, in an early online case, *Cubby v. CompuServe,* a Federal Court for the Southern District of New York held that CompuServe was not a "publisher" because it exercised no editorial control. Therefore the online service could not be held liable for defamatory content posted on its service by a third party.

Four years later a New York trial court rejected the online service Prodigy's argument that it was not a publisher. Because Prodigy monitored and edited some of its content, the court held that Prodigy functioned as an editor (see *Stratton Oakmont Inc. v. Prodigy Services Co. (1995)*).

Statutory law also addressed the issue of liability. The Communications Decency Act of 1996 specifically absolved interactive computer services of direct liability (see 47 U.S.C.A. § 230(c)(1)). What if, however, an online service receives notice that defamatory material has been posted on its site?

Zeran v. America Online Inc. (1997)

□ Kenneth Zeran brought this action against America Online, Inc. ("AOL"), arguing that AOL unreasonably delayed in removing defamatory messages posted by an unidentified third party, refused to post retractions of those messages, and failed to screen for similar postings thereafter. The district court granted judgment for AOL on the grounds that the Communications Decency Act of 1996 ("CDA")—47 U.S.C. § 230— bars Zeran's claims. Zeran appeals, arguing that § 230 leaves intact liability for interactive computer service providers who possess notice of defamatory material posted through their services. He also contends that § 230 does not apply here because his claims arise from AOL's alleged negligence prior to the CDA's enactment. Section 230, however, plainly immunizes computer service providers like AOL from liability for information that originates with third parties. Furthermore, Congress clearly expressed its intent that § 230 apply to lawsuits, like Zeran's, instituted after the CDA's enactment. Accordingly, we affirm the judgment of the district court.

I

☐ "The Internet is an international network of interconnected computers," currently used by approximately 40 million people worldwide. *Reno v. ACLU*, 117 S. Ct. 2329, 2334 (1997). One of the many means by which individuals access the Internet is through an interactive computer service. These services offer not only a connection to the Internet as a whole, but also allow their subscribers to access information communicated and stored only on each computer service's individual proprietary network. *Id.* AOL is just such an interactive computer service. Much of the information transmitted over its network originates with the company's millions of subscribers. They may transmit information privately via electronic mail, or they may communicate publicly by posting messages on AOL bulletin boards, where the messages may be read by any AOL subscriber . . .

On April 25, 1995, an unidentified person posted a message on an AOL bulletin board advertising "Naughty Oklahoma T-Shirts." The posting described the sale of shirts featuring offensive and tasteless slogans related to the April 19, 1995, bombing of the Alfred P. Murrah Federal Building in Oklahoma City. Those interested in purchasing the shirts were instructed to call "Ken" at Zeran's home phone number in Seattle, Washington. As a result of this anonymously perpetrated prank, Zeran received a high volume of calls, comprised primarily of angry and derogatory messages, but also including death threats. Zeran could not change his phone number because he relied on its availability to the public in running his business out of his home. Later that day, Zeran called AOL and informed a company representative of his predicament. The employee assured Zeran that the posting would be removed from AOL's bulletin board but explained that as a matter of policy AOL would not post a retraction. The parties dispute the date that AOL removed this original posting from its bulletin board.

On April 26, the next day, an unknown person posted another message advertising additional shirts with new tasteless slogans related to the Oklahoma City bombing. Again, interested buyers were told to call Zeran's phone number, to ask for "Ken," and to "please call back if busy" due to high demand. The angry, threatening phone calls intensified. Over the next four days, an unidentified party continued to post messages on AOL's bulletin board, advertising additional items including bumper stickers and key chains with still more offensive slogans. During this time period, Zeran called AOL repeatedly and was told by company representatives that the individual account from which the messages were posted would soon be closed. Zeran also reported his case to Seattle FBI agents. By April 30, Zeran was receiving an abusive phone call approximately every two minutes. Meanwhile, an announcer for Oklahoma City radio station KRXO received a copy of the first AOL posting. On May 1, the announcer related the message's contents on the air, attributed them to "Ken" at Zeran's phone number, and urged the listening audience to call the number. After this radio broadcast, Zeran was inundated with death threats and other violent calls from Oklahoma City residents. Over the next few days, Zeran talked to both KRXO and AOL representatives. He also spoke to his local police, who subsequently surveilled his home to protect his safety. By May 14, after an Oklahoma City newspaper published a story exposing the shirt advertisements as a hoax and after KRXO made an on-air apology, the number of calls to Zeran's residence finally subsided to fifteen per day.

Zeran first filed suit on January 4, 1996, against radio station KRXO in the United States District Court for the Western District of Oklahoma. On April 23, 1996, he filed this separate suit against AOL in the same court. Zeran did not bring any action against the party who posted the offensive messages. After Zeran's suit against AOL was transferred to the Eastern District of Virginia pursuant to 28 U.S.C. § 1404(a), AOL answered Zeran's complaint and interposed 47 U.S.C. § 230 as an affirmative defense. AOL then moved for judgment on the pleadings pursuant to Fed. R. Civ. P. 12(c). The district court granted AOL's motion, and Zeran filed this appeal.

II

A

☐ Because § 230 was successfully advanced by AOL in the district court as a defense to Zeran's claims, we shall briefly examine its operation here. Zeran seeks to hold AOL liable for defamatory speech initiated by a third party. He argued to the district court that once he notified AOL of the unidentified third party's hoax, AOL had a duty to remove the defamatory posting promptly, to notify its subscribers of the message's false nature, and to effectively screen future defamatory material. Section 230 entered this litigation as an affirmative defense pled by AOL. The company claimed that Congress immunized interactive computer service providers from claims based on information posted by a third party. The relevant portion of § 230 states: "No provider or user of an interactive computer service shall be treated as the publisher or speaker of any information provided by another information content provider." 47 U.S.C. § 230(c)(1) . . . By its plain language, § 230 creates a federal immunity to any cause of action that would make service providers liable for information originating with a third-party user of the service. Specifically, § 230 precludes courts from entertaining claims that would place a computer service provider in a publisher's role. Thus, lawsuits seeking to hold a service provider liable for its exercise of a publisher's traditional editorial functions—such as deciding whether to publish, withdraw, postpone or alter content—are barred. The purpose of this statutory immunity is not difficult to discern. Congress recognized the threat that tort-based lawsuits pose to freedom of speech in the new and burgeoning Internet medium. The imposition of tort liability on service providers for the communications of others represented, for Congress, simply another form of intrusive government regulation of speech. Section 230 was enacted, in part, to maintain the robust nature of Internet communication and, accordingly, to keep government interference in the medium to a minimum. In specific statutory findings, Congress recognized the Internet and interactive computer services as offering "a forum for a true diversity of political discourse, unique opportunities for cultural development, and myriad avenues for intellectual activity." . . . It also found that the Internet and interactive computer services "have flourished, to the benefit of all Americans, *with a minimum of government regulation*." Congress further stated that it is "the policy of the United States . . . to preserve the vibrant and competitive free market that presently exists for the Internet and other interactive computer services, *unfettered by Federal or State regulation*." . . . None of this means, of course, that the original culpable party who posts defamatory messages would escape accountability. While Congress acted to keep government regulation of the Internet to a minimum, it also found it to be the policy of the United States "to ensure vigorous enforcement of Federal criminal laws to deter and punish trafficking in obscenity, stalking, and harassment by means of computer." . . . Congress made a policy choice, however, not to deter harmful online speech through the separate route of imposing tort liability on companies that serve as intermediaries for other parties' potentially injurious messages. Congress' purpose in providing the § 230 immunity was thus evident. Interactive computer services have millions of users. *See Reno v. ACLU*, 117 S. Ct. at 2334 (noting that at time of district court trial, "commercial online services had almost 12 million individual subscribers"). The amount of information communicated via interactive computer services is therefore staggering. The specter of tort liability in an area of such prolific speech would have an obvious chilling effect. It would be impossible for service providers to screen each of their millions of postings for possible problems. Faced with potential liability for each message republished by their services, interactive computer service providers might choose to severely restrict the number and type of messages posted. Congress considered the weight of the speech interests implicated and chose to immunize service providers to avoid any such restrictive effect.

Another important purpose of § 230 was to encourage service providers to self-regulate the dissemination of offensive material over their services. In this respect, § 230 responded to a New York state court decision, *Stratton Oakmont, Inc. v. Prodigy Servs. Co.*, 1995 WL 323710 (N.Y. Sup. Ct. May 24, 1995). There, the plaintiffs sued Prodigy—an interactive computer service like AOL—for defamatory comments made by an unidentified party on one of Prodigy's 6 bulletin boards. The court held Prodigy to the strict liability standard normally applied to original publishers of defamatory statements, rejecting Prodigy's claims that it should be held only to the lower "knowledge" standard usually reserved for distributors. The court reasoned that Prodigy acted more like an original publisher than a distributor both because it advertised its practice of controlling content on its service and because it actively screened and edited messages posted on its bulletin boards. Congress enacted § 230 to remove the disincentives to self regulation created by the *Stratton Oakmont* decision. Under that court's holding, computer service providers who regulated the dissemination of offensive material on their services risked subjecting themselves to liability, because such regulation cast the service provider in the role of a publisher. Fearing that the specter of liability would therefore deter service providers from blocking and screening offensive material, Congress enacted § 230's broad immunity "to remove disincentives for the development and utilization of blocking and filtering technologies that empower parents to restrict their children's access to objectionable or inappropriate online material." 47 U.S.C. § 230(b)(4). In line with this purpose, § 230 forbids the imposition of publisher liability on a service provider for the exercise of its editorial and self-regulatory functions.

B

☐ Zeran argues, however, that the § 230 immunity eliminates only publisher liability, leaving distributor liability intact. Publishers can be held liable for defamatory statements contained in their works even absent proof that they had specific knowledge of the statement's inclusion . . . According to Zeran, interactive computer service providers like AOL are normally considered instead to be distributors, like traditional news vendors or book sellers. Distributors cannot be held liable for defamatory statements contained in the materials they distribute unless it is proven at a minimum that they have actual knowledge of the defamatory statements upon which liability is predicated. . . . Zeran contends that he provided AOL with sufficient notice of the defamatory statements appearing on the company's bulletin board. This notice is significant, says Zeran, because AOL could be held liable as a distributor only if it acquired knowledge of the defamatory statements' existence. Because of the difference between these two forms of liability, Zeran contends that the term "distributor" carries a legally distinct meaning from the term "publisher." Accordingly, he asserts that Congress' use of only the term "publisher" in § 230 indicates a purpose to immunize service providers only from publisher liability. He argues that distributors are left unprotected by § 230 and, therefore, his suit should be permitted to proceed against AOL. We disagree. Assuming *arguendo* [as a matter of argument] that Zeran has satisfied the requirements for imposition of distributor liability, this theory of liability is merely a subset, or a species, of publisher liability, and is therefore also foreclosed by § 230. The terms "publisher" and "distributor" derive their legal significance from the context of defamation law. Although Zeran attempts to artfully plead his claims as ones of negligence, they are indistinguishable from a garden variety defamation action. Because the publication of a statement is a necessary element in a defamation action, only one who publishes can be subject to this form of tort liability . . . Publication does not only describe the choice by an author to include certain information. In addition, both the negligent communication of a defamatory statement and the failure to remove such a statement when first communicated by another party— each alleged by Zeran here under a negligence label—constitute publication . . . In fact, every repetition of a defamatory statement is considered a publication . . . In this case, AOL is legally considered to be a publisher. "[E]very one who takes part in the publication . . . is charged with publication." . . . Even distributors are considered to be publishers for purposes of defamation law: Those who are in the business of making their facilities available to disseminate the writings composed, the speeches made, and the information gathered by others may also be regarded as participating to such an extent in making the books, newspapers, magazines, and information available to others as to be regarded as publishers. They are intentionally making the contents available to others, sometimes without knowing all of the contents— including the defamatory content—and sometimes without any opportunity to ascertain, in advance, that any defamatory matter was to be included in the matter published . . . AOL falls squarely within this

traditional definition of a publisher and, therefore, is clearly protected by §
230's immunity. Zeran contends that decisions like *Stratton Oakmont* and
Cubby, Inc. v. CompuServe Inc., 776 F. Supp. 135 (S.D.N.Y. 1991), recognize
a legal distinction between publishers and distributors. He
misapprehends, however, the significance of that distinction for the legal
issue we consider here. It is undoubtedly true that mere conduits, or
distributors, are subject to a different standard of liability. As explained
above, distributors must at a minimum have knowledge of the existence
of a defamatory statement as a prerequisite to liability. But this distinction
signifies only that different standards of liability may be applied *within*
the larger publisher category, depending on the specific type of publisher
concerned . . . To the extent that decisions like *Stratton* and *Cubby* utilize
the terms "publisher" and "distributor" separately, the decisions correctly
describe two different standards of liability. *Stratton* and *Cubby* do not,
however, suggest that distributors are not also a type of publisher for
purposes of defamation law. Zeran simply attaches too much importance
to the presence of the distinct notice element in distributor liability. The
simple fact of notice surely cannot transform one from an original
publisher to a distributor in the eyes of the law. To the contrary, once a
computer service provider receives notice of a potentially defamatory
posting, it is thrust into the role of a traditional publisher. The computer
service provider must decide whether to publish, edit, or withdraw the
posting. In this respect, Zeran seeks to impose liability on AOL for
assuming the role for which § 230 specifically proscribes liability—the
publisher role. Our view that Zeran's complaint treats AOL as a publisher
is reinforced because AOL is cast in the same position as the party who
originally posted the offensive messages. According to Zeran's logic, AOL
is legally at fault because it communicated to third parties an allegedly
defamatory statement. This is precisely the theory under which the
original poster of the offensive messages would be found liable. If the
original party is considered a publisher of the offensive messages, Zeran
certainly cannot attach liability to AOL under the same theory without
conceding that AOL too must be treated as a publisher of the statements.
Zeran next contends that interpreting § 230 to impose liability on service
providers with knowledge of defamatory content on their services is
consistent with the statutory purposes outlined in Part II A. Zeran fails,
however, to understand the practical implications of notice liability in the
interactive computer service context. Liability upon notice would defeat
the dual purposes advanced by § 230 of the CDA. Like the strict liability
imposed by the *Stratton Oakmont* court, liability upon notice reinforces
service providers' incentives to restrict speech and abstain from self-
regulation. If computer service providers were subject to distributor

liability, they would face potential liability each time they receive notice of
a potentially defamatory statement—from any party, concerning any
message. Each notification would require a careful yet rapid investigation
of the circumstances surrounding the posted information, a legal
judgment concerning the information's defamatory character, and an on-
the-spot editorial decision whether to risk liability by allowing the
continued publication of that information. Although this might be feasible
for the traditional print publisher, the sheer number of postings on
interactive computer services would create an impossible burden in the
Internet context . . . Because service providers would be subject to liability
only for the publication of information, and not for its removal, they would
have a natural incentive simply to remove messages upon notification,
whether the contents were defamatory or not. See Philadelphia
Newspapers, Inc. v. Hepps, 475 U.S. 767, 777 (1986) (recognizing that fears
of unjustified liability produce a chilling effect antithetical to First
Amendment's protection of speech). Thus, like strict liability, liability upon
notice has a chilling effect on the freedom of Internet speech. Similarly,
notice-based liability would deter service providers from regulating the
dissemination of offensive material over their own services. Any efforts by
a service provider to investigate and screen material posted on its service
would only lead to notice of potentially defamatory material more
frequently and thereby create a stronger basis for liability. Instead of
subjecting themselves to further possible lawsuits, service providers
would likely eschew any attempts at self-regulation. More generally,
notice-based liability for interactive computer service providers would
provide third parties with a no-cost means to create the basis for future
lawsuits. Whenever one was displeased with the speech of another party
conducted over an interactive computer service, the offended party could
simply "notify" the relevant service provider, claiming the information to
be legally defamatory.

In light of the vast amount of speech communicated through
interactive computer services, these notices could produce an impossible
burden for service providers, who would be faced with ceaseless choices
of suppressing controversial speech or sustaining prohibitive liability.
Because the probable effects of distributor liability on the vigor of Internet
speech and on service provider self-regulation are directly contrary to §
230's statutory purposes, we will not assume that Congress intended to
leave liability upon notice intact. Zeran finally contends that the
interpretive canon favoring retention of common law principles unless
Congress speaks directly to the issue counsels a restrictive reading of the
§ 230 immunity here. . . . This interpretive canon does not persuade us to
reach a different result. Here, Congress has indeed spoken directly to the

issue by employing the legally significant term "publisher," which has traditionally encompassed distributors and original publishers alike . . . As explained above, interpreting § 230 to leave distributor liability in effect would defeat the two primary purposes of the statute and would certainly "lessen the scope plainly intended" by Congress' use of the term "publisher." Section 230 represents the approach of Congress to a problem of national and international dimension. The Supreme Court underscored this point in *ACLU v. Reno*, finding that the Internet allows "tens of millions of people to communicate with one another and to access vast amounts of information from around the world. [It] is a unique and wholly new medium of worldwide human communication" . . . Application of the canon invoked by Zeran here would significantly lessen Congress' power, derived from the Commerce Clause, to act in a field whose international character is apparent. While Congress allowed for the enforcement of "any State law that is consistent with [§ 230]," 47 U.S.C. § 230(d)(3), it is equally plain that Congress' desire to promote unfettered speech on the Internet must supersede conflicting common law causes of action . . .

III

☐   The CDA was signed into law and became effective on February 8, 1996. Zeran did not file his complaint until April 23, 1996. Zeran contends that even if § 230 does bar the type of claim he brings here, it cannot be applied retroactively to bar an action arising from AOL's alleged misconduct prior to the CDA's enactment. We disagree. Section 230 applies by its plain terms to complaints brought after the CDA became effective. As noted in Part IIB, the statute provides, in part: "No cause of action may be brought and no liability may be imposed under any State or local law that is inconsistent with this section." 47 U.S.C. § 230(d)(3). Initially, it is doubtful that a retroactivity issue is even presented here. Congress clearly expressed its intent that the statute apply to any complaint instituted after its effective date, regardless of when the relevant conduct giving rise to the claims occurred. Other circuits have interpreted similar statutory language to clearly express Congress' intent that the relevant statutes apply to bar new actions under statutorily specified conditions . . . Congress decided that free speech on the Internet and self-regulation of offensive speech were so important that § 230 should be given immediate, comprehensive effect. . . . Zeran cannot point to any action he took in reliance on the law prior to § 230's enactment. Because § 230 has no untoward retroactive effect, even the presumption against statutory retroactivity absent an express directive from Congress is of no help to Zeran here.

IV

☐   For the foregoing reasons, we affirm the judgment of the district court.

Libel Insurance

As we have seen, libel suits can result from relatively routine situations. Failure to double-check facts, the writing of a "sexy" headline, the zeal of an investigative reporter to "nail" a social offender, or the lack of a budget to hire properly schooled reporters can all be costly. Responsible publishers do not usually begin a day's work with the intention of libeling someone. Although most complaints do not go to trial, daily news gathering often brings the threat of a libel suit. The cost of defending against even a threat of a libel suit can be extremely high. If a dispute actually goes to court, it may cost a newspaper or broadcaster more than $150,000 in attorney's fees and court costs alone. Damage awards have averaged in the millions of dollars since the early 1980s. These costs can have a chilling effect on the media's willingness to publish some stories. Small publications and broadcast stations may choose to shy away from controversial stories rather than risk a lawsuit.

Many publishers and broadcasters carry libel insurance to guard against a potentially devastating libel suit. Although prohibited in some states, libel insurance policies are offered both by private underwriters and the major trade organizations such as the American Newspaper Publishers Association and the National Association of Broadcasters.

Premiums are generally based on a percentage of the overall revenue of a broadcast station or publication and, like all insurance, on the risk of a particular medium. For example, some states have a higher percentage of libel suits and some publications tend to be involved in more libel suits than others. Obviously, in these cases, premiums will be higher.

Not all libel insurance policies are alike. There are differences in coverage, exclusions, and conditions. Many do not cover punitive damage awards. Some cover only judgments and not defense costs. But, like automobile or health insurance, various libel policies are available to protect the responsible publisher or broadcaster from financial ruin. Libel insurance may also serve to lessen the chilling effect that rising damage awards and defense costs have had on the media.

Summary

Libel is, essentially, the publication of material that is injurious to the personal reputation of an individual or the business reputation of a corporation. No libel suit can succeed unless the three elements of libel are met—identification, defamation, and publication. In addition, the plaintiff must establish some degree of fault. Private individuals may recover damages by demonstrating a lesser standard of fault than public figures. Though public figures must show that a publisher or broadcaster acted with actual malice, most states require that a private individual establish only negligence on the part of the media defendant.

The traditional defenses against a libel suit are truth, privilege, and fair comment. Media defendants usually seek a constitutional defense if the plaintiff is a public figure. Minor defenses include statutes of limitations and consent. The publication of a retraction may mitigate damages but will not usually serve as a complete defense. If judges believe that a jury cannot reasonably find in favor of a libel plaintiff, they will grant a summary judgment in favor of the defendant. Depending on the jurisdiction, successful libel plaintiffs may recover compensatory damages, special or actual damages, or punitive damages.

Though opinion is generally protected, if defamatory opinion can be proved true or false, it may not be protected by the First Amendment.

Notes/References

1. Donald M. Gillmor and Jermome A. Barton, *Mass Communication Law*, 4th ed. (St. Paul: West Publishing, 1984), 185.
2. Sir Frederick Pollack and Frederic William Maitland, *The History of English Law*, vol. II (Cambridge: University Press, 1968), 537.
3. *Bindrim v. Mitchell*, 92 Cal.App.2d 61,155 Cal.Rptr. 29 (1979).
4. *Gertz v. Robert Welch Inc.*, 418 U.S. 323, 33940; 94 S.Ct. 2997, 3007 (1974).
5. *McCall v. Courier Journal* (KY Sup.Ct., 1981) 7 Med.L.Rptr. 2118 at 2121.
6. 411.061(6) Kentucky Code (Sept. 1979 Replacement).
7. Indiana Code, 34-4-14-2 Civil Procedure (1982).
8. *Beacon Journal v. Lansdowne* (OH Ct.Comm.Pleas, 1984) 11 Med.L.Rptr. at 1096.
9. *Falwell v. Penthouse* (DC VA, 1981) 7 Med.L.Rptr. at 1896.
10. *New York Times v. Sullivan*, 376 U.S. 279–80 (1964).
11. "Heed Their Rising Voices," *New York Times* (Tuesday, March 29, 1960): L-25.
12. *New York Times v. Sullivan*, 376 U.S. 279–80 (1964).
13. *Curtis Publishing Co. v. Butts* and *Associated Press v. Walker*, 388 U.S. 130 (1967).
14. Ibid.

15. *Rosenblatt v. Baer*, 383 U.S. 75 (1966).

16. *Rosenbloom v. Metromedia*, 403 U.S. 29 (1971) at 57.

17. *Gertz v. Robert Welch Inc.*, 418 U.S. 323, 33940; 94 S.Ct. 2997, 3007 (1974).

18. *Milkovich v. Lorain Journal* (U.S. Sup.Ct., 1990) 17 Med.L.Rptr. 2009.

19. *Philadelphia Newspapers v. Hepps* (U.S. Sup.Ct., 1986) 12 Med.L.Rptr. 1977.

20. *KARK-TV v. Simon* (Ark. Sup.Ct., 1983) 10 Med.L.Rptr. 1050.

21. Ibid.

22. *St. Amant v. Thompson*, 390 U.S. 731 (1968).

23. *Liberty Lobby v. Anderson* (U.S. App.Ct. DC, 1984) 11 Med.L.Rptr. at 1010.

24. *Anderson v. Liberty Lobby* (U.S. Sup.Ct., 1986) 12 Med.L.Rptr. 2303.

25. *McCullough v. Cities Service* (Okla. Sup.Ct., 1984) 10 Med.L.Rptr. 1411.

26. *West's Annotated Indiana Code* (St. Paul: West Publishing, 1985), 398, 35-1–59-1 (1985).

27. *Garrison v. State of Louisiana*, 379 U.S. 64 (1964).

28. *Franklin v. Friedman* (NY Sup.Ct., 1985) 12 Med.L.Rptr. 1146.

29. *Brooks v. Stone* (Ga. Ct.App., 1984) 10 Med.L.Rptr. 1517.

Cases

Action Repair v. ABC (CA 7, 1985) 12 Med.L.Rptr. 1809

Anderson v. Liberty Lobby (U.S. Sup.Ct., 1986) 12 Med.L.Rptr. 2297

Baia v. Jackson Newspapers (Conn. Sup.Ct., 1985) 12 Med.L.Rptr. 1780

Barry v. Time (DC N.Cal., 1984) 10 Med.L.Rptr. 1809

Beacon Journal v. Lansdowne (OH Ct.Comm.Pleas, 1984) 11 Med.L.Rptr. 1096

Bindrim v. Mitchell, 92 Cal.App.2d 61, 155 Cal.Rptr. 29 (1979)

Bose Corporation v. Consumers Union (Sup.Ct., 1985) 10 Med.L.Rptr. 1625

Brady v. Ottaway Newspapers, Inc., (NYS 2d, 1981) 8 Med.L.Rptr. 1671

Brauer v. Globe Newspaper Co., 217 N.E.2d 736, 739 (1966)

Brooks v. Stone (Ga. Ct.App., 1984) 10 Med.L.Rptr. 1517

Buratt v. Capital City Press (La. Ct.App., 1981) 7 Med.L.Rptr. 1856

Cardillo v. Doubleday & Co. Inc., 518 F.2d 638 (2d Cir., 1975)

Catalfo v. Jensen (DC NH, 1986) 12 Med.L.Rptr. 1867

Charlottesville Newspapers Inc. v. Debra C. Matthews (Va. Sup.Ct., 1986) 11 Med.L.Rptr. 1621

Cubby Inc. v. CompuServe Inc. 19 Med.L.Rptr 1525 (S.D.N.Y. 1991)

Curtis Publishing Co. v. Butts and Associated Press v. Walker, 388 U.S. 130 (1967)

Donaldson v. Washington Post Co. (DC Sup.Ct., 1977) 3 Med.L.Rptr. 1436

Edwards v. National Audubon Society, 566 F.2d 113 (2d Cir., 1977)

Falwell v. Penthouse (DC VA, 1981) 7 Med.L.Rptr. 1891

Fawcett Publications v. Mortis, Okla. 1962, 377 P.2d 42, appeal dismissed, cert. denied 376 U.S. 513, 84 S.Ct. 964, 11 L.Ed.2d 968, rehearing denied 377 U.S. 925, 84 S.Ct. 1218, 12 L.Ed. 2d 217

Fleming v. Kane County (DC N.Ill., 1986)13 Med.L.Rptr. 1014

Franklin v. Friedman (NY Sup.Ct., 1985) 12 Med.L.Rptr. 1146

Garrison v. State of Louisiana, 379 U.S. 64 (1964)

Gertz v. Robert Welch Inc., 418 U.S. 323, 339–40; 94 S.Ct. 2997, 3007 (1974)

Green v. Alton Telegraph, 8 Med.L.Rptr. (1982)

Guccione v. Hustler (CA 2, 1986) 13 Med.L.Rptr. 1316

Guccione v. Hustler (DC S.NY, 1986) 12 Med.L.Rptr. 2042

Herbert v. Lando, 60 L.Ed.2d 115 (1979)

Herron v. King Broadcasting Co. (Wash Sup.Ct., 1988) 14 Med.L.Rptr. 2017

J. V. Peters v. Knight-Ridder (Ohio Ct.App., 1984) 10 Med.L.Rptr. 1576

Jackson v. Longcope, 394 Mass. 577, 580; 476 N.E.2d 617 (1985)

Journal Publishing Co. v. McCullough, 743 So.2d 352 (1999)

KARK-TV v. Simon (Ark. Sup.Ct., 1983) 10 Med.L.Rptr. 1049

Keeton v. Hustler (U.S. Sup.Ct., 1984) 10 Med.L.Rptr. 1409–10

Keller v. Miami Herald (DC SD FL, 1984) 11 Med.L.Rptr. 1032

Kerwick v. Orange County Publications (NY Ct.App., 1982) 7 Med.L.Rptr. 1152

Lasky v. ABC (DC So.NY, 1986) 13 Med.L.Rptr. 1379

Liberty Lobby v. Anderson (U.S. App.Ct. DC, 1984) 11 Med.L.Rptr. 1010

Logan v. District of Columbia, 447 F.Supp. 1328 (DC DC, 1978)

McCall v. Courier Journal (KY Sup.Ct., 1981) 7 Med.L.Rptr. 2118

McCullough v. Cities Service (Okla. Sup.Ct., 1984) 10 Med.L.Rptr. 1411

Milkovich v. Lorain Journal (U.S. Sup.Ct., 1990) 17 Med.L.Rptr. 2009

Neiman-Marcus Co. v. Lait, 13 F.R.D. 311 (D NY, 1952)

New York Times v. Sullivan, 376 U.S. 279–80 (1964)

Newton v. NBC (DC Nev., 1987) 114 Med.L.Rptr. 1914

Pelzer v. Minneapolis Tribune (Minn. Dist.Ct., 1982) 7 Med.L.Rptr. 2507

Philadelphia Newspapers v. Hepps (U.S. Sup.Ct., 1986) 12 Med.L.Rptr. 1977

Pitts v. Spokane Chronicle Co., 388 P.2d 976 (1964)

Pring v. Penthouse (DC WY, 1981) 7 Med.L.Rptr. 1101

Ray v. Time Inc., 582 F.2d 1280 (6th Cir., 1978)

Redco Corporation v. CBS (U.S. Ct.App.3d, 1985) 11 Med.L.Rptr. 1861

Rosenblatt v. Baer, 383 U.S. 75 (1966)

Rosenbloom v. Metromedia, 463 U.S. 29 (1971)

Schiavone Construction v. Time (DC NJ, 1985) 12 Med.L.Rptr. 1153

Schiavone Construction v. Time, (DC NJ, 1986) 13 Med.L.Rptr. 1664

St. Amant v. Thompson, 390 U.S. 731 (1968)

Stratton Oakmont, Inc. v. Prodigy Services Co., 23 Med.L.Rptr. 1794
    (N.Y.Sup.Ct. 1995)

Tavoulareas v. Washington Post (CA DC, 1985) 11 Med.L.Rptr. 1777

Time Inc. v. Firestone, 424 U.S. 448 (1976)

Torres v. Playboy (DC So.TX, 1980) 7 Med.L.Rptr. 1185

Weatherland v. Globe International (CA 10, 1987) 14 Med.L.Rptr. 1949

Zeran v. America Online Inc. 129 F.3d 327 (1997)
    http://serv5.law.emory.edu/4circuit/nov97/971523.p.html

11 □□□
    □□□
    □□□
    □□□

Free Press–Fair Trial Issues and the Electronic Media: A Conflict of Rights

Selecting an Impartial Jury

Although the First Amendment guarantees the rights of freedom of speech and press, these rights are not absolute. With freedom comes the knowledge that irresponsible actions can lead to the regulation of that freedom by others. As is often the case, the protection against outside regulation of freedoms lies in self-restraint. When one Constitutionally-guaranteed right comes into conflict with another, the courts must attempt to balance the two rights. Such is the case regarding press coverage of criminal trials. Irresponsible behavior by press, bench, and bar led to an imbalance between First and Sixth Amendment rights.

The Sixth Amendment to the Constitution guarantees to those accused of criminal actions a right to a speedy and public trial by an impartial jury. These rights of a defendant often conflict with rights also guaranteed to the press under the First Amendment. Because a jury is selected after pretrial proceedings, media coverage of the arrest and pleadings of a criminal suspect may prejudice the opinion of prospective jurors. The media have always claimed a First Amendment right to cover trials. Historically, however, this coverage has sometimes compromised the conduct of trials. The courts reserve the right to preserve judicial discipline, while citizens and the press maintain a right to comment on and view the judicial process. When these rights collide, conflict and inequities result. Uncontrolled publicity about a criminal trial can result in an innocent person's conviction or a guilty person's acquittal. In either case, justice is not served. For the First and Sixth

Amendments to function as intended, the press and the judiciary must respect each other's role in American society.

News coverage of crimes and criminal proceedings may create prejudice in prospective jurors and bias jurors who have already been selected. Reports of crimes, arrests, and evidence that has been admitted at trial usually pose no problem. Two areas that pose the greatest problem are the publication of confessions and prior criminal records of defendants when neither are admissible as evidence.

Criminal defendants are entitled to a speedy and public trial by an impartial jury. Pretrial publicity is assumed to have an effect on the impartiality of that jury. Therefore, it would appear that every effort should be made to insulate prospective jurors from publicity that might influence their decision. Critics argue that our system assumes a truly impartial juror is one who is totally ignorant of the facts surrounding a case. An impartial juror has cynically been described as an uninformed moron who does not read the newspapers, watch television news, or listen to the radio. Of course, this is not the case. Since the early days of our republic, it has been recognized that an impartial juror need not be completely unaware of the defendant or of the crime. In *United States v. Burr (1807)*, Chief Justice John Marshall defined an impartial juror as one holding "light impressions which may be supposed to yield to testimony"[1] (i.e., one who is willing to listen to arguments and base any final decision on testimony).

The American Bar Association (ABA) has suggested that the publication of certain types of information may influence potential jurors and may make a fair trial impossible. The ABA recommended that the following material not be published:

- Opinions about the character, guilt, or innocence of the accused
- Admissions or confessions of guilt by the defendant
- References to the results of any examinations or tests, such as lie detectors or laboratory tests
- Statements about the credibility of witnesses or anticipated testimony
- Opinions concerning evidence or arguments in a case and the likelihood that such evidence will be used at trial
- Prior charges and convictions, even though such information may be part of the public record[2]

These recommendations, although by no means universally followed, are the result of a long struggle between the press and the judiciary. This struggle began in the early nineteenth century and is by no means over. Now judges regularly attempt to control prejudicial pretrial publicity by granting a change of venue or a continuance, or by sequestering the jury. A change of venue moves the location of the trial away from an area in which prospective jurors are likely to hold preconceived opinions about the guilt or innocence of an accused person. A continuance postpones the starting date of a trial so that the strong emotions felt by a community, often accompanying the arrest of a suspect, have had time to subside. Sequestering the jury means limiting jurors' contact with the outside world during a trial. This is done in the hope that jurors will not be influenced by media reports of the proceedings or by others desiring to affect the outcome of the trial. A judge may also limit the number of reporters allowed in the courtroom or may seal the past records of a defendant. In rare instances, the judge may actually close pretrial proceedings to reporters. However, recent rulings have made this practice even less likely.

The relationship between the media and the courts is built on a rocky foundation of crime reporting in America, as illustrated by the infamous murder trials of Leslie Irvin and Dr. Sam Sheppard. The fallout from these two cases set the stage for a difficult period in the history of the free press–fair trial debate.

The Tradition of Crime Reporting

The reporting of crime news in the United States has been a staple of journalism since the 1830s when Benjamin Day's *New York Sun* revolutionized the American newspaper by publishing for the masses instead of the elite. Crime news later contributed to the success of such papers as Pulitzer's *World* and Hearst's *Journal.*

The growth of the tabloid press in the early part of this century led to a sensationalistic form of journalism in the 1920s often dubbed jazz journalism. Publications such as the *New York World*, the *Illustrated Daily News*, and Bernard MacFadden's notorious *Graphic* built readerships on reports of crime, sex, and gossip. Competition among the tabloids was fierce and each attempted to out-sensationalize the other in order to boost circulation.

One of the more egregious examples of this sensationalism occurred during and after the 1927 trial of a corset salesman named Judd Gray and his sweetheart, Ruth Snyder. The two were on trial for the murder of Snyder's husband. Not only was the trial covered in great detail, but the execution of Ruth Snyder in the electric chair at Sing Sing prison became one of the most outrageous examples of the bad taste exhibited by the tabloid press of that era. The *Graphic* teased its readers with the following:

> Don't fail to read tomorrow's *Graphic*. An installment that thrills and stuns! A story that fairly pierces the heart and reveals Ruth Snyder's last thoughts on earth; that pulses the blood as it discloses her final letters. Think of it! A woman's final thoughts just before she is clutched

in the deadly snare that sears and burns and FRIES AND KILLS! Her very last words! Exclusively in tomorrow's *Graphic*.[3]

Not to be outdone, the *News* sent photographer Tom Howard into the execution chamber (with a tiny camera strapped to his ankle) where he photographed Snyder's execution. The gruesome picture made up page one of the January 14, 1928, *Daily News* and was captioned "When Ruth Paid Her Debt to the State." The *News* sold 250,000 extra copies of that edition.[4]

The 1930s saw the demise of the tabloids, and a somewhat more responsible form of reporting emerged. However, crime stories continued to be a staple of American journalism. Questionable behavior by journalists in search of a scoop still outraged press critics. The 1935 trial of Bruno Hauptmann, tried for the kidnapping and murder of aviator Charles Lindbergh's baby, drew more than 800 reporters who wrote during a 28-day period. Reporters were joined at the trial by show business personalities, politicians, and an estimated 20,000 members of the general public. The jury was photographed in the jury box, vendors sold souvenir "kidnap ladders," and regular reports about the guilt of Hauptmann appeared in newspapers across the country.

These excesses were not without consequence, however. Although Hauptmann was found guilty, the judge was criticized for permitting a "trial by newspaper." Thereafter, judges were more careful to control the atmosphere of a trial and the conduct of reporters and others present in the courtroom. As a result of the conduct of the press during the Hauptmann trial, the American Bar Association adopted Canon 35 of professional ethics, which prohibited the taking of pictures in the courtroom.

The Road to the Supreme Court

After the Second World War, a string of murders and other sensationalistic stories hit the news wires. The stage was set for another conflict between the press and the judiciary, centering on the public's right to be informed and a defendant's right to a fair trial by an impartial jury.

In 1951, the Supreme Court considered the first of several cases concerning jury prejudice fostered by the news media. It would be eight years, however, before the Court would order a new trial solely on the grounds that pretrial publicity made a fair trial impossible.

In *Shepherd v. Florida (1951)*, four black men were accused of the rape of a white girl in Lake County, Florida. Two were convicted and sentenced to death. During the trial, community prejudice was pervasive. The defendants had been threatened with lynching, one of their parents' homes had been burned, and the National Guard had been called out to protect other blacks living in the community. Some blacks left the community after threats on their lives.

The newspapers had quoted the local sheriff as saying that the defendants had confessed, but no confession was offered at the trial. The papers published several prejudicial articles during the investigation of the crime, including a cartoon picturing four electric chairs that were headed "No Compromise—Supreme Penalty." Although there had been motions for both a change of venue and continuance, they had been denied.

A mistrial was declared; however, it was so declared not on grounds of pretrial publicity but on racial prejudice. Justice Jackson did note that if racial discrimination had not been a factor, the defendants probably would not have received a fair trial anyway.

□   . . . [P]rejudicial influences outside the courtroom, becoming all too typical of a highly publicized trial, were brought to bear on this jury with such force that the conclusion is inescapable that these defendants were prejudged as guilty and the trial was but a legal gesture to register a verdict already dictated by the press and the public opinion which it generated.[5]

The following year, the Supreme Court heard another case in which a confession was published and newspaper reports were somewhat sensationalistic. This time the Court did not order a new trial. In *Stroble v. State of California (1952)*, the Court did require Stroble to demonstrate that pretrial publicity had hurt his case—a requirement to which the Court would return 24 years later in *Nebraska Press*.

The defendant, Stroble, was charged with the first-degree murder of a six-year-old girl. The Los Angeles newspapers published excerpts from an alleged confession. The district attorney also had offered his opinion of the defendant's guilt to the press. Newspaper articles referred to Stroble as a "werewolf," a "fiend," and a "sex-mad killer." Stroble pleaded not guilty to the murder charge. The trial itself was covered by the papers and no objection to press coverage was entered by Stroble, except for the newspapers' occasional reference to him as a "werewolf."

Stroble was convicted by the trial court and the Supreme Court affirmed the conviction. The Court rejected claims that Stroble was deprived of a fair trial because of prejudicial newspaper coverage. The Court noted,

□   The matter of prejudicial newspaper accounts was first brought to the trial court's attention after petitioner's conviction, as one of the grounds in support of a motion for a new trial. At that time petitioner's present

attorney urged that petitioner had been "deprived of the presumption of
innocence by premature release by the District Attorney's office of the
details of the confession," and offered in support of that allegation certain
Los Angeles newspapers published at the time of petitioner's arrest. . . .

. . . [A]t no stage of the proceedings has petitioner offered so much as
an affidavit to prove that any juror was in fact prejudiced by the
newspaper stories. He asks this Court simply to read those stories and
then to declare . . . that [two state courts] deprived him of due process.
That we cannot do, at least where, as here, the inflammatory newspaper
accounts appeared approximately six weeks before the beginning of
petitioner's trial, and there is no affirmative showing that any community
prejudice ever existed or in any way affected the deliberation of the jury.[6]

The majority of the Court established that potentially prejudicial, pretrial publicity, in and of itself, does not automatically result in an unfair trial.
The Court ruled that for a mistrial to be declared, there had to be a strong
showing by the defendant that community prejudice had affected the jury's
verdict.

Justices Douglas and Frankfurter wrote dissents, however, that would
later serve as foundations for a policy favoring a lesser showing by a defendant. Justice Frankfurter wrote,

☐   . . . I cannot agree to uphold a conviction which affirmatively treats
newspaper participation instigated by the prosecutor as part of the
"traditional concept of the American way of the conduct of a trial." Such
passion as the newspapers stirred in this case can be explained (apart
from mere commercial exploitation of revolting crime) only as want of
confidence in the orderly course of justice.[7]

Essentially, Justice Frankfurter's position was that if the press cannot act
responsibly voluntarily, it is up to the trial judge to ensure that they do. This
line of thinking would dominate rulings following the Court's *Sheppard* decision in 1966.

Between 1952 and 1961, the Supreme Court heard several cases in which
defendants claimed to have been denied a fair trial as a result of pretrial publicity. None of the cases resulted in a strong call for a reversal based on the
conduct of the media. In both *Marshall v. United States (1959)* and *Janko v.
United States (1961)*, the Supreme Court did call for new trials. However,
because the Supreme Court acted only in a supervisory capacity and did not
attempt to determine whether the defendant had been denied due process,
these cases had little impact on the conduct of trials at the state and local
levels.

Trial by Newspaper: "Mad Dog Irvin" and "Dr. Sam"

In 1961, the Supreme Court agreed to hear the case of Leslie Irvin, who had been convicted of murder. *Irvin v. Dowd* would be the first state case in which a mistrial was declared by the Supreme Court solely on grounds of prejudicial pretrial publicity. *Marshall v. United States* was the first conviction in a federal court that was reversed solely on grounds of pretrial publicity.

Irvin v. Dowd (1961)

On December 24, 1954, the news media in the southwestern Indiana city of Evansville began reporting on what was to become one of the most highly publicized murder trials in Indiana. The Irvin trial focused attention on the way in which criminal trials were reported and conducted. Ultimately, it changed the practices of both journalists and judges.

At issue was the way in which the news media reported information about Irvin before his arrest and trial. This included the publication of his past criminal record and references to him as a "maniac killer" and a "mad dog." A second problem involved a state law that allowed a change of venue only one county away. Although Irvin's trial was moved from Vanderburgh to Gibson County, most potential jurists had been exposed to the same barrage of pretrial publicity, because the predominate media were the same in both counties. Effectively, the media and the court had failed to safeguard Leslie Irvin's Sixth Amendment right to a fair trial.

The road to the Supreme Court began on Christmas Eve, 1954, when the Evansville Press bannered "Police All Out in Hunt for 'Mad Dog' Killer." Two very similar murders had occurred within a three-week period. On December 2, 1954, Mary Holland, a 33-year-old expectant mother and clerk at the Bellemeade Liquor Store, was forced to kneel over the commode and was shot in the head. On December 23, 1954, Whitney Wesley Kerr, an attendant at a gas station, was found shot in a similar manner. The cash registers at both businesses had been emptied, netting $318.11.

The news reports contributed to a growing siege mentality in the city. The papers warned that a "mad dog killer" was on the prowl. They noted that off-duty policemen had given up their Christmas shopping to join the hunt for what was described as a "maniac killer." A $1000 reward was offered to the public for information leading to the arrest of the killer, and one headline advised, "Your Tip May Help Police Trap Killer." Evansville's police chief described the slayings as "acts of cold-blooded murder" and the "act of a homicidal maniac."

No killer was found, and it appeared that the Christmastime murders did not signal a reign of terror after all. All was calm until the spring of 1955. Then, within a week, four persons were killed in their homes within the greater Evansville area. As in the December slayings, the motive seemed to be burglary, with money, jewelry, and guns missing from each of the homes.

On March 21, 1955, Mrs. Wilhelmina Sailer was murdered in Posey County, and on March 28, three members of the Duncan family were killed in Henderson County, Kentucky. In both incidents, the victims had been shot through the head, with their hands bound. The community once again was gripped by fear. Residents were afraid to walk alone at night, and they kept their doors locked tightly during the day.

Finally, on April 9, the *Evansville Press* reported that police had apprehended a suspect. The headline read, "Tight Secrecy Screens Quiz of 'Hottest' Murder Suspect, Evansville Ex-Convict." The chief of detectives issued a statement to the media in which he said that a suspect was being held for questioning. He added that the suspect had admitted some burglaries, but he refused to divulge the suspect's name. The detective expressed concern that to give any more information might "mess up the case." The article continued by stating that the suspect had left his "trademark" in the burglaries. The Henderson County sheriff told reporters that the trademark was the manner in which the suspect entered the houses of the victims. The article also stated that a two-year-old child was found near the body of her mother in the Duncan home. The *Press* ran a photo of the child and indicated that the toddler had picked the suspect out of a police line-up. The photo caption read, "Although the testimony of a two-year-old couldn't be used in court, it may aid the police." The police would neither confirm nor deny the existence of the two-year-old witness.

Leslie Irvin's name was first associated with the killings on April 10th, when the *Press* headline read, "Junior Sheriffs Spotted Irvin's Black Sedan." The article continued,

> It was the two young sheriffs' patrol members who first got the license number of the car of Leslie Irvin, 30-year-old parolee, whom police have been questioning since last Friday in connection with the slayings. . . .[8]

Although thus far Irvin had not been charged formally with the slayings, the article pointed out that Irvin had "admitted more than two dozen burglaries in Vanderburgh, Posey, Warrick and Gibson counties." The article also noted that Irvin's method of operation matched the way the Duncan home had been broken into either the night before or the morning of the triple slayings.

A subheading in the April 10th article called Irvin "emotionally unstable." An investigating officer is quoted as saying,

The suspect says he threw the gun away which he stole. . . . The method of operation of the subject has been the same in all cases of burglary and his car fits the description of the car that has been seen in the neighborhoods where the burglaries have been committed, some of the burglaries being in the murder area. . . . it should be again pointed out that evidence which is being worked cannot be made public until such evidence has been completely worked.[9]

The next day, readers were treated to a triple headline that read, "Murder Suspect Named by Police," "Leslie Irvin Taking Lie Detector Test," "Parole Violator Arrested Near Yankeetown; Car Matches One Seen at Duncan Home." Accompanying this headline was a full-length police line-up photograph of Irvin, showing the suspect with a police ID tag hanging from his waist.

Statements of Irvin's prior criminal record appear throughout the article. Police are quoted as saying that "Irvin is a parolee sentenced for first-degree burglary from Indianapolis. He served approximately nine years before being paroled and has approximately nine years to serve on his parole."[10] The article also mentions that Irvin had agreed to submit to a lie detector test, that he had admitted numerous burglaries, and that the prosecutor believed enough evidence was available to convict Irvin of first-degree burglary.

On April 12th, there appeared an article that again reported Irvin as "emotionally unstable." More circumstantial evidence was reported in the article, noting that Irvin was absent from work on the days the killings took place.

On Wednesday, April 13th, the *Press* headline read, "Irvin Placed at Murder Scene: Reported Seeking to Make Deal." The subheading stated, "Car Seen Turning into Duncan Lane." A subsequent headline read, "Henderson Sheriff Ready to Ask for Extradition; Local Police Deny Earlier Report of 'Confession.'" Irvin still had not been charged with the murders; however, there was little doubt in the minds of Evansville citizens that the killer had been caught.

Finally, on Thursday, April 14th, Leslie Irvin was charged officially with two counts of murder. He was held without bond. Although he had not been convicted yet, the *Press* was so convinced of his guilt that it ran a headline that boldly asked, "What Made Leslie Irvin a Killer? Known as 'Likeable Fellow' with 'No Problems.'" Once again, a confession was published. The paper reported that Irvin had told Kentucky state police that he had killed three members of the Duncan family and left another for dead. A sidebar to this article contained a clipping from the June 2, 1939, *Press*, which was a news report headed, "Boy, 15, Admits Starting Fires at Bosse High." That "boy" was, of course, Leslie Irvin. The Press noted that this was his "first brush with the law."

Subsequent news coverage of the trial preparations included references to Irvin's assistance in the recovery of a gun from a ditch, and an admission that he shot three members of the Duncan family and killed Wilhelmina Sailer.

The April 28 Press headline read, "2 Innocent Pleas Entered by Irvin." The story goes on to say,

> The 31-year-old parolee, who led police to the murder weapons and told them how he killed six persons, will be examined by court-appointed doctors to determine if he is mentally competent to stand trial.[11]

Irvin's trial began in November and was moved from Vanderburgh County, where he was charged, to adjoining Gibson County. His attorneys objected, stating that Irvin could not receive a fair trial so close to the counties of the crimes. However, as previously mentioned, Indiana law limited a change of venue merely to one county away, and the trial proceeded even though 8 of the 12 jurors seated thought Irvin was guilty. The Gibson County jury found Irvin guilty of murder and sentenced him to death by electrocution.

On January 19, 1956, he was to have returned to court formally to request a new trial, but instead he became the first prisoner to escape from the newly constructed Gibson County jail. In February, he was found in San Francisco and brought back to Indiana. Irvin's attorneys appealed his conviction on grounds that he had not received a fair trial by an impartial jury. Eventually the case was reviewed by the Supreme Court. Justice Clark delivered the opinion of the Court.

☐   . . . it is not required that jurors be totally ignorant of the facts and issues involved. . . . To hold that the mere existence of any preconceived notions as to the guilt or innocence of an accused, without more, is sufficient to rebut the presumption of a prospective juror's impartiality would be to establish an impossible standard. It is sufficient if the juror can lay aside his impression or opinion and render a verdict based on the evidence presented in court.

   . . . Here the build up of prejudice is clear and convincing. An examination of the then current community pattern of thought as indicated by the popular news media is singularly revealing. For example, petitioner's first motion for a change of venue from Gibson County alleged that the trial of petitioner had become the cause celebre of this small community—so much so that curbstone opinions, not only as to the petitioner's guilt but even as to what punishment he should receive, were solicited and recorded on the public streets by a roving reporter, and later were broadcast over the local stations. A reading of the 46 exhibits which petitioner attached to his motion indicates that a barrage of newspaper headlines, articles, cartoons and pictures was unleashed against him during the six or seven months preceding his trial. The motion further alleged that the newspapers in which the stories appeared were delivered regularly to approximately 95% of the dwellings in Gibson County and that, in addition, the Evansville radio and TV stations, which likewise blanketed that county, also carried extensive newscasts covering the same incidents.

. . . It cannot be gainsaid that the force of this continued adverse publicity caused a sustained excitement and fostered a strong prejudice among the people of Gibson County. In fact, on the second day devoted to the selection of the jury, the newspapers reported that "strong feelings," often bitter and angry, "rumbled to the surface," and that "the extent to which the multiple murders—three in one family—have aroused feelings throughout the area was emphasized Friday when 27 of the 35 prospective jurors questioned were excused for holding biased pretrial opinions. . . . Spectator comments, as printed by the newspapers, were "my mind is made up"; "I think he is guilty"; and "he should be hanged."

Finally, and with remarkable understatement, the headlines reported that "impartial jurors are hard to find" . . . An examination of the 2,783-page *voir dire* record shows that 370 prospective jurors or almost 90% of those examined . . . entertained some opinion as voir to guilt—ranging in intensity from mere suspicion to absolute certainty.

. . . Here the "pattern of deep and bitter prejudice" shown to be present throughout the community, was clearly reflected in the sum total of the *voir dire* examination of a majority of the jurors finally placed in the jury box. . . . Eight of the 12 thought petitioner was guilty. . . . With his life at stake, it is not requiring too much that petitioner be tried in an atmosphere undisturbed by so huge a wave of public passion and by a jury other than one in which two-thirds of the members admit, before hearing testimony, to possessing a belief in his guilt.[12]

Leslie Irvin was eventually granted a new trial in a less emotional atmosphere. He was found guilty of murder and sentenced to life in prison. He died of cancer in the Indiana State Penitentiary in 1983.

Six months before the first murders attributed to Irvin, a Cleveland, Ohio, osteopath became the chief suspect in the bludgeon slaying of his wife. The classic "trial by newspaper" case of Dr. Sam Sheppard would reach the Supreme Court five years after the Irvin decision and have even wider-reaching effects.

Sheppard v. Maxwell (1966)

Dr. Sam Sheppard was convicted of second-degree murder in the July 4, 1954, slaying of his pregnant wife, Marilyn. His conviction was upheld by the Ohio Supreme Court, and the U.S. Supreme Court refused to hear his appeal. Sheppard served ten years of a life sentence in the Ohio State Penitentiary. Throughout this time, Sheppard maintained that he was innocent and, ultimately, his attorneys were able to bring a *habeas corpus* proceeding to a federal court. The proceeding argued that Sheppard had been denied a fair trial because of the conduct of the press before and during the trial. In *Sheppard v. Maxwell (1964)*, the federal district court agreed, calling Sheppard's first trial a "mockery of justice."

The appellate court disagreed and ordered Sheppard to continue serving his sentence. However, Sheppard once again appealed to the Supreme Court. Sheppard's attorneys argued that the conduct of the press denied Sheppard his constitutional right to be tried by a fair and impartial jury. The Supreme Court agreed to hear this most bizarre case. This time, Sheppard was defended by F. Lee Bailey. Justice Clark delivered the opinion of the Court.

☐ . . . On the day of the tragedy, July 4, 1954, Sheppard pieced together for several local officials the following story: He and his wife had entertained neighborhood friends, the Ahrens, on the previous evening at their home. After dinner they watched television in the living room. Sheppard became drowsy and dosed off to sleep on a couch. Later, Marilyn partially awoke him saying that she was going to bed. The next thing he remembered was hearing his wife cry out in the early morning hours. He hurried upstairs and in the dim light from the hall saw a "form" standing next to his wife's bed. As he struggled with the "form" he was struck on the back of the neck and rendered unconscious. On regaining his senses he found himself on the floor next to his wife's bed. He raised up, looked at her, took her pulse and "felt that she was gone." He then went to his son's room and found him unmolested. Hearing a noise he hurried downstairs. He saw a "form" running out the door and pursued it to the lake shore. He grappled with it on the beach and again lost consciousness. Upon his recovery he was laying face down with the lower portion of his body in the water. He returned to his home, checked the pulse on his wife's neck, and "determined or thought that she was gone." He then went downstairs and called a neighbor, Mayor Houk of Bay Village. The Mayor and his wife came over at once, found Sheppard slumped in an easy chair downstairs and asked, "What happened?" Sheppard replied: "I don't know but somebody ought to try to do something for Marilyn." Mrs. Houk immediately went up to the bedroom. . . . After Mrs. Houk discovered the body, the Mayor called local police, Dr. Richard Sheppard, petitioner's

brother, and Ahrens. The local police were the first to arrive. . . . Richard
Sheppard then arrived, determined that Marilyn was dead, examined his
brother's injuries, and removed him to the nearby clinic operated by the
Sheppard family. . . . The Sheppard home and premises were taken into
"protective custody" and remained so until after the trial.

From the outset officials focused suspicion on Sheppard. . . . Dr.
Gerber, the Coroner, is reported—and it is undenied—to have told his
men, "Well, it is evident the doctor did this, so let's go get the confession
out of him. . . . The newspapers played up Sheppard's refusal to take a lie
detector test and the "protective ring" thrown up by his family. . . . More
stories appeared when Sheppard would not allow authorities to inject him
with "truth serum."

On the 20th, the "editorial artillery" opened fire with a front page
charge that somebody is "getting away with murder." The following day
. . . another page-one editorial was headed: "Why No Inquest? Do It Now,
Dr. Gerber." The Coroner called an inquest the same day and subpoenaed
Sheppard. It was staged the next day in a school gymnasium. . . . In the
front of the room was a long table occupied by reporters, television and
radio personnel and broadcasting equipment. The hearing was broadcast
with live microphones placed at the Coroner's seat and at the witness
stand. . . . Sheppard was brought into the room by police who searched
him in view of several hundred spectators. Sheppard's counsel were
present during the three-day inquest but were not permitted to
participate. When Sheppard's chief counsel attempted to place some
documents in the record, he was forcibly ejected from the room by the
Coroner, who received cheers, hugs, and kisses from ladies in the
audience. Sheppard was questioned for five and one-half hours about his
actions on the night of the murder, his married life, and a love affair with
Susan Hayes. At the end of the hearing the Coroner announced that he
"could" order Sheppard held for the grand jury, but did not do so.

Throughout this period the newspapers emphasized evidence that
tended to incriminate Sheppard and pointed out discrepancies in his
statements to authorities. At the same time, Sheppard made many public
statements to the press and wrote feature articles asserting his
innocence.

. . . On July 28, an editorial entitled "Why Don't Police Quiz Top
Suspect" demanded that Sheppard be taken to police headquarters. It
described him in the following language:

> Now proved under oath to be a liar, still free to go about his
> business, shielded by his family, protected by a smart lawyer
> who has made monkeys of the police and authorities,

carrying a gun part of the time, left free to do whatever he pleases . . .

☐ A front-page editorial on July 30 asked: "Why Isn't Sam Sheppard in Jail?" It was later titled "Quit Stalling—Bring Him In." . . .

That night at 10 o'clock Sheppard was arrested at his father's home on a charge of murder. He was taken to the Bay Village City Hall where hundreds of people, newscasters, photographers and reporters were awaiting his arrival.

. . . The publicity then grew in intensity until his indictment [by a grand jury] on August 17. . . . Headlines announced . . . that: "Doctor Evidence Is Ready for Jury," "Corrigan Tactics Stall Quizzing," "Sheppard 'Gay Set' Is Revealed by Houk," "Blood Is Found, Police Claim," "Dr. Sam Faces Quiz at Jail on Marilyn's Fear of Him."

With this background the case came on for trial two weeks before the November general election at which the chief prosecutor was a candidate for municipal judge and the presiding judge, Judge Blythin, was a candidate to succeed himself. Twenty-five days before the case was set, a list of 75 veniremen were called as prospective jurors. This list, including the addresses of each venireman, was published in all three Cleveland newspapers. . . . [A]nonynous letters and telephone calls . . . regarding the impending prosecution were received by all of the prospective jurors.

The courtroom in which the trial was held measured 26 by 48 feet. A long temporary table was set up inside the bar, in back of the single counsel table. . . . Approximately 20 representatives of newspapers and wire services were assigned seats at this table by the court. Behind the bar railing there were four rows of benches. . . . The first row was occupied by representatives of television and radio stations, and the second and third rows by reporters from out-of-town newspapers and magazines. . . . Representatives of the news media also used all the rooms on the courtroom floor, including the room where cases were ordinarily called and assigned for trial. . . . Station WSRS was permitted to set up broadcasting facilities on the third floor of the courthouse next door to the jury room . . .

. . . In the corridors outside the courtroom there was a host of photographers and television personnel with flash cameras, portable lights and motion picture cameras. This group photographed the prospective jurors during selection of the jury.

. . . The jurors themselves were constantly exposed to the news media. Every juror, except one, testified at *voir dire* to reading about the case in the Cleveland papers or to having heard broadcasts about it. . . . During the trial, pictures of the jury appeared over 40 times in the

Cleveland papers alone. . . . The day before the verdict was rendered—while the jurors were at lunch and sequestered by two bailiffs—the jury was separated into two groups to pose for photographs which appeared in the newspapers.

We now reach the conduct of the trial. While the intense publicity continued unabated, it is sufficient to relate only the more flagrant episodes: . . .

On the second day of *voir dire* examination a debate was staged and broadcast live over WHK radio. The participants, newspaper reporters, accused Sheppard's counsel of throwing roadblocks in the way of the prosecution and asserted that Sheppard conceded his guilt by hiring a prominent criminal lawyer. Sheppard's counsel objected to this broadcast and requested a continuance, but the judge denied the motion. When counsel asked the court to give some protection from such events the judge replied that "WHK doesn't have much coverage . . . "

On November 24, a story appeared under an eight-column headline: "Sam Called a 'Jekyll-Hyde' by Marilyn, Cousin to Testify.". . . No such testimony was ever produced at the trial. . . . Defense counsel made motions for change of venue, continuance and mistrial, but they were denied.

. . . When the trial was in its seventh week, Walter Winchell broadcast over WXEL television and WJW radio that Carole Beasley, who was under arrest in New York City for robbery, had stated that, as Sheppard's mistress, she had borne him a child. The defense asked that the jury be queried on the broadcast. Two jurors admitted in open court that they had heard it. The judge asked each: "Would that have any effect on your judgement?" Both replied "No." This was accepted by the judge as sufficient; he merely asked the jury to "pay no attention whatever to that type of scavenging . . ."

. . . After the case was submitted to the jury, it was sequestered for its deliberations, which took five days and four nights. After the verdict, defense counsel ascertained that the jurors had been allowed to make telephone calls to their homes every day while they were sequestered in the hotel. . . . The calls were placed by the jurors themselves; no record was kept of the jurors who made calls, the telephone numbers or the parties called. The bailiffs sat in the room where they could hear only the jurors' end of the conversation. The court had not instructed the bailiffs to prevent such calls. . . . [D]efense counsel urged that this ground alone warranted a new trial, but the motion was overruled and no evidence was taken on the question.

The principle that justice cannot survive behind walls of silence has long been reflected in the "Anglo-American distrust for secret trials" . . . A responsible press has always been regarded as the handmaiden of effective judicial administration, especially in the criminal field. . . . The press does not simply publish information about trials but guards against the miscarriage of justice by subjecting the police, prosecutors, and judicial processes to extensive public scrutiny and criticism. . . . But the Court has also pointed out that "[l]egal trials are not like elections, to be won through the use of the meeting hall, the radio, and the newspaper." . . . [O]ur system of law has always endeavored to prevent even the probability of unfairness."

. . . Sheppard was not granted a change of venue to a locale away from where the publicity originated; nor was his jury sequestered. . . . [J]urors were subjected to newspaper, radio and television coverage of the trial while not taking part in the proceedings. They were allowed to go their separate ways outside the courtroom, without adequate directions not to read or listen to anything concerning the case. . . . Moreover the jurors were thrust into the role of celebrities by the judge's failure to insulate them from reporters and photographers.

. . . [W]e believe that arrangements made by the judge with the news media caused Sheppard to be deprived of that "judicial serenity and calm to which [he] was entitled."

. . . The carnival atmosphere at trial could easily have been avoided since the courthouse premises are subject to the control of the court.

Sam Sheppard was released from prison and was tried a second time for the murder of Marilyn Sheppard in 1966. This time he was acquitted—a murder weapon had never been found and the case was difficult to prosecute 12 years after the fact. The ten years in the Ohio State Penitentiary had taken their toll on Sheppard. He found it difficult to readjust to society. He had married a German immigrant with whom he had corresponded while in prison. When he tried to resume his medical practice, several malpractice suits ended his career. His second marriage ended in divorce. With no hope of resuming his medical practice and surrounded by the notoriety of his past, Sheppard became a professional wrestler. Billed as "Dr. Sam," he married the daughter of his promoter and adopted the lifestyle of a biker. He died in 1970 at the age of 46.

The Sheppard case served as the impetus for the 1960s television series *The Fugitive* and the 1993 motion picture of the same name, starring Harrison Ford and Tommy Lee Jones. Sheppard's attorney, F. Lee Bailey, would go on to defend Patty Hearst in the 1970s and serve as part of O.J. Simpson's defense team in 1995.

In 1997 Dr. Sheppard's son, Sam Reese-Sheppard, began steps to clear his father's name. Reese-Sheppard began collecting evidence that would prove that Marilyn Sheppard's real murderer was Richard Eberling, the family's window washer at the time of the killing. Eberling was serving a life term in prison for another murder, however he died before an Ohio Court of claims could render a decision on possible DNA tests.[13]

The Impact of Sheppard

Justice Clark faulted Judge Blythin for failure to control the conduct of reporters and photographers in the courtroom. Early in the trial, Judge Blythin stated that neither he nor anyone else could restrict prejudicial news accounts. Clark disagreed and made several suggestions for curbing the excessive behavior of the news media. These suggestions included limiting the number of reporters in the courtroom, insulating the witnesses from the press, controlling the release of leads and gossip to the press by police, witnesses, and counsel for both sides, and proscribing extrajudicial statements by anyone involved in the trial. Clark also suggested that judges should consider continuance, change of venue, and sequestering of the jury as means of safeguarding the trial process from outside influence.

Justice Clark did not blame the press for Sheppard's lack of a fair trial but blamed Judge Blythin for not ensuring that a fair trial was obtained. Clark did not suggest that courtrooms be closed to the press. In fact, he noted that nothing prevented the press from reporting the events that transpired in the courtroom. However, as we shall see, the fallout from Sheppard ranged from the issuance of prior restraints against the media to the closing of the courtroom as a means of preserving "judicial serenity." No judge wanted to risk becoming the next "Judge Blythin," and the backlash against media coverage of trials was swift in coming.

As a result of *Sheppard*, judges began looking for effective ways to control publicity about trials and the conduct of reporters in the courtroom. The suggestions made by Justice Clark in *Sheppard* and the recommendations made by the Warren Commission in investigating President Kennedy's assassination prompted the American Bar Association to adopt the Reardon Report in 1968. The report resulted from a study by the ABA Advisory Committee on Fair Trial, headed by Massachusetts Supreme Court Justice Paul Reardon. Essentially, the report attempted to define acceptable bench, bar, and press conduct that would ensure that a defendant received a fair trial. It incorporated Justice Clark's *Sheppard* suggestions with others promulgated by the committee. Although not legally binding, enforcement of these recommendations was to act as a standing order against members of the bar under the code of professional responsibility. Law enforcement agencies would regulate the conduct of their personnel, and court personnel were to be controlled by rules of the court.

The most controversial aspect of this agreement involved the means of controlling the news media and other "outside" agencies. The report recommended that judges use their somewhat questionable power of contempt citation against actions committed outside of the courtroom. This meant that members of the press could be cited for printing stories designed to influence the outcome of a trial. A press threatened by the use of this power would be less likely to print stories that might be construed as containing prejudicial material. This possibility created a chilling effect on First Amendment rights. Additionally, the report recommended closing pretrial hearings to the press and public if the judge deemed that ensuring a fair trial was in jeopardy. The pendulum had begun to swing in a direction favoring Sixth Amendment rights over those of the First Amendment.

Examples of information that should not to be published about a defendant included prior criminal records, character references, confessions, test results, and out-of-court speculation on guilt, innocence, or the merits of evidence. Obviously, all of these prohibitions were violated in *Irvin* and *Sheppard*.

The Reardon Report allowed the publication of facts and the circumstances of an arrest, identity of the person arrested, name of the arresting officer or agency, descriptions of physical evidence in hand, and the next step in the judicial process.

Needless to say, the Reardon Report was not well received by the press. It was also criticized by certain elements of the bench and bar. The out-of-court contempt power was never used. However, in the years following *Sheppard*, prior restraints (otherwise known as gag orders) became a relatively common practice. Gag orders are restrictive orders against the media designed to limit the impact of publication on the trial process. In other words, the court prohibits the news media from publishing certain information about a trial. If a news medium violates the order, they are held in contempt of court.

The Reardon Report did foster dialogue between the press and bar. In the interest of harmony, lawyers, judges, and journalists in many states began formulating voluntary guidelines designed to alleviate the conflict between free press and fair trial. These guidelines were fashioned after the Reardon Report and the suggestions found in the Katzenbach rules. The Katzenbach rules, a set of guidelines formulated by U.S. Attorney General Nicholas Katzenbach in 1965, were designed to govern the release of potentially prejudicial information by federal law enforcement officials. Although less controversial than the Reardon Report, the rules prohibited Justice Department officials from releasing information voluntarily about a defendant's guilt or innocence, past criminal record, confessions or alibis, and the results of polygraph, ballistic, or other laboratory tests. For a period, the voluntary guidelines seemed to be alleviating much of the tension between the press and bar. In 1971, however, tensions resumed with a vengeance.

United States v. Dickinson (1972) was set against the backdrop of racial unrest in the South during the early 1970s. A young VISTA worker was charged with conspiracy to murder the mayor of Baton Rouge, Louisiana. (VISTA stands for Volunteers in Service to America, a government program begun in 1964 that sends volunteers into poor areas to teach various job skills and improve living conditions.) VISTA workers often were viewed as "outside agitators" by white southerners and sometimes were harassed. Hence the possibility in *Dickinson* that the VISTA worker had been framed.

A preliminary hearing was set in U.S. district court to determine whether the state had a legitimate case or whether its action was based on racial prejudice.

Judge E. Gordon West, who would conduct the hearing, knew that the prosecution would offer evidence against the civil rights worker that, although damaging, might not be admissible in court. Although the hearing was to be public, Judge West ordered reporters not to publish any of the testimony heard during the preliminary hearing. Two reporters, Larry Dickinson of the *Baton Rouge State Times* and Gibbs Adams of the *Baton Rouge Morning Advocate*, felt that the order was in violation of the First Amendment and chose to write stories that included testimony offered at the hearing. When the stories were published, Judge West found the two reporters in contempt and fined each $300. They appealed the decision.

Appellate Judge John R. Brown noted that while Judge West's gag order violated the First Amendment, the reporters were not free simply to ignore the order. Chief Judge Brown wrote,

☐ The conclusion that the District Court's order was constitutionally invalid does not necessarily end the matter of the validity of the contempt convictions. There remains the very formidable question of whether a person may with impunity knowingly violate an order which turns out to be invalid. We hold that in the circumstances of this case he may not.

We begin with the well-established principle in proceedings for criminal contempt that an injunction duly issuing out of a court having subject matter and personal jurisdiction must be obeyed, irrespective of the validity of the order. Invalidity is no defense to criminal contempt. . . . Court orders have to be obeyed until they are reversed or set aside in an orderly fashion.

. . . Where the thing enjoined is publication and the communication is "news," this condition presents some thorny problems. Timeliness of publication is the hallmark of "news," and the difference between "news" and "history" is merely a matter of hours. Thus, where the publishing of news is sought to be restrained, the incontestable inviolability of the order may depend on the immediate accessibility of orderly review. . . . But newsmen are citizens too. They too may sometimes have to wait. They are not yet wrapped in immunity or given the absolute right to decide with impunity whether a judge's order is to be obeyed. . . .

Under the circumstances, reporters took a chance. As civil disobedients have done before they ran a risk. . . . Having disobeyed the Court's decree, they must, as civil disobeyers, suffer the consequences for having rebelled at what they deem injustice, but in a manner not authorized by law.[14]

The case was returned to the district court, where Dickinson and Adams were once again convicted and fined $300. In *Dickinson v. United States*, the U.S. Supreme Court refused to review the case in 1973.

Dickinson gave rise to an increasing number of prior restraints against the press. Until 1976, judges wishing to control media publicity about a trial often considered some form of restrictive order to be a regular part of the arsenal for maintaining courtroom "sanctity."

Four years after Dickinson, the Supreme Court took up the question of the constitutionality of a trial court's issuance of a gag order against the press so as to ensure a fair trial. In *Nebraska Press Assn. v. Stuart (1976)*, the Court opposed the use of prior restraints against the media.

On the night of October 18, 1975, Erwin Charles Simiants killed six members of the James Kellie family in Sutherland, Nebraska. Simiants then confessed the killings to his family. His father told him to turn himself in to the police. Instead, Simiants stopped by a local bar and had a drink before hiding out in some high weeds behind his victims' house. Sutherland is a town of 840 people located in Lincoln County, which has 36,000 residents. The largest city is North Platte, with a population of 24,000. Needless to say, the news of the crime spread quickly that night. Before long, reporters and cameramen were pouring into tiny Sutherland from as far away as Denver. At 8:00 the next morning, Simiants walked into the home of his uncle, where he was immediately arrested by state police and the local sheriff.

By 9:00 A.M., Simiants had been booked and had confessed to police. Although that confession had not been witnessed by the media, the chief prosecutor was quoted by the Associated Press as saying Simiants apparently walked into his father's home after the shooting and told his father he was responsible for the "deaths."[15]

News coverage of the crime was pervasive. A report on NBC's *Today* program noted that "Simiants reportedly confessed to his father and fled."[16] Additionally, the *North Platte Telegraph* included a report that quoted Simiant's father as saying "My son killed five or six people here."[17]

Because of the wide news coverage, both the county attorney and the defense counsel asked the county court to close the preliminary hearing to the public and issue a restrictive order against further news coverage so that an impartial jury could be selected. County Judge Ronald Ruff refused to close the hearing but ordered the news media not to report on any testimony or evidence taken at the hearing.

The news media, represented by the Nebraska Press Association, appealed the order to the U.S. district court in Lincoln. After all, argued the Press Association, the state of Nebraska had already drawn up a set of press-bar guidelines, patterned after the Sheppard decision, designed to deal with just this sort of matter. The gag order would have to stand, however, until overturned by a higher court.

Judge Hugh Stuart heard the Press Association's appeal and modified the order. Acknowledging the Nebraska press-bar voluntary guidelines, Judge Stuart made the guidelines mandatory in this case. Stuart noted that because of the nature of the crimes, pretrial publicity could present a clear and present danger to Simiants' right to a fair trial. Judge Stuart's order would apply only until a jury was selected, and it prohibited the reporting of the existence or contents of a confession, statements made by Simiants to other persons, the contents of a note written by Simiants on the night of the crime, the results of medical testimony taken at the preliminary hearing, and the identity of victims who had been sexually assaulted during the crime.[18] Stuart then ordered the media not to report that they were operating under a gag order. In essence, Judge Stuart had issued a "gag on a gag." Any news medium reporting on the five issues listed above or informing the public that they were under a restraining order, would be cited for contempt of court.

Again, appeals were filed, and after much legal maneuvering, the U.S. Supreme Court agreed to hear the Nebraska Press case. In the meantime, *State v. Simiants* continued. Before the Supreme Court decided on the constitutionality of the "gag on a gag," Simiants' trial was over. Simiants was found guilty of six counts of murder and sentenced to death. In 1979, Simiants was awarded a new trial on a technicality (not related to the media coverage of his first trial) and was found innocent by reason of insanity.

In *Nebraska Press*, Chief Justice Burger delivered the opinion of the Court.

☐   . . . Our review of the pretrial record persuades us that the trial judge was
   justified in concluding that there would be intense and pervasive publicity
   concerning this case. He could also reasonably conclude, based on
   common human experience, that publicity might impair the defendant's
   right to a fair trial. He did not purport to say more, for he found only a

"clear and present danger that pretrial publicity could impinge on a fair trial." His conclusion as to the impact of such publicity on prospective jurors was of necessity speculative, dealing as he was with factors unknown and unknowable.

We find little in the record that goes to another aspect of our task, determining whether measures short of an order restraining all publication would have insured the defendant a fair trial. Although the entry of the order might be read as a judicial determination that other measures would not suffice, the trial court made no express findings to that effect. . . .

. . . There is no finding that alternative measures would not have protected Simiants' rights. . . .

. . . [W]e note that the events disclosed by the record took place in a community of 850 people. It is reasonable to assume that, without any news accounts being printed or broadcast, rumors would travel swiftly by word of mouth. One can only speculate on the accuracy of such reports, given the generative propensities of rumors; they could well be more damaging than reasonably accurate news accounts. But plainly a whole community cannot be restrained from discussing a subject intimately affecting life within it. . . .

. . . Our analysis ends as it began, with a confrontation between prior restraint imposed to protect one vital constitutional guarantee and the explicit command of another that freedom to speak and publish shall not be abridged. We reaffirm that the guarantees of freedom of expression are not an absolute prohibition under all circumstances, but the barriers to prior restraint remain high and the presumption against its use continues intact. We hold that, with respect to the order entered in this case prohibiting reporting or commentary on judicial proceedings held in public, the barriers have not been overcome; to the extent that this order restrained publication of such material, it is clearly invalid. To the extent that it prohibited publication of information gained from other sources we conclude that the heavy burden imposed as a condition to securing a prior restraint was not met. . . .[19]

In *Nebraska Press*, the Supreme Court said that three elements must be met before a judge can issue a valid restraining order against the press so as to ensure a fair trial. First, there must be a likelihood of widespread prejudicial publicity. Second, all other methods of controlling such publicity must have been exhausted. This includes rigorous *voir dire*, change of venue, and continuance. Finally, there must be a showing that a restraining order will control prejudicial publicity. All three of these guidelines must be met to render a restraining order constitutional. Obviously, meeting these criteria is difficult—hence the "heavy presumption against prior restraint" by the Supreme Court.

One year later, the Supreme Court once again struck down prior restraints against the media. In *Oklahoma Publishing v. District Court*, the Court noted that although the press could be barred from attending juvenile proceedings, if the press were allowed to attend, they could not be prohibited from publishing information obtained at such proceedings.

In the years following *Nebraska Press* and *Oklahoma Publishing*, the number of restraining orders against the press declined. However, some judges still felt compelled to issue prior restraints. In 1983, a federal district court judge issued a restraining order against CBS. The order forbade the broadcast of videotapes of former automobile manufacturer John DeLorean's conversations with federal undercover narcotics agents during his investigation for alleged cocaine dealing. The judge said that broadcast of the tapes would prejudice potential jurors. CBS appealed the order and won the right to broadcast the videotapes. In *CBS v. U.S. District Court*, in a decision based on *Nebraska Press*, the U.S. court of appeals said that the district court had not exhausted all other alternatives available for protecting DeLorean's right to a fair trial.

Closing the Courtroom

Though *Nebraska Press* addressed the issue of prior restraint, the closing of pretrial hearings to the press and public continued to be a major issue into the 1980s. Because of the unlikelihood that a prior restraint order would be upheld after Nebraska Press, some courts sought to control potentially prejudicial news coverage by limiting access to the courtroom. In *Gannett v. DePasquale (1979)*, the Supreme Court first gave apparent support to the concept that there is no First Amendment right on the part of the press to attend pretrial proceedings. In a 5-4 decision, the Court upheld a New York judge's order excluding a *Gannett* newspaper reporter from a pretrial hearing in a second-degree murder case. Writing for the majority, Justice Potter Stewart's opinion was unclear as to whether reporters had no constitutional right to attend pretrial hearings or trials themselves. Not only did the confusion created by *Gannett* lead to an outcry by the press, it also led to a number of courtroom closings. Between July and September of 1979, more than 50 courtrooms were closed for some or all portions of pretrial or trial proceedings.

The *Gannett* decision was weakened only a year later in *Richmond Newspapers v. Virginia (1980)*, when the Court ruled that trials were presumptively open to the public. Chief Justice Burger used language in writing the majority opinion in *Richmond Newspapers* to emphasize that *Gannett* dealt with pretrial hearings and that, in *Richmond Newspapers*, the issue was trial proceedings.

The defendant in Richmond was about to be tried for a fourth time for the murder of a hotel manager. The first trial had been reversed on appeal, and the two subsequent trials had ended in mistrials. Because of the great deal of publicity surrounding the case and the unusual circumstances of two mistrials, the defense counsel moved that the trial be closed to the public. The prosecution did not object, and the judge granted the motion. Two newspaper reporters objected and filed a motion to vacate the closure order. The motion was denied, the press appealed, and the case eventually found its way to the Supreme Court. The Court used this case to clarify language in *Gannett* and to establish that there is a First Amendment right to attend trials and that there is no right to a private trial. The pendulum had begun to swing back toward the center. Chief Justice Burger delivered the opinion of the Court.

☐   . . . In *Gannett Co. v. DePasquale* . . . the Court was not required to decide
whether a right of access to trials, as distinguished from pretrial motions,
was guaranteed. The Court held that the Sixth Amendment's guarantee to
the accused of a public trial gave neither the public nor the press an
enforceable right of access to a pretrial suppression hearing. One
concurring opinion specifically emphasized that a hearing on a motion
before trial to suppress evidence is not a trial. . . . Moreover, the Court did
not decide whether the First and Fourteenth Amendments guarantee a
right of the public to attend trials. . . .
. . . We hold that the right to attend criminal trials is implicit in the
guarantees of the First Amendment; without the freedom to attend such
trials, which people have exercised for centuries, important aspects of
freedom of speech and "of the press could be eviscerated."
. . . [A]lthough the Sixth Amendment guarantees the accused a right
to a public trial, it does not give a right to a private trial. . . . Absent an
overriding interest articulated in findings, the trial of a criminal case must
be open to the public. . . .[20]

The Court emphasized that this right of access applies only to criminal trials. It did not apply the right to civil proceedings.

Two years later, the Supreme Court reaffirmed the *Richmond Newspapers* holding in *Globe Newspaper Co. v. Superior Court (1982)*. At issue was a Massachusetts statute that required closure of all trials dealing with certain sex crimes. The defendant was on trial for forcible rape against two juveniles. When the judge closed the trial, reporters from the *Boston Globe* appealed the order. Eventually, the Supreme Court found that Massachusetts' mandatory closure statute violated the First Amendment right of access to criminal trials recognized in *Richmond Newspapers*.

By the mid 1980s, the Supreme Court had further rejected the Reardon Report's suggestion that a trial might be closed on a motion from the defendant if there is reason to believe a fair trial may be in jeopardy. In two cases involving Press-Enterprise, the Supreme Court dealt serious blows to this concept and returned to a more balanced position regarding First and Sixth Amendment rights.

In *Press-Enterprise I (1984)*, the Supreme Court extended the *Richmond Newspapers* ruling by mandating that jury selection, like trials, should be conducted in public. Chief Justice Burger also provided an interesting history of the jury selection process and its role in the guarantee of a fair trial. Chief Justice Burger delivered the opinion of the Court:

☐ . . . Albert Greenwood Brown, Jr. was tried and convicted of the rape and murder of a teenage girl, and was sentenced to death in California Superior Court. Before the *voir dire* examination of prospective jurors began, petitioner, Press-Enterprise Co., moved that *voir dire* be open to the public and to the press. Petitioners contend that the public had an absolute right to attend the trial, and asserted that the trial commenced with the *voir dire* proceedings. The State opposed petitioner's motion, arguing that if the press were present juror responses would lack the candor necessary to assure [sic] a fair trial.

The trial judge agreed and permitted petitioner to attend only the "general *voir dire*." He stated that counsel would conduct the "individual *voir dire* with regard to death qualifications and any other special areas that counsel may feel some problem with . . ." The *voir dire* consumed six weeks and all but approximately three days was closed to the public.

After the jury was empaneled, petitioner moved the trial court to release a complete transcript of the *voir dire* proceedings. . . . The court denied petitioner's motion. . . . After Brown had been convicted and sentenced to death, petitioner again applied for release of the transcript. In denying this application, the judge stated:

> The jurors were questioned in private relating to past experiences, and while most of the information is dull and boring, some of the jurors had special experiences in sensitive areas that do not appear to be appropriate for public discussion.

☐ Petitioner then sought in the California Court of Appeal a writ of mandate to compel the Superior Court to release the transcript and vacate the order closing the *voir dire* proceedings. The petition was denied. The California

Supreme Court denied petitioner's request for a hearing. We granted certiorari. . . . We reverse.

. . . The roots of open trials reach back to the days before the Norman Conquest when cases in England were brought before "moots," a town meeting kind of body such as the local court of the hundred or the county court.[21] Attendance was virtually compulsory on the part of free men of the community . . . in rendering a judgement. The public aspect thus was "almost a necessary incident of jury trials since the presence of a jury. . . already insured the presence of a large part of the public."[22]

As the jury system evolved in the years after the Norman Conquest, and the jury came to be but a small segment representing the community, the obligation of all free men to attend criminal trials was relaxed; however, the public character of the proceedings, including jury selection, remained unchanged. . . .

The presumptive openness of the jury selection process in England, not surprisingly, carried over into proceedings in Colonial America. . . . Public jury selection thus was the common practice in America when the Constitution was adopted.

. . . No right ranks higher than the right of the accused to a fair trial. But the primacy of the accused's right is difficult to separate from the right of everyone in the community to attend the *voir dire* which promotes fairness.

The open trial thus plays as important a role in the administration of justice today as it did for the centuries before our separation from England. The value of openness lies in the fact that people not actually attending trials can have confidence that standards of fairness are being observed. . . .

"People in an open society do not demand infallibility from their institutions, but it is difficult for them to accept what they are prohibited from observing." *Richmond Newspapers*, supra, at 572. Closed proceedings, although not absolutely precluded, must be rare and only for cause shown that outweighs the value of openness. . . .

The presumption of openness may be overcome only by an overriding interest based on findings that closure is essential to preserve higher values and is narrowly tailored to serve that interest. . . .

To preserve fairness and at the same time protect legitimate privacy . . . those individuals believing public questioning will prove damaging because of embarrassment, may properly request an opportunity to present the problem to the judge in camera but with counsel present and on the record.

By requiring the prospective juror to make an affirmative request the trial judge can ensure that there is in fact a valid basis for a belief that disclosure infringes a significant interest in privacy.

The judge at this trial closed an incredible six weeks of *voir dire* without considering alternatives to closure. Later the court declined to release a transcript of the *voir dire* even while stating that "most of the information" in the transcript was "dull and boring". . . . Those parts of the transcript reasonably entitled to privacy could have been sealed without such a sweeping order; a trial judge should explain why the material is entitled to privacy.

Thus not only was there a failure to articulate findings with requisite specificity, but there was also a failure to consider alternatives to closure and to the total suppression of the transcript.[23]

In *Press-Enterprise II*, in a 7-2 vote, the Court said that defendants wishing to close a preliminary hearing must demonstrate that an open courtroom would have a "substantial probability" of endangering their right to a fair trial. This case all but overrules the validity of *Gannett* and continues movement toward opening the entire judicial process begun in *Nebraska Press* and developed in *Richmond Newspapers, Globe Newspaper,* and *Press-Enterprise I.* In *Press-Enterprise Co. v. Riverside County Superior Court (1986),* Chief Justice Burger delivered the opinion of the Court.

☐   On December 23, 1981, the State of California filed a complaint . . . charging Robert Diaz with 12 counts of murder and seeking the death penalty. The complaint alleged that Diaz, a nurse, murdered 12 patients by administering massive doses of the heart drug, lidocaine. The preliminary hearing commenced on July 6, 1982. Diaz moved to exclude the public from the proceedings. . . . [24] The Magistrate granted the motion, finding that closure was necessary because the case had attracted national publicity and "only one side may get reported in the media."

The preliminary hearing continued for 41 days. Most of the testimony and the evidence presented by the State was medical and scientific; the remainder consisted of testimony by personnel who worked with Diaz on the shifts when the 12 patients died. Diaz did not introduce any evidence, but his counsel subjected most of the witnesses to vigorous cross-examination. Diaz was held to answer on all charges. At the conclusion of the hearing, Press-Enterprise Company asked that the transcript of the proceedings be released. The Magistrate refused and sealed the record.

On January 21, 1983, the State moved in Superior Court to have the transcripts of the hearing released to the public; petitioner later joined in support of the motion. Diaz opposed the motion, contending the release of the transcripts would result in prejudicial pretrial publicity. The Superior Court found that . . . there was . . . "a reasonable likelihood that the release of all or any part of the transcript might prejudice defendant's right to a fair and impartial trial." [Cited from California's statute.]

Petitioner then filed a peremptory writ of mandate with the Court of Appeal. That court originally denied the writ but, after being so ordered by the California Supreme Court, set the matter for a hearing. Meanwhile, Diaz waived his right to a jury trial and the Superior Court released the transcript. After holding that the controversy was not moot, the Court of Appeal denied the writ of mandate.

The California Supreme Court thereafter denied petitioner's peremptory writ of mandate. . . .

. . . We granted certiorari. . . . We reverse.

. . . In *Press-Enterprise I*, we summarized the holdings of prior cases, noting that openness in criminal trials, including the selection of jurors "enhances both the fairness of the criminal trial and the appearance of fairness so essential to public confidence in the system." 464 U.S. at 501

. . . The considerations that led the Court to apply the First Amendment right of access to criminal trials in *Richmond Newspapers* and Globe and the selection of jurors in *Press-Enterprise I* lead us to conclude that the right of access applies to preliminary hearings as conducted in California.[25]

Once again, the Court did not rule out closing some pretrial hearings, but the standards were clearly defined. In *Press-Enterprise II*, the Court reiterated criteria established in *Press-Enterprise I* and *Richmond Newspapers*—that there must be a substantial probability that closure will prevent publicity prejudice of the defendant's right to a fair trial, and that reasonable alternatives to closure cannot adequately protect the defendant's trial rights.

Shortly after the *Press-Enterprise* cases, several state and federal courts were quick to apply the Supreme Court's "presumption of openness" policy.

In *Associated Press v. Bell*, a New York court of appeals reversed a district court ruling that closed a pretrial hearing. The court based the reversal on the fact that the defendant did not note specifically how his trial would be prejudiced if the hearing remained open. On similar grounds, the New York Supreme Court ruled in *Orange County Publications v. Dallow* that a lower court erred in closing a hearing to decide whether a 5-year-old boy accused of the murder of a 9-year-old girl should be held for a grand jury. In *In Re: New York Times (1987)* the Court of Appeals for the Second Circuit found a First Amendment right of access by the press to pretrial motions and procedures filed under seal in criminal proceedings. Finally, in *U.S. v. Raffoul*, a U.S. court of appeals ruled that federal courts must grant a pre-closure hearing before ruling on closure motions made at criminal trials. This, said the court, is a "matter of right" to those persons actually present in the courtroom. Personal notice to the news media is not required.

Former Reagan aid Michael Deaver was charged with perjury as a result of lobbying activities conducted after leaving President Reagan's staff. Federal Judge Thomas Penfield Jackson ordered the *voir dire* closed to protect the privacy of potential jurors. The judge gave prospective jurors the option to be questioned in open court, but only 5 of the 30 to be questioned agreed to do so. In *CNN v. United States (1987)*, the Cable News Network and other news organizations appealed the order, requesting that jury selection be conducted in open court. The appeal was denied, but a Washington, D.C., appellate court swiftly granted a summary reversal of Judge Jackson's order. The court cited the three conditions for closing *voir dire* set forth in *Press-Enterprise I*.

1. Specific findings that open *voir dire* would jeopardize the defendant's fair trial interests or the jurors legitimate privacy interests.
2. Jurors suspecting that privacy interests may be damaged by open *voir dire* must make "affirmative requests" for closure.
3. "Alternatives to closure" must be considered.

The appellate court noted that Judge Jackson's closure order met none of the conditions. The Supreme Court denied review of the case on October 19, 1987.

These rulings do not affect the secrecy of grand jury deliberations. The Court acknowledged that "the proper functioning of our grand jury system depends upon the secrecy of grand jury proceedings."[26] There are five reasons commonly given for the policy of grand jury secrecy. In essence, they are to

1. Prevent the escape of someone who may be indicted
2. Protect deliberations from outside influence
3. Prevent tampering with witnesses
4. Encourage free disclosures by potential witnesses
5. Protect the innocent accused who is later exonerated

Although *Globe Newspaper Co.* struck down the Massachusetts statute that automatically closed trials dealing with certain sex crimes, the Michigan Supreme Court upheld a statute that suppresses the names of persons involved and the details relating to criminal sexual conduct cases. In *Midland Publishing v. District Court Judge*, the court held that such information may be withheld until the defendant is arraigned or the case is dismissed or otherwise concluded. Unlike the unconstitutional Massachusetts statute, the press eventually is granted access to the information.

Similarly, in *In Re: Pacific & Southern Co.* the Georgia Supreme Court ruled that the news media did not have a right of access to criminal trial evidence consisting of videotapes of a crime scene and a convicted murder defendant's statement to police. The basis of the holding was that the appeals process had not been completed, and broadcast of the material could, if a new trial were granted, deny the defendant a fair trial.

The Camera in the Courtroom

The movement toward opening the judicial process more to the press has resulted in an increasing number of states that permit videotaping and broadcasting trial proceedings. The gradual acceptance of cameras in the courtroom has come about in much the same manner as that seen in the "opening" of the courts. The excessive practices of the press with cameras during the Hauptmann trial resulted directly in ABA Canon 35, which banned photographic equipment from the courts. Experiences with the new medium of television in the 1950s and 1960s resulted in that medium's expulsion as well. The primary argument for keeping cameras—both moving and still—out of courts centered around their intrusive nature. The need for bright lights and the bulkiness of early television hardware was cited as depriving defendants of "judicial serenity." Other concerns about the broadcast of trials included the possibility of negative effects on witnesses, "grandstanding" by lawyers and judges up for re-election, and harassment of witnesses who might now be seen on television. Although there was no scientific evidence to support these concerns, the *Hauptmann* and *Sheppard* cases stood as examples of the possible abuse by cameras and broadcasting. Still, cameras found their way into the trial process.

In 1961, Wilbert Rideau was arrested in Lake Charles, Louisiana, during a bank robbery in which a bank employee was killed. Without counsel present, Rideau confessed to the local sheriff in his jail cell while a local TV news crew filmed the confession. This confession was broadcast by KPLC-TV to the Lake Charles area for a total of three times in two days. An estimated 106,000 of the 150,000 residents of Calcasieu Parish saw the broadcast. Rideau's request for a change of venue was denied. Rideau was found guilty and sentenced to death. Subsequent appeals resulted in the case being heard by the Supreme Court.

In *Rideau v. Louisiana (1963)*, the Supreme Court ordered a new trial. Coming on the heels of *Irvin*, the Court held that the broadcast confession had made the selection of an impartial jury impossible. Justice Stewart wrote:

☐　For anyone who has ever watched television, the conclusion cannot be avoided that this spectacle, to the tens of thousands of people who saw and heard it, in a very real sense was Rideau's trial—at which he pleaded guilty of murder. Any subsequent court proceedings in a community so pervasively exposed to such a spectacle could be but a hollow formality.[27]

Rideau was granted a new trial, where he was convicted and sentenced to life in prison. Like Leslie Irvin, prejudicial media coverage had spared him from capital punishment. Irvin had been denied a fair trial because jurors testified that they had been influenced by media coverage. This became known as the "Irvin test."

Rideau extended the Irvin test even further. Now the defense did not have to prove that any jurors were actually influenced by the broadcast, only that they were probably influenced by it. As in *Sheppard*, a change of venue was denied in *Rideau* and a continuance was not considered. The courts preferred that the media bear the brunt of ensuring the fairness of a trial.

During this period, the thinking regarding the potential harm that cameras might bring to the judicial process was similar to the attitudes of the time toward the open courtroom. It was better to err on the side of the Sixth Amendment than on the side of the First Amendment. So, when the Supreme Court heard its first television-cameras-in-court case, a list of potential harm to the fair trial process was generated. Once again, this list was based only on speculation and was not supported by any testimony of fact. *Estes v. State of Texas (1965)* was television journalism's *Sheppard*.

Billie Sol Estes, a Texas financier closely associated with Lyndon Johnson, was tried in 1962 on charges of theft, swindling, and embezzlement. Although Estes objected, the trial judge permitted television coverage of the pretrial hearing and portions of the trial itself. Estes was convicted and appealed on grounds that the television coverage denied him a fair trial. The case reached the Supreme Court, which agreed that the Texas court had not adhered to Canon 35 and that Estes had not received a fair trial. Justice Clark delivered the opinion of the Court.

☐   The question presented here is whether the petitioner . . . was deprived of his right under the Fourteenth Amendment to due process by televising and broadcasting of his trial. Both the trial court and the Texas Court of Criminal Appeals found against the petitioner. We hold to the contrary and reverse his conviction.

While petitioner recites his claim in the framework of Canon 35 of the Judicial Canons of the American Bar Association he does not contend that we should enshrine Canon 35 in the Fourteenth Amendment, but only that the time-honored principles of a fair trial were not followed in his case and that he was thus convicted without due process of law.

. . . Petitioner's case was originally called for trial on September 24, 1962, in Smith County after a change of venue from Reeves County, some

500 miles west. Massive pretrial publicity totaling 11 volumes of press clippings . . . had given it national notoriety. All available seats in the courtroom were taken and some 30 persons stood in the aisles. However, at that time a defense motion to prevent telecasting, broadcasting by radio and news photography and a defense motion for continuance were presented, and after a two-day hearing the former was denied and the latter granted.

These initial hearings were carried live by both radio and television, and news photography was permitted throughout. The videotapes of these hearings clearly illustrate that the picture presented was not one of that judicial serenity and calm to which petitioner was entitled. Indeed, at least 12 cameramen were engaged in the courtroom throughout the hearing taking motion and still pictures and televising the proceedings. Cables and wires were snaked across the courtroom floor, three microphones were on the judge's bench and others were beamed at the jury box and the counsel table. It is conceded that the activities of the television crews and news photographers led to considerable disruption of the hearings.

. . . When the case was called for trial on October 22 the scene had been altered. A booth had been constructed at the back of the courtroom which was painted to blend with the permanent structure of the room. It had an aperture to allow the lens of the cameras an unrestricted view of the courtroom. All television cameras and newsreel photographers were restricted to the area of the booth when shooting film or telecasting.

Because of continual objection, the rules governing live telecasting, as well as radio and still photos, were changed as the exigencies of the situation seemed to require. As a result, live telecasting was prohibited during a great portion of the actual trial. Only the opening and closing arguments of the State, the return of the jury's verdict and its receipt by the trial judge were carried live with sound. . . .

. . . Because of varying restrictions placed on sound and live telecasting, the telecasts of the trial were confined largely to film clips shown on the stations' regularly scheduled news programs. The news commentators would use the film of a particular part of the day's trial activities as a backdrop for their reports. Their commentary included excerpts from testimony and the usual reportorial remarks. On one occasion the videotapes of the September hearings were rebroadcast in place of the "late movie." . . .

We start with the proposition that it is a "public trial" that the Sixth Amendment guarantees to the accused. The purpose of the requirement of a public trial was to guarantee that the accused would be fairly dealt with and not unjustly condemned. . . .

It is said, however, that freedoms granted in the First Amendment extend a right to the news media to televise from the courtroom, and that a refusal to honor this privilege is to discriminate between the newspapers and television. This is a misconception of the rights of the press. . . . The news reporter is not permitted to bring his typewriter or printing press. When the advances in these arts permit reporting by printing press or by television without their present hazards to a fair trial we will have another case. . . .

As has been said, the chief function of our judicial machinery is to ascertain the truth. The use of television, however, cannot be said to contribute materially to this objective. Rather its use amounts to the injection of an irrelevant factor into court proceedings. In addition, experience teaches that there are numerous situations in which it might cause actual unfairness—some so subtle as to defy detection by the accused or controlled by the judge.[28]

The Court then listed four components of the trial that might be adversely affected if trials were telecast:

1. The jury might feel pressure from outside forces, knowing that a trial will be televised. Additionally, television might affect the attentiveness of the jury in the jury box. They may pay attention to cameras and not to details of the case. They might also feel self-conscious on television and be "preoccupied with the telecasting rather than the testimony." They may return home and see the broadcasts of the day's proceedings and be influenced by that. Finally, said the Court, new trials would be jeopardized because potential jurors might have seen the original trial on television.

2. Witnesses might be influenced by televised trials. Some may be "demoralized and frightened, some cocky and given to overstatement; memories may falter," and accuracy may be undermined. Witnesses may be harassed on the street by those having seen their testimony on television and some witnesses may refuse to testify at all, for fear of being on television. Finally, the Court noted that upcoming witnesses may watch the testimony of others on television and change their testimony accordingly.

3. Judges would be saddled with an additional burden while performing the task of controlling the decorum of the courtroom. Judges up for re-election might also be tempted to use television as a means of reaching the electorate.

4. The defendant might be subjected to undue pressures, knowing that there will be "inevitable close ups of his gestures and expressions during the ordeal of his trial."[29]

Reading these potential concerns today gives the impression that the Supreme Court was grasping at straws in an effort to keep television out of the courtrooms. Just as Sheppard spawned the closing of courtrooms, *Estes* signaled the demise of cameras in court. By 1974, all states except Colorado had banned cameras from the courtroom.

Though there is no question that intrusive and irresponsible behavior by television in the coverage of trials would probably affect the outcome of the proceedings, most of the previous arguments can be refuted easily and the abuses cited can be controlled. Cooperation between bench and broadcasters has alleviated much of the tension, and most of these four arguments are no longer serious impediments to a fair trial today. A key to understanding *Estes*, however, lies in the statement that references the technological developments that may permit television coverage without the intrusiveness of the bulky equipment used in 1962. Technological advancements began to reduce "the hazards to a fair trial" to which Justice Clark referred, and television slowly made its way back into the courtroom.

In the late 1970s, states such as Alabama, Texas, New Hampshire, and Florida experimented with cameras in the courtrooms. The Supreme Court upheld Florida's use of cameras in the courtroom in *Chandler v. Florida (1981)*. The court ruled that the mere presence of cameras did not result automatically in an unfair trial.

By the 1990s, a majority of states had experimented with cameras in the courtroom, but federal courts and the Supreme Court remained off-limits. In September 1990, the U.S. Judicial Conference adopted a general policy statement that allowed the use of photography and electronic media in federal courtrooms for a three-year period, but the prohibition returned in 1994.

By 1994, all states except Indiana, Mississippi, and South Dakota allowed cameras in the courtroom. The District of Columbia courts, federal courts, and the Supreme Court do not allow cameras in their proceedings.

The Challenges of Today

The pervasive nature of the electronic media continues to strain the boundaries between the defendant's right to a fair trial and the right to gather news. Can defendants involved in nationally publicized cases be guaranteed a trial by an impartial jury? The question has often been asked: Could Lee Harvey Oswald, arrested in the assassination of President John F. Kennedy, have been assured of a fair trial? The trial of former Panamanian President Manuel Noriega in the fall of 1991 was another prime example of a public figure who is so well known that no change of venue can guarantee an impartial jury. The notoriety of Jeffrey Dahmer, accused of a series of bizarre murders in Milwaukee in 1991, gained more national attention than Sam

Sheppard in his day. Finally, the popularity of "reality" programs like *Cops* and *America's Most Wanted* often cast a disparaging shadow on individuals not yet convicted of a crime. Do these kinds of programs interfere with the delicate balance between First and Sixth Amendment rights?

The televised trial of William Kennedy Smith, who was accused of raping a woman on the grounds of the Kennedy estate in Florida, seems to indicate that a highly publicized trial can be televised without compromising judicial standards. The rape trial of boxer Mike Tyson proceeded in a media-intensive atmosphere without a change of venue. The Tyson jury was sequestered and a fair trial ensued.

Certainly the most sensational pretrial and trial proceedings of the 1990s was the O.J. Simpson murder case. The former football star was charged in the double murder of his ex-wife, Nicole Brown Simpson, and her acquaintance Ronald Goldman. Graphic pictures of the murder scene were televised repeatedly. There were accusations of leaks to the press by police, prior to Simpson's arrest, which was followed by the dramatic televised "low-speed chase" by police through the streets of Los Angeles.[30] Pretrial proceedings were televised and drew network ratings higher than the soap operas that the proceedings preempted.[31] Both prosecution and defense regularly appeared on television to discuss aspects of the case, until both voluntarily agreed to limit such appearances.

Angered by inaccurate reports by KNBC-TV in Los Angeles, Judge Lance Ito barred TV cameras from *voir dire*. After the publication of a book written by a friend of Nicole Brown Simpson accusing O.J. Simpson of murdering his former wife, Judge Ito barred all reporters from *voir dire*. Both prosecution and defense supported Ito's move. A written transcript of the closed proceedings was to be made available to reporters after the jury was selected.[32] The following day, however, Judge Ito lifted the ban on reporters in the court.

Ito received more than 15,000 letters from the public, most of which urged him to ban television from his court. After careful consideration, he allowed one television camera to remain in court. During pretrial hearings Ito warned of the perils of televised coverage. He cited the *Sheppard* and *Estes* trials as examples to be avoided. Ito's decision to allow a single, remote-controlled camera to cover the proceedings was based on his belief that the most irresponsible reporting had taken place outside of the courtroom. Given the public's right to attend trials, and the fact that no more than 15 seats were available in the courtroom, television represented the only way the general public could view the trial. He also felt that the presence of the camera could check and correct irresponsible reporting. Both prosecution and defense supported the decision to televise the trial, noting that such coverage could help "legitimize" the final verdict.[33]

As the trial began Judge Ito, once again, threatened to remove television from his court. This time a *Court-TV* camera panned too far left and an alternate juror was briefly visible on the screen. The judge allowed the camera to remain, but with the understanding that the view would be limited to counsel, bench, and witness stand.

The Simpson trial proceeded with cameras in the courtroom. As a result of the long ordeal, defense council Johnnie Cochran and prosecutors Marcia Clark and Christopher Darden achieved celebrity status in their own right. O.J. Simpson was acquitted. Cochran and Clark went on to become television show hosts, while Darden wrote a "tell-all" book about the trial. Simpson went back to court.

The Goldman and Brown families were successful in a wrongful death civil suit brought against Simpson in 1996. No cameras were permitted in court during the second Simpson trial.

Summary

The Sixth Amendment to the Constitution guarantees those accused of criminal actions a right to a speedy and public trial by an impartial jury. These rights of a defendant often conflict with rights also guaranteed to the press under the First Amendment.

Judges regularly attempt to control prejudicial pretrial publicity by granting a change of venue, a continuance, or sequestering the jury. A change of venue moves the location of the trial away from an area where prospective jurors are likely to hold preconceived opinions about the guilt or innocence of an accused person. A continuance postpones the starting date of a trial so that the strong emotions felt by a community, often accompanying the arrest of a suspect, have had time to subside. Sequestering the jury means limiting jurors' contact with the outside world during a trial. This is done in the hope that jurors will not be influenced by media reports of the proceedings or by others desiring to affect the outcome of the trial.

By the 1990s, a majority of states had experimented with cameras in the courtroom, but federal courts and the Supreme Court remained off-limits. In September 1990, the U.S. Judicial Conference adopted a general policy statement that allowed the use of photography and electronic media in federal courtrooms for a three-year period The use of cameras in federal courtrooms came to an end in 1994, however most states permit some form of televised court coverage. High-profile trials, like the O.J. Simpson murder case have developed new strains on the relationship between the electronic media and the judiciary.

Notes/References

1. *United States v. Burr,* 24 Fed. Cas. 49 No. 14692g (1807).
2. *Fair Trial/Free Press Voluntary Agreements* (Chicago: Legal Advisory Committee on Fair Trial and Free Press, 1974), 7–8.
3. Helen M. Hughes, *News and the Human Interest Story* (Chicago: University of Chicago Press, 1940), 235.
4. Edwin Emery, *The Press and America,* 2nd ed. (Englewood Cliffs, NJ: Prentice-Hall, 1962), 629–30.
5. *Shepherd v. Florida,* 341 U.S. 50 (1951), 71 S.Ct. 549.
6. Stroble v. State of California, 343 U.S. 181 (1952), 72 S.Ct. 599.
7. Ibid., 609.
8. *The Evansville Press* (April 10, 1955): 1.
9. Ibid.
10. "Murder Suspect Named by Police," *The Evansville Press* (April 11, 1955): 1.
11. "Two Innocent Pleas Entered by Irvin," *The Evansville Press* (April 28, 1955): 1.
12. Irvin v. Dowd, 366 U.S. 717 (1961).
13. See Cynthia L. Cooper and Sam Reese Sheppard, *Mockery of Justice* (New York: Onyx, 1997).
14. United States v. Dickinson, 465 F.2d 496 (5th Cir., 1972).
15. Fred W. Friendly and Martha J. H. Elliot, *The Constitution: That Delicate Balance* (New York: Random House, 1984), 150.
16. Ibid., 151.
17. Ibid.
18. Dale Spencer, Katharin P. Darrow, Richard U. Schmidt, Jr., *Free Press and Fair Trial* (Washington, D.C.: American Society of Newspaper Editors/American Newspaper Publishers Association Foundation, 1982), 48.
19. *Nebraska Press Assn. v. Stuart,* 427 U.S. 539 (1976).
20. *Richmond Newspapers, Inc. v. Commonwealth of Virginia,* 448 U.S. 555 (1980) at 560.
21. Citing Pollack, *English Law before the Norman Conquest, 1: Select Essays in Anglo-American Legal History* (1907), 88, 89.
22. Citing Radin, *The Right to a Public Trial,* 6 Temp. L.Q. (1932), 381, 388.
23. *Press-Enterprise v. Riverside County Superior Court,* No. 82–556 (1984) 10 Med.L.Rptr. 1161.
24. California law provided that a trial could be closed if such action would protect the defendant's right to a fair and impartial trial.

25. *Press-Enterprise Co. v. Riverside County Superior Court* (S.Ct., 1986) 13 Med.L.Rptr. 1002.
26. "News Notes," (November, 1987) 14 *Med.L.Rptr.* 21.
27. *Rideau v. Louisiana*, 373 U.S. 723 at 726,83 S.Ct. 1417 (1963).
28. Estes v. State of Texas, 381 U.S. 532 (1965).
29. Ibid.
30. Jon Lafayette, "Chasing the Juice," *Electronic Media* (June 27, 1994), 1. See also, Steve McClellan and Steve Coe, "TV Chase Another Hot Story," *Broadcasting & Cable* (June 27, 1994): 8.
31. Jon Lafayette, "O.J. Case Uproots TV Schedules, Nabs Viewers," *Electronic Media* (July 11, 1994): 3.
32. Robin Clark, "Ito Bars Reporters from Court During Jury Selection," *Indianapolis Star* (October 21, 1994): A2.
33. The *New York Times*, "Simpson Trial Will Be on the Air," *Indianapolis Star* (November 8, 1994): 1.

Cases

Associated Press v. Bell (NY Ct.App., 1987) 14 Med.L.Rptr. 1156

CBS v. U.S. District Court (CA 9, 1984) 10 Med.L.Rptr. 1529

Chandler v. Florida, 449 U.S. 560 (1981)

CNN v. United States (DC Ct.App., 1987) 14 Med.L.Rptr. 1334

Dickinson v. United States, cert. denied 414 U.S. 979 (1973)

Estes v. State of Texas, 381 U.S. 532 (1965)

Gannett v. DePasquale, 443 U.S. 368 (1979)

Globe Newspaper Co. v. Superior Court, County of Norfolk, 457 U.S. 596 (1982)

In Re: New York Times (CA 2, 1987) 14 Med.L.Rptr. 1625

In Re: Pacific & Southern Co. (GA Sup.Ct., 1987) 14 Med.L.Rptr. 1764

Irvin v. Dowd, 366 U.S. 717 (1961)

Janko v. United States, 366 U.S. 716 (1961)

Marshall v. United States, 360 U.S. 310 (1959)

Midland Publishing v. District Court Judge (Mich Sup.Ct., 1984) 11 Med.L.Rptr. 1337

Nebraska Press Assn. v. Stuart, 427 U.S. 539 (1976)

Oklahoma Publishing v. District Court, 430 U.S. 308 (1977)

Orange County Publications v. Dallow (NY Sup.Ct., 1987) 14 Med.L.Rptr. 1311

Press-Enterprise Co. v. Riverside County Superior Court, No. 82–556 (1984) 10 Med.L.Rptr. 1161

Press-Enterprise Co. v. Riverside County Superior Court (S.Ct., 1986) 13 Med.L.Rptr. 1002

Richmond Newspapers v. Commonwealth of Virginia, 488 U.S. 555 (1980)

Rideau v. Louisiana, 373 U.S. 723, 83 S.Ct. 1417 (1963)

Shepherd v. Florida, 341 U.S. 50 (1951) 71 S.Ct. 549 (1951)

Sheppard v. Maxwell, 231 F.Supp. 37 (S.D. OH, 1964)

Sheppard v. Maxwell, 384 U.S. 333 (1966)

State v. Simiants, 194 Neb. 783, 236 N.W.2d 794 (1975)

Stroble v. State of California, 343 U.S. 181(1952), 72 S.Ct. 599 (1952)

United States v. Burr, 24 Fed.Cas. 49 No. 14692g (1807)

United States v. Dickinson, 465 F.2d 496 (5th Cir., 1972)

U.S. v. Raffoul (CA 3, 1987) 14 Med.L.Rptr. 1534

12 □ □ □
□ □ □
□ □ □

Communications Regulation: New Technologies and the Internet

> . . . [T]he experimenter went through the looking glass, to a never-never land . . . where the rules for behavior couldn't be enforced—in fact, were not yet established. [Those] who entered . . . heard things others did not, and . . . did things maybe [they] should not have done. [He/she] could please [his/her] parents by acquiring this instructive hobby, and . . . could defy them by using it, without fear of being discovered, to misbehave.[1]

The epigraph to this chapter could describe concerns voiced today about controversial material available on the Internet. Instead, it refers to the hobby of listening to "profane" wireless radio transmissions from ships in the early part of the twentieth century. The similarity of concern is interesting. What is ironic is that many of the underlying assumptions, policies, and laws that were applied to early radio, remain today—in spite of the passage of the 1996 Telecommunications Act.

This chapter discusses the evolving landscape of telecommunications regulation and addresses some of the issues and possibilities facing the industry, regulators, and the courts.

Changes

In 1996 Congress passed the Telecommunications Act, but the future promises many more changes in the regulatory structure of broadcasting, cable, and developing technologies. Traditional broadcasting continues to be threatened by the growth of cable television and other distribution systems. In 1997 the FCC approved rules for the conversion to digital television.[2] By 2006 or at such time that 85 percent of the American public has access to DTV, television broadcasters will surrender their analog channels. They will have converted to digital transmission. In the meantime, the audiences of the traditional broadcast networks continue to erode while cable audiences have increased. Both industries face challenges posed by alternative distribution systems. Direct broadcast satellites (DBS), home satellite dishes, interactive video systems, digital audio broadcasting (DAB), and the Internet have begun to play a greater role in changing the way we receive information that for many decades was distributed by traditional broadcast and cable technology. Indeed, some see the Internet as the answer to the unlimited channel TV universe. This would certainly make the limited spectrum rationale for broadcast regulation and the bottleneck monopoly argument for cable regulation obsolete.

By the end of the 1990s the Big Three networks' share had fallen below 50 percent.[3] Industry analysts predict that interactive media will replace basic cable, home video, and recorded music as the fastest growing industry in the first decade of the twenty-first century. However, direct broadcast satellites (DBS) have begun to make a dent in cable penetration and threaten further competition as the field grows.[4] Some in government, including members of the FCC, spoke of the need to revisit the "social compact" between broadcasting and the public in the new digital universe. Specifically, in exchange for spectrum space, broadcasters would be expected to serve the needs of women and minorities, children, localism, and diversity of programming. Others expressed concern over the amount of violence on television. Consequently, deregulation of business matters continued, with potential new regulation, at least for broadcasters, in the area of children's programming, violence, and political programming.

The Telecommunications Act of 1996

The passage of the 1996 Telecommunications Act was heralded as "the first major overhaul of telecommunications law since Marconi was alive and the crystal set was state of the art."[5] This hyperbole ignores the fact that Marconi, the inventor of wireless radio, died in 1937, three years after the passage of the Communications Act and long after the crystal set was state of the art. It is true that this is the first major overhaul of the Communications Act of 1934. Although certainly the new law radically changes the way the telecommunications industry does business, questions about the overall scope of the law and the constitutionality of some its provisions remain. In reality, much of the 1934 act remains in place. Broadcasters continue to have fewer First Amendment freedoms than cablecasters.

The deregulatory thrust is essentially an economic one, while some of the most disturbing regulations come with First Amendment concerns. The Communications Decency Act (CDA), which would have regulated indecent material on the Internet in the same manner as it is regulated on broadcast television, was declared unconstitutional in *Reno v. ACLU.* In addition, the V-chip provision has potential for further First Amendment scrutiny. It is significant, however, that the Internet was included in regulation primarily affecting the more traditional media.

Convergence

Convergence is the disintegration of distinctions between different technologies. New combinations of technologies have emerged and promise to challenge the way the electronic media are regulated. In the 1990s, computers and digital technologies blended with traditional broadcast technology. This convergence has accelerated. Digital Television, CD-ROM, and Digital Video Disks (DVD) that store and retrieve video information, break down the differences between the role of the computer and the television set. As the Internet became available on television sets as well as computers, distinctions between broadcasting and cyberspace blurred. The Supreme Court's *Reno* helped renew the legal distinction between the two.

Emerging Distribution Systems

High-Definition Television (HDTV) and Advanced Television (ATV)

High-Definition Television (HDTV) provides a superior picture to the current standard of television serving the United States today. The current U.S. standard (NTSC) consists of 525 lines of resolution and a 4:3 screen aspect ratio. HDTV uses more lines of resolution and a 16:9 aspect ratio—more like the shape of a cinemascope movie screen.

Japan began experimenting with HDTV broadcasts in 1979 and began regular service in 1991. This system is not compatible with the U.S. NTSC standard, therefore implementation would require a complete replacement of transmitting and receiving equipment currently in use.

In order to protect the existing broadcast system in the United States, the FCC decided that any Advanced Television (ATV) system adopted for use in the United States should be NTSC compatible. In other words, an NTSC signal would be simulcast along with an ATV signal so that individuals unable to afford to buy new digital televisions could continue to enjoy television service. The Commission also reasoned that by establishing a separate standard for U.S. ATV, American electronics manufacturers would gain a *hardware* edge over foreign manufacturers, to accompany the existing *software* edge—since much of the world's television programming is produced in the United States.

The FCC treated ATV and HDTV as an upgrade of an existing service and as part of the conversion from analog to digital transmission. In April 1997 the Commission assigned digital channels to all existing full-power television stations. Stations would surrender their analog channels within nine years and transmit only a digital signal. Broadcasters would be able to transmit one HDTV signal, or up to four lower resolution ATV signals on a single channel.[6]

The Changing Climate and Regulation

The changing technological climate promises new challenges for electronic media regulation in both traditional and nontraditional forms of information distribution. Developing technologies like Direct Broadcast Satellite (DBS), Satellite Master Antenna Television (SMATV), and Multichannel Multipoint Distribution Systems (MMDS) (wireless cable) may either be poised for wider acceptance or face extinction, depending on congressional and FCC policy. The much delayed entry of telephone companies into the video distribution market could have the greatest effect on the regulatory climate.

Direct Broadcast Satellites (DBS)

DBS provides subscribers with a programming service beamed from a high-powered satellite to a small receive-only dish placed on the subscriber's roof or other suitable location. Although originally authorized in 1982, DBS did not become readily available until 1994 when DirectTV and USSB began offering service and Thomson Consumer Electronics massproduced home-receiving equipment under the RCA name. By 1997, nearly two million receivers had been sold. By the end of the decade, DirecTV emerged as a leader in the industry, buying competitors like USSB and PrimeStar. In 2001, however, the field began to narrow further when EchoStar, the operator of the DishNetwork, planned to buy DirecTV and merge the two services. On December 3, 2001, the Commission received applications requesting consent to the transfer of control of licenses and authorizations held by Hughes Electronics Corporation, owner of DirecTV, and its subsidiaries and affiliates, and by EchoStar Communications Corporation and its subsidiaries and affiliates to EchoStar Communications Corporation.

Other Distribution Systems

Satellite Master Antenna Television (SMATV)

Satellite Master Antenna TV (SMATV) systems provide programming to apartment buildings, hotels, office buildings, and other multi-unit buildings. This is accomplished through the use of a large satellite-receiving dish whose signal is routed to the various units in the building via wire. Provided a SMATV system does not use any public right of way to transmit its signal, the FCC does not consider it a cable system. Therefore, most SMATV operations are not subject to franchising requirements and other regulations that apply to cable television.

Telephone Company (Telco) Entry into Video Distribution

The modified final judgment (MFJ), results from an out of court settlement between AT&T and the Department of Justice. In 1984, this set the terms for the breakup of AT&T. The MFJ prohibited the seven regional Bell operating companies (RBOCs) (which are Ameritech, Bell Atlantic, Bell South, NYNEX, Pacific Telesis, Southwestern Bell, and U.S. West) from engaging in information services. These services included video newspapers, video classified ads, and video program services outside their regional service areas. In 1991, District Court Judge Harold Greene lifted the ban on information services.

Telcos are regulated as common carriers under Title II of the Communications Act of 1934. As such, telcos exercise no editorial control over messages transmitted on their facilities. Telcos provide access to a communications conduit on a nondiscriminatory, first-come-first-served, basis to customers for a fee. Therefore, the content regulations that apply to broadcasters, cablecasters, and other electronic mass media do not apply to telcos.

Instead, regulation has been developed to ensure that service is available to a wide number of people at a fair price. Since telcos are by nature monopolistic services, in the absence of "effective competition," rate regulation is a major component of government oversight. Regulation may occur at both the federal and state levels. Interstate service falls under the jurisdiction of the FCC, while intrastate service is usually regulated by state agencies, such as public utilities commissions.

The advent of fiber-optic cable and video compression has made telco delivery of video programming an attractive alternative to broadcast, cable, and other sources. Utilizing a broadband-switched fiber network, telcos can deliver to subscribers a digital quality, program-on-demand service. But this technology cannot economically be introduced on a wide scale at this time.

In July 1992 the FCC relaxed the ban on cable–telco cross-ownership and allowed telephone companies to distribute video programming to households. Telephone companies were permitted to transmit video programming without having to obtain a municipal franchise as required for cable systems. The 1996 Telecommunications Act paved the way for telephones to enter the video distribution business, full scale.

Open Video Systems

Sections 651 to 653 of the 1996 Telecommunications Act call for the FCC to promulgate regulations for open video systems, or OVS.[7] This replaces the FCC's Video Dialtone concept, which never really developed. The new act now refers to the old video dialtone concept as "interactive on-demand services." OVS allows telephone companies to deliver video without incurring common carrier and some cable regulations. In exchange for this loosening of regulation, telcos must guarantee that they will carry unaffiliated program providers at reasonable rates. Telcos will be free to select programming on only one-third of active channels when total demand for channel capacity is reached.

Digital Audio Broadcasting (DAB)

Digital Audio Broadcasting allows a broadcast audio signal to be transmitted and received with the quality of a digital compact disc. DAB can be transmitted terrestrially, via satellite, through cable or over fiber-optic lines.

Terrestrial Delivery

In 1991 the National Association of Broadcasters favored the development of a digital system called Acorn DAB. This system proposed using part of the radio spectrum now occupied by existing radio stations, thereby eliminating the need for additional spectrum allocation. The system was also seen as complementing the analog radio stations already in place. Although much discussion has ensued, at this writing a terrestrial system of DAB has not materialized, although in 1998 the FCC initiated a *Notice of Proposed Rule Making* to study the feasibility of this service.

Satellite Delivery

This system of DAB proposes to transmit digital radio broadcasts directly from satellites to special radio receivers. By late 1994 four companies had applied to begin satellite DAB service, however the FCC had not yet allocated the additional 50 MHz of spectrum space required for the service. Broadcasters have always opposed satellite DAB, fearing its impact on existing radio stations, but in 2001 a company called XM Radio began a satellite-delivered subscription service that threatens to modify the economic model of commercial radio in the United States. (See http://www.xmradio.com.)

Cable or Wired Delivery

Some cable systems offer digital audio services through their existing cable lines, while the development of open video services creates the potential for fiber optic delivery of DAB into the home. Wired systems can provide a variety of music formats, allowing subscribers to choose a daily program of music. Naturally, no additional spectrum space is required for this service, however most are transmitted to cable systems via satellite.

The Internet

The Internet, much like both radio and television in their early days, has captured the interest of those with the means to afford the technology. Web pages began as experiments, but are now considered essential for businesses and educational institutions. Access to Web pages began as a free service (after purchasing access to the Internet through a provider). Now, an increasing number of sites charge for access. Many have obtained commercial sponsorship. As Websites have become more sophisticated and access speeds faster, the Web looks more and more like television and the line between TV and the computer continues to blur. Indeed, cable systems now bring the Internet into many of our homes with high-speed cable modems. But a fundamental difference remains in how we utilize the two media. Television, with its large screen, high-quality audio, and entertainment-based programming, is conducive to a more social environment than the personalized experience of the computer. People often watch television in groups—with family and friends. Surfing the Internet remains largely a solitary activity, although as films and other media are streamed online, this will likely change. This difference also impacts the ways in which the two media are treated under the law. The Internet is a pure information provider voluntarily brought into the home by a subscriber, making it more like a newspaper or a magazine than like television.

Legal Issues

As a rapidly developing medium of communication, many questions about how laws are applied to the Internet remain unanswered.

Privacy and copyright matters on the Net are areas of growing concern. Also at issue is whether the Internet should be treated more like the print media, with full First Amendment protection, or more like broadcast media, with limited freedoms. Case law currently would suggest that the Internet enjoys the broad First Amendment rights of print. When Congress sought to apply broadcast-like indecency standards to the Internet as part of the 1996 Telecommunications Act, the Supreme Court ruled the standards unconstitutional. It should be noted that the Court specifically refused to apply the *Red Lion* spectrum scarcity argument to the Internet.

Reno v. American Civil Liberties Union (1997)

☐ . . . Two provisions of the Communications Decency Act of 1996 (CDA or Act) seek to protect minors from harmful material on the Internet, an international network of interconnected computers that enables millions of people to communicate with one another in "cyberspace" and to access vast amounts of information from around the world. Title 47 U. S. C. A. §223(a)(1)(B)(ii) (Supp. 1997) criminalizes the "knowing" transmission of "obscene or indecent" messages to any recipient under 18 years of age. Section 223(d) prohibits the "knowin[g]" sending or displaying to a person under 18 of any message "that, in context, depicts or describes, in terms patently offensive as measured by contemporary community standards, sexual or excretory activities or organs." Affirmative defenses are provided for those who take "good faith, . . . effective . . . actions" to restrict access by minors to the prohibited communications, §223(e)(5)(A), and those who restrict such access by requiring certain designated forms of age proof, such as a verified credit card or an adult identification number, §223(e)(5)(B). A number of plaintiffs filed suit challenging the constitutionality of §§223(a)(1) and 223(d). After making extensive findings of fact, a three-judge District Court convened pursuant to the Act entered a preliminary injunction against enforcement of both challenged provisions. The court's judgment enjoins the Government from enforcing §223(a)(1)(B)'s prohibitions insofar as they relate to "indecent" communications, but expressly preserves the Government's right to investigate and prosecute the obscenity or child pornography activities prohibited therein. The injunction against enforcement of §223(d) is unqualified because that section contains no separate reference to obscenity or child pornography. The Government appealed to this Court under the Act's special review provisions, arguing that the District Court erred in holding that the CDA violated both the First Amendment because it is overbroad and the Fifth Amendment because it is vague.

Held: The CDA's "indecent transmission" and "patently offensive display" provisions abridge "the freedom of speech" protected by the

First Amendment. . . . (b) A close look at the precedents relied on by the Government—*Ginsberg v. New York*, 390 U.S. 629; *FCC v. Pacifica Foundation*, 438 U.S. 726; and *Renton v. Playtime Theatres, Inc.*, 475 U.S. 41—raises, rather than relieves, doubts about the CDA's constitutionality. The CDA differs from the various laws and orders upheld in those cases in many ways, including that it does not allow parents to consent to their children's use of restricted materials; is not limited to commercial transactions; fails to provide any definition of "indecent" and omits any requirement that "patently offensive" material lack socially redeeming value; neither limits its broad categorical prohibitions to particular times nor bases them on an evaluation by an agency familiar with the medium's unique characteristics; is punitive; applies to a medium that, unlike radio, receives full First Amendment protection; and cannot be properly analyzed as a form of time, place, and manner regulation because it is a content based blanket restriction on speech. These precedents, then, do not require the Court to uphold the CDA and are fully consistent with the application of the most stringent review of its provisions. . . . (c) *The special factors recognized in some of the Court's cases as justifying regulation of the broadcast media—the history of extensive government regulation of broadcasting, see, e.g., Red Lion Broadcasting Co. v. FCC, 395 U.S. 367, 399–400; the scarcity of available frequencies at its inception, see, e.g., Turner Broadcasting System, Inc. v. FCC, 512 U.S. 622, 637–638; and its "invasive" nature, see Sable Communications of Cal., Inc. v. FCC, 492 U.S. 115, 128—are not present in cyberspace. Thus, these cases provide no basis for qualifying the level of First Amendment scrutiny that should be applied to the Internet.* [Emphasis added.]

. . . (e) The CDA lacks the precision that the First Amendment requires when a statute regulates the content of speech. Although the Government has an interest in protecting children from potentially harmful materials, see, e.g., Ginsberg, 390 U. S., at 639, the CDA pursues that interest by suppressing a large amount of speech that adults have a constitutional right to send and receive . . . Its breadth is wholly unprecedented. The CDA's burden on adult speech is unacceptable if less restrictive alternatives would be at least as effective in achieving the Act's legitimate purposes. . . . The Government has not proved otherwise. On the other hand, the District Court found that currently available user based software suggests that a reasonably effective method by which parents can prevent their children from accessing material which the parents believe is inappropriate will soon be widely available. Moreover, the arguments in this Court referred to possible alternatives such as requiring that indecent material be "tagged" to facilitate parental control, making exceptions for messages with artistic or educational value, providing some tolerance for parental choice, and regulating some portions of the Internet differently than others. Particularly in the light of the absence of any detailed congressional findings, or even hearings addressing the CDA's special problems, the Court is persuaded that the CDA is not narrowly tailored.

(f) The Government's three additional arguments for sustaining the CDA's affirmative prohibitions are rejected. First, the contention that the Act is constitutional because it leaves open ample "alternative channels" of communication is unpersuasive because the CDA regulates speech on the basis of its content, so that a "time, place, and manner" analysis is inapplicable . . . Second, the assertion that the CDA's "knowledge" and "specific person" requirements significantly restrict its permissible application to communications to persons the sender knows to be under 18 is untenable, given that most Internet forums are open to all comers and that even the strongest reading of the "specific person" requirement would confer broad powers of censorship, in the form of a "heckler's veto," upon any opponent of indecent speech. Finally, there is no textual support for the submission that material having scientific, educational, or other redeeming social value will necessarily fall outside the CDA's prohibitions. . . .

. . . The Government's argument that transmitters may take protective "good faith actio[n]" by "tagging" their indecent communications in a way that would indicate their contents, thus permitting recipients to block their reception with appropriate software, is illusory, given the requirement that such action be "effective": The proposed screening software does not currently exist, but, even if it did, there would be no way of knowing whether a potential recipient would actually block the encoded material. The Government also failed to prove that §223(b)(5)'s verification defense would significantly reduce the CDA's heavy burden on adult speech. . . .

Consolidation of Ownership Issues

Since the 1930s, the FCC has been concerned about diversity of ownership in broadcasting. That same concern has carried over to the newer media as well. An economy of scale has led to an increasing number of mergers and consolidations of media companies and poses a dilemma for regulators. On the one hand, the public interest is served by a number of independent voices in the media—a marketplace of ideas. On the other hand, media companies must be large enough to survive and take advantage of economy of scale. In the same way that "mom and pop" grocery stores were supplanted by large supermarket chains, so have "mom and pop" broadcasters and small cable systems been replaced by media giants. As mergers and consolidations continue, the number of media companies gets smaller and the number of media outlets in the hands of one owner gets larger. Regulators must rationalize the impact that this situation has upon media consumers and society at large. The FCC considers media mergers from a public interest standard, while the Federal Trade Commission (FTC) reviews potential mergers and their effect on competition. The Department of Justice has jurisdiction over antitrust matters.

One argument against consolidation is that the public is deprived of a multiplicity of voices; that only information favorable to the large media company will be transmitted. A counterargument states that larger, more financially stable media companies, might be willing to take more risks than smaller less profitable companies, thereby actually increasing the variety of media programming.

The Time Warner/America Online Merger

The conditional approval of the 2001 merger of Time Warner and America Online by the FCC articulates many of the concerns just discussed. The full text of the FCC approval is available online at http://www.fcc.gov/transaction/aol-tw-decision.html. The Commission's public notice provides a summary of the major issues and considerations.

FCC 01–11
Released: January 11, 2001
SUBJECT TO CONDITIONS, COMMISSION APPROVES
MERGER BETWEEN AMERICA ONLINE, INC. AND TIME WARNER, INC.
The Commission today approved the joint application ("Application") filed by America Online, Inc. ("AOL") and Time Warner Inc. ("Time Warner") (collectively the "Applicants") for approval to transfer control of certain licenses and authorizations to AOL Time Warner, Inc., a newly created company, subject to the conditions stated below. A Memorandum Opinion and Order (the "Order") explaining in further detail the Commission's reasoning and the conditions will be issued shortly.

INTERNET SERVICES
Although the Commission found that the FTC consent decree with AOL Time Warner would substantially ensure that unaffiliated ISPs are able to offer their services over AOL Time Warner's cable system on non-discriminatory terms and conditions, the Commission found that AOL Time Warner might have insufficient incentives to enter contracts with local or regional ISPs that are unaffiliated with AOL Time Warner. The

Commission noted that the FTC consent decree requires AOL Time Warner to negotiate in good faith with any unaffiliated ISP seeking access to its cable systems and, thus, reiterated that AOL Time Warner must engage with local and regional ISPs in a good faith, nondiscriminatory manner. The conditions set forth below regarding choice of ISPs, first screen, billing, technical performance, and disclosure of contracts are particularly relevant to the ability of smaller ISPs to negotiate carriage arrangements on non-discriminatory terms and we expect that AOL Time Warner will negotiate in good faith to reach contract provisions that are consistent with the commercial viability of these entities. The Internet access conditions that the Commission adopted with regard to AOL Time Warner are as follows:

A. Choice of ISPs: AOL Time Warner shall not restrict the ability of any current or prospective ISP customers to select and initiate service from any unaffiliated ISP which, pursuant to a contract with AOL Time Warner, has made its service available over AOL Time Warner's cable facilities ("Participating ISP"). AOL Time Warner must allow customers to select a Participating ISP by a method that does not discriminate in favor of AOL Time Warner's affiliates on the basis of affiliation. At a minimum, AOL Time Warner must allow customers to obtain a list of Participating ISPs by calling their local AOL Time Warner cable system and requesting such a list. Whenever a customer requests a listing of Participating ISPs, AOL Time Warner shall provide the list in a reasonable and timely manner. Such list shall not discriminate in favor of AOL Time Warner's affiliates on the basis of affiliation. AOL Time Warner may not prohibit ISPs from marketing their services to AOL Time Warner cable customers.

B. First Screen: AOL Time Warner must permit each Participating ISP to determine the contents of its subscribers' first screen and may not require a Participating ISP to include any content as a condition of obtaining access to AOL Time Warner cable systems; provided that AOL Time Warner and any Participating ISP may agree that the ISP will include specified content or links on its first screen. AOL Time Warner may not require any high-speed Internet access cable customer to go through an affiliated ISP to reach any Participating ISP from which the customer purchases service.

C. Billing: AOL Time Warner must permit each ISP to have a direct billing arrangement with those high-speed Internet access subscribers to whom the ISP sells service. AOL Time Warner may offer a billing service to any Participating ISP, but may not require any ISP to purchase this service as a condition of obtaining access.

D. Technical Performance: All contracts between AOL Time Warner and unaffiliated ISPs for access to Time Warner's cable systems shall contain a clause warranting that, to the extent AOL Time Warner provides any Quality of Service mechanisms, caching services, technical support customer services, multicasting capabilities, address management and other technical functions of the cable system that affect customers' experience with their ISP, AOL Time Warner must provide them in a manner that does not discriminate in favor of AOL Time Warner's affiliated ISPs on the basis of affiliation.

E. Rights to Disclose Contracts to the Commission: AOL Time Warner may not enter into any contract with any ISP for connection with AOL Time Warner's cable systems that prevents that ISP from disclosing the terms of the contract to the Commission under the Commission's confidentiality procedures.

F. Enforcement: With respect to any dispute concerning AOL Time Warner's compliance with these conditions, the following procedures shall apply. These procedures are designed to resolve any disputes within sixty (60) days of the filing of the Complaint and to have them resolved by the Chief, Cable Services Bureau ("Chief").

1. No less than ten (10) business days before filing a complaint with the Commission, the complainant shall notify AOL Time Warner of its intention to file the complaint. This is intended to afford the parties a final opportunity to resolve their dispute without resort to our processes.

2. Within twenty (20) days after public notice of the filing of the complaint, any interested party shall file an answer. Within ten (10) days after the filing of the answer, the complainant may file its reply. The complainant and AOL Time Warner shall each, with its first filing, furnish a detailed report, technical or otherwise, describing the conduct or events that are the subject of the filing. All filings shall be made with Commission Secretary and shall be concurrently served on the Chief.

3. In resolving these filings, the Chief will apply the following principles: (a) the general pleading rules set forth in Parts 1 and 76 of our rules will apply to the extent they are consistent with the specific requirements of the proceedings provided for herein; (b) complaints of misconduct by AOL shall be filed within one year of the occurrence of the alleged misconduct; (c) discovery shall be at the discretion of the Chief and may be requested by a party in one of its filings provided for above; and (d) the complainant shall bear the burden of proof in the proceeding it commences.

The Chief shall sustain or dismiss the complaint within sixty (60) days of the filing of the complaint.

INSTANT MESSAGING

Given AOL Time Warner's likely domination of the potentially competitive business of new, IM-based services, especially advanced, IM-based high-speed services ("AIHS") applications such as videoconferencing, the Commission concluded that a condition to prevent that merger-specific harm was merited. AOL Time Warner may not offer an AIHS application that includes the transmission and reception, utilizing a names and presence directory ("NPD") over the Internet Protocol path of AOL Time Warner broadband facilities, of one- or two-way streaming video communication using NPD protocols—including live images or tape—that are new features, functions, and enhancements beyond those offered in current offerings such as AIM 4.1 or ICQ 2000b, unless and until AOL Time Warner has successfully demonstrated it has complied with one of the following grounds for relief.

Grounds for Relief. Option One. AOL Time Warner may file a petition demonstrating that it has implemented a standard for server-to-server interoperability of NPD-based services that has been promulgated by the IETF or a widely recognized standard-setting body that is recognized as complying with National Institute of Standard Testing or Industry Standard Organization requirements for a standard setting body. At a minimum, AOL Time Warner must demonstrate that the adopted protocol makes available to another provider of NPD-based services such data in AOL Time Warner's NPD(s) as will enable the other provider's users to know the addresses of AOL Time Warner users and detect their presence online, to the same extent that AOL Time Warner's users know each others' addresses and detect each others' presence online. AOL Time Warner must also demonstrate that the protocol makes available to other IM providers any other information used by AOL Time Warner to implement and process transaction of AIHS services, to the extent allowed by law. The adopted standard shall also ensure that AOL Time Warner shall afford the same quality and speed in processing transactions to and from the other provider as it affords to its own transactions of the same type. Other than specifying server-to-server interoperability as described above, we do not set any technical criteria for interoperability.

Option Two. AOL may file a petition demonstrating that it has entered into written contracts providing for server-to-server interoperability with significant, unaffiliated, actual or potential competing providers of NPD-based services offered to the public. AOL must execute the first such contract prior to offering the video AIHS service described above. After

AOL Time Warner executes the first contract, an officer of AOL Time Warner shall certify to the Commission that it is prepared to promptly negotiate in good faith, with any other requesting provider of NPD-based services.

Within 180 days of executing the first contract, AOL must demonstrate that it has entered into two additional contracts with significant, unaffiliated, actual or potential competing providers. The interoperability achieved under these contracts shall be identical to that described under Option 1 above with identical terms and conditions for technical interoperability. All parties to a contract shall agree not to alter the technical protocol without the consent of all parties providing interoperable IM services under these agreements. The contracts may contain different provisions for business considerations. AOL Time Warner must submit copies of these agreements for server-to-server interoperability into the record of this proceeding within 10 days of execution of such agreement. AOL Time Warner may redact any proprietary information or terms not related to technical interoperability.

Option Three. AOL Time Warner may seek relief from the condition on offering AIHS video services by filing a petition demonstrating that imposition of the condition no longer serves the public interest, convenience and necessity because there has been a material change in circumstance, including new evidence that renders the condition on offering AIHS video services no longer necessary in the public interest, convenience, and necessity. If AOL Time Warner proffers market share information as evidence that the condition no longer is necessary in the public interest, convenience, and necessity, AOL Time Warner must demonstrate that it has not been a dominant provider of NPD services for at least four (4) consecutive months.

Procedure for Submission of Petition to the Commission. To receive authorization to offer AIHS video services pursuant to Options 1–3 above, AOL Time Warner shall submit a Petition to the Commission. The Petition shall be filed with the Secretary's office and shall contain the factual and legal bases demonstrating satisfaction of one of the three options set forth above. The Commission shall put the Petition out for Notice and Comment with a maximum of 30 days for receipt of such comments. Petitioner may submit a reply not more than 15 days after the closure of the comment period. Upon the timely filing of Petitioner's reply, the Petition, comments and reply shall be submitted to the Commission for disposition. The Commission shall issue its findings and conclusions not more than 60 days after receipt of the matter. This timeline may be altered at the discretion of the Commission upon a timely submitted request of the Petitioner. The findings of the Commission shall be made upon clear and convincing evidence, and in the absence of such an evidentiary showing, the condition shall not be eliminated.

Reporting Requirement. The Commission shall require AOL Time Warner to file a progress report with the Commission, 180 days after the release of the Order and every 180 days thereafter, describing in technical depth, the actions it has taken to achieve interoperability of its IM offerings and others' IM offerings. Such reports will be placed on public notice for comment. Any confidential or proprietary information contained in the reports may be submitted to the Commission pursuant to the terms of the protective order in this proceeding.

Enforcement. The Commission shall retain jurisdiction over the licensees or their successors for the purpose of enforcing the terms of this condition, for a period not to exceed five years. The terms of this condition shall be enforced pursuant to the Commission's powers under the Communication Act. Any party to the Order, or their successor in interest, may petition this Commission at any time for relief from the condition on offering AIHS video services imposed pursuant to the Order.

In the event that any person wishes to bring to us a dispute about AOL's compliance with this condition, the Commission shall require that the following procedures be followed. These procedures are designed to resolve any disputes within sixty (60) days of the first filing. Within twenty (20) days after public notice is given of either the filing of a complaint or a showing by AOL Time Warner, any interested party shall file a response (AOL Time Warner's answer to the complaint, another person's response to AOL Time Warner's alleged showing). Within ten (10) days after the filing of the responses, the party that made the first filing may file its reply. The complainant and AOL Time Warner shall each, with its first filing, furnish a detailed report, technical or otherwise, describing the conduct or events that are the subject of the filing. All these filings shall be made with the Commission Secretary and shall be concurrently served on the Chief, Cable Service Bureau. The complaint or showing, as the case may be, shall be dismissed or sustained within sixty (60) days of its filing.

Sunset. Five (5) years after the date of release of the Order, the condition set forth in the preceding paragraphs shall expire and shall not restrain AOL Time Warner from offering video AIHS . . .

OWNERSHIP INTEREST IN GENERAL MOTORS AND HUGHES ELECTRONICS

In response to arguments that AOL Time Warner's indirect ownership interest in DirecTV, Inc. might raise anticompetitive concerns by permitting a cable operator to own part of a DBS provider, the Commission ordered that the Applicants shall notify the Chiefs of the Commission's Cable Services Bureau and International Bureau, in writing, of any transactions that increase the Applicants' ownership interest in General Motors Corporation and/or Hughes Electronics Corporation (the parent companies of DirecTV), no later than 30 days after the transaction.

CONTRACTUAL RELATIONSHIPS WITH AT&T

To mitigate the adverse effects of potential coordination, as a result of the merger, between AT&T and AOL Time Warner, the Commission imposed the following additional conditions:

AOL Time Warner shall be prohibited from entering into any agreement with AT&T, tacit or otherwise, that gives any AOL Time Warner ISP exclusive access to any AT&T cable system for the purpose of offering high-speed Internet access service.

AOL Time Warner shall be prohibited from entering into any agreement with AT&T, tacit or otherwise, that affects AT&T's ability to offer any rates, terms or conditions of access to ISPs that are not affiliated with AOL Time Warner.

AOL Time Warner, by its General Counsel, shall certify to the Commission upon the merger's closing and annually thereafter that it is in compliance with the foregoing two conditions.

MISCELLANEOUS PROVISIONS

The Commission ordered that compliance with all conditions imposed in the Order is a non-severable condition of the grant of the Application.

All references to AOL and Time Warner in the order shall also refer to their respective officers, directors, and employees, as well as to any affiliated companies, and their officers, directors, and employees, except as otherwise noted.

The Commission denied the Petition to Deny filed by the Consumers Union, Consumer Federation of America, and Media Access Project, the Petition to Deny of Thomas Lewis Bonge, the Petitions to Condition filed by RCN Telecom Services and Gemstar, and all similar petitions except as otherwise discussed in this public notice.[ ]

The Commission denied the motion to consolidate this proceeding with the AT&T–MediaOne license transfer proceeding, which was filed by the Consumers Union, Consumer Federation of America, and Media Access Project.

EFFECTIVE DATE OF THE MERGER APPROVAL

The Commission ordered that the grant of the approval of the Application with conditions is effective today, January 11, 2001.

Action by the Commission on January 11, 2001, Commissioners Furchtgott-Roth and Powell, concurring in part and dissenting in part. —FCC—

Conclusion

Critics of telecommunications policy and the regulatory process charge that Congress and the Commission have applied limited and archaic regulatory schemes to new technologies, some of which have been declared unconstitutional. Why would we apply broadcast indecency standards to new technology like the World Wide Web? This would be the same approach as applying the indecency standard of "wireless" to broadcast radio. How can a policy of diversity in media be reconciled with the economic need for media industries to consolidate and grow larger and larger? The public interest standard, developed in the 1890s for railroad regulation, remains a specter in the regulation of new systems. This standard has remained elusive for more than seventy-five years, yet the 1996 Telecommunications Act does not modify or address this standard. Consequently, the United States still lacks a coherent, rational telecommunications regulatory scheme. Perhaps new legislation, able to pass constitutional muster, will be passed. Or, perhaps case law will eventually determine how new technologies and systems will be integrated into our regulatory and legal system. In any case it is safe to say that the legal environment affecting the electronic media will remain a dynamic arena.

Notes/References

1. Susan Douglas, *Inventing American Broadcasting* (Baltimore: Johns Hopkins University Press, 1987): 191–92.
2. See http://www.fcc.gov/dtv/ for text of the FCC rules.
3. "HUTs Continue to Fall," *Broadcasting & Cable* (April 21, 1997): 11.
4. "The Sky Is Rising," *Broadcasting & Cable* (March 17, 1997): 30.
5. Christopher Stern, "New Law of the Land," *Broadcasting & Cable* (February 5, 1996): 8.
6. See http://www.fcc.gov/Bureaus/Engineering_Technology/Orders/1997/fcc97115.html.
7. See http://www.fcc.gov/Bureaus/Cable/Orders/fcc96334.txt.

1 □ □ □
□ □ □
□ □ □

Copyright Forms

Form SR (For a Sound Recording)
Form PA (For a Work of the Performing Arts)

⊗ Application Form SR ⊗

Detach and read these instructions before completing this form.
Make sure all applicable spaces have been filled in before you return this form.

BASIC INFORMATION

When to Use This Form: Use Form SR for registration of published or unpublished sound recordings. It should be used when the copyright claim is limited to the sound recording itself, and it may also be used where the same copyright claimant is seeking simultaneous registration of the underlying musical, dramatic, or literary work embodied in the phonorecord.

With one exception, "sound recordings" are works that result from the fixation of a series of musical, spoken, or other sounds. The exception is for the audio portions of audiovisual works, such as a motion picture soundtrack or an audio cassette accompanying a filmstrip. These are considered a part of the audiovisual work as a whole.

Deposit to Accompany Application: An application for copyright registration must be accompanied by a deposit consisting of phonorecords representing the entire work for which registration is to be made.

Unpublished Work: Deposit one complete phonorecord.

Published Work: Deposit two complete phonorecords of the best edition, together with "any printed or other visually perceptible material" published with the phonorecords.

Work First Published Outside the United States: Deposit one complete phonorecord of the first foreign edition.

Contribution to a Collective Work: Deposit one complete phonorecord of the best edition of the collective work.

The Copyright Notice: Before March 1, 1989, the use of copyright notice was mandatory on all published works, and any work first published before that date should have carried a notice. For works first published on and after March 1, 1989, use of the copyright notice is optional. For more information about copyright notice, see Circular 3, "Copyright Notices."

For Further Information: To speak to an information specialist, call (202) 707-3000 (TTY: (202) 707-6737). Recorded information is available 24 hours a day. Order forms and other publications from Library of Congress, Copyright Office, 101 Independence Avenue, S.E., Washington, D.C. 20559-6000 or call the Forms and Publications Hotline at (202) 707-9100. Most circulars (but not forms) are available via fax. Call (202) 707-2600 from a touchtone phone. Access and download circulars, forms, and other information from the Copyright Office Website at www.loc.gov/copyright.

LINE-BY-LINE INSTRUCTIONS

Please type or print neatly using black ink. The form is used to produce the certificate.

1 SPACE 1: Title

Title of This Work: Every work submitted for copyright registration must be given a title to identify that particular work. If the phonorecords or any accompanying printed material bears a title (or an identifying phrase that could serve as a title), transcribe that wording completely and exactly on the application. Indexing of the registration and future identification of the work may depend on the information you give here.

Previous, Alternative, or Contents Titles: Complete this space if there are any previous or alternative titles for the work under which someone searching for the registration might be likely to look, or under which a document pertaining to the work might be recorded. You may also give the individual contents titles, if any, in this space or you may use a Continuation Sheet. Circle the term that describes the titles given.

2 SPACE 2: Author(s)

General Instructions: After reading these instructions, decide who are the "authors" of this work for copyright purposes. Then, unless the work is a "collective work," give the requested information about every "author" who contributed any appreciable amount of copyrightable matter to this version of the work. If you need further space, request additional Continuation Sheets. In the case of a collective work such as a collection of previously published or registered sound recordings, give information about the author of the collective work as a whole. If you are submitting this Form SR to cover the recorded musical, dramatic, or literary work as well as the sound recording itself, it is important for space 2 to include full information about the various authors of all of the material covered by the copyright claim, making clear the nature of each author's contribution.

Name of Author: The fullest form of the author's name should be given. Unless the work was "made for hire," the individual who actually created the work is its "author." In the case of a work made for hire, the statute provides that "the employer or other person for whom the work was prepared is considered the author."

What is a "Work Made for Hire"? A "work made for hire" is defined as: (1) "a work prepared by an employee within the scope of his or her employment"; or (2)

"a work specially ordered or commissioned for use as a contribution to a collective work, as a part of a motion picture or other audiovisual work, as a translation, as a supplementary work, as a compilation, as an instructional text, as a test, as answer material for a test, or as an atlas, if the parties expressly agree in a written instrument signed by them that the work shall be considered a work made for hire." If you have checked "Yes" to indicate that the work was "made for hire," you must give the full legal name of the employer (or other person for whom the work was prepared). You may also include the name of the employee along with the name of the employer (for example: "Elster Record Co., employer for hire of John Ferguson").

"Anonymous" or "Pseudonymous" Work: An author's contribution to a work is "anonymous" if that author is not identified on the copies or phonorecords of the work. An author's contribution to a work is "pseudonymous" if that author is identified on the copies or phonorecords under a fictitious name. If the work is "anonymous" you may: (1) leave the line blank; or (2) state "anonymous" on the line; or (3) reveal the author's identity. If the work is "pseudonymous" you may: (1) leave the line blank; or (2) give the pseudonym and identify it as such (for example: "Huntley Haverstock, pseudonym"); or (3) reveal the author's name, making clear which is the real name and which is the pseudonym (for example: "Judith Barton, whose pseudonym is Madeline Elster"). However, the citizenship or domicile of the author **must** be given in all cases.

Dates of Birth and Death: If the author is dead, the statute requires that the year of death be included in the application unless the work is anonymous or pseudonymous. The author's birth date is optional, but is useful as a form of identification. Leave this space blank if the author's contribution was a "work made for hire."

Author's Nationality or Domicile: Give the country in which the author is a citizen, or the country in which the author is domiciled. Nationality or domicile **must** be given in all cases.

Nature of Authorship: Sound recording authorship is the performance, sound production, or both, that is fixed in the recording deposited for registration. Describe this authorship in space 2 as "sound recording." If the claim also covers the underlying work(s), include the appropriate authorship terms for each author, for example, "words," "music," "arrangement of music," or "text."

Generally, for the claim to cover both the sound recording and the underlying work(s), every author should have contributed to both the sound recording **and** the underlying work(s). If the claim includes artwork or photographs, include the appropriate term in the statement of authorship.

SPACE 3: Creation and Publication

General Instructions: Do not confuse "creation" with "publication." Every application for copyright registration must state "the year in which creation of the work was completed." Give the date and nation of first publication only if the work has been published.

Creation: Under the statute, a work is "created" when it is fixed in a copy or phonorecord for the first time. Where a work has been prepared over a period of time, the part of the work existing in fixed form on a particular date constitutes the created work on that date. The date you give here should be the year in which the author completed the particular version for which registration is now being sought, even if other versions exist or if further changes or additions are planned.

Publication: The statute defines "publication" as "the distribution of copies or phonorecords of a work to the public by sale or other transfer of ownership, or by rental, lease, or lending"; a work is also "published" if there has been an "offering to distribute copies or phonorecords to a group of persons for purposes of further distribution, public performance, or public display." Give the full date (month, date, year) when, and the country where, publication first occurred. If first publication took place simultaneously in the United States and other countries, it is sufficient to state "U.S.A."

SPACE 4: Claimant(s)

Name(s) and Address(es) of Copyright Claimant(s): Give the name(s) and address(es) of the copyright claimant(s) in the work even if the claimant is the same as the author. Copyright in a work belongs initially to the author of the work (including, in the case of a work made for hire, the employer or other person for whom the work was prepared). The copyright claimant is either the author of the work or a person or organization to whom the copyright initially belonging to the author has been transferred.

Transfer: The statute provides that, if the copyright claimant is not the author, the application for registration must contain "a brief statement of how the claimant obtained ownership of the copyright." If any copyright claimant named in space 4a is not an author named in space 2, give a brief statement explaining how the claimant(s) obtained ownership of the copyright. Examples: "By written contract"; "Transfer of all rights by author"; "Assignment"; "By will." Do not attach transfer documents or other attachments or riders.

SPACE 5: Previous Registration

General Instructions: The questions in space 5 are intended to show whether an earlier registration has been made for this work and, if so, whether there is any basis for a new registration. As a rule, only one basic copyright registration can be made for the same version of a particular work.

Same Version: If this version is substantially the same as the work covered by a previous registration, a second registration is not generally possible unless: (1) the work has been registered in unpublished form and a second registration is now being sought to cover this first published edition; or (2) someone other than the author is identified as copyright claimant in the earlier registration and the author is now seeking registration in his or her own name. If either of these two exceptions applies, check the appropriate box and give the earlier registration number and date. Otherwise, do not submit Form SR. Instead, write the Copyright Office for information about supplementary registration or recordation of transfers of copyright ownership.

Changed Version: If the work has been changed and you are now seeking registration to cover the additions or revisions, check the last box in space 5, give the earlier registration number and date, and complete both parts of space 6 in accordance with the instructions below.

Previous Registration Number and Date: If more than one previous registration has been made for the work, give the number and date of the latest registration.

SPACE 6: Derivative Work or Compilation

General Instructions: Complete space 6 if this work is a "changed version," "compilation," or "derivative work," and if it incorporates one or more earlier works that have already been published or registered for copyright, or that have fallen into the public domain, or sound recordings that were fixed before February 15, 1972. A "compilation" is defined as "a work formed by the collection and assembling of preexisting materials or of data that are selected, coordinated, or arranged in such a way that the resulting work as a whole constitutes an original work of authorship." A "derivative work" is "a work based on one or more preexisting works." Examples of derivative works include recordings reissued with substantial editorial revisions or abridgments of the recorded sounds, and recordings republished with new recorded material, or "any other form in which a work may be recast, transformed, or adapted." Derivative works also include works "consisting of editorial revisions, annotations, or other modifications" if these changes, as a whole, represent an original work of authorship.

Preexisting Material (space 6a): Complete this space **and** space 6b for derivative works. In this space identify the preexisting work that has been recast, transformed, or adapted. The preexisting work may be material that has been previously published, previously registered, or that is in the public domain. For example, the preexisting material might be: "1970 recording by Sperryville Symphony of Bach Double Concerto."

Material Added to This Work (space 6b): Give a brief, general statement of the **additional** new material covered by the copyright claim for which registration is sought. In the case of a derivative work, identify this new material. Examples: "Recorded performances on bands 1 and 3"; "Remixed sounds from original multitrack sound sources"; "New words, arrangement, and additional sounds." If the work is a compilation, give a brief, general statement describing both the material that has been compiled **and** the compilation itself. Example: "Compilation of 1938 Recordings by various swing bands."

SPACE 7, 8, 9: Fee, Correspondence, Certification, Return Address

Deposit Account: If you maintain a Deposit Account in the Copyright Office, identify it in space 7a. Otherwise, leave the space blank and send the filing fee of $30 (effective through June 30, 2002) with your application and deposit. (See space 8 on form.)

Correspondence (space 7b): This space should contain the name, address, area code, telephone number, fax number, and email address (if available) of the person to be consulted if correspondence about this application becomes necessary.

Certification (space 8): This application cannot be accepted unless it bears the date and the **handwritten signature** of the author or other copyright claimant, or of the owner of exclusive right(s), or of the duly authorized agent of the author, claimant, or owner of exclusive right(s).

Address for Return of Certificate (space 9): The address box must be completed legibly since the certificate will be returned in a window envelope.

MORE INFORMATION

"Works": "Works" are the basic subject matter of copyright; they are what authors create and copyright protects. The statute draws a sharp distinction between the "work" and "any material object in which the work is embodied."

"Copies" and "Phonorecords": These are the two types of material objects in which "works" are embodied. In general, **"copies"** are objects from which a work can be read or visually perceived, directly or with the aid of a machine or device, such as manuscripts, books, sheet music, film, and videotape. **"Phonorecords"** are objects embodying fixations of sounds, such as audio tapes and phonograph disks. For example, a song (the "work") can be reproduced in sheet music ("copies") or phonograph disks ("phonorecords"), or both.

"Sound Recordings": These are "works," not "copies" or "phonorecords." "Sound recordings" are "works that result from the fixation of a series of musical, spoken, or other sounds, but not including the sounds accompanying a motion picture or other audiovisual work." Example: When a record company issues a new release, the release will typically involve two distinct "works": the "musical work" that has been recorded, and the "sound recording" as a separate work in itself. The material objects that the record company sends out are "phonorecords": physical reproductions of both the "musical work" and the "sound recording."

Should You File More Than One Application? If your work consists of a recorded musical, dramatic, or literary work and if both the "work" and the sound recording are eligible for registration, the application form you should file depends on the following:

File Only Form SR if: The copyright claimant is the same for both the musical, dramatic, or literary work and for the sound recording, and you are seeking a single registration to cover both of these "works."

File Only Form PA (or Form TX) if: You are seeking to register only the musical, dramatic, or literary work, not the sound recording. Form PA is appropriate for works of the performing arts; Form TX is for nondramatic literary works.

Separate Applications Should Be Filed on Form PA (or Form TX) and on Form SR if: (1) The copyright claimant for the musical, dramatic, or literary work is different from the copyright claimant for the sound recording; or (2) You prefer to have separate registrations for the musical, dramatic, or literary work and for the sound recording.

Fees are effective through June 30, 2002. After that date, check the Copyright Office Website at www.loc.gov/copyright or call (202) 707-3000 for current fee information.

FORM SR
For a Sound Recording
UNITED STATES COPYRIGHT OFFICE

REGISTRATION NUMBER

_____

SR _____ SRU _____

EFFECTIVE DATE OF REGISTRATION

Month _____ Day _____ Year _____

DO NOT WRITE ABOVE THIS LINE. IF YOU NEED MORE SPACE, USE A SEPARATE CONTINUATION SHEET.

1

TITLE OF THIS WORK ▼

PREVIOUS, ALTERNATIVE, OR CONTENTS TITLES (CIRCLE ONE) ▼

2 a

NAME OF AUTHOR ▼

DATES OF BIRTH AND DEATH
Year Born ▼   Year Died ▼

Was this contribution to the work a "work made for hire"?
☐ Yes
☐ No

AUTHOR'S NATIONALITY OR DOMICILE
Name of Country
OR { Citizen of ▶_____
Domiciled in ▶_____

WAS THIS AUTHOR'S CONTRIBUTION TO THE WORK
Anonymous?   ☐ Yes ☐ No
Pseudonymous? ☐ Yes ☐ No
If the answer to either of these questions is "Yes," see detailed instructions.

NATURE OF AUTHORSHIP   Briefly describe nature of material created by this author in which copyright is claimed. ▼

NOTE

Under the law, the "author" of a "work made for hire" is generally the employer, not the employee (see instructions). For any part of this work that was "made for hire," check "Yes" in the space provided, give the employer (or other person for whom the work was prepared) as "Author" of that part, and leave the space for dates of birth and death blank.

b

NAME OF AUTHOR ▼

DATES OF BIRTH AND DEATH
Year Born ▼   Year Died ▼

Was this contribution to the work a "work made for hire"?
☐ Yes
☐ No

AUTHOR'S NATIONALITY OR DOMICILE
Name of Country
OR { Citizen of ▶_____
Domiciled in ▶_____

WAS THIS AUTHOR'S CONTRIBUTION TO THE WORK
Anonymous?   ☐ Yes ☐ No
Pseudonymous? ☐ Yes ☐ No
If the answer to either of these questions is "Yes," see detailed instructions.

NATURE OF AUTHORSHIP   Briefly describe nature of material created by this author in which copyright is claimed. ▼

c

NAME OF AUTHOR ▼

DATES OF BIRTH AND DEATH
Year Born ▼   Year Died ▼

Was this contribution to the work a "work made for hire"?
☐ Yes
☐ No

AUTHOR'S NATIONALITY OR DOMICILE
Name of Country
OR { Citizen of ▶_____
Domiciled in ▶_____

WAS THIS AUTHOR'S CONTRIBUTION TO THE WORK
Anonymous?   ☐ Yes ☐ No
Pseudonymous? ☐ Yes ☐ No
If the answer to either of these questions is "Yes," see detailed instructions.

NATURE OF AUTHORSHIP   Briefly describe nature of material created by this author in which copyright is claimed. ▼

3 a

YEAR IN WHICH CREATION OF THIS WORK WAS COMPLETED
_____ Year   This information must be given in all cases.

b DATE AND NATION OF FIRST PUBLICATION OF THIS PARTICULAR WORK
Complete this information ONLY if this work has been published.
Month ▶_____ Day ▶_____ Year ▶_____
_____ ◀ Nation

4 a

See instructions before completing this space.

COPYRIGHT CLAIMANT(S) Name and address must be given even if the claimant is the same as the author given in space 2. ▼

b

TRANSFER If the claimant(s) named here in space 4 is (are) different from the author(s) named in space 2, give a brief statement of how the claimant(s) obtained ownership of the copyright. ▼

DO NOT WRITE HERE / OFFICE USE ONLY

APPLICATION RECEIVED

ONE DEPOSIT RECEIVED

TWO DEPOSITS RECEIVED

FUNDS RECEIVED

MORE ON BACK ▶ • Complete all applicable spaces (numbers 5-9) on the reverse side of this page.
• See detailed instructions.   • Sign the form at line 8.

DO NOT WRITE HERE
Page 1 of _____ pages

EXAMINED BY	FORM SR
CHECKED BY	
CORRESPONDENCE ❑ Yes	FOR COPYRIGHT OFFICE USE ONLY

DO NOT WRITE ABOVE THIS LINE. IF YOU NEED MORE SPACE, USE A SEPARATE CONTINUATION SHEET.

PREVIOUS REGISTRATION Has registration for this work, or for an earlier version of this work, already been made in the Copyright Office?

❑ **Yes** ❑ **No** If your answer is "Yes," why is another registration being sought? (Check appropriate box) ▼

a. ❑ This work was previously registered in unpublished form and now has been published for the first time.

b. ❑ This is the first application submitted by this author as copyright claimant.

c. ❑ This is a changed version of the work, as shown by space 6 on this application.

If your answer is "Yes," give: **Previous Registration Number** ▼   **Year of Registration** ▼

5

DERIVATIVE WORK OR COMPILATION
Preexisting Material Identify any preexisting work or works that this work is based on or incorporates. ▼

a

Material Added to This Work Give a brief, general statement of the material that has been added to this work and in which copyright is claimed. ▼

b

6

See instructions
before completing
this space.

DEPOSIT ACCOUNT If the registration fee is to be charged to a Deposit Account established in the Copyright Office, give name and number of Account.
     Name ▼   **Account Number** ▼

a

CORRESPONDENCE Give name and address to which correspondence about this application should be sent.   Name/Address/Apt/City/State/ZIP ▼

b

Area code and daytime telephone number ▶   Fax number ▶
Email ▶

7

CERTIFICATION* I, the undersigned, hereby certify that I am the

Check only one ▼

❑ author   ❑ owner of exclusive right(s)

❑ other copyright claimant   ❑ authorized agent of _____
                                     Name of author or other copyright claimant, or owner of exclusive right(s) ▲

of the work identified in this application and that the statements made by me in this application are correct to the best of my knowledge.

Typed or printed name and date ▼ If this application gives a date of publication in space 3, do not sign and submit it before that date.

                                                Date▶ _____

       ☞   **Handwritten signature (x)** ▼
          X _

8

Certificate will be mailed in window envelope to this address	Name ▼
	Number/Street/Apt ▼
	City/State/ZIP ▼

YOU MUST:
• Complete all necessary spaces
• Sign your application in space 8
**SEND ALL 3 ELEMENTS
IN THE SAME PACKAGE:**
1. Application form
2. Nonrefundable filing fee in check or money order payable to *Register of Copyrights*
3. Deposit material
MAIL TO:
Library of Congress
Copyright Office
101 Independence Avenue, S.E.
Washington, D.C. 20559-6000

As of
July 1, 1999,
the filing fee
for Form SR
is $30.

9

*17 U.S.C. § 506(e): Any person who knowingly makes a false representation of a material fact in the application for copyright registration provided for by section 409, or in any written statement filed in connection with the application, shall be fined not more than $2,500.

June 1999—50,000
WEB REV: June 1999   ♻ PRINTED ON RECYCLED PAPER   ☆U.S. GOVERNMENT PRINTING OFFICE: 1999-454-879/48

✆ Form PA ✆

Detach and read these instructions before completing this form.
Make sure all applicable spaces have been filled in before you return this form.

━━━━━━━━━━━━━━ BASIC INFORMATION ━━━━━━━━━━━━━━

When to Use This Form: Use Form PA for registration of published or unpublished works of the performing arts. This class includes works prepared for the purpose of being "performed" directly before an audience or indirectly "by means of any device or process." Works of the performing arts include: (1) musical works, including any accompanying words; (2) dramatic works, including any accompanying music; (3) pantomimes and choreographic works; and (4) motion pictures and other audiovisual works.

Deposit to Accompany Application: An application for copyright registration must be accompanied by a deposit consisting of copies or phonorecords representing the entire work for which registration is made. The following are the general deposit requirements as set forth in the statute:
Unpublished Work: Deposit one complete copy (or phonorecord).
Published Work: Deposit two complete copies (or one phonorecord) of the best edition.
Work First Published Outside the United States: Deposit one complete copy (or phonorecord) of the first foreign edition.
Contribution to a Collective Work: Deposit one complete copy (or phonorecord) of the best edition of the collective work.
Motion Pictures: Deposit *both* of the following: (1) a separate written description of the contents of the motion picture; and (2) for a published work, one complete copy of the best edition of the motion picture; or, for an unpublished work, one complete copy of the motion picture or identifying material. Identifying material may be either an audiorecording of the entire soundtrack or one frame enlargement or similar visual print from each 10-minute segment.

The Copyright Notice: Before March 1, 1989, the use of copyright notice was mandatory on all published works, and any work first published before that date should have carried a notice. For works first published on and after March 1, 1989, use of the copyright notice is optional. For more information about copyright notice, see Circular 3, "Copyright Notice."

For Further Information: To speak to an information specialist, call (202) 707-3000 (TTY: (202) 707-6737). Recorded information is available 24 hours a day. Order forms and other publications from the address in space 9 or call the Forms and Publications Hotline at (202) 707-9100. Most circulars (but not forms) are available via fax. Call (202) 707-2600 from a touchtone phone. Access and download circulars, forms, and other information from the Copyright Office website at *www.copyright.gov.*

━━━━━━━━━━━━━━ LINE-BY-LINE INSTRUCTIONS ━━━━━━━━━━━━━━
Please type or print using black ink. The form is used to produce the certificate.

1 SPACE 1: Title

Title of This Work: Every work submitted for copyright registration must be given a title to identify that particular work. If the copies or phonorecords of the work bear a title (or an identifying phrase that could serve as a title), transcribe that wording *completely* and *exactly* on the application. Indexing of the registration and future identification of the work will depend on the information you give here. If the work you are registering is an entire "collective work" (such as a collection of plays or songs), give the overall title of the collection. If you are registering one or more individual contributions to a collective work, give the title of each contribution, followed by the title of the collection. For an unpublished collection, you may give the titles of the individual works after the collection title.

Previous or Alternative Titles: Complete this space if there are any additional titles for the work under which someone searching for the registration might be likely to look, or under which a document pertaining to the work might be recorded.

Nature of This Work: Briefly describe the general nature or character of the work being registered for copyright. Examples: "Music"; "Song Lyrics"; "Words and Music"; "Drama"; "Musical Play"; "Choreography"; "Pantomime"; "Motion Picture"; "Audiovisual Work."

2 SPACE 2: Author(s)

General Instructions: After reading these instructions, decide who are the "authors" of this work for copyright purposes. Then, unless the work is a "collective work," give the requested information about every "author" who contributed any appreciable amount of copyrightable matter to this version of the work. If you need further space, request additional Continuation Sheets. In the case of a collective work such as a songbook or a collection of plays, give information about the author of the collective work as a whole.

Name of Author: The fullest form of the author's name should be given. Unless the work was "made for hire," the individual who actually created the work is its "author." In the case of a work made for hire, the statute provides that "the employer or other person for whom the work was prepared is considered the author."

What is a "Work Made for Hire"? A "work made for hire" is defined as: (1) "a work prepared by an employee within the scope of his or her employment"; or (2) "a work specially ordered or commissioned for use as a contribution to a collective work, as a part of a motion picture or other audiovisual work, as a translation, as a

supplementary work, as a compilation, as an instructional text, as a test, as answer material for a test, or as an atlas, if the parties expressly agree in a written instrument signed by them that the work shall be considered a work made for hire." If you have checked "Yes" to indicate that the work was "made for hire," you must give the full legal name of the employer (or other person for whom the work was prepared). You may also include the name of the employee along with the name of the employer (for example: "Elster Music Co., employer for hire of John Ferguson").

"Anonymous" or "Pseudonymous" Work: An author's contribution to a work is "anonymous" if that author is not identified on the copies or phonorecords of the work. An author's contribution to a work is "pseudonymous" if that author is identified on the copies or phonorecords under a fictitious name. If the work is "anonymous" you may: (1) leave the line blank; or (2) state "anonymous" on the line; or (3) reveal the author's identity. If the work is "pseudonymous" you may: (1) leave the line blank; or (2) give the pseudonym and identify it as such (example: "Huntley Haverstock, pseudonym"); or (3) reveal the author's name, making clear which is the real name and which is the pseudonym (for example: "Judith Barton, whose pseudonym is Madeline Elster"). However, the citizenship or domicile of the author **must** be given in all cases.

Dates of Birth and Death: If the author is dead, the statute requires that the year of death be included in the application unless the work is anonymous or pseudonymous. The author's birth date is optional, but is useful as a form of identification. Leave this space blank if the author's contribution was a "work made for hire."

Author's Nationality or Domicile: Give the country of which the author is a citizen, or the country in which the author is domiciled. Nationality or domicile **must** be given in all cases.

Nature of Authorship: Give a brief general statement of the nature of this particular author's contribution to the work. Examples: "Words"; "Coauthor of Music"; "Words and Music"; "Arrangement"; "Coauthor of Book and Lyrics"; "Dramatization"; "Screen Play"; "Compilation and English Translation"; "Editorial Revisions."

3 SPACE 3: Creation and Publication

General Instructions: Do not confuse "creation" with "publication." Every application for copyright registration must state "the year in which creation of the work was completed." Give the date and nation of first publication only if the work has been published.

Creation: Under the statute, a work is "created" when it is fixed in a copy or phonorecord for the first time. Where a work has been prepared over a period of time, the part of the work existing in fixed form on a particular date constitutes the created work on that date. The date you give here should be the year in which the author completed the particular version for which registration is now being sought, even if other versions exist or if further changes or additions are planned.

Publication: The statute defines "publication" as "the distribution of copies or phonorecords of a work to the public by sale or other transfer of ownership, or by rental, lease, or lending"; a work is also "published" if there has been an "offering to distribute copies or phonorecords to a group of persons for purposes of further distribution, public performance, or public display." Give the full date (month, day, year) when, and the country where, publication first occurred. If first publication took place simultaneously in the United States and other countries, it is sufficient to state "U.S.A."

4 SPACE 4: Claimant(s)

Name(s) and Address(es) of Copyright Claimant(s): Give the name(s) and address(es) of the copyright claimant(s) in this work even if the claimant is the same as the author. Copyright in a work belongs initially to the author of the work (including, in the case of a work made for hire, the employer or other person for whom the work was prepared). The copyright claimant is either the author of the work or a person or organization to whom the copyright initially belonging to the author has been transferred.

Transfer: The statute provides that, if the copyright claimant is not the author, the application for registration must contain "a brief statement of how the claimant obtained ownership of the copyright." If any copyright claimant named in space 4 is not an author named in space 2, give a brief statement explaining how the claimant(s) obtained ownership of the copyright. Examples: "By written contract"; "Transfer of all rights by author"; "Assignment"; "By will." Do not attach transfer documents or other attachments or riders.

5 SPACE 5: Previous Registration

General Instructions: The questions in space 5 are intended to show whether an earlier registration has been made for this work and, if so, whether there is any basis for a new registration. As a general rule, only one basic copyright registration can be made for the same version of a particular work.

Same Version: If this version is substantially the same as the work covered by a previous registration, a second registration is not generally possible unless: (1) the work has been registered in unpublished form and a second registration is now being sought to cover its first published edition; or (2) someone other than the author is identified as copyright claimant in the earlier registration, and the author is now seeking registration in his or her own name. If either of these two exceptions applies, check the appropriate box and give the earlier registration number and date. Otherwise, do not submit Form PA; instead, write the Copyright

Office for information about supplementary registration or recordation of transfers of copyright ownership.

Changed Version: If the work has been changed and you are now seeking registration to cover the additions or revisions, check the last box in space 5, give the earlier registration number and date, and complete both parts of space 6 in accordance with the instructions below.

Previous Registration Number and Date: If more than one previous registration has been made for the work, give the number and date of the latest registration.

6 SPACE 6: Derivative Work or Compilation

General Instructions: Complete space 6 if this work is a "changed version," "compilation," or "derivative work," and if it incorporates one or more earlier works that have already been published or registered for copyright or that have fallen into the public domain. A "compilation" is defined as "a work formed by the collection and assembling of preexisting materials or of data that are selected, coordinated, or arranged in such a way that the resulting work as a whole constitutes an original work of authorship." A "derivative work" is "a work based on one or more preexisting works." Examples of derivative works include musical arrangements, dramatizations, translations, abridgments, condensations, motion picture versions, or "any other form in which a work may be recast, transformed, or adapted." Derivative works also include works "consisting of editorial revisions, annotations, or other modifications" if these changes, as a whole, represent an original work of authorship.

Preexisting Material (space 6a): Complete this space **and** space 6b for derivative works. In this space identify the preexisting work that has been recast, transformed, or adapted. For example, the preexisting material might be: "French version of Hugo's 'Le Roi s'amuse'." Do not complete this space for compilations.

Material Added to This Work (space 6b): Give a brief, general statement of the **additional** new material covered by the copyright claim for which registration is sought. In the case of a derivative work, identify this new material. Examples: "Arrangement for piano and orchestra"; "Dramatization for television"; "New film version"; "Revisions throughout; Act III completely new." If the work is a compilation, give a brief, general statement describing both the material that has been compiled **and** the compilation itself. Example: "Compilation of 19th Century Military Songs."

7, 8, 9 SPACE 7, 8, 9: Fee, Correspondence, Certification, Return Address

Deposit Account: If you maintain a Deposit Account in the Copyright Office, identify it in space 7a. Otherwise, leave the space blank and send the fee of $30 with your application and deposit.

Correspondence (space 7b): This space should contain the name, address, area code, telephone number, fax number, and email address (if available) of the person to be consulted if correspondence about this application becomes necessary.

Certification (space 8): The application cannot be accepted unless it bears the date and the **handwritten signature** of the author or other copyright claimant, or of the owner of exclusive right(s), or of the duly authorized agent of the author, claimant, or owner of exclusive right(s).

Address for Return of Certificate (space 9): The address box must be completed legibly since the certificate will be returned in a window envelope.

MORE INFORMATION

How to Register a Recorded Work: If the musical or dramatic work that you are registering has been recorded (as a tape, disk, or cassette), you may choose either copyright application Form PA (Performing Arts) or Form SR (Sound Recordings), depending on the purpose of the registration.

Form PA should be used to register the underlying musical composition or dramatic work. Form SR has been developed specifically to register a "sound recording" as defined by the Copyright Act—a work resulting from the "fixation of a series of sounds," separate and distinct from the underlying musical or dramatic work. Form SR should be used when the copyright claim is limited to the sound recording itself. (In one instance, Form SR may also be used to file for a copyright registration for both kinds of works—see (4) below.) Therefore:

(1) File **Form PA** if you are seeking to register the musical or dramatic work, not the "sound recording," even though what you deposit for copyright purposes may be in the form of a phonorecord.

(2) File **Form PA** if you are seeking to register the audio portion of an audiovisual work, such as a motion picture soundtrack; these are considered integral parts of the audiovisual work.

(3) File **Form SR** if you are seeking to register the "sound recording" itself, that is, the work that results from the fixation of a series of musical, spoken, or other sounds, but not the underlying musical or dramatic work.

(4) File **Form SR** if you are the copyright claimant for both the underlying musical or dramatic work and the sound recording, *and* you prefer to register both on the same form.

(5) File both forms **PA and SR** if the copyright claimant for the underlying work and sound recording differ, or you prefer to have separate registration for them.

"Copies" and "Phonorecords": To register for copyright, you are required to deposit "copies" or "phonorecords." These are defined as follows:

Musical compositions may be embodied (fixed) in "copies," objects from which a work can be read or visually perceived, directly or with the aid of a machine or device, such as manuscripts, books, sheet music, film, and videotape. They may also be fixed in "phonorecords," objects embodying fixations of sounds, such as tapes and phonograph disks, commonly known as phonograph records. For example, a song (the work to be registered) can be reproduced in sheet music ("copies") or phonograph records ("phonorecords"), or both.

Copyright Office fees are subject to change.
For current fees, check the Copyright Office
website at *www.copyright.gov*, write the Copyright Office, or call (202) 707-3000.

FORM PA

For a Work of the Performing Arts
UNITED STATES COPYRIGHT OFFICE

REGISTRATION NUMBER

_____

PA   PAU
EFFECTIVE DATE OF REGISTRATION

_____

Month   Day   Year

DO NOT WRITE ABOVE THIS LINE. IF YOU NEED MORE SPACE, USE A SEPARATE CONTINUATION SHEET.

1

TITLE OF THIS WORK ▼

PREVIOUS OR ALTERNATIVE TITLES ▼

NATURE OF THIS WORK ▼ See instructions

2 **a**

NAME OF AUTHOR ▼

DATES OF BIRTH AND DEATH
Year Born ▼   Year Died ▼

Was this contribution to the work a "work made for hire"?
☐ Yes
☐ No

AUTHOR'S NATIONALITY OR DOMICILE
Name of Country
OR { Citizen of _____
Domiciled in _____

WAS THIS AUTHOR'S CONTRIBUTION TO THE WORK
Anonymous? ☐ Yes ☐ No
Pseudonymous? ☐ Yes ☐ No
If the answer to either of these questions is "Yes," see detailed instructions.

NATURE OF AUTHORSHIP Briefly describe nature of material created by this author in which copyright is claimed. ▼

NOTE

Under the law, the "author" of a "work made for hire" is generally the employer, not the employee (see instructions). For any part of this work that was "made for hire" check "Yes" in the space provided, give the employer (or other person for whom the work was prepared) as "Author" of that part, and leave the space for dates of birth and death blank.

b

NAME OF AUTHOR ▼

DATES OF BIRTH AND DEATH
Year Born ▼   Year Died ▼

Was this contribution to the work a "work made for hire"?
☐ Yes
☐ No

AUTHOR'S NATIONALITY OR DOMICILE
Name of Country
OR { Citizen of _____
Domiciled in _____

WAS THIS AUTHOR'S CONTRIBUTION TO THE WORK
Anonymous? ☐ Yes ☐ No
Pseudonymous? ☐ Yes ☐ No
If the answer to either of these questions is "Yes," see detailed instructions.

NATURE OF AUTHORSHIP Briefly describe nature of material created by this author in which copyright is claimed. ▼

c

NAME OF AUTHOR ▼

DATES OF BIRTH AND DEATH
Year Born ▼   Year Died ▼

Was this contribution to the work a "work made for hire"?
☐ Yes
☐ No

AUTHOR'S NATIONALITY OR DOMICILE
Name of Country
OR { Citizen of _____
Domiciled in _____

WAS THIS AUTHOR'S CONTRIBUTION TO THE WORK
Anonymous? ☐ Yes ☐ No
Pseudonymous? ☐ Yes ☐ No
If the answer to either of these questions is "Yes," see detailed instructions.

NATURE OF AUTHORSHIP Briefly describe nature of material created by this author in which copyright is claimed. ▼

3 **a**

YEAR IN WHICH CREATION OF THIS WORK WAS COMPLETED This information must be given Year in all cases.

b DATE AND NATION OF FIRST PUBLICATION OF THIS PARTICULAR WORK
Complete this information ONLY if this work has been published.
Month _____ Day _____ Year _____
Nation _____

4

See instructions before completing this space.

COPYRIGHT CLAIMANT(S) Name and address must be given even if the claimant is the same as the author given in space 2. ▼

TRANSFER If the claimant(s) named here in space 4 is (are) different from the author(s) named in space 2, give a brief statement of how the claimant(s) obtained ownership of the copyright. ▼

DO NOT WRITE HERE
OFFICE USE ONLY

APPLICATION RECEIVED

ONE DEPOSIT RECEIVED

TWO DEPOSITS RECEIVED

FUNDS RECEIVED

MORE ON BACK ▶ • Complete all applicable spaces (numbers 5-9) on the reverse side of this page.
• See detailed instructions.   • Sign the form at line 8.

DO NOT WRITE HERE
Page 1 of _____ pages

EXAMINED BY	FORM PA
CHECKED BY	
☐ CORRESPONDENCE Yes	FOR COPYRIGHT OFFICE USE ONLY

DO NOT WRITE ABOVE THIS LINE. IF YOU NEED MORE SPACE, USE A SEPARATE CONTINUATION SHEET.

PREVIOUS REGISTRATION Has registration for this work, or for an earlier version of this work, already been made in the Copyright Office?

☐ **Yes** ☐ **No** If your answer is "Yes," why is another registration being sought? (Check appropriate box.) ▼ If your answer is No, do **not** check box A, B, or C.

a. ☐ This is the first published edition of a work previously registered in unpublished form.

b. ☐ This is the first application submitted by this author as copyright claimant.

c. ☐ This is a changed version of the work, as shown by space 6 on this application.

If your answer is "Yes," give: **Previous Registration Number** ▼   **Year of Registration** ▼

5

DERIVATIVE WORK OR COMPILATION Complete both space 6a and 6b for a derivative work; complete only 6b for a compilation.
Preexisting Material Identify any preexisting work or works that this work is based on or incorporates. ▼

a

6

See instructions before completing this space.

Material Added to This Work Give a brief, general statement of the material that has been added to this work and in which copyright is claimed. ▼

b

DEPOSIT ACCOUNT If the registration fee is to be charged to a Deposit Account established in the Copyright Office, give name and number of Account.
Name ▼   **Account Number** ▼

a

7

CORRESPONDENCE Give name and address to which correspondence about this application should be sent. Name / Address / Apt / City / State / ZIP ▼

b

Area code and daytime telephone number   (   )   Fax number   (   )

Email

CERTIFICATION* I, the undersigned, hereby certify that I am the

Check only one ▶
{
☐ author
☐ other copyright claimant
☐ owner of exclusive right(s)
☐ authorized agent of
}

Name of author or other copyright claimant, or owner of exclusive right(s) ▲

of the work identified in this application and that the statements made by me in this application are correct to the best of my knowledge.

8

Typed or printed name and date ▼ If this application gives a date of publication in space 3, do not sign and submit it before that date.

Date

Handwritten signature (X) ▼

☞   x

Certificate will be mailed in window envelope to this address:	Name ▼
	Number/Street/Apt ▼
	City/State/ZIP ▼

YOU MUST:
• Complete all necessary spaces
• Sign your application in space 8

SEND ALL 3 ELEMENTS IN THE SAME PACKAGE:
1. Application form
2. Nonrefundable filing fee in check or money order payable to *Register of Copyrights*
3. Deposit material

MAIL TO:
Library of Congress
Copyright Office
101 Independence Avenue, S.E.
Washington, D.C. 20559-6000

Fees are subject to change. For current fees, check the Copyright Office website at www.copyright.gov, write the Copyright Office, or call (202) 707-3000.

9

Rev: June 2002—20,000   Web Rev: June 2002   ♻ Printed on recycled paper   U.S. Government Printing Office: 2000-461-113/20,021

FCC Forms

FCC 302-DTV Application for Digital Television Broadcast License
FCC 303-S Application for Renewal of License for AM, FM, TV,
Translator or LPTV Station
FCC 323 Ownership Report for Commercial Broadcast Stations
FCC 396-A Broadcast Equal Employment Opportunity Model Program
Report
FCC 398 Children's Television Programming Report

Federal Communications Commission
Washington, D.C. 20554

Approved by OMB
3060-0837

APPLICATION FOR DIGITAL TELEVISION BROADCAST STATION LICENSE

GENERAL INSTRUCTIONS

A. This FCC Form is to be used to apply for a new or modified noncommercial educational or commercial digital television (DTV) broadcast station license. It **may be used**:

- To cover an authorized construction permit (or auxiliary antenna), provided that the facilities have been constructed in compliance with the provisions and conditions specified on the construction permit.

- To implement modifications to existing licenses as permitted by 47 C.F.R. Sections 73.1675(c) or 73.1690(c).

The form **may not be used**:

- To change location of the tower structure. Any such relocation requires the prior filing and approval of FCC Form 301 or 340, as appropriate. See 47 C.F.R. Section 73.1690(b)(2).

- To alter licensed directional radiation characteristics or to exceed the composite antenna pattern authorized in an underlying construction permit. Any such alteration requires the prior filing and approval of FCC Form 301, as appropriate. See 47 C.F.R. Section 73.1690(b)(3).

- To change the operating power or ERP from that specified in the station authorization, except as permitted by 47 C.F.R. Section 73.1690(c). Any other such change requires the prior filing and approval of FCC Form 301 or 340, as appropriate. See 47 C.F.R. Section 73.1690(b)(7).

- To increase the height of the antenna radiation center by more than two meters or decrease radiation center height by more than four meters from the value specified in the station's current construction permit or license. Any such modification requires the prior filing and approval of FCC Form 301 or 340, as appropriate. See 47 C.F.R. Section 73.1690(c).

The form consists of the following sections:

I.   General Information
II. Legal Qualifications

III. Preparer's Certification (for preparer of engineering sections of the application) and Engineering Data

B. This application form makes references to FCC rules. Applicants should have on hand and be familiar with current broadcast rules in Title 47 of the Code of Federal Regulations (C.F.R.):

(1) Part 0   "Commission Organization"
(2) Part 1   "Practice and Procedure"
(3) Part 73 "Radio Broadcast Services"

FCC Rules may be purchased from the Government Printing Office. Current prices may be obtained from the GPO Customer Service Desk at (202) 512-1803. For payment by credit card, call (202) 512-1800, M-F, 8 a.m. to 4 p.m. e.s.t; facsimile orders may be placed by dialing (202) 518-2233, 24 hours a day. Payment by check may be made to the Superintendent of Documents, Attn: New Orders, P.O. Box 371954, Pittsburgh, PA 15250-7954.

C. Electronic Filing of Application Forms. The Commission is currently developing electronic versions of various broadcast station application and reporting forms, such as this application form. As each application form and report goes online, the Commission will by Public Notice announce its availability and the procedures to be followed for accessing and filing the application form or report electronically via the Internet. For a six-month period following the issuance of the Public Notice, the subject application form or report can be filed with the Commission either electronically or in a paper format. Electronic filing will become mandatory, on a form-by-form basis, six months after each application form or report becomes available for filing electronically.

D. Applicants that prepare this application in paper form should file an original and two copies of this application and all exhibits. Applicants should follow the procedures set forth in Part 0 and Part 73 of the Commission's Rules. Amendments to previously filed applications should be prepared, signed and filed in the same manner as the original application, and should contain the following information to identify the associated application:

(1)   Applicant's name.
(2)   Service.
(3)   Call letters.

All previous editions obsolete.

FCC 302-DTV Instructions
September 2001

(4) Channel number.
(5) Community of license.
(6) File number of application being amended (if known).

(7) Date of filing of application being amended (if file number is not known).

E. A copy of the completed application and all related documents shall be made available for inspection by the public in the applicant's public inspection file pursuant to 47 C.F.R. Section 73.3526 for commercial stations and 47 C.F.R. Section 73.3527 for noncommercial educational stations.

F. Applicants should provide all information requested by this application. No section may be omitted. If any portions of the application are not applicable, the applicant should so state. **Defective or incomplete applications will be returned without consideration.** Inadvertently accepted applications are also subject to dismissal.

G. In accordance with 47 C.F.R. Section 1.65, applicants have a continuing obligation to advise the Commission, through amendments, of any substantial and material changes in the information furnished in this application. This requirement continues until the FCC action on this application is no longer subject to reconsideration by the Commission or review by any court.

H. This application requires applicants to certify compliance with many statutory and regulatory requirements. Detailed instructions provide additional information regarding Commission rules and policies. These materials are designed to track the standards and criteria which the Commission applies to determine compliance and to increase the reliability of applicant certifications. They are not intended to be a substitute for familiarity with the Communications Act and the Commission's regulations, policies, and precedent. While applicants are required to review all application instructions, they are not required to complete or retain any documentation created or collected to complete the application.

I. This application is presented primarily in a "Yes/No" certification format. However, it contains appropriate places for submitting explanations and exhibits where necessary or appropriate. Each certification constitutes a material representation. Applicants may only mark the "Yes" certification when they are certain that the response is correct. A "No" response is required if the applicant is requesting a waiver of a pertinent rule and/or policy, or where the applicant is uncertain that the application fully satisfies the pertinent rule and/or policy. Thus, a "No" response to any of the certification items **will not** cause the immediate dismissal of the application

provided that an appropriate exhibit is submitted.

J. **The applicant, and the applicant's authorized engineering representative, if any, must sign the application.** Depending on the nature of the applicant, the application should be signed as follows: if a sole proprietorship, personally; if a partnership, by a general partner; if a corporation, by an officer; for an unincorporated association, by a member who is an officer; if a governmental entity, by such duly elected or appointed official as is competent under the laws of the particular jurisdiction. Counsel may sign the application for his or her client, but only in cases of the applicant's disability or absence from the United States. If the application is filed electronically, the signature will consist of the electronic equivalent of the typed name of the individual. See Report and Order in MM Docket No. 98-43, 13 FCC Rcd 23056, 23064 (1998).

INSTRUCTIONS FOR SECTION I: GENERAL INFORMATION

A. **Item 1: Applicant Name.** The legal name of the applicant must be stated exactly in Item 1. If the applicant is a corporation, the applicant should list the exact corporate name; if a partnership, the name under which the partnership does business; if an unincorporated association, the name of an executive officer, his/her office, and the name of the association; and, if an individual applicant, the person's full legal name.

Applicants should use only those state abbreviations approved by the U.S. Postal Service.

Facility ID Number. Radio and TV Facility ID Numbers can be obtained at the FCC's Internet Website at www.fcc.gov/mmb. Once at this website, scroll down and select CDBS Public Access. You can also obtain your facility number by calling: Radio (202) 418-2700; TV (202) 418-1600. Further, the Facility ID Number is now included on all Radio and TV authorizations and postcards.

B. **Item 2: Contact Representative.** If the applicant is represented by a third party (for example, legal counsel), that person's name, firm or company, mailing address and telephone/ electronic mail address may be specified in Item 2.

C. **Item 3: Fees.** The Commission is statutorily required to collect charges for certain regulatory services to the public. Generally, applicants seeking a license to cover the facility authorized by, and constructed pursuant to, an outstanding permit are required to pay and submit a fee with the filing of FCC 302-DTV. However, governmental entities, which include any possession, state, city, county, town, village, municipal corporation

2

or similar political organization or subpart thereof controlled by publicly elected and/or duly appointed public officials exercising sovereign direction and control over their respective communities or programs, are exempt from the payment of this fee. Also exempted from this fee are licensees and permittees of noncommercial educational broadcast stations seeking a license to cover authorized facilities. See 47 C.F.R. Section 1.1114.

When filing a fee-exempt application, an applicant must complete Item 3 and provide an explanation as appropriate. Applications **NOT** subject to a fee may be hand-delivered or mailed to the FCC at its Washington, D.C. offices. See 47 C.F.R. Section 0.401(a). Fee-exempt applications should not be sent to the Mellon Bank Lockbox; so doing will result in a delay in processing the application.

The Commission's fee collection program utilizes a U.S. Treasury lockbox bank for maximum efficiency of collection and processing. Prior to the institution of electronic filing procedures, all FCC Form 302-DTV applications requiring the remittance of a fee, or for which a waiver or deferral from the fee requirement is requested, must be submitted to the appropriate post office box address. See 47 C.F.R. Section 0.401(b). A listing of the required fee and the address to which FCC Form 302-DTV should be mailed or otherwise delivered are also set forth in the "Mass Media Services Fee Filing Guide." This document can be obtained either by writing to the Commission's Form Distribution Center, 9300 E. Hampton Drive, Capital Heights, Maryland 20743, or by calling 1-800-418-FORM and leaving a request on the answering machine provided for this purpose. See also 47 C.F.R. Section 1.1104. The Fee Filing Guide also contains a list of the Fee Type Codes needed to complete this application.

Payment of any required fee must be made by check, bank draft, money order, or credit card. If payment is made by check, bank draft, or money order, the remittance must be denominated in U.S. dollars, drawn upon a U.S. institution, and made payable to the Federal Communications Commission. No postdated, altered, or third-party checks will be accepted. **DO NOT SEND CASH.** Additionally, checks dated six months or older will not be accepted.

FCC Form 159 must be submitted with any application subject to a fee received at the Commission.

Procedures for payment of application fees when applications are filed electronically will be announced by subsequent Public Notice. See General Instruction C above. Payment of application fees may also be made by Electronic Payment **prior to** the institution of electronic

filing, provided that prior approval has been obtained from the Commission. Applicants interested in this option must first contact the Credit and Debt Management Center at (202) 418-1995 to make the necessary arrangements.

Applicants hand-delivering FCC Forms 302-DTV may receive dated receipt copies by presenting copies of the applications to the acceptance clerk at the time of delivery. For mailed-in applications, a "return copy" of the application should be furnished and clearly marked as a "return copy." The applicant should attach this copy to a stamped, self-addressed envelope. Only one piece of paper per application will be stamped for receipt purposes.

For further information regarding the applicability of a fee, the amount of the fee, or the payment of the fee, applicants should consult the "Mass Media Services Fee Filing Guide."

D.   **Item 4: Facility Information**. This question asks the applicant to specify: (1) whether commercial or noncommercial educational operation is proposed; (2) whether the license covers the main or auxiliary transmitter; and (3) the community to which the station will be licensed.

E.   **Item 5: Program Test Authority**. The permittee of an DTV station with a nondirectional antenna may commence program testing upon completion of construction and notification to the Video Services Division of the Commission's Mass Media Bureau, **provided** that: (1) an FCC Form 302-DTV is filed within 10 days of the commencement of program tests; and (2) the permit does not contain any special operating conditions that prohibit automatic program test authority. Accordingly, this question asks whether the applicant is operating pursuant to automatic program test authority or requesting program test authority.

F.   **Item 6: Purpose of Application**. This question asks whether the FCC Form 302-DTV is being filed to cover an outstanding construction permit or to modify an authorized license without first obtaining a construction permit pursuant to the Report and Order in MM Docket No. 96-58, 12 FCC Rcd 12371 (1997). It also requires that the applicant identify the permit covered or license being modified.

INSTRUCTIONS FOR SECTION II: LEGAL INFORMATION

A.   **Item 1: Certification**. Each applicant is responsible for the information that the application instructions convey. As a key element in the Commission's streamlined licensing process, a certification that these materials have been reviewed and that each question response is based on the applicant's review is required.

B. **Item 2: Permit Conditions**. This question requires the applicant to certify that all terms, conditions, and obligations set forth in the underlying construction permit have been fully met. Each applicant should review its underlying construction permit carefully prior to making its certification to confirm that the facility was constructed exactly in accordance with the permit. If any such term, condition, or obligation has not been fulfilled, the applicant should respond "No" to Section II, Item 2 and provide an appropriate explanatory exhibit. See 47 C.F.R. Section 73.1690.

C. **Item 3: Changed Circumstances**. This question requires the applicant to certify that all information provided in the underlying construction permit application remains correct. If any circumstance has arisen which would cause any statement or representation contained in the construction permit application to be incorrect, the applicant should respond "No" to Section II, Item 3 and provide an appropriate explanatory exhibit.

D. **Items 4 and 5: Character Issues/Adverse Findings**. Item 4 requires the applicant to certify that neither it nor any party to the application has had any interest in or connection with an application that was or is the subject of unresolved character issues. An applicant must disclose in response to Item 5 whether the applicant or any party to the application has been the subject of a final adverse finding with respect to certain relevant non-broadcast matters. The Commission's character policies and litigation reporting requirements for broadcast applicants focus on misconduct which violates the Communications Act or a Commission rule or policy and on certain specified non-FCC misconduct. In responding to Items 4 and 5, applicants should review the Commission's character qualifications policies, which are fully set forth in Character Qualifications, 102 FCC 2d 1179 (1985), reconsideration denied, 1 FCC Rcd 421 (1986), as modified, 5 FCC Rcd 3252 (1990) and 7 FCC Rcd 6564 (1992).

NOTE: As used in this question, the term "party to the application" includes any individual or entity whose ownership or positional interest in the applicant is attributable. An attributable interest is an ownership interest in or relation to an applicant or licensee which will confer on its holder that degree of influence or control over the applicant or licensee sufficient to implicate the Commission's multiple ownership rules. In responding to Items 4 and 5, applicants should review the Commission's multiple ownership attribution policies and standards which are set forth in the Notes to 47 C.F.R. Section 73.3555, as revised and explained in

Review of the Commission's Regulations Governing Attribution of Broadcast and Cable/MDS Interests, 14 FCC Rcd 12559 (1999), reconsideration granted in part, 16 FCC Rcd 1097 (2000). See also Report and Order in MM Docket No. 83-46, 97 FCC 2d 997 (1984), reconsideration granted in part, 58 RR 2d 604 (1985), further modified on reconsideration, 61 RR 2d 739 (1986).

Where the response to Item 4 is "No," the applicant must submit an exhibit that includes an identification of the party having had the interest, the call letters and location of the station or file number of the application or docket, and a description of the nature of the interest or connection, including relevant dates. The applicant should also fully explain why the unresolved character issue is not an impediment to a grant of this application.

In responding to Item 5, the applicant should consider any relevant adverse finding that occurred within the past ten years. Where that adverse finding was fully disclosed to the Commission in an application filed on behalf of this station or in another broadcast station application and the Commission, by specific ruling or by subsequent grant of the application, found the adverse finding not to be disqualifying, it need not be reported again and the applicant may respond "Yes" to this item. However, an adverse finding that has not been reported to the Commission and considered in connection with a prior application would require a "No" response.

Where the response to Item 5 is "No," the applicant must provide in an exhibit a full disclosure of the persons and matters involved, including an identification of the court or administrative body and the proceeding (by dates and file numbers), and the disposition of the litigation. Where the requisite information has been earlier disclosed in connection with another pending application, or as required by 47 U.S.C. Section 1.65(c), the applicant need only provide an identification of that previous submission by reference to the file number in the case of an application, the call letters of the station regarding which the application or Section 1.65 information was filed, and the date of filing. The applicant should also fully explain why the adverse finding is not an impediment to a grant of this application.

E. **Item 6: Anti-Drug Abuse Act Certification**. This question requires the applicant to certify that neither it nor any party to the application is subject to denial of federal benefits pursuant to the Anti-Drug Abuse Act of 1988, 21 U.S.C. Section 862.

Section 5301 of the Anti-Drug Abuse Act of 1988 provides federal and state court judges the discretion to deny federal benefits to individuals convicted of offenses consisting of the distribution or possession of controlled substances. Federal benefits within the scope of the statute include FCC authorizations. A "Yes" response to Item 9 constitutes a certification that neither the applicant nor any party to this application has been convicted of such an offense or, if it has, it is not ineligible to receive the authorization sought by this application because of Section 5301.

NOTE: With respect to this question, the term "party to the application" includes if the applicant is an individual, that individual; if the applicant is a corporation or unincorporated association, all officers, directors, or persons holding 5 percent or more of the outstanding stock or shares (voting and/or non-voting) of the applicant; all members if a membership association; and if the applicant is a partnership, all general partners and all limited partners,

including both insulated and non-insulated limited partners, holding a 5 percent or more interest in the partnership.

INSTRUCTIONS FOR SECTION III: ENGINEERING DATA AND PREPARER'S CERTIFICATION

A. **Notification Requirements**. All applicants must comply with the requirements of Section 73.1030. Specifically, applicants must notify United States Government radio astronomy installations, radio receiving installations, and FCC monitoring stations of the proposed facility and its possible impact on their operations. The Commission need not be informed of the date of such notification.

B. **Tech Box:** The applicant must specify the information requested in Items 1 through 3 of the Tech Box. The data should accurately reflect the specifications set forth in the underlying construction permit.

C   **Item 4: Main Studio Location.** The applicant must certify that its main studio location complies with the requirements of Section 73.1125. In order to answer "Yes" to this question, the applicant's proposed main studio must be **either** (1) within the principal community contour of **any AM FM or TV station** licensed to that community; **or** (2) less than 25 miles from the reference coordinates of the center of its community of license. A community's reference coordinates are generally the coordinates listed in the United States Department of the Interior publication entitled Index to the National Atlas of the United States. An alternative reference point, if none is listed in the Atlas, is the coordinates of the community's main Post Office.

In order to qualify as a "main studio," the proposed location must be equipped with type-accepted equipment and capable of originating programming at any time. Additionally, the studio must be staffed by **at least** one management-level employee **and** one staff-level employee at all times during regular business hours. See Jones, Eastern of the Outer Banks, Inc., 6 FCC Rcd 3615 (1991), clarified, 7 FCC Rcd 6800 (1992), aff'd 10 FCC Rcd 3759 (1995). Additionally, each AM, FM, and TV broadcast station must at all times maintain a toll-free telephone line from its community of license to its main studio, wherever located.

D   **Item 5: Constructed Facility.** The applicant must certify that the facility was constructed as authorized in the underlying construction permit. If there are any differences between the facilities constructed compared with those authorized in the construction permit, the applicant may need to seek approval for the change on FCC Form 301 or 340. See Section 73.3572.

E. **Item 6: Special Operating Conditions:** The special operating conditions are located on the final pages of the construction permit. Attach exhibits, if required, to document compliance with the special operating conditions.

NOTE: Special operating conditions may prohibit automatic program test authority.

F. **Item 7. Transmitter.** A permittee or licensee installing as a main transmitter one that is not included on the FCC's "Radio Equipment List, Equipment Acceptable for Licensing," must have first obtained authority to use such a transmitter through the filing and grant of FCC Form 301 or 340.

Applications filed pursuant to Sections 73.1675(c) or 73.1690(c). Items 8-11 set forth a series of certifications concerning applications filed pursuant to Sections 73.1675(c) or 73.1690(c). All appropriate exhibits must be submitted as required. Applicants should refer to the appropriate rule sections, as referenced in the Form. See Report and Order in MM Docket No. 96-58, 12 FCC Rcd 12371 (1997).

G. **Item 8: Changing transmitter power output.** Applicants proposing to replace an omnidirectional antenna with another omnidirectional antenna or change transmitter output power as a result of modifying the transmission line system must check "Yes" for Item 8.

NOTE: If the applicant is proposing to replace an omnidirectional antenna with another omnidirectional antenna, the new antenna must be mounted not more than two meters above nor four meters below the

Appendix 2 **399**

authorized values. See 47 C.F.R. Section 73.1690(c)(1). If the applicant is proposing to change transmitter output power by replacing its transmission line, the station's effective radiated power must not change. See 47 C.F.R. Section73.1690(c)(10). If the proposal meets these requirements, program test operations may commence at full power pursuant to Section 73.1620(a)(1)

Item 9: Replacing a directional antenna. Item 9 is to be answered by applicants replacing a directional antenna with another directional antenna. See 47 C.F.R Section 73.1690(c)(3).

Item 9a requires the applicant to certify and provide an exhibit demonstrating that: (1) the proposed theoretical antenna pattern will not exceed the licensed directional pattern at any azimuth and no change in effective radiated power will result; and (2) the requested modification of license complies with 47 C.F.R. Section 73.685(f).

NOTE: The new antenna must be mounted not more than two meters above nor four meters below the authorized values.

Item 10: Use a formerly licensed main facility as an auxiliary facility. Items 10a – 10b set forth a series of certifications for applicants proposing the use of a formerly licensed main facility as an auxiliary facility. All such applicants must complete both Items 10a and 10b.

Item 10a. This question requires the applicant to certify and submit an exhibit showing that the proposed auxiliary facilities will not extend beyond the Grade B coverage area of the main antenna after the change in ERP has been effectuated. See 47 C.F.R. Section 73.1675(a).

Item 10b. **Environmental Protection Act**. License modifications authorized by the Report and Order in MM Docket No. 96-58 will necessitate an analysis under the Commission's environmental rules for the first time, as they are authorized without the prior approval of an FCC Form 301 or Form 340.

The National Environmental Policy Act of 1969 requires all federal agencies to ensure that the human environment is given consideration in all agency decision-making. Since January 1, 1986, applications for new broadcast stations, modifications of existing stations, and license renewals must contain either an environmental assessment that will serve as the basis for further Commission review and action, or an indication that operation of the station will not have a significant environmental impact. See Section 1.1307(b). in this

regard, applicants are required to look at eight environmental factors. These factors are relatively self-explanatory, except for the evaluation of whether the station adequately protects the public and workers from potentially harmful radiofrequency (RF) electromagnetic fields.

New RF Exposure Requirements. In 1996, the Commission adopted new guidelines and procedures for evaluating environmental effects of RF emissions. All applications subject to environmental processing filed on or after October 15, 1997 must demonstrate compliance with the new requirements. These new guideline incorporate two tiers of exposure limits:

General population/uncontrolled exposure limits apply to situations in which the general public may be exposed or in which persons who are exposed as a consequence of their employment may not be made fully aware of the potential for exposure or cannot exercise control over their exposure. Members of the general public are always considered under this category when exposure is not employment-related.

Occupational/controlled exposure limits apply to human exposure to RF fields when persons are exposed as a consequence of their employment and in which those persons who are exposed have been made fully aware of the potential for exposure and can exercise control over their exposure. These limits also apply where exposure is of a transient nature as a result of incidental passage through a location where exposure levels may be above the general populations/uncontrolled limits as long as the exposed person has been made fully aware of the potential for exposure and can exercise control over his or her exposure by leaving the area or some other appropriate means.

The new guidelines are explained in more detail in OET Bulletin 65, entitled Evaluating Compliance with FCC Guidelines for Human Exposure to Radiofrequency Electromagnetic Fields, Edition 97-01, released August, 1997, and Supplement A: Additional Information for Radio and Television Broadcast Stations (referred to here as "OET Bulletin 65" and "Supplement A," respectively). Both OET Bulletin 65 and Supplement A can be viewed and/or downloaded from the FCC Internet site at http://www.fcc.gov/oet/rfsafety. Copies can also be purchased from the Commission's duplicating/research contractor, International Transcription Services, Inc., 1231 20th Street, N.W., Washington, D.C. 20036 (telephone: (202) 857-3800; fax: (202) 857-3805. Additional information may be obtained from the RF Safety Group at rfsafety@fcc.gov or (202) 418-2464 or from the FCC Call Center at 1-888-CALL FCC (225-5322).

6

Should the applicant be unable to conclude that its proposal will have no significant impact on the quality of the human environment, it must submit an Environmental Assessment containing the following information:

1. A description of the facilities as well as supporting structures and appurtenances, and a description of the site as well as the surrounding area and uses. If high-intensity white lighting is proposed or utilized within a residential area, the EA must also address the impact of this lighting upon the residents.

2. A statement as to the zoning classification of the site, and communications with, or proceedings before and determinations (if any) by zoning, planning, environmental and other local, state, or federal authorities on matters relating to environmental effects.

3. A statement as to whether construction of the facilities has been a source of controversy on environmental grounds in the local community.

4. A discussion of environmental and other considerations that led to the selection of the particular site and, if relevant, the particular facility; the nature and extent of any unavoidable adverse environmental effects; and any alternative sites or facilities that have been or reasonably might be considered.

5. If relevant, a statement why the site cannot meet the FCC guidelines for RF exposure with respect to the public and workers.

NOTE: Even if the applicant concludes that human RF electromagnetic exposure is consistent with the Commission's guidelines, each site user must also meet requirements with respect to "on-tower" or other exposure by workers at the site (including RF exposure on one tower caused by sources on another tower or towers). These requirements include, but are not limited to, the reduction or cessation of transmitter power when persons have access to the site, tower, or antenna. Such procedures must be coordinated among all tower users. See OET Bulletin 65 for details.

Item 11: Change the license status. Applicants may change their license status from commercial to noncommercial or from noncommercial to commercial. However, if changing from commercial to noncommercial educational status, the applicant must submit as an exhibit a completed Section II of FCC Form 340, establishing its qualifications to operate the subject facility as a noncommercial educational station. See 47 C.F.R. Section 73.1690(c)(9).

H. **Preparer's Certification.** When someone other than the applicant has prepared the engineering section of FCC Form 302-DTV, Section III requires that person to certify, to the best of his/her knowledge and belief, the veracity of the technical data supplied. The Section III preparer's certification in FCC Form 302-DTV need not be completed if the engineering portion of the application has been prepared by the applicant. In that event, the applicant's certification in Section II of FCC Form 302-DTV will encompass both the legal and engineering sections of the application.

FCC NOTICE TO INDIVIDUALS REQUIRED BY THE PRIVACY ACT AND THE PAPERWORK REDUCTION ACT

The FCC is authorized under the Communications Act of 1934, as amended, to collect the personal information we request in this form. We will use the information provided in the application to determine whether approving this application is in the public interest. If we believe there may be a violation or potential violation of a FCC statute, regulation, rule or order, your application may be referred to the Federal, state or local agency responsible for investigating, prosecuting, enforcing or implementing the statute, rule, regulation or order. In certain cases, the information in your application may be disclosed to the Department of Justice or a court or adjudicative body when (a) the FCC or (b) any employee of the FCC; or (c) the United States Government is a party to a proceeding before the body or has an interest in the proceeding. In addition, all information provided in this form will be available for public inspection.

If you owe a past due debt to the federal government, any information you provide may also be disclosed to the Department of Treasury Financial Management Service, other federal agencies and/or your employer to offset your salary, IRS tax refund or other payments to collect that debt. The FCC may also provide this information to these agencies through the matching of computer records when authorized.

If you do not provide the information requested on this form, the application may be returned without action having been taken upon it or its processing may be delayed while a request is made to provide the missing information. Your response is required to obtain the requested authorization.

We have estimated that each response to this collection of information will take 1 hour and 30 minutes. Our estimate includes the time to read the instructions, look through existing records, gather and maintain the required data, and actually complete and review the form or response. If you have any comments on this estimate, or on how we can improve the collection and reduce the burden it causes you, please write the Federal Communications Commission, AMD-PERM, Paperwork Reduction Project (3060-0837), Washington, DC 20554. We will also accept your comments via the Internet if you send them to jboley@fcc.gov. Please DO NOT SEND COMPLETED APPLICATIONS TO THIS ADDRESS. Remember - you are not required to respond to a collection of information sponsored by the Federal government, and the government may not conduct or sponsor this collection, unless it displays a currently valid OMB control number of if we fail to provide you with this notice. This collection has been assigned an OMB control number of 3060-0837.

THE FOREGOING NOTICE IS REQUIRED BY THE PRIVACY ACT OF 1974, P.L. 93-579, DECEMBER 31, 1974, 5 U.S.C. 552a(e)(3), AND THE PAPERWORK REDUCTION ACT OF 1995, P.L. 104-13, OCTOBER 1, 1995, 44 U.S.C. Section 3507.

Federal Communications Commission
Washington, D. C. 20554

Approved by OMB
3060-0837

FOR
FCC
USE
ONLY

FCC 302-DTV

APPLICATION FOR DIGITAL TELEVISION BROADCAST STATION LICENSE

FOR COMMISSION USE ONLY

FILE NO.

Section I - General Information

1.	Legal Name of the Licensee/Permittee		
	Mailing Address		
	City	State or Country (if foreign address)	ZIP Code
	Telephone Number (include area code)	E-Mail Address (if available)	
	Call Sign	Facility Identifier	

2.	Contact Representative (if other than licensee/permittee)	Firm or Company Name	
	Mailing Address		
	City	State or Country (if foreign address)	ZIP Code
	Telephone Number (include area code)	E-Mail Address (if available)	

3. If this application has been submitted without a fee, indicate reason for fee exemption (see 47 C.F.R. Section 1.1114):

☐ Governmental Entity   ☐ Noncommercial Educational Licensee   ☐ Other _____

4. Facility Information:

   a. ☐ Commercial   ☐ Noncommercial

   b. ☐ Main   ☐ Auxiliary

   c. Community of License: | City | State |

5. **Program Test Authority:**

   ☐ Requesting program test authority.

   ☐ Station operating pursuant to automatic program test authority (47 C.F.R. Section

All previous editions obsolete.

FCC 302-DTV
September 2001

6.   **Purpose of Application:**

     ☐   Cover construction permit (list original construction permit file number -- starts with the prefix BPCDT, BPEDT, BMPCDT or BPMEDT):   ———————

     ☐   Modify an authorized license (list license file number -- starts with the prefix BLCDT, BLEDT, BMLCDT or BMLEDT):   ———————

     ☐   Amend a pending application

        If an amendment, **submit as an Exhibit** a listing by Section and Question Number the portions of the pending application that are being revised.

Exhibit No.

NOTE: **In addition to the information called for in this section, an explanatory exhibit providing full particulars must be submitted for each question for which a "No" response is provided.**

Section II - Legal

1. **Certification.** Licensee/Permittee certifies that it has answered each question in this application based on its review of the application instructions and worksheets. Licensee/Permittee further certifies that where it has made an affirmative certification below, this certification constitutes its representation that the application satisfies each of the pertinent standards and criteria set forth in the application instructions and worksheets.   ☐ Yes ☐ No

2. Licensee/Permittee certifies that all terms, conditions, and obligations set forth in the underlying construction permit have been fully met.   ☐ Yes ☐ No | See Explanation in Exhibit No. |

3. Licensee/Permittee certifies that, apart from changes already reported, no cause or circumstance has arisen since the grant of the underlying construction permit which would result in any statement or representation contained in the construction permit application to be now incorrect.   ☐ Yes ☐ No | See Explanation in Exhibit No. |

4. **Character Issues.** Licensee/Permittee certifies that neither licensee/permittee nor any party to the application has or has had any interest in, or connection with: ☐ Yes ☐ No | See Explanation in Exhibit No. |
   a. any broadcast application in any proceeding where character issues were left unresolved or were resolved adversely against the applicant or party to the application; or
   b. any pending broadcast application in which character issues have been raised.

5. **Adverse Findings.** Licensee/Permittee certifies that, with respect to the licensee/permittee and any party to the application, no adverse finding has been made, nor has an adverse final action been taken by any court or administrative body in a civil or criminal proceeding brought under the provisions of any law related to the following: any felony; mass media-related antitrust or unfair competition; fraudulent statements to another governmental unit; or discrimination.   ☐ Yes ☐ No | See Explanation in Exhibit No. |

6. **Anti-Drug Abuse Act Certification.** Licensee/Permittee certifies that neither licensee/permittee nor any party to the application is subject to denial of federal benefits pursuant to Section 5301 of the Anti-Drug Abuse Act of 1988, 21 U.S.C. Section 862.   ☐ Yes ☐ No

I certify that the statements in this application are true, complete, and correct to the best of my knowledge and belief, and are made in good faith. I acknowledge that all certifications and attached Exhibits are considered material representations. I hereby waive any claim to the use of any particular frequency as against the regulatory power of the United States because of the previous use of the same, whether by license or otherwise, and request an authorization in accordance with this application. (See Section 304 of the Communications Act of 1934, as amended.)

Typed or Printed Name of Person Signing	Typed or Printed Title of Person Signing
Signature	Date

Section III - Engineering

TECHNICAL SPECIFICATIONS
Ensure that the specifications below are accurate. Contradicting data found elsewhere in this application will be disregarded. All items must be completed. The response "on file" is not acceptable.

TECH BOX

1. Channel _____

2. Operating Constants

Transmitter power output (average power at input to transmission line, after any filter attached to the transmitter, if used)		Transmission line power loss	
kW	dBk		dB

Antenna Input power	Maximum antenna power gain	Effective radiated power (average power)	
dBk	dB	kW	dBk

3. Antenna Data

Manufacturer	Model

NOTE: In addition to the information called for in the Certification Checklist, an explanatory exhibit providing full particulars must be submitted for each question for which a "No" response is provided.

CERTIFICATION

4. **Main Studio Location.** The main studio location complies with 47 C.F.R. Section 73.1125.   ☐ Yes ☐ No [See Explanation in Exhibit No.]

5. **Constructed Facility.** The facility was constructed as authorized in the underlying construction permit or complies with 47 C.F.R. Section 73.1690.   ☐ Yes ☐ No [See Explanation in Exhibit No.]

6. **Special Operating Conditions.** The facility was constructed in compliance with all special operating conditions, terms, and obligations described in the construction permit.   ☐ Yes ☐ No [See Explanation in Exhibit No.]

[Exhibit No.]

An exhibit may be required. Review the underlying construction permit.

7. **Transmitter.** The transmitter complies with 47 C.F.R. Section 73.1660.   ☐ Yes ☐ No [See Explanation in Exhibit No.]

PREPARER'S CERTIFICATION ON PAGE 6 MUST BE COMPLETED AND SIGNED.

APPLICATION FILED PURSUANT TO 47 C.F.R. SECTIONS 73.1675(c) or 73.1690(c).
Only applicants filing this application pursuant to 47 C.F.R. Sections 73.1675(c) or 73.1690(c) must complete the following

8. **Changing transmitter power output.** Is this application being filed to authorize a change in transmitter power output caused by the replacement of an omnidirectional antenna with another omnidirectional antenna or an alteration of the transmission line system? See 47 C.F.R. Sections 73.1690(c)(1) and (c)(10). ☐ Yes ☐ No

9. **Replacing a directional antenna.** Is this application being filed pursuant to 47 C.F.R. Section 73.1690(c)(3) to replace a directional antenna with another directional antenna? ☐ Yes ☐ No

    If "Yes" to the above, the applicant certifies the following:

    a. **Pattern of Directional Antenna.** The proposed theoretical antenna pattern complies with 47 C.F.R. Section 73.1690(c)(3). **Exhibit is required.** ☐ Yes ☐ No   See Explanation in Exhibit No. ___   Exhibit No. ___

10. **Use a formerly licensed main facility as an auxiliary facility.** Is this application being filed pursuant to 47 C.F.R. Section 73.1675(c)(1) to request authorization to use a formerly licensed main facility as an auxiliary facility and/or change the ERP of the proposed auxiliary facility? ☐ Yes ☐ No

    If "Yes" to the above, the applicant certifies the following:

    a. **Auxiliary antenna service area.** The proposed auxiliary facility complies with 47 C.F.R. Section 73.1675(a). **Exhibit is required.** ☐ Yes ☐ No   See Explanation in Exhibit No. ___

    b. **Environmental Protection Act.** The proposed facility is excluded from environmental processing under 47 C.F.R. Section 1.1306 (*i.e.,* the facility will not have a significant environmental impact and complies with the maximum permissible radiofrequency electromagnetic exposure limits for controlled and uncontrolled environments). ☐ Yes ☐ No   See Explanation in Exhibit No. ___

        By checking "Yes" above, the applicant also certifies that it, in coordination with other users of the site, will reduce power or cease operation as necessary to protect persons having access to the site, tower or antenna from radiofrequency electromagnetic exposure in excess of FCC guidelines.

11. **Change the license status.** Is this application being filed pursuant to 47 C.F.R. Section 73.1690(c)(9) to change the license status from commercial to noncommercial or from noncommercial to commercial? ☐ Yes ☐ No   Exhibit No. ___

    If "Yes" to the above, submit an exhibit providing full particulars. For applications changing license status from commercial to noncommercial, include Section II of FCC Form 340 as an exhibit to this application.

PREPARER'S CERTIFICATION ON PAGE 6 MUST BE COMPLETED AND SIGNED.

SECTION III PREPARER'S CERTIFICATION

I certify that I have prepared Section III (Engineering Data) on behalf of the applicant, and that after such preparation, I have examined and found it to be accurate and true to the best of my knowledge and belief.

Name	Relationship to Applicant (e.g., Consulting Engineer)	
Signature	Date	
Mailing Address		
City	State or Country (if foreign address)	ZIP Code
Telephone Number (include area code)	E-Mail Address (if available)	

WILLFUL FALSE STATEMENTS ON THIS FORM ARE PUNISHABLE BY FINE AND/OR IMPRISONMENT (U.S. CODE, TITLE 18, SECTION 1001), AND/OR REVOCATION OF ANY STATION LICENSE OR CONSTRUCTION PERMIT (U.S. CODE, TITLE 47, SECTION 312(a)(1)), AND/OR FORFEITURE (U.S. CODE, TITLE 47, SECTION 503).

Federal Communications Commission
Washington, D. C. 20554

FCC 303-S

Approved by OMB
3060-0110

| FOR
| FCC
| USE
| ONLY

**APPLICATION FOR
RENEWAL OF LICENSE
FOR AM, FM, TV,
TRANSLATOR OR
LPTV STATION**

FOR COMMISSION USE ONLY
FILE NO.

AM, FM and TV APPLICANTS MUST COMPLETE AND SUBMIT SECTIONS I, II, III AND V ONLY.

FM TRANSLATOR, TV TRANSLATOR and LPTV APPLICANTS MUST COMPLETE AND SUBMIT SECTIONS I, II, IV AND V ONLY.

IF APPLICATION IS FOR RENEWAL OF LICENSES FOR BOTH A PRIMARY STATION and A CO-OWNED TRANSLATOR WHICH REBROADCASTS THE PRIMARY STATION'S SIGNAL, APPLICANT MUST COMPLETE AND SUBMIT SECTIONS I, II, III, IV AND V.

SECTION I (FEE INFORMATION) - TO BE COMPLETED BY ALL APPLICANTS

1. PAYOR NAME (Last, First, Middle Initial)

MAILING ADDRESS (Line 1) (Maximum 35 characters)

MAILING ADDRESS (Line 2) (Maximum 35 characters)

CITY	STATE OR COUNTRY (if foreign address)	ZIP CODE
TELEPHONE NUMBER (include area code)	CALL LETTERS	OTHER FCC IDENTIFIER (IF APPLICABLE)

2. A. Is a fee submitted with this application? ☐ Yes ☐ No

  B. If No, indicate reason for fee exemption (see 47 C.F.R. Section 1.1114):

  ☐ Governmental Entity   ☐ Noncommercial educational licensee   ☐ Other (Please explain):

  C. If Yes, provide the following information:

Enter in Column (A) the correct Fee Type Code for the service you are applying for. Fee Type Codes may be found in the "Mass Media Services Fee Filing Guide." Column (B) lists the Fee Multiple applicable for this application. Enter in Column (C) the result obtained from multiplying the value of the Fee Type Code in Column (A) by the number listed in Column (B).

| | (A)
FEE TYPE
CODE | (B)
FEE MULTIPLE
(if required) | (C)
FEE DUE FOR FEE
TYPE CODE IN
COLUMN (A) | FOR FCC USE ONLY |
| --- | --- | --- | --- | --- |
| (1) | | | $ | |

To be used only when you are requesting concurrent actions which result in a requirement to list more than one Fee Type Code.

	(A)	(B)	(C)	FOR FCC USE ONLY
(2)			$	

| ADD ALL AMOUNTS SHOWN IN COLUMN C, LINES (1) AND (2), AND ENTER THE TOTAL HERE. THIS AMOUNT SHOULD EQUAL YOUR ENCLOSED REMITTANCE. | TOTAL AMOUNT REMITTED WITH THIS APPLICATION
$ | FOR FCC USE ONLY |
| --- | --- | --- |

June 1995/June 1997 edition usable with TV supplements.

CLEAR ALL PAGES

FCC 303-S
October 1997

SECTION II - TO BE COMPLETED BY ALL APPLICANTS

1. NAME OF LICENSEE OF AM, FM OR TV STATION	NAME OF LICENSEE OF FM OR TV TRANSLATOR OR LOW POWER TV STATION
MAILING ADDRESS	

CITY	STATE	ZIP CODE

2. This application is for: ☐ Commercial ☐ Noncommercial

                (a) ☐ AM ☐ FM ☐ TV

Call Letters	Community of License	
	City	State

                (b) ☐ FM Translator ☐ TV Translator ☐ Low Power TV

Call Letters	Area Licensed to Serve	
	City	State

Call Letters	Area Licensed to Serve	
	City	State

3. Attach as an Exhibit an identification of any FM booster or TV booster station for which renewal of license is also requested.

    Exhibit No.

4. Is the applicant in compliance with the provisions of Section 310 of the Communications Act of 1934, as amended, relating to interests of aliens and foreign governments?

    ☐ Yes ☐ No

    If No, attach as an Exhibit an explanation.

    Exhibit No.

5. Since the filing of the applicant's last renewal application or any other application for the subject station(s), has an adverse finding been made or final action been taken by any court or administrative body with respect to the applicant or parties to the application in a civil or criminal proceeding, brought under the provisions of any law relating to the following: any felony; mass media related antitrust or unfair competition; fraudulent statements to another governmental unit; or discrimination?

    ☐ Yes ☐ No

    If the answer is Yes, attach as an Exhibit a full disclosure concerning the persons and matters involved, including an identification of the court or administrative body and the proceeding (by dates and file numbers), and the disposition of the litigation. Where the requisite information has been earlier disclosed in connection with another application or as required by 47 U.S.C. Section 1.65(c), the applicant need only provide: (i) an identification of that previous submission by reference to the file number in the case of an application, the call letters of the station regarding which the application or Section 1.65 information was filed, and the date of filing; and (ii) the disposition of the previously reported matter.

    Exhibit No.

6. Would a Commission grant of this application come within 47 C.F.R. Section 1.1307, such that it may have a significant environmental impact, including exposure of workers or the general public to levels of RF electromagnetic fields exceeding identified health and safety guidelines adopted by the FCC?

    ☐ Yes ☐ No

    NOTE: Licensees of FM translator stations operating with an effective radiated power (ERP) of 100 watts or less are excluded from the RF exposure requirements in 47 C.F.R. Section 1.1307. All other requirements of the rule must be met.

    If Yes, attach as an Exhibit an Environmental Assessment, as required by 47 C.F.R. Section 1.1311.

    Exhibit No.

    If No, explain briefly why not.

    ☐ **Explanation attached**

CLEAR ALL PAGES

SECTION III: TO BE COMPLETED BY COMMERCIAL AND NONCOMMERCIAL AM, FM and TV APPLICANTS ONLY

1. Have the following reports been filed with the Commission:

    (a) The Broadcast Station Annual Employment Reports (FCC Form 395-B), as required by 47 C.F.R. Section 73.3612?   ☐ Yes ☐ No

    > Exhibit No.

    If No, attach as an Exhibit an explanation.

    (b) The applicant's Ownership Report (FCC Form 323 or 323-E), as required by 47 C.F.R. Section 73.3615?   ☐ Yes ☐ No

    If No, give the following information:

    > Date last ownership report was filed: _____

    > Call letters of station for which it was filed: _____

2. Has the applicant placed in its public inspection file at the appropriate times the documentation required by 47 C.F.R. Section 73.3526 and 73.3527?   ☐ Yes ☐ No

    > Exhibit No.

    If No, attach as an Exhibit a complete statement of explanation.

3. **FOR COMMERCIAL AM, FM AND TV APPLICANTS ONLY:**

    Is the station currently on the air?   ☐ Yes ☐ No

    If No, attach as an Exhibit a statement of explanation, including the steps the applicant intends to take to restore service to the public.

    > Exhibit No.

4. **FOR COMMERCIAL AND NONCOMMERCIAL TV APPLICANTS**

    > Exhibit No.

    Attach as an Exhibit a summary of written comments and suggestions received from the public, if any, that comment on the station's programming and characterize that programming as constituting violent programming.

5. **FOR COMMERCIAL TV APPLICANTS ONLY:**

    (a) For the period of time covered by this report, has the applicant complied with the limits on commercial matter as set forth in 47 C.F.R. Section 73.670? (The limits are no more than 12 minutes of commercial matter per hour on weekdays, and no more than 10.5 minutes of commercial matter per hour during children's programming on weekends. The limits also apply pro rata to children's programs which are 5 minutes or more and which are not part of a longer block of children's programming.)   ☐ Yes ☐ No

    > Exhibit No.

    (b) If No, submit as an Exhibit a list of each segment of programming 5 minutes or more in duration designed for children 12 years old and under and broadcast during the license period which contained commercial matter in excess of the limits. For each programming segment so listed, indicate the length of the segment, the amount of commercial matter contained therein, and an explanation of why the limits were exceeded.

> **CLEAR ALL PAGES**

FOR COMMERCIAL TV APPLICANTS ONLY

6. For the license period prior to September 1, 1997, attach as an Exhibit a summary of the applicant's programming response, nonbroadcast efforts and support for other stations' programming directed to the educational and informational needs of children 16 years old and under, and reflecting the most significant programming related to such needs which the licensee has aired, as described in 47 C.F.R. Section 73.3526(a)(8)(iii).

Exhibit No.

7. For the period from September 1, 1997, to the filing of the applicant's license renewal application, state the average number of hours of **Core Programming** per week broadcasts by the station. See 47 C.F.R. Section 73.671(c).

Does the licensee identify each **Core Program** at the beginning of the airing of each program as required by 47 C.F.R. Section 73.673? ☐ Yes ☐ No

Does the licensee provide information identifying each **Core Program** aired on its station, including an indication of the target child audience, to publishers of program guides as required by 47 C.F.R. Section 73.673? ☐ Yes ☐ No

8. Complete the following for each **Core Program** that you aired on or after September 1, 1997, that meets the definition of **Core Programming**, including **each** composite element of such programming. Complete chart below for each **Core Program**. (Use supplemental page for additional programs.)

Title of Program:			Origination		
			Local	Network	Syndicated
Days/Times Program Regularly Scheduled:	Total times aired	Number of Preemptions	If preempted and rescheduled, list date and time aired.		
			Dates	Times	
Length of Program: (minutes)					
Age of Target Child Audience: from _____ years to _____ years.					
Describe the educational and informational objective of the program and how it meets the definition of Core Programming.					

CLEAR ALL PAGES

9. Complete the following for each **Non-Core Educational and Informational Programs** that you aired on or after September 1, 1997, that is specifically designed to meet the educational and informational needs of children 16 and under, but does not meet one or more of the composite elements of the definition of **Core Programming.** See 47 C.F.R. Section 73.671. Complete chart below for each additional such educational and informational program. (Use supplemental page for additional programs.)

Title of Program:	Origination		
	Local	Network	Syndicated

Dates/Times Program Aired:	Total times aired	Number of Preemptions	If preempted and rescheduled, list date and time aired.	
			Dates	Times
Length of Program: (minutes)				
Age of Target Child Audience (if applicable): from __ years to __ years.				

Describe the program.

	Yes	No
Does the program have educating and informing children ages 16 and under as a significant purpose?	☐	☐
If Yes, does the licensee identify each program at the beginning of its airing consistent with 47 C.F.R. Section 73.673?	☐	☐
If Yes, does the licensee provide information regarding the program, including an indication of the target child audience, to publishers of program guides consistent with 47 C.F.R. Section 73.673?	☐	☐

10. List **Core Programs**, if any, aired by other stations that are sponsored by the licensee and that meet the criteria set forth in 47 C.F.R. Section 73.671. Also indicate whether the amount of total **Core Programming** broadcast by another station increased.

Name of Program	Call Letters of Station Airing Sponsored Program	Channel Number of Station Airing Sponsored Program	Did total programming increase?
			☐ Yes ☐ No
			☐ Yes ☐ No
			☐ Yes ☐ No

For each **Core Program** sponsored by the licensee, complete the chart below.

Title of Program:	Origination		
	Local	Network	Syndicated

Days/Times Program Regularly Scheduled:	Total times aired	Number of Preemptions	If preempted and rescheduled, list date and time aired.	
			Dates	Times
Length of Program: (minutes)				
Target Child Audience: from ____ years to ____ years.				

Describe the educational and informational objective of the program and how it meets the definition of **Core Programming.**

CLEAR ALL PAGES

11. Does the licensee publicize the existence and location of the station's Children's Television Programming Reports (FCC 398) as required by 47 C.F.R. Section 73.3526(a)(8)(iii)?   ☐ Yes ☐ No

If No, attach as an Exhibit a statement of explanation, including the specific steps the applicant intends to implement to ensure compliance in the future. | Exhibit No. |

12. Include as an Exhibit any other comments or information you want the Commission to consider in evaluating your compliance with the Children's Television Act. This may include information on any other non-core educational and informational programming that you aired or plan to air, or any existing or proposed non-broadcast efforts that will enhance the educational and informational value of such programming to children. See 47 C.F.R. Section 73.671, NOTE 2. | Exhibit No. |

NOTE: Where applicable, applicants in responding to Questions 3, 4 and 5 may submit or incorporate by reference any previously filed FCC Form 398s setting forth the information sought to be elicited in this supplement to FCC Form 303-S.

WILLFUL FALSE STATEMENTS MADE ON THIS FORM ARE PUNISHABLE BY FINE AND/OR IMPRISONMENT (U.S. CODE, TITLE 18, SECTION 1001), AND/OR REVOCATION OF ANY STATION LICENSE OR CONSTRUCTION PERMIT (U.S. CODE, TITLE 47, SECTION 312(a)(1)), AND/OR FORFEITURE (U.S. CODE, TITLE 47, SECTION 503).

I certify that the statements in this application are true, complete, and correct to the best of my knowledge and belief, and are made in good faith.

Name of Licensee	Signature
Date	

CLEAR ALL PAGES

Core Programming Supplemental Page

Title of Program:			Origination		
			Local	Network	Syndicated

Days/Times Program Regularly Scheduled:	Total times aired	Number of Preemptions	If preempted and rescheduled, list date and time aired.	
			Dates	Times
Length of Program: (minutes)				
Age of Target Child Audience: from _____ years to _____ years.				

Describe the educational and informational objective of the program and how it meets the definition of Core Programming.

Title of Program:			Origination		
			Local	Network	Syndicated

Days/Times Program Regularly Scheduled:	Total times aired	Number of Preemptions	If preempted and rescheduled, list date and time aired.	
			Dates	Times
Length of Program: (minutes)				
Age of Target Child Audience: from _____ years to _____ years.				

Describe the educational and informational objective of the program and how it meets the definition of Core Programming.

Title of Program:			Origination		
			Local	Network	Syndicated

Days/Times Program Regularly Scheduled:	Total times aired	Number of Preemptions	If preempted and rescheduled, list date and time aired.	
			Dates	Times
Length of Program: (minutes)				
Age of Target Child Audience: from _____ years to _____ years.				

Describe the educational and informational objective of the program and how it meets the definition of Core Programming.

FCC 303-S (Page 7)
October 1997

CLEAR ALL PAGES

Non-Core Programming Supplemental Page

Title of Program:		Origination		
		Local	Network	Syndicated

Dates/Times Program Aired:	Total times aired	Number of Preemptions	If preempted and rescheduled, list date and time aired.	
			Dates	Times

Length of Program: _____ (minutes)

Age of Target Child Audience (if applicable): from __ years to __ years.

Describe the program.

Does the program have educating and informing children ages 16 and under as a significant purpose?	☐ Yes ☐ No
If Yes, does the licensee identify each program at the beginning of its airing consistent with 47 C.F.R. Section 73.673?	☐ Yes ☐ No
If Yes, does the licensee provide information regarding the program, including an indication of the target child audience, to publishers of program guides consistent with 47 C.F.R. Section 73.673?	☐ Yes ☐ No

Title of Program:		Origination		
		Local	Network	Syndicated

Dates/Times Program Aired:	Total times aired	Number of Preemptions	If preempted and rescheduled, list date and time aired.	
			Dates	Times

Length of Program: _____ (minutes)

Age of Target Child Audience (if applicable): from __ years to __ years.

Describe the program.

Does the program have educating and informing children ages 16 and under as a significant purpose?	☐ Yes ☐ No
If Yes, does the licensee identify each program at the beginning of its airing consistent with 47 C.F.R. Section 73.673?	☐ Yes ☐ No
If Yes, does the licensee provide information regarding the program, including an indication of the target child audience, to publishers of program guides consistent with 47 C.F.R. Section 73.673?	☐ Yes ☐ No

CLEAR ALL PAGES

FCC 303-S (Page 8)
October 1997

SECTION IV : TO BE COMPLETED BY FM TRANSLATOR, TV TRANSLATOR and LPTV APPLICANTS ONLY

1. Is the applicant's station currently operating and rebroadcasting the signal of an FM, TV or LPTV station?

☐ Yes ☐ No

   If Yes, identify the station being rebroadcast:

Call Sign	Channel No.	City of License/Area Served

   If No, attach as an Exhibit a statement of explanation, including the steps the applicant intends to take to resume operations.

   Exhibit No.

2. Is the station being rebroadcast licensed to either the applicant or a commonly controlled entity?

☐ Yes ☐ No

   If No, has the required retransmission consent been obtained?

☐ Yes ☐ No

   If No, attach as an Exhibit an explanation.

   Exhibit No.

3. Is the station being rebroadcast the same station as previously notified?

☐ Yes ☐ No

   If No, attach as an Exhibit an explanation, including an identification of the station that was previously rebroadcast.

   Exhibit No.

4. **FOR LOW POWER TV APPLICANTS ONLY:**

   Have the Broadcast Station Annual Employment Reports (FCC Form 395-B) been filed with the Commission as required by 47 C.F.R. Section 73.3612?

☐ Yes ☐ No

   Exhibit No.

   If No, attach as an Exhibit an explanation.

5. **FOR FM TRANSLATOR APPLICANTS ONLY:**

   (a) Is the applicant in compliance with 47 C.F.R. Section 74.1232(d) which prohibits the common ownership of a commercial primary station and an FM translator station whose coverage contour extends beyond the protected contour of the commercial primary station being rebroadcast? This restriction also applies to any person or entity having any interest in, or any connection with, the primary FM station.

☐ Yes ☐ No

   If No, attach as an Exhibit an explanation.

   Exhibit No.

   (b) Is the applicant in compliance with 47 C.F.R. Section 74.1232(e) which prohibits an FM translator station whose coverage contour extends beyond the protected contour of the commercial primary station being rebroadcast from receiving any support (except for specified technical assistance), before, during or after construction, directly or indirectly, from the primary station or any person or entity having any interest in, or any connection with, the primary station?

☐ Yes ☐ No

   If No, attach as an Exhibit an explanation.

   Exhibit No.

FCC303-S (Page 9)
October 1997

CLEAR ALL PAGES

SECTION V: TO BE COMPLETED BY ALL APPLICANTS

FOR AM, FM OR TV APPLICANTS ONLY: Applicant has attached Sections I, II, III, and V only.   ☐ Yes ☐ No

FOR FM TRANSLATOR, TV TRANSLATOR OR LPTV APPLICANTS ONLY: Applicant has attached Sections I, II, IV and V only.   ☐ Yes ☐ No

FOR CO-OWNED TRANSLATOR AND PRIMARY STATION APPLICANTS ONLY: Applicant has attached Sections I, II, III, IV and V.   ☐ Yes ☐ No

The APPLICANT hereby waives any claim to the use of any particular frequency or of the electromagnetic spectrum as against the regulatory power of the United States because of the previous use of the same, whether by license or otherwise, and requests an authorization in accordance with this application. (See Section 304 of the Communications Act of 1934, as amended.)

The APPLICANT acknowledges that all the statements made in this application and attached exhibits are considered material representations and that all the exhibits are a material part hereof and are incorporated herein as set out in full in the application.

CERTIFICATION

1. By checking Yes, the applicant certifies, that, in the case of an individual applicant, he or she is not subject to a denial of federal benefits that includes FCC benefits pursuant to Section 5301 of the Anti-Drug Abuse Act of 1988, 21 U.S.C. Section 862, or, in the case of a non-individual applicant (e.g., corporation, partnership or other unincorporated association), no party to the application is subject to a denial of federal benefits that includes FCC benefits pursuant to that section. For the definition of a "party" for these purposes, see 47 C.F.R. Section 1.2002(b).   ☐ Yes ☐ No

2. I certify that the statements in this application are true, complete, and correct to the best of my knowledge and belief, and are made in good faith.

Name	Signature
Title	Date

WILLFUL FALSE STATEMENTS MADE ON THIS FORM ARE PUNISHABLE BY FINE AND/OR IMPRISONMENT (U.S. CODE, TITLE 18, SECTION 1001), AND/OR REVOCATION OF ANY STATION LICENSE OR CONSTRUCTION PERMIT (U.S. CODE, TITLE 47, SECTION 312(a)(1)), AND/OR FORFEITURE (U.S. CODE, TITLE 47, SECTION 503))

CLEAR ALL PAGES

FCC 303-S (Page 10)
October 1997

Federal Communications Commission
Washington, D. C. 20554

Approved by OMB
3060-0010

FCC 323
INSTRUCTIONS FOR OWNERSHIP REPORT

GENERAL INSTRUCTIONS - Section I

1. This report is to be filed by commercial AM, FM and Television broadcast stations and by International broadcast stations as indicated below (see 47 C.F.R. Section 73.3615).

    (a) By licensee at two-year intervals on the anniversary date of the station's renewal application filing date. Where the licensee, however, is a partnership that is composed entirely of natural persons, the biennial reporting requirement does not apply. Similarly, sole proprietorships (i.e., where the station is licensed to an individual(s)) are not required to file biennially.

    If information submitted is equally applicable to each listed station, one biennial report may be filed for all such stations; otherwise, a separate report shall be filed for each station on the appropriate filing date.

    If there has been no change since the filing of the last biennial report, a certification may be filed in lieu of a new report, stating that the previously filed report has been examined and is currently accurate.

    (b) By permittee or licensee following the consummation, pursuant to Commission consent, of a transfer of control or an assignment.

    (c) By permittee within 30 days after the grant of a construction permit for a new commercial radio or television broadcast station. The permittee is also required to update its initial report or to certify the continuing accuracy and completeness of that report when the permittee applies for a station license for that new station.

2. **Electronic Filing of Application Forms.** The Commission is currently developing electronic versions of various broadcast station application and reporting forms, such as this report form. As each application form and report goes online, the Commission will by Public Notice announce its availability and the procedures to be followed for accessing and filing the application form or report electronically via the Internet. For a six-month period following the issuance of the Public Notice, the subject application form or report can be filed with the Commission either electronically or in a paper format. Electronic filing will become mandatory, on a form-by-form basis, six months after each application form or report becomes available for filing electronically.

3. File one copy of this report with the Federal Communications Commission. Form 323's not involving the payment of a fee can be hand-delivered or mailed to the FCC's Washington, D.C. offices. See 47 C.F.R. Section 0.401(a). For "biennial" ownership reports that must be submitted with a fee, see 47 C.F.R. Section 0.401(b) and Fee Instructions below.

4. This form is not to be used to report or request a transfer of control or assignment of license or construction permit (except to report a transfer of control or assignment made pursuant to prior Commission consent). The appropriate forms for use in connection with such transfers or assignments are FCC Forms 314, 315 and 316. See 47 C.F.R. Sections 73.3540 and 73.3541. It is the responsibility of the licensee or permittee to determine whether a given transaction constitutes a transfer of control or an assignment. However, for purposes of example only, and for the convenience of interested persons, there are listed below some of the more common types of transfers.

A transfer of control takes place when:

    (a) An individual stockholder gains or loses affirmative or negative (50%) control. (Affirmative control consists of control of more than 50% of voting stock; negative control consists of control of exactly 50% of voting stock.)

    (b) Any family group or any individual in a family group gains or loses affirmative or negative (50%) control. (See also Instruction 6, Section II.)

    (c) Any group in privity gains or loses affirmative or negative (50%) control.

The following are examples of transfers of control or assignments requiring prior Commission consent:

    (a) A, who owns 51% of the licensee's or permittee's stock, sells 1% or more thereof. A transfer has been effected.

    (b) X corporation, wholly owned by Y family, retires outstanding stock which results in family member A's individual holdings being increased to 50% or more. A transfer has been effected.

    (c) A and B, husband and wife, each owns 50% of the licensee's or permittee's stock. A sells any of his stock to B. A transfer has been effected.

    (d) A is the partner in the licensee. A sells any part of his

All previous editions obsolete.

FCC 323 Instructions
September 2000

interest to newcomer B or existing partner C. An assignment has been effected.

(e) X partnership incorporates. An assignment has been effected.

(f) Minority stockholders form a voting trust to vote their 50% or more combined stockholdings. A transfer has been effected.

(g) A, B, C, D, and E each own 20% of the stock of X corporation. A, B, and C sell their stock to F, G, and H at different times. A transfer is effected at such time as 50% or more of the stock passes out of the hands of the stockholders who held stock at the time the original authorization for the licensee or permittee corporation was issued.

5. **Names/Addresses.** The name of the licensee or permittee should be stated exactly as it appears on the station's existing license or construction permit. The current street address or post office box used by the licensee or permittee for receipt of Commission correspondence should be set forth.

Any change in the name of the licensee or permittee, which does not involve a change in ownership requiring prior Commission approval, can be communicated to the Commission by letter. To report any changes in the mailing address previously used by the licensee or permittee, FCC Form 5072, entitled "Change in Official Mailing Address for Broadcast Station", should be promptly transmitted to the Commission. See 47 C.F.R. Section 1.5.

Facility ID Number. Radio and TV Facility ID Numbers can be obtained at the FCC's Internet Website at www.fcc.gov/mmb/asd/seacall.html or by calling: Radio - (202)-418-2730; TV - (202)-418-1600. Further, the Facility ID Number is now included on all Radio and TV authorizations and postcards.

6. If the licensee or permittee is directly or indirectly controlled by another entity or if another entity has an attributable interest in such licensee or permittee, a separate Form 323 should be submitted for such entity. For successive entities, interests are multiplied. See Ownership Instructions, 3.

7. **FEES.** By law, the Commission is required to collect charges for certain of the regulatory services it provides to the public. A fee is required to be paid and submitted with the filing of a license's "biennial" ownership report **only**. The "biennial" ownership report is the Form 323, or the aggregate Form 323's as the case may be when the licensee is directly or indirectly controlled by another entity or if another entity has an attributable interest in the licensee, that is submitted on behalf of the individual AM, FM, or TV

broadcast station. Further, where there has been no change in information since the last filing of a station's "biennial" ownership report, a certification may be filed on behalf of the station in lieu of a new report, stating that the previously filed "biennial" ownership report has been examined and is currently accurate and complete. Such certification constitutes the station's "biennial" ownership report for that year and the required fee must also be submitted with the certification. The "biennial" ownership report (whether on Form 323 or as a certification) is filed on an individual station basis and the required fee is calculated thereon. It is the number of stations for which a report is filed that determines the total fee due; not the number of Form 323's filed in connection therewith.

When filing a fee-exempt FCC Form 323, the licensee/permittee must complete Question 4 and provide an explanation as appropriate.

FCC Form 323's NOT involving the payment of a fee must be hand-delivered or mailed to the FCC's Washington, D.C. offices. See 47 C.F.R. Section 0.401(a). Do not send fee-exempt applications to Mellon Bank because it will result in a delay in processing the report.

FCC Form 159 must be submitted with any application or report subject to a fee received at the Commission. Licensees or permittees who wish to pay for more than one filing in the same lockbox with a single payment can do so by submitting FCC Form 159. When paying for multiple filings in the same lockbox with a single payment instrument, you must list each filing as a separate item on FCC Form 159 (Remittance Advice). If additional entries are necessary, please use FCC Form 159C (Continuation Sheet).

The Commission's fee collection program utilizes a U.S. Treasury lockbox bank for maximum efficiency of collection and processing. All "biennial" ownership reports, which require the remittance of a fee, must be submitted to the appropriate post office box address. See 47 C.F.R. Section 0.401(b). A listing of the required fee, a copy of a Remittance Advice Form (FCC Form 159) and the addresses to which the "biennial" ownership report should be mailed or otherwise delivered is also set forth in the Mass Media Services Fee Filing Guide," which is obtainable either by writing to the Commission's Form Distribution Center, 9300 E. Hampton Drive, Capital Heights, Maryland 20743, or by calling Telephone No. 1-800-418-FORM and leaving your request on the answering machine provided for this purpose. See also 47 C.F.R. Section 1.1104.

Payment of any required fee must be made by check, bank draft, money order or credit card. If paying by check, bank draft or money order, your remittance must be denominated in U.S. dollars, and drawn upon a U.S. financial institution and made payable to the Federal Communications Commission. No postdated, altered or third-party checks will be accepted. DO NOT SEND CASH. Checks dated six months or older will not be acceptable for filing.

Procedures for payment of fees when applications and reporting forms are filed electronically will be announced by subsequent public notice. See General Instructions, 2. Payment of fees may also be made by Electronic Payment prior to the institution of electronic filing procedures, provided prior approval has been obtained from the Commission. Licensees interested in this option must first contact the Credit and Debt Management Center at (202) 418-1995 to make the necessary arrangements.

Parties hand-delivering "biennial" ownership reports may receive dated receipt copies by presenting copies to the acceptance clerk at the time of delivery. For mailed-in "biennial" ownership reports, a "return copy" of the report can be furnished provided the licensee clearly identifies the "return copy" and attaches to it a stamped, self-addressed envelope. Only one piece of paper per report will be stamped for receipt purposes. The "return copy" should be placed on top of the reporting form package. Failure to do so may result in your copy not being returned.

For further information regarding fees and payment procedures licensees should consult the "Mass Media Services Fee Filing Guide." Also see the Commission's Public Notice of June 6, 1990, entitled "Broadcast Annual Ownership Reports (Fee Requirements)", 67 RR 2d 1227.

OWNERSHIP INSTRUCTIONS - SECTION II

1. As used in Question 6, the term "respondent" refers either to the licensee or permittee or to an entity controlling or holding an "attributable" interest in the licensee or permittee, as defined in Instruction 3 below.

2. Any contract or modification of contract relating to the ownership, control, or management of the licensee or permittee or to its stock must be filed with the Commission, as required by 47 C.F.R. Section 73.3613. Attention is directed to the fact that Section 73.3613 requires the filing of all contracts of the types specified and is not limited to executed contracts, but includes options, pledges, and other executory agreements and contracts relating to ownership, control, or management.

3. As used in Question 9, an "attributable" interest is an ownership interest in or relationship to a licensee or permittee which will confer on its holder that degree of influence or control over the licensee or permittee sufficient to implicate the Commission's multiple ownership rules. In responding to Question 9, licensees/permittees should review the Commission's multiple ownership attribution policies and standards which are set forth in the Notes to 47

C.F.R. Section 73.3555, as revised and explained in Review of the Commission's Regulations Governing Attribution of Broadcast and Cable/MDS Interests, FCC 99-207, released August 6, 1999. See also Report and Order in MM Docket No. 83-46, 97 FCC 2d 997 (1984), reconsideration granted in part, 58 RR 2d 604 (1985), further modified on reconsideration, 61 RR 2d 739 (1986).

The following interests are attributable and the holder of such interest and should be reported in response to Question 9(a):

If a Corporation: Each officer, director and owner of stock accounting for 5% or more of the issued and outstanding voting stock of the respondent is considered the holder of an attributable interest. Where the 5% stock owner is itself a corporation, each of its stockholders, directors and "executive" officers (president, vice-president, secretary, treasurer or their equivalents) is considered a holder of an attributable interest, **UNLESS** the respondent submits as an exhibit a statement establishing that an individual director or officer will not exercise authority or influence in areas that will affect the corporate respondent or the station. In this statement, the respondent should identify the individual by name and title, describe the individual's duties and responsibilities, and explain the manner in which such individual is insulated from the corporate applicant and should not be attributed an interest.

A person or entity holding an ownership interest in the corporate stockholder of the corporate respondent is considered a party to this application ONLY IF that interest, when multiplied by the corporate stockholder's interest in the respondent, would account for 5% or more of the issued and outstanding voting stock of the applicant. For example, where Corporation X owns stock accounting for 25% of the applicant's votes, only Corporation X shareholders holding 20 percent or more of the issued and outstanding voting stock of Corporation X have a 5% or more indirect interest in the respondent (.25 x .20 = .05) and, therefore, are considered holders of attributable interests. In applying the multiplier, any entity holding more than 50% of its subsidiary will be considered a 100% owner. Where the 5% stock owner is a partnership, each general partner and any limited partner that is not insulated, regardless of the partnership interest, is considered a party to the application.

Stock subject to stockholder cooperative voting agreements accounting for 5% or more of the votes in a corporate respondent will be treated as if held by a single entity and any stockholder holding 5% or more of the stock in that block is considered a holder of an attributable interest.

If a single entity holds more than 50% of the voting stock, and a simple majority is all that is required to control corporate affairs, no other stockholder need be reported, unless that entity's interest is attributable under the Commission's Equity/Debt Plus attribution standard described below.

An investment company, insurance company or trust department of a bank is not considered a holder of an attributable interest, and a respondent may properly certify that such entity's interest is non-attributable in response to Question 9(b), **IF** its aggregated holding accounts for less than 20% of the outstanding votes in the applicant **AND IF** such entity exercises no influence or control over the corporation, directly or indirectly; and such entity has no representatives among the officers and directors of the corporation.

If a PARTNERSHIP: Each partner, including all limited partners. However, a limited partner in a limited partnership is **not** considered a holder of an attributable interest **IF** the limited partner is not materially involved, directly or indirectly, in the management or operation of the media-related activities of the partnership and the respondent so certifies in response to Question 9(b). Sufficient insulation of a limited partner for purposes of this certification would be assured if the limited partnership arrangement:

(1) specifies that any exempt limited partner (if not a natural person, its directors, officers, partners, etc.) cannot act as an employee of the limited partnership if his or her functions, directly or indirectly, relate to the media enterprises of the company;

(2) bars any exempt limited partner from serving, in any material capacity, as an independent contractor or agent with respect to the partnership's media enterprises;

(3) restricts any exempted limited partner from communicating with the licensee or the general partner on matters pertaining to the day-to-day operations of its business;

(4) empowers the general partner to veto any admissions of additional general partners admitted by vote of the exempt limited partners;

(5) prohibits any exempt limited partner from voting on the removal of a general partner or limits this right to situations where the general partner is subject to bankruptcy proceedings, as described in Sections 402 (4)-(5) of the Revised Uniform Limited Partnership Act, is adjudicated incompetent by a court of competent jurisdiction, or is removed for cause, as determined by an independent party;

(6) bars any exempt limited partner from performing any services to the limited partnership materially relating to its media activities, with the exception of making loans

to, or acting as a surety for, the business; and

(7) states, in express terms, that any exempt limited partner is prohibited from becoming actively involved in the management or operation of the media businesses of the partnership.

Notwithstanding conformance of the partnership agreement to these criteria, however, the requisite certification **cannot** be made **IF** the limited partner's interest is attributable under the Commission's **Equity/Debt Plus** attribution standard described below; or **IF** the respondent has actual knowledge of a material involvement of a limited partner in the management or operation of the media-related businesses of the partnership. In the event that the respondent cannot certify as to the noninvolvement of a limited partner, the limited partner will be considered as a holder of an attributable interest.

If a LIMITED LIABILITY COMPANY: The Commission treats a LLC as a limited partnership, each of whose members is considered to be a party to the application. However, where a LLC member is insulated in the manner specified above with respect to a limited partnership and where the relevant state statute authorizing the LLC permits a LLC member to insulate itself in accordance with the Commission's criteria, that LLC member is not considered a holder of an attributable interest. In such a case, the applicant should certify "Yes" in response to Question 9(b).

Equity/Debt Plus Attribution Standard. Certain interests held by substantial investors in, or creditors of, the respondent may also be attributable and the investor reportable as a holder of an attributable interest, if the interest falls within the Commission's **EDP** attribution standard. Under the **EDP** standard, the interest held, aggregating both equity and debt, must exceed 33% of the total asset value (all equity plus all debt) of the respondent, a broadcast station licensee, cable television system, daily newspaper or other media outlet subject to the Commission's broadcast multiple ownership rules **AND** the interest holder must either also hold an attributable interest in a media outlet in the same market or supply over 15% of the total weekly broadcast programming hours of the station in which the interest is held. For example, the equity interest of an insulated limited partner in a limited partnership respondent would normally not be considered attributable. However, under the **EDP** standard, that interest would be attributable if the limited partner's interest exceeded 33% of the respondent's total asset value **AND** the limited partner also held a 5% voting interest in a radio or television station licensee in the same market.

4. Among other things, Question 9(a) seeks information as to those persons to which the Commission's minority and

female ownership policies have historically applied. In addition to gender information, the race/ethnic categories are:

a. **American Indian or Alaska Native.** A person having origins in any of the original peoples of North and South America (including Central America), and who maintains tribal affiliation or community attachment.

b. **Asian.** A person having origins in any of the original peoples of the Far East, Southeast Asia, or the Indian Subcontinent including, for example, Cambodia, China, India, Japan, Korea, Malaysia, Pakistan, the Philippine Islands, Thailand, and Vietnam.

c. **Black or African American.** A person having origins in any of the black racial groups of Africa.

d. **Hispanic or Latino.** A person of Cuban, Mexican, Puerto Rican, South or Central American, or other Spanish Culture or origin, regardless of race.

e. **Native Hawaiian or Other Pacific Islander.** A person having origins in any of the original peoples of Hawaii, Guam, Samoa, or other Pacific Islands.

f. **White.** A person having origins in any of the original peoples of Europe, the Middle East, or North Africa.

CERTIFICATION INSTRUCTIONS - SECTION III

1. The person certifying the accuracy of the information in this report must be the individual licensee or permittee, a general partner in the licensee or permittee partnership, or an appropriate officer in the licensee or permittee corporation or association. If this report is filed for a respondent and not for a licensee or permittee, the person certifying the accuracy of the information must be a general partner in the respondent partnership or an appropriate officer in the respondent corporation or association.

FCC NOTICE TO INDIVIDUALS REQUIRED BY THE PRIVACY ACT AND THE PAPERWORK REDUCTION ACT

The FCC is authorized under the Communications Act of 1934, as amended to collect the personal information requested in this report. We will use the information provided in this report to assess compliance with the Commission's regulations and policies. If we believe there may be a violation or potential violation of a FCC statute, regulation, rule or order, your application may be referred to the Federal, state or local agency responsible for investigating, prosecuting, enforcing or implementing the statute, rule, regulation or order. In certain cases, the information in your report may be disclosed to the Department of Justice or a court or adjudicative body when (a) the FCC; (b) any employee of the FCC; or (c) the United States

Government is a party to a proceeding before the body or has an interest in the proceeding. In addition, all information provided in this form will be available for public inspection.

If you owe a past due debt to the federal government, any information you provide may also be disclosed to the Department of Treasury Financial Management Service, other federal agencies and/or your employer to offset your salary, IRS tax refund or other payments to collect that debt. The FCC may also provide this information to these agencies through the matching of computer records when authorized.

If you do not provide the information requested on this form, the report may be returned without action having been taken upon it or its processing may be delayed while a request is made to provide the missing information. Your response is required to obtain the requested authorization.

We have estimated that each response to this collection of information will take 7.5 hours. Our estimate includes the time to read the instructions, look through existing records, gather and maintain the required data, and actually complete and review the form or response. If you have any comments on this estimate, or on how we can improve the collection and reduce the burden it causes you, please write the Federal Communications Commission, AMD-PERM, Paperwork Reduction Project (3060-0010), Washington, DC 20554. We will also accept your comments via the Internet if your send them to jboley@fcc.gov. Please DO NOT SEND COMPLETED APPLICATIONS TO THIS ADDRESS. Remember - you are not required to respond to a collection of information sponsored by the Federal government, and the government may not conduct or sponsor this collection, unless it displays a currently valid OMB control number of if we fail to provide you with this notice. This collection has been assigned an OMB control number of 3060-0010.

THE FOREGOING NOTICE IS REQUIRED BY THE PRIVACY ACT OF 1974, P.L. 93-579, DECEMBER 31, 1974, 5 U.S.C. 552a(e)(3), AND THE PAPERWORK REDUCTION ACT OF 1995, P.L. 104-13, OCTOBER 1, 1995, 44 U.S.C. 3507.

Federal Communications Commission Washington, D. C. 20554 **FCC 323** **OWNERSHIP REPORT** **FOR** **COMMERCIAL BROADCAST STATIONS**	Approved by OMB 3060-0010	FOR FCC USE ONLY

SECTION I - GENERAL INFORMATION

FOR COMMISSION USE ONLY
FILE NO.

1. Legal Name of the Licensee/Permittee

   Mailing Address

City	State or Country (if foreign address)	ZIP Code

Telephone Number (include area code)	E-Mail Address (if available)

	Facility ID Number	Call Sign

2. | Contact Representative (if other than Licensee/Permittee) | Firm or Company Name |
   |---|---|
   | Telephone Number (include area code) | E-Mail Address (if available) |

3. Name of entity, if other than licensee
   or permittee, for which report is filed

   Mailing Address

City	State or Country (if foreign address)	ZIP Code

Telephone Number (include area code)	E-Mail Address (if available)

4. If this application has been submitted without a fee, indicate reason for fee exemption (see 47 C.F.R. Section 1.1114):

   ☐ Governmental Entity   ☐ Fee-exempt Report   ☐ Other _____

SECTION II - OWNERSHIP INFORMATION

5. All of the information furnished in this Report is accurate as of _____
   (Date must comply with 47 C.F.R. Section 73.3615(a), i.e., information must be current within 60 days of filing of this report, when 5(a) below is checked.)

   This Report is filed for *(check one)*

   a. ☐ Biennial   b. ☐ Transfer of Control or Assignment of License/ Permit   c. ☐ Other

   for the following stations:

Call Letters	Facility ID Number	Location	Class of service

All previous editions obsolete.

CLEAR ALL PAGES

FCC 323
September 2000

6. Respondent is:

_____ Sole proprietorship   _____ Not-for-profit corporation   _____ Limited partnership

_____ For-profit corporation   _____ General partnership   _____ Other

If "Other," describe the nature of the respondent in an Exhibit.

Exhibit No.

7. List all contracts and other instruments required to be filed by 47 C.F.R. Section 73.3613. (Only licensees, permittees, or a reporting entity with a majority interest in or that otherwise exercises <u>de facto</u> control over the subject licensee or permittee shall respond.)

Description of contract or instrument	Name of person or organization with whom contract is made	Date of Execution	Date of Expiration

8. Capitalization (Only licensees, permittees, or a reporting entity with a majority interest in or that otherwise exercises <u>de facto</u> control over the subject licensee or permittee shall respond.)

Class of stock (preferred, common or other)	Voting or Non-voting	Number of Shares			
		Authorized	Issued and Outstanding	Treasury	Unissued

9. a. List the respondent, and, if other than a natural person, its officers, directors, stockholders and other entities with attributable interests, non-insulated partners and/or members. If a corporation or partnership holds an attributable interest in the respondent, list separately its officers, directors, stockholders and other entities with attributable interests, non-insulated partners and/or members. Create a separate row for each individual or entity. Attach supplemental pages, if necessary.

(Read carefully - The numbered items below refer to line numbers in the following table.)

1. Name and address of respondent and each party to the respondent holding an attributable interest (if other than individual also show name, address and citizenship of natural person authorized to vote the stock or holding the attributable interest). List the respondent first, officers next, then directors and, thereafter, remaining stockholders and other entities with attributable interests, and partners.

2. Gender (male or female).

3. Ethnicity (check one).

4. Race (select one or more).

5. Citizenship.

6. Positional interest: Officer, director, general partner, limited partner, LLC member, investor/creditor attributable under the Commission's **equity/debt plus** standard, etc.

7. Percentage of votes.

8. Percentage of total assets (equity debt plus).

CLEAR ALL PAGES

1.			
2.			
3.	☐ Hispanic or Latino ☐ Not Hispanic or Latino	☐ Hispanic or Latino ☐ Not Hispanic or Latino	☐ Hispanic or Latino ☐ Not Hispanic or Latino
4.	☐ American Indian or Alaska Native ☐ Asian ☐ Black or African American ☐ Native Hawaiian or Other Pacific Islander ☐ White	☐ American Indian or Alaska Native ☐ Asian ☐ Black or African American ☐ Native Hawaiian or Other Pacific Islander ☐ White	☐ American Indian or Alaska Native ☐ Asian ☐ Black or African American ☐ Native Hawaiian or Other Pacific Islander ☐ White
5.			
6.			
7.			
8.			

CLEAR ALL PAGES

Supplemental Page for Question 9(a)

1.			
2.			
3.	☐ Hispanic or Latino ☐ Not Hispanic or Latino	☐ Hispanic or Latino ☐ Not Hispanic or Latino	☐ Hispanic or Latino ☐ Not Hispanic or Latino
4.	☐ American Indian or Alaska Native ☐ Asian ☐ Black or African American ☐ Native Hawaiian or Other Pacific Islander ☐ White	☐ American Indian or Alaska Native ☐ Asian ☐ Black or African American ☐ Native Hawaiian or Other Pacific Islander ☐ White	☐ American Indian or Alaska Native ☐ Asian ☐ Black or African American ☐ Native Hawaiian or Other Pacific Islander ☐ White
5.			
6.			
7.			
8.			

CLEAR ALL PAGES

(b) Respondent certifies that equity and financial interests not set forth in response to Question 9(a) are non-attributable.

[ ] Yes [ ] No [See Explanation in Exhibit No.]

[ ] N/A

(c) Is the respondent or any party holding an attributable interest in the respondent also the holder of an attributable interest in any other broadcast station or in any cable or newspaper entities in the same market or with overlapping signals in the same broadcast service, as described in 47 C.F.R. Sections 73.3555 and 76.501?

[ ] Yes [ ] No

If "Yes," submit an Exhibit identifying the holder of that other attributable interest, listing the call signs, locations and facilities identifiers of such other broadcast stations, and describing the nature and size of the ownership interest and the positions held in the other broadcast, cable or newspaper entities.

[Exhibit No.]

(d) Are any of the individuals listed in response to Question 9(a) related as parent-child, husband-wife, brothers and sisters?

[ ] Yes [ ] No

If "Yes," submit an Exhibit setting forth full information as to the family relationship.

[Exhibit No.]

(e) Is respondent seeking an attribution exemption for any officer or director with duties unrelated to the licensee or permittee?

[ ] Yes [ ] No

If "Yes," submit an Exhibit identifying that individual by name and title, fully describing that individual's duties and responsibilities, and explaining why that individual should not be attributed an interest.

[Exhibit No.]

SECTION III - CERTIFICATION

I certify that I am _____

(Official Title)

of _____

(Exact legal title or name of respondent)

and that I have examined this Report and that to the best of my knowledge and belief, all statements in this Report are true, correct and complete.

(Date of certification must be within 60 days of the date shown in Question 5, Section II and in no event prior to that date.)

Signature	Date
Telephone Number of Respondent (Include area code)	

WILLFUL FALSE STATEMENTS ON THIS FORM ARE PUNISHABLE BY FINE AND/OR IMPRISONMENT (U.S. CODE, TITLE 18, SECTION 1001), AND/OR REVOCATION OF ANY STATION LICENSE OR CONSTRUCTION PERMIT (U.S. CODE, TITLE 47, SECTION 312(a)(1)), AND/OR FORFEITURE (U.S. CODE, TITLE 47, SECTION 503).

CLEAR ALL PAGES

Federal Communications Commission
Washington, D. C. 20554

Approved by OMB
3060-0120

BROADCAST EQUAL EMPLOYMENT OPPORTUNITY
MODEL PROGRAM REPORT

Legal Name of the Applicant		
Mailing Address		
City	State or Country (if foreign address)	ZIP Code
Telephone Number (include area code)	E-Mail Address (if available)	
	Facility ID Number	Call Sign

☐ Application for Construction Permit for New Station   ☐ Application for Assignment of License

☐ Application for Transfer of Control

    a. Service Type: ☐ AM ☐ FM ☐ TV ☐ Other (specify) _____

    b. Community of License: | City | State |

INSTRUCTIONS

Applicants seeking authority to construct a new commercial, noncommercial or international broadcast station, applicants seeking authority to obtain assignment of the construction permit or license of such a station, and applicants seeking authority to acquire control of an entity holding such construction permit or license are required to afford equal employment opportunity to all qualified persons and to refrain from discrimination in employment and related benefits on the basis of race, color, religion, national origin or sex. See 47 C.F.R. Section 73.2080. Pursuant to these requirements, an applicant who proposes to employ five or more full-time employees must establish a program designed to assure equal employment opportunity for women and minority groups (that is, Blacks not of Hispanic origin, Asians or Pacific Islanders, American Indians or Alaskan Natives and Hispanics). This is submitted to the Commission as the Model EEO Program. For purposes of this form, a station employment unit is a station or a group of commonly owned stations in the same market that share at least one employee.

Guidelines for a Model EEO Program and a Model EEO Program are attached.

NOTE: Check appropriate box, sign the certification below and return to FCC:

☐ Station employment unit will employ fewer than 5 full-time employees; therefore no written program is being submitted.

☐ Station employment unit will employ 5 or more full-time employees. Our Model EEO Program is attached. (You must complete all sections of this form.)

I certify that the statements made herein are true, complete, and correct to the best of my knowledge and belief, and are made in good faith.

Signed	Name of Respondent
Title	Date

WILLFUL FALSE STATEMENTS ON THIS FORM ARE PUNISHABLE BY FINE AND/OR IMPRISONMENT
(U.S. CODE, TITLE 18, SECTION 1001), AND/OR REVOCATION OF ANY STATION LICENSE OR CONSTRUCTION PERMIT
(U.S. CODE, TITLE 47, SECTION 312(a)(1)), AND/OR FORFEITURE (U.S. CODE, TITLE 47, SECTION 503).

FCC 396-A
April 2000

GUIDELINES TO THE MODEL EEO PROGRAM

The model EEO program adopted by the Commission for construction permit applicants, assignees, and transferees contains five sections designed to assist the applicant in establishing an effective EEO program for its station. The specific elements which should be addressed are as follows:

I. GENERAL POLICY

The first section of the program should contain a statement by the applicant that it will afford equal employment opportunity in all personnel actions without regard to race, color, religion, national origin or sex, and that it has adopted an EEO program which is designed to fully utilize the skills of qualified persons.

II. RESPONSIBILITY FOR IMPLEMENTATION

This section calls for the name (if known) and title of the official who will be designated by the applicant to have responsibility for implementing the station's program.

III. POLICY DISSEMINATION

The purpose of this section is to disclose the manner in which the station's EEO policy will be communicated to employees and prospective employees. The applicant's program should indicate whether it: (a) intends to utilize an employment application form which contains a notice informing job applicants that discrimination is prohibited and that persons who believe that they have been discriminated against may notify appropriate governmental agencies; (b) will post a notice which informs job applicants and employees that the applicant is an equal opportunity employer and that they may notify appropriate governmental authorities if they believe that they have been discriminated against; and (c) will seek the cooperation of labor unions, if represented at the station, in the implementation of its EEO program and in the inclusion of nondiscrimination provisions in union contracts. The applicant should also set forth any other methods it proposes to utilize in conveying its EEO policy (e.g., orientation materials, on-air announcements, station newsletter) to employees and prospective employees.

IV. RECRUITMENT

The applicant should specify the recruitment sources and other techniques it proposes to use to attract qualified job applicants. The purpose of the listing is to assist the applicant in developing specialized referral sources to ensure wide dissemination of vacancy information as job opportunities occur. Sources which subsequently prove to be nonproductive should not be relied on and new sources should be sought.

V. RECRUITMENT ELECTION

Our EEO Rule requires broadcasters to select from two approaches how they will choose to ensure the success of their outreach. Specifically, as one option, broadcasters may adopt two supplemental recruitment measures specified in Section 73.2080 of the Commission's Rules. As a second option, broadcasters may forego the supplemental recruitment measures and design their own broad and inclusive outreach program, as long as they are able to demonstrate success in achieving broad outreach to all segments of the community, including minorities and females, based upon an analysis of the recruitment source, race, national origin, and gender of applicants attracted by their outreach efforts. See 47 C.F.R. Section 73.2080.

MODEL EQUAL EMPLOYMENT OPPORTUNITY PROGRAM

I. GENERAL POLICY

It will be our policy to provide equal employment opportunity to all qualified individuals without regard to race, color, religion, national origin or sex in all personnel actions including recruitment, evaluation, selection, promotion, compensation, training and termination.

It will also be our policy to promote the realization of equal employment opportunity through a positive, continuing program of specific practices designed to ensure the full realization of equal employment opportunity without regard to race, color, religion, national origin or sex.

To make this policy effective, and to ensure conformance with the Rules and Regulations of the Federal Communications Commission, we have adopted an Equal Employment Opportunity Program which includes the following elements:

II. RESPONSIBILITY FOR IMPLEMENTATION

Name/Title

will be responsible for the administration and implementation of our Equal Employment Opportunity Program. It will also be the responsibility of all persons making employment decisions with respect to the recruitment, evaluation, selection, promotion, compensation, training and termination of employees to ensure that our policy and program is adhered to and that no person is discriminated against in employment because of race, color, religion, national origin or sex.

III. POLICY DISSEMINATION

To assure that all members of the staff are cognizant of our equal employment opportunity policy and their individual responsibilities in carrying out this policy, the following communication efforts will be made:

☐ The station's employment application forms will contain a notice informing prospective employees that discrimination because of race, color, religion, national origin or sex is prohibited and that they may notify the appropriate local, State or Federal agency if they believe they have been the victims of discrimination.

☐ Appropriate notices will be posted informing applicants and employees that the station is an Equal Opportunity Employer and of their right to notify an appropriate local, State or Federal agency if they believe they have been the victims of discrimination.

☐ We will seek the cooperation of unions, if represented at the station, to help implement our EEO program and all union contracts will contain a nondiscrimination clause.

☐ Other (specify)

IV. RECRUITMENT

To ensure that information concerning each full-time vacancy is widely disseminated, we propose to use the following list of recruitment sources consistent with the requirements of 47 C.F.R. Section 73.2080:

V. RECRUITMENT ELECTION

Please indicate which option the station will utilize for the next two years.

☐ Supplemental Recruitment Measures (Option A)   ☐ Alternative Recruitment Option (Option B)

430 FCC Forms

Federal Communications Commission
Washington, D.C. 20554

Approved by OMB
3060-0754

Instructions for FCC 398
Children's Television Programming Report
(FCC Form 398 attached)

GENERAL INSTRUCTIONS

Introduction
This FCC Form is to be used to provide information on the efforts of commercial television broadcast stations to provide children's educational television programming as required by the Children's Television Act of 1990, Pub. L. No. 101-437, 104 Stat. 996-1000, codified at 47 U.S.C. §§ 303a, 303b, 394, and the Commission's regulations implementing that statute. See Report and Order in MM Docket No. 93-48, 11 FCC Rcd 10660 (1996).

Applicable Rules and Regulations
Before this form is prepared, the licensee should review the relevant portions of Sections 73.671, 73.673, and 73.3526(e)(11)(iii) in Title 47 of the Code of Federal Regulations (C.F.R.). Copies of Title 47 may be purchased from the Superintendent of Documents, Government Printing Office, Washington, D.C. 20402. You may telephone the GPO Customer Service Desk at (202) 512-1800 for current prices. Licensees should make every effort to file complete forms in compliance with the rules.
Replies to questions on this form and the licensee's statements constitute representations on which the FCC will rely in considering the renewal of the licensee's television broadcast authorization. Thus, time and care should be devoted to all replies, which should reflect accurately the licensee's efforts to provide children's educational television programming as required by the Children's Television Act of 1990 and the Commission's rules.

Preparation and Retention of Reports
Pursuant to 47 C.F.R. Section 73.3526(e)(11)(iii), each commercial television broadcast licensee must prepare a Children's Television Programming Report for each calendar quarter reflecting efforts made by the licensee during the quarter, as well as efforts planned for the next quarter, to serve the educational and informational needs of children. The licensee must place a copy of each quarterly report in its station's public inspection file by the tenth day of the succeeding calendar quarter (i.e., by April 10 for the first quarterly report; by July 10 for the second quarterly report; by October 10 for the third quarterly report; and by January 10 for the fourth quarterly report). All entries on the report must be typed or legibly printed in ink. The signed original of each report should be retained in the station's non-public files, and a copy placed in the public inspection file. The reports must be separated from other material in the public inspection file, and the licensee must publicize in an appropriate manner the existence and location of these reports.

Filing Reports with the Commission
For the year 2000, licensees must file their quarterly Children's Television Programming Reports with the Commission on an annual basis (i.e., four quarterly reports filed jointly once a year) on January 10, 2001. This annual FCC Form 398 must be filed electronically. The Commission will **not** accept either a computer diskette or a paper copy of this report.

Commencing with the submission for the first quarter of 2001, due to be filed April 10, 2001, the FCC Form 398 must be filed electronically with the Commission on a **quarterly** basis on the following dates: April 10 for the first quarter report; July 10 for the second quarter report; October 10 for the third quarter report; and January 10 of the succeeding year for the last quarter report.

FCC Form 398 can be file electronically over the Internet by accessing the FCC Web site at http://www.fcc.gov, selecting Electronic filing from the menu (above the Headlines banner), then selecting the Children's Television Programming Report (FCC Form 398). Follow the instructions on that page for the electronic preparation and filing of the FCC 398 report.

No fee is required to file this report.

Incorporation by Reference
Licensees may **NOT** incorporate by reference data, documents, exhibits, or other showings already on file with the FCC. All applicable items on this form must be answered without reference to a previous filing.

Children's Television Act Program Requirements
Pursuant to the Children's Television Act and 47 C.F.R. Section 73.671(a), each television broadcast station licensee has an obligation to serve, over the term of its license, the educational and informational needs of children through both the licensee's overall programming and programming specifically designed to serve such needs. Licensees are required to publicize the availability of their programming specifically designed to educate and inform children in accord with 47 C.F.R. Section 73.673 and to report on these programs and related matters in accord with 47 C.F.R. Section 73.3526 (e)(11)(iii).

Educational and informational television programming is defined in 47 C.F.R. Section 73.671(c) as programming that furthers the educational and informational needs of children 16 years of age and under in any respect, including the child's intellectual/cognitive or social/emotional needs. **Core Programming** is defined as educational and informational programming that is specifically designed to serve the educational and informational needs of children and that also satisfies the following criteria:

(1) the program has serving the educational and informational needs of children ages 16 and under as a significant purpose;
(2) the program is aired between the hours of 7:00 a.m. and 10:00 p.m.;
(3) the program is a regularly scheduled weekly program;
(4) the program is at least 30 minutes in length;
(5) the educational and informational objective of the program and the target child audience are specified in writing in the licensee's Children's Television Programming Report, as described in 47 C.F.R. Section 73.3526(e)(11)(iii); and
(6) instructions for listing the program as educational/informational, including an indication of the age group for which the program is intended, are provided to publishers of program guides.

For Assistance
For assistance with FCC Form 398, contact the Video Services Division of the Mass Media Bureau at the FCC, Washington, D.C. 20554, Telephone Number (202) 418-1600.

INSTRUCTIONS FOR SPECIFIC ITEMS ON FCC FORM 398

Question 1. The licensee should provide its current call sign, channel number, and community of license, including city, state, county, and zip code, as set forth in its license authorization. The licensee should also provide its licensee name, indicate the station's license renewal expiration date, indicate the call sign used on the preceding Children's Television Programming Report prepared for the station (if different from the current call sign), check the appropriate box indicating whether it is a network affiliate (if so, identify the affiliated network) or

2

an independent station, and indicate the name of the Nielsen DMA in which the station is located. In addition, if the licensee has a World Wide Web home page, it should provide the address. The licensee should also provide the station's facility ID number.

Question 2. Indicate the average number of hours per week of core programming broadcast by the station over the past calendar quarter.

Question 3. Indicate whether the licensee identifies each core program at the beginning of the program as required by 47 C.F.R. Section 73.673.

Question 4. Indicate whether the licensee provides information identifying each core program and its target child audience to publishers of program guides and, if so, list those program guide publishers.

Question 5. For each core program aired by the station during the calendar quarter for which this report is being prepared, set forth in Form Question 5 the following information: the title of the program; whether the program is originated by the station or its affiliated network, or is syndicated; the days and times the station regularly schedules the program; the program length (in minutes); the total number of times the program aired at its regularly scheduled time during the quarter; and the number of times the program was preempted during the quarter. If the program was preempted during the quarter, the station should complete a "Preemption Report," included in this form, for each preempted core program. The licensee should also indicate the ages of the target child audience; and include a description of the educational and informational objective of the program, as well as a discussion of how the program meets the definition of core programming set forth in 47 C.F.R. Section 73.671(c). For a qualifying regular series a general description of the series should be sufficient so long as the description is adequate to provide the public with enough information about

how the series is specifically designed to meet the educational and informational needs of children.

Question 6. For each program aired by the station during the preceding calendar quarter that is specifically designed to meet the educational and informational needs of children ages 16 and under, but does not meet one or more elements of Core Programming, set forth in Form Question 6 the following information: the title of the program; whether the program is originated by the station, its affiliated network, or is syndicated; the days and times the program aired during the quarter; the program length (in minutes); the total number of times the program aired during the quarter; if preempted and rescheduled during the quarter, the date and time the program aired; the ages of the target child audience (if applicable); a description of the program; and, beginning September 1, 1997, an indication of whether the program has educating and informing children ages 16 and under as a significant purpose. For any such program, state whether the licensee identifies the program at the beginning of the program and whether information is provided to publishers of program guides consistent with 47 C. F.R. Section 73.673.

Question 7. For each program the station plans to air during the next calendar quarter that meets the definition of core programming, set forth in Form Question 7 the following information: the title of the program; whether the program will be originated by the station or its affiliated network, or will be syndicated; the days and times the program will be regularly scheduled; the program length (in minutes); the total number of times the program will be aired during the quarter; the ages of the target child audience; and a description of the educational and informational objective of the program, as well as a discussion of how it meets the definition of core programming set forth in 47 C.F.R. Section 73.671(c).

Question 8. Indicate whether the licensee publicizes the existence and location of the station's Children's Television Programming

3

Reports as required by 47 C.F.R. Section 73.3526(e)(11)(iii).

Question 9. Pursuant to 47 C.F.R. Section 73.671(b), in addition to airing core and non-core educational and informational children's programming a licensee may contribute to satisfying its obligation under the Children's Television Act by engaging in special efforts to produce and support educational and informational television programming aired by another station in the licensee's marketplace. List the name(s) of any core program(s) aired by other stations that are sponsored by the licensee, and identify the call letters and channel number of the station(s) airing the sponsored core program(s).

Indicate whether the amount of total core programming aired on the other station(s) has increased as a result of the sponsored programming. A licensee will receive credit for special sponsorship efforts only if it can demonstrate that its production or support of such core programming aired on another station in its market increased the amount of core programming on the other station. In addition, for each core program sponsored by the licensee, set forth in Question 9 the following information: the title of the program; whether the program is originated by the station for which this report is filed or its affiliated network, or is syndicated; the days and times the program was regularly scheduled; the program length (in minutes); the total number of times the program aired during the quarter; the number of times the program was preempted during the quarter; if the program was preempted and rescheduled during the quarter, the dates and times the program aired; the ages of the target child audience; and a description of the educational and informational objective of the program, as well as a discussion of how the program meets the definition of core programming in 47 C.F.R. Section 73.671(c).

Question 10. Pursuant to 47 C.F.R. Section 73.3526(e)(11)(iii), licensees must identify the individual at the station responsible for collecting comments on the station's compliance with the Children's Television Act. Provide the name, address, telephone number, and the internet mail address (if available) of this individual.

Question 11. Provide any other comments or information you wish the Commission to consider in evaluating whether the licensee has met its obligations under the Children's Television Act and the Commission's rules. This may include, but is not limited to, information on any non-core educational and informational programming that the station plans to air during the next calendar quarter, as well as information on any existing or proposed non-broadcast activities that the licensee believes enhance the educational and informational value to children of the licensee's educational programming.

Preemption Report. As indicated in Question 5, if a core program was preempted during the quarter for any reason, the licensee should complete a Preemption Report for each preempted core program. The Report should include the following information: the title of the program; the total number of times the program was aired during the quarter (including the number of times the program aired at its regularly scheduled date and time and the number of times any rescheduled programs aired); the number of preemptions during the quarter; and the number of preemptions rescheduled during the quarter. The Report should also indicate, for each preempted episode of the core program: the date the episode was preempted; if rescheduled, the date and time the episode was rescheduled; if rescheduled, whether promotional efforts were made to notify the public of the rescheduled date and time; and whether the rescheduled date is the program's "second home" as described in letters, dated July 11, 1997, from Roy J. Stewart, Chief, Mass Media Bureau, to: Martin D. Franks, Senior Vice President, Washington, CBS, Inc.; Alan Braverman, Senior Vice President and General Counsel, ABC, Inc.; Rick Cotton and Diane Zipurky, NBC, Inc. The Report should also indicate for each preempted episode the reason for the preemption.

4

FCC NOTICE TO INDIVIDUALS REQUIRED BY THE PRIVACY ACT AND THE PAPERWORK REDUCTION ACT

The solicitation of personal information requested in this form is authorized by the Communications Act of 1934, as amended. The Commission will use the information provided in this form to evaluate licensees' renewal applications, monitoring industry progress toward meeting the goals of the Children's Television Act. In reaching that determination, or for law enforcement purposes, it may become necessary to refer personal information contained in this form to another government agency. In addition, all information provided in this form will be available for public inspection. Your response is required to ensure compliance with the Children's Television Act.

We have estimated that each response to this collection of information will take 6.0 hours. Our estimate includes the time to read the instructions, look through existing records, gather and maintain the required data, and actually complete and review the form or response. If you have any comments on this estimate, or on how we can improve the collection and reduce the burden it causes you, please write the Federal Communications Commission, AMD-PERM, Paperwork Reduction Project (3060-0754), Washington, DC 20554. We will also accept your comments via the Internet if your send them to jboley@fcc.gov. Please DO NOT SEND COMPLETED APPLICATIONS TO THIS ADDRESS. Remember - you are not required to respond to a collection of information sponsored by the Federal government, and the government may not conduct or sponsor this collection, unless it displays a currently valid OMB control number of if we fail to provide you with this notice. This collection has been assigned an OMB control number of 3060-0754.

THE FOREGOING NOTICE IS REQUIRED BY THE PRIVACY ACT OF 1974, P.L. 93-579, DECEMBER 31, 1974, 5 U.S.C. Section 552a(e)(3), AND THE PAPERWORK REDUCTION ACT OF 1995, P.L. 104-13, OCTOBER 1, 1995, 44 U.S.C. Section 3507.

5

Federal Communications Commission
Washington, D. C. 20554

Approved by OMB
3060-0754

FCC 398
Children's Television Programming Report

Report reflects information for quarter ending (mm/dd/yy) _____

1. Call Sign	Channel Number	Community of License				
		City	State	County		ZIP Code
Licensee						

☐ Network Affiliation: _____	☐ Independent	Nielsen DMA	World Wide Web Home Page Address (if applicable)
Facility ID Number	Previous call sign (if applicable)	LicenseRenewal Expiration Date (mmddyy)	

Core Programming

2. State the average number of hours of Core Programming per week broadcast by the station. See 47 C.F.R. Section 73.671(c).

3. Does the licensee identify each Core Program at the beginning of the airing of each program as required by 47 C.F.R. Section 73.673?   ☐ Yes   ☐ No

4. a. Does the licensee provide information identifying each Core Program aired on its station, including an indication of the target child audience, to publishers of program guides as required by 47 C.F.R. Section 73.673?   ☐ Yes   ☐ No

    b. Identify publishers who were sent information in 4.a.

5. Complete the following for each program that you aired during the past three months that meets the definition of Core Programming.   Complete chart below for each Core Program.

Title of Program:			Origination		
			Local	Network	Syndicated
Days/Times Program Regularly Scheduled:		Total times aired at regularly scheduled time	Number of Preemptions	If preempted, complete Preemption Report	
Length of Program: (minutes)					
Age of Target Child Audience: from ____ years to ____ years.					
Describe the educational and informational objective of the program and how it meets the definition of Core Programming.					

Non-Core Educational and Informational Programming

6. Complete the following for each program that you aired during the past three months that is specifically designed to meet the educational and informational needs of children ages 16 and under, but does not meet one or more elements of the definition of Core Programming.   See 47 C.F.R. Section 73.671.   Complete chart below for each additional such educational and informational program.

Title of Program:			Origination		
			Local	Network	Syndicated

Dates/Times Program Aired:	Total times aired	Number of Preemptions	If preempted and rescheduled, list date and time aired.	
			Dates	Times

| Length of Program: (minutes) | | |
| Age of Target Child Audience (if applicable): from __ years to __ years. | | |

Describe the program.

Does the program have educating and informing children ages 16 and under as a significant purpose?	☐ Yes ☐ No
If Yes, does the licensee identify each program at the beginning of its airing consistent with 47 C.F.R. Section 73.673?	☐ Yes ☐ No
If Yes, does the licensee provide information regarding the program, including an indication of the target child audience, to publishers of program guides consistent with 47 C.F.R. Section 73.673?	☐ Yes ☐ No

Other Matters

7. Complete the following for each program that you plan to air for the next quarter that meets the definition of Core Programming.   Complete chart below for each Core Program.

Title of Program:			Origination		
			Local	Network	Syndicated

| Days/Times Program Regularly Scheduled: | Total times to be aired | Length of Program: (minutes) | Age of Target Child Audience: from ____ years to____ years. |

Describe the educational and informational objective of the program and how it meets the definition of Core Programming.

8. Does the licensee publicize the existence and location of the station's Children's Television Programming Reports (FCC 398) as required by 47 C.F.R. Section 73.3526(e)(11)(iii)?   ☐ Yes ☐ No

9. List Core Programs, if any, aired by other stations that are sponsored by the licensee and that meet the criteria set forth in 47 C.F.R. Section 73.671. Also indicate whether the amount of total Core Programming broadcast by another station increased.

Name of Program	Call Letters of Station Airing Sponsored Program	Channel Number of Station Airing Sponsored Program	Did total programming increase?
			☐ Yes ☐ No
			☐ Yes ☐ No
			☐ Yes ☐ No

For each Core Program sponsored by the licensee, complete the chart below.

Title of Program:			Origination		
			Local	Network	Syndicated

Days/Times Program Regularly Scheduled:	Total times aired	Number of Preemptions	If preempted and rescheduled, list date and time aired.	
			Dates	Times

Length of Program: _____ (minutes)

Target Child Audience: from _____ years to _____ years.

Describe the educational and informational objective of the program and how it meets the definition of Core Programming.

10. Name of children's programming liaison:	
Name	Telephone Number (include area code)
Address	Internet Mail Address (if applicable)
City	State

11. Include any other comments or information you want the Commission to consider in evaluating your compliance with the Children's Television Act (or use this space for supplemental explanations). This may include information on any other non-core educational and informational programming that you aired this quarter or plan to air during the next quarter, or any existing or proposed non-broadcast efforts that will enhance the educational and informational value of such programming to children. See 47 C.F.R. Section 73.671, NOTE 2.

I certify that the statements in this application are true, complete, and correct to the best of my knowledge and belief, and are made in good faith.

Name of Licensee	Signature
Date	

PREEMPTION REPORT

Complete the chart below for each core program listed in Question 5 of FCC 398 that was preempted during the past three months.

<table>
<tr><td colspan="3">Title of Program:</td></tr>
<tr><td>Total Times to be Aired</td><td>Number of Preemptions</td><td>Number of Preemptions Rescheduled</td></tr>
<tr><td>Date Preempted/Episode #</td><td>If rescheduled, date and time rescheduled</td><td>Is the rescheduled date the second home?
☐ Yes ☐ No</td></tr>
<tr><td colspan="3">If rescheduled, were promotional efforts made to notify public of rescheduled date and time? ☐ Yes ☐ No</td></tr>
<tr><td colspan="3">Reason for Preemption:
☐ Breaking News ☐ Sports ☐ Other
☐ Other News ☐ Public Interest</td></tr>
</table>

FCC 398 (Page 4)
April 2001

Bibliography

"ABC Relaxes Advertising Guidelines," *Broadcasting* (September 9, 1991): 25.

"ACT Challenges Children's TV Rules," *Broadcasting* (May 20, 1991): 62.

Bessie, Simon Michael. *Jazz Journalism*. New York: E.P. Dutton & Co., 1938.

Biederman, Donald E., Edward Pierson, Martin Silfin, Jeanne A. Glasser, Robert C. Berry, Lionel S. Sobel. *Law and Business of the Entertainment Industries*, 3rd ed. Westport, CT: Praeger, 1996.

Blackstone, William. *Commentaries on the Laws of England*. Edited by Charles M. Haar. Boston: Beacon Press, 1962.

Bosmajian, Haig A., ed. *The Principles and Practices of Freedom of Speech*. Boston: Houghton Mifflin, 1971.

Brunel, Andre. "Trademark Protection for Internet Domain Names" in *The Internet and Business: A Lawyer's Guide to Emerging Legal*. Fairfax, VA: Computer Law Association, 1996, 2. (www.cla.org/RuhBook/chp3.htm, Feb. 17, 1999.)

Buranelli, Vincent. *The Trial of Peter Zenger*. New York: New York University Press, 1957.

"Cable Rereg Bill Bogs Down," *Broadcasting* (July 15, 1991): 15.

Carter, T. Barton, Marc A. Franklin, Jay B. Wrisht. *The First Amendment and the Fifth Estate: Regulation of Electronic Mass Media*, 5th ed. Westbury, NY: Foundation Press, 1999.

"Case Dismissed," *Broadcasting* (October 14, 1991): 52.

Chafee, Jr., Zechariah. *Free Speech in the United States*. Cambridge, MA: Harvard University Press, 1964.

Chafee, Jr., Zechariah. *Thirty-Five Years with Freedom of Speech*. New York: Roger N. Baldwin, Civil Liberties Foundation, 1952.

Cole, Barry G., and Mal Gettinger. *Reluctant Regulators: The FCC and the Broadcast Audience*. Reading, MA: Addison-Wesley, 1978.

"Congress All Shook Up Over Rock Lyrics," *Broadcasting* (September 23, 1985): 28.

Cooper, Cynthia L., and Sam Reese Sheppard. *Mockery of Justice*. New York: Onyx Press, 1997.

Copyright Basics, Circular 1. Washington, D.C.: Copyright Office, Library of Congress, 1987.

"Costly Mistake," *Broadcasting* (October 14, 1991): 52.

"Court Throws Out FCC's 24-Hour Indecency Ban," *Broadcasting* (May 20, 1991): 33.

Creech, Kenneth C. "An Historical and Descriptive Analysis of Low-Power Educational Radio Broadcasting in the United States." Ph.D. dissertation, Wayne State University, 1978.

"Disney Facing Hurdle in Effort to Relax PTAR," *Broadcasting* (December 10, 1990): 102.

"Divided Commission Eases Fin-Syn Restrictions," *TV Today* (April 15, 1991): 2.

Douglas, Susan. *Inventing American Broadcasting*. Baltimore: Johns Hopkins University Press, 1987.

Downs, Donald Alexander. *Nazis in Skokie: Freedom, Community and the First Amendment*. Notre Dame, IN: University of Notre Dame Press, 1985.

Educational Radio: The Hidden Medium. Washington, DC: National Association of Educational Broadcasters, 1967.

"EEO Forfeitures and Short-Term License Renewals Continue," *Haley, Bader & Potts Information Memorandum* 16 (February 14, 1991): 6.

Emery, Edwin. *The Press and America*, 2nd ed. Englewood Cliffs, NJ: Prentice-Hall, 1962.

Eshelman, David. "The Emergence of Educational FM Broadcasting," *NAEB Journal* 26 (March/April 1967): 57.

"Fairness Doctrine Legislation Re-Emerges," *Broadcasting* (January 12, 1991): 43.

Fair Trial/Free Press Voluntary Agreements. Chicago: Legal Advisory Committee on Fair Trial and Free Press, 1974.

"False Radio Broadcast Evokes FCC Investigation," *Broadcasting* (February 4, 1991): 29.

"FCC Allocates Interactive Video Spectrum," *Broadcasting* (January 20, 1992): 11.

"FCC Broadens Area Considered for License Character," *Broadcasting* (May 14, 1990): 32.

"FCC Considers Restoring Must-Carry Rules," *Broadcasting* (July 22, 1991): 32.

"FCC Creates Adult Country: Midnight–6 A.M.," *Broadcasting* (November 30, 1987): 51.

"FCC Gets Tough on Political and EEO Violations, Sets Record Fines," *TV Today* (May 21, 1990): 3.

"FCC Hears Little Support for 24-Hour Broadcasting Indecency Ban," *Broadcasting* (February 26, 1990): 48.

"FCC Launches Attack on Indecency," *Broadcasting* (April 30, 1987): 35.

"FCC Report Concedes TV's Future to Cable," *Broadcasting* (July 1, 1991): 19.

"FCC Revamping Comparative Hearings Process," *Broadcasting* (May 14, 1990): 31.

"FCC Takes Action on Process Abuse, Station Licensing Character Policy," *TV Today* (May 14, 1990): 4.

"FCC Takes Tentative Step Toward TV Dereg," *Broadcasting* (July 15, 1991): 13.

"FCC Tells TV Station It May Have Violated Indecency Law," *Broadcasting* (January 18, 1988): 46.

"FCC to Delay Children's Ad Time Limits Until '92," *Broadcasting* (July 29, 1991): 68.

"FCC to Investigate Murder Hoax," *Broadcasting* (April 22, 1991): 48.

"FCC Turns Up the Heat on Indecency," *Broadcasting* (August 28, 1989): 27.

Federal Communications Commission. *Annual Report, 1945.* Washington, DC: U.S. Government Printing Office, 1946.

"A Foot in the Door for Telcos," *Broadcasting* (July 29, 1991): 23.

"Fox Wins 18 1/2 Hour, One Year Fin-Syn Waiver," *Broadcasting* (May 7, 1990): 28.

Francois, William E. *Mass Media Law and Regulation*, 3rd ed. Columbus, OH: Grid Publishing Co., 1982.

Friedrich, C.J., and J. Sayer Smith. "Radio Broadcasting and Higher Education," in *Studies in the Control of Radio*, Numbers 1–6, History of Broadcasting: Radio to Television Series. Edited by Christopher Sterling. New York: Arno Press and the New York Times, 1971.

Friendly, Fred W., and Martha J.H. Eliot. *The Constitution: That Delicate Balance.* New York: Random House, 1984.

Frost, S.E. *Education's Own Stations.* Chicago: University of Chicago Press, 1937.

"FTC Takes Action on 'Infomercials,'" *Electronic Media* (May 21, 1990): 32.

Geller, Henry. *Fiber Optics: An Opportunity for a New Policy.* Washington, DC: The Annenberg Washington Program, 1991.

Gillmor, Donald M., Jerome A. Barron, Joddf. Simon, Herbeit A. Jerry. *Mass Communication Law: Cases and Comment*, 5th ed. St. Paul: West Publishing Co., 1990.

"Gleam in Fowler's Regulatory Eye," *Broadcasting* (September 14, 1981): 27.

Goodale, James, ed. *Communications Law 1982.* New York: Practicing Law Institute, 1982.

"Group Ownership on the Rise," *Broadcasting* (February 11, 1991): 69.

Hamlin, David. *The Nazi/Skokie Conflict: A Civil Liberties Struggle.* Boston: Beacon Press, 1980.

Harless, James D. *Mass Communication: An Introductory Survey.* Dubuque, IA: William C. Brown, 1985.

Head, Sydney, and Christopher Sterling. *Broadcasting in America*, 6th ed. Boston: Houghton-Mifflin Company, 1990.

Hernandez, Ruel Torres. "ECPA and Offline Computer Privacy," *Federal Communications Law Journal* 41:1 (1990): 17.

"High Court Strikes Blow for Investigative Journalism," *Broadcasting* (October 12, 1987): 79.

"Hill, FCC Face Full Agenda After August Vacation," *Broadcasting* (September 12, 1991): 14.

Hilliard, Robert L. *The Federal Communications Commission: A Primer.* Boston: Focal Press, 1991.

"Hoax Fallout," *Broadcasting* (April 29, 1991): 7.

Holmes, Oliver W. *The Common Law.* Boston: Little, Brown, 1881.

Holonen, Doug. "Big 3, Hollywood Rips Fin-Syn," *Electronic Media* (April 15, 1991): 1, 52.

Hudon, Edward G. *Freedom of Speech and Press in America.* Washington, DC: Public Affairs Press, 1963.

Hughes, Helen M. *News and the Human Interest Story.* Chicago: University of Chicago Press, 1940.

"Imaging: The Merger of Computer and TV," *Broadcasting* (January 27, 1992): 41.

"In Brief," *Broadcasting* (April 29, 1991): 72.

"Indecency Ban Comes Under Fire: Appeals Court Judge Criticizes FCC's 24-Hour Indecency Prohibition Challenging Commission's Contention That It Is 'Narrowly Tailored,'" *Broadcasting* (February 4, 1991): 40–41.

"Indecency Ban Mixed," *Electronic Media* (May 20, 1991): 1.

"Indecency Effort Set," *Electronic Media* (April 22, 1991): 1.

"Infinity Fights Indecency Ban," *Broadcasting* (February 18, 1991): 60.

"Is Wireless Cable 'Cable'?" *Broadcasting* (July 15, 1991): 31.

"Janet Steiger: The FTC's Vigilant Enforcer," *Broadcasting* (February 5, 1990): 76.

Johnson, Nicholas, and John Jay Dystel. "A Day in the Life: The Federal Communications Commission," *The Yale Law Journal* 82:8 (July 1973): 1574.

Keeton, W. Page, Dan B. Dobbs, Robert E. Keeton, David G. Owen. *Prosser and Keeton on Torts*, 5th ed. St. Paul: West Publishing Co., 1984.

"Kellner Presses Fox's Case for Fin-Syn Exemption," *Broadcasting* (November 19, 1990): 50.

Kovner, Victor. "Recent Developments in Intrusion, Private Facts, False Light and Commercialization Claims," in *Communications Law 1982*. Edited by James C. Goodale. New York: Practicing Law Institute, 1982.

Krasnow, Erwin G., and Lawrence D. Longley. *The Politics of Broadcast Regulation*, 2nd ed. New York: St. Martin's Press, 1978.

"The Laissez Faire Legacy of Charles Ferris," *Broadcasting* (January 19, 1981): 37.

Le Duc, Don R. *Beyond Broadcasting: Patterns in Policy and Law*. New York: Longman, 1987.

"License Pulled for Drug Conviction," *Broadcasting* (January 28, 1991): 49.

Lowery, Shearon A., and Melvin L. DeFleur. "The Invasion from Mars: Radio Panics America," in *Milestones in Mass Communication Research*, 2nd ed. New York: Longman, 1988.

"Making Life a Bit Easier; Reregulation Gets Under Way," *Broadcasting* (November 6, 1972): 19.

Mason, Alpheus Thomas, and William M. Beaney. *American Constitutional Law: Introductory Essays and Selected Cases*, 4th ed. Englewood Cliffs, NJ: Prentice-Hall, 1968.

McCrory, James. "Developments in Libel Law," in *Communications Law 1982*. Edited by James Goodale. New York: Practicing Law Institute, 1982.

Mermigas, Diane. "Networks Study Prime-Time Cuts," *Electronic Media* (April 29, 1991): 31.

Mill, J.S. *On Liberty Etc.* London: Oxford University Press, 1969.

Miller, Arthur R., and Michael H. Davis. *Intellectual Property: Patents, Trademarks and Copyright*. St. Paul: West Publishing Co., 1991.

Milton, John. *Areopagitica and Of Education*. Edited by George H. Sabine. New York: Appleton-Century-Crofts, 1951.

Mott, Frank Luther. *American Journalism*, 3rd ed. New York: Macmillan, 1962.

National Association of Broadcasters. "FCC Streamlines Comparative Hearings," *TV Today* (December 17, 1990): 1.

Nelson, Harold L., Dwight L. Teeter, Jr., and Don R. Le Duc. *Law of Mass Communications: Freedom and Control of Print and Broadcast Media*, 6th ed. Westbury, NY: The Foundation Press, 1990.

Paper, Lewis J. *Brandeis*. New York: Citadel Press, 1983.

Pollock, Sir Frederick, and Frederic William Maitland. *The History of English Law*, Vol. II. Cambridge: Cambridge University Press, 1968.

"Record Labeling Could Have Radio Fallout?" *Broadcasting* (April 30, 1990): 58.

Saettler, Paul. *A History of Instructional Technology*. New York: McGraw-Hill, 1968.

Sayre, Jeanette. "An Analysis of the Radio Broadcasting Activities of Federal Agencies," in *Studies in the Control of Radio*, Numbers 1–6, History of Broadcasting: Radio to Television Series. Edited by Christopher Sterling. New York: Arno Press and the New York Times, 1971.

Scofield, Coral. *A Study of the Court of Star Chamber*. New York: Burt Franklin, 1969.

Shientag, Bernard L. *Moulders of Legal Thought*. Port Washington, NY: Kennikat Press Inc., 1968.

"Sikes Looks to Strengthen Broadcasters' Hand," *Broadcasting* (July 8, 1991): 23.

"Sikes: Repeal Compulsory License, Take Another Look at PTAR," *Broadcasting* (January 27, 1992): 14.

"Sikes the Enforcer," *Broadcasting* (February 12, 1990): 24.

"So Many Technologies, So Little Space," *Broadcasting* (May 6, 1991): 52.

Spencer, Dale, Katharine P. Darrow, Richard M. Schmidt, Jr. *Free Press and Fair Trial*. Washington, DC: American Society of Newspaper Editors/American Newspaper Publishers Association Foundation, 1982.

Sponseller, Diane. "Who's Got Your Number? Regulators Confront the New Caller ID Services," *Public Utilities Fortnightly* (February 15, 1990): 55.

"Station Stunts Tread Fine Line of Humor and Hoax," *Broadcasting* (April 8, 1991): 55.

Sterling, Christopher H., and John M. Kittross. *Stay Tuned: A Concise History of American Broadcasting*, 2nd ed. Belmont, CA: Wadsworth, 1990.

Stevens, George E. "Mass Media and the 'Libel Proof' Doctrine," *Journalism Quarterly* 66:1 (Spring 1989): 177.

Stover, Dawn. "Look Who's Calling," *Popular Science* (July 1990): 76.

"Supreme Court Upholds Noriega Tape Ban," *Broadcasting* (November 26, 1990): 52.

Timmer, Joel. "When a Commercial Is Not a Commercial: Advertising of Violent Entertainment and the First Amendment," 7 *Commercial Law and Policy* 157–86 (2002).

Tresolini, Rocco J., and Martin Shapiro. *American Constitutional Law*, 3rd ed. New York: Macmillan, 1970.

"TV Answer Puts Money Down on Infrastructure for Interactive Consumer Service," *Broadcasting* (September 30, 1991): 46.

"Two More Stations Fined for Indecency Violations," *Radio and Records* (April 26, 1991): 12, 22.

"Under Way," *Broadcasting* (October 22, 1990): 6.

Warren, Samuel D., and Lewis D. Brandeis. "The Right of Privacy," *Harvard Law Review* 4 (December 15, 1890): 193.

Weiler, Paul C. *Entertainment, Media, and the Law: Text, Cases, Problems.* St. Paul: The West Group, 1997.

West's Indiana Law Encyclopedia, Vol. 18. St. Paul: West Publishing Co., 1959.

White, Llewellyn. *The American Radio.* Chicago: University of Chicago Press, 1947.

Youm, Kyu Ho. "The Impact of People v. Croswell on Libel Law," *Journalism Monographs* 113 (June, 1989): 6.

Glossary

Administrative law judge an individual who presides over hearings for administrative agencies such as the Federal Communications Commission

Amici curiae literally, "friends of the court." Individuals or organizations not part of a legal action, permitted to submit briefs to a court to help the court reach a decision. The American Civil Liberties Union often submits friends of the court briefs in First Amendment cases.

Appellant the party who appeals a decision of a lower court

Appellee the party against whom an appeal is filed

Brief the written legal argument submitted to the court by attorneys as part of a lawsuit

Civil suit a legal action seeking monetary damages as a result of a private wrong or injury. Criminal actions are brought by a public prosecutor to redress a crime against society

Common law law that has evolved over the years as accepted practice. Originating in England, common law is the application of the decisions of judges over time. Common law is often called "discovered law" because judges look to the past to discover a solution to a problem.

Construction permit (CP) authorization to build or make changes to a broadcast facility, issued by the FCC

Conversion the unauthorized assumption of ownership over goods or personal property belonging to another; using someone else's goods or property to the exclusion of the owner's rights

Defendant the party against whom a criminal or civil action is brought

Deposition a sworn statement made by a party outside of the court in answer to questions posed by an attorney

Discovery the exchange of information between two parties to a lawsuit prior to the beginning of a trial

Grand jury a group of citizens appointed to decide whether enough evidence exists to indict an individual or individuals for the commission of a crime. An indictment by the grand jury will result in charges being filed, and a trial may follow.

In camera   in a judge's chambers without the public present

Indictment   a written accusation by a grand jury charging an individual or individuals with a serious crime

Information highway   a term coined during the 1992 Presidential campaign by Vice Presidential candidate Al Gore. It generally refers to the convergence of television, telephone, and computer technologies providing consumers with interactive data, entertainment, and personal communications services.

Injunction   a court order that commands a party to refrain from doing something, or an order to perform a specific act

Inquest   an investigation by a coroner or medical examiner as to the manner in which an individual has died when death occurs under suspicious or violent circumstances. Sometimes a jury assists in the investigation.

Memorandum decision   a court ruling issued without opinions or reasons given

Mistrial   a trial that is stopped because of a major procedural defect. For example, extensive, prejudicial pretrial publicity may result in the declaration of a mistrial based on the grounds that the defendant may not receive a fair trial.

Notice of Inquiry (NOI)   a statement by the FCC that describes a problem or issue and asks for public comments on how the problem should be solved. An NOI is published in the *Federal Register.* (*See* Report and Order.)

Notice of Proposed Rule Making (NPRM)   an FCC statement that describes how it plans to change its rules. An NPRM is published in the Federal Register and public comments are accepted. (*See* Report and Order.)

Per curiam   a court ruling that is an unsigned opinion representing the collective thinking of all justices on the court

Petitioner   the party seeking review of a lower court ruling or other judicial relief by seeking a hearing by a higher court

Plaintiff   the party who initiates a lawsuit

Preliminary hearing   a hearing held before a judge to determine whether there is enough evidence to proceed to trial

Prima facie   literally, "on the face of it." A *prima facie* fact is presumed to be true unless it is disproved by evidence to the contrary.

Remand   an order of a higher court that instructs a lower court to take some further action

Remittitur   the process by which an excessive jury award is reduced. A judge may order a portion of what is determined to be an excessive jury award to be returned by the plaintiff.

Renewal expectancy the assumption that the FCC will favor existing broadcast licenses over competitive applications at license renewal time, all other things being equal. Codified by the Telecommunications Act of 1996.

Report and Order (R & O) an FCC statement explaining how its rules and regulations have been changed. The Commission may use an R & O to adopt a new rule, modify an existing rule, or explain why a proposed rule has not been changed. It may also be issued to terminate a proceeding. An R & O is published in the *Federal Register*. (*See* Notice of Inquiry; Notice of Proposed Rule Making.)

Respondent the party opposed to judicial relief requested by the petitioner

Restraining order synonymous with injunction

Sequester to quarantine a jury from influences of the outside world during the course of a trial to ensure that the jury remains impartial

Slip opinion a copy of a court opinion circulated immediately after the opinion is decided

Stare decisis to abide by or hold to. When a court establishes a series of principles over time, they will be applied *stare decisis* in future cases where the facts are substantially the same.

Strict scrutiny content-based restrictions on speech protected by the First Amendment are given "strict scrutiny" by the Courts. This means that the government must show that restricting the speech serves a compelling government interest and is narrowly drawn to achieve that interest.

Summary judgment a pretrial motion that, if successful, will result in a judgment for a party without the necessity of going to trial

Tort a private civil wrong or injury

Venireman a member of a jury

Venue the location of a trial. When there has been substantial media coverage of a case, it is common practice for a judge to issue a change of venue to ensure that an impartial jury can be selected from the population.

Voir dire the process of questioning prospective jurors for the purpose of eliminating those who are unlikely to render an unbiased verdict

Writ of certiorari a discretionary order issued by the Supreme Court asking to hear a case from a lower court

Index